DATE DUE			
ILL			
#1772712			
COW			
3-13-06			

GAYLORD 234   PRINTED IN U.S.A.

Green Accounting

International Library of Environmental Economics and Policy

General Editors: *Tom Tietenberg and Wendy Morrison*

Titles in the Series

Green Accounting

Edited by

Peter Bartelmus and Eberhard K. Seifert

Wuppertal Institute for Climate, Environment and Energy GmbH, Germany

ASHGATE

Published by
Ashgate Publishing Limited
Gower House
Croft Road
Aldershot
Hants GU11 3HR
England

Ashgate Publishing Company
Suite 420
101 Cherry Street
Burlington, VT 05401-4405
USA

Ashgate website: http://www.ashgate.com

British Library Cataloguing in Publication Data
Green accounting. – (International library of environmental economics and policy)
   1. Environmental auditing 2. Industries – Environmental aspects – Accounting
   I. Bartelmus, Peter, 1942– II. Seifert, Eberhard
   657

Library of Congress Cataloging-in-Publication Data
Green accounting / edited by Peter Bartelmus and Eberhard Seifert.
      p. cm. — (International library of environmental economics and policy)
   Includes bibliographical references.
   ISBN 0-7546-2232-0 (alk. paper)
      1. Natural resources—Accounting. 2. Environmental economics. 3. Sustainable development. I. Bartelmus, Peter. II. Seifert, E. K. (Eberhard K.) III. Series.

HF5686.N3 G74 2002
657—dc21

2002026132

ISBN 0 7546 2232 0

Printed in Great Britain by The Cromwell Press, Trowbridge, Wiltshire

Contents

PART III   GREENING THE NATIONAL ACCOUNTS

PART IV   CORPORATE ENVIRONMENTAL ACCOUNTING

PART V   POLICY USE AND ANALYSIS

Acknowledgements

The editors and publishers wish to thank the following for permission to use copyright material.

AMBIO – Royal Swedish Academy of Sciences for the essay: Mark T. Brown and Sergio Ulgiati (1999), 'Emergy Evaluation of the Biosphere and Natural Capital', *Ambio*, **28**, pp. 486–93. Copyright © 1999 Royal Swedish Academy of Sciences.

Blackwell Publishing Limited for the essay: François Quesnay (1759), 'The "Third Edition" of the *Tableau Économique*', in M. Kuczynski and R.L. Meek (eds) (1972), *Quesnay's Tableau Économique* (facsimile reproduction and English translation), London: Macmillan, pp. title page, i–xij.

Cambridge University Press for the essay: Peter Bartelmus (1997), 'Whither Economics? From Optimality to Sustainability?', *Environment and Development Economics*, **2**, pp. 323–45. Copyright © 1997 Cambridge University Press.

Edward Elgar for the essay: Stefan Bringezu and Yuichi Moriguchi (2002), 'Material Flow Analysis', in Robert U. Ayres and Leslie W. Ayres (eds), *A Handbook of Industrial Ecology*, Cheltenham, UK and Northampton MA, USA: Edward Elgar, pp. 79–90, pp. 572–7.

Elsevier Science for the essay: Arieh A. Ullmann (1976), 'The Corporate Environmental Accounting System: A Management Tool for Fighting Environmental Degradation', *Accounting, Organizations and Society*, **1**, pp. 71–9.

International Association for Research in Income and Wealth for the essays: Peter Bartelmus, Carsten Stahmer and Jan van Tongeren (1991), 'Integrated Environmental and Economic Accounting: Framework for a SNA Satellite System', *Review of Income and Wealth*, **37**, pp. 111–48; Mark de Haan and Steven J. Keuning (1996), 'Taking the Environment into Account: The NAMEA Approach', *Review of Income and Wealth*, **42**, pp. 131–48.

Interscience Enterprises Ltd for the essay: Roy Brouwer, Martin O'Connor and Walter Radermacher (1999), 'GREEned National STAtistical and Modelling Procedures: The GREENSTAMP Approach to the Calculation of Environmentally Adjusted National Income Figures', *International Journal of Sustainable Development*, **2**, pp. 7–31. Copyright © 1999 Interscience Enterprises Ltd.

Kluwer Academic Publishers for the essays: J. Steven Landefeld and Stephanie L. Howell (1998), 'USA: Integrated Economic and Environmental Accounting: Lessons from the IEESA', in K. Uno and P. Bartelmus (eds), *Environmental Accounting in Theory and Practice*, Dordrecht, Boston and London: Kluwer Academic Publishers, pp. 113–29. Copyright © 1998 Kluwer

Series Preface

The *International Library of Environmental Economics and Policy* explores the influence of economics on the development of environmental and natural resource policy. In a series of twenty five volumes, the most significant journal essays in key areas of contemporary environmental and resource policy are collected. Scholars who are recognized for their expertise and contribution to the literature in the various research areas serve as volume editors and write an introductory essay that provides the context for the collection.

Volumes in the series reflect the broad strands of economic research including 1) Natural and Environmental Resources, 2) Policy Instruments and Institutions and 3) Methodology. The editors, in their introduction to each volume, provide a state-of-the-art overview of the topic and explain the influence and relevance of the collected papers on the development of policy. This reference series provides access to the economic literature that has made an enduring contribution to contemporary and natural resource policy.

TOM TIETENBERG
KATHLEEN SEGERSON
General Editors

Editors' Preface

Since the first Earth Summit in Rio de Janeiro there has been general agreement: sustainable development is the solution to fostering socioeconomic progress while protecting our life-supporting environment. Yet, consensus springs from the opacity of the concept rather than a convincing strategy of implementing the paradigm. A confusing array of definitions and indicators of sustainable or human development, genuine progress, ecological footprints or quality of life has been the outcome.

In our Introduction we argue that integrated environmental and economic accounting, popularly termed 'green accounting', is our best bet for capturing the elusive paradigm. Modifying established accounting systems will lead us away from rhetoric and ad hoc index compilation that lacks transparency and comparability with standard economic indicators. The essays selected for this volume show that the expansion of empirical analysis by green accounting points to a radical change of conventional economics whose abstract modelling has demonstrated limited 'real-world' relevance.

We are not there yet. As expected, resistance to such change is strong. Conventional neoclassical economists prefer to live with the 'semi-fiction' (as Robert Solow once put it) of optimizing an ideal world of perfectly competitive markets – and they have a point, as long as alternative analyses and policies have not proven their superiority in enhancing long-term wealth and welfare. National accountants echo this adherence to established approaches. At least for now, they have relegated any modifications of the national accounts to 'satellites' or preferably to 'research'. Their argument that the reputation of 'official' statistics has to be protected against the vagaries of analytical debates should also be taken seriously.

We have therefore to demonstrate convincingly, and hence quantitatively, that environmental and social concerns need to be factored into mainstream economic analysis and policy. This volume shows that the tools are available and could be included in the toolboxes of decision-makers and national and corporate accountants. However, green accounting is still work in progress. For instance, the unfortunate polarization between physical/ecological and monetary/economic accounting persists, as do other methodological 'dichotomies'. We have selected, therefore, the contributions to this volume with a view to conveying the wide range of approaches to measuring the interaction between environment and economy.

Part I sets out from a historical *aperçu*, revealing roots of environmental accounting in Quesnay's *Tableau Économique*. Surprisingly, it took about 150 years to rediscover environmental concerns and tackle them as external effects of economic activity. The next two chapters address the prevailing dichotomy of ecological versus economic measurement and analysis. Part II describes how ecological sustainability can be accounted for by measuring the material and energy flows that impair the carrying capacity of natural systems. Part III, in contrast, shows the possibilities of linking physical and monetary accounts for the assessment of economic sustainability as produced and natural capital maintenance. The greening of the national accounts thus provides a framework for overcoming the physical–monetary dichotomy. Part IV gives a first impression of the rapidly expanding field of corporate environmental accounting. The greened national accounts should provide a useful framework for linking micro- and macro-accounts and analyses. The final Part shows that various accounting dichotomies carry over into the use of accounting indicators, either directly in policy-making or through the filter of modelling.

Our introduction to this volume attempts to flesh out the necessarily judgemental selection of essays through reference to related areas and publications. We took care to present a comprehensive overview of the main environmental accounting approaches but were bound, of course, by limits of space, time and knowledge. Any oversight of important work is inadvertent and reflects our ignorance rather than ulterior motives. We hope that this volume will encourage interdisciplinary research, testing and implementation of green accounting at corporate, national and international levels.

Peter Bartelmus and Eberhard K. Seifert
Wuppertal, 3 February 2003

Introduction: Accounting for Sustainability

As no selection of essays can do full justice to the broad and rapidly developing field of environmental accounting, this Introduction provides context and perspective to the different chapters through references to related fields of research and methodologies.[1] The reader should be able to identify the place and connotation of particular concepts and approaches of environmental accounting within the overall subject of assessing sustainable development.[2] A brief outlook on open questions is to indicate where unresolved issues call for further investigation and testing of green accounting concepts and methods.

1 Sustainable Development: From Paradigm to Measurement

1.1 Environment and Development: The International Debate

High-profile pollution incidents in the 1960s brought about gloom,[3] generating a sense of urgency for tackling global environmental problems. As a result, the first of a number of United Nations conferences focused on the Human Environment (Stockholm, 5–16 June 1972). This conference established the United Nations Environment Programme (UNEP) and requested the development of a global environmental monitoring system. Principle 13 of the Conference Declaration on 'an integrated and co-ordinated approach to development planning' (United Nations, 1973) went, however, largely unheeded.

National and international data systems took their cue from the Stockholm Conference and focused on physical (non-monetary) data for monitoring the state of the environment. Owing to the lack of a common unit of measurement, relatively loose frameworks were advanced for organizing and presenting an unwieldy amount of environmental data. For instance, the United Nations (1984) Framework for the Development of Environment Statistics (FDES) and related technical reports (United Nations, 1988, 1991) presented long lists of statistics and indicators under activity-impact-response categories.[4]

Calls for integrating environment and development increased with the realization of failure in both tackling global environmental problems and implementing international development strategies. It is to the merit of the Brundtland Commission on Environment and Development (WCED, 1987) that it drew attention to 'interdependences' of environmental, social and economic concerns, inconsistently addressed by compartmentalized line ministries and agencies.

Acting on the Brundtland Report, the United Nations convened a Conference on Environment and Development in Rio de Janeiro (3–14 June 1992). This first 'Earth Summit' propagated *sustainable development* as the key to integrating the main (social, economic and environmental) dimensions of development in planning and policy-making. The Action Plan of the Rio Summit,

Agenda 21, considered integrated environmental and economic accounting as 'a first step towards the integration of sustainability into economic management' (United Nations, 1994, para. 8.41). In Europe, the 1997 Amsterdam Treaty of the European Union proclaimed sustainable development as its 'preeminent goal', and the 2001 Gothenburg session of the European Council called for a 'horizontal strategy' across all three dimensions of sustainable development.

The 2002 Johannesburg Summit on Sustainable Development of the United Nations reaffirmed the member states' commitment to the Rio principles and the full implementation of Agenda 21. Anticipating the review of Agenda 21 in the Johannesburg Summit, the Secretary-General of the United Nations identified, in his Millennium Report, green accounting as 'the surest way' of better integrating the environment into mainstream economic policy.

1.2   Fuzzy Measures for a Fuzzy Concept

The Brundtland Commission also offered the popular definition of sustainable development as 'development that meets the needs of the present without compromising the ability of future generations to meet their own needs' (WCED, 1987, p. 43). The definition is vague: it does not specify the categories of human needs, gives no clear time frame for analysis (future generations!), nor does it indicate particular roles for the environment or social concerns.

Opaque definitions such as the above or the economists' favourite of non-declining welfare (Pezzey, 1989) provided fertile ground for numerous measures of social progress, environmental impact, and sustainable or human development. These measures include, in particular, a genuine progress indicator (GPI) (Cobb, Halstead and Rowe, 1995), ecological footprints (Wackernagel and Rees, 1996), total (including natural) wealth (World Bank, 1997), indices of human development (UNDP, annual), sustainable development (Nováček and Mederly, 2002) and environmental sustainability.[5]

These compound indices deserve some attention because they all take the environment 'into account'. They do not apply, however, a systematic accounting *procedure* with its well-known properties of double or quadruple (entry) checking.[6] They are therefore discussed critically in a historical context only – as precursors or complements to more rigorous and systematic accounting (see section 2.3).

1.3   Environmental Accounting: Tackling Environmental Sustainability

The elusive notion of sustainability needs to be operationalized in a systemic context of economy–environment interaction. To this end, natural science offers basic principles for the nature–economy interface, and economics provides the tool of accounting for this interface. Thermodynamic laws of matter and energy conservation and dissipation govern the use of natural resources. Formal double-entry accounting can then be applied to assess the use (input) and dispersion (output) of these resources from/to the natural environment.

Figure 1 illustrates this 'throughput' of materials (including energy carriers) through the economy and its positive and negative welfare effects on human beings. The figure also shows the two basic functions of the environment: (1) resource supply of raw materials, space and energy to the economy (source function); and (2) waste assimilation (sink function). The fortunate coincidence of physical laws, ensuring the equality of inputs and outputs of energy and materials, and input–output-based economic accounting points to an obvious approach of

Figure 1   Environment–economy interaction and effects

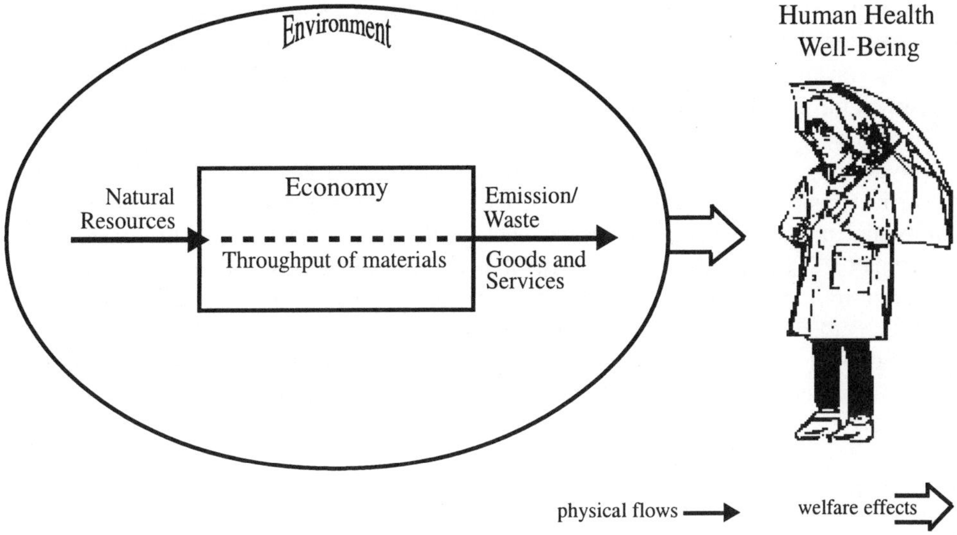

Source: Bartelmus (2001).

applying the latter to the former. The result is 'green accounting'[7] – that is, the extension of conventional economic accounts into the physical world of natural resource use and abuse by economic activity.

Unfortunately, agreement on the need for integrative accounting ends with implementation. The application of environmental accounting tools requires the aggregation of physical data by means of a common measuring rod. The dissent is on whether to use physical measures – notably the 'natural' mass unit, weight – or the prices and costs of economic accounts for weighting the importance of environmental impacts. The roots of this dissent lie in different world-views of economists and environmentalists. Environmental economists rely on individual preferences, expressed or simulated in markets (and market prices), to value economic products and environmental assets and services. In contrast, environmentalists consider the environment as an indivisible (public) good on whose value markets should not have a say.[8]

With measurability in mind, both views focus on the interaction of environment and economy and hence on concepts of 'environmental' (at the expense of social and other concerns) sustainability of economic activity. Two operational sustainability concepts can thus be distinguished according to the economic and ecological outlook (see also section 5.2):

* *Economic sustainability* aims at keeping (produced as well as natural) capital intact as a necessary condition for continuing economic performance and growth.
* *Ecological sustainability* is to diminish pressure on the carrying capacities of natural systems by reducing material throughput to tolerable levels by 'dematerializing' the economy.

Two main accounting systems show most promise in capturing the two notions of environmental sustainability. They make use of, or build upon, official, national or internationally endorsed systems of environmental and economic statistics and accounting. Material flow accounts (MFA) aim at measuring actual and potential environmental impacts in physical units. The United Nations (1993) System for integrated Environmental and Economic Accounting (SEEA) embraces both physical and monetary accounts, seeking compatibility with the worldwide adopted System of National Accounts, the SNA (United Nations *et al.*, 1993). The SEEA thus succeeds in overcoming the environmental–economic dichotomy, at least from an empirical point of view.

The narrow focus on the *environmental* sustainability of economic growth by greened economic accounts does not do justice to the much broader paradigm of sustainable development. 'Development' itself encompasses social, ecological, cultural and political objectives, besides economic ones. The corresponding sustainability notion would therefore have to incorporate, in addition to economic and ecological criteria, social, institutional and other targets (Bartelmus, 1994, ch. 3.2). The problem with these additional concerns is measurability in a comparable (integrative) fashion. The final 'outlook' section (6) will refer to attempts at incorporating at least some services of social and human capital into the accounting framework.

2   A Historical Review

For the review of path-breaking publications we looked back at the paths taken, less travelled or abandoned. However, we cannot present here a full evaluation of all the tracks and deviations of environmental and sustainability assessments. Some are outlined below as introductions to the different approaches presented in this book. Others, like Georgescu-Roegen's (Chapter 4) thermodynamic analysis of the physical basis of the economy (see section 3.1), themselves represent a historical step forward. We will trace, rather, one particular line of historical development, represented by the three chapters of Part I, which together are indicative of the ups and downs of 'accounting for nature' in connection with assessments of economic performance.

2.1   The Tableau Économique: *Accounting of the 'Natural Order'*

Historically, double-entry bookkeeping was both a result of, and stimulus for, flourishing commerce in the Italian Renaissance. It took the impending societal crisis of declining French feudalism in the mid-eighteenth century to open eyes to concerns beyond conventional commerce and accounting. With a view to halting this decline and possibly preserving the economic and social interests of the feudal class of landowners, the physiocratic movement of the time focused on the use of nature by 'agriculture'. In this context, agriculture has to be seen in a broad sense. It includes activities of farming, forestry, fishery and mining, and was considered as the only productive force in the 'natural order' of society and economy.

Against this background François Quesnay (1694–1774) (Chapter 1), the private physician of Madame Pompadour at the court of Louis XV, attempted a justification of this order from an economic angle and by means of a quantitative analysis of the national economy. His famous *Tableau Économique* sets out from a normative distribution of income and wealth as annual 'advances' to 'productive' farmers, landowners and the 'sterile' class of industry and commerce. Criss-crossing flows between the productive and sterile classes then describe the circular flows (*calcul itératif*) of money and products. Quesnay modified his *Tableau* several times. Chapter 1 displays the original zigzag table, but it was the later (condensed) version which revealed more clearly characteristics of an input–output table (Phillips, 1955; Leontief, 1987). Broader views see the *Tableau* and its concomitant analysis as a precursor of the Keynesian multiplier and of Sraffa's price system (Vaggi, 1987, p. 23), or simply as the 'most brilliant idea . . . the political economy so far had generated' (Marx, 1894, 1965 edn, p. 319).

For all the praise and critique it generated, and for all we know, the *Tableau* has never been claimed as a forerunner of green accounting. However, a number of facets of physiocratic thought and its expression in a quantitative scheme suggests tracing back the origins of green accounting to an approach that accounts for the power (gr. *kratos*) of nature (gr. *physis*) in the management of the 'national household' (gr. *oikonomia*).[9] These facets include the accounting for:

- the availability of natural and produced assets, the *avances*, as the starting point for all periodic economic (notably agricultural) activity
- 'sustainability', as expressed in the basic ideas of interrelationships between society and the economic system, and their reproduction and maintenance in accordance with the 'natural order'
- the creation of new wealth through 'net' product (surplus) as the means of attaining sustainable (continuing) economic growth.

With reference to the *Tableau*'s capacity of 'representing the wealth of nations', Adam Smith (1776, 1991 edn, p. 463) had to admit that 'this system, however, with all its imperfections, is, perhaps, the nearest approximation to the truth that has yet been published upon the subject of political œconomy . . .'. However, it was his derisive critique of the French (physiocratic) 'Political Œconomy' as 'that system which . . . exists only in the speculation of a few men of great learning and ingenuity in France' (*ibid.*, p. 446)[10] and the success of industrialization which sent Quesnay's *Tableau* – and, in fact, environmental concerns in economics and accounting – into oblivion. Notable exceptions such as Jevons's (1865, 1965 edn) warning of the depletion of a key natural resource (coal) left no mark on dominant capitalist and socialist economic theories, at least until the doomsday warnings of the 1960s and early 1970s.[11]

2.2   *Environmental Disruption and Social Cost Assessment*

In the wake of unprecedented economic growth in industrialized countries, classical and neoclassical economic theory could not be bothered with real-world deviations from their perfect-competition and general-equilibrium paradigms. These paradigms could be formalized with mathematical rigour in models where disturbances from less-than-perfect markets or localized pollution incidents could be 'externalized'. If need be, such externalities could be easily 'internalized' into mainstream economics by appropriate Pigovian taxation (Pigou, 1920, 1932 edn). *De facto* they were ignored as marginal.

It took a further – environmental – crisis to generate the above-mentioned doom and gloom of the 1960s and 1970s, and the visionary intellect of K. William Kapp (1910–1976) (Chapter 2) to overcome the marginalization of (Pigovian) externalities in economic analysis. In his 1950 classic, *The Social Costs of Private Enterprise* and further editions, Kapp (1950,

1963, 1971) identified environmental disruptions of pollution, erosion, loss of species and other natural resources as threats to human survival. As a consequence, assessing the causes and magnitude of these impacts was, in his view, beyond the capacities of both neoclassical welfare analysis and national income accounting.

Kapp's essay in this volume conveys a condensed view of these thoughts with some insight on how the 'staggering' social costs could be assessed. These costs are deemed to be the result of a 'complex process of interaction of social and physical factors' (p. 33), which 'compartmentalized' (p.36) disciplines were unable to tackle. Lacking a theory for this interaction, Kapp calls for an empirical (quantitative) assessment of environmental impacts by means of an 'inventory' of environmental damages. Considering the monetary assessment of social (damage) costs 'doomed to failure', the inventory is to assess the physical state of the environment. Knowledge gained by such an inventory would facilitate the setting of standards and targets for purposes of environmental control. Controversial monetary damage valuation could thus be circumvented. The introduction of environmental and further standards of 'existential minimum needs' into input–output models would help promote environmentally sound production techniques ('input mixes') and land use zoning. About two decades later these ideas were taken up again by the so-called Greenstamp research group with similar arguments as to social cost measurement (see section 5.1).

Kapp also anticipates the distorting role of 'defensive expenditures', pointing out that the 'increasing amounts and proportions of outlays . . . spent on nothing else but work designed to protect and keep intact the substance of our environment' render GNP 'inadequate and unreliable' (p. 39, n. 12) as a measure of growth and development. He is content, however, to point out the deficiencies of the accounting indicator while shying away from its modification – as suggested by the proponents of extended welfare measurement.

2.3   Welfare versus Quality-of-Life Measurement

Not everybody shared Kapp's view about the non-measurability of social (environmental) costs and benefits. Stung by the criticism of the key indicator of economic growth, GNP, economists William D. Nordhaus and James Tobin (1918–2002) (Chapter 3) were among the first to attempt a correction of this epitome of economic performance. The idea was to better reflect the ultimate objective of economic activity – social welfare. Their Measure of Economic Welfare (MEW)[12] adds 'desirables' of leisure and outputs of subsistence activities to net domestic product and deducts 'regrettables' of instrumental (defensive) expenditures, growth requirements and environmental externalities. While admitting the imperfections of GNP, the authors nevertheless consider the conventional aggregate as capable of conveying 'the broad picture of secular progress' (p. 72).

Disagreement with this analysis came from 'ecological' economists who criticized the scope and coverage of the MEW measure, and environmentalists who rejected any monetary assessment of environmental concerns.

Ecological economists viewed the enormous additions to GNP from imputations for leisure and non-market activities, compared to relatively small deductions for regrettables and disamenities, as preconceived faith in economic growth. In their opinion, MEW simply overstates, through doubtful valuation and coverage, the importance of leisure and non-market activity and understates welfare losses from environmental and social deterioration. Hence they advanced their own improved measures, presenting a broader list of 'defensive expenditures' (Leipert, 1989) and environmental damages. Daly and Cobb (1989) incorporated these detractions from the human quality of life in an Index of Sustainable Economic Welfare (ISEW); Hueting (1993) suggested a Sustainable National Income (SNI) measure. Their principal intention was to show that national income and product are indeed deceptive indicators of prosperity and social progress.

As is to be expected, the modified ISEW, called the 'Genuine Progress Indicator' (GPI), differed dramatically from conventional GDP: America appeared to be 'down' despite an upward trend of GDP (Cobb, Halstead and Rowe, 1995). Other studies of the GPI obtained different results. Australia, for example, showed a similar increase in GDP but also a 25 per cent increase of the GPI (Hamilton, 1999). This may be either the result of a more sustainable economic performance or, more probably, of considerable differences in scope, coverage, valuation and estimations, and deviations from standard classifications and definitions of economic indicators (Bartelmus, 2002).

As an alternative to the monetary evaluation of economic growth and its impacts on environmental and social concerns, the social indicator movement of the 1970s brought about non-monetary (social) indicators of the human quality of life (OECD, 1973; Drewnowski, 1970, 1974). However, the failure in reaching international consensus on social concerns and basic human needs confined the quality-of-life and social-indicator movement to local activities.

About 20 years later, environmentalists voiced again a strong rejection of GDP as a distorted and misleading measure of social progress. In their opinion, monetary measures of economic growth conceal violations of natural thresholds, which undermine economic development (for example, Brown, 1993, p. 4; van Dieren, 1995, pp. xi, 7; Daly, 1996, p. 64). It remains to be seen if renewed efforts of developing indicators of sustainable development (Moldan, Billharz and Matravers, 1997; United Nations, 2001), of quality of life (Fergany, 1994; Henderson, Lickerman and Flynn, 2000) or human development (UNDP, annual) signal a comeback of the quality-of-life discussion. Given the lack of a common framework that would reflect an accepted sustainability notion, the odds are against such a comeback as an international standard for measuring sustainability.

Neither the GDP corrections nor the indicator movements could dethrone national income and product as the leading measures of economic performance. The reasons may be that eclectic data and indicator selection, inconsistencies with established economic concepts and definitions, and non-transparent valuation and weighting in ad hoc index calculations impair the comparability of economic and environmental effects and may open the door to data manipulation. More systematic physical and monetary accounting – the topic of this volume – is needed.

3 Getting Physical or Monetary?

Several accounting systems were built around the above-discussed dichotomy of physical and monetary assessments of sustainability. Figure 2 illustrates this dichotomy within an overall accounting framework. The framework distinguishes, besides physical and monetary accounting, an intermediate, mixed (hybrid) physical–monetary approach. The figure also indicates the

Figure 2   Framework for environmental and economic accounting

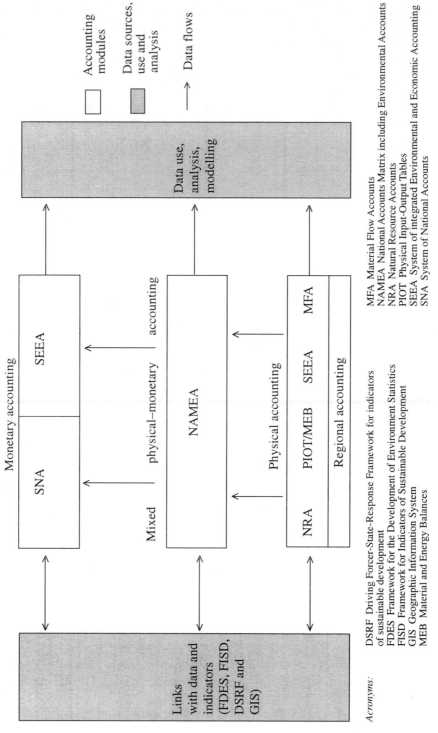

Acronyms: DSRF Driving Forcer-State-Response Framework for indicators
of sustainable development
FDES Framework for the Development of Environment Statistics
FISD Framework for Indicators of Sustainable Development
GIS   Geographic Information System
MEB   Material and Energy Balances

MFA   Material Flow Accounts
NAMEA National Accounts Matrix including Environmental Accounts
NRA   Natural Resource Accounts
PIOT Physical Input-Output Tables
SEEA System of integrated Environmental and Economic Accounting
SNA   System of National Accounts

Source: Bartelmus (2001).

links of the accounting systems to data sources, represented by international data frameworks, and to the use of accounting indicators in modelling and policy-making. This section follows Parts II and III of the volume in discussing, first, the main physical approaches and then possibilities of integrating or linking the different accounting systems.

3.1 Physical Accounting

The work of Nicholas Georgescu-Roegen (1906–1994) (Chapter 4) provides the rationale for measuring the environment–economy interaction in material and energy flow accounts (Seifert, 1993; Mayumi, 2001). His merit is not only to relate the physics of thermodynamics, and in particular entropy, to economics, but also to extend the entropy law beyond energy to matter. In his essay he asserts that, with regard to the depletion of terrestrial deposits of matter, 'for all practical purposes, the Earth is a closed thermodynamic system' (p. 101): 'matter matters' (p. 91).[13] His suggestion to 'keep separate books for matter and energy' (p. 92), at the macro-level, is indeed an invitation to develop national material and energy accounts.

Approaches to capturing the process of dissipation of low-entropy matter into high-entropy waste range from relatively simple natural resource accounts (NRA) to complex material and energy balances (MEB) and even more ambitious natural patrimony accounts (NPA). At the micro-economic (product/process) level they have become known as cradle-to-grave or life-cycle analyses (see section 4).

NRA, pioneered by Norway (Alfsen, Bye and Lorentsen, 1987), describe the natural resource stocks and their use during an accounting period in a fairly aggregate fashion. Only selected resource accounts were prepared, however, probably because of the aggregation problem posed by the use of different units of measurement. This might also be the reason why Statistics Norway largely abandoned this approach and developed instead – quite unusually for a national statistical service – a national general equilibrium model (Alfsen, 1996). In contrast to the Norwegian NRA, the French NPA attempt to link all kinds of institutional (economic agents) and environmental (natural resources, sinks, biota, land use, ecosystems) components in a complex statistical system (Weber, 1983; Theys, 1989). Only parts of this system were implemented in France and a few other countries, with NPA remaining largely a French speciality.

MEB are to monitor the material throughput depicted in Figure 1. They aim to provide information on material and energy inputs from the environment into the economy, their transformation in economic production and consumption processes, and their return to the environment as wastes and residuals. Robert Ayres (Chapter 5) presented the MEB system he had earlier developed with his colleagues (Ayres and Kneese, 1969; Kneese, Ayres and d'Arge, 1970) to the international community in 1976. However, the United Nations Statistical Commission rejected this presentation as 'a good paper for the long term' (United Nations, 1977, para. 112). This rejection delayed the further development of MEB for about 20 years – that is, until material and energy flows were incorporated in the SEEA, and in somewhat modified form, in material flow accounts (MFA).

Blinded possibly by the suggestive power of environmentally modified monetary indicators like a 'green GDP', it is often overlooked that the United Nations' SEEA also contains fully-fledged physical accounts (United Nations, 1993, ch. III). In fact these accounts are a combination of NRA and MEB. NRA provide the asset (stock and changes in stock) accounting methods, and MEB the link to economic transformation processes. The MEB were, however, not included in the SEEA in the detail suggested by Ayres because data needs and lack of knowledge about a multitude of production and consumption processes would render the implementation of MEB 'unrealistic' (United Nations, 1993, para. 200).

The MFA (Steurer, 1992; Bringezu, 1993; Schmidt-Bleek, 1994; Fischer-Kowalski, 1998; Fischer-Kowalski and Hüttler, 1999) are a somewhat simplified, pragmatic approach to assessing the material throughput through the economy. Stefan Bringezu and Yuichi Moriguchi (Chapter 6) describe the MFA as a tool for assessing society's physical metabolism. As in the SEEA and MEB, these accounts include primary resource extraction, product and residual flows, as well as ('bulk') material balances. The authors distinguish between 'type I' analysis of different substances, materials and products and 'type II' analysis of throughput through firms, sectors and regions. The former serve to support strategies of 'detoxification', the latter focus on the 'dematerialization' of the economy (see section 5.2). The accounts generate a number of input and output indicators to support these strategies. The total material requirement (TMR) indicator, in particular, includes hidden 'ecological rucksacks' (p. 158) which are production impacts on natural resources that did not become a physical part of the product (erosion, gangue and so on). The purpose is to measure comprehensively the material base of the economy. International guidelines and applications indicate growing interest in material flow analysis by data users and producers (Adriaanse *et al.*, 1997; Matthews *et al.*, 2000; Eurostat, 2001).

Physical input–output tables (PIOT) can be extended to include some of the material flows of MEB and MFA (Stahmer, Kuhn and Braun, 1998). The PIOT link these flows to the different economic sectors, in consistency with the national accounts, which represents a first step towards adjusting ('greening') the national accounts. On their own, PIOT are typically used for Leontief-type analyses (see section 5.1).

Günter Strassert (Chapter 7), a bioeconomist, introduces Georgescu-Roegen's ideas into an input–output framework. He suggests a further extension of input–output tabulations into the realm of ecological accounting. Focusing on physical flows in both the input–output and eco-systems, final (human) consumption becomes immaterial – as 'human enjoyment' – with consumption goods as input into such enjoyment and waste as its output. This is a considerable deviation from national accounts concepts of income, production and consumption, and hence the conventional (and quantifiable) goals of economic activity.

A major drawback of physical indicators is their use of different units of measurement, preventing aggregation and comparison of the availability and use of different natural assets. The above-mentioned MFA and PIOT attempt to resolve this problem by measuring material and substance flows in tons per time period. Weighting different environmental impacts by weight has been criticized as 'ton ideology' (Gawel, 1998). Counterarguments point out that selected indicators of emissions cannot capture the large number of known and unknown environmental damages. What is needed is an overall 'rule of thumb', like the trend of the above-described TMR aggregate, to 'help us to move in the right direction' (Hinterberger, Luks and Schmidt-Bleek, 1997, p. 7).

Energy economists (Cottrell, 1970; Odum, 1971; Slesser, 1975; Costanza, 1980) laid the foundation for expressing the value of nature, and possibly economic output, in terms of energy requirements. Mark T. Brown and Sergio Ulgiati (Chapter 8) thus use solar energy units as equivalent measures for environmental resource flows and natural capital ('emergy') stores. They apply an environmental accounting approach developed by Odum (1996). The idea is to assess emergy as the total direct and indirect energy used in the production of a particular, or *the* national, product. Note that Georgescu-Roegen (Chapter 4) takes a critical view of aggregation in energy units as a substitute for (or linked to) economic valuation.[14] In his view, a clear relationship between matter, energy and human tastes and preferences cannot be established, despite a common root of scarcity.

3.2   Integrated Physical and Monetary Accounting

Physical accounts alert us to undesirable trends of environmental impacts and provide useful data for the management of particular natural resources. They do not possess, however, the integrative power of monetary environmental accounts. Monetary valuation is indeed the only possible way of fully integrating environmental concerns into the economic accounting system while ensuring consistency and comparability of 'greened' with conventional economic indicators.

The pricing of 'priceless' environmental goods and services, which are not valued in markets but are essential for generating and maintaining human wealth and welfare, is not without controversy. Welfare or utility maximization, the core tenet of economic theory, calls for including the *damage* (negative utility) to humans from environmental 'externalities' of economic activities. To maintain economic efficiency (in the sense of Pareto optimality) economic agents have to account for the loss of formerly abundant benefits of nature – that is, new scarcities of environmental services, in their plans and budgets. However, damage valuation is already a problem for cost-benefit analyses of particular projects and programmes and poses near-insurmountable problems at the national (accounting) level (Bartelmus, 1998). Nonetheless, some economists experimented with damage valuations in regional and national accounts (delos Angeles and Peskin, 1998; Markandya and Pavan, 1999).

Taking their cue from practical approaches to measuring externalities as the cost of attaining environmental quality standards (Baumol and Oates, 1971), Peter Bartelmus, Carsten Stahmer and Jan van Tongeren (Chapter 9) favour a 'maintenance (of natural assets) costing' approach. They define the maintenance costs as those 'which would be necessary to avoid, restore or replace decreases of environmental quantities and qualities during the reference period' (pp. 214–15). Such costing permits accounting for the depletion and degradation of natural assets as natural capital consumption, in consistency with the (produced) capital consumption concept of the national accounts. In this manner, the *economic sustainability* principle of capital maintenance (see section 1.3) is extended into the field of environmental assets.

Contrary to any damage valuation, this approach is compatible with the basic objective of the national accounts, which is to measure economic performance rather than welfare (United Nations *et al.*, 1993, ch. I.J).[15] The result is an integrated accounting system which later became the United Nations (1993, 2000a) System for integrated Environmental and Economic Accounting (SEEA). Deducting the environmental maintenance costs from value added and capital formation thus obtains environmentally modified accounting indicators, notably Environmentally-adjusted net Value Added (EVA), Domestic Product (EDP) and Capital Formation (ECF). As already indicated, the SEEA also elaborated physical accounts as counterparts of and data source for the monetary ones. Such compatibility of physical and monetary accounting could make an important contribution to settling the ecological–economic dispute on assessing the sustainability of economic activity.

Agenda 21 of the Rio Summit took up the proposed green accounting system and requested that 'integrated environmental and economic accounting . . . be established in all member States at the earliest date . . .' (United Nations, 1994, para. 8.42). As a first reaction, the revised SNA 1993 incorporated an outline of the proposed SEEA as a 'satellite' account in a special chapter (United Nations *et al.*, 1993, ch. XXI.D). As indicated below in section 6, 'Outlook', the current revision of the SEEA (United Nations *et al.*, in prep.) seems to have abandoned some of the systemic features in favour of a less stringent modular framework.

Two case studies by Steven Landefeld and Stephanie Howell (for the USA) (Chapter 10) and by Seung-Woo Kim, Jan van Tongeren and Alessandra Alfieri (for the Republic of Korea) (Chapter 11) demonstrate the feasibility and limitations of integrative monetary accounting *à la* SEEA. Peter Bartelmus presents the results of such accounting for other countries in Chapter 20. For industrialized countries, environmental costs range between 2–5 per cent of NDP. The good news is that the (maintenance or avoidance) cost of environmental impacts appears to be relatively low; the bad news is that the actual damage (to health and well-being) value can be much higher.[16]

The imputation of monetary values on non-market transactions and processes has been criticized on principle not only by environmentalists but also by conservative national accountants. Especially in industrialized countries, these accountants have been quite recalcitrant in implementing environmental satellite accounts in monetary terms. Some 'official' statisticians seem to believe that they might lose their long-standing goodwill if they let in controversial concepts and valuations, even through the back door of supplementary (satellite) systems. As a result, more cautious approaches of mixed, physical (for the environment) and monetary (for economic indicators) accounting seem to prevail for now, at least in Europe.

Mark de Haan and Steven J. Keuning (Chapter 12) present the prototype of such accounting, the Dutch National Accounting Matrix including Environmental Accounts (NAMEA). The matrix refrains from any monetary valuation of environmental impacts. Rather, it places physical impacts (mainly emissions) next to the conventional economic aggregates of those sectors that caused the impacts. NAMEA facilitates thus the linkage of physical impacts with their immediate causes which is a necessary intermediate step towards integrated monetary accounting. The matrix does attempt aggregation of environmental impacts up to a point – that is, for selected environmental 'policy themes'.[17] NAMEA can be seen as a hybrid input–output tabulation which, of course, lends itself to various types of input–output analyses (see section 5.1).

4   Corporate Accounting – Tailing Big Brother?

National accountants have three major advantages over their micro-economic (corporate) sisters and brothers: first, they are less confined by accountancy laws and rules; second, they are not directly affected by their own calculations; and third, their macro-economic vantage-point gives them a broader view and earlier recognition of changing socioeconomic concerns. This may explain why corporate accounting has lagged behind national accounting in addressing information needs on the human quality of life and the natural environment.

Linking micro- and macro-accounting in a common framework would be beneficial for corporate accountants who could use national environmental accounting conventions and experiences as a starting point for their own ventures into environmental concerns. National accountants would also benefit from such linkage since the standardization and implementation of their system depends on grassroots practices and data availability. To further micro–macro links in environmental accounting – rather than giving a comprehensive history or description of corporate environmental accounting – is thus the purpose of Part IV of this volume.

4.1 Getting Physical or Monetary?

The inclusion of non-economic, social concerns in corporate accounts was triggered in Europe by the social indicator movement of the 1970s (see section 2.3). The Swiss–German 'social balances' (*Sozialbilanzen*) (Hoffmann-Nowotny, 1981) were short-lived, however, because of measurement and aggregation problems of quality of life components, on the one hand, and conflicting interests between corporate-economic and social objectives, on the other hand. Nonetheless, social accounting can be seen as the 'Trojan horse' which opened the walls of conventional corporate accounting to the 'accountability' of corporations for their social and environmental impacts (Gray, 1992, p. 400).

It is thus not surprising that scholars at the university of St Gall (Switzerland) used the breach made into economic accounting by extending the social balances into 'ecological bookkeeping' (Müller-Wenck, 1978). Arieh Ullmann (Chapter 13) is one of the protagonists of this approach. His essay identifies the fundamental dichotomies of physical versus monetary and input- versus output-oriented accounting that still haunt micro- and macro-level accounting. He also alerts us to the problems of aggregating physical indicators in – extended – social accounts, and of monetary valuation of phenomena that are essentially 'external' to corporate activities. Ullmann opts, therefore, for a physical input–output approach in his environmental accounting system. The solution to the aggregation problem is 'equivalent factors' (similar to those of the above-described NAMEA) with which to evaluate 'environmental scarcity' of source and sink functions of the environment.

It took a long time and inspiration from the environmentalist and sustainable development movements to widely acknowledge the relevance of environmental concerns for the accountancy profession. Gray (1990, 1992) has been among the first to call for introducing notions such as carrying capacity and capital maintenance into corporate accounts. Contrary to the Swiss physical/ecological approach, Gray recognized the value of both physical impact accounting in non-financial accounts and 'sustainable cost' accounting in financial 'shadow' accounts. He stopped short, however, of advancing an accounting system to this end, considering the difficulties of doing so 'monumental' (Gray, 1992, p. 420).

Stefan Schaltegger (Chapter 14) tackled the monumental task. His essay conveys the basic ideas that were later presented in a comprehensive publication on 'contemporary environmental accounting' (Schaltegger and Burritt, 2000). This book has been seminal to a wide range of international activities and studies on 'Environmental Management Accounting' (EMA).[18] Schaltegger also distinguishes between financial (monetary) and ecological (physical) accounting and suggests taking the two together in a modular presentation of an environmental accounting framework (p. 291). This categorization mirrors the conservative modular approach to green accounting, favoured by 'official' statistics (see section 6, below):

- including only internal costs of outlays for environmental protection in the monetary accounts

- assessing environmental impacts through physical input–output accounts
- 'integrating' accounts by means of calculating eco-efficiency indicators, notably as the ratio of (monetary) value added and (physical) environmental impact.

Except for the less controversial compilation of environmental expenditures, the focus is thus on physical material flows with three different types of efficiency measure. This distinction permits the categorization of a number of popular accounting approaches:

- 'Ecological product efficiency' appears to be the objective of product- or process-oriented life-cycle (cradle-to-grave) analyses (LCA).
- 'Ecological function efficiency' relates to ultimate services of products as proposed by the Wuppertal Institute's MIPS (Material Intensity per Service) indicator (Schmidt-Bleek, 1993, 1994).
- 'Eco-efficiency' (economic-ecological efficiency) corresponds to the resource–productivity indicators underlying the Factor 4 sustainability target (von Weizsäcker, Lovins and Lovins, 1997; see also section 5.2).

Schaltegger considers the mixing of environmental externalities with internal cost as a 'distortion of actual figures' of economic performance. Like Ullman, he advocates assessing the environmental impacts of the company in physical terms by means of input–output accounts of natural resource use, and emissions and wastes. This type of accounting has become popular among environment-minded businesses for meeting stakeholders' demand for environmental information.

The 'eco-balances' of the Kunert Group of Companies (Chapter 15) are therefore shown in this volume as one of the first (and outstanding) examples of corporate environmental accounting and reporting.[19] The balances include not only input and output flows of materials and substances but also stocks of environmental and produced assets, as well as environmental performance indicators. The objective is to provide information for internal environmental management and external communication. Moreover, a pilot project on 'environmental cost management' indicates a considerable potential for 'non-value-added cost saving' by reducing the purchases of environmentally noxious substances. Such avoidance costing is a first step towards maintenance costing as advocated by the SEEA.

4.2   Financial Accounting and the Micro–Macro Link

Peter Letmathe and Roger K. Doost (Chapter 16) elaborate on such environmental cost accounting. They seek greater efficiency in complying with environmental legislation through material and energy cost-saving techniques. To this end, they propose an internal pricing system for environmental impacts that goes beyond reducing the costs of complying with environmental law by including environmental risks and 'additional' costs of potential externalities. This costing would reflect company policies and goals beyond commercial interest, such as the health of ecosystems and the welfare of future generations. However, the authors appear to stop short of recommending the full internalization of externalities. They see the purpose of environmental cost accounting mainly in monitoring the causes and effects of environmental impacts for possible cost reduction rather than in full-cost pricing of the company's products.

Others ventured straight into costing environmental externalities. The British Association of Chartered Certified Accountants (ACCA) (Bebbington *et al.*, 2001) issued a study on introducing environmental externalities into corporate accounts for the purposes of 'full cost accounting' (FCA). The Canadian Institute of Chartered Accountants (1997) and the Center for Waste Reduction Technologies (1999) have made similar proposals. They take international recommendations on the implementation of sustainable development by means of market instruments as mandates for such external environmental cost accounting.[20] The ACCA study thus proposes to compile parallel (shadow) accounts that display environmental (maintenance) costs without affecting the core financial accounts. This is analogous to the 'satellite' approach taken by the SEEA, although no reference is made to the United Nations (1993 and 2000a) editions of the SEEA.

On the monetary side of corporate accounting, the less problematic assessment of environmental protection expenditures (EPE) has so far made greater strides than the valuation of environmental externalities and natural capital. It is clearly more attractive for a firm to present its environmental protection efforts than to cost its impacts on the outside world. The German Union of Engineers (Verein Deutscher Ingenieure, 2001) thus presented detailed guidelines on costing EPE, defining and classifying end-of-pipe and integrated environmental protection measures. The guidelines do not refer to the detailed Eurostat (1994) recommendations for compiling EPE accounts in a European System for the Collection of Economic Information on the Environment (SERIEE). The reason for this might be a reluctance to alert corporations to potential uses of their data in the national accounts.

The apparent disregard of 'big brother's' national green accounting concepts and methods points to another unfortunate dichotomy between micro- and macro-accounting (besides the monetary–physical one). Linking the two is urgently needed if only to avoid duplication of work, but more importantly to harmonize concepts and methods for comparable bottom-up and top-down environmental reporting and sustainability analysis. For corporations the benefits of such a 'micro–macro link' (MML)[21] include:

- 'a more robust and widely accepted approach to FCA' (as recommended by the ACCA study, Bebbington *et al.*, 2001, p. 134) – in other words, internationally standardized measurement and reporting of environmental sustainability cost
- enhanced compatibility of physical material flow and monetary environmental cost accounts at enterprise, household, regional and national levels
- consistent micro- and macro-economic strategies and policy with regard to the sustainability of production and consumption patterns of economic sectors, corporations and households, and of the overall development of regions and countries.

The integrated – environmental and economic, physical and monetary – accounting system of the SEEA appears to provide, at least for now, the best framework for developing the MML.

5   Policy Use and Analysis

Environmental accounts, just as conventional accounts, serve two basic functions, 'scorekeeping and management' (Peskin, 1998, p. 375). Scorekeeping – that is, the summary assessment of economic performance – has received, perhaps unduly so, the greatest attention from policy-makers and the general public. Policy-makers, in particular, prefer highly aggregated indices to get the picture of the forest rather than being bogged down by looking at trees. Most of the above-discussed 'fuzzy' indices of sustainable development or genuine progress (see section 1.2) cater to this preference. This section looks, however, at the use of more transparent accounting indicators, either directly in policy-making or indirectly through the filter of modelling.

5.1   Modelling versus Accounting

Some national accountants and model-builders consider modelling as a tool of avoiding controversial monetary valuations, especially of environmental externalities (for example, van Dieren, 1995; Vanoli, 1998; Meyer, 1999). De Haan and Keuning express this view clearly in Chapter 12 by assigning a 'zero transaction value' to pollutants and replacing this 'trivial value' (p. 258) by physical units in their accounting matrix. They thus refute any corrections of value added and net or gross domestic product. Instead, they propose Leontief-type input–output analyses of direct and indirect emissions per unit of Dutch guilder of final demand for NAMEA applications (Keuning and de Haan, 1998).

Economic accounting and analysis/modelling are closely related in a chicken-and-egg fashion. On the one hand, the concepts, definitions and structure of the national accounts are derived from analytical macro-variables such as income, consumption, capital, investment and their functional relationships. On the other hand, national accounts concepts deviate from theoretically desirable notions in order to compile observable data from statistical sources; nonetheless, standard economic indicators are widely used in, and thus shape, economic analysis and decision-making. This is particularly evident for the key indicator of the national accounts, national product, and for its use as a welfare measure in optimal growth theory (cf. Weitzman, 1976).[22]

Karl-Göran Mäler (Chapter 17) extends Weitzman's approach to investigate the welfare relevance of environmental expenditures, environmental degradation and natural resource depletion, and to draw conclusions about their role in the national accounts. He shows that sustainable development, defined as constant (non-declining) welfare, requires the preservation of the services of produced capital *and* natural resource stocks. The decrease in these services is accounted for by costing and deducting environmental *damage* from net national product and adding all capital increase. These findings are similar to those of other studies that advocate the internalization of environmental damage for generating an optimal (maximum) national product for the present and future generations (Solow, 1974; Hartwick, 1977; Dasgupta and Mäler, 1991). Thus, neoclassical economic theory seems to support the costing of environmental impacts in greened national accounts.

Note, however, that these analyses call for the valuation of the – damage – costs *borne* by individuals rather than the more practical and consistent (with national accounting standards) – maintenance – costs *caused* by economic agents. Moreover, any rational application of cost-internalization instruments (see section 5.2) requires knowledge about where and when environmental costs were incurred, according to the user/polluter-pays principles. Damage to health and other amenities may occur much later than the physical impacts, may be the result of various synergistic environmental impacts and may affect a large number of persons and institutions. The causes of damage are thus difficult to trace back to specific time periods and responsible economic agents. Mäler himself admits that the theoretical welfare analysis of environmental effects stands little chance of implementation, but serves conceptual clarification.

For the operational purposes of steering the economy on to a sustainable path, the sectors and actors responsible for non-sustainabilities – that is, for particular environmental impacts – need to be identified. National accounts are well suited for providing such sectoral detail, especially through input–output tabulations (United Nations *et al.*, 1993, ch. XV). Wassily Leontief (1906–1999) (Chapter 18) not only pioneered the by now conventional input–output analysis but also extended it into the environmental field. He shows how external effects (of pollution) can be incorporated, first in physical terms, and then – via costing the elimination or prevention of 'intolerable' pollution levels – in money values. He thus avoids the welfare-measurement trap of optimal growth theories and utility maximization. By focusing on environmental cost caused, rather than damage borne, he also sets the stage for maintenance costing applied in the SEEA. Furthermore, his essay illustrates the transition from descriptive compilation and calculation (of missing data for instance by means of emissions coefficients) to the analysis of the effects of environmental cost internalization.

It is thus only a small but significant step to move from costing actual pollution to modelling tolerable pollution levels expressed as standards or targets in input–output models. Roy Brouwer, Martin O'Connor and Walter Radermacher (Chapter 19) propose such modelling in the so-called 'Greenstamp' project.[23] The result is a (hypothetical) 'greened GDP' that would be generated in an economy that complies with these standards. To this end, the authors propose applying a cost-effectiveness analysis which determines the least cost of compliance – quite similar to SEEA's maintenance costing, but 'at various scales of analysis and timeframes' (p. 395). The explicit purpose of modelling the greened GDP is thus to assess 'performance potential . . . that a national economy would be able to achieve while simultaneously respecting specified environmental quality and resource husbandry requirements' (p. 395). Admittedly, such modelling of alternative (in terms of different sets of standards) scenarios 'leads to many sets of time-series for possible greened GDPs' (p. 415).

It might not be easy for policy-makers to choose from these options, given the usually difficult-to-assess underlying model assumptions. There is a lot of merit, though, in Greenstamp's linkage of modelling to environmental accounts. However, the categorical denial of costing environmental impacts in the national accounts themselves may be questioned. For instance, an international panel of renowned experts in the field, established by the US National Academy of Sciences, comes to the conclusion that 'for valuation, BEA [the US Bureau of Economic Analysis] should rely whenever possible on market and behavioral data. However, novel valuation techniques will be necessary for the development of a comprehensive set of nonmarket accounts' (Nordhaus and Kokkelenberg, 1999, p. 7).

5.2 *Policy Use of Accounting Indicators*

Some models make good use of accounting indicators in a more rigorous manner than the intuitive interpretation of data by policy-makers. Direct data use has the advantage, however, of avoiding the analytical straightjacket of model assumptions and simplifications. Conventional economic models have indeed been criticized as puzzle-solving games that ignore real-world social, ecological and moral concerns (Funtowicz and Ravetz, 1991, p. 138).

Direct data use of multi-purpose statistical systems like the national accounts is difficult to determine since these systems are designed to serve the largest possible number of decision-makers (United Nations *et al.*, 1993, paras 1.29–43). Peter Bartelmus (Chapter 20) focuses therefore on particular uses of environmental accounting data, including alerting to undesirable trends of environmental impacts, determining priorities for environmental and economic policies, and setting policy instruments according to the significance (cost value) of environmental impacts. He distinguishes two categories of environmental sustainability of economic performance and growth, viz. ecological and economic sustainability.

Ecological sustainability can be measured in terms of reduced material throughput, i.e. 'dematerialization' of the economy which is a proxy for reduced pressures on natural carrying capacities. Estimates of material intensities of economic performance in industrialized countries (in terms of GDP) indicate a (relative) delinking of environmental pressures from economic growth. Recent results of material flow analyses indicate that such delinkage does not necessarily mean a decrease in absolute levels of material flows because of compensatory GDP increase (Adriaanse *et al.*, 1997; Bringezu, 2002).

On their own, material throughputs cannot answer the question of 'how much' dematerialization is sustainable. Reduction targets for overall natural resource flows by a 'Factor 4' (or even 10) indicate the amount of dematerialization deemed to be necessary for achieving ecological sustainability at a 'desirable' rate of economic growth.[24] A constant high level of natural resource requirements in industrialized nations is thus a far cry from an absolute dematerialization of the economy and reflects a non-sustainable economic performance. The step from assessment to management of dematerialization requires the translation of overall targets into particular standards and 'management rules' (Daly, 1990) for the 'eco-efficient' use of different natural resources. The idea is to increase resource productivity by lowering material inputs and using resources within regenerative and absorptive capacities.

With regard to *economic sustainability*, Bartelmus presents results of SEEA applications which indicate 'weak' sustainability for industrialized countries in terms of overall (produced and natural) capital maintenance. Negative Environmentally-adjusted net Capital Formation (ECF) for some developing countries indicates that these countries failed in maintaining their capital base, impairing the sustainability of future economic growth. He also describes how environmental cost calculations can be used to set the initial level of market instruments in order to attain environmental sustainability of economic activity. Market instruments such as eco-taxes or tradable pollution permits are to prompt economic agents into internalizing environmental costs into their plans and budgets. The objective is to bring about environmentally sound production and consumption patterns, and to encourage technological innovation.

6   Outlook

The 1992 Rio Summit proclaimed sustainable development as the solution to world poverty and environmental decline. Ten years later there is widespread disappointment about the implementation of Rio's Agenda 21. In fact, the weak results of the 2002 Johannesburg Summit appear to confirm a renewed focus on economic growth, thinly veiled by sustainability rhetoric.[25] At the national level, countries tend to relegate the presumably integrative concept of sustainable development to weak environmental ministries and agencies. Difficulties in implementing the complex paradigm of multi-dimensional development and undeniable successes in pollution control could be the reasons. What is overlooked, of course, is that much of the environmental success in industrialized countries is achieved by importing sustainability from other countries through natural resource purchase and translocation of dirty industries.

The reductionist return to conventional economic growth needs to be monitored and reversed. Systemic accounting approaches seem to be our best bet for assessing the relevance of impacts and repercussions between environment and economy; they facilitate the setting of priorities for integrative policies and of applying market instruments according to polluter/user-pays principles.

However, such comprehensive accounting is still work in progress. Various 'dichotomies' mentioned above reflect open questions that future research and methodological development need to address. They include:

- monetary versus physical accounting, and corresponding valuation and evaluation of environmental impacts
- the need for linking corporate and national accounting
- regional (subnational) versus national accounting and corresponding sustainability analyses
- economic (weak) versus ecological (strong) sustainability, captured by monetary and physical indicators, respectively
- systems versus modular frameworks of environmental accounting.

If anything, the acrimonious debate of one daring attempt at questioning the current measurement of environmental impacts (Lomborg, 2001)[26] reveals the crucial role of more transparent and comparative assessments of economic performance and its environmental trade-offs. Such comparison requires the kind of 'weighting' and 'valuing' offered by the main green accounting systems.

The time seems to have come now when official statisticians ought to overcome their reluctance to incorporating such accounts in the repertoire of regular statistical reporting and analysis. This could be facilitated by parallel ('satellite') accounts. Such accounts give data users a choice between conventional and greened accounts in deciding what they need for assessing the sustainability of economic activity. Should we not get the information we need (even at the price of some rough estimation), rather than get accurate statistics we do not need? International efforts at standardizing green accounting (Eurostat, 2001; United Nations, 1993, 2000a, and the ongoing revision of the SEEA) can be expected to overcome some of the qualms of national accountants.

The current revision of the SEEA is, however, ambivalent with regard to the physical–monetary dichotomy. On the one hand, the draft of the revised SEEA (United Nations *et al.*, in prep.) incorporates hardly applicable (at national levels) welfare valuations (see section 3.2). On the other hand, recurrent warnings against any monetary valuation indicate a predilection for physical accounting. As a result, the integrative systemic character of the original SEEA cannot be kept up.[27]

Finally, we should be aware that to date, for reasons of measurability, green accounting has focused on the immediate interface between environment and economy, and hence on the sustainability of economic performance and growth. Such accounting ignores important dimensions of the sustainable *development* paradigm. Some of these dimensions, like health, security or biodiversity, do not (yet?) fit into the accounting frameworks. Non-economic needs and values could however be specified as exogenous targets and thresholds of a normative policy framework, as suggested by Bartelmus (Chapter 20). Within this framework, conventional and environmentally sustainable economic strategies could be played out. Appropriate 'social' indicators would have to monitor violations of, or compliance with, the social restrictions posed by the framework.

There are, though, some promising attempts at extending the accounting boundaries for the assessment of the formation and use of human and social capital (van Tongeren and Becker, 1995; Bos, 1996). Another attempt at 'nearly comprehensive' accounting is the compilation of a 'magic triangle' of input–output tables in monetary, physical and time units (Stahmer, 2000). The time accounts, in particular, are well suited to assessing human capital inputs and investment. These approaches need to be nurtured and tested, with a view to making them an instrument of regular reporting on sustainable development. The sustainability of the paradigm might depend on it.

Acknowledgements

Comments by Stefan Bringezu of the Wuppertal Institute are gratefully acknowledged.

Notes

1   Authors of the essays presented in the book are cited with chapter numbers in parentheses; other references are shown in usual (author and year of publication) form.
2   Such placement and interpretation necessitates some evaluation of the different tools of measuring sustainability. The views expressed in this regard are thus those of the authors and not necessarily those of their current or former affiliations.
3   Reflected in well-known publications such as *Silent Spring* (Carson, 1965), *Death of Tomorrow* (Loraine, 1972), or the Club of Rome's *Limits to Growth* (Meadows *et al.*, 1972). The latter predicted a 'rather sudden and uncontrollable decline in both population and industrial capacity' for this century.
4   The FDES was later picked up by the Organisation for Economic Co-operation and Development (OECD) as a 'stress-response' framework for environmental indicators (OECD, 1994).
5   The environmental sustainability index was advanced by a consortium of US research institutes (Global Leaders of Tomorrow, 2002).
6   Quadruple-entry accounting is a feature of the established national accounts where 'transactions between economic agents are recorded simultaneously for each agent from a debit and credit angle' (United Nations *et al.*, 1993, para. 1.58).
7   Green accounting is a popular term for 'environmental accounting' or more exactly 'integrated environmental and economic accounting'. All these terms include accounting in physical and/or monetary units. They are used interchangeably in the following, even if some authors seem to distinguish physical – material flow – accounts from monetary 'environmental' ones.
8   This crude distinction between holistic views of the human environment and mainstream (neoclassical) economic approaches to the environment–economy interface is, of course, a simplification of existing schools of thought. For instance, 'ecological economists' can be placed somewhere in-between, while the 'bioeconomists'' focus on biological processes is close to the ecological world-view.
9   Quesnay himself called his *Tableau* 'booklet of housekeeping' (*livret de ménage*) (Kuczynski, 1971, p. 382).

10   Smith (1776, 1991 edn, p. 448) was particularly piqued by the physiocrats' honouring the farmers 'with the peculiar appellation of the productive class' while degrading 'artificers, manufacturers and merchants by the humiliating appellation of the barren or unproductive class'.

11   See note 3. For a 'rediscovery' of some largely ignored precursors of environmental and ecological economics, see Seifert (1985) and Martinez-Alier (1987).

12   Later renamed Net Economic Welfare (NEW) by Samuelson and Nordhaus (1992, pp. 429–31) in their textbook. See Eisner (1988) for a review of this and other measures to better reflect economic welfare in 'extended national income and product accounts'.

13   See also Georgescu-Roegen (1971). Boulding (1966) vividly expressed similar ideas by the metaphor of the 'cowboy economy' which exploits the closed system of 'spaceship earth'. A critical review of Georgescu-Roegen's contribution to the field of ecological economics is given in a special issue of *Ecological Economics* 22/3 (1997).

14   As do others: see for a brief critical review of the 'energy theory of value' Söllner (1997, pp. 190–92).

15   Note that the original SEEA did allow for 'contingent valuation' (a particular form of damage valuation) in a separate version, albeit for 'experimentation' only (United Nations, 1993, para. 322). However, actual damage estimates were typically conducted outside the national accounts system, suffering from similar flaws as the above-described (section 1.2) indices of sustainable development.

16   Or lower at that: for example, in the Philippines the costs of water pollution control were estimated at nearly 10 times the benefits on health, ecosystems and economic productivity (delos Angeles and Peskin, 1998, p. 99). In Germany, environmental damage estimates range between 100 and 1000 billion DM (Wicke, 1993, pp. 60 *et seq.*), depending on the definition, coverage and valuation mix of the damages.

17   'Equivalent factors' estimate the contribution of individual indicators to the policy themes of the greenhouse effect, ozone layer depletion, acidification or waste accumulation. However, such calculations still do not permit inter-theme comparisons.

18   An assessment of the recent burst of activities in this area is beyond this volume. See for an overview, United Nations (2000c).

19   The Kunert AG report was chosen as the 'world-best' by SustainAbility Ltd., a London-based research institute, on behalf of the United Nations Environment Programme (UNEP) in 1995.

20   The European Union's Fifth Action Programme (European Commission, 1992, p. 72) considers that, with a view to getting the prices right, 'valuations, pricing and accounting mechanisms have a pivotal role to play in the achievement of sustainable development'. Similarly, Agenda 21 of the United Nations recommends that 'governments, business and industry, . . . academia and international organizations should work towards . . . the internalization of environmental costs into accounting and pricing mechanisms' (United Nations, 1993, para. 30.9).

21   For a more general description of the MML in national accounting, see the SNA (United Nations *et al.*, 1993, paras 1.58–67) and a handbook on SNA implementation (United Nations, 2000b).

22   Cf. the above-described (section 3.2) valuation controversy where economists call for damage valuation and pragmatic accountants settle for maintenance costing. Another issue is the treatment of Hicksian income in the SNA (United Nations *et al.*, 1993, para. 8.15) where *ex ante* and *ex post* views of the income concept seem to clash.

23   A research group, consisting of the statistical offices of the Netherlands and Germany, the University of Paris-Versailles, the German Institute for Ecological-Economic Research (IÖW) and the Wuppertal Institute for Climate, Environment and Energy, carried out the EU-sponsored project.

24   The Factor 4 goal of halving material input while doubling wealth and welfare (von Weizsäcker, Lovins and Lovins, 1997) is derived from the need of maintaining the 'long-term ecological equilibrium of the planet'. Under current production and consumption patterns, global Factor 4 corresponds to a Factor 10 for industrialized countries. The assumption is that equal access to environmental services should be reached by all in about 50 years while permitting a limited increase of material use in developing countries (Schmidt-Bleek, 1994, p. 168).

25   The Monterrey Consensus (of 22 March 2002) of the International Conference on Financing for Development, whose focus on public-private partnerships was taken up by the Johannesburg Summit, is quite revealing in its goals to '*achieve* sustained economic growth and *promote* sustainable development' (United Nations document A/CONF. 198/3, para. 1), our emphasis.

26 See the overview given in *The Economist* of 2–8 February 2002, pp. 15–16 and 71–72.
27 In fact, the last draft of the revised SEEA (United Nations *et al.*, in prep.) seems to have dropped 'System' from its title.

References

Adriaanse, A. *et al.* (1997), *Resource Flows: The Material Basis of Industrial Economies*, Washington, DC: World Resources Institute.

Alfsen, K.H. (1996), 'Macroeconomics and the Environment: Norwegian Experience', in V.P. Gandhi (ed.), *Macroeconomics and the Environment*, Washington, DC: International Monetary Fund.

Alfsen, K.H., Bye, T. and Lorentsen, L. (1987), *Natural Resource Accounting and Analysis in Norway*, Oslo: Central Bureau of Statistics.

Ayres, R.U. and Kneese, A. (1969), 'Production, Consumption, and Externalities', *American Economic Review*, **59**, pp. 282–97.

Bartelmus, P. (1994), *Environment, Growth and Development: The Concepts and Strategies of Sustainability*, London and New York: Routledge.

Bartelmus, P. (1998), 'The Value of Nature – Valuation and Evaluation in Environmental Accounting', in K. Uno and P. Bartelmus (eds), *Environmental Accounting in Theory and Practice*, Dordrecht, Boston and London: Kluwer Academic Publishers.

Bartelmus, P. (2001), 'Accounting for Sustainability: Greening the National Accounts', in M.K. Tolba (ed.), *Our Fragile World, Challenges and Opportunities for Sustainable Development*, Forerunner to the Encyclopedia of Life Support Systems, Vol. II, Oxford: EOLSS Publishers.

Bartelmus, P. (2002), 'Unveiling Wealth – Accounting for Sustainability', in P. Bartelmus (ed.), *Unveiling Wealth – On Money, Quality of Life and Sustainability*, Dordrecht, Boston and London: Kluwer Academic Publishers.

Baumol, W.J. and Oates, W.E. (1971), 'The Use of Standards and Prices for Protection of the Environment', *Swedish Journal of Economics*, **73**, pp. 42–54.

Bebbington, J., Gray, R., Hibbitt, C. and Kirk, E. (2001), *Full Cost Accounting: An Agenda for Action*, ACCA Research Report No. 73, London: The Association of Chartered Certified Accountants.

Bos, F. (1996), 'Human Capital and Economic Growth: A National Accounting Approach', Paper presented at the 1996 IARIW Conference in Lillehammer.

Boulding, K.E. (1966), 'The Economics of the Coming Spaceship Earth', in H. Jarret (ed.), *Environmental Quality in a Growing Economy*, Baltimore: Johns Hopkins Press for Resources for the Future.

Bringezu, S. (1993), 'Towards Increasing Resource Productivity: How to Measure the Total Material Consumption of Regional or National Economies?', *Fresenius Environmental Bulletin*, **2**, pp. 437–42.

Bringezu, S. (2002), 'Industrial Ecology: Analyses for Sustainable Resource and Materials Management in Germany and Europe', in R.U. Ayres and L.W. Ayres (eds), *A Handbook of Industrial Ecology*, Cheltenham, UK and Northampton MA, USA: Edward Elgar.

Brown, L.R. (1993), 'A New Era Unfolds', in L.R. Brown *et al.* (eds), *State of the World 1993 – A Worldwatch Institute Report on Progress Toward a Sustainable Society*, New York and London: Norton.

Canadian Institute of Chartered Accountants (1997), *Full Cost Accounting from an Environmental Perspective*, Toronto: CICA.

Carson, R. (1965), *Silent Spring*, London: Penguin.

Center for Waste Reduction Technologies (1999), *Total Cost Assessment Methodology: Internal Managerial Decision Making Tool*, New York: CWRT.

Cobb, C., Halstead, T. and Rowe, J. (1995), 'If the GDP is Up, Why is America Down?', *The Atlantic Monthly*, October, pp. 59–78.

Costanza, R. (1980), 'Embodied Energy and Economic Valuation', *Science*, **210**, pp. 1219–24.

Cottrell, W.F. (1970, first edn 1955), *Energy and Society*, Westport: Greenwood Press.

Daly, H.E. (1990), 'Towards Some Operational Principles of Sustainable Development', *Ecological Economics*, **2**, pp. 1–6.

Daly, H.E. (1996), *Beyond Growth*, Boston: Beacon Press.

Daly, H.E. and Cobb, J.B. Jr (1989), *For the Common Good: Redirecting the Economy Towards Community, the Environment, and a Sustainable Future*, Boston, Mass.: Beacon Press.

Dasgupta, P. and Mäler, K.-G. (1991), *The Environment and Emerging Development Issues*, Beijer Reprint Series No. 1, Stockholm: Beijer.

delos Angeles, M.S. and Peskin, H. (1998), 'Philippines: Environmental Accounting as Instrument of Policy', in K. Uno and P. Bartelmus (eds), *Environmental Accounting in Theory and Practice*, Dordrecht, Boston and London: Kluwer Academic Publishers.

Drewnowski, J. (1970), *Studies in the Measurement of Levels of Living and Welfare*, Geneva: UNRISD.

Drewnowski, J. (1974), *On Measuring and Planning the Quality of Life*, Publications of the Institute of Social Studies, The Hague and Paris: Mouton.

Eisner, R. (1988), 'Extended Accounts for National Income and Product', *Journal of Economic Literature*, **XXVI**, pp. 1611–84.

European Commission (1992), *The Fifth Action Programme*, Brussels: European Commission.

Eurostat (1994), *SERIEE. The European System for the Collection of Economic Information on the Environment*, Luxembourg: European Communities.

Eurostat (2001), *Economy-wide Material Flow Accounts and Derived Indicators: A Methodological Guide*, Luxembourg: European Communities.

Fergany, N. (1994), 'Quality of Life Indicators for Arab Countries in an International Context', *International Statistical Review*, **62** (2), pp. 187–202.

Fischer-Kowalski, M. (1998), 'Society's Metabolism: The Intellectual History of Materials Flow Analysis, Part I, 1860–1970', *Journal of Industrial Ecology*, **2** (1), pp. 61–78.

Fischer-Kowalski, M. and Hüttler, W. (1999), 'Society's Metabolism: The Intellectual History of Materials Flow Analysis, Part II, 1970–1998', *Journal of Industrial Ecology*, **2** (4), pp. 107–36.

Funtowicz, S.O. and Ravetz, J.R. (1991), 'A New Scientific Methodology for Global Environmental Issues', in R. Costanza (ed.), *Ecological Economics: The Science and Management of Sustainability*, New York: Columbia University Press.

Gawel, E. (1998), 'Das Elend der Stoffstromökonomie – Eine Kritik [The misery of material flow economics – a critique]', *Konjunkturpolitik*, **44** (2), pp. 173–206.

Georgescu-Roegen, N. (1971), *The Entropy Law and the Economic Process*, Cambridge, MA: Harvard University Press.

Global Leaders of Tomorrow Environment Task Force, World Economic Forum, Annual Meeting (2002), *2002 Environmental Sustainability Index*, New Haven: Yale Center for Environmental Law and Policy.

Gray, R.H. (1990), *The Greening of Accountancy: The Profession after Pearce*, London: Association of Chartered Certified Accountants.

Gray, R.H. (1992), 'Accounting and Environmentalism: An Exploration of the Challenge of Gently Accounting for Accountability, Transparency and Sustainability', *Accounting Organisations and Society*, **17** (5), pp. 399–425.

Hamilton, C. (1999), 'The Genuine Progress Indicator, Methodological Developments and Results from Australia', *Ecological Economics*, **30**, pp. 13–28.

Hartwick, J.M. (1977), 'Intergenerational Equity and the Investing of Rents from Exhaustible Resources', *American Economic Review*, **67** (3), pp. 972–74.

Henderson, H., Lickerman, J. and Flynn, P. (eds) (2000), *Calvert-Henderson Quality of Life Indicators*, Bethesda, MD: Calvert Group.

Hinterberger, F., Luks, F. and Schmidt-Bleek, F. (1997), 'Material Flows vs. "Natural Capital": What Makes an Economy Sustainable?', *Ecological Economics*, **23**, pp. 1–14.

Hoffmann-Nowotny, H.-J. (1981), *Sozialbilanzierung [Social accounting]*, Vol. VIII, Ser. *Soziale Indikatoren-Konzepte und Forschungsansätze*, Frankfurt/Main: Campus.

Hueting, R. (1993), 'Calculating a Sustainable National Income: A Practical Solution for a Theoretical Dilemma', in A. Franz and C. Stahmer (eds), *Approaches to Environmental Accounting: Proceedings of the IARIW Conference on Environmental Accounting* (Baden, Austria, 27–29 May 1991), Heidelberg: Physica.

Jevons, W.S. (1865, 1965 edn), *The Coal Question: An Inquiry Concerning the Progress of the Nation, and the Probable Exhaustion of Our Coal Mines*, reprint of the 3rd edn, New York: Augustus Kelly.

Kapp, K.W. (1950), *The Social Costs of Private Enterprise*, Boston, Mass.: Harvard University Press.

Kapp, K.W. (1963), *The Social Costs of Business Enterprise*, 2nd and enlarged edn, Bombay and London: Asia Publishing House.

Kapp, K.W. (1971), *The Social Costs of Private Enterprise*, New York: Schocken Books.

Keuning, S.J. and de Haan, M. (1998), 'Netherlands: What's in a NAMEA? Recent Results', in K. Uno and P. Bartelmus (eds), *Environmental Accounting in Theory and Practice*, Dordrecht, Boston and London: Kluwer Academic Publishers.

Kneese, A.V., Ayres, R.U. and d'Arge, R.C. (1970), *Economics and the Environment. A Material Balance Approach*, Baltimore, ML and London: Johns Hopkins University Press.

Kuczynski, M. (1971), 'Quesnay', in *Ökonomische Schriften*, Bd. 1, Berlin: Akademie-Verlag.

Leipert, C. (1989), 'National Income and Economic Growth: The Conceptual Side of Defensive Expenditures', *Journal of Economic Issues*, **23**, pp. 843–56.

Leontief, W. (1987), 'Quesnays "Tableau économique" und die Einsatz–Ausstoß-Analyse [Quesnay's *Tableau Économique* and the Input–Output Analysis]', in W. Leontief and H.C. Recktenwald (eds), *Über François Quesnays 'Physiokratie'* (Vademecum zu einem frühen Klassiker der ökonomischen Wissenschaft), Düsseldorf: Wirtschaft und Finanzen.

Lomborg, B. (2001), *The Skeptical Environmentalist – Measuring the Real State of the World*, Cambridge: Cambridge University Press.

Loraine, J.A.C. (1972), *The Death of Tomorrow*, London: Heinemann.

Markandya, A. and Pavan, M. (eds) (1999), *Green Accounting in Europe – Four Case Studies*, Dordrecht, Boston and London: Kluwer Academic Publishers.

Martinez-Alier, J. (1987), *Ecological Economics, Energy, Environment and Society*, Oxford: Basil Blackwell.

Marx, K. (1894, 1965 edn), 'Theorien über den Mehrwert [Theories of Surplus Value]', in Institut für Marxismus-Leninismus beim ZK der SED (ed.), *Karl Marx, Friedrich Engels*, Band 26, erster Teil, Berlin: Dietz.

Matthews, E. *et al.* (2000), *The Weight of Nations. Material Outflows from Industrial Economies*, Washington, DC: World Resources Institute.

Mayumi, K. (2001), *The Origins of Ecological Economics. The Bioeconomics of Georgescu-Roegen*, London and New York: Routledge.

Meadows, D.H., Meadows, D.L., Randers, J. and Behrens III, W.W. (1972), *The Limits to Growth*, New York: Universe Books.

Meyer, B. (1999), 'Research-Statistical-Policy Co-operation in Germany: Modelling with Panta Rhei', in European Commission, *From Research to Implementation: Policy-driven Methods for Evaluating Macro-economic Environmental Performance*, EU RTD in Human Dimensions of Environmental Change Report Series, European Commission.

Moldan, B., Billharz, S. and Matravers, R. (eds) (1997), *Sustainability Indicators: A Report on the Project on Indicators of Sustainable Development*, Chichester: Wiley.

Müller-Wenck, R. (1978), *Die ökologische Buchhaltung. Ein Informations- und Steuerungsinstrument für umweltkonforme Unternehmenspolitik [Ecological Bookkeeping. An Information and Control Instrument for Environmentally Sound Corporate Policy]*, Frankfurt/Main and New York: Campus.

Nordhaus, W.D. and Kokkelenberg, E.C. (eds) (1999), *Nature's Numbers – Expanding the National Accounts to Include the Environment*, Washington, DC: National Academy Press.

Nováček, P. and Mederly, P. (2002), *Global Partnership for Development*, Olomouc: Palacky University.

Odum, H.T. (1971), *Environment, Power and Society*, New York: Wiley.

Odum, H.T. (1996), *Environmental Accounting. Energy and Environmental Decision Making*, New York: Wiley.

Organisation for Economic Co-operation and Development (OECD) (1973), *List of Social Concerns Common to Most OECD Countries*, Paris: OECD.

Organisation for Economic Co-operation and Development (OECD) (1994), *Environmental Indicators*, Paris: OECD.

Peskin, H.M. (1998), 'Alternative Resource and Environmental Accounting Approaches and their Contribution to Policy', in K. Uno and P. Bartelmus (eds), *Environmental Accounting in Theory and Practice*, Dordrecht, Boston and London: Kluwer Academic Publishers.

Pezzey, J. (1989), 'Economic Analysis of Sustainable Growth and Sustainable Development', Environment Department Working Paper No. 15, Washington, DC: The World Bank.

Phillips, A. (1955), 'The Tableau Économique as a Simple Leontief Model', *Quarterly Journal of Economics*, **69**, pp. 137–44.

Pigou, A.C. (1920, 1932 edn), *The Economics of Welfare*, 4th edn, London: Macmillan.

Samuelson, P.A. and Nordhaus, W.D. (1992), *Economics*, 14th edn, New York: McGraw-Hill.

Schaltegger, S. and Burritt, R. (2000), *Contemporary Environmental Accounting. Issues, Concepts and Practice*, Sheffield: Greenleaf Publishing.

Schmidt-Bleek, F. (1993), 'MIPS – A Universal Ecological Measure?', *Fresenius Environmental Bulletin*, **2**, pp. 306–11.

Schmidt-Bleek, F. (1994), *Wieviel Umwelt braucht der Mensch? MIPS, das Maß für ökologisches Wirtschaften [How Much Environment Do We Need? MIPS, the Measure for Ecologically Sound Economic Performance]*, Berlin, Basel and Boston: Birkhäuser.

Seifert, E.K. (1985), 'Zur "Naturvergessenheit" ökonomischer Theorien [Ignoring Nature in Economic Theories]', in R. Pfriem (ed.), *Ökologische Unternehmenspolitik*, Frankfurt/Main: Campus.

Seifert, E.K. (1993), 'Georgescu-Roegen', in G. Hodgson, W. Samuels and M. Tool (eds), *International Handbook for Institutional Economics*, Aldershot and Vermont: Edward Elgar.

Slesser, M. (1975), 'Accounting for Energy', *Nature*, **254**, pp. 170–72.

Smith, A. (1776, 1991 edn), *Wealth of Nations*, Amherst, NY: Prometheus Books.

Söllner, F. (1997), 'A Reexamination of the Role of Thermodynamics for Environmental Economics', *Ecological Economics*, **22** (3), pp. 175–201.

Solow, R.M. (1974), 'Intergenerational Equity and Exhaustible Resources', *Review of Economic Studies*, Symposium, pp. 29–46.

Stahmer, C. (2000), 'The Magic Triangle of I-O Tables', in S. Simon and J. Proops (eds), *Greening the Accounts*, Cheltenham: Edward Elgar.

Stahmer, C., Kuhn, M. and Braun, N. (1998), 'Physical Input–Output Tables for Germany 1990', *Eurostat Working Paper*, No. 2/1998/B/1, Luxembourg: Eurostat.

Steurer, A. (1992), *Stoffstrombilanz Österreich 1988* [Material Flow Balance Austria 1988], Schriftenreihe Soziale Ökologie, Vol. 26, Vienna: Institut für interdisziplinäre Forschung und Fortbildung der Universitäten Innsbruck, Klagenfurt und Wien.

Theys, J. (1989), 'Environmental Accounting in Development Policy: The French Experience', in Y.J. Ahmad, S. El Serafy and E. Lutz (eds), *Environmental Accounting for Sustainable Development*, Washington, DC: The World Bank.

United Nations (1973), *Report of the United Nations Conference on the Human Environment, Stockholm, 5–16 June 1972*, New York: United Nations (sales no. E.73.II.A.14).

United Nations (1977), *Statistical Commission, Report of the Nineteenth Session*, New York: United Nations.

United Nations (1984), *A Framework for the Development of Environment Statistics*, New York: United Nations (sales no. E.84.XVII.12).

United Nations (1988), *Concepts and Methods of Environment Statistics: Human Settlement Statistics – A Technical Report*, New York: United Nations (sales no. E.88.XVII.14).

United Nations (1991), *Concepts and Methods of Environment Statistics: Statistics of the Natural Environment – A Technical Report*, New York: United Nations (sales no. E.91.XVII.18).

United Nations (1993), *Integrated Environmental and Economic Accounting*, New York: United Nations (sales no. E.93.XVII.12).

United Nations (1994), *Earth Summit, Agenda 21, the United Nations Programme of Action from Rio*, New York: United Nations (sales no. E.93.I.11).

United Nations (2000a), *Integrated Environmental and Economic Accounting – An Operational Manual*, New York: United Nations (sales no. E.00.XVII.17).

United Nations (2000b), *Links Between Business Accounting and National Accounting*, New York: United Nations (sales no. E.00.XVII.13).

United Nations (2000c), *Improving Governments' Role in the Promotion of Environmental Managerial Accounting*, New York: United Nations (sales no. E.00.II.A.2).

United Nations (2001), *Indicators of Sustainable Development, Guidelines and Methodologies*, New York: United Nations (sales no. E.01.II.A.6).

United Nations Development Programme (UNDP) (annual), *Human Development Report*, Oxford: Oxford University Press.

United Nations *et al.* (1993), *System of National Accounts 1993*, New York and others: United Nations (sales no. E.94.XVII.4) and others.

United Nations *et al.* (in prep.), *Integrated Environmental and Economic Accounting, 2003*, New York and others: United Nations and others.

Vaggi, G. (1987), 'Quesnay, François', in J. Eatwell, M. Millgate and P. Newman (eds), *The New Palgrave, A Dictionary of Economics*, Vol. 4, Q–Z, London and Basingstoke: Macmillan.

van Dieren, W. (ed.) (1995), *Taking Nature Into Account*, New York: Springer.

Vanoli, A. (1998), 'Modelling and Accounting Work in National and Environmental Accounts', in K. Uno and P. Bartelmus (eds), *Environmental Accounting in Theory and Practice*, Dordrecht, Boston and London: Kluwer Academic Publishers.

van Tongeren, J. and Becker, B. (1995), 'Integrated Satellite Accounting, Socio-economic Concerns and Modelling', DESIPA Working Paper Series, No. 10, New York: United Nations.

Verein Deutscher Ingenieure (VDI) (2001), *Determination of Costs for Industrial Environmental Protection Measures* (VDI guideline 3800), Berlin: Beuth.

von Weizsäcker, E.U., Lovins, A. and Lovins, H. (1997), *Factor Four: Doubling Wealth – Halving Resource Use*, London: Earthscan.

Wackernagel, M. and Rees, W. (1996), *Our Ecological Footprint, Reducing Human Impact on Earth*, Gabriola Island, BC and Philadelphia, PA: New Society Publishers.

Weber, J-L. (1983), 'The French Natural Patrimony Accounts', *Statistical Journal of the United Nations ECE*, **1**, pp. 419–44.

Weitzman, M. (1976), 'On the Welfare Significance of National Product in a Dynamic Economy', *Quarterly Journal of Economics*, **90**, pp. 156–62.

Wicke, L. (1993), *Umweltökonomie: Eine praxisorientierte Einführung* [*Environmental Economics: A Practical Introduction*], Munich: Franz Vahlen.

World Bank (1997), *Expanding the Measure of Wealth, Indicators of Environmentally Sustainable Development*, Washington, DC: The World Bank.

World Commission on Environment and Development (WCED) (1987), *Our Common Future*, Oxford: Oxford University Press.

Part I
Taking Environment into Account: A Historical Perspective

[1]

François Quesnay

The 'Third Edition' of the
TABLEAU ÉCONOMIQUE

Facsimile Reproduction and
English Translation

TABLEAU ÉCONOMIQUE.

Objets à considérer, 1.º Trois sortes de dépenses ; 2.º leur source ; 3.º leurs avances ; 4.º leur distribution ; 5.º leurs effets ; 6.º leur reproduction ; 7.º leurs rapports entr'elles ; 8.º leurs rapports avec la population ; 9.º avec l'Agriculture ; 10.º avec l'industrie ; 11.º avec le commerce ; 12.º avec la masse des richesses d'une Nation.

DÉPENSES PRODUCTIVES *relatives à l'Agriculture &c.*	DÉPENSES DU REVENU, *l'Impôt prélevé, se partage aux Dépenses productives et aux Dépenses stériles.*	DÉPENSES STÉRILES *relatives à l'industrie, &c*
Avances annuelles pour produire un revenu de 600.ᵗᵗ sont 600.ᵗᵗ	*Revenu annuel de*	*Avances annuelles pour les Ouvrages des Dépenses Stériles, sont*
600.ᵗᵗ produisent net............	600.ᵗᵗ	300.ᵗᵗ

Productions............................ *moitié passe ici* Ouvrages, &c.

300.ᵗᵗ reproduisent net........300.ᵗᵗ	*moitié*	300.ᵗᵗ
150. reproduisent net.........150.	*passe icy*	150.
75. reproduisent net..........75.		75.
37..10.ˢ reproduisent net......37..10.		37..10
18..15. reproduisent net........18..15.		18..15
9...7...6.ᵈ reproduisent net......9...7...6.		9...7...6.
4..13...0. reproduisent net......4..13...9.		4..13...9
2..6..10. reproduisent net.......2..6..10.		2...6...10
1...3...5. reproduisent net.........1...3...5.		1...3...5
0..11...8. reproduisent net......0...11...8.		0..11....8
0...5..10. reproduisent net.........0...5..10.		0...5...10
0...2..11. reproduisent net........0...2...11.		0...2...11
0....1...5 reproduisent net..........0...1...5		0...1....5

&c.

REPRODUIT TOTAL..............600.ᵗᵗ *de revenu ; de plus, les frais annuels de 600.ᵗᵗ et les interêts des avances primitives du Laboureur, de 300.ᵗᵗ que la terre restitue. Ainsi la réproduction est de 1500.ᵗᵗ compris le revenu de 600.ᵗᵗ qui est la base du calcul, abstraction faite de l'impôt prélevé, et des avances qu'exige sa reproduction annuelle, &c. Voyez l'Explication à la page suivante.*

TABLEAU ÉCONOMIQUE[1]

Objects to be considered: (1) three kinds of expenditure; (2) their source; (3) their advances; (4) their distribution; (5) their effects; (6) their reproduction; (7) their relations with one another; (8) their relations with the population; (9) with agriculture; (10) with industry; (11) with trade; (12) with the total wealth of a nation.

PRODUCTIVE EXPENDITURE	EXPENDITURE OF THE REVENUE	STERILE EXPENDITURE
relative to agriculture, etc.	after deduction of taxes, is divided between productive expenditure and sterile expenditure	relative to industry, etc.
Annual advances required to produce a revenue of 600^l are 600^l	Annual revenue	Annual advances for the works of sterile expenditure are

600^l produce net .... 600^l .... 300^l

Products *one-half goes here* .... *one-half goes here* Works, etc.

300^l reproduce net ...... *one-half* ..... 300^l ..... *one-half* ..... 300^l
goes here .... *goes here*

150 reproduce net .... 150 ..... *one-half, etc.* 150
..... *one-half, etc.* .....

75 reproduce net 75 75

37..10^s reproduce net .... 37..10 ....37..10

18..15 reproduce net .... 18..15 ....18..15

9...7...6^d reproduce net ....9...7...6^d ....9...7...6^d

4..13...9 reproduce net ....4..13...9 ....4..13...9

2...6..10 reproduce net ....2...6..10 ....2...6..10

1...3...5 reproduce net ....1...3...5 ....1...3...5

0..11...8 reproduce net ....0..11...8 ....0..11...8

0...5..10 reproduce net ....0...5..10 ....0...5..10

0...2..11 reproduce net ....0...2..11 ....0...2..11

0...1...5 reproduce net ....0...1...5 ....0...1...5

etc.

TOTAL REPRODUCED ...... 600^l of revenue; in addition, the annual costs of 600^l and the interest on the original advances of the husbandman amounting to 300^l, which the land restores. Thus the reproduction is 1500^l, including the revenue of 600^l which forms the base of the calculation, abstraction being made of the taxes deducted and of the advances which their annual reproduction entails, etc. See the Explanation on the following page.

EXPLICATION
DU TABLEAU ÉCONOMIQUE.

LES *Dépenses productives* font employées à l'agriculture, prairies, pâtures, forêts, mines, pêche, &c. pour perpétuer les richeffes, en grains, boiffons, bois, beftiaux, matières premières des ouvrages de main-d'œuvre, &c.

Les *Dépenses stériles* fe font en marchandifes de main-d'œuvre, logemens, vêtemens, intérêts d'argent, domeftiques, frais de commerce, denrées étrangères, &c.

La vente du produit net que le Cultivateur a fait naître l'année précédente, par le moyen des *Avances annuelles* de 600 liv. employées à la culture par le Fermier, fournit au Propriétaire le payement d'un *revenu* de 600 livres.

Les *avances annuelles* de 300 liv. des dépenfes ftériles font employées pour les fonds & les frais du commerce, pour les achats de matière première d'ouvrage de main-d'œuvre, & pour la fubfiftance & autres befoins de l'artifan, jufqu'à ce qu'il ait achevé & vendu fon ouvrage.

Les *600 liv. de revenu* font dépenfées par le Propriétaire, moitié à la claffe des dépenfes productives en pain, vin, viande, &c. & l'autre moitié à la claffe des dépenfes ftériles en vêtemens, emmeublemens, uftenfiles, &c.

Ces dépenfes peuvent fe porter plus ou moins d'un côté ou de l'autre, felon que celui qui les fait fe livre plus ou moins au luxe de fubfiftance, ou au luxe de décoration. On a pris ici l'état moyen où les dépenfes reproductives renouvellent d'année en année le même revenu. Mais on

a

EXPLANATION

OF THE *TABLEAU ÉCONOMIQUE*

Productive expenditure is employed in agriculture, grasslands, pastures, forests, mines, fishing, etc., in order to perpetuate wealth in the form of corn, drink, wood, livestock, raw materials for manufactured goods, etc.

Sterile expenditure is on manufactured commodities, house-room, clothing, interest on money, servants, commercial costs, foreign produce, etc.

The sale of the net product which the cultivator has generated in the previous year, by means of the *annual advances* of 600 livres employed in cultivation by the farmer, results in the payment to the proprietor of a *revenue* of 600 livres.

The *annual advances* of the sterile expenditure class, amounting to 300 livres, are employed for the capital and costs of trade, for the purchase of raw materials for manufactured goods, and for the subsistence and other needs of the artisan until he has completed and sold his work.

Of the *600 livres of revenue*, one-half is spent by the proprietor in purchasing bread, wine, meat, etc., from the productive expenditure class, and the other half in purchasing clothing, furnishings, utensils, etc., from the sterile expenditure class.

This expenditure may go more or less to one side or the other, according as the man who engages in it goes in more or less for luxury in the way of subsistence or for luxury in the way of ornamentation. We assume here a medium situation in which the reproductive expenditure renews the same revenue from year to year. But it is easy to estimate the changes which

ij

peut juger facilement des changemens qui arriveroient dans la reproduction annuelle du revenu, felon que les dépenfes ftériles ou les dépenfes productives l'emporteroient plus ou moins l'une fur l'autre: on peut, dis-je, en juger facilement par les changemens mêmes qui arriveroient dans l'ordre du tableau. Car fuppofé que le luxe de décoration augmentât d'un fixième chez le Propriétaire, d'un fixième chez l'Artifan, d'un fixième chez le Cultivateur, la reproduction du revenu de 600 liv. fe réduiroit à 500 liv. Si au contraire l'augmentation de dépenfe étoit portée à ce degré du côté de la confommation, ou de l'exportation des denrées du cru, la reproduction du revenu de 600 liv. monteroit à 700 liv. ainfi progreffivement. On voit par-là que l'excès du luxe de décoration peut très-promptement ruiner avec magnificence une Nation opulente.

Les 300 livres du revenu qui dans l'ordre du tableau ont paffé aux dépenfes productives, y rendent en argent des *avances*, lefquelles reproduifent net 300 liv. qui font partie de la reproduction du revenu du Propriétaire: Et par le refte de la diftribution des fommes qui reviennent à cette même claffe, le revenu total eft reproduit annuellement. Ces 300 liv. dis-je, qui reviennent d'abord à la claffe des dépenfes productives par la vente des productions que le Propriétaire y achette, font dépenfées par le Fermier, moitié en confommation de productions fournies par cette même claffe, & l'autre moitié en entretien de vêtemens, uftenfiles, inftrumens, &c. qu'il paye à la claffe des dépenfes ftériles. Et elles renaiffent avec le produit net.

Les 300 liv. du revenu du Propriétaire, qui ont paffé à la claffe des dépenfes ftériles, font dépenfées par l'artifan,

would take place in the annual reproduction of revenue, according as
sterile expenditure or productive expenditure preponderated to a greater
or lesser degree. It is easy to estimate them, I say, simply from the changes
which would occur in the order of the *tableau*. Suppose, for example, that
luxury in the way of ornamentation increased by one-sixth in the case of
the proprietor, by one-sixth in the case of the artisan, and by one-sixth in
the case of the cultivator. Then the revenue reproduced, which is now
600 livres, would be reduced to 500 livres. Suppose, on the other hand,
that an increase of the same degree took place in expenditure on the consumption or export of raw produce. Then the revenue reproduced would
increase from 600 to 700 livres, and so on in progression. Thus it can be
seen that an opulent nation which indulges in excessive luxury in the way
of ornamentation can very quickly be overwhelmed by its sumptuousness.

The 300 livres of revenue which according to the order of the *tableau*
have passed into the hands of the class of productive expenditure, return
to this class its *advances* in the form of money. These advances reproduce
300 livres net, which represents the reproduction of part of the proprietor's
revenue; and it is by means of the remainder of the distribution of the
sums of money which are returned to this same class that the total revenue
is reproduced each year. These 300 livres, I say, which are returned at the
beginning of the process to the productive expenditure class, by means of
the sale of the products which the proprietor buys from it, are spent by the
farmer, one-half in the consumption of products provided by this class
itself, and the other half in keeping itself in clothing, utensils, implements,
etc., for which it makes payment to the sterile expenditure class. And the
300 livres are regenerated with the net product.

The 300 livres of the proprietor's revenue which have passed into the
hands of the sterile expenditure class are spent by the artisan, as to one-

moitié à la claſſe des dépenſes productives en achats de productions pour la ſubſiſtance, pour les matières premières des ouvrages, & pour le commerce extérieur; & l'autre moitié eſt partagée pour l'entretien, & pour la reſtitution des *avances*, à la claſſe même des dépenſes ſtériles. Cette circulation & cette diſtribution réciproque ſe continuent dans le même ordre par ſoudiviſions juſqu'au dernier denier des ſommes qui paſſent réciproquement d'une claſſe de dépenſes à l'autre claſſe de dépenſes.

La circulation porte 600 liv. à la claſſe des dépenſes ſtériles, ſur quoi il faut en retirer 300 livres pour les *avances annuelles;* il reſte 300 livres pour le ſalaire. Ce ſalaire eſt égal aux 300 liv. que cette claſſe reçoit de la claſſe des dépenſes productives, & les avances ſont égales aux 300 liv. du revenu qui paſſe à cette même claſſe de dépenſes ſtériles.

Les productions de l'autre claſſe ſont de 1200 livres, diſtraction faite de l'impôt, de la dixme, & de l'intérêt des avances du Laboureur, qui ſeront conſidérées à part, pour ne pas trop compliquer l'ordre des dépenſes. Dans la dépenſe des 1200 livres de productions, le Propriétaire du revenu en achette pour 300 liv. il en paſſe pour 300 liv. à la claſſe des dépenſes ſtériles, dont la moitié qui eſt de 150 liv. eſt conſommée pour la ſubſiſtance dans cette claſſe; l'autre moitié qui eſt de 150 liv. eſt enlevée pour le commerce extérieur qui ſe rapporte à cette même claſſe. Enfin il y en a pour 300 livres qui ſont conſommées dans la claſſe des dépenſes productives, par les hommes qui les font naître, & pour 300 liv. employées pour la nourriture & entretien des beſtiaux. Ainſi des 1200 livres de

half, in the purchase of products for his subsistence, for raw materials for his work, and for foreign trade, from the productive expenditure class; and the other half is distributed among the sterile expenditure class itself for its maintenance and for the restitution of its *advances*. This circulation and mutual distribution are continued in the same way by means of sub-divisions down to the last penny of the sums of money which mutually pass from the hands of one expenditure class into those of the other.

Circulation brings 600 livres to the sterile expenditure class, from which 300 livres have to be kept back for the *annual advances,* which leaves 300 livres for wages. These wages are equal to the 300 livres which this class receives from the productive expenditure class, and the advances are equal to the 300 livres of revenue which pass into the hands of this same sterile expenditure class.

The products of the other class amount to 1200 livres, abstracting from taxes, tithes, and interest on the husbandman's advances, which will be considered separately in order not to complicate the order of expenditure too much. The 1200 livres' worth of product are disposed of as follows: The proprietor of the revenue buys 300 livres' worth of them. 300 livres' worth passes into the hands of the sterile expenditure class, of which one-half, amounting to 150 livres, is consumed for subsistence within this class, and the other half, amounting to 150 livres, is taken for external trade, which is included in this same class. Finally, 300 livres' worth are con-sumed within the productive expenditure class by the men who cause them to be generated; and 300 livres' worth are used for the feeding and maintenance of livestock. Thus of the 1200 livres' worth of product, 600

iv

productions, cette claſſe en dépenſe 600 liv. & ſes *avances* de 600 liv. lui ſont rendues en argent par les ventes qu'elle fait au Propriétaire & à la claſſe des dépenſes ſtériles. Un huitième du total de ces productions entre dans le commerce extérieur en exportation, ou en matières premières & nourriture pour les ouvriers du pays qui vendent leurs ouvrages aux autres Nations, où les ventes du Commerçant contrebalancent les achats des marchandiſes, & de la matière d'or & d'argent que l'on tire de l'étranger.

Tel eſt l'ordre diſtributif de la conſommation des productions du cru entre les claſſes de citoyens, & telle eſt l'idée que l'on doit ſe former de l'uſage & de l'étendue du commerce extérieur d'une Nation agricole floriſſante.

Le débit réciproque d'une claſſe de dépenſe à l'autre diſtribue le revenu de 600 livres de part & d'autre; ce qui donne 300 livres de chaque côté, outre les avances qui ſont conſervées. Le Propriétaire ſubſiſte par les 600 livres qu'il dépenſe. Les 300 livres diſtribuées a chaque claſſe de dépenſes, ajoûtées aux produits de l'impôt, de la dixme, &c. qui y ſont annexés, peuvent y nourrir un homme dans l'une & dans l'autre: ainſi 600 liv. de revenu & les dépendances peuvent faire ſubſiſter trois hommes chefs de famille. Sur ce pied, 600 millions de revenu peuvent faire ſubſiſter trois millions de familles eſtimées à quatre perſonnes, de tout âge, par famille.

Les frais fournis par les *avances annuelles* de la claſſe des dépenſes productives qui renaiſſent auſſi chaque année, & dont environ la moitié eſt dépenſée pour la nourriture des beſtiaux, & l'autre moitié en payement de ſalaire pour les hommes occupés aux travaux de cette claſſe, ajoûtent

300

are consumed by this class, and its *advances* of 600 livres are returned to it in the form of money through the sales which it makes to the proprietor and to the sterile expenditure class. One-eighth of the total of this product enters into external trade, either as exports or as raw materials and sub-sistence for the country's workers who sell their goods to other nations. The sales of the merchant counterbalance the purchases of the com-modities and bullion which are obtained from abroad.

Such is the order of the distribution and consumption of raw produce as between the different classes of citizens; and such is the view which we ought to take of the use and extent of external trade in a flourishing agricultural nation.

Mutual sales from one expenditure class to the other distribute the revenue of 600 livres to both sides, giving 300 livres to each, in addition to the advances which are maintained intact. The proprietor subsists by means of the 600 livres which he spends. The 300 livres distributed to each expenditure class, together with the product of the taxes, the tithes, etc., which is added to them, can support one man in each: thus 600 livres of revenue together with the appurtenant sums can enable three heads of families to subsist. On this basis 600 millions of revenue can enable three million families to subsist, estimated at four persons of all ages per family.

The costs provided for by the *annual advances* of the productive expendi-ture class, which are also regenerated each year, and of which one-half is spent on the feeding of livestock and the other half in paying wages to the men engaged in the work carried on by this class, add 300 millions of

ʒoo millions de dépenſes qui peuvent, avec la part des autres produits qui y ſont annexés, faire ſubſiſter encore un million de chefs de familles.

Ainſi ces 900 millions qui, abſtraſtion faite de l'impôt, de la dixme, & des intérêts des avances annuelles & des avances primitives du Laboureur, renaîtroient annuellement des biens-fonds, pourroient faire ſubſiſter ſeize millions de perſonnes de tout âge, conformément à cet ordre de cir-culation & de diſtribution des revenus annuels.

Par circulation, on entend ici les achats de la première main, payés par le revenu qui ſe partage à toutes les claſſes d'hommes, diſtraſtion faite du commerce, qui mul-tiplie les ventes & les achats, ſans multiplier les choſes, & qui n'eſt qu'un ſurcroît de dépenſes ſtériles.

Les *richeſſes de la claſſe des Dépenſes produſtives* d'une Nation où les Propriétaires des terres ont conſtamment 600 millions de revenu, peuvent être évaluées ainſi.

Un revenu de 600 millions pour les Propriétaires ſup-poſe en outre ʒoo millions d'impôts; & 1ʒo millions pour la dixme du produit annuel, total frais compris, qui ſe lèvent ſur les parties de culture décimables: Ce qui forme en total 1 milliard ʒo millions, le revenu compris: De plus, la reproduſtion de 1 milliard ʒo millions d'avances annuelles, & 110 millions d'intérêt pour ces avances à 10 pour 100: Le tout enſemble eſt ... 2,210,000,000ˡ.

Dans un royaume où il y auroit beaucoup de vignes, de bois, de prés, &c. il n'y auroit qu'environ les deux tiers de ces 2 milliards 210 millions, qui s'obtiendroient par le travail de la charrue. Cette partie exigeroit, dans un bon Etat de grande culture exécutée par des chevaux,

expenditure to the total; and this, together with the share of the other products which are added to them, can enable another one million heads of families to subsist.

Thus these 900 millions, which, abstracting from taxes, tithes, and interest on the annual advances and original advances of the husbandman, would be annually regenerated from landed property, could enable 16 million people of all ages to subsist according to this order of circulation and distribution of the annual revenue.

By circulation is here meant the purchases at first hand, paid for by the revenue which is shared out among all classes of men, abstracting from trade, which multiplies sales and purchases without multiplying things, and which represents nothing but an addition to sterile expenditure.

The *wealth of the productive expenditure class*, in a nation where the proprietors of land regularly receive a revenue of 600 millions, can be wo rked out as follows:

A revenue of 600 millions for the proprietors presupposes an extra 300 millions for taxes; and 150 millions for tithes on the annual product, all charges included, which are levied on the tithable branches of cultivation. This makes a total of 1050 millions, including the revenue. Add to these the reproduction of 1050 millions of annual advances, and 110 millions of interest on these advances at 10 per cent, and the grand total becomes

. . . . 2,210,000,000 livres.

In a kingdom with many vineyards, forests, meadows, etc., only about two-thirds of these 2210 millions would be obtained by means of ploughing. Assuming a satisfactory state of affairs in which large-scale cultivation was being carried on with the aid of horses, this portion would require

D

vi

l'emploi de trois cens trente-trois mille, trois cens trente-
quatre charrues à 1 2 o arpens de terre par charrue; trois
cens trente-trois mille, trois cens trente-quatre hommes
pour les conduire; & 4 o millions d'arpens de terre.

Cette culture pourroit, avec 5 ou 6 milliards d'avances,
s'étendre en France à plus de 6 o millions d'arpens.

On ne parle pas ici de la petite culture exécutée avec
des bœufs, où il faudroit plus d'un million de charrues, &
environ 2,000,000 d'hommes pour exploiter 4 o millions
d'arpens de terre, qui ne rapporteroient que les deux
cinquièmes du produit que donne la grande culture. Cette
petite culture à laquelle les Cultivateurs font réduits, faute
de richeffes pour établir les avances primitives, s'exécute
aux dépens des biens-fonds mêmes, employés en grande
partie pour les frais, & par des dépenfes annuelles excef-
fives pour la fubfiftance de la multitude d'hommes occupés
à ce genre de culture, qui abforbent prefque tout le produit. Cette culture ingrate, qui décèle la pauvreté & la
ruine des Nations où elle domine, n'a aucun rapport à
l'ordre du Tableau, qui eft réglé fur l'état de la moitié de
l'emploi d'une charrue, où les avances annuelles peuvent,
au moyen du fond des avances primitives, produire cent
pour cent.

Les avances primitives bien complettes de l'établiffe-
ment d'une charrue dans la grande culture, pour le pre-
mier fond des dépenfes en beftiaux, inftrumens, femence,
& nourriture, entretien, falaire, &c. dans le cours du
travail de deux ans, avant la première récolte, font efti-
mées 1 o,000 liv. ainfi le total pour trois cens trente-trois
mille, trois cens trente-quatre charrues, eft 3,333,340,000[1],

the employment of 333,334 ploughs at 120 *arpents* of land per plough; 333,334 men to drive them; and 40 million *arpents* of land.

With advances amounting to five or six milliards, it would be possible for this type of cultivation to be extended in France to more than 60 million *arpents*.

We are not speaking here of small-scale cultivation carried on with the aid of oxen, in which more than a million ploughs and about two million men would be required to work 40 million *arpents* of land, and which would bring in only two-fifths of the product yielded by large-scale cultivation. This small-scale cultivation, to which cultivators are reduced owing to their lack of the wealth necessary to make the original advances, and in which the land is largely employed merely to cover the costs, is carried on at the expense of landed property itself, and involves an excessive annual expenditure for the subsistence of the great numbers of men engaged in this type of cultivation, which absorbs almost the whole of the product. This thankless type of cultivation, which reveals the poverty and ruin of those nations in which it predominates, has no connection with the order of the *tableau*, which is worked out on the basis of half the employment of a plough of land, where the annual advances are able, with the aid of the fund of original advances, to produce 100 per cent.

The full total of the original advances required for putting a plough of land under large-scale cultivation, for the first fund of expenditure on livestock, implements, seed, food, upkeep, wages, etc., in the course of two years' labour prior to the first harvest, is estimated at 10,000 livres. Thus the total for 333,334[13] ploughs is 3,333,340,000 livres. (*See the articles* FARM,[14] FARMERS,[15] CORN[16] *in the Encyclopedia.*)

Voyez dans l'Encyclopédie les art. FERMÉ, FERMIERS, GRAINS.

L'intérêt de ces avances doit rendre au moins 10 pour 100, parce que les produits de l'agriculture font expofés à des accidens ruineux qui, en dix ans, enlèvent au moins la valeur de la récolte d'une année. Ces avances exigent d'ailleurs beaucoup d'entretien & de renouvellemens; ainfi le total des intérêts des avances primitives de l'établiffe-ment des Laboureurs, eft . . . . 333,322,000$^{liv.}$

Les prés, les vignes, les étangs, les bois, &c. deman-dent peu d'avances primitives de la part des Fermiers. La valeur de ces avances peut être réduite, en y comprenant les dépenfes primitives des plantations & autres ouvrages exécutés aux dépens des Propriétaires, à 1,000,000,000^l.

Mais les vignes & le jardinage exigent beaucoup d'avan-ces annuelles qui, rapportées en commun avec celles des autres parties, peuvent du fort au foible, être comprifes dans le total des avances annuelles expofées ci-deffus.

La reproduction totale annuelle en pro-
duit net, en avances annuelles avec leurs
intérêts, & en intérêts des avances primi-
tives, évaluée conformément à l'ordre du
tableau, eft . . . . 2,543,322,000^l.

Le territoire de la France pourroit, avec des avances & du débit, produire autant & même beaucoup plus.

De cette fomme de 2,543,322,000^l, il y a 525 mil-lions, qui font la moitié de la reproduction des avances annuelles, employées à la nourriture des beftiaux: Il refte, (fi tout l'impôt rentre dans la circulation, & s'il ne porte pas fur les avances des Laboureurs.) . . 2,018,322,000^l.

The interest on these advances ought to amount to 10 per cent at least, since the products of agriculture are subject to disastrous accidents which, over a period of ten years, destroy at least the value of one year's harvest. Moreover, these advances require a great deal of upkeep and renewal. Thus the total interest on the original advances required for setting up the husbandmen is . . . . 333,322,000 livres.

Meadows, vineyards, ponds, forests, etc., do not require very great original advances on the part of the farmers. The value of these advances, including in them the original expenditure on plantations and other work carried out at the expense of the proprietors, can be reduced to 1,000,000,000 livres.

But vineyards and gardens require large annual advances which, taken together with those of the other branches, may on the average be included in the total of annual advances set out above.

The total annual reproduction of
net product, of annual advances with
the interest thereon, and of interest
on the original advances, worked out
in accordance with the order of the
tableau, *is* . . . . 2,543,322,000 livres.

The territory of France, given advances and markets, could produce as much as this and even a great deal more.

Of this sum of 2,543,322,000 livres,   525 millions constitutes that half of the reproduction of the annual advances which is employed in feeding livestock. There remains (if the whole of the taxes go back into circulation, and if they do not encroach upon the advances of the husbandmen)   . . . . 2,018,322,000 livres.

viii

C'eſt, POUR LA DÉPENSE DES HOMMES , *du fort au foible,* 504,580,500¹ *pour chaque million de chef de famille, ou pour un chef de famille* 562 *liv. que les accidens réduiſent environ à* 530¹. Sur ce pied un Etat eſt puiſſant en tribut & en reſſources ; & les hommes y ſubſiſtent dans l'aiſance.

Le fond des terres qui produit annuellement au profit des hommes, 2,018,322,000¹, dont 1,050,000,000¹ ſont en produit net, étant eſtimé ſur le pied du denier 30, eſt dans ce point de vûe une richeſſe de 33,455,000,000¹, auquel il faut ajoûter les 4,333,340,000¹ d'avances primitives ; le total eſt 36,788,340,000¹. En y réuniſſant les 2,543,322,000¹ du produit annuel,

LE TOTAL , FRAIS COMPRIS ,
DES RICHESSES DE LA CLASSE DES
DÉPENSES PRODUCTIVES SERA... 40,331,662,000¹.

On n'a pas eſtimé à part la valeur & le produit des beſtiaux, parce qu'on les a compris dans les avances des Fermiers, & dans le total des produits annuels.

Nous plaçons ici les terres, parce que, relativement à leur valeur vénale, on peut les regarder en quelque ſorte comme des richeſſes mobiliaires, en ce que leur prix eſt aſſujéti aux variations de l'état des autres richeſſes néceſſaires pour la culture. Car les terres ſe détériorent, & les Propriétaires perdent ſur la valeur vénale de leurs biens-fonds, à proportion que les richeſſes de leurs Fermiers dépériſſent.

Les *richeſſes de la claſſe des Dépenſes ſtériles* ſont 1.º le fond des avances annuelles ſtériles . . . 525,000,000ˡⁱᵛ⋅

2.º Avances primitives de cette claſſe pour établiſſemens de manufactures, pour

inſtrumens

That makes, FOR MEN'S EXPENDITURE, *504,580,500 livres on the average for each million heads of families, or 562 livres for each individual head of family, which accidents reduce to about 530 livres.* On this basis a state is strong in taxable capacity and resources, and its people live in easy circumstances.

The stock of land which annually produces for the benefit of men 2,018,322,000 livres, of which 1,050,000,000 take the form of net product, when evaluated at the rate of one in 30, constitutes from this point of view wealth amounting to 33,455,000,000 livres, to which must be added the original advances of 4,333,340,000 livres, making a total of 36,788,340,000. Adding to this the 2,543,322,000 livres of annual product,

THE TOTAL, COSTS INCLUDED, OF

THE WEALTH OF THE PRODUCTIVE

EXPENDITURE CLASS WILL BE: . . . . 40,331,662,000 livres.

The value and the product of livestock have not been separately calculated, since they have been included in the advances of the farmers and in the total of the annual product.

We include the land here because, relatively to its market value, it can be considered in something the same way as movable property, since its price is dependent upon changes in the other items of wealth required for cultivation. For land deteriorates, and the proprietors lose on the market value of their landed property, to the extent that the wealth of their farmers is wasted away.

The *wealth of the sterile expenditure class* consists of 1. The total of the annual sterile advances . . . . 525,000,000 livres.

2. The original advances of this class for setting up manufactures, for tools,

inftrumens, machines, moulins, forges
ou autres ufances, &c. . . . . 2,000,000,000^l

3.° L'argent monnoyé ou le pécule
d'une Nation agricole opulente, eft à
peu près égal au produit net qu'elle
retire annuellement de fes biens-fonds
par l'entremife du commerce. Ainfi . . . 1,000,000,000*

* Ou environ 18,600,000 de marcs d'argent. On remarque que le pécule de l'Angleterre refte fixé à peu près à cette proportion, qui, dans l'état préfent de fes richeffes, fe foûtient environ à 26 millions fterlins, ou à 11 millions de marcs d'argent. Si cette Nation s'eft trouvée expofée par fes guerres à des befoins preffans, & à des emprunts exceffifs, ce n'étoit pas par le défaut de l'argent, c'étoit par les dépenfes qui excédoient les revenus de l'Etat : Quand l'argent fourniroit aux emprunts, les revenus n'en feroient pas moins furchargés par les dettes ; & la Nation feroit ruinée, fi la fource même des revenus en fouffroit un dépériffement progreffif, qui diminuât la reproduction annuelle des richeffes. C'eft fous ce point de vûe qu'il faut envifager l'état des Nations ; parce que le pécule eft toûjours renaiffant dans une Nation où les richeffes fe renouvellent continuellement & fans dépériffement. Pendant environ un fiècle, c'eft-à-dire, depuis 1450 jufqu'à 1550, il y a eu en Europe une grande diminution dans la quantité de l'argent, comme on peut en juger par le prix des marchandifes en ce temps-là ; mais cette moindre quantité de pécule étoit indifférente aux Nations ; parce que la valeur vénale de cette richeffe étoit la même par-tout, & que, par rapport au pécule, leur état étoit le même relativement à leurs revenus, qui étoient par-tout également mefurés par la valeur uniforme de l'argent. Dans ce cas, il vaut mieux, pour la commodité des hommes, que ce foit la valeur qui fupplée à la maffe, que fi la maffe fuppléoit à la valeur. On eft porté à croire que c'eft la découverte de l'Amérique qui a procuré en Europe une plus grande abondance d'or & d'argent ; cependant la valeur de l'argent avoit baiffé vis-à-vis les marchandifes, au degré où elle eft aujourd'hui, avant l'arrivée de l'or

& de l'argent de l'Amérique en Europe. Mais toutes ces variétés générales ne changent rien à l'état du pécule de chaque Nation, y étant toûjours proportionné aux revenus des biens-fonds & aux gains du commerce extérieur. Dans le fiècle précédent, fous Louis XIV, le marc d'argent monnoyé valoit 28 liv. Ainfi 18,600,000 de marcs valoient alors environ 500 millions. C'étoit à peu près l'état du pécule de la France dans ce temps où le Royaume étoit beaucoup plus riche qu'il n'étoit fur la fin du règne de ce Monarque.

En 1716, la refonte générale des efpèces ne monta pas à 400 millions ; le marc d'argent monnoyé étoit à 43 liv. 12 fols ; ainfi la maffe des efpèces de cette refonte ne montoit pas à neuf millions de marcs ; c'étoit plus de moitié moins que dans les refontes générales de 1683 & 1693. Cette maffe de pécule n'aura pû augmenter par les fabrications annuelles d'efpèces, qu'autant que le revenu de la Nation aura augmenté : Quelque confidérable que foit le total de ces fabrications annuelles depuis cette refonte, il aura moins fervi à augmenter la maffe d'argent monnoyé, qu'à reparer ce qui en eft enlevé annuellement par la contrebande, par les diverfes branches de commerce paffif, & par d'autres emplois de l'argent chez l'étranger ; car depuis 44 ans, le total de ces tranfmiffions annuelles bien calculé, fe trouveroit fort confidérable. L'augmentation du numéraire qui eft fixée depuis long-temps à 54 livres, ne prouve pas que la quantité du pécule de la Nation ait beaucoup augmenté. Ces eftimations font peu conformes aux opinions du vulgaire, fur la quantité d'argent monnoyé d'une Nation ; le peuple croit que c'eft dans l'argent que confifte la richeffe d'un Etat : mais l'argent, comme toutes les autres productions, n'eft richeffe qu'à raifon

machines, mills, forges, and other works,

etc. . . . . 2,000,000,000 livres.

3. The coined money or money stock of an opulent agricultural nation is about equal to the net product which it obtains annually from its landed property through the medium of trade. Thus it is . . . . . 1,000,000,000 livres.*

---

* Or about 18,600,000 marks of silver. It is to be noted that the money stock of England remains fixed at about this proportion, which in the present state of its wealth maintains it at approximately 26 millions sterling, or 11 million marks of silver. If this nation has found itself in urgent need through its wars, and has been obliged to contract excessive loans, this was not due to a lack of money, but to the fact that the state's expenditure exceeded its revenue. When money is provided for loans, the debts add no less of a burden to the revenue, and the nation is ruined, if the very source of the revenue is progressively wasted away, causing a reduction in the annual reproduction of wealth. It is from this point of view that the state of a nation should be considered; for the money stock is always renascent in a nation where wealth is being renewed continually and without abatement. For about a century, i.e. from 1450 to 1550, there was a great reduction in the quantity of money in Europe, as can be seen from the prices of commodities in those times. But this smaller quantity of money was a matter of indifference to the nations, because the market value of this form of wealth was the same everywhere, and because, in proportion to the money stock, their condition was the same relatively to their revenues, which were everywhere measured alike in terms of the uniform value of silver. In such a case it conduces more to men's convenience that it should be value which makes up for quantity rather than quantity which makes up for value. We are led to believe that it was the discovery of America which procured a greater abundance of gold and silver in Europe; yet the value of silver had fallen relatively to commodities, to the level at which it stands today, before the arrival of the American gold and silver in Europe. But all these general variations have no effect at all on the state of the money stock of each

nation, which is always proportionate to the revenue from its landed property and to the gains from its external trade. In the last century, under Louis XIV, the mark of coined silver was worth 28 livres. Thus 18,600,000 marks were then worth about 500 million livres. This was roughly the size of the money stock in France in those times, when the kingdom was much wealthier than it was towards the end of the reign of this monarch.

In 1716, the general recoinage of specie did not amount to 400 millions; the mark of coined silver was at 43 livres 12 sous; thus the total amount of specie involved in this recoinage did not amount to nine million marks; and this was more than one-half less than the amounts involved in the general recoinages of 1683 and 1693. This total money stock can have been increased as a result of the annual production of specie only to the extent that the nation's revenue has been increased. However great the total of this annual production may have been since this recoinage, it will have served less to increase the total stock of coined money than to make up for what has been abstracted from it annually as a result of smuggling, the various branches of passive trade, and other methods of employing money in foreign countries; for over a period of 44 years the total of these annual transfers, if properly calculated, would be found to be very considerable. The rise in the money unit, which has been fixed for a long time at 54 livres, does not prove that the quantity of the nation's money stock has greatly increased. These views are hardly consistent with the notions vulgarly held concerning the quantity of coined money in a nation. The people believe that it is in money that the wealth of a state consists. But money, like all other products, constitutes wealth only in proportion to its market value; and it is

x

4.º La valeur foncière de 4 millions de maifons ou logemens pour 4 millions de familles, chaque maifon eftimée du fort au foible 1500 liv. eft . . . . . . 6,000,000,000.

5.º La valeur de l'emmeublement & uftenfiles de 4 millions de maifons efti-mées du fort au foible environ à une année du revenu ou du gain de 4 mil-lions de chefs de familles, eft . . . . . 3,000,000,000.

6.º La valeur de l'argenterie, bijoux, pierreries, glaces, tableaux, livres & autres ouvrages de main-d'œuvre du-rables, qui s'achettent ou fe tranf-mettent par fucceffion, peut être, dans une Nation riche, de . . . . 3,000,000,000.

7.º La valeur des vaiffeaux mar-chands & militaires, & leurs dépen-dances, fi la Nation eft maritime ; de plus, l'artillerie, les inftrumens & autres ouvrages durables pour la guerre de terre. Les édifices, décorations & au-tres ouvrages durables publics : tous ces objets enfemble peuvent être évalués à... 2,000,000,000.

On ne parle pas des marchandifes de main-d'œuvre

de fa valeur vénale, & n'eft pas plus difficile à acquérir que toute autre marchandife, en le payant par d'autres richeffes. Sa quantité dans un Etat y eft bornée à fon ufage, qui y eft réglé par les ventes & les achats dans fes dé-penfes annuelles ; & les dépenfes annuelles y font réglées par les revenus. Une Nation ne doit donc avoir d'argent monnoyé qu'à raifon de fes revenus ; une plus grande quantité lui feroit inutile ; elle en échangeroit le fuperflu avec les autres Nations, pour d'autres richeffes qui lui feroient plus avantageufes, ou plus fa-tisfaifantes ; car les poffeffeurs de l'argent, même les plus économes, font toûjours attentifs à en retirer quelque profit. Si on trouve à le prêter dans le pays à un haut intérêt, c'eft une preuve qu'il n'y eft tout au plus que dans la proportion que nous avons obfervée, puifqu'on en paye l'ufage ou le befoin à fi haut prix.

4. The capital value of four million houses or dwelling-places for four million families, each house being valued on the average at 1500 livres, comes to . . . . . 6,000,000,000 livres.

5. The value of the furnishings and utensils of four million houses, estimated on the average at about one year's revenue or gain of four million heads of families, comes to . . . . 3,000,000,000 livres.

6. The value of silver plate, jewellery, precious stones, mirrors, pictures, books, and other durable manufactured products, which are purchased or inherited, may in a wealthy nation amount to . . . . 3,000,000,000 livres.

7. The value of merchant and military shipping, and their appurtenances, in the case of a maritime nation; in addition, the artillery, weapons, and other durable products required for land warfare; the buildings, ornamental structures, and other durable public works: all these things taken together can be valued at . . . . . . 2,000,000,000 livres.

We do not take account here of the manufactured commodities and

no harder to acquire, by paying over other kinds of wealth for it, than any other commodity. Its quantity in a state is limited by the uses to which it can be put; these are regulated by the sales and purchases which take place in its annual expenditure; and its annual expenditure is regulated by its revenue. Thus a nation's stock of coined money should be no more than proportionate to its revenue; a greater quantity would be of no use to it; it would exchange the surplus with other nations in order to obtain other items of wealth which would be of greater benefit to it or which would afford it more satisfaction; for those who possess money, even the most thrifty of them, are always concerned with getting some profit from it. If it is found that money is being lent at a high rate of interest in a country, this is proof that the quantity of money is at most only in the proportion we have described, since those who need it or want the use of it are paying such a high price for it.

& denrées exportées ou importées, & renfermées dans les boutiques & magafins des Commerçans, deftinées à l'ufage ou confommation annuelle, parce qu'elles font comprifes & comptées dans l'état des productions & dépenfes annuelles, conformément à l'ordre expofé dans le Tableau.

Le Total des richesses de la classe des Dépenses stériles peut être environ . . . . . . 18,000,000,000[1]

Total général . . . . 59,000,000,000.

Suppofez erreur de $\frac{1}{20}$.ᵉ de plus ou de moins, c'eft . . . . 55 à 60,000,000,000.

Nous parlons d'une Nation opulente qui poffede un territoire & des avances qui lui rendent annuellement & fans dépériffement 1 milliard 50 millions de produit net; mais toutes ces richeffes entretenues fucceffivement par ce produit annuel, peuvent fe détruire ou perdre leur valeur, dans la décadence d'une Nation agricole, par le fimple dépériffement des avances pour les dépenfes productives, lequel peut faire de grands progrès en peu de temps par huit caufes principales.

1.º Mauvaife forme d'impofition, qui porteroit fur les avances des Cultivateurs, *Noli me tangere;* c'eft la devife de ces avances.

2.º Surcharges de l'impôt en dépenfes de perception.

3.º Excès de luxe de décoration.

4.º Excès de dépenfes litigieufes.

5.º Défaut de commerce extérieur des productions des biens-fonds.

produce which are exported and imported, and which are stored in the shops and warehouses of the merchants and destined for annual use or consumption, since they are included and taken account of in the figures of annual product and expenditure, in conformity with the order set out in the *tableau*.

THE TOTAL OF THE WEALTH OF

THE STERILE EXPENDITURE CLASS

may amount to about . . . . 18,000,000,000 livres.

GRAND TOTAL . . . . 59,000,000,000 livres.

That is, assuming a possible error of

one-twentieth either way . . . . . 55 to 60,000,000,000 livres.

We are speaking here of an opulent nation with a territory and advances which yield it annually and without any abatement a net product of 1050 millions. But all these items of wealth, which are successively maintained by this annual product, may be destroyed or lose their value if an agricultural nation falls into a state of decline, simply through the wasting away of the advances required for productive expenditure. This wasting away can make considerable headway in a short time for eight principal reasons:

1. A bad system of tax-assessment, which encroaches upon the cultivators' advances. *Noli me tangere* – that is the motto for these advances.

2. An extra burden of taxation due to the costs of collection.

3. An excess of luxury in the way of ornamentation.

4. Excessive expenditure on litigation.

5. A lack of external trade in the products of landed property.

xij

6.° Défaut de liberté dans le commerce intérieur des denrées du crû, & dans la culture.

7.° Vexations perfonnelles des habitans de la campagne.

8.° Défaut du retour du produit net annuel à la claffe des dépenfes productives.

EXTRAIT

xij

6. A lack of freedom of internal trade in raw produce, and in culti-vation.

7. The personal harassment of the inhabitants of the countryside.

8. Failure of the annual net product to return to the productive expenditure class.

[2]

K. WILLIAM KAPP

Environmental disruption:
General issues and methodological problems *

1. Introduction

Since the task of presenting the opening statement to this international symposium has been assigned to me, I should like to preface my paper by one or two introductory observations. I consider it as particularly appropriate that this first international symposium on the disruption and possible destruction of man's environment takes place in a country that had to endure the horrors of Hiroshima and Nagasaki. Moreover, Japan today has one of the most rapid rates of industrialization and of economic development with all its disruptive consequences on the environment. This is another reason which makes the choice of Tokyo as the geographical site for this international discussion of a world-wide problem highly appropriate.

The impairment of man's environment has a long history; some of the phenomena even antedate the Industrial Revolution; they can be observed in varying forms and intensities in pre-industrial societies and less developed economies. However, while deforestation, soil erosion and even air and water pollution are anything but new phenomena, their role and significance as threats to human well-being and in fact to human survival tend to become cumulative with the progress of modern industrial techniques and their indiscriminate application under conditions of increasing rates of population growth and settlement density. In fact, the rapid advance of science and technology in such fields as energy production from atomic and thermo-nuclear sources,

* This is the revised version of a paper presented at the " International Symposium on Environmental Disruption in the Modern World : A Challenge to Social Scientists ". The symposium, held in Tokyo, March 8-14, 1970, was organized by the Standing Committee on Environmental Disruption of the International Social Science Council. A volume of conference papers has now appeared under the title *Proceedings of International Symposium on Environmental Disruption: A challenge to social scientists*, S. Tsuru (ed.), The book is not distributed commercially but can be obtained at cost from the International Social Council.

Soc. sci. inform. 9(4), pp. 15-32.

16   *Man and his environment*

the unresolved problem of the disposal of radio-active waste material, the indiscriminate use of pesticides and " hard " detergents, new means of transportation at super-sonic speeds with their detrimental effects of noise, the ever increasing use of automobiles, the steady growth of agglomerations with their congested and unsanitary living conditions, new techniques of communication and of storing data and centralizing knowledge of all sorts together with their potential use for purposes of controlling and manipulating human behavior and human choices — all this introduces new hazards into man's natural and socio-political environment which are bound to undermine his physical and mental health [1] and ultimately to threaten human civilization and survival. I do not regard it as my task to analyze these actual and potential consequences, which, indeed, has been done by more competent scholars working both in the natural and social sciences. However, we need to remind ourselves that the impairment of our environment has reached not only a new quantitative dimension but a new quality as a result of the combined and cumulative effects of the complex interaction of a multitude of factors. While pre-industrial societies have been threatened by man-made deforestation, erosion and natural catastrophes of various sorts, and while air and water pollution could perhaps still be regarded as limited dangers a few decades ago, the causes and effects of the disruption of man's environment have multiplied to such an extent that it is necessary to view them as immediate threats and typical phenomena which transform the world upon which human life and survival depend.

The disruption of man's natural and social environment has been discussed and to some extent systematically investigated for more than two decades. However, the growing realization of the magnitude of the dangers involved has given the problem of environmental disruption a new urgency which makes it one of the most challenging issues which mankind has ever faced and calls for practical action which does not permit further postponement. The social sciences must develop more adequate perspectives and concepts for the analysis of the causal chain which leads to environmental disruption and thus prepare the ground for more effective methods of control.

The analysis and control of the impairment of the environment in modern society is not the special province of any particular scientific discipline or group of disciplines. No single discipline and indeed neither the social nor the natural sciences of and by themselves are able to come to grips with the problem of environmental disruption. For, this disruption is the outcome of

---

1. "The problem of the psychological pressure of crowding [...] the development of stress syndromes in some mammals leads to death, increases frustrations and neurotic behaviour [...] it is bound to engender violence if it goes on too long [...] crowding means you are going to have an increasing amount of regimentation, which can very readily go over to authoritarianism if you are not careful." From Sir Julian Huxley, "On population", *The Center Diary*, July 4, 1946.

a complex process of interaction of social and physical factors which cannot be adequately analyzed in terms of the concepts, theories and perspectives of any of the conventional disciplines. The disruption of man's environment by his own activities and decisions is a particularly complex process which transcends the scope and the points of view of any of today's highly compartmentalized fields of study. For this and other reasons which, I hope, will become more persuasive in the course of the subsequent analysis, I feel that many of the terms and concepts developed by particular disciplines (as, *e.g.*, externalities, diseconomies, nuisances, ecological imbalance, biospheric disruption, etc.), useful as they may have been and perhaps still are for particular theoretical purposes, are no longer adequate. In fact, the increasing disruption of man's natural and social environment raises the most far-reaching problems not only with respect to the proper methodological and theoretical procedures but also, and particularly with regard to the proper modes of control and policy-making. The solution of these theoretical and practical problems calls for the closest possible collaboration of social and natural scientists, including technologists. With this end in view I would indeed endorse Professor Tsuru's suggestion to use the term "environmental disruption" as a broad and general concept designed to cover all those phenomena which either singly or together affect the character and quality of the natural and the social environment of man. The use of the term environmental disruption should serve as a recognition of the fact that we are concerned with matters that touch the core of human existence and which in their complexity transcend the scope and competence of any particular discipline.

2. Circular causation

This brings me back to the fundamental issue of the causal process which gives rise to the disruption of the physical and social environment. Only if we view the process of causation correctly can we hope to make headway with the urgent task of controlling this disruption or at least limiting its most destructive effects. Nothing would be more misleading than to over-simplify this process of causation and view it in a superficial and uncritical way.

Of course, it is true that the increase of population alone is bound to give rise to an impairment of man's environment. It is also correct that some disruption may be caused by natural catastrophes without man's intervention. And nobody can deny that evidence of environmental disruption antedated modern industrial societies. Air pollution was reported in London as early as the 13th century and deforestation of steep slopes and valleys with its increased incidence of destructive snow and stone avalanches — not to mention erosion — has been present in Switzerland long before the Industrial Revolution and before this country developed a predominantly industrial structure during the 19th and 20th centuries. Similarly, destructive effects of defores-

18   *Man and his environment*

tation have been characteristic features of other pre-industrial economies including many of today's less developed Asian countries, as for instance the Philippines, Indonesia and India [2].

However, these earlier examples should not divert our attention from the important fact that in modern societies disruptive effects are set in motion by the often indiscriminate use of industrial techniques under specific conditions of institutionalized legal relations and patterns of action and investment. Hence to concentrate only on the physical chain of causation or to view the problem in isolation from the institutional framework in which it takes place can convey only an incomplete and therefore a false picture.   In short, the causal chain is at the same time a physical and a social process [3].   Speaking as an economist, I have long held the view and continue to believe that the institutionalized system of decision-making in a market economy has a built-in tendency of disregarding those negative effects (*e.g.*, air and water pollution) which are "external" to the decision-making unit.   Even if an individual firm intended to and would be in a financial position, as many oligopolists obviously are, to avoid the negative effects of their applied technology, it could do so only by raising its costs; that is by deliberately reducing its profit margin and its profit earning capacity.   Thus, a system of decision-making, operating in accordance with the principle of investment for profit, cannot be expected to proceed in any other way but to try to reduce its costs whenever possible by shifting them to the shoulders of others or to society at large.   Two points may be raised in opposition to this view.   In the first place it may be argued that these affected persons or society will defend themselves by legal action if they consider the damages of sufficient importance.   If they do not defend themselves, this must be proof of the fact that the damages are not important enough to warrant such action.   This argument overlooks that *a*) the damage may be gradual in building up until it becomes cumulative in character and comes to light only after considerable delays, and *b*) it may be difficult to prove damages and impossible to impute them to the action or lack of action of any particular economic unit.

In the second place, it may be argued — in opposition to my view that the institutional system of decision-making in a market economy has a built-in tendency of disregarding all negative effects — that the decisions of municipalities and public authorities in general are also responsible for the disruption

2. See K. W. Kapp, "Social costs in economic development", in: G. P. Sicat *et al.* (eds.), *Economics and development: An introduction*, Quezon City, 1965 (Reprint n° 49, Institut für Sozialwissenschaften, Universität Basel, Switzerland), and C. Uhlig, *Das Problem der "social costs" in der Entwicklungspolitik*, Stuttgart, 1966.

3. Professor Tsuru has made the point that "superimposed upon the physical chain of causation are the socio-economic and legal relations which could make a great deal of difference to the impact of physical factors upon human welfare". *Cf.* "Environmental pollution control in Japan", paper presented to the International Symposium on Environmental Disruption in the Modern World, p. 1.

of the environment. This is doubtless correct. One may even be inclined to go a step further and argue that socialist planning agencies will act in a similar way. Perhaps this is so, although it is not self-evident why.

But let us review these cases a little more closely. In the first place there is no doubt that municipalities also contribute to the disruption of the environment. However, apart from the problem of the relative importance of public sources of environmental disruption (in comparison to private sources) [4], does this refute the thesis advanced earlier? If municipalities and public or planning authorities set the stage for an impairment of the environment, for instance when they attract industries in order to increase their tax income regardless of possible negative effects they sacrifice the quality of the environment for revenues by choice, that is their action is identical to that of a private firm operating under the "constraints" of the principles of rentability. Both try to maintain an artificial, purely formal short-run financial solvency by ignoring the social costs of development. Some of the current attempts to render public decision-making more "rational" in terms of market costs and returns may carry the danger that the disregard of some or all of the negative effects of decisions may become even more general and typical. Instead of reducing the incidence of social costs connected with environmental disruption, such attempts are likely to increase them.

Rather than pursuing this perhaps controversial line of reasoning, let me suggest a more general framework of analysis in order to deal with the explanation of the process of causation which underlies the disruption of man's environment. Human action, including public decision-making, takes place within, and has repercussions on our natural-physical environment which has its own ecological structure and is subject to specific laws [5]. If these structures and regularities are left out of account, either due to ignorance or deliberately, the outcome of any decision may differ from one's intended objectives or, even if the original goal is attained, there may be additional effects of a negative character. Viewed in this way, the disruption of the environment can be interpreted as the outcome of human action which, while apparently rational within a given institutionalized framework of socio-economic and legal relations, nevertheless gives rise to a particularly destructive (social) irrationality because its repercussions on the physical, biological, psychological and social environment are ignored or neglected.

The result is an inefficient use of economic means and resources in the sense that socially more important values and objectives are sacrificed and remain unsatisfied in favor of less important ones. More specifically, formerly

4. "According to some estimates in some fields, and with respect to some kinds of discharges, industrial wastes exceed by a multiple the discharge by all municipalities, quite apart from the fact that industrial plants discharge vastly different amounts of waste." A. V. Kneese, "Research goals and progress towards them", in: H. Jarret (ed.), *Environmental quality in a growing economy*, Baltimore, Md., 1966, p. 79.

5. The same applies *pari passu* to the disruption of the social environment.

20 *Man and his environment*

"free" goods like clean air and water have become scarce. Moreover, by
shifting the costs of environmental disruption to third persons or to society,
we add to the distortion of an already imperfect market and price structure
and of the distribution process. Some economic units are able to acquire
benefits by disrupting our environment. It is not that they get something
for nothing, which is problematical enough from the point of view of any
hoped for and frequently alleged correlation between income and output,
but they get something by causing damages to the others.

We may go one step further: by viewing human action as taking place
within, and with repercussions on a physical and social environment with
specific structures and regularities, it becomes clear that the various spheres
of man's environment which are affected by his action are interdependent.
Moreover, the interaction of the socio-economic with the physical and biological spheres (or systems of relationships) is much more complex and much
less explored than the operation of any of the various systems which the
conventional academic disciplines have isolated for separate study in the
light of their particular objectives. If we look in this way upon the causal
chain which gives rise to disruption it must be evident that its causal analysis
cannot be carried on successfully in terms of one or the other of the compartmentalized social, physical and biological disciplines. Neither social nor
natural scientists nor engineers and public health experts, trained in their
limited disciplines and familiar only with their narrow concepts and theories
today are able to focus attention on the whole relevant pattern of interaction
which must be the "unit of investigation" — if we are to make headway with
the causal analysis of the impairment of our environment. It is true, we
still lack such a theory and/or science which is capable of elucidating the mode
and outcome of the complex interaction of several systems. Hence, our
knowledge of the causes and extent of environmental disruption is incomplete
and we continue to feed this imperfect knowledge into data-processing
computers. In other words, we must act on the basis of imperfect knowledge as
we have in the past and may have to, even though to a lesser extent, in the future.

However, there is one important aspect we do know about the causal chain
which gives rise to the disruption of man's natural and social environment:
in many (if not in most) instances it is a process of circular causation which
has a tendency of becoming cumulative unless some deliberate action is taken
to arrest or redirect it. The effects for instance of air and water pollution are
typically the result of the interaction of several factors. Thus, the effects of
any single discharge of pollutants varies with its frequency and concentration as
well as the capacity of the environment to absorb the pollutants without
harmful effects.

"Up to a certain level of concentration, disposal of wastes, disfigurement
of the landscape, and congestions are, at worst, local irritations. Air, water
and earth room can absorb a lot without great damage. Beyond that point,
real trouble ensues; differences of degree of frequency and concentration

create differences in kind." [6] In short, there is a threshold beyond which further discharges of waste cause not constant but cumulative changes and disproportionate damages. The disruption of man's natural and social environment is cumulative in still another way. Not only will different kinds of pollutants from different sources combine in chemical reactions but a whole series of intervening environmental variables such as weather, wind, topography and even design of construction of dwellings in large cities may combine to bring about varying degrees of deterioration of the quality of the environment. Such cumulative tendencies apply not only to air but also to water pollution. What is frequently overlooked is the fact that the quality of our environment as indeed that of society is always an aggregate: that is to say, the actual effects in terms of damage to human health and vitality, and actually experienced discomfort caused by any particular type of environmental disruption is always a function of the combined effects of all sources of disruption which may include, in addition to air and water pollution, other factors such as excessive noise, urban concentration, long hours spent in travel to and from work in metropolitan areas under chaotic traffic conditions and inadequate, congested transport facilities with high accident and death rates, inadequate time for leisure and recreation and the progressive absorption of free space and open landscapes [7]. Future hazards to man are such more or less dimly visualized developments as sonic booms, radio-active contamination, damage to the genetic structure and mutations, to name only a few [8].

3. Increasing disruption of the environment and increasing social costs

Before dealing with some of the more specific issues raised by the control and maintenance of the quality of man's environment, I would like to advance the thesis that we are faced with a tendency of an increasing impairment of the environment and hence of increasing social costs resulting therefrom. The thesis is advanced tentatively and substantiated here in a deductive-systematic manner but I am sure that it can be and will be substantiated also in terms of empirico-quantitative data as soon as we put our mind to developing the proper statistics and quantitative indicators. With population rising at prevailing rates, with output (as measured in terms of GNP) rising

6. Jarret (ed.), op. cit., pp. ix-x.

7. A more complete picture would have to include such perhaps less tangible but no less important factors as the effects of increasingly sedentary working conditions in an expanding service-sector of the economy, changes in the rhythm of work and rest, increasing specialization and monotony of work in some, and requirements of hectic performances in other professions, which in their combined effects are manifest in specific occupational morbidity and mortality rates and new characteristic civilization diseases. (Cf. M. Hochrein, J. Schleicher, Herz-Kreislauferkrankungen, 1959.)

8. Cf. H. J. Barnett, "Pressure of growth upon environment", in: Jarret (ed.),op. cit., p. 16.

22 _Man and his environment_

at higher rates than rates of population growth, with time (as measured in travel time) and space shrinking, not only congestion but input and hence residual waste products and the need for their disposal tend to increase disproportionately. Under these circumstances, the resulting disruption of the environment is likely to increase disproportionately also unless inputs could be converted fully into outputs and consumption of final outputs took the form of a final "destruction" of such outputs or, alternatively, if the capacity of the environment to assimilate residual waste products could be shown to be unlimited or could be increased without running into increasing real costs. None of these conditions is fulfilled or can be expected to hold as has been shown recently [9].

The capacity of the environment to assimilate residual waste products is limited and can be expanded only at increasing costs; inputs cannot be converted fully into outputs and the so-called consumption of final products, far from being a process in which such outputs are fully used up or "destroyed", leaves undesirable waste products to be discharged and disposed of in one way or in another. After a certain threshold has been reached, such discharge tends to lead to a growing impairment of the environment with resulting negative consequences on human health and life which can be counteracted and controlled only at increasing costs. In the light of these considerations it must be clear that increasing population, rapid progress of science and an indiscriminate application of new technology, increasing outputs and hence inputs, while increasing "productivity" (in a narrow sense), nevertheless are giving rise to increasing social costs understood either in physical terms (_i.e._, in terms of the negative social effects represented by the impairment of the environment, human health and life) or in terms of the real outlays measured in terms of labor required to prevent or remedy damages caused by the disposal of residual waste products. Until quite recently, modern industrial economies have not held their producers accountable for the widespread damages caused by increasing outputs (and inputs) and their practice of disposing of residual waste products more or less indiscriminately with the resulting impairment of the quality of the environment.

Today we are witnessing a growing awareness of the character of the damages caused and of the losses sustained. As long as this awareness was absent or could be played down by general references to the advantages of growth and development and also to the obvious difficulties surrounding all exact measurement and evaluation of losses, it was possible to take a "calculated risk" [10] with regard to these losses or to disregard them by shifting them to

9. R. U. Ayres and A. V. Kneese, "Production, consumption, and externalities", _American economic review_ 59 (3), June 1969, pp. 282-284.

10. The term "calculated risk" is, of course, a popular cliché which appeals to our age of calculation and measurement; actually nobody "calculated" anything and there was at first no empirical experience in terms of which probabilities could be measured. _Cf._ L. A. Chambers, "Risk versus cost in environmental health", in: H. Wolozin (ed.), _The economics_

the economically and politically weaker sections of society. Such a willingness to take "calculated risks" with man's environment and hence with human health and life was and is, of course, in open violation to all those systems of ethics which do not condone the sacrifice of human health and life either to increased output or to some abstract notion of the common good[11]. Today with the growing awareness of the threat and the magnitude of the actual and potential damages, the deterioration of man's environment is a public and hence a political issue. Thus, it becomes evident that economic practice and economic theory have systematically underestimated the costs of production, that the unpaid or social costs unaccounted for in traditional entrepreneurial outlays have been staggering and that the real costs (measured in terms of labor required to remedy or prevent the deterioration of the environment) are assuming increasing proportions of total costs and outputs[12].

But whether the principle of increasing environmental disruption and increasing social costs is accepted or not one conclusion can hardly be denied: under the impact of human action and decision-making and under the influence of a rapidly advancing technology and science, our environment is being transformed to an ever increasing extent. To be sure, man has always changed and adapted his environment in accordance to his own requirements. In this sense the present disruption represents an acceleration of a trend which has been present in the past. However, what must not be overlooked is the fact that we are confronted with a change of quantity into quality. Today's transformation of the environment is no longer an expression of an increasing mastery over the world we live in but is instead a sign of a loss of such mastery. We have reached the point where a steadily growing quantity of disruption turns into a serious impairment of the quality of the environment. It is this impairment with its manifest threats to human health and human life which has created an entirely novel situation. Its novelty is precisely the fact that the more the environment becomes the product of our action the less can we escape with impunity the responsibility of controlling and maintaining it. This brings us first to the problems of measurement and evaluation.

---

of air pollution, New York, 1966, pp. 51-60. On the illusions underlying the cliché of a "calculated risk" and probability calculations in contemporary social and military sciences, including capital and investment theory and business administration, see A. Rappoport, *Strategy and conscience*, New York, 1964, p. 22 *sq.*

11. Chambers, *op. cit.*, p. 52.

12. I cannot deal here with the implications of the foregoing analysis for future rates of growth except to emphasize that our traditional measures of output and growth in terms of GNP are likely to become progressively inadequate and unreliable as indicators of growth and development if increasing amounts and proportions of outlays are spent on nothing else but work designed to protect and keep intact the substance of our environment.

24　*Man and his environment*

4. Issues of measurement and evaluation

In view of the extent of the deterioration of man's environment nothing seems
to be more important than to develop reliable indicators designed to assess,
measure and evaluate, to the fullest possible extent, the degree and consequences of this deterioration in its various manifestations. This issue is
directly related to the problem of environmental control. In the first place,
the assessment of the negative consequences of environmental disruption is
an important desideratum of and, indeed, the first step toward an evaluation
of the benefits obtainable from the control, protection and improvement of
the quality of the environment. The two tasks: assessment of negative
consequences and estimates of benefits, are closely interrelated. In the second
place, it has long been argued that measures of control are economically justified only if their total benefits exceed or equal their costs. For this reason
too, problems of assessment and measurement are obviously important.

And yet, problems of measuring costs and benefits belong to the thorniest
and most controversial issues. Nor is this surprising. Both the costs of
environmental disruption and the benefits of environmental 'control and
improvement are predominantly non-market in character. Many of the
costs and benefits cannot be quantified and still less be adequately measured
in terms of prices. Some may be measurable in this way, or ways and means
may be found to arrive at some indirect form of quantification in monetary
terms. For example, when air and water pollution affect property values,
any improvement of the quality of air and water may be reflected in higher
land or real estate values. But even here problems arise. Suppose we were
able to devise a technique to establish and impute the causal contribution
which a particular source of water or air pollution has made to the loss of
value of a particular site, this would still not be a reliable and unambiguous
measure of social costs nor of benefits of control. Just as the decreased land
and property value caused by air and water pollution affects third persons
who may have had nothing to do with the productive process responsible
for the pollution, the increased property value resulting from air and water
pollution control are in many instances "unearned" increments. To identify
such unearned increments with the social benefits of environmental control
is highly questionable, even on theoretical grounds, which most social scientists, and especially economists, would have to reject as problematical even
though, or more precisely because, such identification may be found acceptable
by the real estate lobby [13].

Any suggestion to decide the justification of control measures in terms
of a willingness to pay for them, or by assuming a capacity to compensate

13. It is possible to justify such identification of social benefits with unearned increments
on the basis of some arbitrary and highly unrealistic assumptions as to market structure;
on the whole subject see M. Mason Gaffney, "Welfare economics and the environment",
in: Jarret (ed.), *op. cit.*, p. 91 *sq.* and 99.

those who have to bear the costs of control out of increments of property values or other monetary values accruing to others fails to take sufficient account of three factors: *a*) actual markets are far from perfect — in fact they are "oligopolistic" in character —, *b*) the consequences of environmental disruption are highly heterogeneous and cannot be compared quantitatively with one another, and *c*) the benefits obtainable from environmental control are equally heterogeneous and can neither be compared quantitatively with one another nor with the outlays for control. To quantify them nevertheless by means of some arbitrary monetary standard is at best problematical and at worst contradictory to logic if not in violation of our ethics. For what is the monetary value of human health and human life? What is the value of the quality of urban life or the beauty of a landscape that is being sacrificed in the process of urban expansion? The fact of the matter is that both, disruption and improvement of our environment, involve us in decisions which have the most heterogeneous long-term effects and which, moreover, are decisions made by one generation with consequences to be borne by the next. To place a monetary value on and apply a discount rate (which?) to future utilities or disutilities in order to express their present capitalized value may give us a precise monetary calculation, but it does not get us out of the dilemma of a choice and the fact that we take a risk with human health and survival. For this reason, I am inclined to consider the attempt of measuring social costs and social benefits simply in terms of monetary or market values as doomed to failure. Social costs and social benefits have to be considered as extra-market phenomena; they are borne by and accrue to society as a whole; they are heterogeneous and cannot be compared quantitatively among themselves and with each other, not even in principle.

More specifically, the social benefits sought by environmental control are social or public goods and must be dealt with as such. That is to say, they are above all goods or services which diffuse themselves throughout society; no one can nor should be excluded from their enjoyment; they are "non-rival" that is, their use or enjoyment by one does not necessarily reduce their supply. For this reason we will have to look for other methods of assessment than those available or suggested in terms of market values. We will have to face political decisions based on evaluations arrived at outside the market under conditions of possible disagreements and lack of unanimous consent. Such decisions are similar to those which were made in the past and continue to be made with regard to labor legislation (including workmen's compensation for accidents and occupational diseases), to social security legislation and legislation regulating standards of food and drugs, provisions of educational facilities, etc. No cost-benefit analysis helps us in these instances and no market values and indeed no compensatory principle and no Pareto optimum can help us now in deciding whether and which controls are to be adopted. As in all decisions of this kind, we will have to act even if some industries may be worse off or fail to give their consent initially as was the case with regard

26 *Man and his environment*

to the aforementioned cases of legislation.   In fact, the more we admit that *all* benefits (secondary, indirect, intangible, etc.) of control measures ultimately have to be included in benefit-cost calculations the more problematical becomes any evaluation in terms of one single monetary standard.   In short, I fail to see that cost-benefit analyses as they stand today have a solution of the problem of evaluating either the social costs of the disruption, or the social benefits of the improvement of our environment by control measures [14].

And yet, my position should not be interpreted as a counsel in favor of arbitrary action; nor should economists who hold similar views be accused of preaching a gospel of license.   In order to act rationally, we must know and assess the consequences of our action or non-action.   To this effect we will have to draw the necessary inferences from what I have called the complex and cumulative character of the causal chain and to make an inventory of the actual and potential damages and losses caused by investment decision and government action or non-action.   To this effect, we need a cooperative multi-disciplinary research effort on a national and perhaps an international basis [15].   In fact, in modern industrial societies it has always been important and is steadily becoming more urgent to anticipate the actual and potential effects of damages *before* investment decisions are taken.   What are needed are inventories of the fullest possible range of the consequences which new technologies and inputs are likely to have on man and his environment. There can be no rational action and decision-making any more without systematic prior scientific analysis and prognosis.   Many (though perhaps not all) of the unanticipated negative consequences and social costs which confront us today could have been anticipated by prior research and adequate outlays for scientific analysis.   Today when we can build upon the accumulated experiences and lessons of the past, the pay-off of such prior research and prognosis is likely to be considerable.

14. Musgrave and others have made the point that the situation is more "manageable" when we deal with multipurpose water development projects, for in this case we are confronted not with a final social benefit but with an intermediate (social or public) good which contributes to final goods with market values, R. A. Musgrave, "Cost benefit analysis and the theory of public finance", *Journal of economic literature* 3 (3), September 1969, p. 800.   While this is true up to a certain point I doubt whether the case is in fact much easier and more manageable.   Because even in this case it is not evident that the current market values (*e.g.*, of crops or electricity) are such as to provide (especially in less developed countries) a sufficiently reliable and meaningful indicator of the relative importance of the goods and services which can be produced with the aid of such intermediate social goods or projects — quite apart from such thorny problems as to the choice of the capital inputs (*e.g.*, seed varieties) and hence yield data to be used not to speak of the selection of the interest rate to be applied as the relevant discount rate in order to arrive at current values of benefits.

15. It may well be that this research effort calls for an institutionalization in the form of national and international research institutes whose primary task it would be to develop methods of study and collect relevant data related to the deterioration of man's environment by various types of investment decisions under specific conditions.

Analysis and prognosis, by assessing the consequences of decision-making, will provide us with an inventory of the nature of the damages and social costs of private and public investments; it will at the same time yield the necessary data and facts in the light of which it will be possible to evaluate and revise our aims and objectives and thereby to improve our policy-making. However, far from denying that measurement is important and that science is measurement (and all that), I want to emphasize that what is even more important than precision in measurement is the selection of the goals, *i.e.*, the distinction of what is essential and what is less essential; this indeed will call for more than data and facts concerning the possible consequences of alternative courses of action. It calls above all for some general standards in terms of which it may be possible to agree on and select the social goals we seek. Once agreed and stipulated, it would then be necessary to compare the real costs of attaining such stipulated ends by different courses of action or methods of control.

5. Environmental control

The data and relationship established by analysis and their possible future consequences are directly relevant for the elaboration of the policies and methods of control which we are looking for. Implicit in this suggestion is the thesis that such data and relationships point to norms of action and facilitate the formulation of explicit value premises. By telling us what we have to expect; by showing us the dangers and threats which the disruption of the environment implies for human health and survival, analysis and prognosis define the choices before us and are thus part of the process of arriving at intelligent and reasoned decisions. In short, they are indispensable parts of the logic of formulating aims, policy objectives and methods of control.

The standards in terms of which it may be possible to stipulate specific social goals remain, of course, subject to *bona fide* differences of opinion. For this reason it is essential to work out objective standards in the form of appropriate limits of maximum tolerable or acceptable levels of concentrations of contaminants, *e.g.*, in such fields as air and water pollution or minimum requirements for the maintenance of human health and survival. The object of such safety limits is to determine the extent to which any type of disruption becomes a threat to the environment and to man. We cannot concern ourselves here with the specific techniques of elaborating such limits [16]. This is the task of natural scientists, technologists, public health experts and social

---

16. In the light of our analysis of the cumulative nature of the causal chain it goes without saying that such limits or safety standards cannot be identical for all localities and all countries. Thus, the multiplicity of the sources of air and water pollution, of the intervening environmental variables, of the conditions of climate, topography and the nature of the cumulative process would call for a variety of standards.

28 *Man and his environment*

psychologists. What concerns us is the role and significance of safety limits in connection with the problem of controlling the disruption of the environment. Such limits fulfill several functions in addition to providing standards for measuring (in physical terms) the state of the disruption of the environment at a given time and place, thus serving also as indicators of dangers. They define what may be called the fundamental existential minimum requirements of individual life (or social needs). As such they may be regarded as the individual and social welfare minima directly relevant for the formulation of social goals or objectives. That is to say, while such safety limits do not represent automatically social goals — indeed they have not been social goals in all those countries which have tolerated the present disruption of the environment — and while the selection of policy objectives will continue to call for choices, such choices will have to be taken as a function of the social or existential minimum needs on the one hand and the community's productive potentialities on the other [17]. Furthermore, such social minima would be relevant for the selection of what is important in the light of objectives derived from individual human requirements and would bring us closer to a substantive concept of economic rationality measured in terms of actual satisfaction of human needs in contrast to a purely formal concept of rationality which underlies our contemporary abstract models.

It must be admitted, however, that social minima do not define an ideal or perfect state or, for that matter, an "optimal" use of resources. In fact, they provide only a modest and imperfect answer to the problem — but they would offer at least operational criteria or indicators for policy-making in terms of increments of improvements. Such operational indicators would be a considerable advance over optima formulated in terms of market outlays and returns which take inadequate account of social costs and benefits, and which despite their obvious questionable character have again and again been advocated as criteria of action [18]. Once safety limits, as for instance maximum permissible levels of concentration of pollutants, have been stipulated by the political process of decision-making, they can then be translated into a broad production function (or physical investment pattern), in the form of an input-output model designed to identify the inputs and techniques as well as the outputs called for by our existential minimum needs [19].

17. C. Bettelheim, *Studies in the theory of planning*, Bombay, 1959, p. 14. It goes without saying that social minima and existential minimum needs must not be considered as static but are subject to change depending upon the state of our knowledge, our technology and the level of productivity.

18. For a recent denunciation of this "vice of vulgar economics", *cf.* J. Robinson, *Essays in the theory of economic growth*, London, 1962, p. 27.

19. I realize that I am using the concept of an input-output relationship in a broader fashion than it was originally developed but I think that this extension of the concept can be justified, see W. Leontief, "The problem of quality and quantity in economics", in: *Essays in economic theories and theorizing*, London, 1966.

The emphasis must be placed on a direct *ex-ante* approach to control in contrast to current attempts at remedial action by such indirect measures as tax-exemptions, subsidies and the levying of charges according to the flow of pollutants. *Ex-post* remedial measures designed to check the impairment may have the advantage of leaving the choice of input and techniques to the individual economic unit. This method, which has been relied upon in the past, is becoming hazardous and in many instances irrational and potentially suicidal. Penalties, tax exemptions, subsidies or charges in accordance with the volume of contaminants discharged have very different incentive (or disincentive) effects on different firms depending upon their market power and their income and income tax position [20]. A penalty of $ 100 for each violation is ineffective and invites pollution if several hundred thousand dollars worth of costs (if not millions) can be avoided by the discharge of untreated waste materials. Similarly, small subsidies may offer little incentives for the installation of the required equipment. In view of the fact that expenditures for such equipment can anyway be treated as costs and hence are tax deductible, the resulting incentive effect has apparently not worked in the past. Massive subsidies and hence public expenditures may have to be called for in order to be effective and the outcome would be additional taxes levied on Peter to pay Paul [21]. In short, tax reductions and incentives alone will not be effective, quite apart from the fact that they tend to distort further an already imperfectly working price system.

The magnitude of the threat and the values at stake seem to me to call for a line of attack which must be directed towards the design and technique of production. What needs to be changed and controlled are the "input mix", the technical process and the location and concentration of the process of production. This is perhaps best illustrated by a concrete example: if we want to avoid the destruction of plants by insects and pests, we can use insecticides and pesticides. We have done so in the past only to discover that the insects and disease carriers develop immunity and that the increasing amounts of chemicals or their residues pollute our environment and tend to become serious health hazards to man. Instead of developing more and "better" pesticides which, moreover, tend to attack not only pests but insects in general, plant geneticists and plant breeders are experimenting today with breeding plants with greater resistance to attacks by insects and pests. This type of control, by changing the nature of capital inputs, may be more economical and more effective in the long run than the use of chemicals, while at the same time avoiding the dangers of the pollution of the environment [22].

20. On this point see Gaffney, *op. cit.*, p. 91.

21. Time and space do not permit a consideration of the question as to the proper allocation of costs of remedying past damage and preventing future disruption.

22. *Cf.* S. S. Chase, "Anti-famine strategy, genetic engineering for foods", *Bulletin of the atomic scientists* 25 (8), October 1969, p. 4.

30 *Man and his environment*

Similarly, the control of air pollution by automobiles seems to me to be more economical and more certain by the design of new and more effective engines and/or by substitutes for gasoline than by indirect controls or better law enforcement.

Another illustration of the possibilities of controlling pollution by a new input mix and design is the installation of a central heating unit for a new residential district in the Northwest of Frankfurt (Germany), following earlier experiments in Lausanne (Switzerland). This heating unit uses as inputs the garbage collected in the residential district, which is burned at high temperatures (900° C). This not only prevents odorous compounds of the garbage from entering the atmosphere but tends to avoid the impairment of the atmosphere of the residential area thanks to the installation of one single smoke stack of special height (110 m), equipped with an electric filter. Moreover, the site for the smoke stack was selected after careful study of climatic conditions with respect to prevailing wind direction and velocity. The case of the Northwest City of Frankfurt is mentioned here as an illustration of a simultaneous disposal of waste material and its utilization as input for a central heat generating unit designed and located in accordance with the relevant technical and meteorological considerations [23]. While even this approach does not solve all problems of air pollution [24], it does show that the choice of a rational input mix necessarily calls for a deliberate choice of location.

In fact, this brings me to the final observations I wish to make in this context. Since the disruption of the environment is clearly a function of the location and relative congestion of an area it is imperative to consider these factors in all future decisions concerning industrial and residential sites. In other words, a rational determination of land use requires that we extend the unit of investigation and the area of environmental control in accordance with the actual physical interdependencies in an area as determined by its waterways, its topography, its climatic and meteorological conditions as well as its density of settlement. This broader perspective in location theory will become more and more urgent with the growing exposure to the dangers of pollution from radioactive waste materials and possible accidents from radioactive sources such as atomic reactors. Instead of purely local zoning regulations, a rational location policy requires planning based upon a complete inventory of physical conditions and existing population densities on a regional, national and perhaps even international basis. In short, choices of site and location problems in general, whether residential, commercial or industrial can no longer be made

---

23. H. Kampffmeyer *et al.*, *Die Nordweststadt in Frankfurt-am-Main*, Frankfurt-am-Main, 1968, and personal communications.

24. It does not because it is not feasible to reduce completely or destroy all effluents of a noxious character (*e.g.*, sulphur dioxyde, SO_2). Furthermore "the leeside of one city may be the windward side of another city", *cf.* J. R. Taylor *et al.*, "Control of air pollution by site selection and zoning", in: World Health Organization (ed.), *Air pollution*, Geneva, 1961, p. 294 (Monograph series, 46).

solely with reference to traditional market factors and costs such as outlays for transportation, materials and labor. Here too, costs and benefits will have to be evaluated in the light of inventories of hazards established by multidisciplinary research efforts. Whether the practical implications of such studies will be a dispersal or a concentration of industries and residential areas and which methods of control will be called for is today an open question.

6. Conclusions

We are thus led to the conclusion that while science and technology and their application under given institutional arrangements have led to a serious deterioration of man's environment, the mastery and control of the resulting hazards to human health and life can be achieved if at all only by making science and technology accountable to society. At the same time, social policy and decision-making must themselves be shaped by scientific research. So far we have applied science and technology without paying attention to their human and social consequences. If we want to reverse this process and bring it under social and political control, we will have to pay greater attention to the imperatives of human life and survival in making use of science and technology.

Unless we succeed in this endeavor even at the price of substantial changes in our institutional arrangements, the disruption of man's environment is likely to assume increasing dimensions. In fact, this disruption is becoming the dominant problem of the outgoing 20th century — equal if not surpassing in importance the recurrent threats to human health and survival in the Middle Ages by diseases of epidemic proportions, the exposure of the individual to arbitrary and despotic rule and exploitation, and the human and material losses caused by mass unemployment which preoccupied economists during the last decades.

From the perspective of modern biology and anthropology man has been described as an endangered being whose survival and development into a functioning member of his culture constitutes an achievement against many odds. In the light of the cumulative effects of an uncontrolled use of modern technologies on the quality of man's natural and social environment, man in addition endangers himself because his action and his uncontrolled productive activities threaten his health and actually his survival as a species. Ultimately the disruption of man's environment by his own action and the human and social costs created thereby call for more than remedial action here and there; they call for *ex-ante* measures of control. The destructive transformation of the world we live in will neither be stopped nor reversed as long as responsibility for the maintenance of the quality of the environment in the interest of present and future generations does not find an unequivocal expression in

32   *Man and his environment*

our system of morals and ultimately in ethical and political imperatives which
guide individual and social action.   It seems to me that such a system of
social and ethical responsibilities for the maintenance of man's environment
also confronts the social sciences and is one of the challenges which we have
jto face.

The modern problems of the disruption of man's environment and of the
social costs and consequences of such impairment, and the search for ways
and means of controlling and improving the quality of man's environment,
constitute not only a challenge to our intellectual and practical ingenuity
but could open opportunities for joining those early social critics and dis-
senters, who were concerned with these issues.   And, if I may add one conclud-
ing remark: perhaps it is this urgent task of preventing a further disruption
of man's natural and social environment and of improving the quality of
the conditions of human life which could bridge the gap between the disaffected
parts of the younger generation and those among the older ones whose critical
udgments have not been eroded by a positivistic acceptance of the *status quo.*

*K. William Kapp, Professor of Economics at the University of Basle, Switzerland, is
engaged in research on problems of environmental disruption, developing economies and
theory of institutional economics. Among his publications:* Hindu culture, economic
development and economic planning: A collection of essays *(1962);* Social costs of
business enterprise *(1962);* "Nationalökonomie und rationaler Humanismus", Kyklos *21,
1968;* "On the nature and significance of social costs", Kyklos *22, 1969.*

[3]

Is Growth Obsolete?

WILLIAM D. NORDHAUS AND JAMES TOBIN

YALE UNIVERSITY

A long decade ago economic growth was the reigning fashion of political economy. It was simultaneously the hottest subject of economic theory and research, a slogan eagerly claimed by politicians of all stripes, and a serious objective of the policies of governments. The climate of opinion has changed dramatically. Disillusioned critics indict both economic science and economic policy for blind obeisance to aggregate material "progress," and for neglect of its costly side effects. Growth, it is charged, distorts national priorities, worsens the distribution of income, and irreparably damages the environment. Paul Erlich speaks for a multitude when he says, "We must acquire a life style which has as its goal maximum freedom and happiness for the individual, not a maximum Gross National Product."

Growth was in an important sense a discovery of economics after the Second World War. Of course economic development has always been the grand theme of historically minded scholars of large mind and bold concept, notably Marx, Schumpeter, Kuznets. But the mainstream of economic analysis was not comfortable with phenomena of change and progress. The stationary state was the long-run equilibrium of classical and neoclassical theory, and comparison of alternative static equilibriums was the most powerful theoretical tool. Technological change and population increase were most readily accommodated as one-time exogenous shocks; comparative static analysis could be used to tell how they altered the equilibrium of the system. The obvious fact that these "shocks" were occurring continuously, never allowing the

NOTE: The research described in this paper was carried out under grants from the National Science Foundation and the Ford Foundation. The paper and its appendixes were originally published in *Economic Growth*, Fiftieth Anniversary Colloquium V, New York, National Bureau of Economic Research, 1972; the paper is reproduced here as it appeared in the colloquium volume. All references to the appendixes pertain to that publication.

The paper is published in this volume upon recommendation of the Executive Committee and approval by the National Bureau of Economic Research because it stimulated considerable discussion at the conference, some of which is reproduced here. It was invited for presentation when an earlier paper by another author was not forthcoming, and most importantly because of its special relevance to the subject of this conference.

We would like to express our appreciation to Walter Dolde, James Pugash, Geoffrey Woglom, Hugh Tobin, and especially Laura Harrison, for assistance in the preparation of this paper. We are grateful to Robin Matthews for pointing out some problems in our treatment of leisure in the first draft.

510 *Amenities and Disamenities of Economic Growth*

system to reach its equilibrium, was a considerable embarrassment. Keynesian theory fell in the same tradition, attempting rather awkwardly, though nonetheless fruitfully, to apply static equilibrium theory to the essentially dynamic problem of saving and capital accumulation.

Sir Roy Harrod in 1940 began the process, brought to fruition by many theorists in the 1950s, of putting the stationary state into motion. The long-run equilibrium of the system became a path of steady growth, and the tools of comparative statics could then be applied to alternative growth paths rather than to alternative stationary states. Neo-Keynesian macroeconomics began to fall into place as a description of departures from equilibrium growth, although this task of reinterpretation and integration is still far from a satisfactory completion.

By now modern neoclassical growth theory is well enough formulated to have made its way into textbooks. It is a theory of the growth of potential output, or output at a uniform standard rate of utilization of capacity. The theory relates potential output to three determinants: the labor force, the state of technology, and the stock of human and tangible capital. The first two are usually assumed to grow smoothly at rates determined exogenously by noneconomic factors. The accumulation of capital is governed by the thrift of the population, and in equilibrium the growth of the capital stock matches the growth of labor-*cum*-technology and the growth of output. Simple as it is, the model fits the observed trends of economic growth reasonably well.

The steady equilibrium growth of modern neoclassical theory is, it must be acknowledged, a routine process of replication. It is a dull story compared to the convulsive structural, technological, and social changes described by the historically oriented scholars of development mentioned above. The theory conceals, either in aggregation or in the abstract generality of multisector models, all the drama of the events — the rise and fall of products, technologies, and industries, and the accompanying transformations of the spatial and occupational distribution of the population. Many economists agree with the broad outlines of Schumpeter's vision of capitalist development, which is a far cry from growth models made nowadays in either Cambridge, Massachusetts, or Cambridge, England. But visions of that kind have yet to be transformed into a theory that can be applied in everyday analytic and empirical work.

In any case, growth of some kind is now the recognized economic norm. A symptom of the change in outlook can be found in business cycle semantics. A National Bureau *recession* was essentially a period

Is Growth Obsolete? 511

in which aggregate productive activity was declining. Since 1960 it has become increasingly customary to describe the state of the economy by the gap between its actual output and its growing potential. Although the word recession is still a source of confusion and controversy, almost everyone recognizes that the economy is losing ground — which will have to be recaptured eventually — whenever its actual rate of expansion is below the rate of growth of potential output.

In the early 1960s growth became a proclaimed objective of government policy, in this country as elsewhere. Who could be against it? But like most value-laden words, growth has meant different things to different people and at different times. Often growth policy was simply identified with measures to expand aggregate demand in order to bring or keep actual output in line with potential output. In this sense it is simply stabilization policy, only more gap-conscious and growth-conscious than the cycle-smoothing policies of the past.

To economists schooled in postwar neoclassical growth theory, growth policy proper meant something more than this, and more debatable. It meant deliberate effort to speed up the growth of potential output itself, specifically to accelerate the productivity of labor. Growth policy in this meaning was not widely understood or accepted. The neoclassical model outlined above suggested two kinds of policies to foster growth, possibly interrelated: measures that advanced technological knowledge and measures that increased the share of potential output devoted to accumulation of physical or human capital.[1] Another implication of the standard model was that, unless someone could find a way to accelerate technological progress permanently, policy could not raise the rate of growth permanently. One-shot measures would speed up growth temporarily, for years or decades. But once the economy had absorbed these measures, its future growth rate would be limited once again by constraints of labor and technology. The level of its path, however, would be permanently higher than if the policies had not been undertaken.

Growth measures nearly always involve diversions of current resources from other uses, sacrifices of current consumption for the benefit of succeeding generations of consumers. Enthusiasts for faster

---

[1] The variety of possible measures, and the difficulty of raising the growth rate by more than one or two percentage points, have been explored by Edward Denison in his influential study, *The Sources of Economic Growth in the United States and the Alternatives Before Us,* New York, Committee for Economic Development, January 1962, Supplementary Paper No. 13.

512   *Amenities and Disamenities of Economic Growth*

growth are advocates of the future against the present. Their case rests
on the view that in a market economy left to itself, the future would be
shortchanged because too small a fraction of current output would be
saved. We mention this point now because we shall return later to the
ironical fact that the antigrowth men of the 1970s believe that it is they
who represent the claims of a fragile future against a voracious present.

    Like the enthusiasts to whom they are a reaction, current critics
of growth are disenchanted with both theory and policy, with both the
descriptive and the normative implications of the doctrines of the previous decade. The sources of disenchantment are worth considering
today, because they indicate agenda for future theoretical and empirical research.

    We have chosen to direct our attention to three important prob-
lems raised by those who question the desirability and possibility of
future growth: (a) How good are measures of output currently used for
evaluating the growth of economic welfare? (b) Does the growth process inevitably waste our natural resources? (c) How does the rate of
population growth affect economic welfare? In particular, what would
be the effect of zero population growth?

MEASURES OF ECONOMIC WELFARE

A major question raised by critics of economic growth is whether we
have been growing at all in any meaningful sense. Gross national product statistics cannot give the answers, for GNP is not a measure of
economic welfare. Erlich is right in claiming that maximization of GNP
is not a proper objective of policy. Economists all know that, and yet
their everyday use of GNP as the standard measure of economic performance apparently conveys the impression that they are evangelistic
workshipers of GNP.

    An obvious shortcoming of GNP is that it is an index of produc-
tion, not consumption. The goal of economic activity, after all, is consumption. Although this is the central premise of economics, the profession has been slow to develop, either conceptually or statistically,
a measure of economic performance oriented to consumption, broadly
defined and carefully calculated. We have constructed a primitive and
experimental "measure of economic welfare" (MEW), in which we attempt to allow for the more obvious discrepancies between GNP and
economic welfare. A complete account is given in Appendix A. The
main results will be discussed here and summarized in Tables 1 and 2.

Is Growth Obsolete? 513

In proposing a welfare measure, we in no way deny the importance of the conventional national income accounts or of the output measures based upon them. Our MEW is largely a rearrangement of items of the national accounts. Gross and net national product statistics are the economists' chief tools for short-run analysis, forecasting, and policy and are also indispensable for many other purposes.

Our adjustments to GNP fall into three general categories: reclassification of GNP expenditures as consumption, investment, and intermediate; imputation for the services of consumer capital, for leisure, and for the product of household work; correction for some of the disamenities of urbanization.

1. Reclassification of GNP Final Expenditures

Our purposes are first, to subtract some items that are better regarded as instrumental and intermediate than as final output, and second, to allocate all remaining items between consumption and net investment. Since the national accounts do not differentiate among government purchases of goods and services, one of our major tasks will be to split them among the three categories: intermediate, consumption, and net investment. We will also reclassify some private expenditures.

Intermediate products are goods and services whose contributions to present or future consumer welfare are completely counted in the values of other goods and services. To avoid double counting they should not be included in reckoning the net yield of economic activity. Thus all national income accounts reckon as final consumption the bread but not the flour and as capital formation the finished house but not the lumber. The more difficult and controversial issues in assigning items to intermediate or final categories are the following:

Capital Consumption. The depreciation of capital stocks is a cost of production, and output required to offset the depreciation is intermediate as surely as materials consumed in the productive process. For most purposes, including welfare indexes, NNP is preferable to GNP. Only the difficulties and lags in estimating capital consumption have made GNP the popular statistic.

However, NNP itself fails to treat many durable goods as capital, and counts as final their entire output whether for replacement or accumulation. These elementary points are worth repeating because some of our colleagues are telling the public that economists glorify wasteful "through-put" for its own sake. Focusing on NNP, and accounting for

514   *Amenities and Disamenities of Economic Growth*

all durables as capital goods, would avoid such foolish paradoxes as the implication that deliberate efforts to make goods more perishable raise national output. We estimate, however, that proper treatment of consumer durables has little quantitative effect (see Table 1, lines 3 and 5).

The other capital consumption adjustments we have made arise from allowing for government capital and for the educational and medical capital embodied in human beings. In effect, we have reclassified education and health expenditures, both public and private, as capital investments.

Growth Requirements.   In principle net national product tells how much consumption the economy could indefinitely sustain. GNP does not tell that; consuming the whole GNP in any year would impair future consumption prospects. But *per capita* rather than aggregate consumption is the welfare objective; neither economists nor other observers would as a rule regard sheer increase in the numbers of people enjoying the same average standard of living as a gain in welfare. Even NNP exaggerates sustainable *per capita* consumption, except in a society with stationary population—another example of the pervasiveness of the "stationary" assumption in the past. Per capita consumption cannot be sustained with zero net investment; the capital stock must be growing at the same rate as population and the labor force. This capital-widening requirement is as truly a cost of staying in the same position as outright capital consumption.[2]

This principle is clear enough when growth is simply increase in population and the labor force. Its application to an economy with technological progress is by no means clear. Indeed, the very concept of national income becomes fuzzy. Should the capital-widening requirement then be interpreted to mean that capital should keep pace with output and technology, not just with the labor force? If so, the implied sustainable consumption per capita grows with the rate of technological progress. This is the point of view which we have taken in what follows. On the other hand, a given level of consumption per capita could be

---

[2] Consider the neoclassical model without technological change. When labor force is growing at rate g, the capital-labor ratio is k, gross product per worker is $f(k)$, net product per worker is $f(k) - \delta k$, then the net investment requirement is gk, and sustainable consumption per worker is $f(k) - \delta k - gk$. Denoting the capital-output ratio as $\mu = [k/f(k)]$, sustainable consumption per worker can also be written as $f(k)[1 - \mu(\delta + g)]$. Although NNP embodies in principle the depreciation deduction δk, it does not take account of the capital-widening requirement gk.

Is Growth Obsolete? 515

sustained with a steady decline in the capital-output ratio, thanks to technological progress.[3]

The growth requirement is shown on line 7 of Table 2. This is clearly a significant correction, measuring about 16 per cent of GNP in 1965.

Our calculations distinguish between actual and sustainable per capita consumption. *Actual MEW* may exceed or fall short of *sustainable MEW,* the amount that could be consumed while meeting both capital consumption and growth requirements. If these requirements are met, per capita consumption can grow at the trend rate of increase in labor productivity. When actual MEW is less than sustainable MEW, the economy is making even better provision for future consumers; when actual MEW exceeds sustainable MEW, current consumption in effect includes some of the fruits of future progress.

Instrumental Expenditures. Since GNP and NNP are measures of production rather than of welfare, they count many activities that are evidently not directly sources of utility themselves but are regrettably necessary inputs to activities that may yield utility. Some consumer outlays are only instrumental, for example, the costs of commuting to work. Some government "purchases" are also of this nature—for example, police services, sanitation services, road maintenance, national defense. Expenditures on these items are among the necessary overhead costs of a complex industrial nation-state, although there is plenty of room for disagreement as to the necessary amounts. We are making no judgments on such issues in classifying these outlays as intermediate rather than final uses of resources. Nevertheless, these decisions are difficult and controversial. The issues are clearly illustrated in the important case of national defense.

We exclude defense expenditures for two reasons. First, we see no direct effect of defense expenditures on household economic welfare. No reasonable country (or household) buys "national defense" for its own sake. If there were no war or risk of war, there would be no need

---

[3] As is well known, the whole concept of equilibrium growth collapses unless progress is purely labor-augmenting, "Harrod-neutral." In that case the rate g above is $n + \gamma$, where n is the natural rate of increase and γ is the rate of technological progress, and "labor force" means effective or augmented labor force. In equilibrium, output and consumption per natural worker grow at the rate γ, and "sustainable" consumption per capita means consumption growing steadily at this rate. Clearly, level consumption per capita can be sustained with smaller net investment than $g\mu f(k)$; so μ and k steadily decline. See section A.2.3, below.

516   *Amenities and Disamenities of Economic Growth*

for defense expenditures and no one would be the worse without them. Conceptually, then, defense expenditures are gross but not net output.

The second reason is that defense expenditures are input rather than output data. Measurable output is especially elusive in the case of defense. Conceptually, the output of the defense effort is national security. Has the value of the nation's security risen from $0.5 billion to $50 billion over the period from 1929 to 1965? Obviously not. It is patently more reasonable to assume that the rise in expenditure was due to deterioration in international relations and to changes in military technology. The cost of providing a given level of security has risen enormously. If there has been no corresponding gain in security since 1929, the defense cost series is a very misleading indicator of improvements in welfare.

The economy's ability to meet increased defense costs speaks well for its productive performance. But the diversion of productive capacity to this purpose cannot be regarded simply as a shift of national preferences and the product mix. Just as we count technological progress, managerial innovation, and environmental change when they work in our favor (consider new business machines or mineral discoveries) so we must count a deterioration in the environment when it works against us (consider bad weather and war). From the point of view of economic welfare, an arms control or disarmament agreement which would free resources and raise consumption by 10 per cent would be just as significant as new industrial processes yielding the same gains.

In classifying defense costs—or police protection or public health expenditures—as regrettable and instrumental, we certainly do not deny the possibility that given the unfavorable circumstances that prompt these expenditures consumers will ultimately be better off with them than without them. This may or may not be the case. The only judgment we make is that these expenditures yield no direct satisfactions. Even if the "regrettable" outlays are rational responses to unfavorable shifts in the environment of economic activity, we believe that a welfare measure, perhaps unlike a production measure, should record such environmental change.

We must admit, however, that the line between final and instrumental outlays is very hard to draw. For example, the philosophical problems raised by the malleability of consumer wants are too deep to be resolved in economic accounting. Consumers are susceptible to influence by the examples and tastes of other consumers and by the sales efforts of producers. Maybe all our wants are just regrettable necessities; maybe productive activity does no better than to satisfy the wants which it generates; maybe our net welfare product is tautologically zero. More seriously, we cannot measure welfare exclusively by the quantitative flows of goods and services. We need other gauges of the health of individuals and societies. These, too, will be relative to the value systems which determine whether given symptoms indicate health or disease. But the "social indicators" movement of recent years still lacks a coherent, integrative conceptual and statistical framework.

We estimate that overhead and regrettable expenses, so far as we have been able to define and measure them, rose from 8 per cent to 16 per cent of GNP over the period 1929–65 (Table 2, line 4).

2. Imputations for Capital Services, Leisure, and Nonmarket Work

In the national income accounts, rent is imputed on owner-occupied homes and counted as consumption and income. We must make similar imputations in other cases to which we have applied capital accounting. Like owner-occupied homes, other consumer durables and public investments yield consumption directly, without market transactions. In the case of educational and health capital, we have assumed the yields to be intermediate services rather than direct consumption; that is, we expect to see the fruits of investments in education and health realized in labor productivity and earnings, and we do not count them twice. Our measure understates economic welfare and its growth to the extent that education and medical care are direct rather than indirect sources of consumer satisfaction.

The omission of leisure and of nonmarket productive activity from measures of production conveys the impression that economists are blindly materialistic. Economic theory teaches that welfare could rise, even while NNP falls, as the result of voluntary choices to work for pay fewer hours per week, weeks per year, years per lifetime.

These imputations unfortunately raise serious conceptual questions, discussed at some length in section A.3, below. Suppose that in calculating aggregate dollar consumption the hours devoted to leisure and nonmarket productive activity are valued at their presumed opportunity cost, the money wage rate. In converting current dollar consumption to constant dollars, what assumption should be made about the unobservable price indexes for the goods and services consumed during those hours? The wage rate? The price index for marketed con-

518   *Amenities and Disamenities of Economic Growth*

TABLE 1
Measures of Economic Welfare, Actual and
Sustainable, Various Years, 1929–65
(billions of dollars, 1958 prices, except lines 14–19, as noted)

	1929	1935	1945	1947	1954	1958	1965
1 Personal consumption, national income and product accounts	139.6	125.5	183.0	206.3	255.7	290.1	397.7
2 Private instrumental expenditures	−10.3	−9.2	−9.2	−10.9	−16.4	−19.9	−30.9
3 Durable goods purchases	−16.7	−11.5	−12.3	−26.2	−35.5	−37.9	−60.9
4 Other household investment	−6.5	−6.3	−9.1	−10.4	−15.3	−19.6	−30.1
5 Services of consumer capital imputation	24.9	17.8	22.1	26.7	37.2	40.8	62.3
6 Imputation for leisure							
B	339.5	401.3	450.7	466.9	523.2	554.9	626.9
A	339.5	401.3	450.7	466.9	523.2	554.9	626.9
C	162.9	231.3	331.8	345.6	477.2	554.9	712.8
7 Imputation for nonmarket activities							
B	85.7	109.2	152.4	159.6	211.5	239.7	295.4
A	178.6	189.5	207.1	215.5	231.9	239.7	259.8
C	85.7	109.2	152.4	159.6	211.5	239.7	295.4
8 Disamenity correction	−12.5	−14.1	−18.1	−19.1	−24.3	−27.6	−34.6
9 Government consumption	0.3	0.3	0.4	0.5	0.5	0.8	1.2
10 Services of government capital imputation	4.8	6.4	8.9	10.0	11.7	14.0	16.6
11 Total consumption = actual MEW							
B	548.8	619.4	768.8	803.4	948.3	1,035.3	1,243.6
A	641.7	699.7	823.5	859.3	968.7	1,035.3	1,208.0
C	372.2	449.4	649.9	682.1	902.3	1,035.3	1,329.5
12 MEW net investment	−5.3	−46.0	−52.5	55.3	13.0	12.5	−2.5
13 Sustainable MEW							
B	543.5	573.4	716.3	858.7	961.3	1,047.8	1,241.1
A	636.4	653.7	771.0	914.6	981.7	1,047.8	1,205.5
C	366.9	403.4	597.4	737.4	915.3	1,047.8	1,327.0
14 Population (no. of mill.)	121.8	127.3	140.5	144.7	163.0	174.9	194.6

(continued)

Is Growth Obsolete? 519

Table 1 (concluded)

		1929	1935	1945	1947	1954	1958	1965
	Actual MEW per capita							
15	Dollars							
	B	4,506	4,866	5,472	5,552	5,818	5,919	6,391
	A	5,268	5,496	5,861	5,938	5,943	5,919	6,208
	C	3,056	3,530	4,626	4,714	5,536	5,919	6,832
16	Index (1929 = 100)							
	B	100.0	108.0	121.4	123.2	129.1	131.4	141.8
	A	100.0	104.3	111.3	112.7	112.8	112.4	117.8
	C	100.0	115.5	151.4	154.3	181.2	193.7	223.6
	Sustainable MEW per capita							
17	Dollars							
	B	4,462	4,504	5,098	5,934	5,898	5,991	6,378
	A	5,225	5,135	5,488	6,321	6,023	5,991	6,195
	C	3,012	3,169	4,252	5,096	5,615	5,991	6,819
18	Index (1929 = 100)							
	B	100.0	100.9	114.3	133.0	132.2	134.3	142.9
	A	100.0	98.3	105.0	121.0	115.3	114.7	118.6
	C	100.0	105.2	141.2	169.2	186.4	198.9	226.4
19	Per capita NNP							
	Dollars	1,545	1,205	2,401	2,038	2,305	2,335	2,897
	1929 = 100	100.0	78.0	155.4	131.9	149.2	151.1	187.5

Note: Variants A, B, C in the table correspond to different assumptions about the bearing of technological progress on leisure and nonmarket activities. See section A.3.2, below, for explanation.

Source: Appendix Table A.16.

sumption goods? Over a period of forty years the two diverge substantially; the choice between them makes a big difference in estimates of the growth of MEW. As explained in Appendix A, the market consumption "deflator" should be used if technological progress has augmented nonmarketed uses of time to the same degree as marketed labor. The wage rate should be the deflator if no such progress has occurred in the effectiveness of unpaid time.

In Tables 1 and 2 we provide calculations for three conceptual alternatives. Our own choice is variant B of MEW, in which the value of leisure is deflated by the wage rate; and the value of nonmarket activity, by the consumption deflator.

520 *Amenities and Disamenities of Economic Growth*

TABLE 2

Gross National Product and MEW, Various Years, 1929–65

(*billions of dollars, 1958 prices*)

	1929	1935	1945	1947	1954	1958	1965
1. Gross national product	203.6	169.5	355.2	309.9	407.0	447.3	617.8
2. Capital consumption, NIPA	−20.0	−20.0	−21.9	−18.3	−32.5	−38.9	−54.7
3. Net national product, NIPA	183.6	149.5	333.3	291.6	374.5	408.4	563.1
4. NIPA final output reclassified as regrettables and intermediates							
a. Government	−6.7	−7.4	−146.3	−20.8	−57.8	−56.4	−63.2
b. Private	−10.3	−9.2	−9.2	−10.9	−16.4	−19.9	−30.9
5. Imputations for items not included in NIPA							
a. Leisure	339.5	401.3	450.7	466.9	523.2	554.9	626.9
b. Nonmarket activity	85.7	109.2	152.4	159.6	211.5	239.7	295.4
c. Disamenities	−12.5	−14.1	−18.1	−19.1	−24.3	−27.6	−34.6
d. Services of public and private capital	29.7	24.2	31.0	36.7	48.9	54.8	78.9
6. Additional capital consumption	−19.3	−33.4	−11.7	−50.8	−35.2	−27.3	−92.7
7. Growth requirement	−46.1	−46.7	−65.8	+5.4	−63.1	−78.9	−101.8
8. Sustainable MEW	543.6	573.4	716.3	858.6	961.3	1,047.7	1,241.1

NIPA = national income and product accounts.

Note: Variants A, B, C in the table correspond to different assumptions about the bearing of technological progress on leisure and nonmarket activities. Variant A assumes that neither has benefited from technological progress at the rate of increase of real wages; variant C assumes that both have so benefited; variant B assumes that leisure has not been augmented by technological progress but other nonmarket activities have benefited. See section A.3.2, below, for explanation.

Source: Appendix Table A.17.

3. Disamenities of Urbanization

The national income accounts largely ignore the many sources of utility or disutility that are not associated with market transactions or measured by the market value of goods and services. If one of my neighbors cultivates a garden of ever-increasing beauty, and another makes more and more noise, neither my increasing appreciation of the one nor my growing annoyance with the other comes to the attention of the Department of Commerce.

Is Growth Obsolete? 521

Likewise there are some socially productive assets (for example, the environment) that do not appear in any balance sheets. Their services to producers and consumers are not valued in calculating national income. By the same token no allowance is made for depletion of their capacity to yield services in the future.

Many of the negative "externalities" of economic growth are connected with urbanization and congestion. The secular advances recorded in NNP figures have accompanied a vast migration from rural agriculture to urban industry. Without this occupational and residential revolution we could not have enjoyed the fruits of technological progress. But some portion of the higher earnings of urban residents may simply be compensation for the disamenities of urban life and work. If so we should not count as a gain of welfare the full increments of NNP that result from moving a man from farm or small town to city. The persistent association of higher wages with higher population densities offers one method of estimating the costs of urban life as they are valued by people making residential and occupational decisions.

As explained in section A.4, below, we have tried to estimate by cross-sectional regressions the income differentials necessary to hold people in localities with greater population densities. The resulting estimates of the disamenity costs of urbanization are shown in Table 1, line 8. As can be seen, the estimated disamenity premium is quite substantial, running about 5 per cent of GNP. Nevertheless, the urbanization of the population has not been so rapid that charging it with this cost significantly reduces the estimated rate of growth of the economy.

The adjustments leading from national accounts "personal consumption" to MEW consumption are shown in Table 1, and the relations of GNP, NNP, and MEW are summarized in Table 2. For reasons previously indicated, we believe that a welfare measure should have the dimension *per capita*. We would stress the per capita MEW figures shown in Tables 1 and 2.

Although the numbers presented here are very tentative, they do suggest the following observations. First, MEW is quite different from conventional output measures. Some consumption items omitted from GNP are of substantial quantitative importance. Second, our preferred variant of per capita MEW has been growing more slowly than per capita NNP (1.1 per cent for MEW as against 1.7 per cent for NNP, at annual rates over the period 1929–65). Yet MEW has been growing. The progress indicated by conventional national accounts is not just a myth that evaporates when a welfare-oriented measure is substituted.

522   *Amenities and Disamenities of Economic Growth*

GROWTH AND NATURAL RESOURCES

Calculations like the foregoing are unlikely to satisfy critics who believe that economic growth per se piles up immense social costs ignored in even the most careful national income calculations. Faced with the finiteness of our earth and the exponential growth of economy and population, the environmentalist sees inevitable starvation. The specter of Malthus is haunting even the affluent society.

There is a familiar ring to these criticisms. Ever since the industrial revolution pessimistic scientists and economists have warned that the possibilities of economic expansion are ultimately limited by the availability of natural resources and that society only makes the eventual future reckoning more painful by ignoring resource limitations now.

In important part, this is a warning about population growth, which we consider below. Taking population developments as given, will natural resources become an increasingly severe drag on economic growth? We have not found evidence to support this fear. Indeed, the opposite appears to be more likely: Growth of output per capita will accelerate ever so slightly even as stocks of natural resources decline.

The prevailing standard model of growth assumes that there are no limits on the feasibility of expanding the supplies of nonhuman agents of production. It is basically a two-factor model in which production depends only on labor and reproducible capital. Land and resources, the third member of the classical triad, have generally been dropped. The simplifications of theory carry over into empirical work. The thousands of aggregate production functions estimated by econometricians in the last decade are labor-capital functions. Presumably the tacit justification has been that reproducible capital is a near-perfect substitute for land and other exhaustible resources, at least in the perspective of heroic aggregation customary in macroeconomics. If substitution for natural resources is not possible in any given technology, or if a particular resource is exhausted, we tacitly assume that "land-augmenting" innovations will overcome the scarcity.

These optimistic assumptions about technology stand in contrast to the tacit assumption of environmentalists that no substitutes are available for natural resources. Under this condition, it is easily seen that output will indeed stop growing or will decline. It thus appears that the substitutability (or technically, the elasticity of substitution) between the neoclassical factors, capital and labor, and natural resources is of crucial importance to future growth. This is an area needing extensive further research, but we have made two forays to see what the evidence is. Details are given in Appendix B, below.

First we ran several simulations of the process of economic growth in order to see which assumptions about substitution and technology fit the "stylized" facts. The important facts are: growing income per capita and growing capital per capita; relatively declining inputs and income shares of natural resources; and a slowly declining capital-output ratio. Among the various forms of production function considered, the following assumptions come closest to reproducing these stylized facts: (a) Either the elasticity of substitution between natural resources and other factors is high — significantly greater than unity — or resource-augmenting technological change has proceeded faster than overall productivity; (b) the elasticity of substitution between labor and capital is close to unity.

After these simulations were run, it appeared possible to estimate directly the parameters of the preferred form of production function. Econometric estimates confirm proposition (a) and seem to support the alternative of high elasticity of substitution between resources and the neoclassical factors.

Of course it is always possible that the future will be discontinuously different from the past. But if our estimates are accepted, then continuation of substitution during the next fifty years, during which many environmentalists foresee the end to growth, will result in a small increase — perhaps about 0.1 per cent per annum — in the growth of per capita income.

Is our economy, with its mixture of market processes and governmental controls, biased in favor of wasteful and shortsighted exploitation of natural resources? In considering this charge, two archetypical cases must be distinguished, although many actual cases fall between them. First, there are appropriable resources for which buyers pay market values and users market rentals. Second, there are inappropriable resources, "public goods," whose use appears free to individual producers and consumers but is costly in aggregate to society.

If the past is any guide for the future, there seems to be little reason to worry about the exhaustion of resources which the market already treats as economic goods. We have already commented on the irony that both growth men and antigrowth men invoke the interests of future generations. The issue between them is not whether and how much provision must be made for future generations, but in what form

524 *Amenities and Disamenities of Economic Growth*

it should be made. The growth man emphasizes reproducible capital and education. The conservationist emphasizes exhaustible resources —minerals in the ground, open space, virgin land. The economist's initial presumption is that the market will decide in what forms to transmit wealth by the requirement that all kinds of wealth bear a comparable rate of return. Now stocks of natural resources—for example, mineral deposits—are essentially sterile. Their return to their owners is the increase in their prices relative to prices of other goods. In a properly functioning market economy, resources will be exploited at such a pace that their rate of relative price appreciation is competitive with rates of return on other kinds of capital. Many conservationists have noted such price appreciation with horror, but if the prices of these resources accurately reflect the scarcities of the future, they must rise in order to prevent too rapid exploitation. Natural resources *should* grow in relative scarcity—otherwise they are an inefficient way for society to hold and transmit wealth compared to productive physical and human capital. Price appreciation protects resources from premature exploitation.

How would an excessive rate of exploitation show up? We would see rates of relative price increase that are above the general real rate of return on wealth. This would indicate that society had in the past used precious resources too profligately, relative to the tastes and technologies later revealed. The scattered evidence we have indicates little excessive price rise. For some resources, indeed, prices seem to have risen more slowly than efficient use would indicate ex post.

If this reasoning is correct, the nightmare of a day of reckoning and economic collapse when, for example, all fossil fuels are forever gone seems to be based on failure to recognize the existing and future possibilities of substitute materials and processes. As the day of reckoning approaches, fuel prices will provide—as they do not now—strong incentives for such substitutions, as well as for the conservation of remaining supplies. On the other hand, the warnings of the conservationists and scientists do underscore the importance of continuous monitoring of the national and world outlook for energy and other resources. Substitutability might disappear. Conceivably both the market and public agencies might be too complacent about the prospects for new and safe substitutes for fossil fuels. The opportunity and need for fruitful collaboration between economists and physical scientists has never been greater.

Possible abuse of public natural resources is a much more serious problem. It is useful to distinguish between *local* and *global* ecological disturbances. The former include transient air pollution, water pollution, noise pollution, visual disamenities. It is certainly true that we have not charged automobile users and electricity consumers for their pollution of the skies, or farmers and housewives for the pollution of lakes by the runoff of fertilizers and detergents. In that degree our national product series have overestimated the advance of welfare. Our urban disamenity estimates given above indicate a current overestimate of about 5 per cent of total consumption.

There are other serious consequences of treating as free things which are not really free. This practice gives the wrong signals for the directions of economic growth. The producers of automobiles and of electricity should be given incentives to develop and to utilize "cleaner" technologies. The consumers of automobiles and electricity should pay in higher prices for the pollution they cause, or for the higher costs of low-pollution processes. If recognition of these costs causes consumers to shift their purchases to other goods and services, that is only efficient. At present overproduction of these goods is uneconomically subsidized as truly as if the producers received cash subsidies from the Treasury.

The mistake of the antigrowth men is to blame economic growth per se for the misdirection of economic growth. The misdirection is due to a defect of the pricing system — a serious but by no means irreparable defect and one which would in any case be present in a stationary economy. Pollutants have multiplied much faster than the population or the economy during the last thirty years. Although general economic growth has intensified the problem, it seems to originate in particular technologies. The proper remedy is to correct the price system so as to discourage these technologies. Zero economic growth is a blunt instrument for cleaner air, prodigiously expensive and probably ineffectual.

As for the danger of global ecological catastrophes, there is probably very little that economics alone can say. Maybe we are pouring pollutants into the atmosphere at such a rate that we will melt the polar icecaps and flood all the world's seaports. Unfortunately, there seems to be great uncertainty about the causes and the likelihood of such occurrences. These catastrophic global disturbances warrant a higher priority for research than the local disturbances to which so much attention has been given.

526   *Amenities and Disamenities of Economic Growth*

POPULATION GROWTH

Like the role of natural resources, the role of population in the standard
neoclassical model is ripe for re-examination. The assumption is that
population and labor force grow exogenously, like compound interest.
Objections arise on both descriptive and normative grounds. We know
that population growth cannot continue forever. Some day there will
be stable or declining population, either with high birth and death rates
and short life expectancies, or with low birth and death rates and long
life expectancies. As Richard Easterlin argues in his National Bureau
book,[4] there surely is some adaptation of human fertility and mortality
to economic circumstances. Alas, neither economists nor other social
scientists have been notably successful in developing a theory of fertility that corresponds even roughly to the facts. The subject deserves
much more attention from economists and econometricians than it has
received.

On the normative side, the complaint is that economists should
not fatalistically acquiesce in whatever population growth happens.
They should instead help to frame a population policy. Since the costs
to society of additional children may exceed the costs to the parents,
childbearing decisions are a signal example of market failure. How to
internalize the full social costs of reproduction is an even more challenging problem than internalizing the social costs of pollution.

During the past ten years, the fertility of the United States population has declined dramatically. If continued, this trend would soon
diminish fertility to a level ultimately consistent with zero population
growth. But such trends have been reversed in the past, and in the absence of any real understanding of the determinants of fertility, predictions are extremely hazardous.

The decline may be illustrated by comparing the 1960 and 1967
net reproduction rates and intrinsic (economists would say "equilibrium") rates of growth of the United States population. The calculations of Table 3 refer to the asymptotic steady-state implications of
indefinite continuation of the age-specific fertility and mortality rates
of the year 1960 or 1967. Should the trend of the 1960s continue, the
intrinsic growth rate would become zero, and the net reproduction rate
1.000, in the 1970s. Supposing that the decline in fertility then stopped.
The actual population would grow slowly for another forty or fifty

---

[4] *Population, Labor Force, and Long Swings in Economic Growth: The American
Experience,* New York, NBER, 1968.

Is Growth Obsolete? 527

TABLE 3
U.S. Population Characteristics in Equilibrium

	Intrinsic Growth Rate (per cent per year)	Net Reproduction Rate	Median Age
1960 fertility-mortality	2.1362	1.750	21–22
1967 fertility-mortality	0.7370	1.221	28
Hypothetical ZPG	0.0000	1.000	32

years while the inherited bulge in the age distribution at the more fertile years gradually disappeared. The asymptotic size of the population would be between 250 million and 300 million.

One consequence of slowing down the rate of population growth by diminished fertility is, of course, a substantial increase in the age of the equilibrium population, as indicated in the third column of Table 3. It is hard to judge to what degree qualitative change and innovation have in the past been dependent on quantitative growth. When our institutions are expanding in size and in number, deadwood can be gracefully bypassed and the young can guide the new. In a stationary population, institutional change will either be slower or more painful.

The current trend in fertility in the United States suggests that, contrary to the pessimistic warnings of some of the more extreme anti-growth men, it seems quite possible that ZPG can be reached while childbearing remains a voluntary private decision. Government policy can concentrate on making it completely voluntary by extending the availability of birth control knowledge and technique and of legal abortion. Since some 20 per cent of current births are estimated to be unintended, it may well be that intended births at present are insufficient to sustain the population.

Once the rate of population growth is regarded as a variable, perhaps one subject to conscious social control, the neoclassical growth model can tell some of the consequences of its variation. As explained above, sustainable per capita consumption (growing at the rate of technological progress) requires enough net investment to increase the capital stock at the natural rate of growth of the economy (the sum of the

528 *Amenities and Disamenities of Economic Growth*

rate of increase of population and productivity). Given the capital-output ratio, sustainable consumption per capita will be larger the lower the rate of population increase; at the same time, the capital-widening requirement is diminished.

This is, however, not the only effect of a reduction of the rate of population growth. The equilibrium capital-output ratio itself is altered. The average wealth of a population is a weighted average of the wealth positions of people of different ages. Over its life cycle the typical family, starting from low or negative net worth, accumulates wealth to spend in old age, and perhaps in middle years when children are most costly. Now a stationary or slow-growing population has a characteristic age distribution much different from that of a rapidly growing population. The stationary population will have relatively fewer people in the early low-wealth years, but relatively more in the late low-wealth

TABLE 4

Illustrative Relationship of Sustainable Per Capita Consumption to Marginal Productivity of Capital and to Capital-Output Ratio

Marginal Productivity of Capital					Index of Consumption Per Capita (c)		
Gross (R)	Net of Depreciation ($R - \delta$)	Ratio of Capital to GNP (μ')	Ratio of Capital to NNP (μ)	Index of NNP per Capita (y)	1960 Pop. Growth	1967 Pop. Growth	ZPG
(1)	(2)	(3)	(4)	(5)	(6)	(7)	(8)
.09	.05	3.703	4.346	1.639	1.265	1.372	1.426
.105	.065	3.175	3.637	1.556	1.265	1.344	1.386
.12	.08	2.778	3.125	1.482	1.245	1.309	1.343
.15	.11	2.222	2.439	1.356	1.187	1.233	1.257

Note: A Cobb-Douglas production function is assumed for GNP, with constant returns to scale, with an elasticity of output with respect to capital (α) of $1/3$, and with the rate (γ) of labor-augmenting technological progress 3 per cent per year. The depreciation rate (δ) is assumed to be 4 per cent per year. GNP per capita (Y) is $ae^{\gamma t}k^\alpha$ and NNP per capita (y) is $Y - \delta k$, where k is the capital-labor ratio.
  Column 3: Since $Rk = \alpha Y$, $\mu' = k/Y = \alpha/R$.
  Column 4: $\mu = \mu'/(1 - \delta\mu')$.
  Column 5: $y = (1 - \delta\mu')Y$. For the index, $ae^{\gamma t}$ is set equal to 1.
  Columns 6, 7, and 8: $c = [1 - (n + \gamma)\mu]y$. Given $\gamma = 0.03$, $n + \gamma$ is 0.0513 for 1960, 0.0374 for 1967, 0.0300 for ZPG.

Is Growth Obsolete? 529

TABLE 5

Desired Wealth-Income Ratios Estimated
for Different Rates of Population Growth
(and for Different Equivalent Adult Scales
and Subjective Discount Rates [a])

Net Interest Rate $(R - \delta)$	Desired Wealth-Income Ratio (μ)		
	1960 Pop. Growth (.021)	1967 Pop. Growth (.007)	ZPG
Teenagers, 1.0; Children, 1.0; Discount, 0.02			
.05	−1.70	−1.46	−1.24
.065	0.59	0.91	1.16
.08	2.31	2.70	2.90
.11	4.31	4.71	4.95
Teenagers, 0.8; Children, 0.6; Discount, 0.01			
.05	0.41	0.74	0.97
.065	2.36	2.75	3.00
.08	3.74	4.16	4.41
.11	5.17	5.55	5.75
Teenagers, 0.8; Children, 0.6; Discount, 0.02			
.05	−1.17	−0.95	−0.75
.065	1.08	1.38	1.60
.08	2.74	3.11	3.34
.11	4.61	4.98	5.18
Teenagers, 0.0; Children, 0.0; Discount, 0.02			
.05	−0.40	−0.15	0.02
.065	1.93	2.20	2.36
.08	3.56	3.85	4.01
.11	5.20	5.47	5.61

Note: The desired wealth-income ratio is calculated for
a given steady state of population increase and the corresponding equilibrium age distribution. It is an aggregation
of the wealth and income positions of households of different ages. As explained in Appendix C it also depends on
the interest rate, the typical age-income profile and the expected growth of incomes ($\gamma = 0.03$), the rate of subjective
discount of future utility of consumption, and the weights
given to teenagers (boys 14–20 and girls 14–18) and other
children in household allocations of lifetime incomes to
consumption in different years. See Appendix C for further
explanation.

[a] Shown in boldface.

530 *Amenities and Disamenities of Economic Growth*

TABLE 6
Estimated Equilibrium Capital-Output Ratios
and Per Capita Consumption Rates [a]

Population Growth Rate	Interest Rate $(R - \delta)$	Capital-Output Ratio (μ)	Consumption Index (c)	Per Cent Increase in c over 1960
Teenagers, 1.0; Children, 1.0; Discount, 0.02				
1960	.089	2.88	1.23	
1967	.085	2.99	1.30	5.62
ZPG	.082	3.07	1.34	9.04
Teenagers, 0.8; Children, 0.6; Discount, 0.01				
1960	.074	3.28	1.25	
1967	.071	3.38	1.33	6.23
ZPG	.069	3.47	1.37	9.74
Teenagers, 0.8; Children, 0.6; Discount, 0.02				
1960	.084	3.00	1.24	
1967	.080	3.11	1.31	5.82
ZPG	.078	3.16	1.35	8.97
Teenagers, 0.0; Children, 0.0; Discount, 0.02				
1960	.077	3.22	1.25	
1967	.074	3.28	1.32	6.42
ZPG	.073	3.33	1.36	9.99

Note: Estimated by interpolation from Tables 4 and 5. See Figure 1.
[a] Equivalent adult scales and subjective discount rate are shown in boldface.

years. So it is not obvious in which direction the shift of weights moves the average.

We have, however, estimated the shift by a series of calculations described in Appendix C. Illustrative results are shown in Tables 4–6 and Figure 1. Evidently, reduction in the rate of growth increases the society's desired wealth-income ratio. This means an increase in the capital-output ratio which increases the society's sustainable consumption per capita.[5]

On both counts, therefore, a reduction in population increase

---

[5] Provided only that the change is made from an initial situation in which the net marginal productivity of capital exceeds the economy's natural rate of growth. Otherwise the increased capital-widening requirements exceed the gains in output.

Is Growth Obsolete? 531

FIGURE 1
Determination of Equilibrium Capital-Output Ratio and Interest Rate
(equivalent adult scale for teenagers and children = 1.0; subjective
discount rate = 0.02)

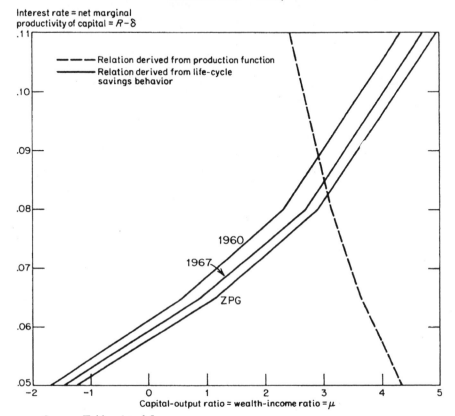

Interest rate = net marginal
productivity of capital = $R - \delta$

- ----- Relation derived from production function
- —— Relation derived from life-cycle savings behavior

1960
1967
ZPG

Capital-output ratio = wealth-income ratio = μ

Source: Tables 4 and 5.

should raise sustainable consumption. We have essayed an estimate
of the magnitude of this gain. In a ZPG equilibrium sustainable consumption per capita would be 9–10 per cent higher than in a steady
state of 2.1 per cent growth corresponding to 1960 fertility and mortality, and somewhat more than 3 per cent higher than in a steady state
of 0.7 per cent growth corresponding to 1967 fertility and mortality.

These neoclassical calculations do not take account of the lower
pressure of population growth on natural resources. As between the
1960 equilibrium and ZPG, the diminished drag of resource limitations
is worth about one-tenth of 1 per cent per annum in growth of per cap-

532 *Amenities and Disamenities of Economic Growth*

ita consumption. Moreover, if our optimistic estimates of the ease of substitution of other factors of production for natural resources are wrong, a slowdown of population growth will have much more important effects in postponing the day of reckoning.

Is growth obsolete? We think not. Although GNP and other national income aggregates are imperfect measures of welfare, the broad picture of secular progress which they convey remains after correction of their most obvious deficiencies. At present there is no reason to arrest general economic growth to conserve natural resources, although there is good reason to provide proper economic incentives to conserve resources which currently cost their users less than true social cost. Population growth cannot continue indefinitely, and evidently it is already slowing down in the United States. This slowdown will significantly increase sustainable per capita consumption. But even with ZPG there is no reason to shut off technological progress. The classical stationary state need not become our utopian norm.

Part II
Physical Accounts: Assessing the Biophysical Base of the Economy

[4]

Energy Analysis and Economic Valuation*

NICHOLAS GEORGESCU-ROEGEN
Regional Research Institute, West Virginia University
and Faculté des Sciences Economiques, Université Louis Pasteur, Strasbourg

I. Introduction

Ever since the oil embargo of 1973–74 everyone speaks of the *energy* crisis. And whether we are "optimists" or "pessimists", by now most of us recognize that what will happen in the end to this crisis is not an idle question. Only economists still refuse to see the indissoluble relationship between the scarcity of natural resources and the economic process as a whole. As an excuse we hear, for example, that the limitations of natural resources cannot lead to any interesting conclusions [72, 43], as if scarcity were not the very element around which the economic system turns and spins. But the "official" position is systematically defended by the decision-makers of the most influential economic associations. No invited paper at the Tokyo World Congress of the International Economic Organization dealt with the limitations of natural resources. As explained by an official communication, the Program Committee was "very selective." Most curiously, the general theme of the Congress was "Economic Growth and Resources" and the year was 1977! All the more we should admire Mogens Boserup's candid verdict at the closing session.

> There was a remarkable degree of consensus in turning down, or rather ignoring, all the 'doomsday' attitudes and opinions on natural resources. And even apart from that particular issue, there was an almost complete absence of sharp confrontation of opinions.
> As we know, a gathering of economists which fails to produce disagreement on essential issues is a rare occurrence—and even a scandal, some would say . . . . A question [thus],immediately comes to my mind: Why do economists agree so largely on the issue of natural resources, not only at an I.E.A. meeting in Tokyo, but in the profession as a whole? [7].

*The author is Professor Emeritus, Vanderbilt University. He is deeply grateful to Jean-Paul Fitoussi, Egon Matzner, and William H. Miernyk for their sympathetic interest in the endeavors summarized in this paper. He wants also to thank the Earhart Foundation for a timely research fellowship.

A contrasting situation prevails in other circles, where new energy experts in ever increasing numbers now expatiate to their hearts' delight on the issue of accessible sources of energy, more often than not contributing to the confusion of both students and policy makers.

Some writers, however, did not have to wait for the warning spelled out by the oil embargo. Long before it, they re-examined with new insights the old problem of the relation between the supply of accessible natural resources, the size of population, and the well-being of the people. But what is highly significant is that, with practically no exception, these writers also argued that energy is the only necessary support of the economic process. This position is not, therefore, a product of the oil embargo; it represents the result of a genuine intellectual endeavor.

It is natural to refer to the belief that energy alone counts as the "energetic" dogma, even though this meaning is slightly different from those used by physics in the past. At first, "energetics"—a term coined by William Macquorn Rankine—denoted the science we now call "thermodynamics". Subsequently, "energetics" was used to denote a school of thought defended by a few illustrious scientists (such as Wilhelm Ostwald and George Helm in Germany and Pierre Duhem in France) influenced in part by the scientific epistemology of Ernst Mach [45]. Against the idea set forth by Ludwig Boltzmann that the laws of energy are the direct consequences of the laws of Newtonian mechanics applied to the motion of *material* particles, the energetic school maintained that, on the contrary, matter must in the ultimate analysis reduce to the only "substance", energy. The current view that only energy matters for mankind's specific mode of existence is not completely identical with that school's position, but at bottom the two are sufficiently similar to justify using the term "energetics" for its label.

The fierce controversy surrounding the old energetic school represented a purely academic issue at the time. The same is not true for the present energetic dogma. Being the currently dominating dogma, it determines the principles that guide policy makers concerned with the energy shortage and technology assessment. Some of us may think that the validity of these principles also constitute only a purely academic issue. For mankind as a whole, however, it is a truly vital matter.

In this paper, I propose, first, to explain in broad terms the technical reasons why the energetic dogma is wrong, why matter matters, too.[1] Second, I shall use the analytical representation of a multi-process for discussing the general problem of energy analysis. On this basis, I shall show where the

---

1. I may explain that from my first analysis of the entropic nature of the economic process I have maintained that both energy *and* matter irrevocably degrade from available into unavailable forms [29, 75, 93–6; 30, 142, 277–80]. At the time, believing that my thesis was common knowledge at least among natural scientists, I did not go into technical details. But the accentuation of the energetic position after the oil embargo convinced me that my belief was wrong; I then began offering specific arguments in support of my thesis [31–38].

recent claims that energy analysis is the rational basis for economic valuation go wrong. Third, on the basis of the impossibility of reducing matter to energy, I shall show that economic choice is a purely economic matter, not a physico-chemical one. Finally, I shall apply some of these results to the problem of what constitutes a *viable* technology, as distinct from *feasible* recipes. As an application, I shall investigate the viability of a technology based on direct use of solar radiation through the recipes known *at present*.[2] Surprising though it might seem to the current energetic temper, the conclusion of this last probing is that such a technology is not *viable*, that any direct use of solar radiation by any present recipe is a "parasite" of the current technology based on other sources. This result calls for a thorough reorientation of our present approach to technology assessment.

II. The Energetic Dogma

Different writers justify the modern dogma of energetics in different, some-times in substantially different, ways. For example, one of the earliest pro-pounders, Fred Cottrell [22] argued that all that mankind needs is to obtain *net energy*. The definition of this concept presents no apparent difficulties. If we use, for example, the energy equivalent of one ton of crude oil to extract ten tons of shale oil, a simple arithmetical substraction tells us that the resulting net energy is the equivalent of nine tons of oil. Twenty years later, one of the ablest American ecologists, H. T. Odum [53], revived Cottrell's idea and raised it to the rank of the only criterion of efficiency: the greater the net energy obtained by a process, the more efficient is that process.[3] Because of its simplicity, the principle has since been widely accepted and also defended with even greater force. Indeed, what could be more senseless than to use one ton of oil to obtain less than one ton of oil and nothing else?

However, this very idea prompts one to ask "why not relate efficiency to *net matter?*" Indeed, we use copper in the process of producing copper; hence, we thereby gain some net matter. Whatever we may do, we are faced with new snags. Copper mining also implies a *negative* net energy, whereas any power plant implies numerous *negative* net matters.

Even though Odum is not as explicit on this point as one would wish, we must grant him that net energy must be computed by subtracting from the gross output not only the energy directly used in the process but also the amount of energy necessary to produce or repair all *material* parts worn out by the process (Sec. VI). With this explanation, however, the slip of the energetic bias is showing badly. For without this bias, one may very well propose, by

2. Even though another official communication affirms that technology assessment is not an accepted preoccupation for the established profession, I owe no apology whatsoever for dealing with that problem in this paper.

3. A different approach focuses instead on gross energy (Sec. VI).

symmetry, to reduce everything to net matter, defined as the excess of matter output over the matter necessary to produce the matter and the energy used up. Such a proposal could point out that matter is used in a power plant to produce energy just as in another process energy is used to produce matter. The truth, as we shall see in time, is that neither net energy by itself nor net matter by itself can constitute a general principle of technology assessment (Sec. VIII).

Another mode of justifying energetics in recent times may be traced back to the now classic volume *The Next Hundred Years*, where we read that "All we need do is to add sufficient energy to the system and we can obtain whatever materials we desire" [11, 90, 95, 114]. The energetic gospel in this plain form has been spread by numberless other authors. But Harrison Brown and his associates have also justified it by the axiom that recycling of matter can, in principle, be complete [11, 90–92]. Interesting also is that they immediately added that "fundamentally there is no lower limit to the grade of an ore which can be processed," which obviously is a necessary implication of that axiom.[4]

The few physicists and chemists who have touched this issue also seem to support energetics. For example, Alvin Weinberg, quoted in [32], described energy as "an ultimate raw material" because "energy is convertible into most of the other requirements of life"—which can only consist of matter. Take also Glenn Seaborg, who argued that science will ultimately eliminate all technical inefficiencies so that with an abundant amount of energy we shall be able "to recycle almost any waste, . . . to extract, transport and return to nature when necessary all materials in an acceptable form, in an acceptable amount, and in an acceptable place so that the natural environment will remain natural and will support the continued growth and evolution of all forms of life" [65].

Taken at its face value, this is quite strong energetic position; it comes near to claiming that the whole planet could be maintained intact forever. But an even more stringent expression of the modern energetic dogma is due to Kenneth Boulding [4]: "There is, fortunately, no law of increasing material entropy."[5] This declaration exposes without any shadows the root of that dogma; matter does not count, only energy counts for mankind's economic struggle.

The foregoing variants seem to cover the entire spectrum of the energetic arguments. However, they all lead to one and the same analytical picture of the economic process in its relation to the environment. It is the picture

4. Energetics also permeates Brown's position in his earlier volume [10]. But, curiously, both volumes cite facts that go directly against the energetic dogma (see below, Sec. V).

5. Years after taking this position and yet arguing that a close relation exists between the Entropy Law and the economic process, Boulding [5], turned to arguing that entropy is a "negative potential" and hence is not a concept fit for explaining evolutionary development. But still more recently he came to realize that materials also are vital environmental elements [6].

represented by the multi-process matrix of flows and funds shown in Table I [30].[6] To avoid irrelevant issues, let us divide the economic process only into those consolidated processes and aggregated categories that are relevant for the present argument:

P_1: produces "controlled" energy, CE, from energy in situ, ES;
P_2: produces "capital" goods, K;
P_3: produces "consumer" goods, C;
P_4: recycles completely the material wastes, W, of all processes into recycled matter, RM;
P_5: maintains the population, H.

The special features of the foregoing picture must be well marked. First, neither a growing nor a declining economy can provide an acid test for the energetic dogma. Material growth cannot feed on an environmental flow of energy alone,[7] whereas a declining economy may very well need no flow of environmental matter. The test case must therefore be a stationary process, or, with Marx's more felicitous terminology, a reproducible one.

But regardless of the actual system, one point is beyond any doubt ever since Lord Kelvin observed more than one hundred years ago that energy is not lost but only becomes unavailable to us [74, 189; 78, 236–39]. All processes, therefore, necessarily produce dissipated (unavailable) energy, DE, which returns to the environment. In the energetic model, however, no matter leaves the economic process; all matter is completely recycled within that process. Thus, no matter has to be brought into the economic process from the environment. The only flows between the economic process and the environment are energy flows, namely, the input flow e_1 and the output flow $d = \Sigma d_i$.

Second, the representation of Table I reflects one elementary aspect of reality that needs unparsimonious emphasis in view of the "flow complex" that seems to dominate modern economic thought [29, 88; 30, 219]. Like all actual processes, the economic process has a material scaffold represented by its fund elements: capital equipment, K_i; people, H_i and H; and Ricardian land, L_i. We can never handle energy without a material lever, a material receptor, or a material transmitter. We ourselves are material structures without which no biological life can exist. In including the material funds (actually, the agents) in the analytical picture, I have assumed—a perfectly fair assump-

---

6. This analytical representation is both simple and safe. It does away with the bewildering flow diagrams used by ecologists and energy analysts (in which funds are ignored), and it avoids the analytical pitfall of "internal flow" that awaits the users of the input-output table [30, 253–62]. Also, the flow-fund model should not be confused with the flow-stock model introduced by Sir John Hicks in the theory of market disequilibriums. The function of the stocks is to accumulate flows and to decumulate themselves into flows. Funds participate in a process but without changing.

7. Obvious though this point may seem, it calls for some technical justifications, which will be provided later (Sec. III).

tion, I think—that the energetic position does not go so far as to claim that actual processes require no material structures of the kind we recognize side by side with energy at the macro-level.

Third, the output flow of capital, x_{22}, is destined to maintain the capital funds K_i in a reproducible condition; their wear-and-tear is thus compensated for by the maintenance flows x_{2i}. Similarly, the flows x_{i5} maintain the population H "intact". These are the elementary conditions for the (P_i)'s to be reproducible. And since in the case under consideration all flows must be expressed in physical units (calories or moles, for instance), the following equalities must always prevail as an aggregated translation of the conservation laws at the macro-level:

$$d_1 = e_1 - x_{11}, \qquad d_i = x_{1i} \qquad\qquad (i = 2, 3, 4, 5),$$

$$w_1 = x_{21}, \qquad w_2 = x_{42} - x_{22}, \qquad w_3 = x_{23} + x_{43} - x_{33}, \qquad (1)$$

$$w_4 = x_{44} - x_{24}, \qquad w_5 = x_{25} + x_{35}.$$

Fourth, every recipe (P_i) is assumed to be *feasible*; that is, it can produce its product provided it is supported by the specified funds and is fed the specified inputs. But the feasibility of every recipe (P_i) does not necessarily

Table I. The Economic Process in Relation to the Environment According to the Energetic Dogma

Product	(P_1)	(P_2)	(P_3)	(P_4)	(P_5)
		Flow Coordinates			
CE	x_{11}	$-x_{12}$	$-x_{13}$	$-x_{14}$	$-x_{15}$
K	$-x_{21}$	x_{22}	$-x_{23}$	$-x_{24}$	$-x_{25}$
C	*	*	x_{33}	*	$-x_{35}$
RM	*	$-x_{42}$	$-x_{43}$	x_{44}	*
ES	$-e_1$	*	*	*	*
W	w_1	w_2	w_3	$-w_4$	w_5
DE	d_1	d_2	d_3	d_4	d_5
		Fund Coordinates			
Capital equipment	K_1	K_2	K_3	K_4	K_5
People	H_1	H_2	H_3	H_4	H_5
Ricardian land	L_1	L_2	L_3	L_4	L_5

imply the *viability* of the *technology* represented by all the processes together (an important point to be retained for further reference). The necessary and sufficient conditions for the viability of the technology of our reproducible economic system is given by the inequalities $x_{i5} \geqslant x^0_{i5}$, x^0_{i5} being a minimum determined by the standard of living, and the well-known relations

$$\sum{}' x_{1i} = x_{11}, \qquad \sum{}' x_{2i} = x_{22}, \qquad x_{35} = x_{33}, \qquad \sum{}' x_{4i} = x_{44},$$

$$\sum{}' w_i = w_4, \tag{2}$$

where the prime accent shows that the variable subscript cannot be equal to the fixed one.[8]

III. Perpetual Motion of the Third Kind

Let us now recall that in the thermodynamic terminology established by Ilya Prigogine a system that can exchange only energy with its surroundings is *closed*. The economic process represented by Table I is therefore a closed system. In addition, this closed system is reproducible—i.e., it is a steady state, to use the thermodynamic terminology. According to the energetic dogma, it can provide internal *mechanical* work at a constant rate as long as a constant flow e_1 of environmental energy is forthcoming. Because of the theoretical importance of such a system for the energetic thesis and for other issues as well, I have proposed to refer to it as *perpetual motion of the third kind*.[9] And since my position is that this perpetual motion is impossible, by analogy with the negation of the other two perpetual motions by the first and second thermodynamic laws we may regard this impossibility as a fourth law of thermodynamics [31; 34–38].[10]

A technical point that must be dealt with before anything else in connection with this proposition concerns the famous Einsteinian equivalence between mass and energy, $E = mc^2$. For as even a Nobel laureate, Hannes Alfvén propounds, "matter, then, can be seen as a form of energy" [1]. The assertion only bespeaks the familiar bias in favor of energy. It is not because matter is not just mass, but some positive amount of mass and some positive

---

8. The case in which all w_i's are null, which does away with any need for recycling, corresponds to Boulding's tenet.

9. To my knowledge, only Zemansky [78, 193] uses the same term for a closely related system—namely, for a system in which work is not dissipated against friction, viscosity, etc. My definition, I believe, is more relevant analytically.

10. This law should not be regarded (as has proved possible quite often) as a corollary of the Entropy Law. According to this law, an *isolated* system—i.e., a system that can exchange neither matter nor energy with its surroundings—tends toward the Heat Death—or toward Chaos if one includes matter under the rule of that law [29, 75; 30, 142; 32, 8]. The confusion may stem from the loose practice of using "closed" instead of "isolated", e.g., [46].

Here it may be well to recall that a system which can exchange both matter and energy is *open*. The fourth logical category, a system that may exchange only matter, is factually impossible since any transport of matter involves energy as well.

amount of energy structured in the definite patterns of the chemical elements
and their compounds, that Einstein's equivalence does not bear out that view.
I wish to submit that there is an intrinsic asymmetry between matter and
energy, which is due to the asymmetry between mass and energy. Indeed, as
long as we do not recognize the irreducible asymmetry between the two
terms of the Einstein formula—which with properly chosen units may be
written in the perfectly symmetrical form $E = m$—we are just as justified to
speak of a "crisis of matter" as of a "crisis of energy".

Energy is converted into mass (and vice versa) in numerous nuclear
reactions which begin and end with some mass. In the familiar relations

Proton + Antineutrino $\rightleftarrows$ *Neutron* + Positron

Neutron + Neutrino $\rightleftarrows$ *Proton* + Electron

where the underlined terms have a positive mass. Pairs of anti-particles with
positive mass may be entirely converted into pure energy, as it happens when
an electron and a positron by colliding turned into a photon. To be sure, the
reverse reaction also is *possible*. Photons may be converted into pairs of
electrons and positrons, as it happened on a large scale immediately after the
Big Bang while the temperature of the universe was still greater than 6 x 10⁹
degrees Kelvin, which is the threshold of that reaction. But since such pairs
are extremely unstable (like all pairs of matter and antimatter), they almost
instantaneously disintegrate into pure energy. This is why positrons exist
only in some intense astronomical phenomena or in high-energy laboratories.
For photons to split into neutrons and antineutrons the temperature must be
higher than 10^{13} degrees Kelvin, which is one hundred times higher than that
believed to prevail at one hundredth of a second after the Big Bang. This last
temperature—about 10^{11} degrees Kelvin—is greater than the hottest stars
[75]. Nothing can be surmised about what happened before that particular
moment, but what we know is that *material* particles—protons and neutrons
were not produced then and cannot be produced now from pure energy.[11]
And since without nucleons there can be no atoms, hence no matter, the
present explanations of the origin of the chemical elements cannot do without
assuming that the combined number of the protons and neutrons has always
been the same as in the initial hot soup [73; 75]. To express the fact that
nowhere in the universe matter can be created out of pure energy, the
Einstein relation should be written $E + mc^2 = E_0 + m_0c^2$, $m_0 > 0$ whenever m
includes some nucleon mass, that is, some matter. (The subscript identifies
initial amounts.)

---

11. Only what is proven to work at the time has a legitimate place in the arguments of the
sort developed here. Speculations have no proof value and may even be dangerous. For example,
were the servants of science to persistently preach that we will certainly learn how to block out
gravitation by some cavorite—the material discovered by Mr. Cavor in one of H. G. Wells's
fantasies—people would be misled in building houses without stairs and without elevators.

Heavier elements are currently fused from lighter ones but only in stars, where the temperature reaches astronomical levels, between 10^7 and 10^{10} degrees Kelvin.[12] But at these temperatures matter exists only in a desaggregated state as plasma. Should a closed system become so hot, it could no longer produce any mechanical work (let alone harbor life).

Nuclear reactions are certainly going on at all times on our planet, too. Radioactive elements continuously decay. However, these phenomena as well as all nuclear reactions set up by us usually convert mass into energy, *not vice versa*. Mass is converted into energy even when we light up a match. This loss of mass is fantastically small because of the large value of c. But the difference between the weight of spent nuclear cores and their initial weight can be shown on ordinary scales. And at the Sun's dimension, 4,200,000 tons of mass are "lost" every second. Certainly, we can also convert energy into additional mass, but only in very special cases (usually, in laboratory installations) and in relatively small amounts and not into *nucleon* mass.

At the temperatures at which mechanical work can be performed, the overwhelming chemical elements are stable. In a closed system the amount of each element remains constant. "Materials are not destroyed",—Slesser, an energy specialist, tells us, "the iron molecule in iron ore is still an iron molecule when it is turned into steel or when it ultimately ends up as rust" [70]. Seaborg also argues that "we have here on earth the same amount of matter we have had since the dawn of history"—in truth, since the earth became a stable planet [65]. Only, both Slesser and Seaborg intended their observations as a support of energetics, in the same way in which Brooks and Andrews claimed that "the literal notion of running out of mineral supplies is ridiculous. The entire planet is composed of minerals" [9].

The simplest way to expose the fallacy of the Brooks-Andrews argument is to note that, by the same token, we could maintain that we cannot possibly run out of energy because the entire planet is full of energy. Indeed, the thermal energy contained in the ocean waters would alone suffice to maintain an undreamed-of industrial activity for billions of years to come. The rub is that all (or practically all) this fantastic amount of energy is unavailable for conversion into mechanical work by an engine of *finite* dimensions, which must by necessity operate in *cycles*. Indeed, as Planck suggested [57; 58], the thermal energy of a bath of constant temperature could be converted into mechanical work by an infinitesimally slow moving piston-and-cylinder of an *infinite* length (on the same familiar principles that govern the isothermal expansion of the gas in a Carnot cycle).[13]

---

12. Despite the immensity of these ovens the material universe still consists mainly of hydrogen, according to some estimations, 92.06 percent, with helium representing 7.82 percent [2].

13. Peculiar thermodynamic ideas such as this bring to mind Dirk ter Haar's statement that the concept of entropy "is not easily understood even by physicists," [30] may seem a severe judgment typical of an authority in a field. However, nowadays most physicists have only a

Certainly, the whole planet is made of matter. But the argument based on this point ignores the fact that, just like the thermal energy of the Earth, not all terrestrial matter is in available form. Matter also continuously degrades into an unavailable form.

Two factors may explain why this last fact is widely ignored. The first is the peculiar attraction our minds feel for all strains of mechanical models. The most probable reason is that we act on the material surroundings mainly by pushing and pulling. The mechanistic dogma had already lost its Laplacean grip on physics, when, in his Baltimore lectures (1894), Lord Kelvin confessed that he could not understand a phenomenon unless he was able to represent it by a mechanical model. It is the attraction of the mechanistic *Weltbild* that induces us to believe that matter cannot be definitively irrecoverable. Indeed, in mechanics, matter can only change its place, not its quality; hence any system may move back and forth without suffering any change.[14]

The second factor is that, curious though it may seem, the foundation of thermodynamics is energetic—as Rankine perceived it—for thermodynamics is concerned only with what happens to energy. To be sure, matter enters into the picture, but only as a support of chemical reactions (because they always involve energy transformations) and in problems of pure (nonchemical) mixtures (because unmixing necessitates work). Both these aspects have been introduced into thermodynamical theory by J. Willard Gibbs, who is thus regarded as the founder of "chemical energetics" [66].

Take the ultra familiar apparatus consisting of a piston-and-cylinder filled with some gas that is generally used to describe and justify the basic laws of thermodynamics and to prove Carnot's fundamental proposition that maximum efficiency is obtained only by a perfectly *reversible* engine. To circumvent the undeniable fact that because of friction no motion can be reversible, thermodynamic theory assumes that any motion is reversible if its speed is infinitesimally slow.[15] Such a speed does eliminate friction from the

---

superficial knowledge of thermodynamics (if any), so that some may go wrong even on the notion of heat (see *Journal of Economic Literature*, December 1972, p. 1268, and note 14, below).

14. A celebrated symptom of our mechanistic propensity was Ludwig Boltzmann's famous endeavor to explain irreversible phenomena by blending the perfect determinism of the reversible laws of Newtonian mechanics with probability . For the economist this hybrid construction presents a crucial interest. By maintaining that the regeneration of unavailable energy is only highly *improbable*, not *impossible*, the propounders of the probabilistic theory foster the belief in the possibility of cheating at the entropy game (just as we may cheat at any game of chance) or, as P. W. Bridgman ridiculed the thought some 50 years ago, of "bootlegging entropy" [29; 30; 32]. It is regrettable therefore that not all physicists know that Boltzmann's construction met with irrefutable criticism from some of the greatest physicists, for which see [25; 30]. Far sadder it is they do not know that through his pathbreaking contributions Ilya Prigogine showed that Boltzmann's "'mechanical theory' of the evolution of matter [is based on] intuitive arguments [and] the program was never realized, despite frequent affirmations to the contrary" [60–62]. If one has not gone beyond Boltzmann, one is apt to proclaim (as Auer does) that the Entropy Law sets no obstacle to endless economic growth [3].

15. It may be well to explain that in thermodynamics a motion is reversible only if the motion and *everything else in its surroundings* can be returned to the original situations [57; 78].

picture, but it introduces an even more essential obstacle. With an infinitesimally slow speed a piston would take an infinite time to move over any finite distance. Time and again, infinity steps in to set things out of bounds for us mortals.[16] Because a reversible engine thus exists on paper only, no actual engine can operate at maximum efficiency.

In the end, thermodynamics had to recognize the existence of friction as well as of a few other germane factors, which account not only for irreversibility in nature, but also for the fact that available energy cannot be completely converted into *useful* work. Part of this energy is always converted into irrecuperable heat.

Friction thus appears as a ghost, so to speak, in the backstage of the thermodynamic setup, a ghost that robs us of available energy. Indeed, thermodynamics did not move further to recognize and analyze the elementary fact that friction robs us of *available matter* as well. It did not tackle even the specific laws of the energy degraded by friction. This task was left to the engineers, but even they have established only tables for the forces of friction of the most frequently used materials. With the help of these tables, we can determine the work against friction W_f, to be used in the (still incomplete) transformation formula:

$$Q_a = W_u + W_f, \tag{3}$$

where Q_a is available energy and W_u is useful work (the internal energy of the system being assumed to remain constant).[17]

About the dissipation of matter by friction we still know practically nothing. One possible explanation of this conspicuous lacuna is the difficulty of explaining the phenomenon of friction. Mechanical laws applied to material particles cannot explain it. Its laws have a purely empirical basis and on closer and closer examination are usually found to be " 'falser' and 'falser' " [27]. And a consummate student of the problem concludes that the subject of friction "remains a highly controversial one, and there are very few statements that can be made in this field which will find no opposition" [63].

But friction is not the "imperfection" only of matter in bulk that robs us of both energy *and* matter. There are neither perfectly rigid nor perfectly elastic materials; there are no perfect insulators and no perfect conductors; nor are there materials for which the force of friction is infinite (the opposite case of frictionless materials). And it is because of these numerous imperfec-

---

16. Recall Planck's infinite piston mentioned earlier.

17. The traditional formula is $Q = W$ because in thermodynamics work is defined only in the absence of friction [24]. Formula (3) was recently proposed by Silver [67]. But he, too, stopped short of mentioning the material effect of friction. Moreover, to cover all energy wastes, the formula should read $Q_a = W_u + W_f + Q_l$, where Q_l is the leakage of thermal energy—i.e., the amount of thermal energy that always descends a temperature gradient *without performing any work*.

tions (the list is not exhaustive) that the robber, the only robber, of energy and matter is matter itself.

All over the material world there is rubbing by friction, cracking and splitting by changes in temperature or evaporation, there is clogging of pipes and membranes, there is metal fatigue and spontaneous combustion. Matter is thus continuously displaced, altered, and scattered to the four corners of the world. It thus becomes less and less available for our own purposes.

The energetic dogma claims that this dissipation can be completely reversed provided there is enough available energy. But the operation must necessarily involve some material instruments. Because there are no perdurable material structures these instruments will necessarily wear out. They will have to be replaced by others produced by some other instruments, which will also wear out and will have to be replaced, and so on, in an unending regress. This regress is a sufficient ground for denying the possibility of complete recycling, just as the same kind of regress is the reason often invoked in thermodynamics against the possibility of completely erasing the changes caused in the *energy* structure by a natural process [24, 24].

Finally, another possible (and important) thought in support of complete recycling must be entertained. It relates to John von Neumann's proof that a universal Turing machine may be so designed that if left in a floating medium together with a large number of each one of its elementary parts it will reproduce itself [52]. Could not then the fund elements of the process represented by Table I constitute such a "machine"? This machine does "float" in a medium that, although closed, contains all the necessary elements for its reproduction, namely, the waste outputs of processes (P_i)'s. Yet the idea that the economic process could be a universal Turing machine must be rejected. Neumann's proof is a very ingenious paper-and-pencil exercise based on a requirement that makes the project impossible in practice. The troublesome requirement for a universal Turing machine is that its capacity for instruction must be limitless [30, 86–93]. And even if we softened this condition to "practically infinite," the machine would still require a practically infinite sequence of time intervals to reproduce itself, since each "move" of the machine requires a duration. Therefore, this last justification of complete recycling runs against the same familiar obstacle as all other ideal schemes: the unreachable infinity.

But the energetic thesis can be examined from still other analytical viewpoints.

IV. The Dissipation of Matter and Planck's Law

I have spoken of some asymmetry between energy and mass and between energy and matter. There is still another asymmetry. Both mass and energy are homogeneous "substances". Energy is the same whether it is associated with a photon or with the force of the wind. This is certainly why the idea of reducing everything to energy has such a strong appeal. But there also is no qualitative difference whatever between the mass, say, of a proton and that of any other elementary particle. However, this last fact is of no value for the relationship between the economic process and the environment. In the economic process it is not mass as such that counts. What counts is matter in bulk (and, of course, energy). And the rub is that unlike mass and energy, matter is a highly heterogeneous category. Every chemical element has at least one property that characterizes it completely and hence renders it indispensable for some technical recipes.

We must therefore expect that, in contrast with the general theory of energy (thermodynamics), the study of the transformations of matter in bulk should be hard going, as we have just seen for the case of friction alone. It is a rather simple problem to understand how energy degrades as heat dissipates from the hotter to the colder bodies of a system, because in this way it becomes less and less available to be converted into mechanical work. Remember the famous Carnot principle: we must have a difference of temperature between the boiler and the condenser in order to obtain mechanical work by a cyclical engine. Without entering into the technical maze, one may see why the increase in the dissipation of energy is measured by the thermodynamic formula for entropy:

$$\Delta S = (\Delta Q / T)_{reversible} \tag{4}$$

where ΔQ is the heat transferred by conduction at the absolute temperature T.[18]

For the entropy of the simple mixture of two *distinct* ideal gases of the same pressure P and temperature T, we have Gibbs's famous formula:

$$S = -R \left[m_1 \ln (m_1/m) + m_2 \ln (m_2/m) \right] + (c_1 m_1 + c_2 m_2) \ln T$$
$$+ (a_1 m_1 + a_2 m_2) - Rm \ln P, \tag{5}$$

where $m_1 + m_2 = m$ are the corresponding moles, R is the gas constant, and a_i, c_i are physical characteristics of the gases. Mixing two gases of the same pressure and temperature thus increases the entropy by[19]

$$\Delta S = -R \left[m_1 \ln (m_1/m) + m_2 \ln (m_2/m) \right], \tag{6}$$

18. Even though "hotness" is one of the most common sensations, the flow of heat (as strictly conceived in thermodynamics) has no direct physical significance and there are no *direct* operations for measuring it [8; 24].

19. Because the same technical detail will come up later in Sec. VI, it may be well to add here that the enthalpy, H, does not change [48; 57; 58]. Enthalpy, which corresponds to the intuitive notion of heat content, is the amount of thermal energy necessary to bring the substance from absolute zero to its temperature state while pressure is kept constant. In practice, enthalpy is the calorific value of a fuel—i.e., the maximum amount of thermal energy that can be obtained by burning it.

a very familiar formula that nowadays is used on both solid and flimsy grounds.

Ordinarily, this formula is mentioned in connection with a paradox pointed out by Gibbs himself [66]. If the two gases are identical, (6) is still positive, although the mixture then causes no entropy change whatsoever. But another aspect of (6), stemming from an observation by Max Planck [58, 104], bears on the present argument. Planck suggested that in the case of (6) "it would be more to the point to speak of a dissipation of matter than of a dissipation of energy".[20]

According to either (6) or (5) the greatest dissipation for a given m occurs when $m_1 = m_2$. But let us consider the case in which $m_1 = 1$ and $m_2 = 10^{100}$. Then, ΔS is completely negligible. Yet, on the basis of the intuitive conception of dissipation, it stands to reason that, *if gas 1 is the valuable one*, from the particular human viewpoint the dissipation is far greater in the latter than in the former case. It is in the latter case that we can properly say that one mole of gas 1 has become unavailable to us. Indeed, to reassemble those molecules would be a task as formidable as reassembling the molecules of a small amount of ink spread over the Atlantic Ocean!

Undoubtedly, we can reassemble the scattered pearls of a necklace that broke in a room, in a theater, even somewhere in Manhattan provided we are prepared to expend enough time, enough energy, and wear out numberless objects in the process. The extrapolation of this macroscopic recipe to the microscopic level of molecules or even of small bits of matter is clearly unwarrented. From all we know, can one believe in the possibility of reassembling not all, but practically all the rubber molecules of our worn-out tires, all the lead dissipated through the exhaust pipes, or all the copper dissipated from our pennies through use? In a reasonably finite time as well? The object lesson is that at the microscopic level the same recipe that succeeds for reassembling the pearls of a broken necklace would require, among other hard-to-conceive facilities, an *infinite* time. The operation belongs therefore to the same category as the irreversible engine and Planck's scheme for using the heat of the oceans. Planck even concludes that, because $\Delta S > 0$, "diffusion like friction and heat conduction is an irreversible process" [57, 113; 58; 78].

The preceding analysis shows, however, that (6) measures in reverse the intensity of diffusion conceived so as to make sense in our actual manipulation of matter. According to that formula, mixing one carload of needles with one carload of hay creates a greater diffusion than losing one important needle in a carload of hay that corresponds to the task of complete recycling or of mining any rock. Although we can easily extract a metal from a rich ore, the

---

20. Understandingly, Planck did not say "dissipation of mass."

task is harder and harder as the metal content decreases, and for a content of, say, 10^{-100} it becomes impossible.

There remains however the issue of the thermodynamic interpretation of (6). For this, we may recall that in thermodynamic theory $T\Delta S$ represents the work necessary to restore the corresponding system to its original position. In the present case, this means to separate again the two gases completely. A theoretical blueprint for performing this separation was imagined by Jakobus Henrikus van't Hoff (the first Nobel Prize winner in chemistry). The device— the van't Hoff box—consists of a perfectly isolated cylinder with two pistons working in opposite directions; each piston consists of a semi-permeable membrane, one permeable only to gas 1, the other only to gas 2. The mixture is placed between the two pistons, which at first are far apart. As the pistons are pushed infinitesimally slowly against each other, the gases are separated since each gas gets behind its own semi-permeable membrane. It is easily shown that the work necessary for this pushing is indeed equal to the product of (6) by T [58; 78]. This result seems to provide a strong support to the purest energetic dogma. If we have enough energy (equal at least to $T\Delta S$), we can extract the entire amount of any gas from any mixture. Several snags, however, beset the actual implementations of this idea.

First, just as in actuality there are no completely frictionless, no perfectly elastic, and no other perfect materials, there are no perfect semi-permeable membranes. The separation therefore cannot be complete.[21] Second, with use all membranes become clogged [57; 58]. They wear out, just as does any other part of a mechanism; in the end they must be replaced, thus starting the endless regress mentioned earlier.[22]

Van't Hoff box constitutes at least an ideal procedure for unmixing gases, but no similar device exists for other mixtures. In practice, each mixture separation is achieved by some particular procedure, by chemical reactions, centrifugal or magnetic forces, etc. To be sure, the absence of a general blueprint does not prove that some ideal blueprint may not exist for each particular mixture. But several arguments plead against this thought.

Let us remember Maxwell's demon, the demon presupposed to separate the fast-moving from the slow-moving molecules of a gas. It is now generally believed that this miraculous demon has been "exorcised," so that, like any other living creature, it must consume a greater amount of available energy than it creates by the separation of "hot" from "cold" molecules. Now, to separate a mixture of, say, nitrogen and oxygen, we need a demon far more miraculous than Maxwell's. Indeed, Maxwell's demon does not have to bring back absolutely every molecule to its initial container. Moreover, it may safely

21. Another imperfection is responsible for the fact that in actuality some mixed gases always remain between the membranes no matter how much the pistons are pressed against each other.

22. Highly pertinent to the topic of this paper is the recent discovery (by R. K. Knoll and S. M. Johnson of NASA, Cleveland) that solar collectors also become progressively clogged.

leave some "hot" or "cold" molecules in the wrong container; it is only the average speed that counts. Our new demon, on the contrary, *must not leave even one single molecule mixed with those of the other kind*. To exorcise it, we must not only supply it with enough energy but also endow it with a material existence. And since matter keeps dissipating, the problem now boils down to whether our demon can recycle itself completely while recycling the gas mixture, also completely. The system of Table I depicts, in fact, such a demon. No wonder that the miraculous features of our demon are tacitly implied in many ideas concerning the unlimited renewability of material resources.

To Brown [10], it seems, belongs the idea of mining the whole crust by utilizing the energy of the radioactive elements thus obtained. Such a miraculous technology would come to an end only after all rocks had been crushed. The sad truth is that no blueprint has been put forward to describe how this technology may work. Instead, the idea is regarded as a real flight of fancy by practically all geologists, who generally support Peter Flawn's dictum that even "the average rock will never be mined" [28; 18; 68]. As Preston Cloud, who is known to have opposed with all his authority all minerological flights of fancy, tried to enlighten the layman, "it is the uncommon features of a rock that make it a candidate for mining!" This is why almost certainly your backyard is not a potential mine.

Brooks and Andrews denounced Flawn's dictum by invoking the fact that titanium is also mined (as a by-product) from presumably sub-average grades. A few other writers also proclaimed that "the world will not run out of geologic resources," assuring us that only the energy limit may prevent the mining of any ordinary rocks [21]. But most have a hard time remaining consistent when faced with such facts, for example, as the existence of a geochemical barrier cutting off the mining of copper at 16 times the average abundance]20, 129].

Let us also observe with necessity that even if the average rock could be mined, this would not entail that the entire mineral content of the crust is accessible. The distribution of grades has a peculiar bimodal shape and is thus very skew [69]. Hence, the overwhelming majority of rocks are much poorer than the average grade. Whether or not a mineral may be mined from a given rock depends on the specific theoretical cutoff for that mineral and for that type of rock, not on its average crustal abundance. Matter, to recall, is heterogeneous, so that for each substance and rock there is some specific mining procedure(s). This is why it seems well nigh impossible to establish a general formula for deciding whether or not a substance is available from a given mixture. In this lies the theoretical difficulty (hinted at earlier) of defining the unavailable form of matter by a general analytical formula.

Curves describing how the amount of rock crushed and the amount of energy used vary with respect to the rock's metal content are readily available in the literature. They all are asymptotic to the vertical axis [56]. Those for energy should actually be asymptotic to a line parallel to that axis, so as to reveal the existence of a theoretical cutoff, however small this may be.

As a last argument we may mention a statement by Planck, which although very important, seems to have passed unnoticed. At the end of an elaborate discussion of all types of mixtures, Planck arrived at a formula which entitled him to conclude that "neither a gas nor a liquid nor a solid body can ever be completely freed from the last traces of foreign contaminating substances" [57, 125; 58, 238]. Exceptions occur, but only at absolute zero [58, 239; 48, 46].

Now, according to the third law of thermodynamics, enunciated by W. Nernst, absolute zero cannot be attained in actuality. Therefore, Nernst's and Planck's negations are mutually bound. They also form a twin package. The former says that matter *in bulk* cannot be "purified" of thermal energy, the latter that it cannot be purified of any contaminant.

And what deserves strong emphasis is that, in contrast with the Entropy Law, the truth of these laws is not subject to any instrumental constraints. They are true in an absolute sense. To explain, *in theory* we can restore a partial system to exactly its original position, if we have a certain amount of energy and some specific apparatus at our disposal. There is no way, however, to circumvent the impossibilities affirmed by either Nernst's law or Planck's.

It is Planck's law for matter than provides us with a very important analytical argument against the energetic dogma, which necessarily implies that *recycling may be complete* and that *any rock can be mined*.

V. Matter Matters, Too

Complete recycling being impossible, even in a steady state the "transactions" between the economic process and the environment must necessarily consist of some available matter as well in order to compensate for the matter dissipated continuously and irrevocably. As Harrison Brown observed, if all the iron produced in the United States between 1870 and 1950 (about 2 billion tons) had still been in use in 1950, there would have been then 13.5 tons per capita, almost double the actual figure [10]. The same difference would be even more impressive were it established on the entire past production. We all know where the difference went. "Oxidation by the air, corrosion by liquids, and other general wear [certainly because of friction and metal fatigue] take heavy tolls" [10]. As is always the case, some iron is also "lost" during production processes. Although it is not possible to estimate the amount of iron "that has been lost never to be recovered", Brown [11] estimates that about 10 percent of the iron used for steel production is lost irrecoverably and that over 100 years the remaining iron becomes unavailable matter. Just to maintain the iron equipment existing in 1954 (without providing for any economic growth), a flow of ore convertible into about 0.3 tons of iron per person had to be mined each year.

Of course, this maintenance flow varies from substance to substance according not only to the changing technology but also to the size of the stock existing in the process. In the case of gold this flow is naturally small for several reasons—its chemical resilience, its particular use, and the relatively small amount of it in existence. Yet it is hardly exact to assert that "most gold ever mined is still available" [68]. The millions and millions of past bracelets, necklaces, coins, etc. have not all been kept at a Fort Knox.

The fact that the flow of dissipated matter increases with the size of the material stock must be recognized as a very important link in the argument of this paper. For it explains, on the one hand, why, even if some cutoffs may be so low that it may be almost impossible to ascertain them by a laboratory experiment, their effect at the scale of the entire planet and in the long run cannot be ignored. On the other hand, it explains why we are apt to believe in the perpetuity of the so-called natural cycles of oxygen, carbon, nitrogen, etc., that adorn all ecological manuals.[23]

As far as the economic process itself is concerned, we must not ignore the substantial dissipation of matter caused not by purely natural phenomena but by some activities of living creatures, of mankind's, above all. It is the dissipation of some vital elements by man's consumption of food and timber in places far away from the farm and the forest that produced those items. The practice—a consequence of the high and growing level of urbanization everywhere in the world—also wastes available energy. Most curiously, we are aware of this waste, but not of the waste of available matter. The difference is responsible for the fallacy that forests can provide "an endless supply of wood" because the flow of sunshine is practically endless [51]. Yet forests cannot be everlasting anymore than topsoil can retain its quality forever without outside intervention [30, 302].[24]

The conclusion of the foregoing analysis is that for the environmental transactions we must keep two separate books—one for matter, one for energy—for at the macro-level no practical procedure exists for converting energy into matter or matter of whatever form into energy. The relation of matter and energy is not like that between, say, dollars and yen, nor even between land and working implements in agricultural production (Sec. VII).

A new multi-process matrix must therefore replace that of Table I. In this

---

23. It is because of the immensity of every one of these stocks that the amount continuously leaving the cycle is not conspicuous over short periods. One of the telling facts is that practically all the carbon deposited as calcium carbonate on the bottom of the oceans will not re-enter the so-called carbon cycle. And this is only a minor troublesome factor of the global circulation of environmental carbon [76].

24. Very likely, it will be the more palpable waste—of the energy consumed by transportation —that, in case of a serious difficulty in obtaining environmental low entropy, will bring about a substantial amount of deurbanization [31].

new matrix (Table II), an additional process, (P_0), transforms matter *in situ*, MS, into controlled matter, CM. All other processes have the same roles as before and are identified by the same notations. But there are several important changes.

First, new flows, s_i, represent the dissipated matter, DM, produced by every process and passed into the environment. Second, the recycling process, (P_4), no longer recycles all material waste, as assumed in the energetic model. Since dissipated matter is irrecoverably lost, (P_4) can recycle only matter that is still available but has no longer a shape useful to us: broken bottles, broken pipes, run-down batteries, worn-out motors, etc. Because recyclable materials belong in garbage cans or in junk yards, for brevity, we may refer to them as "garbojunk", GJ.[25] Third, another inherent aspect of the economic process is represented by a flow of items that also are returned to the environment and are labeled here "refuse", R. This flow consists in large part of available matter and available energy, but in a form that is not potentially useful to us at present. The crushed rock of an open-pit copper mine, most urban waste, and nuclear garbage, for example, belong to this category.[26]

As in the case of Table I, the relations:

$$\Sigma' x_{0i} = x_{00}, \qquad \Sigma' x_{1i} = x_{11}, \qquad \Sigma' x_{2i} = x_{22}, \qquad x_{35} = x_{33}, \tag{7}$$
$$\Sigma' x_{4i} = x_{44}, \qquad \Sigma' w_i = w_4$$

represent the viability of the steady state. However, because R may include both energy and matter, we can no longer write the relations for the conservation of these items separately, as in (1).

VI. Energy Analysis and Economics

My position has been (and still is) that the Entropy Law is the taproot of economic scarcity. In a world in which that law did not operate, the same energy could be used over and over again at any velocity of circulation one pleased and material objects would never wear out. But life could certainly not exist either.[27] In our world, everything that has some usefulness (desirability) for us consists of low entropy. It is for these reasons that the economic process is entropic in all its material fibers [29; 30; 32]. But I have also

---

25. The possibility of recycling garbojunk marks a second asymmetry between energy and matter. Recycling of matter is possible because some material objects are "durable" in the sense that, in contrast with energy, they are not *instantaneously* degraded through their participation in producing mechanical or other types of work. The point bears on the old economic controversy over repeated use versus instantaneous consumption.

26. In order to save space, the fund coordinates are not represented explicitly in Table II.

27. We often connect the Entropy Law with disorder, yet without it there would be no order in actual phenomena. The truth is that the Entropy Law is the law of orderly succession. For—a piquant observation—without the Entropy Law you would not dare take a bath, one half of the water might become *by itself* so hot as to scald your neck and the other so cold as to frostbite your toes.

Table II. The Actual Relationship Between the Economic Process and the Environment

Product	(P_0)	(P_1)	(P_2)	(P_3)	(P_4)	(P_5)
			Flow Coordinates			
CM	x_{00}	*	$-x_{02}$	$-x_{03}$	$-x_{04}$	*
CE	$-x_{10}$	x_{11}	$-x_{12}$	$-x_{13}$	$-x_{14}$	$-x_{15}$
K	$-x_{20}$	$-x_{21}$	x_{22}	$-x_{23}$	$-x_{24}$	$-x_{25}$
C	*	*	*	x_{33}	*	$-x_{35}$
RM	*	*	$-x_{42}$	$-x_{43}$	x_{44}	*
ES	*	$-e_1$	*	*	*	*
MS	$-M_0$	*	*	*	*	*
GJ	w_0	w_1	w_2	w_3	$-w_4$	w_5
DE	d_0	d_1	d_2	d_3	d_4	d_5
DM	s_0	s_1	s_2	s_3	s_4	s_5
R	r_0	r_1	r_2	r_3	r_4	r_5

maintained (without always being read correctly) that although low entropy is a necessary condition for usefulness, it is not also a sufficient one (just as usefulness is a necessary but not sufficient condition for economic value.) Poisonous mushrooms, for example, consist of low entropy [29, 94; 30, 282].

The entropic nature of the economic process notwithstanding, it would be a great mistake to think that it may be represented by a vast system of thermodynamic equations—as has been proposed, for example, by Lichnerowicz [50]. The entropic process moves through an intricate web of anthropomorphic categories, of utility and labor, above all. Its true product is not a physical flow of dissipated matter and energy, but the enjoyment of life—account being also taken of the drudgery of labor [30, ch. x]. And, in spite of some voices to the contrary, pleasure is not related by a definite quantitative law to the low entropy consumed. Nor is labor's "disutility" related by such a law to the expended low entropy. William Petty was right in teaching that nature is the mother and labor the father of wealth—only he ought to have said "of our existence." Therefore, even if we accepted the energetic view, in which the whole economic process is maintained only by the flow of environmental energy e_1, economic value could still not be reduced to energy.[28]

Nevertheless, the possibility of reducing prices to energy units, Btu's instead of dollars, has been in the focus of attention ever since the oil embargo prompted people to think of energy and to attempt an analysis of its circulation in man's activities. Gilliland [42] even argued that energy analysis is the natural way for doing away with the difficulty of adding apples and oranges, which is what economists have to do. Slesser [70] and R. S. Berry (quoted by Slesser) propound the strongest form of this dogma: to measure the cost of things in money "which is after all nothing more than a highly sophisticated value judgment" does not offer a firm basis for economic valuation. Actually, if economists were to look at scarcity in a more complete way, their "estimates would come closer and closer to the estimates [of] the thermodynamicists". This simply means to do away with economics and replace it by thermodynamics.[29] This position is so generally embraced that net energy analysis now constitutes the official criterion for technology assessment and energy policy in the United States [26].

All this is highly surprising in view of the fact that a great confusion still prevails even among the experienced practitioners of energy analysis. There is, first, the controversy concerning the difference between Odum's net energy analysis and the gross energy analysis based on some principles set up by a 1974 meeting of IFIAS, the International Federation of Institutes of Advanced Study (note 2, *supra*). Slesser, a representative of the latter school, claims that one has "yet to see a rigorous definition of net energy" [71]. It is true that even in his latest writings Odum is not sufficiently clear on many important points, such as whether the energy of labor should be taken into account. Moreover, he often confuses the reader by such requirements as that even money must be included in the general flow [54]. However, the situation is not much more enviable in the other camp, as is evidenced by a series of highly critical letters to the editor and small notes which failed to clear the

28. I have myself insisted that prices are parochial elements of the economic system and also that the market mechanism by itself it incapable of preventing environmental catastrophes. But I did not deny the necessity of the market mechanism for the allocation of resources and the distribution of income among the members of the *same generation* [32; 34].

29. Hayek [43, 51], as Keith Wilde recently reminded me, protested long time ago against "the various forms of social 'energetics' [as those propounded by] Ernest Solvay, Wilhelm Ostwald and Frederick Soddy." However, none of these authors held the same position as the modern energetists. What they claimed is that regardless of how economic value is established, the economic process cannot violate any of the natural laws, including the laws of thermodynamics. In fact, Ostwald was the first author to observe that from the dawn of mankind's existence technological progress has always consisted in increasing the power of our biological organs. And contrary to Hayek's accusation, Ostwald [55, 164] explicitly argued that "we would err if we measured value only in proportion to the amount of free energy." Only Soddy plunged into economic matters proper and devoted several works to a solution of the instabilities caused by credit creation. An interesting recent paper by Daly [23] aims at rehabilitating Soddy.

air.[30] One critic charged that because "the energy analysts disagree in their basic ground rules" energy analysis can be used "to prove whatever case you choose" [47]. Even one of the prominent energy analysts, P. F. Chapman, recognized that "there are almost as many methods [of analysis] as there are workers in the field" and energy analysis may follow four different aims and adopt three different methods [13]. Results, as he showed, may even be contradictory. There has been some controversy even over how to measure energy (as we shall presently see).

The issue of whether energy analysis provides an equivalent basis to the price system was recently entertained by David Huettner [46]. But, here again, the letters to the editor that his article provoked suggest that he, too, failed to make his case.[31] In deriving his price equations Huettner followed the fallacious practice in standard economics of ignoring the essential difference between flows—the material elements that are changed by a production process—and funds—the agents that perform the change [31; 32]. As a result, his price equations had exactly the same form as his equations for the presumed energy equivalents. Because of this identity the real difference between economic valuation and energy calculations could not be brought to light so as to settle the question raised by Price, "why energy analysis gives a different answer than the economic analysis" [59]. The flow-fund model used in my tables will settle this issue without much ado.

Let us consider first the simplest case, that of Table I, and begin with the net energy analysis. We must first decide what net energy is in that structure. I think that in the spirit of the Cottrell-Odum conception we may safely assume that net energy aims at determining how much controlled energy, CM, is accessible in all forms to the ultimate consumers. However, few additional observations now appear necessary. First, for the concept of net energy we do not have to distinguish between the various kinds of environmental energy, ES. In other words, it does not matter whether the net energy is derived from fossil fuels or from the wind, for example. Second, the dissipated heat must not be counted at all in computing net energy. That is, we must not add d_1 to the net output of energy x_{11}, or deduct d_i from the gross input x_{1i}. Finally, we must also not count in any way the energy spent by people in performing work or in consuming goods. To do so would be to mix economics with energy analysis. The analysis would then be falsified by a double counting resulting in an extensive cancellation, for in a steady state— which is still our testing ground—the total input flow of any environmental element is exactly equal to the corresponding total output flow.

Four possible definitions of net energy seem to deserve attention: a) x_{11}; b) the difference between x_{11} and the energy equivalent of x_{21}; c) x_{15}; and d) x_{15} plus the energy equivalent of x_{25} and x_{35}. The first suggestion can be easily dis-

---

30. *New Scientist*, 9, 16, and 23 January 1975.
31. *Science*, 15 April 1977, 259–62, especially M. Slesser. See also *Science*, 2 April 1976, 8–12.

carded. If x_{11} is, say, electricity produced from fossil fuels *in situ*, that electricity is not net energy even with respect to the process (P_1). For part of that electricity has been used in a roundabout process to produce, among other things, the material flow x_{21} necessary for compensating the wear and tear of K_1 during the mining of e_1 and its use in a thermoplant.

Suggestion (b) leads to

$$\text{Net energy} = x_{11} - (x_{21})_e, \tag{8}$$

where $(x)_e$ denotes the energy equivalent of x. But this definition raises the troublesome question: what is the energy equivalent of a steel beam?

Here, again, various ideas have been at work. One simple method consists of taking into account only the energy *directly* used by a process because such data are readily available from official statistics. This method leads to

$$(x_{21})_e = x_{21}(x_{12}/x_{22}), \tag{9}$$

and

$$\text{Net energy} = (x_{11}x_{22} - x_{12}x_{21})/x_{22}. \tag{10}$$

Obviously, this represents a substantial underestimation, for the production of x_{22} needs x_{42} units of *RM* as well. We must, therefore, find out $(x_{42})_e$ as well. We are thus involved in an algorithm that will not end until an energy equivalent is established for every type of product.[32] The result is a system of equations which recalls the Leontief system [16; 77].[33] Let us then denote by a_i the energy equivalent per unit of flow product of (P_i). From Table I we obtain:

$$\text{Net energy} = x_{11} - a_2 x_{21},$$
$$-x_{12} + a_2 x_{22} - a_4 x_{42} = 0,$$
$$-x_{13} - a_2 x_{23} - a_4 x_{43} + a_3 x_{33} = 0,$$
$$-x_{14} - a_2 x_{24} + a_4 x_{44} = 0, \tag{11}$$

which by (2) yields

$$\text{Net energy} = x_{15} + a_2 x_{25} + a_3 x_{35}. \tag{12}$$

This relation shows that suggestion (b) is equivalent to suggestion (d) and also that (c) would not do. It also shows that, for example, the average cost of K in units of controlled energy (net energy) is a_2.

32. It may be well to emphasize that the term "energy equivalent" does not imply a physical equivalence in the sense that a pound of copper, for example, may be converted into its energy equivalent or vice versa.

33. This is an almost insuperable task for the analyst even if a detailed input-output table in real terms is available. But this difficulty is wholly irrelevant to the issue under consideration now. Chapman, however, insists that in this method one should in *principle* consider a *subsystem*, not the whole national economy [13]. Moreover, in the illustrative application of this method to the energy sector, it is not clear how the energy equivalence of non-energy items was computed [16]. From repeated remarks on the matter, we may infer that for these items the energy equivalent of the dollar was used, a procedure that is totally incompatible with energy analysis.

Net energy defined by (11) can also be expressed as a function of the flow coordinates alone:

$$\text{Net energy} = \begin{vmatrix} x_1 & -x_{21} & 0 \\ -x_{12} & x_{22} & -x_{42} \\ -x_{14} & -x_{24} & x_{44} \end{vmatrix} \div \begin{vmatrix} x_{22} & -x_{42} \\ -x_{24} & x_{44} \end{vmatrix} \tag{13}$$

This formula proves the extremely curious result that in the case of an energetic system, the net energy does not depend on the flows of the consumer goods industry.

Energy analysts are far from agreeing on whether or not we should attribute an energy equivalent to W. The difficulty is identical to that of attributing a cost to joint products in economics. But if we introduce the w_i's in (11) and denote by a prime the new energy equivalents and by z_w' the energy equivalent of w, by (2) we obtain immediately

$$a_i' - a_w' = a_i, \tag{14}$$

which means that the new equivalents are not completely determined. This result, which in some arguments may be quite troublesome, should have been expected.

We may turn now to the gross energy analysis. The stated aim of this analysis is to determine the amount of energy *in situ* "needed directly and indirectly to deliver a good or a service to the final customer" [49; 71]. However, "a quagmire of confusion" seems to prevail about the precise rules of how to achieve it [49]. Gross energy analysis has in view mainly the fossil fuels. For this reason, the recommended unit of energy is the calorific value, which represents the energy potentially available by burning a given amount of such fuels [16; 59].[34] A difficulty arises because there is no accepted calorific value for nuclear fuels. Nor can one speak of such a value for the energy input of a hydroelectric plant. The principles also provide that solar energy should not be counted as an input since it is "a free good" [19], a position which has its snags (and which does not affect the net energy approach). One author argues that labor and even profits "are also energy inputs" [77]. However, most of the gross energy analysts stick to the rules (also adopted above) according to which neither labor nor waste enter into the calculation [71]. There also are issues that concern both methods and about which no practitioner is explicit. One such issue is what precisely should be included in the capital cost x_{2i}.

Let now X denote the transposed matrix of the first four rows and four col-

---

34. In a more sophisticated form it is explained that we should consider only free energy, which determines the maximum mechanical work obtainable under normal pressure and temperature. Specifically, it is the Gibbs free energy, $G = H - TS$, that is meant [59; 70]. However, the enthalpy, H, is used instead (note 19, above), because in burning fuel under normal conditions ΔG does not differ substantially from ΔH [24, 73].

umns of Table I; let e denote the column vector $(e_1, 0, 0, 0)$; and let $b = (b_1, b_2, b_3, b_4)$ be the column vector of the energy equivalents in units of ES. We have

$$Xb = e .\tag{15}$$

From this and (1) we obtain

$$e_1 = b_1 x_{15} + b_2 x_{25} + b_3 x_{35} ,\tag{16}$$

which shows how much energy *in situ*, b_i, is needed for a unit of every good consumed by the households.[35]

The comparison of (12) and (15) yields

$$Net\ energy = e_1 / b_1 ,\tag{17}$$

or, equivalently,

$$b_i = b_1 a_i , \qquad (i = 2, 3, 4) .\tag{18}$$

These results show, first, why the main issue in gross energy analysis turned around the proper unit for energy. If e_1 consists of fossil fuels, then Champan [13] is vindicated for insisting that one kWh of electricity should be counted as about four kWh's of calorific power, which simply means that $b_1 = 4$.

But the same relations prompt one to wonder why all the fight about which approach is the correct one since the two sets of energy equivalents are related by the simple relations (18). The truth is that, whereas a can be deduced from b, the converse is not true. This does not mean, however, that gross energy analysis is the better approach. According to the rule mentioned earlier, in the case of solar energy $e_1 = 0$, hence $b = 0$[36] and *Net Energy* = ∞. Briefly, within its own scope gross energy cannot discriminate between two technologies based on solar energy alone (also Sec. VIII). On the other hand, net energy analysis completely ignores the efficiency of the technologies by which resources *in situ* are transformed into controlled energy. As far as net energy analysis is concerned, it does not matter whether two tons or one million of tons of oil *in situ* are depleted for abtaining one ton of oil net.

Still reasoning on the basis of Table I, let us turn now to economic valuation, briefly, to what the normal prices would be in such an economic world. The point that can hardly be overemphasized in this connection is that in any economic system both the quantities represented by the flow elements *and* the services provided by the agents have value. Let $p = (p_1, p_2, p_3, p_4)$ be the column vector of the prices of the flow elements, and let P_K, P_H, P_L be the prices of services during their specific periods. The economic equations are

$$Xp = B ,\tag{19}$$

---

35. It is easily seen that only b_3 is affected by the flow coordinates of (P_3). Also, the introduction of an energy equivalent b_w for W will lead to a system identical to (15) in which b is replaced by b', with $b' = b_1$, $b_i' = b_i - b_w$, $i \neq 1$.

36. This is so because if $|X| = 0$, then (15) has no solution.

where B is the column vector (B_1, B_2, B_3, B_4) and

$$B_i = P_K K_i + P_H H_i + P_L L_i. \tag{20}$$

We have further

$$p_1 x_{15} + p_2 x_{25} + p_3 x_{35} = \Sigma B_i. \tag{21}$$

which is the equation of the national budget.

Only in the highly unrealistic case, in which only the services of labor are included in the budgets B_i, can (19) determine all relative prices.[37] In actuality, the indeterminateness is removed by additional factors of a purely economic nature, such as tastes and income distribution.[38]

It is now perfectly clear that in *absolutely* no situation is it possible for the energy equivalents to represent economic valuations. Although the matrix of the price system (19) is the same as that of the systems of energy equivalents, (11) and (15), the former system cannot be equivalent to either of the latter. Actually, reducing economic value to energy is a more extreme position than the purest theory of labor value. To put in a homely way, according to the energetic portion one ounce of black caviar (which is mostly protein) should have the same price as one ounce of spaghetti (mostly carbohydrates) if it would take the same amount of either gross or net energy to produce them. Such an equivalence will never work.

VII. Global Analysis and Economic Choice

The analysis of the realistic case, in which not only energy but also matter counts, proceeds in the same way as for a generalized Leontief system in which there are several but distinct prime factors of production (say, uniform labor and uniform land). This means that the relations pertaining to one factor can be established by assuming that the other factors are in infinite supply [29, ch. 10].

Let us then abstract first from the MS. Let Y denote the transposed matrix of the first five rows and five columns of Table II; let f denote the column vector of the new gross energy equivalents $(f_0, f_1, f_2, f_3, f_4)$ and e the column vector $(0, e_1, 0, 0, 0)$. As before, we have

$$Yf = e, \tag{22}$$

which yields

$$e_1 = f_1 x_{15} + f_2 x_{25} + f_3 x_{35}, \tag{23}$$

---

37. In no actual economy is $P_K = 0$. Moreover, where institutionally $P_L = 0$, differential rent still gives rise to income transfers (illicit, naturally).

38. Should W be attributed a market price, p_w, the new prices, p', will satisfy analogous relations to those of note 35, above.

with

$$f_i = e_1 \Delta_{i1}/\Delta, \tag{24}$$

where Δ is the determinant of Y and Δ_{i1} the minor of the element of subscripts $(i, 1)$.

For gross matter equivalents we shall abstract from the ES. If g denotes the column vector of these equivalents and m the column vector $(M_0, 0, 0, 0, 0)$, then

$$Yg = m \tag{25}$$

from which we obtain

$$M_0 = g_1 x_{15} + g_2 x_{25} + g_3 x_{35}, \tag{26}$$

with

$$g_i = M_0 \Delta_{i0}/\Delta. \tag{27}$$

The corresponding formulae for the net energy follow straightforwardly:

$$\text{Net energy} = e_1/f_1, \qquad \text{Net matter} = M_0/g_0. \tag{28}$$

The conclusion is that to deliver a marginal unit of, say, C to the ultimate consumer we must consume f_2 units of energy *in situ* as well as g_2 units of matter *in situ*.

The upshot of the foregoing considerations is that, whatever the source of the energy used (solar or terrestrial), we must not ignore the depletion of the terrestrial deposits of available matter caused by any productive process. For all practical purposes, the Earth is a closed thermodynamic system, notwithstanding the meteorite fall and the material particles that occasionally escape the gravitation pull. In the very long run, therefore, some material elements will become more critical than energy for an industrial system of the prevailing sort [30; 32]. An increasing number of natural scientists have recently become convinced of this point and now even insist that a number of important elements are already approaching the pressing limit of scarcity [17; 69]. But sad to say, instead of following the old commandment and "beat our swords into plowshares," we keep on forging the plowshares of future generations into our present dreadful "swords".

Let us remember that energy and matter in bulk are not convertible into each other (Sec. VI), i.e., there is no relation $F(M, e) = \text{const}$. We do not have, therefore, a grid of isoquants which could enable us to reduce the economic choice pertaining to natural resources to physico-chemical calculations. Take the case of two technologies, $T_1(M_0^1, e_1^1)$ and $T_2(M_0^2, e_1^2)$, producing the same result and such that $M_0^1 > M_0^2$, $e_1^1 < e_1^2$. If they use terrestial resources, no proposition of physics or chemistry can tell us which technology is *economically* preferable. The nature of the issue is purely economic for it involves a multitude of factors of varying historical uncertainties and imponderabilities.

Since matter also matters, it would be misleading to reduce economic choice to energy alone. Actually, in some cases it is only matter that counts. Assume that the above technologies use "free" solar energy. The choice must now take into account net energy, NE, instead of gross energy. And how to choose between $T_1(M_0^1, NE_1)$ and $T_2(M_0^2, NE^2)$ when $M_0^1 > M_0^2$ and $NE^1 < NE^2$ is again an economic, not a purely technical problem. However, if $NE^1 = NE^2$, matter is decisive, T_2 is preferable, regardless of how much gross energy it uses.

One factor (besides those mentioned earlier) that may explain why matter has been ignored by the modern analysis of entropic transformations is the bonanza of fossil fuels that began about two hundred years ago and is still going on. This bonanza has an immense double advantage. It takes relatively little matter to extract fossil fuels from where they lie in the bowels of the earth *and* even less to convert them into industrial thermal energy. The same is not true for nuclear energy, which requires large installations for refining, enriching and conversion. The difficulties that now stand in the way of the direct use of solar energy by the *presently known* recipes also stem from the immense requirements of matter. From all we can judge now, the necessary amount of matter for a technology varies according to the intensity of the energy used. It is high for weak-intensity energy (as is the solar radiation at ground level) because such energy must be concentrated into a much higher intensity if it is to support the intensive industrial processes as those now supported by fossil fuels. And it is high for high-intensity energy because such energy must be contained (besides being "sifted" first).

VIII. Global Analysis and Technology Assessment

Nowadays we hear over and over again that nothing should stop us from using a technology based on solar energy because solar energy "is free, after all" [19]. However, absolutely every environmental energy *is* free, in the sense that nature does not have a check-out counter at which we should pay for resources *in situ*. Money royalties are instituted by man, not by nature. Perhaps by saying that solar energy is free we simply mean that it is "extremely abundant". And it is indeed abundant: its annual flow reaching the upper atmosphere is some twelve thousand times greater than the world's current consumption of energy from all sources! Unfortunately, abundance of energy *in situ* alone is not necessarily an advantage. This is the case of solar energy, which also has the great shortcoming of being extremely weak when it reaches us.

The direct use of solar energy constitutes now such a highly hopeful topic,[39] that it should be instructive to assess such a technology on the basis

39. E.g., *Congressional Record: Senate*, 31 July 1975 and 10 December 1975; Sylvia Potter, "We

of the ideas developed in this paper. Let us begin by recalling the necessary distinction between "recipe" and "technology" as well as the fact that *feasible* recipes do not necessarily constitute a *viable* technology (Sec. II). Legions of successful experiments represent feasible recipes that *at present* cannot be part of a viable technology. A striking example is the feasible recipe for quarring the Moon, which could not possibly replace now the mining of the Earth. Further, let us confine our argument to a technology based on those recipes for harnessing solar energy directly *that are known to work at present*.[40] We may safely include under the term "collectors" any devices used by these recipes.

For simplicity, we may divide the whole system into only three individual processes: (P_1) produces collected solar energy, SE, with the aid of collectors, CL, and some capital equipment, K; (P_2) produces collectors with the aid of SE and K; (P_3) produces K from mineral deposits by using SE (Table III).[41] Obviously,

$$x_{21} = x_{22},$$ (29)

since collectors have no use outside (P_1).

It is legitimate to assume that all recipes (P_i) are feasible (P_1) is certainly feasible. Collectors also are currently produced, although by other sources of energy—mainly, by fossil fuels energy, FE. The same is true of K. But since energy is a homogeneous "stuff," fossil fuel energy could very well be replaced by collected solar radiation. The only possible snag may concern intensity. Unfortunately, the intensity of energy (expressed by dQ/dt) is another aspect—besides matter—ignored by thermodynamics, which cannot therefore cast any light on the issue.[42] However, we should not overlook the fact that proven recipes can raise the temperature of collected solar radiation to quite impressive levels. The solar oven Odeillo (in the Pyrenees) produces a temperature near to 4,000° centigrade, and has a power of about 65 kW. If we wanted a greater power, we may, conceivably, build as many Odeillos as needed. A solar power plant, however, requires an immense and elaborate installation. The plant projected by ERDA at Barston (California) involves not less than 1,700 polished mirrors, each of 400 square feet—a total of some 18 acres—moved by a very complicated mechanism that turns them so as to follow the sun while focusing on the boiler exactly and continuously. Yet its power is a modest 10 MW.

Stand on Threshold of Solar Energy Era," *News and Observer* (Raleigh, N.C.), 16 September 1975; "European Common Market Heats Up on Solar Energy," *International Herald Tribune*, 25 July 1977.

40. Accordingly, we do not consider the suggestion for collecting solar radiation in outerspace and transmitting the collected energy to the ground level. The recipe is still unproven.

41. Let us note that (P_1) must include a fund of CL besides the fund of K.

42. According to the standard formula $Q = W$, one should be able to send a rocket to the moon by spreading the necessary Q over time so thinly that it would amount to lighting up one match after another. The omission explains why many writers are puzzled by the paradox that solar energy, immensely abundant though it is, seems so very hard to be used directly for our *present industrial* needs.

For the technology depicted by Table III to be viable, we must have

$$y_1 = x_{11} - x_{12} - x_{12} > 0, \qquad y_3 = -x_{31} - x_{32} + x_{33} > 0, \qquad (30)$$

where y_1 and y_2 represent the flows necessary for the *maintenance* of the corresponding fund factors (people and fixed capital).

The underlined term should be clearly understood. A viable technology is like a viable species, that is, once sprung from a previous technology all it needs to do is to maintain itself. To wit, the first bronze hammers were hammered by stone hammers, but during the succeeding age all bronze hammers were hammered by bronze hammers. Undoubtedly, to hammer a bronze hammer by stone hammers was a more demanding task than to hammer a stone hammer. But the threshold from an old to a new technology can be surmounted only by an additional cost *at the old prices*. If we ignore this point, we cannot see the weakness of the argument that solar technology is

Table III. Technology Based on Solar Energy

Product	(P_1)	(P_2)	(P_3)	Net flows
SE	x_{11}	$-x_{12}$	$-x_{13}$	y_1
C	$-x_{21}$	x_{22}	$\star$	$\star$
K	$-x_{31}$	$-x_{32}$	x_{33}	y_3

viable and the only thing necessary to bring it about is to find out how to produce collectors profitably. As the example of the Bronze Age shows, the viability of a technology requires only that its material scaffold be self-supporting, regardless.

Let us now consider the problem of prices. If (30) is fulfilled, there exists a price system that makes the system work. That is, if X denotes now the transposed matrix of Table III and p is the column vector (p_1, p_2, p_3), the system

$$Xp = B \qquad (31)$$

has a positive solution, B being defined as in (20). Therefore, if no such solution exists for $B > 0$, the technology is not viable. But, curiously, the converse is not true: (30) may have a positive solution without the technology being viable.[43] On the other hand, the brute fact that we are not already living in a technology based on solar radiation does not prove that such a

43. See *Mathematical Note* at the end.

technology is not viable. It may very well be less efficient than the fossil fuel technology in current monetary terms or in terms of human effort. The issue is quite involved. However, other absences prevail over this inconclusive standpoint.

The most accepted explanation of why solar energy has not yet replaced other sources of power is that the necessary collectors cost too much. Save for this remediable situation, a solar technology capable of sustaining the modern industrial activity is in fact viable. The difficulty is "a cost problem, not a material problem" [64, 17]. But if the only obstacle were the money deficits incurred by solar recipes, one question would cry for an answer. Over the past five years, at least, hundreds of millions of dollars have been spent for the development of more efficient recipes. ERDA, in particular, has interspersed this country with numberless model homes and experimental windmills. Yet no breakthrough has taken place to increase the confidence in a viable solar technology. None of the richly endowed research outfits have achieved even a workable pilot of a combined (P_1) and (P_2) working in mutual support, let alone a pilot of full-fledged solar technology to prove its viability *independent of prices*. For when it comes to prove that a technical idea is workable, cost does not matter much. Otherwise, we would not have succeeded in proving that we can put a man on the Moon.

The obvious upshot is that at present it is not possible to produce collectors only by the solar energy they collect. Any use of a presently feasible recipe based on solar collectors, therefore, is a parasite of the current technology. And, like any parasite, it could not survive its host [38; 39; 40; 41].

This means that instead of (30), we have[44]

$$x_{11} < x_{12}, \qquad x_{11} < x_{13}, \tag{31}$$

even if we weaken the other condition to

$$-x_{31} - x_{32} + x_{33} = 0. \tag{32}$$

For a global analysis of the way solar energy is now harnessed, we must consider the flow matrix of Table IV, in which (29) and (31) are assumed to hold. The energy necessary to produce collectors by (P_2) now comes from a non-solar (fossil fuels) power plant (P_4^0), which also provides the energy for the production of capital equipment by a new process, (P_3^0). The argument will be even more instructive if we assume that the only net flow is x_{11}.

From the fact that $y_{33} > x_{33} = x_{31} + x_{22}$, it reasonably follows that $y_{43} > x_{13}$. Hence, $y_{44} = x_{12} + y_{43} > x_{12} + x_{13}$, and by (31)

$$y_{44} > 2x_{11}. \tag{33}$$

---

44. The inequality $x_{11} < x_{13}$ is a foregone result of the other inequality, given just the enormous amounts of heat needed to produce metals from ores.

1054   *Nicholas Georgescu-Roegen*

Table IV. The Present Mixed Technology

Product	(P_1)	(P_2)	(P_3^0)	(P_4^0)	Net flows
SE	x_{11}	*	*	*	x_{11}
CL	$-x_{21}$	x_{22}	*	*	*
K	$-x_{31}$	$-x_{32}$	y_{33}	$-y_{34}$	*
FE	*	$-x_{12}$	$-y_{43}$	y_{44}	*

This proves that not only is (P_1) a parasite of fossil fuels, but that *globally the recipe consumes twice as much of the other energy than its net output*.[45]

A further result will clarify the real meaning of non-profitable cost. Since the mixed technology represented by Table IV effectively produces a net output, a system of positive prices exists. If we consolidate the budget equations of (P_1) and (P_2), we obtain

$$B_1 + B_2 + p_3(x_{31} + x_{32}) = p_1 x_1 - p_4 x_2. \qquad (34)$$

Because of the first inequality (31), it follows that $p_1 > p_4$. In other words, in the mixed technology, the price of a BTU obtained from solar energy is higher than that obtained from fossil fuels.[46] It is thus seen that the fact that producing one BTU from solar energy is at present nonprofitable is not due to price; instead, it reflects a hidden waste of the solar recipe.

A successful pilot combination of (P_1) and (P_2) that needs only matter from the outside would constitute a significant achievement, but still not completely conclusive. This combination, which is represented by Table V, still requires process like (P_3^0) and (P_4^0). Instead of (31), we have

$$x_{11} > x_{12}, \qquad x_{11} < x_{13}. \qquad (35)$$

Since even in this case, $y_{33} > x_{33}$, we obtain, as before,

$$y_{44} > x_{13} > x_{11} - x_{12}, \qquad (36)$$

with the same result concerning the global energy deficit [41]. In this case, however, it does not seem necessary for this deficit to lead to $p_1 > p_4$.[47]

45. Even if we believed that because of the superior intensity of FE, y_{43} may not be necessarily greater than x_{13}, (33) would be replaced by a weaker, but still relevant inequality.

46. The fact that people neverhtheless buy home solar installations should not surprise us. People heat their homes with electricity even though this mode consumes more energy than using coal, for example. Also, people buy electric gadgets without necessarily deriving an amount of energy from them comparable with that which was used in the production of those gadgets.

47. Perhaps this result may not stand further probing. For it appears highly curious indeed for a solar BTU depending indirectly on fossil fuels to cost less than an input BTU.

Table V. Collectors Produced by Solar Energy

Product	(P_1)	(P_2)	(P_3^0)	(P_4^0)	Net flows
SE	x_{11}	$-x_{12}$	*	*	$x_{11} - x_{12}$
CL	$-x_{21}$	x_{22}	*	*	*
K	$-x_{31}$	$-x_{32}$	y_{33}	$-y_{34}$	*
FE	*	*	$-y_{43}$	y_{44}	*

The statement by Denis Hayes, that "we can use solar energy now [because] the technology is here" [44], probably reflects the overenthusiasm of a keen student of the problems of energy scarcity. The truth is that only the feasible recipes are here, just as numberless other such recipes are. But a viable technology is not.

The discovery of far more efficient recipes may change the picture radically. However, harnessing solar radiation is not a problem that has just recently confronted us, as was the case of the peaceful use of nuclear energy some forty years ago. At that time, one could have easily gone wrong about the possibility of using the newly discovered energy; none other than Lord Rutherford did. But solar collectors have been used on a substantial scale for almost one hundred years now, and during all this time there has been practically no true breakthrough [12]. Undoubtedly, the Sun is the only steady and completely healthy source of energy whether for a new "Wood Age" or some other kind of solar age. At present, however, it seems very unlikely however that it will enable mankind to fly in jets, to live in sky-scrapers, and to travel in automobiles at one hundred kilometers per hours, for example.

To try persistently to find more efficient recipes is not only legitimate, it is imperative. But to claim that solar technology is here before it actually is, or to preach that "come what may we shall find a way" will only conceal from the public awareness the seriousness of the acute problem of natural resources and thus render any move toward an adequate policy to deal with that problem far more difficult than it actually is.

Mathematical Note

Let X be the matrix of Table III and let the prime accent denote inversion. By (30), the system

$$Xs' = w \tag{37}$$

1056   *Nicholas Georgescu-Roegen*

has a positive solution $s = (1, 1, 1)$ for $w = y \geqslant 0$.[48] By Theorem 5 [29, 324–25], it has a solution $s > 0$ for any $w > 0$. Hence $|X| = 0$,[49] and by Theorem 4 [29, 323], the system

$$X'p' = B',$$

(38)

where $B = (B_1, B_2, B_3) > 0$, has a solution $p > 0$. This proves that for any viable technology and for any fund prices, there exists a set of positive prices for the flow elements.

Let us now assume that (38) has a positive solution. From Theorem 4, again, it follows that

$$X\lambda' = z'$$

has a solution $\lambda > 0$ for any $z > 0$. Hence, $\Omega \in \Gamma$, where Ω is the non-negative quadrant and Γ is the convey cone determined by (P_1), (P_2), and (P_3). Unless $X = I$, there must be some w such that $w \in \Gamma$ but $w \in \Omega$. Nothing warrants that this is not the case for y. For a simple example:

$$X = \begin{bmatrix} 4 & -2 & -3 \\ -1 & +1 & 0 \\ -1 & -2 & 5 \end{bmatrix}$$

48. The vector notation $a \geqslant b$ excludes the of case $a = b$.
49. Direct computation yields $|X| = x_{22}y_1(x_{31} + x_{32}) + x_{22}y_3(x_{11} - x_{12}) > 0$. Incidentally, the number of conditions of Theorem 7 [29, 326, 336] can be further reduced by one unit; if the minor of third order—in the precent case, $|X|$—is positive, so must the minor of second order be.

References

1. Alfvén, Hannes. *Atom, Man and the Universe*. San Francisco: H. F. Freeman, 1969.
2. Allen, C. W. *Astrophysical Quantities*, 3rd ed. London: Athlone, 1973.
3. Auer, Peter L. "Does Entropy Production Limit Economic Growth?" in *Prospects for Growth: Changing Expectations for the Future*, edited by K. D. Wilson. New York: Praeger, 1977, pp. 314–34.
4. Boulding, Kenneth E. "The Economics of the Coming Spaceship Earth," in *Environmental Quality in a Growing Economy*, edited by H. Jarrett. Baltimore: Johns Hopkins University Press, 1966, pp. 3–14.
5. ———. "The Great Laws of Change," in *Evolution, Welfare and Time in Economics*, edited by A. M. Tang, F. M. Westfield and J. S. Worley. Lexington, Mass.: D. C. Heath, 1976, pp. 3–14.
6. ———, "Energy Policy: A Piece of Cake." *Technology Review*, December 1977, 8.
7. Boserup, Mogens, "Chairman's Report on Specialized Session III." Plenary Session, Fifth World Congress of the International Economic Association, Tokyo, 29 August–3 September 1977. (*Proceedings* forthcoming.)
8. Bridgman, P. W. *The Logic of Modern Physics*. New York: Macmillan, 1927.
9. Brooks, David P. and P. W. Andrews, "Mineral Resources, Economic Growth, and World Population." *Science*, 5 July 1974, 13–19.
10. Brown, Harrison. *The Challenge of Man's Future*. New York: Viking Press, 1954.
11. ———, James Bonner, and John Weir. *The Next Hundred Years*. New York: Viking Press, 1957.
12. Butti, Ken and John Perlin, "Solar Water Heaters in California, 1891–1930." *CoEvolution Quarterly*, Fall 1977, 4–13.
13. Chapman, P. F., "Energy Costs: A Review of Methods." *Energy Policy*, June 1974, 91–103.

14. _____, "The Energy Costs of Materials." *Energy Policy*, March 1975, 47–57.

15. _____, "The Ins and Outs of Nuclear Energy." *New Scientist*, December 1977, 866–69.

16. _____, G. Leach and M. Slesser, "The Energy Cost of Fossil Fuels." *Energy Policy*, September 1974, 231–43.

17. Chynoweth, A. G., "Materials Conservation: A Technologist's Viewpoint." *Challenge*, January-February 1976, 34–42.

18. Cloud, Preston. "Realities of Mineral Distribution," in *Man and His Physical Environment*, 2nd ed., edited by G. D. McKenzie and R. O. Utgard. Minneapolis: Burgess, 1974, pp. 185–98.

19. Committee for Economic Development (CED). *Key Elements to a National Energy Strategy*. New York, 1977.

20. Committee on Mineral Resources and the Environment (COMRATE). *Mineral Resources and the Environment*. Washington, D.C., 1975.

21. Cook, Peter, "Mineral Resources, Economic Growth, and World Population," *Science*, 5 July 1974, 13–19.

22. Cottrell, Fred. *Energy and Society*. New York: McGraw Hill, 1953.

23. Daly, Herman. "The Economic Thought of Frederick Soddy." Unpublished essay, 1978.

24. Denbigh, Kenneth. *Principles of Chemical Equilibrium*, 3rd ed. Cambridge, England: University Press, 1971.

25. Ehrenfest, Paul and Tatiana. *The Conceptual Foundations of the Statistical Approach in Mechanics*. Ithaca: Cornell University Press, 1959.

26. Energy Research and Development Agency (ERDA). *A National Plan for Energy Research, Development, and Demonstration: Creating Energy Sources for the Future*. Washington, D.C., 1975.

27. Feyman, R. P., R. B. Leighton and M. Sands. *The Feyman Lectures on Physics*, vol. I. Readings, Mass.: Addison-Wesley, 1966.

28. Flawn, Peter T. *Mineral Resources: Geology, Engineering, Economics, Politics*. Chicago: Rand McNally, 1966.

29. Georgescu-Roegen, Nicholas. *Analytical Economics: Issues and Problems*. Cambridge, Mass.: Harvard University Press, 1966.

30. _____. *The Entropy Law and the Economic Process*. Cambridge, Mass.: Harvard University Press, 1971.

31. _____, "A Different Economic Perspective." Paper read at the Boston Meeting of the American Association for the Advancement of Science, 21 February 1976.

32. _____. *Energy and Economic Myths: Institutional and Analytical Economic Essays*. New York: Pergamon Press, 1976.

33. _____, "Is Perpetual Motion of the Third Kind Possible?" Paper read at the Colloquium of the *Ecole Nationale Supérieure de Transportation*, Paris, 19 November 1976.

34. _____. "Economics and Mankind's Ecological Problem," in *U.S. Economic Growth from 1976 to 1986: Prospects, Problems, and Patterns*, Joint Economic Committee, Congress of the United States, Washington, D.C., vol. 7, pp. 62–91.

35. _____. "Bioeconomics: A New Look at the Nature of the Economic Activity," in *The Political Economy of Food and Energy*, edited by Louis Junker. Ann Arbor: University of Michigan, 1977, pp. 105–34.

36. _____, "The Steady State and Ecological Salvation: A Thermodynamic Analysis," *BioScience*, April 1977, 266–70.

37. _____. "Matter Matters, Too," in *Prospects for Growth: Changing Expectations for the Future*, edited by K. D. Wilson. New York: Praeger, 1977, pp. 293–313.

38. _____. "The Role of Matter in the Substitution of Energies" (Third International Colloquium on Petroleum Economics, Québec, 3–5 November 1977) ni *Resources énergétiques et coopération internationale*. Québec: Presses de l'Université Laval, 1978 (forthcoming).

39. _____, "Myths about Energy and Matter." *Growth and Change*, January 1979, pp. 16–23.

40. _____. "Matter: A Resource Ignored by Thermodynamics," in *Proceedings of the World Conference on Future Sources of Organic Materials* (Toronto, 10–13 July 1978), Toronto: Pergammon Press, 1979 (forthcoming).

41. _____, "Technology Assessment: The Case of the Direct Use of Solar Energy." *Atlantic Economic Journal*, December 1978, pp. 15–21.

42. Gilliland, Martha W., "Energy Analysis and Public Policy." *Science*, 26 September 1975, 1051–56, and 2 April 1976, 8–12.

43. Hayek, F. A. *The Counter-Revolution in Science*. Glencoe, Ill.: The Free Press, 1952.

44. Hayes, Denis, "We Can Use Solar Energy Now." *Washington Post*, 26 February 1978, D1–D4.

45. Hiebert, Erwin H. "The Energetics and the New Thermodynamics," in *Perspectives in the History of Science and Technology*, edited by Duanne H. D. Roller. Norman: University of Oklahoma Press, 1971, pp. 67–86.

46. Huettner, David A., "Net Energy Analysis: An Economic Assessment." *Science*, 9 April 1976, 101–104.

47. Kenward, Michael, "The Analyst's Precedent." *New Scientist*, 9 January 1975, 51.

48. Kirkwood, John G. and Irwin Oppenheim. *Chemical Thermodynamics*. New York: McGraw-Hill, 1961.

49. Leach, Gerald, "Energy Analysis." *New Scientist*, 16 January 1975, 160.

50. Lichnerowicz, Marc, "Economie et thermodynamique: Un modèle d'échange économique." *Economies et Sociétés*, October 1971, 1641–86.

51. Nash, Robert, "The Future of Wilderness: A Problem Statement." *Bulletin of the American Academy of Arts and Sciences*, May 1978, 18–24.

52. Neumann, John von. "The General and Logical Theory of Automata," in *Cerebral Mechanisms in Behavior: The Hixon Symposium*, edited by L. A. Jeffress. New York: Wiley, 1951, pp. 1–31.

53. Odum T. H., "Energy, Ecology, and Economics." *Ambio*, 1973, No. 6, 220–27.

54. _____, "Energy Analysis." *Science*, 15 April 1977, 260.

55. Ostwald, Wilhelm. *Die Energie*. Leipzig: J. A. Barth, 1908.

56. Page, Norman G. and S. C. Creasey, "Ore Grade, Metal Production, and Energy." *Journal of Research, U.S. Geological Survey*, January-February 1975, 9–13.

57. Planck, Max. *Theory of Heat*. London: Macmillan, 1932.

58. _____. *Treatise on Thermodynamics*, 7th ed. New York: Dover, 1945.

59. Price, John H. *Dynamic Energy Analysis and Nuclear Power*. London: Friends of the Earth, 1974.

60. Prigogine, Ilya. "Time, Structure and Entropy," in *Time in Science and Philosophy*, edited by Jiří Zeman. Amsterdam: Elsevier, 1971, pp. 89–100.

61. _____, "Irreversibility as a Symmetry-breaking Process." *Nature*, 9 November 1973, 67–71.

62. _____, C. George, F. Henin and L. Rosenfield, "A Unified Formulation of Dynamics and Thermodynamics." *Chemica Scripta*, 1973, No. 1, 5–32.

63. Rabinowicz, Ernest. *Friction and Wear of Materials*. New York: Wiley, 1965.

64. Rose, David J. "Materials Requirements for Emerging Energy Technology," in [20], Appendix to Section I, D.15–D.23.

65. Seaborg, Glenn T. "The Erehwon Machine: Possibilities for Reconciling Goals by Way of New Technology," in *Energy, Economic Growth and the Environment*, edited by Sam H. Schurr. Baltimore: Johns Hopkins University Press, 1972, pp. 125–38.

66. Seeger, Raymond J. *Men of Physics: J. Willard Gibbs*. New York: Pergamon Press, 1974.

67. Silver, R. S. *Introduction to Thermodynamics*. Cambridge, England: University Press, 1971.

68. Skinner, Brian J. *Earth Resources*, Englewood Cliffs, N.J.: Prentice-Hall, 1969.

69. _____, "A Second Iron Age Ahead?" *American Scientist*, May-June 1976, 258–69.

70. Slesser, Malcom, "Accounting for Energy." *Nature*, 20 March 1975, 170–72.

71. _____, "Energy Analysis." *Science*, 15 April 1977, 259–60.

72. Solow, Robert M., "Is the End of the World at Hand?" *Challenge*, March-April 1973, 39–50.

73. Tayler, R. J. *The Origin of the Chemical Elements*. London: Wykeham, 1972.

74. Thomson, Sir William (Lord Kelvin). *Mathematical and Physical Papers*, vol. I. Cambridge, England: University Press, 1881.

75. Weinberg, Steven. *The First Three Minutes*. New York: Basic Books, 1977.

76. Woodwell, G. M., R. H. Whittacker, W. A. Reiners, G. E. Likens, C. C. Delwiche and D. B. Botkin, "The Biota and the World Carbon Budget." *Science*, 13 January 1978, 141–46.

77. Wright, David J., "Goods and Services: An Input-Output Analysis." *Energy Policy*, December 1974, 307–14.

78. Zemansky, Mark W. *Heat and Thermodynamics*, 5th ed. New York: McGraw-Hill, 1968.

[5]

ENVIRONMENT STATISTICS

Draft guildelines for statistics on materials/energy balances

Report of the Secretary-General

SUMMARY

The Statistical Commission considered a draft system of environment
statistics (E/CN.3/452) at its eighteenth session, and recommended that work
in this area should continue. The present paper deals with one part of the
over-all framework of environment statistics proposed there, namely,
statistics on materials/energy balances, proposing draft guidelines for the
compilation of such statistics. It is designed on the same principles as the
System of National Accounts, and is entirely compatible with the national
accounts. It is also entirely compatible with "Towards a System of Integrated
Energy Statistics" (E/CN.3/476), also before the Commission. Unlike the
latter, which is focused upon short-run possibilities and objectives, the
present paper is concerned with a longer-run statistical programme, one which
may be thought of as an objective towards which to aim, rather than a project
for immediate implementation.

The paper discusses the uses of statistics of this type (chapter II),
design criteria (chapter III) and the structure of the proposed framework
(chapter IV). It then goes on to provide the necessary definitions (chapter V).
Chapter VI contains a short note on the assessment of environmental damages
and abatement costs, and chapter VII suggests possible ways to approach
implementation in the shorter run.

E/CN.3/492
English
Page 2

CONTENTS

E/CN.3/492
English
Page 3

INTRODUCTION

1.　The present paper[1] is a continuation of work on part of the programme outlined in "Statistics of the environment", (E/CN.3/452), considered by the Statistical Commission at its eighteenth session.[2] It contains draft guidelines for
statistics on materials/energy balances, as part of the over-all development of
statistics on the environment. Those elements of these guidelines dealing with
energy statistics are in harmony with the programme outlined in "Towards a System
of Integrated Energy Statistics" (E/CN.3/476), also before the Commission. The
framework proposed is intended to encompass a common core of statistics that would
be suitable both for analysis of the energy economy per se and for energy statistics
pertaining to the environment.

2.　The general character, purposes and possible uses of a system of environmental
statistics has been discussed extensively, both at meetings and seminars[3] and in
previous documents.[4] Hence, only a brief re-capitulation is provided here.
Statistics on materials/energy balances were proposed as part of a phased programme
of work on environmental statistics to be undertaken over the next few years by the
United Nations Statistical Office and the Conference of European Statisticians,
with support from the United Nations Environment Programme. It is thus conceived
as a "module" in a larger system of statistics. The structure and content of the
complete system have not, as yet, been fully defined, pending more extensive interaction between the agencies that would ultimately be responsible for defining
classifications and compiling statistics and potential users thereof, both national
and international. In the case of the materials/energy module, it is felt that
user needs are sufficiently well defined to permit a more detailed level of specification at this time.

3.　Briefly, the primary purpose of a system of environmental statistics (and,
hence, of any module thereof) is to facilitate environmental studies and analysis
with policy implications, particularly by and for Governments and international
agencies. Such studies will, typically, require forecasts of the environmental
consequences of various economic, demographic or technological trends or policies
or, conversely, of the economic and social implications of environmental changes.

4.　Obviously, there is already a large amount of accumulated raw data relevant to
some environmental topics but much more is needed in other areas. Raw data may be
derived from many sources, such as scientific measurements, questionnaires and
sample surveys, administrative records etc. Many of these data have been, or will
be, processed, compiled and published as special-purpose statistical series.

1/　Prepared by R.U. Ayres, acting as consultant to the United Nations.

2/　Official Records of the Economic and Social Council, Fifty-eighth Session,
Supplement No. 2, paras. 86-92.

3/　A meeting on Statistics for Environmental Studies and Policies was held by
the Conference of European Statisticians, Geneva, 19-23 March 1973 ("Report of the
meeting", CES/AC/40/5, 26 March 1973); a Seminar on Environmental Statistics was
held jointly by the Conference of European Statisticians and the Senior Advisors to
ECE Governments on Environmental Problems, Geneva, 15-19 October 1973 ("Conclusions
of the Seminar", CES/Sem. 6/11-Env. Sem 1/11, 27 November 1973).

4/　Conference of European Statisticians, "Statistics for environmental studies
and policies" (CES/AC-40/2) (Geneva, 13 February 1973) and "Steps towards a system
of environmental statistics (CES/Sem 6/2-Env/Sem 1/2) (Geneva, 4 September 1973).

E/CN.3/492
English
Page 4

5. There are also on-going programmes to develop internationally comparable statistics on population, urbanization, health, nutrition, education, social variables, weather and climate, resources, energy, agriculture, trade and so forth.

6. In the context of the existing United Nations programmes, the proposed system of environmental statistics has two important functions. First, it will provide a broad framework for co-ordinating and harmonizing a number of concurrent statistical activities. Secondly, it should provide guidance to both national and international statistical offices in terms of evolving future activities in such a way as to fit into a coherent over-all scheme.

7. It is natural to raise the question as to why a broadly conceived system of environmental statistical is really needed. Why not, in other words, build another set of special statistics encompassing purely environmental changes such as ambient pollution levels and discharges? This question is all the more important, inasmuch as many statisticians have evidently assumed that environmental statistics, would, indeed, be limited to this kind of data. The materials/energy balance module, on the other hand, does not include statistics about the ambient state of the environment but does, very clearly, overlap other existing types of special statistics such as energy and industrial statistics.

8. The answer to this question can be found in the nature of the environment itself--it is all-encompassing by definition--and the requirements imposed by this attribute of comprehensiveness on the analytical tools needed to study or do research on environmental issues. It is not enough to consider biological or ecological effects in isolation. For purposes of environmental policy evaluation and assessment, changes in the biosphere or the climate of the earth must be traced back to social and economic activities of man which, in turn, depend upon resource constraints and technology. It is the causal connexions between these diverse phenomena that matter and for which an international system of statistics is needed. A set of statistics that simply describes the ultimate physical or biological consequences of the causal chain, without incorporating data on the critical dynamic mechanisms, would have a very limited value to policy makers. Its value would not be consonant with the enormous cost of acquiring and processing the necessary data on a worldwide basis.5/

9. In short, special-purpose statistics are a valuable resource in the context of short-range environmental problem-solving, but they are seldom adequate for longer-range analytical studies--a purpose they were after all not designed to serve. For the latter, it is essential to distinguish observed symptoms or effects (which are by far the easiest to measure,and, hence, dominate the existing data), from more

---

5/ The possible scientific value of such data is another question. It must be pointed out, however, that the kind of data most valuable to scientists is often of little or no use to statisticians. For instance, marine biologists interested in the movement of toxic substances (say, mercury) through a "food chain" of biological organisms would like to gather very complete data, covering a large number of organisms, for a specific lake or bay for which mercury inputs could be monitored exactly. On the other hand, environmental policy makers would prefer to collect time-series or cross-sectional data on the mercury content of all fish sold for human consumption. The design of a suitable monitoring system will be completely different in the two cases, and the data gathered for one purpose would generally be of negligible value for the other. It remains to be seen, however, whether data gathering projects can in principle be designed to serve scientific and environmental policy purposes simultaneously.

E/CN.3/492
English
Page 5

fundamental underlying variables or driving forces. While a thorough explanation of this distinction cannot be undertaken here, suffice it to say that the system of environmental statistics--and materials/energy balances, in particular--will be designed to satisfy the broader needs of governmental agencies for a systems approach to the analysis of policy choices with respect to environmental implications of major public projects, technological developments, material substitutions, fuel substitutions and so forth. These purposes require development of analytical tools and models utilizing extensive data on environmental media, resources, processes, and stocks and flows of materials and energy.

10. An important distinction can be made between statistics that are derived entirely from direct measurements (or survey responses) and statistics that are, in part, synthesized from a combination of direct measurements and physical, biological or economic models. The importance of the distinction can best be explained by an example. Let us suppose that it is deemed important to develop uniform statistics on the discharge of pollutants into the atmosphere by region. The most straightforward approach is to sample the atmosphere in a large number of locations, utilizing spectrophotometres, lasers and all other available instruments, and compile the resulting measurements. Of course, the practical difficulty and expense of the method dictates that the number of sampling locations and times will be limited, it being assumed that measurements taken at random times and locations will be typical.6/ An alternative approach would rely on in-depth engineering studies, including detailed measurements where necessary, of each industry, starting with the biggest and most obviously polluting ones, to develop a set of characteristic coefficients relating material and energy inputs, production of useful products and production of waste products. The coefficients can also be statistically related to scale of production, age of facility and other variables. (In short, a model is built for each industry). Estimates of production of pollutants for a region, then, can be generated from a combination of engineering process data and economic statistics on industrial production by commodity, process and location. This alternate strategy is particularly vital in the environmental area and will be a key factor in making basic decisions in the design of the system of environmental statistics, and especially materials/energy balances.

11. The use of partly synthetic statistics and other innovations can help to keep the difficulty and cost of developing the module within reasonable limits, but, - as will be seen, - its ultimate scope is nevertheless quite large. This naturally raises three related questions. First, is it a practical goal to implement such a large system? Secondly, are there ways of implementing it in stages, starting with comparatively small parts of the full system, so as to establish procedures and work out difficulties before a full-scale commitment is made? Thirdly, would a modest part of the complete system have significant value in itself, independent of the rest?

12. It is clear that if the answer to even one of these questions were negative, the probability of success would be slight. Chapter VII argues for affirmative answers to all three questions, however, and proposes a specific strategy for implementation in stages.

6/ This assumption is very likely to be faulty. For obvious reasons, teams of technicians carrying out sample surveys are quite likely to prefer working during ordinary (daylight) business hours. Polluters know this. It is widely rumoured, therefore, that major polluters save their worst pollutants for discharge at night, when visibility is bad.

E/CN.3/492
English
Page 6

I. ACTION BY THE COMMISSION

13. The Statistical Commission may wish to comment upon the scope, feasibility and desirability of the framework described herein, as a basis for organizing statistics on materials and energy balances, in the light of the relationship of that framework to the wider body of environmental statistics, on the one hand, and to the national accounts and balances, on the other hand.

II. USE OF MATERIALS/ENERGY BALANCES IN SIMULATION AND OPTIMIZATION MODELS

14. Probably the major application of statistics on materials/energy balances will be as a basis for constructing large-scale models for environmental forecasting and management purposes, just as there is a natural application of national accounting data to the development of input-output economic models. Indeed, the module will facilitate the natural extension of input-output models to incorporate resource requirements and waste residual outputs and to reflect the fact that the material/energy inputs and outputs for the economy must always balance.

15. Table 2 of the framework displays the origins and destinations of each individual commodity (material or energy). But this information can also be expressed in the form of a commodity input-output table showing the relationships between all materials and forms of energy simultaneously.

16. A table of this kind can be used as an adjunct to a conventional (monetary) input-output table, or it can be used independently in an exactly analogous manner. (Indeed, the basic equations are identical). Thus, if a certain set of "final" material commodities is required, the matrix will immediately tell us the corresponding total quantity of each material or form of energy - including all raw materials and intermediates - that must be produced, based on current technology production. When the matrix is inverted, we can also discover the amount of each material or form of energy that is embodied both directly and indirectly in a unit quantity of any specified final material.

17. Thus, the inverse commodity matrix will tell us exactly how much energy, by type, is consumed both directly and indirectly in producing a given final product commodity - whether it be a loaf of bread or an automobile. Hence, the materials/energy input-output matrix will greatly facilitate answering questions that have sometimes proved vexatious in the past. For example, there has been controversy as to whether or not a hypothetical new technology such as solar cells for direct conversion of solar energy into electricity or direct microbiological conversion of petroleum into protein (by-passing conventional agriculture) would actually conserve more energy than it consumes. These questions can easily be settled by computing the direct and indirect energy required to produce the solar cells and supporting equipment, or the synthetic protein, respectively. These figures can be compared to the expected lifetime electricity output of the solar cells, on the one hand, or direct and indirect energy input to animal protein produced by conventional agriculture, on the other hand.

18. Optimization models may be expected to come into increasing use for purposes of environmental management. Selections must be made among alternative investment and abatement strategies, processes and/or manufacturing technologies, sources of

E/CN.3/492
English
Page 7

raw materials, locations of productive facilities, planting patterns for crops, product mix patterns for refineries and so forth. Models used for dealing with questions of this sort are typically of the "activity analysis" type, with optimization algorithms based on linear programming. Non-linear programming, rank-order enumeration and other methods can also be applied.

19. The formal uses of materials/energy balances in constructing and implementing environmental assessment and/or forecasting models of various types will be discussed below. However, it may be useful to review a typical situation where statistics on materials/energy balances or their equivalent would be helpful to policy-level planners. There have been a number of instances in recent decades where a particular pollutant was suddenly discovered to be potentially dangerous for some reason. Examples include the following:

(a) In 1959 mercury poisoning was tentatively identified as the cause of "Minimata disease", so-called because of a large-scale outbreak near the village of Minimata, Japan, beginning in 1953. Research in the last decade has shown that matallic mercury discharged in industrial wastes is converted by bacterial action to organic methyl mercury which is water soluble and is incorporated into the marine food chain, where it is gradually accumulated and concentrated in the bodies of fish or other higher organisms that are eventually consumed by humans. When this phenomenon was discovered it became apparent that mercury, in any form whatever, is environmentally dangerous.

(b) Also in Japan, a new disease called "Itai-Itai" (the aching disease) appeared starting about 1910 in the villages of the Jinzu River basin down-stream from a copper mine. The cause of the disease was traced eventually to cadmium, discharged with the mine waste. Like mercury, it is apparent that cadmium in the environment is exceedingly toxic and dangerous, regardless of circumstances.

(c) Rachel Carson's landmark book, Silent Spring[7]/ identified DDT (endrin, dieldrin and some other chlorinated hydrocarbons) as environmentally hazardous due to its long residence time in soil and natural organisms. Like methyl mercury, DDT passes through the food chain and is concentrated by organisms at the higher trophic levels, such as fish-eating birds and insectivores. It can also cause harm directly to humans. For these and other reasons DDT, endrin and dieldrin have been banned in the United States of America. The long-term prognosis is not clear at this point.

(d) Evidence has been found that chlorinated biphenyls--another type of persistent chlorinated hydrocarbon were building up in the oceans of the world. It was suggested that this might interfere with the growth of phytoplankton, the primary photosynthetic organisms upon which the entire marine food chain depends--and which also constitutes an important link in the oxygen cycle of the world.

(e) Some evidence has come to light that inert and long-lived chlorine-bearing fluorocarbons, used as propellants for aerosol products may be accumulating in the stratosphere where the chlorine may combine with ozone, thus depleting the "ozone layer". This would allow more intense ultra-violet radiation to reach the surface of the earth, thus potentially increasing the incidence of skin cancer.

7/ New York, Fawcett World, 1962.

E/CN.3/492
English
Page 8

(f) Another organic chlorine chemical, vinyl chloride, has been found to be
highly carcinogenic. This chemical is exclusively used to manufacture the ubiquitous
plastic polyvinyl chloride (which is perfectly safe). However, during the manufacturing process some of the vinyl chloride monomer may escape into the environment.
Workers, in particular, have some chance of exposure to it. Also, there is a possibility that a small quantity of unreacted vinyl chloride may be incorporated in the
finished plastic product where users might be exposed to it.

(g) Carbon dioxide in the earth's atmosphere tends to absorb infra-red radiation from the earth and re-radiate it isotropically, thus acting as a reflector.
This is called the "greenhouse effect", since it tends to warm the surface of the
earth by preventing heat from escaping. Combustion of fossil fuels produces carbon
dioxide and may increase the average concentration in the atmosphere, thus tending
to raise the average temperature of the surface of the earth. On the other hand,
combustion produces small particles, especially in the range of diameters less than
one micron (10^6 metre or 10^3 mm), which reflect visible light very effectively. An
accumulation of particulates in the stratosphere could, thus, lead to a cooling
trend. It is not yet known which of these phenomena is likely to be predominant,
and the over-all climatic consequences of simultaneously injecting both carbon
dioxide and small particulates into the atmosphere via combustion and other processes
is a matter of fierce dispute among the experts.

20. It is evident that, in all such cases, discovery of a potential problem associated with a particular waste residual naturally leads to questions about the overall quantity of the residual, its geographical distribution, and the processes or
industries with which it is associated. This type of information is far from easy
to find, in general. One can say that carbon dioxide results from combustion of
fossil fuels and estimate that approximately all fossil fuels produced in a year are
also consumed in combustion processes. Similarly, all DDT that is produced is presumably dispersed into the environment in one way or another, though the geographical
pattern of use is not so easy to fix. But what about the other cases?

21. Mercury is used in a variety of products, including fungicides, pharmaceuticals,
thermometers, mirrors, mercury vapour lamps and dental alloys. It is also used as
a catalyst in a process for the manufacture of chlorine and acetic anhydride -
probably the major source of leakage into the environment. Cadmium is a by-product
of zinc and is often found in zinc or copper mine or smelter wastes. It is also
used as a plating material, in batteries, as a pigment and as a plasticizer - among
other uses. Some of these uses may lead to environmental problems while others will
not. How can we estimate the current quantities and locations, and the likely future
changes in use and waste-flows?

22. Polychlorinated biphenyls are mainly used as high-temperature coolants for
electrical transformers and similar devices. Chlorinated fluorocarbons are used as
inert aerosol propellants as already noted--and also as refrigerants for household
refrigerators and air-conditioners. Again, how can we estimate present production
and usage patterns and project future changes?

23. Statistics on materials/energy balances are specifically designed to deal with
questions like these.

E/CN.3/192
English
Page 9

III. DESIGN CRITERIA AND PROBLEMS

24. The importance of designing the system of environmental statistics and its various parts, such as materials/energy balances, to be compatible with the existing System of National Accounts (SNA) has been repeatedly stressed. Clearly, the same underlying structure and definitions should be used. Even if one system requires more disaggregation than the other, categories should be consistent with each other as far as possible. Thus SNA definitions and categories will be used unless there is a specific reason not to do so. Any deviation must be explained and justified. Similarly, the framework should be designed to co-ordinate a wide range of existing types of special statistics on energy, resources, industrial production etc.

25. The primary purpose of materials/energy balances is to trace the extractions and transformations of materials and energy from natural resources through various successive stages of processing to final use, and thence back to the environment as waste (or to secondary uses). The statistics must, therefore, deal explicitly with transformations from one form (or category) to another. This introduces a number of difficulties and creates risks of undercounting or overcounting. For instance, coal is used to generate electricity, another form of energy. Clearly, electricity generated from coal-fired boilers cannot be treated as an item in the accounts equivalent to coal itself, even though some users might consider them mutually substitutable. From the statistical viewpoint, processed forms of materials or energy should be kept separate from raw forms. Moreover, each stage of processing must be conceptually distinguished.

26. Another difficulty is posed by the interconvertibility of fuels and materials for other purposes. Natural gas, oil, coal and wood can be burned for heat. Or coal can be converted to coke which is used to reduce iron ore. The chemical energy value contained in the coke is partly wasted in the form of heat and by-products such as carbon dioxide and partly embodied in the product (pig iron). If the pure iron were oxidized (i.e., burned), it would revert to the chemical form of the ore (Fe_2O_3 or Fe_3O_4). Thus reduction is, energetically, the reverse of oxidation.

27. An example which is currently quantitatively insignificant but may be important in the future is the use of refined metals such as lead, zinc and nickel as battery anodes. (In the future lithium, sodium or magnesium may be widely used in this application). As the battery is discharged, the metal in the anode reacts with oxygen or some other element, resulting in a lower available energy content. The process may be reversed by recharging the battery using an external electrical supply. A satisfactory statistical system must be capable of disentangling these energy conversion processes.

28. Another troublesome case arises when natural gas, together with atmospheric air, are converted into ammonia. The hydrogen in the ammonia comes originally from the methane in the gas. Thus, the gas is, in effect, a feedstock for a non-fuel chemical product. (Of course, the ammonia has energy content and could actually be used as a fuel). Natural gas is also the main source of ethane and propane, which are in turn converted to ethylene and propylene, basic building blocks of organic chemistry leading to synthetic fibres, plastics and so forth. In the same way butane, benzene, toluene and xylene are generally obtained from cracking crude oil or, less frequently, from coal tar. These are used, in turn, to manufacture butylene, butadiene, styrene and a host of other synthetic elastomers and polymers.

E/CN.3/492
English
Page 10

29. Obviously, some materials that are manufactured from potential primary fuels later become available again as secondary fuels. This applies especially to organic materials such as paper and paperboard. Similarly, secondary flows of non-fuel materials must be considered. A satisfactory statistical system should explicitly reflect these factors.

30. It is important to note, also, that many processed materials can be derived from alternative - sometimes very diverse - sources. Acetic acid and methyl alcohol can be obtained commercially from destructive distillation (pyrolysis) of wood or from fossil hydrocarbons. Ethyl alcohol for human consumption is derived from distillation of fermented carbohydrates (grain, potatoes, fruit etc.), whereas industrial alcohol is produced - much more cheaply - from natural gas liquids. Benzene and toluene are industrially produced from coal tar or from petroleum. Sodium carbonate (soda ash) is currently obtained mainly from natural deposits (trona), whereas it was formerly synthesized by the Solvay process from sodium chloride (rock salt) and limestone. The reverse is true of aluminium fluoride (cryolite), used in large quantities in the aluminium industry, which was formerly obtained from a natural deposit in Greenland but will, in the future, be manufactured synthetically (unless its use is obviated by a process change).

31. Many industrial chemicals which are now produced directly from raw materials will be derived largely or entirely from waste products in the future. The most obvious example is sulphuric acid, which is currently manufactured from elemental sulphur but will eventually be a by-product of coal or oil desulphurization or stock-gas treatment. Examples are not confined to the chemical and metallurgical industries. For instance, plaster of Paris - used in the building industry - is currently manufactured from the natural mineral gypsum, but will probably be available as a by-product of future stack-gas treatment processes. Future insulation, paving materials and other construction materials will undoubtedly be derived increasingly from recycled wastes. And already many food products and additives are being derived from non-agricultural sources. This is notably true of synthetic beverages and sweeteners, but animal feedstuffs and even synthetic proteins may be manufactured from fossil hydrocarbons in significant quantities before the end of this century.

32. An important consequence of the foregoing, from the standpoint of designing a set of tables, is that groupings that might seem "natural" today may not be so a few years hence. In particular, it cannot be assumed that a given processed material always comes from the same raw material or that a given raw material or ore will always be refined into the same final product. Thus, while it is sometimes useful to distinguish raw (unprocessed) materials from processed materials, this cannot be done meaningfully within a more narrowly defined category such as "agricultural products", "fuels", or "chemical products".

33. The interconversion of materials and forms of energy raises a potentially troublesome set of problems pertaining to units of account. Various inputs to a physical or chemical conversion process may be traditionally measured in different units; similarly, inputs and outputs may be measured in different units. For instance, coal entering a generating plant is normally measured in mass (tonnage) units while electricity output is measured in kwh. The equivalence factor between tons of coal and kwh of electricity is not a natural constant: it depends on the quality of the coal and the efficiency of the generating plant and varies over time. (The "energy balance" between outputs also involves different units--BTU and kwh).

E/CN.3/492
English
Page 11

34. Another example arises in the case of petroleum refineries where simultaneous materials and energy balances are needed. The input crude oil is measured in physical volume (usually in barrels) which is characterized by a certain average heat energy content (BTU/bbl). The outputs are also measured in volume terms, but the energy per unit volume of various refinery fractions (gasoline, naphtha, fuel oil, residual oil) varies quite considerably due to differences in specific gravity. Thus, the total volume of outputs need not be exactly equal to the volume of inputs, but the sum of weights and energies should, of course, balance when losses are considered. The specific gravity of input crude oil will vary from one country to another;[8]/ similarly, the specifications (including specific gravity) of outputs will also vary. Thus a set of supplementary weight/volume/energy equivalences must be supplied for each conversion process and for each country. Many of the indicated equivalence tables will, of course, be required for international energy statistics.

35. It is important to bear in mind that materials/energy balances will not be useful for cataloguing all actual or potential pollutants. They are necessarily concerned with volume pollutants, such as organic wastes or combustion products, plus specific major chemicals and metals. However, some pollutants are not subject to conservation rules. These include noise - (a non-conserved form of waste energy), - visual pollution and litter, carcinogenic, mutagenic, teratogenic or toxic organic chemicals and radio-active wastes. These can only be dealt with by linking the materials/energy balances to supplementary tabulations, such as the proposed International Registry of Toxic Chemicals.[9]/

36. Logically, materials/energy balances could include the "stocks and flows" of some elements such as carbon, nitrogen, phosphorous (and energy) in major environmental reservoirs, such as the atmosphere, soil, forests, surface waters and oceans. At present, this must be regarded as an objective for the distant future, since it is not practically feasible to quantify most of the flows at present. From an environmental point of view, this gap is a major challenge that must be filled, in the first instance, by design of appropriate environmental monitoring systems, such as the Global Environmental Monitoring System (GEMS) currently being developed by the United Nations Environment Programme.

37. Similarly, ecological and health effects associated with pollution cannot now be incorporated into materials/energy balances. Such statistics are currently compiled to a minor extent by national agencies, Food and Agriculture Organization and World Health Organization. Similarly existing industrial and resource statistics must also be co-ordinated. Links can be provided by developing supplementary tables to reconcile relevant definitions and categories. At some future time, it would be desirable for the system of environmental statistics to incorporate these external data on a uniform and consistent basis.

8/ In tropical countries, crude is often "spiked" by addition of naphtha to increase the output of light fractions, since heavy fuel fractions (used for heating) are less required.

9/ See "The International Register of Potentially Toxic Chemicals - components and network", Report of the United Nations Environment Programme Workshop, 20 January 1975, UNEP/WG.1/4/Rev.1. The linkage would be essentially automatic as long as both systems use the same or related classifications.

E/CN.3/492
English
Page 12

IV. STRUCTURE OF STATISTICS ON MATERIALS/ENERGY BALANCES

38. The underlying design principle for the proposed statistics on materials/
energy balances is conservation of materials and energy: all material and energy
inputs to the world economic system, as well as to individual countries, must be
accounted for either as final outputs or as changes in accumulated stocks, including
durable goods in service as well as inventories. Two "balance" concepts are used:
a gross (volume) balance is applied in the case of production, consumption and trade
of major resources and commodities. A more refined materials and energy balance,
by process, is also applied to elucidate the relation between resource/commodity
production and consumption and the generation of waste flows.

39. Some of the categories used are standard ones from national accounts statistics,
namely, domestic output, imports, exports, domestic consumption and sectoral classifications of economic activity. There are two significant additions: (a) physical
stocks and flows, including commodities and wastes; and (b) explicit materials/
energy transformations, that is, processes.

40. The terms "stock" and "flow" are used above in a general and somewhat undefined
sense. Definitions of these terms, as specifically used in the present document,
will be given below. Distinctions must be made between stocks that are physically
distinguishable natural reservoirs, such as ground water or oceans, and stocks that
are essentially accounting categories, differentiated by ownership, production process etc. Similarly, flows may be additions to or subtractions from the quantity
of a physical resource contained in a given natural reservoir; they may be transformations from one physical form to another; or they may represent shifts from one
accounting category to another.

41. All changes of stocks are equivalent to flows, and this accounting identity is
essential in constructing a statistical system. It follows, too, that changes in
a stock can either be determined by direct enumeration and/or direct measurement,
or they can be inferred by measuring and summing the corresponding input and output
flows. Where both possibilities are feasible, one provides a useful check on the
other. Sometimes only one of the two approaches is feasible, however, and it is not
necessary to specify which approach is to be used in any given case.

42. Because of the interconnectedness of materials/energy stocks and flows, it is
natural to employ a schematic matrix form of presentation. This format emphasizes
the structural linkages with SNA; it also facilitates understanding of the differences between the two systems. The structure of the proposed framework is displayed
graphically in figure I and in matrix form in the Annex. (Explanatory notes and a
list of symbols and accounting identities in the system are also included in the
Annex). It will be noted that balances can be defined at two different levels of
aggregation. In the first place, all material and energy input and output flows to
a given category or interaction box in figure I must exactly be accounted for by
depletion or accumulation of some stock. This must hold not only for gross quantities (measured in mass or weight, for instance) but also for specific chemical
elements. For instance, all phosphorus consumed by a sector must be compensated
for exactly by the phosphorus content of production or of accumulation. By extension, of course, the same kinds of balances must also hold for groups of sectors,
or for the economy as a whole. Thus, all sulphur that is extracted from the earth
each year, either directly as sulphur or as a contaminant of petroleum or coal, must
either accumulate in some reservoir or stock of durables, or it must become a
corresponding flow of waste residuals.

E/CN.3/492
English
Page 13

Figure I. Diagrammatic presentation of materials/energy balances

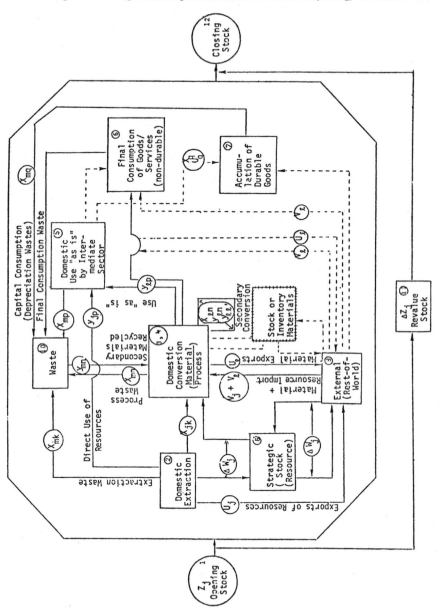

E/CN.3/492
English
Page 14

43. The stock/flow data required to complete the scheme outlined above can be displayed conveniently in four major tabulations. Table 1 displays aggregated data on production, consumption and stocks of resources at all stages of processing, beginning with natural resources and unprocessed commodities and proceeding through all intermediate forms to finished materials and classifiable products. Fuels and forms of energy are also included.

44. It is certainly possible, in principle, to subdivide table 1 into several parts, as has been advocated. For instance, natural resources (not extracted), raw materials, and fuel (as extracted), and processed materials and processed forms of energy could be separated into separate tables for convenience. Similarly, natural resources could be subdivided into renewable and non-renewable categories with separate tables for each. These subdivisions may ultimately be done for convenience, since the combined table will obviously be very large. However, any separations also necessarily introduce some degree of arbitrariness. Is forage or pasture harvested by animals to be regarded as "extracted" or not? Are ground water or top soil "renewable" or not? To avoid fruitless controversy over such questions, it seems advisable to avoid unnecessary boundaries.

45. The purpose of table 1 is to display gross accounting balances for each major natural resource or commodity in large-scale production. In the case of renewable natural resources, such tables would provide a basic management tool, e.g., for adjusting extraction rates to maximize output without depleting the resource. In the case of non-renewable resources, the current extraction rate would typically be measured against the rate of upward revaluation of stocks due to exploratory activity or improvements of extraction technology. Limitations on current production of resources and on its rate of expansion constitute an important input to resource/environmental management and economic forecasting models.

46. Commodity data are included in the same basic tabulation because they provide the necessary link between final demand for goods and services and calls on basic resources. Again, these data would primarily be utilized in resource/environmental management and forecasting models.

47. The resource/commodity balance data in table 1 will generally be derived annually from current government statistics on agriculture, fisheries, forestry, mining, manufacturing and trade. Departments of parks, tourism and urban affairs will also provide some data. While these standard statistical sources are not necessarily of high quality, the over-all figures thus derived will nevertheless constitute a useful means of updating and projecting the more detailed materials/ energy balance-by-process data in table 2, discussed below. Table 1 would include production, consumption, import, and export figures for such materials as DDT, chlorinated biphenyls, fluorocarbons, polyvinyl chloride, mercury and cadmium, thus providing basic data to deal with questions of the type discussed above.

48. Table 2 is an elaboration of table 1, providing breakdowns on material/energy source by extraction or production process, subsequent conversion (if any) by process, utilization as such, by sector and incorporation into various durable goods, by category.

E/CN.3/492
English
Page 15

Table 1. Resource/commodity accounts

Country/year

Account	Resource/ commodity name	Resource No. 1	Resource No. 2	Resource No. 3
		Hectares x 10^3	M^3	Bbl
Opening stock not yet extracted				
Stockpile held for strategic reserve				
Withdrawals from (additions to) strategic reserve				
Domestic production (total)				
Exports				
Imports				
Domestic consumption (total)				
Domestic use for conversion to other commodities				
Domestic utilization in unconverted form				
Additions to, or revaluations of opening stock				
Closing stock				

E/CN.3/492
English
Page 16

Table 2. Conversion/disposition accounts

Accounts	Resource/ commodity (name, unit)	Resource No. 1 (units)					
Sources, by major production process	Production process name	Process 1	Process 2	Process 3	Process 4	Process 5	Other process n.e.c.
	Process type, code						
	Quantity produced						
Disposition by major conversion processes	Conversion process name	Process 1	Process 2	Process 3	Process 4	Process 5	Other process n.e.c.
	Process type, code						
	Quantity converted						
Disposition by incorporation in major commodities	Commodity name	Commodity 1	Commodity 2	Commodity 3	Commodity 4	Commodity 5	Other commodity
	Commodity code						
	Quantity accounted for						
Utilization by sector (final form)	Sector	Agri- culture	Manu- facturing	Construc- tion	Transport	Govern- ment and services	Household
	Quantity						
Utilization by category of durables (final form)	Category	Machinery and equipment	Producer struc- tures	Residen- tial housing	Personal vehicles	Household appliance	Other private
	Quantity						

E/CN.3/492
English
Page 17

49. The purpose of table 2 is to display moderately detailed relationships between inputs and outputs of materials and energy, including wastes, at the successive stages of production and transformation of natural resources into commodities and subsequently into final goods and services. The data will ultimately provide a basis for projecting detailed resource and energy requirements and gross residuals generation prior to abatement processes, consequent to changes in the technological level of industry or the pattern of government regulation. It also permits, in principle, the development of linear-programming or related models to facilitate the optimal choice of industrial development strategy and pollution abatement strategy in terms of resource and conservation and environmental protection criteria.

50. Statistical data for table 2 are not completely available currently in most countries, and would have to be gathered especially, through such sources as a census of manufactures. This is unlikely to be carried out on an annual basis in the foreseeable future and would, in any case, involve significant delays for data processing and checking. Thus, table 2 will normally be compiled several years later than table 1; it will be several years out of data when published - and will be prepared at less frequent intervals. It will constitute a "benchmark" in the same sense as the input-output tables now prepared at intervals by several Govern-ments. Table 2 would include information on key industrial processes. For example, it would show the amount of chlorine that is produced by means of the so-called "mercury-cell" method of electrolysis (as opposed to the "diaphragm cell"). It is only the former which leads to loss of mercury to the environment. It would also show the amount of cadmium that is used for plasticizers, which might ultimately escape to the environment via incineration of combustible solid wastes.

51. The connexion between tables 1 and 2 is not completely defined without a set of supplementary tables displaying the equivalences between weight, volume, heat and elect-trical energy units for inputs and outputs of each conversion process. Typical equiva-lence relationships that must be specified include: density (mass/volume), energy content (BTU/kg or BTU/litre) and generating efficiency (kwh/BTU). As noted pre-viously, these equivalences vary from year to year and from country to country.

52. Table 3 is concerned with production, consumption (depreciation) and stocks of durable goods, by category. A supplementary table must also be developed, indicating typical or average materials content of the various categories of durables.

53. The purpose of table 3 is mainly to develop a record of stocks of durables in use, from which inferences can be drawn with regard to future wastes to be disposed of and materials potentially available for recycling, particularly metals. A gross accounting type of balance is likely to be adequate. Most of the data, except on depreciation and scrappage, are already available from conventional sources. Data on depreciation and scrappage of durables will require some extension of currently available data from such sources as census of households and of manufactures.

54. The table would also be useful in the event that some material already in widespread use was found to be potentially harmful (as, for instance, lead pipe or lead-based paint). Many household appliances or machines contain component elements that may cause environmental hazards when the equipment is eventually discarded, especially if it is incinerated. Examples include fluorocarbon refrigerants, high-temperature coolants, mercury-vapour lamps and mercury-switches. The rapidly

E/CN.3/492
English
Page 18

Table 3. Accumulation accounts

Accounts	Measure	Type of durable					
		Machinery and equipment	Producer structures	Residential housing	Personal vehicles	Household appliances	Other
Opening stock	Value ($)						
	Units						
Domestic production	Value						
	Units						
Exports	Value						
	Units						
Imports	Value						
	Units						
Domestic consumption (addition to stock)	Value						
	Units						
Domestic scrappage (depreciation of stock)	Value						
	Units						
Revaluation of opening stock	Value						
	Units						
Closing stock	Value						
	Units						

E/CN.3/492
English
Page 19

spreading use of synthetic fabrics and plastics for household furnishings and even structural components, combined with an enormous number of different plasticizers, stabilizers, fire retardants, colouring agents, water repellants and so forth, raises strong possibilities that currently unsuspected risks will come to light from time to time. When this occurs, statistical data on the distribution and use of the dangerous substances will obviously be needed.

55. Table 4 is concerned with generation and disposition of waste materials and forms of energy, by type. It lists categories of waste and tabulates sources by production process, by type of end-use, by sector etc. Wastes generated by depreciation of durable goods are also tabulated by category of durable.

56. Table 4 is, in certain respects, the heart of the materials/energy balances, since it is the link between economic activity and the production and disposition of waste residuals which pollute the environment. The statistics will be used, primarily, in forecasting the environmental consequences of economic growth and development, in designing governmental programmes to improve the state of the environment or to minimize the adverse environmental impact of development projects. Explicit links are thus provided to specific resource extraction and commodity manufacturing processes and to various types of consumption. Waste residuals are also linked to aggregate sectors. Waste flows are identified as to environmental media.

57. The basic source of these statistics will be some combination of engineering studies (e.g., of a "typical" plant exemplifying a given extraction or production process) and of survey or monitoring data compiled by responsible monitoring and regulatory agencies. These data are not currently available in adequate detail in most countries, and much attention will have to be given to the problem of designing appropriate methods of measurement and aggregation.

58. Table 4 could include such data as the rate of loss of mercury to the environment from the mercury-cell chlorine manufacturing process, or the cadmium content of wastes from zinc mining and/or smelting. It would also, in principle, show mercury and cadmium residuals resulting from the incineration of paper impregnated with mercury-based fungicides or plastic products containing cadmium-based plasticizer. For DDT, polychlorinated biphenyls and fluorocarbons, it would show waste flows resulting directly from "final" use of these materials.

59. It is important to point out that, while the data in table 4 should be fully consistent in a materials/energy balance sense with data in tables 1, 2 and 3, as a general rule they would be derived independently from measurements of discharges or ambient environmental pollutant concentrations. Discrepancies would normally occur in the process of constructing the tables - as now happens in building input-output tables - and their resolution should help to strengthen the data base as compared to what it would be if based only on production and/or consumption data.

E/CN.3/492
English
Page 20

Table 4. Waste residual accounts

Accounts	Type of waste (name, units)	Waste No. 1 (units)					
Waste source by major materials production/ conversion process a/	Production process name	Process 1	Process 2	Process 3	Process 4	Process 5	Other process n.e.c
	Process type, code						
	Waste quantity generated — Soil / Air / Water / Ocean						
Waste generated by disposition services and consumption b/	Sector	Commercial transport	Utility services	Other commerce	Government	Personal transport	Other household
	Quantity by medium — Soil / Air / Water / Ocean						
Waste generated by sector (total)	Sector	Agriculture	Manufacturing	Construction	Transport	Government and services	Household
	Quantity by medium — Soil / Air / Water / Ocean						
Waste generated by depreciation of durables	Type	Machinery and equipment	Producer structures	Residential housing	Personal vehicles	Household appliance	Other private
	Quantity by medium — Soil / Air / Water / Ocean						

a/ Including airborne wastes from incineration of municipal or industrial solid wastes.

b/ Not including solid wastes that are subsequently incinerated (to avoid double counting).

E/CN.3/492
English
Page 21

V. DEFINITIONS OF NATURAL RESOURCES, COMMODITIES AND WASTES

60. The distinction often made between renewable and non-renewable resources has already been mentioned. In brief, the renewable resources are primarily sunlight, air, water and chemical substances, such as carbohydrates and proteins, which are major constituents of biological systems. These are extensively transported and converted from one form to another via natural, meteorological, biological and geological processes or are extracted by man from natural cyclic systems. Hydrogen/ water, oxygen, carbon/carbon dioxide,[10]/ alkali metals (sodium, potassium and calcium) and nitrogen are chief constituents of such materials.[11]/ Because of the existence of natural cycles, supplies of all of these elements are essentially infinitely renewable. Elements such as silicon, sulphur and chlorine are also present in such large amounts in the earth's crust, relative to their incorporation in living systems, that their possible natural cycles are of somewhat less interest. Land is often regarded as a renewable resource because it too is, in theory, indefinitely reusable, i.e., it is not "used up" by conservative cultivation practices. Obviously, this statement does not apply to specific nutrients in soil, which can be and are used up by some types of agriculture and must be separately replaced. Also, it is evident that some agricultural practices result in irreversible erosion losses of the top soil itself; this should be dealt with by means of supplementary tables.

61. Some elements of the major natural cycles (land, air, water, living systems) are accounted for and distinguished. Thus, if ground water is one source of water for irrigation in a country, the table should include an estimate of the current stock of the underground reservoir available for pumping. It is not necessary to try to estimate the total quantity of ground water available in the country. In the case of tree crops, such as citrus fruits, apples, plums, peaches, nuts, olives, coconuts, coffee, cocoa, natural rubber, and in the case of other perennial producers, such as grape vines or alfalfa, the stock in question may be measured by the number of producing trees or the area of land planted. In the case of dairy products, the stock (number) of producing cows is of considerable interest, especially when significant expansion in the producing stock takes several years. One important use of the statistical system should be to record significant trends, such as the substitution of annual crops, for example, soybeans, for perennial crops in certain countries.

62. The total stock of any renewable resource is fixed by nature, but the amount in any given form or location can vary from time to time and may be affected by the actions of man. The "flows" are transfers from one form, location or category to another. In most instances, the total stock of a renewable resource in its natural state is actually irrelevant (and may be unknown, except to a crude first approximation), because what counts is the amount available in certain forms, locations or times. This is generally a function of the rate of flow rather than the size of the total reservoir.

10/ Hydrogen is biologically derived from water and vice versa; similarly carbon and oxygen are biologically interconvertible. Oxygen is, of course, involved in both cases.

11/ Phosphorus, the other essential ingredient of biological materials, is not cycled except on a geological time-scale. This gives rise to special interest in phosphorus as a potential bottleneck of life on earth.

E/CN.3/492
English
Page 22

63. It is clear, for example, that most of the water on earth is in the deep
oceans, but equally clear that what really counts for human purposes is the amount
of surface run-off and the stored surface fresh water which can be diverted to
agricultural, industrial or municipal use before being returned. Most of the
earth's carbon is in carbon dioxide dissolved in the ocean or in carbonaceous rocks,
such as limestone, whereas only the free carbon dioxide in the atmosphere is available to plants. Similarly, most of the earth's oxygen is tied up with hydrogen in
water or as oxides, but only the free oxygen in the atmosphere is available to
animals. Finally, the free atmospheric nitrogen is not available to plants or animals; not until it is "fixed" as water soluble nitrates (by specialized bacteria)
can it be taken up and utilized by biological organisms.

64. Renewable resources to be accounted for specifically in tables 1 and 2 include
the following:

Water (volume)

    Fresh, surface; underground; ice/snow (water equivalent); saline (land-locked).

Land (area)

    Cultivated; fallow, grazed; grazing only; forest, harvested; forest, unharvested;
desert; tundra; urbanized; parks, urban; parks, natural area; transition zone, salt
marsh; transition zone, dune; transition zone, up-stream valley; transition zone,
alpine meadow; ocean beach, protected; lake/riverside, protected.

Fisheries (annual production, by weight)

    Salmon; tuna; sardines; cod; flounder; sole; oysters; clams.

Orchards and plantations (annual production, volume or weight)

    Grape vines (volume); tree fruit, by type (weight); nuts, by type (weight);
olives, coffee, cacao etc.; pulpwood (weight); softwood (volume); hardwood (volume).

Livestock by type (producing units)

    Cattle; sheep; goats; hogs; horses, mules; water buffalo; oxen.

Assimilative capacity of water (for organic waste)

Assimilative capacity of air for particulates and gaseous wastes

    Oxides of sulphur; oxides of nitrogen; carbon monoxide.

Assimilative capacity of soil for organic wastes (such as sewage sludge)

Sunlight, incident on land per sq km per year

E/CN.3/492
English
Page 23

65. Non-renewable resources are extracted from the earth's crust and not replaced by natural cyclic processes, except, perhaps, over geological time-scales. Non-renewable resources to be accounted for specifically in tables 1 and 2 would include at least the following:

Fossil fuels

Coal; lignite; natural gas; petroleum; other.

Metals and minerals

Alumium; antimony; arsenic; asbestos; barite; bauxite; beryllium; bismuth; bitumen; borax; brines(B, Li, K, Cl, Br, I); cadmium; chromium; clay/kaolin; coal; cobalt; construction stone; copper; diatomite; dolomite; evaporites; feldspar; fluorine; fluorite; gallium; gemstones; gold; granite, building stones; graphite; gypsum; helium; iron; kyanite; lead; limestone and dolomite; lithium, cesium and rubidium; magnesium; manganese; marble; mercury; mica; molybdenum; nickel; niobium; oil shale; phosphate rock; platinum; potash; quartzite; rare-earth elements; rhenium; salt; sand/gravel; scandium; selenium; silica sand; silver; slate; sulphur; talc; tantalum; thallium; thorium; tin; titanium; trona; tungsten; uranium; vanadium; zeolite; zinc; zirconium and hafnium.

66. Commodities, in this context, are simply processed materials, forms of energy or products. Any consistent international classification, such as the International Standard Classification of All Goods and Services (ICGS) can be used as a basis for tables 1 and 2, although some elaboration will be needed. A full list of commodities, cannot be reproduced here, but lists are available in the ICGS, which is before the Commission (E/CN.3/493).

67. The main difficulty with most existing international commodity classifications arises from their use of "basket" categories for chemicals. For the purpose of establishing balances, it is essential to avoid lumping together different chemicals (or other major materials) in groups under general headings such as "cyclic intermediates". Rather, the major tonnage chemicals must be tabulated individually, lumping all others in a not-elsewhere-classified (n.e.c.) category.

68. Categories of waste residuals have not yet been internationally specified, but the following should probably be included, as a minimum:

Waterborne wastes

BOD;[12]/ COD;[13]/ dissolved solids (salts); suspended solids.

Airborne wastes

Particulates; carbon monoxide; carbon dioxide; hydrocarbons; oxides of nitrogen; oxides of sulphur.

---

[12]/ Biological Oxygen Demand in water measured at the end of 5 days. This is a measure of the quantity of biodegradable organic material in the waste water.

[13]/ Chemical Oxygen Demand.

E/CN.3/492
English
Page 24

Solid wastes

    Combustible solids; non-combustible solids.

Heavy metals

    Lead; mercury; cadmium; arsenic; other (chromium, selenium, bismuth, thallium etc.).

Chlorinated hydrocarbons

    DDT; fluorocarbons (chlorinated); chlorinated biphenyls.

Thermal waste

    Heated waste water > 5° above ambient; water vapour (steam).

Nuclear waste

    Plutonium (curies); other high level (curies); other low level (curies).

69. As commented earlier, the System of National Accounts definitions are to be adhered to as closely as possible. There is no difficulty with using SNA definitions for domestic production, exports, imports and domestic consumption.

70. The terms requiring more careful definition (stock not yet extracted, stock in strategic reserve, conversion/utilization as such, conversion process, durable goods, depreciation, waste) are dealt with below.

71. Stock not yet extracted. This term applies most obviously to a non-renewable natural resource such as petroleum or iron ore. However, for consistency, one can also apply the term to natural accumulations of renewable resources such as uncut forests, potentially cultivable farm land or stored fresh water (underground or surface). It does not apply to natural resources that cannot be stored at all, such as sunlight impinging on the surface of the earth or atmospheric water vapour.

72. In the case of non-renewable resources (e.g., minerals or fossil fuels), the obvious definition of "stock" would be the concentrations which can, in principle, be extracted from the earth's crust. However, this is generally not a fixed quantity; it depends on the state of technology and the effort expended on extraction. Moreover, the over-all distribution of mineral concentrations is not known. Much of the partial knowledge that does exist is not available to the public (or Governments). Hence, more limited concepts, such as "proved" reserves and "inferred" reserves have come into use.

73. The proven reserves of minerals or fossil fuels available at a given time depend directly on the rate of discovery, the rate of extraction and the assumed market price of the commodity. The same can also be said for inferred or estimated reserves. A rise in commodity prices will automatically increase the expected economic recovery from existing mines or wells and vice versa. This change can

E/CN.3/492
English
Page 25

realistically be reflected in annual statistical series provided some reasonable price convention is specified. Since mineral commodity prices are notoriously unstable, and true world market prices are not even defined for a number of commodities,[14] it could be highly misleading to use spot prices on a given date each year or in a single location for purposes of estimating recoverable resources. It might, however, be reasonable to use something like an extrapolation of a five-year rolling average of historical prices taken from a number of locations as a basis for estimation. Another possibility is to use the prices on the futures market (appropriately averaged, of course) where such a market exists.

74. Unfortunately, one must recognize a fundamental difficulty in assigning any consistent interpretation to estimates of proven and/or inferred reserves. The problem is that transfers of known deposits from the latter to the former category occur at the time specific mine investments are being planned in detail. This, in turn, occurs as new sources are needed to replace depleted ores. Mining or petroleum companies have no incentive to carry out detailed surveys of known deposits prior to such time. Hence, in many cases there is a marked tendency for proven reserves to hover around the level of 20 years supply at current or extrapolated output, simply because this is the economic lifetime of a typical mine or oil field.

75. An alternative theoretical possibility might be to use inferred reserves. This figure is less sensitive to the economic parameters of the mining or drilling business but, on the other hand, it is intrinsically much more uncertain for two reasons. First, by definition, the ore bodies or deposits counted in this category have not been surveyed in detail; hence, magnitude of yield probably can only be determined on the basis of previous experience in the same region or in similar geological strata. Secondly, much of the underlying data is currently not in the public domain, being proprietary to the various mining and oil drilling concerns. In the near future, at least, publicly available figures are likely to be significantly incomplete and, therefore, highly unreliable. To be sure, it is widely recognized that more and better information in this area is needed and must ultimately be provided under census-type legislation[15] as a matter of necessity for rational public policy making.

76. Stock in strategic reserve. For purposes of these guidelines the "strategic" stockpile is conceptually distinguished from normal commercial inventories of materials. It can be assumed that commercial users of raw and processed materials keep the smallest quantities on hand that are consistent with risks of supply interruption and market fluctuation. These risks do not generally change dramatically from year to year; hence, commercial inventories remain relatively constant.

---

[14] This may be due to the prevalence of either long-term bilateral contracts between producers and consumers or localized sources incapable of supplying markets located far away. The latter may, in turn, be a consequence of lack of facilities for storage and preservation (e.g., for food products) or intrinsically high transport costs (e.g., sand and gravel).

[15] Legitimate proprietary interests can be preserved (as in the census of manufactures for most industrialized countries) by not publishing data for individual producers or narrowly specified locations. However, useful national aggregates could be prepared from individual producers' data.

E/CN.3/492
English
Page 26

77. Strategic stocks, however, are maintained by Governments for both national
security and political reasons. These stocks can and do change dramatically from
one year to the next depending on government policy. Some stockpiles of critical
materials (such as tungsten, chrome and manganese) have amounted to as much as
several years of normal consumption. If this material is sold off quickly - as has
happened - it may have a sharp effect on current production and cause large discrepancies between current production and current consumption.

78. Conversion versus utilization. The distinction here is critical. A resource
or commodity is "converted" if, and only if, it is physically or chemically incorporated into another commodity or product. Thus, chemical feedstocks are incorporated into synthetic rubber, plastics or fibres. Fibres (synthetic or natural)
are incorporated into woven or knitted fabrics, which are in turn converted into
textile products. Similarly pulpwood is converted into pulp, thence to paper and
finally to paper products. Metal ores are converted to concentrates, then to crude
pigs or ingots, then to more refined alloys in castings, bars, sheet, foil, wire,
tube and finally (after cutting, shaping, machining, welding etc.) to metal products,
structures etc. The chemical energy of coal or residual oil is also "incorporated"
into a successor product by electrical generating plants.

79. It is important to note, however, that many important materials and energy
fuels are not physically or chemically incorporated into successor products. On
the contrary, they are used up, and discarded as wastes, at intermediate processing
or manufacturing stages. This applies for example, to cleaning agents, lubricants,
coolants, dispersants, bleaches, anti-freezes, fluxes, solvents and numerous other
items. It is notably true of fuels and electricity used in industry and commerce
(except as noted above, where the fuel energy is simply converted to electricity).
It also applies to many products such as maintenance items and capital goods that
are not sold to final demand but used as intermediate inputs in industry. All of
these may be said to be used "as such", in that they are not physically or chemically incorporated into successor products.

80. Conversion process. In view of the foregoing definition, the meaning of "conversion" is probably sufficiently clear. In general, there are a number of different, accepted methods of producing a given commodity or product. These may start
from different input materials or they may proceed by different routes. For example,
ethane can be produced either from petroleum by fractional distillation or from
natural gas by separation. Similarly, ethylene can be produced from naphtha, ethane,
propane or from other hydrocarbons by thermal cracking. Again, ethylene dichloride
(EDC) can be manufactured from ethylene by direct chlorination or by oxychlorination.
Similarly, vinyl chloride monomer can be produced either by pyrolysis of EDC or by
direct chlorination of ethane (see figure II). All of the above constitute distinct
processes.

81. On the other hand, differences in scale or in detailed plant design do not constitute different processes - only variations on a basic theme. In the basic materials industries (e.g., chemicals, metals) the number of different conversion processes in use is small enough so that there is wide agreement among engineers as to
their specific identities and characterization in terms of inputs, outputs, capital
equipment and labour requirements. Obviously, there is some room for disagreement

E/CN.3/492
English
Page 27

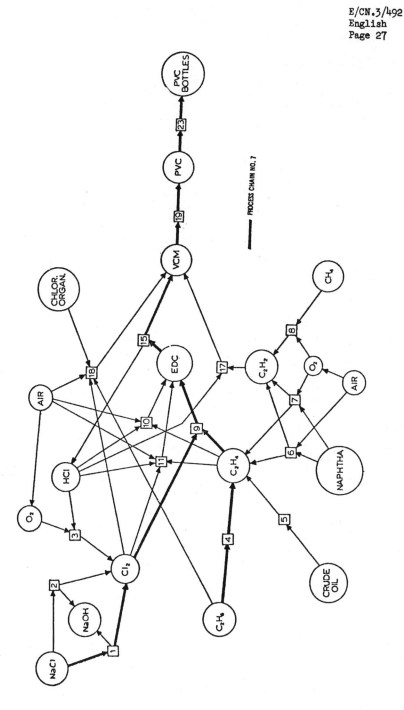

Figure II. Process network leading to PVC bottles

E/CN.3/492
English
Page 28

Notes to figure II

Processes 12, 13, 14 and 16 are pictorially identical to processes 9, 10, 11 and 15, respectively, except that processes 13 and 14 use oxygen instead of air.

Unit processes participating in bottle manufacture are:

1.	Chlorine via salt electrolysis - mercury cell
2.	Chlorine via salt electrolysis - diaphragm cell
* 3.	Chlorine via HCl oxidation using HNO_3 (Kel-Chlor)
4.	Ethylene from ethane pyrolysis
* 5.	Ethylene via autothermic cracking
6.	Acetylene/ethylene via Wulff process (naphtha feed)
* 7.	Acetylene/ethylene from naphtha by partial oxidation
8.	Acetylene from methane by partial oxidation
9.	EDC via ethylene chlorination (vapour)
*10.	EDC via ethylene oxychlorination (vapour)
11.	EDC via ethylene chlorination/oxychlorination (vapour)
*12.	EDC via ethylene chlorination (liquid)
*13.	EDC via ethylene oxychlorination (liquid)
*14.	EDC via ethylene chlorination/oxychlorination (liquid)
15.	VCM from EDC pyrolysis
16.	VCM from EDC pyrolysis with waste treatment
17.	VCM from concentrated acetylene
*18.	VCM from ethane oxychlorination (Transcat) - part waste feed
19.	PVC from VCM - bulk process
23.	PVC bottle manufacture

*Processes not presently in domestic production.

as to exact definitions, but an international group of experts should be able to arrive at a satisfactory resolution of most difficulties. More serious problems arise in the industries which fabricate products or structures from finished materials. Here the processes are not well-defined because the number and range of final products is extremely large and processes can only be defined functionally (e.g., cutting, drilling, weaving, assembly, painting) rather than in terms of specific input/output combinations. Thus, in practice, a high degree of aggregation of processes must be accepted in these industries.

82. This would be a serious drawback but for the fact that fabrication and assembly operations do not generate large waste flows (except for cumbustion products and scrap, which is largely recycled) and thus do not have significant adverse environmental effects. Combustion of fuel in heating plants or stationary engines can be regarded as distinct and reasonably well-defined processes.

83. Durable goods. The term "durable" is used here in essentially the same way as it is used in national accounts. The distinction between durable and non-durable goods is based on average lifetime in service. A one-year criterion is normally

E/CN.3/492
English
Page 29

assumed. Most producer goods (machines, tools, structures) are durable by this standard. Consumer goods are more divided. Houses, cars, household appliances, recreational goods, furnishings and most clothing are durables. Food, beverages, cleaning supplies, cosmetics, pharmaceuticals, newspapers, magazines and sundries are clearly consumables, along with some items of clothing.

84. The distinction is useful because consumables are converted immediately to waste (in varying forms), whereas durables only contribute to waste-streams as they are discarded. Regrettably, direct data on scrappage of durables is almost non-existent. In some cases, e.g., automobiles, annual scrappage may be inferred for many countries by comparing new registrations of vehicles with changes in total registrations, although this procedure is far from foolproof. In some countries, registration fees are so large in comparison with the value of the vehicle that old vehicles are never scrapped, but perpetually rebuilt. This is, to some extent, tantamount to piece-meal scrappage spread over a long period of time. But reliable data are unavailable as to the details of this process.

85. For other durable goods, even less information on scrappage is typically available. Consequently, it is necessary to estimate scrappage by assuming that it occurs when goods have depreciated to negligible economic value. Thus, depreciation data are needed.

86. Waste versus recycling. In most cases, the term "waste" is not ambiguous in practice. The only source of ambiguity arises in connexion with recycling. Specifically, any by-product of an industrial process is a waste product if there is no immediate market for it and if it must be stored indefinitely or disposed of through an environmental medium (atmosphere, surface water, soil etc.). All consumables become wastes at the point where they are discarded by their users and collected for disposal.

87. By this definition, primary scrap material - metal, paper or plastic - that is generated in a factory, and collected and sold commercially to a specialist processor is not classified as a waste stream, because this material was never actually discarded or disposed of through an environmental medium. On the other hand, so-called secondary scrap material that is separated from mixed municipal or other refuse (after collection from the original users) is counted initially as part of a waste stream, notwithstanding later re-use. In the present context, the term "recycling" refers only to the recovery and re-use of secondary scrap.

88. A possible ambiguity arises in connexion with material that is discarded as waste, which accumulates in one spot, and which is subsequently found to have commercial value for some purpose. This has recently happened, for instance, in the case of some nineteenth-century mine tailings, which constitute viable ore based on present-day technology. Such an eventuality can de dealt with by appropriate re-valuation of the stock of the resource in question.

E/CN.3/492
English
Page 30

VI. ENVIRONMENTAL DAMAGES AND ABATEMENT COSTS[16]

89. One of the types of information most frequently needed by policy analysts concerned with environmental problems is data on costs, both paid and unpaid. In the category of paid costs one would include expenditures - either by producers or by consumers - directly or indirectly attributable to pollution abatement and/or environmental management activities. The actual expenditures by affected parties may often not be directly known, since they are not part of a government budget.

90. It is clear that information on actual expenditures on pollution control and abatement should, in principle, be derivable from the national accounts. Expenditures by Governments attributable to environmental management could be explicitly separated. On the production side, a separate industry to produce pollution abatement or environmental management goods and services would also need to be distinguished from the other sectors. Purchases of such services by Governments, or by other production sectors, would constitute revenues to that sector.

91. The practical difficulty in compiling this information arises from the fact that it is very difficult to distinguish between goods and services purchased for various purposes by firms. Even the standard distinction between capital and operating costs is an essentially artificial one, though sanctified through long recognition by the tax regulations of most countries and familiarity on the part of accountants and auditors. But to distinguish between different kinds of capital and different kinds of operating costs would be very troublesome. Most firms would have difficulty documenting the internal allocation of expenditures in this manner, and outsiders still more so.

92. The most plausible way out of this difficulty would be for certain categories of capital and operating expenditures to be explicitly designated as for environmental purposes by the tax authorities. (For example, purchases of electrostatic precipitators, complete water treatment plants, complete desulphurization plants, catalytic convertors for automobiles etc.). An accelerated depreciation schedule or some other form of tax concession could be made available on condition that the expenditures were properly documented. The information thus accumulated would constitute a potential data base for statistics on the paid costs of environmental control.

93. The problem of determining unpaid environmental damage costs is even more difficult, since most of these costs are unpaid, at least in part, precisely because there is no impersonal market mechanism for fixing their appropriate prices. A number of economists have attempted to develop cost-benefit methodologies for estimating real or potential damages.[17] Whatever their respective merits, all these methods have the common disadvantage (from a statistical point of view) of being indirect and theoretical. That is, there is no set of empirically derived damage costs that could be compared on an international basis at this time.

16/ The present chapter should be read in conjunction with chapter IV in "The feasibility of welfare-oriented measures to complement the national accounts and balances" (E/CN.3/477), also before the Statistical Commission.

17/ For a comprehensive summary of the relevant methods, see Government of the United States of America, Department of Transportation, Economic and Social Measures of Biologic and Climatic Change, edited by R.C. d'Arge, CIAP Monograph No. 6 (Washington, D.C., September 1975).

E/CN.3/492
English
Page 31

94. In the near future, unfortunately, it seems unlikely that any fully satisfactory resolution of these difficulties will be achieved. What can be done short of such an ideal solution? As regards paid costs, the only possibility that strongly suggests itself at this stage is the systematic use of engineering information to estimate costs, and of survey data to estimate the extent of pollution abatement activity. In water-pollution control, for instance, the following three-tiered classification of water-treatment processes has been established by wide usage:

   (a) <u>Primary treatment</u>. Settling and filtration; removing most suspended solids and 30 per cent of BOD.<u>18</u>/

   (b) <u>Secondary treatment</u>. Bacterial treatment of the output of the primary treatment process, leading to cumulative removal of 90 per cent of BOD, 50 per cent of nitrogen, 20 per cent of phosphorus and 5 per cent of dissolved salts.

   (c) <u>Tertiary treatment</u>. Various additional steps leading to cumulative removal of 95 per cent of BOD, 98 per cent of nitrogen, 97 per cent of phosphorus and 50 per cent of dissolved salts.

95. It is feasible to classify all industrial or other waste-water discharges according to the highest level of treatment, for example, 10 per cent tertiary and 80 per cent secondary. Data of this sort could be broken down by region and source category (industry, agriculture, industry). Unfortunately, the classification into primary, secondary, tertiary levels of treatment is applicable mainly to municipal wastes or process industries utilizing organic materials (pulp and paper, food processing etc.). It is not very relevant for chemical or metallurgical wastes.

96. In a similar vein, it is feasible to classify levels of treatment of smoke for major industrial or municipal steam-electric power plants, incinerators, coke ovens, blast furnaces etc. Particulate removal by means of electrostatic precipitation can be estimated in percentage terms. Levels of treatment of motor vehicle exhaust can also be estimated by engineering analysis and dynamometer tests on a cross-sectional sample of each year's new vehicle output, combined with longitudinal surveys on a few vehicles over their lifetimes to determine the effect of aging. Fractional removal of sulphur and ash from coal and from fuel oil are fairly well-known and can be determined by comparing samples of raw and finished fuels. Fractional removal of sulphur dioxide from stack gases would be a known function of the efficiency of the treatment process (if any). Disposition of municipal solid wastes via land fill, incinerator or by other means is not as well documented as might be expected, but good estimates are available in many localities.

97. With regard to other pollutants, however, treatment or abatement methods are generally not yet standardized and levels and costs of treatment will prove more difficult to compile. This problem is particularly troublesome where trace contaminants or wastes from metallurgical or chemical processes are concerned. No immediate solution seems available.

   <u>18</u>/ Biological Oxygen Demand - that is, the amount of oxygen that will be consumed by aerobic decay organisms in five days. It is a measure of the amount of biodegradable organic material in the waste mater.

E/CN.3/492
English
Page 32

VII. POSSIBILITIES FOR INITIAL IMPLEMENTATION

98. It is highly desirable to segment the framework proposed in these guidelines
so as to permit gradual construction of the full system in smaller stages. Both
horizontal and vertical cuts are possible. A horizontal cut would begin with one
reasonably well-defined stage of materials flow (say, extraction of raw materials)
and identify all the relevant flows into and out of box 2 in figure I. This would
be a relatively simple extension of production and trade statistics already available in many countries. The two added features would be specification of waste
flows from primary extraction processes (by process) and specification of subsequent
utilization according to whether further conversion processes are involved or not.
The system could not, of course, be "closed" in any sense and materials/energy
balances could only be struck for the extractive activities per se.

99. In a similar manner, other sectors in figure I could be dealt with successively.
Thus, all imports and exports of raw materials, commodities and finished goods
could be compiled to obtain a balance for the rest-of-world sector. Balances for
consumption of non-durables and accumulation of durables could be arrived at by a
combination of direct survey data and indirect (synthetic) methods. The same is
true for conversion industries and manufacturing industries. Here census-type data
would have to be supplemented by engineering studies. The inputs and outputs to
the waste sector (presumably left to the last) would then be completely specified.

100. The weaknesses of this approach are clear: first, the piecemeal approach does
not yield a very useful result until it has been completed. Moreover, by far the
largest and most difficult segments are perhaps still indigestibly massive projects.

101. The vertical approach offers more promise. Here one would identify a single
element (or group of related materials) and follow it through the economy from raw
material to final consumption, taking account of all waste flows. At a later time,
one could aggregate the results to obtain a complete system. Meanwhile, the partial
results are still potentially quite useful.

102. In fact, it would make sense to begin with a set of the most environmentally
critical materials, such as toxic heavy metals (lead, cadmium, mercury etc.). Most
of these metals have a fairly restricted set of uses. Experience acquired in compiling the process-waste-consumption flow data on these metals would be helpful in
dealing with the more widely used and more complex flow patterns of the major
metals. Moreover, the data sets for many metals overlap significantly. For instance, cadmium is a coproduct of zinc refining. In compiling necessary data on
cadmium, one would necessarily obtain quite a lot of relevant data on zinc, thus
simplifying the task for zinc. Similarly, zinc and lead often occur together,
along with copper, silver, arsenic and other metals.

103. The logic of a vertical approach beginning with the more toxic metals and then
gradually extending to other materials can also be seen from the fact that some
materials or elements are far more critical than others, both from conservationist
and environmentalist standpoints. A disproportionate amount of environmental
damage is caused by a small number of processes (e.g. combustion of fossil fuels)
and by chemical compounds composed of a small number of especially potent elements.

E/CN.3/492
English
Page 33

104. In this context, it is noteworthy that the major elements of biological
systems (hydrogen, carbon, oxygen) are relatively innocuous when combined with each
other, but that four minor elements of living systems (nitrogen, sulphur, phosphorus
and chlorine) combine with these three, singly or all together, to form a large
variety of toxic or carcinogenic compounds from oxides of nitrogen and sulphur to
cyanides, mercaptans, nitrosamines, nerve gases such as phosgene, peracyl acetic
nitrate, bacteriocides, algicides, fungicides, herbicides, insecticides, food pre-
servatives, vinyl chloride and polychlorinated biophenyls. Clearly, monitoring
these four elements and their uses should take precedence over monitoring the other
three.

105. Similarly, a group of minor metals, including lead, cadmium, mercury, arsenic
and chromium, are far more dangerous to the environment than the more widely used
elements such as compounds or alloys of aluminium, calcium, iron, silicon and sodium.
Again, even though the latter are far more important economically, priority in
monitoring should go to the former.

E/CN.3/492
English
Annex
Page 1

Annex

MATRIX REPRESENTATION OF STATISTICS ON MATERIALS/ENERGY BALANCES

	1	2	3	4	5	6	7	8	9	10	11	12
1. Opening stock	Z_j											
2. Domestic extraction		X_{jk}	y_{jn}	y_{j1}		-	-	ΔW_j	U_j	X_{mk}		
3. Domestic conversion (process)		NT	NT	y_{1n}	NT	NT	NT	-	NT	X_{nm}		
3'. Domestic conversion (material)		-	y_{1n}	$X_{11'}$		y_{1p}	y_{1q}	-	U_1	NT		
4. Intermediate production					-	NT	NT	-	-	X_{mp}		
5. Final consumption, non-durables					-	NT	NT	-	NT	-		
6. Accumulation, durables					-	-	W_q	-	-	X_{mq}		
7. Strategic stock of resources		-	ΔW_j	-	-	-	-	W_j	ΔW_j	-		
9. External sector		V_j	V_1	NT	NT	NT	V_q	ΔW_j	-	-		
10. Waste		-	y_{mn}	-	-	-	-	-	-	W_m		
11. Revaluation											ΔZ_j	
12. Closing stock												Z_j

NT = Not tabulated

E/CN.3/492
English
Annex
Page 2

Notes to matrix display

1. The matrix display corresponds essentially to boxes 1 to 12 and connecting lines in figure I in chapter IV above (see notes below, however). Tabulations (or sub-matrices) are shown symbolically. An explanation of indices and nomenclature follows these notes.

2. In figure I, intermediate use (box 5) and final consumption of non-durable goods and services (box 6) are separated. However, these are combined in some tables, e.g., $y_{lp}(t)$, $X_{mp}(t)$.

3. Current production of durable goods $W_q(t)$ in material terms cannot be derived from the other elements of the matrix. This is, strictly speaking, a supplementary table. In principle, however, it must be the sum of material flows from finished materials y_{lp} and intermediate products (flows from box 5 to box 7 in figure I, not tabulated). Note that current depreciation of durable goods $y_q(t)$ in material terms corresponds to the consumption of such goods and their abandonment or demolition. This is, essentially, a waste stream and can be defined as such (hence $y_q = \sum_m X_{mq}$).

4. Some useful aggregate variables do not correspond directly with either stocks or flows in the diagrammatic presentation (figure I). Examples include:

    y_j (domestic supply of jth resource);

    y_l (domestic supply of lth material or commodity);

    X_m (total waste of mth type).

5. Some flows (lines) in figure I have no corresponding tables (see note 3 above), either due to relative unimportance or lack of data. These are denoted NT (Not Tabulated) in the matrix, and are shown as lines of dashes in figure I.

6. The stockpile of finished or partly processed materials has been tentatively omitted. However, this omission should be considered for possible future inclusion. It is shown in figure I as a broken-line box (not numbered).

E/CN.3/492
English
Annex
Page 3

LIST OF SYMBOLS AND DEFINITIONS

Symbol	Definition	Range of Indices
(All letters J ... q, except o)		(All letters, J ... Q, except 0)
j	Natural resource type	$j=1, \ldots J$
$k(j)$	Extraction process (mode) for j^{th} type of resource [a]	$k(j)=1, \ldots K(J)$
ℓ	Processed material or commodity	$\ell=1, \ldots L$
m	Waste residual type	$m=1, \ldots M$
n	Conversion process type	$n=1, \ldots N$
p	Production or consumption sector	$p=1, \ldots P$
q	Type of tangible capital asset	$q=1, \ldots Q$

Symbol	Definition (Stock)	Maximum Number of Quantities
Z_j	Stock of jth resource not yet extracted	J
W_j	Stock of jth resource held for strategic reserves	<< J
W_m	Stock of mth type of waste available for possible recovery	<< M
V_q	Stock of qth type of tangible capital asset "in use"	Q

Symbol	Definition (Flow)	Maximum Number of Quantities
Y_j	Domestic consumption of jth resource	J
X_{jk}	Domestic output of resource j by k^{th} process	$\sum_j K(j)$
U_j	Exports of jth resource (unprocessed)	J
V_j	Imports of jth resource (unprocessed)	J
ΔW_j	Stockpile withdrawals [c], j^{th} resource	J
ΔZ_j	Stock additions [b] or revaluations, j^{th} resource	J
Y_ℓ	Domestic supply of ℓth material/commodity	L
$X_{\ell n}$	Output of ℓth material/commodity by n^{th} process	<< L x N
U_ℓ	Exports of ℓth material/commodity	L
V_ℓ	Imports of ℓth material/commodity	L
$Y_{j\ell}$	Input of jth resource to ℓ^{th} material/commodity	J x L
Y_{jn}	Input of jth resource to n^{th} process	J x N
Y_{jp}	Utilization of jth resource *as such* by p^{th} sector	J x P
$Y_{\ell\ell'}$	Conversion of ℓth material to ℓ'^{th} material ($Y_{\ell\ell} = 0$)	L x L
$Y_{\ell n}$	Input of ℓth material/commodity to n^{th} process	L x N
$Y_{\ell,p}$	Utilization of material/commodity ℓ *as such* in sector p	L x P
$Y_{\ell,q}$	Utilization of material/commodity ℓ *as such* in capital q	L x Q
X_q	Current production of capital of type q	Q
Y_q	Current depreciation (consumption) of stock of type q	Q
X_m	Total waste generated of type m	M
X_{mk}	Waste of type m produced by $k(j)^{th}$ resource extraction process	$\sum_j k(j)$ x M
X_{mn}	Waste of type m produced by n^{th} conversion or consumption process	N x M
X_{mp}	Waste of type m produced by consumption use (as such) in p^{th} sector. (d)	P x M
X_{mq}	Waste of type m produced by depreciation (consumption) of capital goods (e) of type q	Q x M
Y_{mn}	Input of mth waste type to n^{th} process (recycling)	M x N
U_q	Export of qth capital	
V_q	Import of qth capital	

E/CN.3/492
English
Annex
Page 4

LIST OF SYMBOLS AND DEFINITIONS (Continued)

Accounting Identities	Interpretation
$Y_j = \sum_{k(j)} X_{jk} - U_j + V_j + \Delta W_j$	Domestic supply equals production less exports plus imports plus stockpile withdrawals.
$Y_\ell = \sum_n X_{\ell n} - U_\ell V_\ell$	Same as above.
$V_j = \sum_\ell Y_{j\ell} + \sum_p Y_{jp}$ $= \sum_n Y_{jn} + \sum_p Y_{jp}$	Consumption of jth resource equals the amount of that resource converted to all other forms plus the amount of the resource used as such (without further conversion). By definition resource supply equals current consumption.
$\left[\sum_\ell Y_{j\ell} = \sum_n Y_{jn}\right]$	Resources allocated among all conversion processes (n) must equal resources converted to processed materials (ℓ), by definition.
$V_\ell = \sum_{\ell' \neq \ell} Y_{\ell\ell'} + \sum_p Y_{\ell p} + \sum_q Y_{\ell q}$ $= \sum_n Y_{\ell n} + \sum_p Y_{\ell p} + \sum_q Y_{\ell q}$ $\left[\sum_{\ell' \neq \ell} Y_{\ell\ell'} = \sum_n Y_{\ell n}\right]$	Consumption of ℓth material or commodity equals the amount of the material converted to other materials, plus the amount utilized as such (without further conversion) for intermediate production (e.g. of services), final consumption goods and durable (capital) goods. The quantity of material/commodity allocated among all (other) conversion *processes* must equal the quantity converted to other materials and processes.
$X_m = \sum_m X_{mk} + \sum_n X_{mn} + \sum_p X_{mp}$ $+ \sum_q X_{mq}$	Total waste generated of type m must equal waste produced by extraction, conversion, consumption and depreciation, respectively.

MATERIALS BALANCE BY PROCESS

$\sum_j Y_{jn} + \sum_\ell Y_{\ell n} + \sum_m Y_{mn}$ $= \sum_\ell X_{\ell n} + \sum_n X_{mn}$	The sum of all materials entering a process must equal the sum of all useful products plus wastes. Care must be exercised to include environmental resources (air,water) on both sides of the equation.

(a) It is convenient (and reasonable) to assume that each resource has a *unique* set of associated extraction processes and that each process results in only *one* product. If a given extraction process (say strip mining) is applicable to more than one resource, it is simply counted as a separate process in each case. This procedure is *not* followed for conversion processes because of the problem of joint products. That is, each process yields several products. Hence processes must be separately indexed.

(b) Additions to stock are defined as gross annual production in the case of renewable natural resources. In the case of non-renewable resources, effective additions to stock arise from revised estimates of recoverable fraction of existing ore-bodies due to price changes or technological improvements, discoveries of new sources of standard types of ores and development of practical methods of utilizing known but hitherto unutilizable ores such as oil shale, ocean nodules, etc.

(c) Stockpile accumulation is regarded as a *negative withdrawal*.

(d) Conversion wastes are excluded, being separately accounted for in the extraction and conversion stages.

(e) Capital goods in this context specifically include consumer durables (automobile, housing) as well as producer durables and structures.

[6]

Material flow analysis

Stefan Bringezu and Yuichi Moriguchi

Understanding the structure and functioning of the industrial or societal metabolism is at the core of industrial ecology (Ayres 1989a; see also Chapters 1, 2 and 3). Material flow analysis (MFA) refers to the analysis of the throughput of process chains comprising extraction or harvest, chemical transformation, manufacturing, consumption, recycling and disposal of materials. It is based on accounts in physical units (usually in terms of tons) quantifying the inputs and outputs of those processes. The subjects of the accounting are chemically defined substances (for example, carbon or carbon dioxide) on the one hand and natural or technical compounds or 'bulk' materials (for example, coal, wood) on the other hand. MFA has often been used as a synonym for material flow accounting; in a strict sense the accounting represents only one of several steps of the analysis, and has a clear linkage to economic accounting.

MFA has become a fast-growing field of research with increasing policy relevance. All studies are based on the common paradigm of industrial metabolism and use the methodological principle of mass balancing. However, there are various methodological approaches which are based on different goals, concepts and target questions, although each study may claim to contribute to knowledge of the industrial metabolism. In 1996, the network ConAccount was established to provide a platform for information exchange on MFA (*www.conaccount.net*). A first inventory on MFA projects and activities was provided (Bringezu *et al.* 1998a). Several meetings took place (Bringezu *et al.* 1997, 1998b; Kleijn *et al.* 1999) and a research and development agenda was defined through an interactive process (Bringezu *et al.* 1998c).

The diversity of MFA approaches derives from different conceptual backgrounds. The basic concept common to many studies is that the industrial system together with its societal interactions is embedded in the biogeosphere system, thus being dependent upon factors critical for the coexistence of both systems (Ayres and Simonis 1994; Baccini and Brunner 1991, see also Chapter 2). The paradigm vision of a sustainable industrial system is characterized by minimized and consistent physical exchanges between human society and the environment, with the internal material loops being driven by renewable energy flows (for example, Richards *et al.* 1994). However, different strategies have been pursued to develop industrial metabolism in a sustainable fashion.

One basic strategy may be described as *detoxification* of the industrial metabolism. This refers to the mitigation of the releases of critical substances to the environment by pollution reduction. In a wider sense, this relates to any specific environmental impact such as toxicity to human beings and other organisms, eutrophication, acidification, ozone depletion, global warming and so on. Regulatory governmental actions in terms of substance bans and restrictions of use represented the first measures of environmental policy (see Chapter 6). The concept of cleaner technology is aimed primarily towards the mitigation of critical releases to the environment (see Chapter 4). It is possible that, as a consequence of the effectiveness of such measures, pollution problems in the spatial–temporal short range could be solved. Transregional and global problems and problem shifting to future generations, however, as well as the complexity of the industrial metabolism, made it necessary to analyze the flows of hazardous substances, selected materials or products in a systems-wide approach; that is, from cradle to grave, and with respect to the interlinkage of different flows.

Another complementary strategy may be regarded as *dematerialization* of the industrial metabolism. Considering the current quantity of primary resource use by industrial economies, an increase of resource efficiency by a factor of 4 to 10 was proposed (Schmidt-Bleek 1994a, 1994b; Weizsäcker *et al.* 1997). This goal has been adopted by a variety of international organizations and national governments. On the program level the factor 4/10 concept was adopted by the special session of the United Nations (UNGASS 1997) and the World Business Council for Sustainable Development (WBCSD 1998). The environmental ministers of the OECD (1996a) urged progress towards this end. Several countries included the aim in political programs (for example, Austria, the Netherlands, Finland and Sweden; see also Gardener and Sampat 1998). In Scandinavian countries research was launched to test the broad-scale feasibility of factor 4/10 (Nordic Council of Ministers 1999). In Germany a draft for an environmental policy program (BMU 1998) refers to a factor of a 2.5 increase in productivity of non-renewable raw materials (1993 to 2020). An increase in eco-efficiency is now considered essential by the environmental ministers of the European Union (1999). The review of the Fifth (environmental) Action Programme (Decision No 2179/98/EC) emphasizes resource use and efficiency.

The factor concept aims at the provision of increased services and value-added with reduced resource requirements. Dematerialization of the economy may imply a diminution of all hardware products and thus the throughput of the economy as a whole, comprising the use of primary *and* secondary materials. However, dematerialization may also be directed more specifically to the reduction of the primary inputs and/or final waste disposal. The concept of eco-efficiency includes not only the major inputs (materials, energy, water, area) but also the major outputs to the environment (emissions to air, water, waste) and relates them to the products, services or benefits produced (EEA 1999a; OECD 1998b; Verfaillie and Bidwell 2000). However, for the environment the reduction of the absolute impacts through material flows is essential. Thus, the quantity of human-induced material flows through the industrial system must also be adjusted to adequate levels of exchange between the economy and the environment.

TYPES OF ANALYSIS

In the above context, two basic types of material flow-related analyses may be distinguished according to their primary focus; although in practice a continuum of different approaches exists (Table 8.1). Neither type I nor type II is strictly coincident with the above-mentioned two paradigmatic strategies. However, the importance of the detoxification concept seems highest in Ia and lowest in IIc. In contrast, the intention to support dematerialization seems highest in analyses of IIc and lowest in Ia. Nevertheless both complementary strategies are increasingly being combined, especially in Ic and IIa. Whereas type I analyses are often performed from a technical engineering perspective, type II analyses are more directed to socioeconomic relationships.

Table 8.1   Types of material flow-related analysis

Type of analysis	I		
	a	b	c
Objects of primary interest	Specific environmental problems related to certain impacts per unit flow of:		
	substances e.g. Cd, Cl, Pb, Zn, Hg, N, P, C, CO_2, CFC	materials e.g. wooden products, energy carriers, excavation, biomass, plastics	products e.g. diapers, batteries, cars
	within certain firms, sectors, regions		
	II		
	a	b	c
	Problems of environmental concern related to the throughput of:		
	firms e.g. single plants, medium and large companies	sectors e.g. production sectors, chemical industry, construction	regions e.g. total or main throughput, mass flow balance, total material requirement
	associated with substances, materials, products		

Source: Adapted from Bringezu and Kleijn (1997).

Type Ia

Substance flow analysis (SFA) has been used to determine the main entrance routes to the environment, the processes associated with these emissions, the stocks and flows within the industrial system as well as the trans-media flows, chemical, physical, biological transformations and resulting concentrations in the environment (see Chapter 9). Spaciotemporal distribution is of high concern in SFA. Results from these analyses are often used as inputs to further analyses for quantitatively assessing risks to substance-specific endpoints.

A variety of studies have been conducted on toxic heavy metals such as arsenic, cadmium, chromium, copper, mercury, lead and zinc (Ayres, Ayres and Tarr 1994; Ayres and Ayres 1996; Ayres and Ayres 1999a; Reiner *et al.* 1997; Dahlbo and Assmuth 1997; Maag *et al.* 1997; Hansen 1997; Maxson and Vonkeman 1996; Voet *et al.* 1994; see also Chapters 27 and 28).

Nutrients such as nitrogen and phosphorus are taken into account mainly because of eutrophication problems and the search for effective mitigation measures (Ayres and Ayres 1996; Voet 1996).

The flow of carbon is studied because it is linked to global warming due to current fossil fuel dependence. The accounting for carbon dioxide and other greenhouse gas emissions and the study of trends, sources, responsible technologies, possible sinks and measures for abatement have been increasingly reported by statistical services.

The flow of chlorine and chlorinated substances has been subject to various studies owing to the toxic potential and various pollution problems through chlorinated solvents and persistent organochlorines (Ayres and Ayres 1999a; Kleijn *et al.* 1997), the ozone-depleting effect of CFCs (Obernosterer and Brunner 1997) and a controversial debate over risks incurred through incineration of materials such as PVC (Tukker 1998).

Type Ib

Selected bulk material flows have been studied for various reasons. Resource extraction by mining and quarrying was studied to assess the geomorphic and hydrological changes due to urbanization (see Chapter 28). The flow of biomass from human production has been studied to relate it to biomass production in natural ecosystems in order to evaluate the pressure on species diversity (Vitousek *et al.* 1986; Haberl 1997).

On the one hand, metals like aluminum, timber products like pulp and paper, and construction aggregates represent important base materials for industrial purposes. On the other hand these flows – although per se rather harmless – may be *linked* with other flows significantly burdening the environment, for example, the 'red mud' problem with alumina production and the energy-intensive production of aluminum (Ayres and Ayres 1996). Base materials such as plastics have been subject to various studies on the potentials and environmental consequences of recycling and cascading use (for example, Fehringer and Brunner 1997; Patel 1999).

Possible effects of alternative technologies and materials management on global warming potential have been studied, for example for construction materials (Gielen 1999). This kind of analysis is related to studies of types Ic and IIb.

Type Ic

When the environmental impacts of certain products and services is the primary interest, the approach is normally denoted life cycle assessment (LCA). The product LCA literature is reviewed in Chapter 12. In general, the system boundary of LCA ('cradle to grave') corresponds with the systems perspective of the anthroposphere, technosphere or physical economy. Some methods of evaluation may be used for LCA and MFA as well (see Chapter 13).

From type Ia to type Ic the primary interest becomes increasingly comprehensive and complex (Table 8.1). It commences with the analysis of selected substances, considered compound materials and progresses to products consisting of several materials. Not only the number of potential objects but also the number of potential impacts per study object increases by several orders of magnitude. The complexity of the associated chain net also grows.

Type IIa

The primary interest may lie in the metabolic performance of a firm or household, a sector or a region. In this case, there may be no or insufficient information about specific environmental problems. Often the main task is to evaluate the throughput of those entities in order to find the major problems, support priority setting, check the possibilities for improvement measures and provide tools for monitoring their effectiveness.

Accounting for the physical throughput of a firm is becoming more and more common-place, at least for bigger companies. It is found in corporate environmental reporting. Materials accounts are used for environmental management (see Orbach and Liedtke 1998 for a review for Germany). Eco-efficiency at the firm level has been indicated in reports (for example, WBCSD 1998, 1999 – method overview and pilot study results; Verfaillie and Bidwell 2000 – program activities). Flow analyses of materials have been applied for optimization within companies (Spengler 1998). However, the limited scope of firm accounts calls for complementary analyses with a wider systems perspective, either through LCA-type analyses for infrastructures (Bringezu *et al.* 1996) and main products (for example, Liedtke *et al.* 1998) or by analyses of higher aggregates of production and consumption, that is analyses of total production sectors or whole economies.

Type IIb

When the primary interest is devoted to certain industrial sectors or fields of activity, MFA may be used to identify the most critical fluxes in terms of quality and/or quantity. For instance, different industrial sectors may be compared with regard to various inputs and outputs either from other sectors or from the environment (Ayres and Ayres 1998; Hohmeyer *et al.* 1997; Windsperger *et al.* 1997). When the analysis comprises all sectors of a region or national economy in a comparative manner, the accounting is closely related to type IIc; in that case the main interest may still be devoted to the national economy as a whole and the sectoral analysis serves to indicate those sectors which are of prior importance regarding criteria of specific interest (for example, CO_2 emission intensity or resource intensity). In those cases, a top-down approach is usually applied. Certain sectors or activities may be analyzed in detail, for example, the construction sector (Glenck and Lahner 1997; Schandl and Hüttler 1997) or activities such as nutrition, cleaning, maintaining a dwelling and working, transport and communication (Baccini and Brunner 1991). Analyses of this type may have strong interrelations to type Ib, as when for instance construction material flows are accounted for in a comprehensive manner (Bringezu and Schütz 1998; Kohler *et al.* 1999).

Type IIc

A major field of MFA represents the analysis of the metabolism of cities, regions and national or supranational economies. The accounting may be directed to selected substances and materials or to total material input, output and throughput.

The metabolism of cities was analyzed in early studies by Wolman (1965) and Duvigneaud and Denayer-DeSmet (1977) and thoroughly for the case of Hong Kong (Boyden 1980; Koenig 1997) and Vienna (Obernosterer *et al.* 1998). For a review, see Einig (1998). At the regional level a comprehensive milestone study was performed by Brunner *et al.* (1994) for the Swiss valley, Bünztal. The flow of pollutants was analyzed by Stigliani and Anderberg (1994) for the Rhine basin. The metabolism of the old industrialized German Ruhr region was studied by Bringezu and Schütz (1996b). Economy-wide MFA at the national level has attracted special attention (see below). The main interest lies in the overall characterization of the metabolic performance of the studied entities, in order to understand the volume, structure and quality of the throughput and to assess the status and trend with regard to sustainability.

The term 'MFA' has usually referred to analyses of types Ia, Ib, IIb and IIc. Studies of type Ic are generally considered to fall under the heading of LCA. Accounting of type IIa is mainly related to environmental management. There are also combinations of regional and product-oriented analyses. Accounting for the hidden flows of imports (and exports), that is upstream resource requirements of imported (or exported) products, may be combined with the domestic resource requirements of a regional or national economy in order to provide the total material requirements (TMR) (and total material consumption – TMC) indicators (Bringezu *et al.* 1994; Adriaanse *et al.* 1997). Nevertheless, all of these analyses use the accounting of material inputs and outputs of processes in a quantitative manner, and many of them apply a systems or chain perspective.

USE OF MATERIAL FLOW-RELATED ANALYSES

In general MFA provides a system-analytical view of various interlinked processes and flows to support the strategic and priority-oriented design of management measures. In line with environmental protection policy as it has evolved since the 1960s, type Ia analyses have been applied to control the flow of hazardous substances. The results contributed to public policy in different ways (Bovenkerk 1998; Hansen 1998):

- The analyses assisted in finding a consensus on the data which is an important prerequisite for policy measures.
- MFA has led to new insights and to changes in environmental policy (for example, abandoning the aim of closed chlorine cycling in favor of controlling the most hazardous emissions).
- The analyses discovered new problems (for example, the mercury stocks in chlorine plants).
- They also contributed to finding new solutions (for example, source-oriented input reduction in the case of non-degradable substances).

The use and policy relevance of type II analyses have been increased in recent years in the following ways (Bringezu 2000b):

- support for policy debate on goals and targets, especially with regard to the resource and eco-efficiency debate and the integration of environmental and economic policies,
- number of companies providing firm and product accounts,
- provision of economy-wide material flow accounts for regular use in official statistical compilations,
- derivation of indicators for progress towards sustainability.

PROCEDURE AND ELEMENTS OF THE ANALYSIS

Although there is no general consensus on a methodological framework for materials accounting and flow analysis, the procedure and some elements of the studies have essential features in common (see reports of the ConAccount focus groups 'Towards a general framework for MFA' in Bringezu *et al.* 1997, pp. 309–22). The procedure usually comprises four steps: goal and systems definition, process chain analysis, accounting and balancing, modeling and evaluation.

The *systems definition* comprises the formulation of the target questions, the definition of scope and systems boundary. *Target questions* are defined according to the primary objectives. In all types of analysis, it has to be determined which flow categories will have to be accounted in order to quantify volume and path of the flows, and to find out those flows which are most relevant and crucial for the problems of primary interest, and those factors most responsible for these flows. The *scope* defines the spatial, temporal and sometimes functional extent of the studied objects. The categorized flows are studied along their path that is related to spatially defined compartments or regions or to functionally defined industrial sectors. The flows are always accounted on the basis of a temporally defined period. The scope may be similar for type I and type II. The system boundary defines the start and the end of the material flows which are accounted. It is – at least – partly determined by the scope but may comprise additional functional elements, such as the borderline between the environment and the economic sectors of a region. Scope and system boundary are not necessarily identical, especially when regionally oriented accounts are combined with product chain-oriented accounts. For instance, if the transnational material requirement of a national economy is determined (for example, as part of TMR, see below) the scope remains national while the system boundary is defined functionally on a larger scale.

At a certain level of detail the *process chain analysis* defines the processes for which the inputs and outputs are to be determined quantitatively by *accounting and balancing*. Here the fundamental principle of mass conservation is used to balance inputs and outputs of processes and (sub)systems (Ayres and Ayres 1999a). The balancing is used to check accuracy of empirical data, to improve consistency and to 'fill in' missing data. This is usually performed on the basis of stoichiometric or technical coefficients (for example, Windsperger *et al.* 1997; Bringezu *et al.* 1998a) and may be assisted by computer simulation (Ayres and Ayres 1999a), based on mathematical modeling (Baccini and Bader 1996).

Modeling may be applied in the basic form of 'bookkeeping' or with increasing complexity as static and dynamic modeling (see Chapter 9). The *evaluation* of the results is related to the primary interest and basic assumptions. The criteria may focus on the indication of (a) specifically known impacts per unit of flow. Here impact coefficients can be applied, for example for ozone depletion (see Chapter 13). The criteria may (b) indicate a generic environmental pressure potential. In this case, the volume[1] of flows (for example, water consumption, materials extraction) may be used to monitor certain pressures over time. More elaborate, but still generic, criteria can be based on energy flow-based parameters such as exergy (Ayres and Ayres 1999a) or emergy (Odum 1996).

ECONOMY-WIDE MFA

Material flow accounts may quantify the physical exchange of national economies with the environment. After the first approaches of Ayres and Kneese (1969), domestic MFAs were established independently for Austria (Steurer 1992), Japan (Japanese Environmental Agency 1992) and Germany (Schütz and Bringezu 1993). Aggregated material flow balances comprise domestic resource extraction and imports (inputs) and domestic releases to the environment and exports (outputs), as shown in Table 8.2. Upstream or downstream flows associated with imports and exports (resource requirements or emissions) may also be taken into account. A sectoral disaggregation can be provided by physical input–output tables (see Chapter 10).

Table 8.2   Economy-wide material balance with derived indicators

Inputs (origin)	Outputs (destination)
Domestic extraction	Emissions and wastes
Fossil fuels (coal, oil etc.)	Emissions to air
Minerals (ores, gravel etc.)	Waste landfilled
Biomass (timber, cereals etc.)	Emissions to water
	Dissipative use of products
Imports	(Fertilizer, manure, compost, seeds etc.)
Direct material input (DMI)	*Domestic processed output to nature (DPO)*
Unused domestic extraction	Disposal of unused domestic extraction
From mining/quarrying	From mining/quarrying
From biomass harvest	From biomass harvest
Soil excavation	Soil excavation
Total material input (TMI)	*Total domestic output to nature (TDO)*
	Exports
	Total material output (TMO)
	Net additions to stock (NAS)
	Infrastructures and buildings
Upstream flows associated with imports	Other (machinery, durable goods etc.)
Total material requirements (TMR)	Upstream flows associated with exports

Note: Excludes water and air flows (unless contained in other materials).

Source: Adapted from Eurostat (2000).

MFA has also entered official statistical compendia within the framework of integrated environmental and economic accounting (Radermacher and Stahmer 1998; see also Chapter 14). A methodological guide has been prepared by Eurostat (2000). National material accounts exist for Austria (Schandl 1998; Gerhold and Petrovic 2000; Matthews *et al.* 2000), Denmark (Pedersen 1999), Germany (see Chapter 23), Finland (Muukkonen 2000; Statistics Finland 1999; Mäenpää *et al.* 2000), Italy (De Marco *et al.* 1999; Femia 2000), Japan (see Chapter 24), the Netherlands (Matthews *et al.* 2000), Sweden (Isacsson *et al.* 2000), the UK (Vaze and Barron 1998; see also Chapter 26) and the USA (see

Chapter 22). Work is going on for Australia (see Chapter 25), China (a continuation of the work of Chen and Qiao 2000), Egypt (see el Mahdi 1999) and Amazonia (for Brazil see Machado and Fenzl 2000).

ATTRIBUTION TO SECTORS, ACTIVITIES AND FUNCTIONS

The throughput of the whole economy can be disaggregated and attributed to specific industrial sectors by 'top-down' approaches. This attribution[2] can be oriented towards economic or functional criteria. Usually on the basis of economic input–output (I/O) classification throughput of sectors may be determined by I/O analysis (see Chapter 10). This allows for an overall comparison of all industrial sectors. The sum of individual sectoral flows in general equals the economy-wide sum. Economic I/O tables are used to attribute physical inputs (Bringezu *et al.* 1998b) or outputs (Hohmeyer *et al.* 1997) of the national economy to the sectors of intermediate or final demand. Physical I/O tables (PIOT) provide a much more elaborate picture of sectoral product supply and delivery as well as resource inputs from the environment and waste disposal and emissions to the environment. PIOT have been established for Germany (Stahmer *et al.* 1998) and Denmark (Pedersen 1999).

The overall throughput may also be attributed to metabolic functions of the anthroposphere such as energy supply, nutrition, construction and maintenance (Bringezu 1997a). The attribution to 'activity fields' such as food supply, energy supply, construction, water supply and transport may be more actor-oriented but cannot simply be aggregated into one national account (Schandl and Hüttler 1997).

A 'bottom-up' approach may be applied to analyze the material flows of a specific sector. For instance, the flows of the construction sector had been approximated on the basis of various construction types. A comparison between 'bottom-up' and 'top-down' reveals significant differences (Friege 1997; Kohler *et al.* 1999). MFA of specific sectors often uses a combination of 'bottom-up' and 'top-down' methods and related data sources (for example, Glenck and Lahner 1997).

MFA-BASED INDICATORS

Material flow accounts provide an important basis for the derivation of environmental indicators and indicators for sustainability (Berkhout 1999; Jimenez-Beltran 1998; FME 1999). In order to monitor and assess the environmental performance of national and regional economies, a variety of indicator systems have been proposed (Moldan *et al.* 1997). The Driving Force-Pressure-State-Impact-Response (DPSIR) scheme was established as a framework (EEA 1999a, 1999b; OECD 1998a). (It had been used since the early 1990s as 'PSR' by the OECD.) The extraction of resources on the input side and the release of emissions and waste on the output side relate to environmental pressures, (sectoral) activities represent driving forces. The flows may change the state of environment which gives rise to various impacts and the societal or political response may influence the metabolic situation towards sustainability.

Corresponding to the different objectives in Table 8.1, indicators may focus on the specific impact per unit of flow (for example, emission of substances contributing to global warming) or on the volume of flows which exert a certain generic pressure (for example, consumption of water, energy, materials). MFA-based indicators have been introduced in official reports to provide an overview on the headline issues of resource use, waste disposal and emissions to air and water as well as eco-efficiency (EEA 2000; UKDETR 1999, Hoffrén 1999).

On the one hand, economy-wide material flow accounts provide a more comprehensive picture of the industrial metabolism than single indicators. On the other hand, they can be used to derive several parameters which – when taken in time series and for international comparison – provide certain aggregated information on the metabolic performance of national or regional economies (Figure 8.1). First international comparisons have been provided on input and resource efficiency indicators by Adriaanse *et al.* (1997) and on output and balance indicators by Matthews *et al.* (2000). (See also Chapters 15 to 17.)

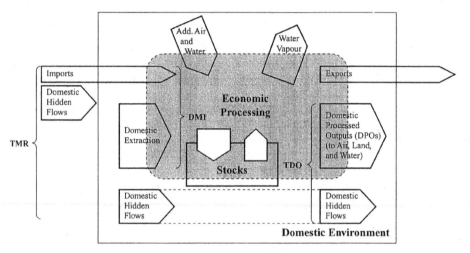

Source: Matthews *et al.* (2000).

Figure 8.1   Economy-wide material flows

Input Indicators

Direct material input (DMI) measures the input of used materials into the economy, that is all materials which are of economic value and used in production and consumption activities; DMI equals domestic (used) extraction plus imports. Materials which are extracted by economic activities but that do not normally serve as input for production or consumption activities (mining overburden and so on) have been termed 'hidden flows' or 'ecological rucksacks'. Hidden flows (Adriaanse *et al.* 1997), or rucksack flows (Schmidt-Bleek *et al.* 1998; Bringezu *et al.* 1996) comprise the primary resource requirement not entering the product itself. Hidden flows of primary production are defined as unused domestic extraction or 'indirect material flows' (Eurostat 2000). Hidden flows of imports equal unused and used predominantly foreign extraction associated with the production and delivery of the imports. These are not used for further processing and are usually without economic value. DMI plus unused domestic extraction comprises total (domestic) material input.

Total material requirement (TMR)[3] includes, in addition to TMI, the upstream hidden material flows which are associated with imports and which predominantly burden the environment in other countries. It measures the total 'material base' of an economy, that is the total primary resource requirements of the production activities. Adding the upstream flows converts imports into their 'primary resource extraction equivalent'.

Data for TMR and DMI (including composition, that is input structure of the industrial metabolism) have been provided for China (Chen and Qiao 2000), Germany, the Netherlands, Japan, USA (Adriaanse *et al.* 1997), Poland (Mündl *et al.* 1999), Finland (Juutinen and Mäenpää 1999; Muukkonen 2000; FME 1999) and the European Union (Bringezu and Schütz 2001). DMI is available for Sweden (Isacsson *et al.* 2000). Work is going on for Italy (de Marco *et al.* 1999) and Amazonia (Machado and Fenzl 2000). TMI, although termed TMR, has been accounted for in Australia (Poldy and Foran 1999).

Output Indicators

Domestic processed output (DPO) represents the total mass of materials which have been used in the domestic economy before flowing into the environment. These flows occur at the processing, manufacturing, use and final disposal stages of the economic production–consumption chain. Exported materials are excluded because their wastes occur in other countries. Included in DPO are emissions to air from commercial energy combustion and other industrial processes, industrial and household wastes deposited in landfills, material loads in wastewater, materials dispersed into the environment as a result of product use (dissipative flows) and emissions from incineration plants. Material flows recycled in industry are not included in DPO.

Total domestic output (TDO) is the sum of DPO and disposal of unused domestic extraction. This indicator represents the total quantity of material outputs to the environment released in domestic territory by economic activity. *Direct material output* (DMO) is the sum of DPO and exports. This parameter represents the total quantity of direct material outputs leaving the economy after use, either into the environment or to the rest of the world. *Total material output* (TMO) also includes exports and therefore measures the total of material that leaves the economy; TMO equals TDO plus exports.

Consumption Indicators

Domestic material consumption (DMC) measures the total amount of material directly used in an economy, excluding hidden flows (for example, Isacsson *et al.* 2000). DMC equals DMI minus exports.

Total material consumption (TMC) measures the total primary material requirement associated with domestic consumption activities (Bringezu *et al.* 1994). TMC equals TMR minus exports and their hidden flows.

Balance Indicators

Net additions to stock (NAS) measures the physical growth rate of an economy. New materials are added to the economy's stock each year (gross additions) in buildings and other infrastructure, and materials incorporated into new durable goods such as cars, industrial machinery and household appliances, while old materials are removed from stock as buildings are demolished, and durable goods disposed of. NAS may be calculated indirectly as the balancing item between the annual flow of materials that enter the economy (DMI), plus air inputs (for example, for oxidization processes), minus DPO, minus water vapor, minus exports. NAS may also be calculated directly as gross additions to stock, minus the material outputs of decommissioned building materials (as construction and demolition wastes) and disposed durable goods, minus materials recycled.

Physical trade balance (PTB) measures the physical trade surplus or deficit of an economy. PTB equals imports minus exports. Physical trade balances may also be defined including hidden flows associated with imports and exports (for example, on the basis of TMC accounts).

Efficiency Indicators

Services provided or economic performance (in terms of value-added or GDP) may be related to either input or output indicators to provide efficiency measures. For instance, GDP per DMI indicates the direct materials productivity. GDP per TDO measures the economic performance in relation to material losses to the environment. Setting the value-added in relation to the most important inputs and outputs provides information on the eco-efficiency of an economy. The interpretation of these relative measures should always consider the trends of the absolute parameters. The latter are usually also provided on a per capita basis to support international comparisons.

Increasingly, MFA and its indicators will be used to provide the basis for political measures and to evaluate the effectiveness of such measures. For that purpose bulk material flow analyses and substance flow analyses can be combined and the monitoring of progress towards sustainability can be gradually improved by taking a stepwise approach (see Bringezu *et al.* 1998a).

NOTES

1. The indicative value depends on the relation to (a) other flows, (b) assessment parameters such as critical levels, and (c) system properties of the accounting (for example, systems borders from cradle to grave) (Bringezu 2000a).
2. To conform to LCA usage, attribution is sometimes called 'allocation'.
3 In studies prior to Adriaanse *et al.* (1997), TMR had been defined as total material input, TMI (for example, Bringezu 1997b).

References

Adriaanse, Albert (1993), *Environmental Policy Performance Indicators: A Study on the Development of Indicators for Environmental Policy in the Netherlands*, The Hague: Sdu Uitgeverij Koninginnegracht.

Adriaanse, Albert, Stefan Bringezu, Allen Hammond, Yuichi Moriguchi, Eric Rodenburg, Donald G. Rogich and Helmut Schütz (1997), *Resource Flows: The Material Basis of Industrial Economies*, Washington, DC: World Resources Institute.

Ayres, Robert U. (1989a), 'Industrial metabolism', in Jesse H. Ausubel and Hedy E. Sladovich (eds), *Technology and Environment*, Washington, DC: National Academy Press.

Ayres, Robert U. and Leslie W. Ayres (1996), *Industrial Ecology: Closing the Materials Cycle*, Cheltenham, UK and Lyme, MA: Edward Elgar.

Ayres, Robert U. and Leslie W. Ayres (1998), *Accounting For Resources 1: Economy-wide Applications of Mass-balance Principles to Materials and Waste*, Cheltenham, UK and Lyme, MA: Edward Elgar.

Ayres, Robert U. and Leslie W. Ayres (1999a), *Accounting For Resources 2: The Life Cycle of Materials*, Cheltenham, UK and Lyme, MA: Edward Elgar.

Ayres, Robert U. and Allen V. Kneese (1969), Production, consumption and externalities', *American Economic Review*, 59(3), 282–97.

Ayres, Robert U. and Udo E. Simonis (eds) (1994), *Industrial Metabolism: Restructuring for Sustainable Development*, Tokyo, New York, Paris: United Nations University Press.

Ayres, Robert U., Leslie W. Ayres and Joel A. Tarr (1994), 'Consumptive uses and losses of toxic heavy metals in the United States, 1880–1980', in Robert U. Ayres and Udo E. Simonis (eds), *Industrial Metabolism: Restructuring for Sustainable Development*, Tokyo: United Nations University Press. pp. 259–95.

Baccini, Peter and Hans-Peter Bader (1996), *Regionaler Stoffhaushalt: Erfassung, Bewertung und Steuerung*, Heidelberg, Berlin, Oxford: Spektrum Akademischer Verlag.

Baccini, Peter and Paul H. Brunner (1991), *Metabolism of the Anthroposphere*, Berlin and Heidelberg: Springer-Verlag.

Berkhout, Franz G. (1999), *The Concept of Industrial Metabolism and its Implications for Statistics*, Eurostat Working Papers 2/1999/B/2, Luxembourg.

BMU: see Bundesministerium für Umwelt, Naturschutz und Reaktorsicherheit.

Bovenkerk, Michiel (1998), 'The use of material flow accounting in environmental policy making in the Netherlands', in Stefan Bringezu, Marina Fischer-Kowalski, René Kleijn and Viveka Palm (eds), *Proceedings of the ConAccount Conference, September 11–12 1997*, Wuppertal Special Report 6, Wuppertal, Germany: Wuppertal Institut, pp. 28–37.

Boyden, Stephen (1980), 'Ecological study of human settlements', *Nature and Resources*, 16(3), 2–9.

Bringezu, Stefan (1997a), 'From quality to quantity: Material Flow Analysis', in Stefan Bringezu, Marina Fischer-Kowalski, René Kleijn and Viveka Palm (eds), *Proceedings of the ConAccount Workshop, January 21–23, 1997*, Wuppertal Special 4, Wuppertal, Germany: Wuppertal Institut, pp. 43–57.

Bringezu, Stefan (1997b), 'Accounting for the physical basis of national economies: material flow indicators', in B. Móldan, S. Billharz and R. Matravers (eds), *Sustainability Indicators: A Report on the Project on Indicators of Sustainable Development*, SCOPE 58, Chichester: John Wiley and Sons, pp. 181–8.

Bringezu, Stefan (2000a), *Ressourcennutzung in Wirtschaftsräumen . . . Stoffstromanalysen für eine nachhaltige Raumentwicklung*, (Resource use in economic regions . . . material flow analyses for sustainable development), Berlin: Springer Verlag (in German).

Bringezu, Stefan (2000b), 'Industrial ecology and material flow analysis', *Proceedings of the international symposium 'Industrial ecology and sustainability'*, Troyes, France, Technical University of Troyes, September 22–25, 1999.

Bringezu, Stefan and René Kleijn (1997), 'Short review of the MFA work presented', in *Proceedings of the ConAccount Workshop; Regional and National Material Flow Accounting*, Leiden and Wuppertal, Germany: Wuppertal Institute Special Report 4, 306–8.

Bringezu, Stefan and Helmut Schütz (1996b), 'Die stoffliche Basis des Wirtschaftsraumes Ruhr. Ein Vergleich mit Nordrhein-Westfalen und der Bundesrepublik Deutschland', *Zeitschrift für Raumforschung und Raumordnung*, 6/1996, 433–41.

Bringezu, Stefan and Helmut Schütz (1998), *Material Flows Accounts–Part II–Construction, Materials, Packaging*, Luxembourg: Eurostat – Statistical Office of the European Communities. Doc. MFS/97/7. (*http://www.wupperinst.org/download/index.html*).

Bringezu, Stefan and Helmut Schütz (2001), *Total Material Requirement of the European Union*, Copenhagen: European Environment Agency Technical Report nos. 55 and 56.

Bringezu, Stefan, Marina Fischer-Kowalski, René Kleijn and Viveka Palm (eds) (1997), 'Regional and national material flow accounting: from paradigm to practice of sustainability', *Proceedings of the ConAccount Workshop January 21–23, 1997*, Leiden The Netherlands, Wuppertal Special 4, Wuppertal, Germany: Wuppertal Institut.

Bringezu, Stefan, Marina Fischer-Kowalski, René Kleijn and Viveka Palm (eds) (1998a), *The ConAccount Inventory: A Reference List for MFA Activities and Institutions*, Wuppertal Special 9, Wuppertal, Germany: Wuppertal Institut.

Bringezu, Stefan, Marina Fischer-Kowalski, René Kleijn and Viveka Palm (eds) (1998b), 'Analysis for action: support for policy towards sustainability by regional and national material flow accounting', *Proceedings of the ConAccount Conference September 11–12 1997*, Wuppertal Special 6, Wuppertal, Germany: Wuppertal Institut.

Bringezu, Stefan, Marina Fischer-Kowalski, René Kleijn and Viveka Palm (eds) (1998c), *The ConAccount Agenda: The Concerted Action on Material Flow Analysis and First Research and Development Agenda*, Wuppertal Special 8, Wuppertal, Germany: Wuppertal Institut.

Bringezu, Stefan, Friedrich Hinterberger and Helmut Schutz (1994), 'Integrating sustainability into the system of national accounts: the case of interregional material flows', in *Proceedings of Papers Presented at the International AFCET Symposium: Models of Sustainable Development: Exclusive or Complementary Approaches to Sustainability*, Paris, March, pp. 669–80.

Bringezu, Stefan, H. Stiller and Friedrich B. Schmidt-Bleek (1996), 'Material intensity analysis–a screening step for LCA: concept, method and applications', *Proceedings of the Second International Conference on EcoBalance, November 18–20, 1996*, Tsukuba, Japan, pp. 147–52.

Brunner, Paul H., Hans Daxbeck and Peter Baccini (1994), 'Industrial metabolism at the regional and local level: A case study on a Swiss region', in Robert U. Ayres and Udo E. Simonis (eds), *Industrial Metabolism: Restructuring for Sustainable Development*, Tokyo: United Nations University Press, pp. 163–93.

Bundesministerium für Umwelt, Naturschutz und Reaktorsicherheit (BMU) (1998), *Nachhaltige Entwicklung in Deutschland – Entwurf eines umweltpolitischen Schwerpunktprogramms*, Bonn: BMU.

Chen, X. and L. Qiao, (2000), 'Material flow analysis of Chinese economic-environmental system', *Journal of Natural Resources*, **15**(1), 17–23.

Dahlbo, Helena and T.W. Assmuth (1997), 'Analysis of lead fluxes in municipal solid waste systems for identification of waste prevention and recycling potential', in Stefan Bringezu, Marina Fischer-Kowalski, René Kleijn and Viveka Palm (eds), *Proceedings of the ConAccount Workshop, January 21–23, 1997*, Wuppertal Special 4, Wuppertal, Germany: Wuppertal Institut, pp. 227–32.

de Marco, Ottilie G. Lagoia and E. Pizzoli Mazzacane (1999), 'Material flow analysis of the Italian economy: preliminary results',in René Kleijn, Stefan Bringezu, Marina Fischer-Kowalski and Viveka Palm (eds), *Ecologizing societal metabolism. Designing scenarios for sustainable materials management; Proceedings of the ConAccount Workshop November 21, 1998*, CML Report 148, Leiden: Leiden University, pp. 3–14.

Duvigneaud, Paul and S. Denayer-DeSmet (1977), 'L'écosystème urbs. L'écosystème urbaine bruxellois', in Paul Duvigneaud and P. Kestemont, *Productivité biologique en Belgique*, Gembloux, France: SCOPE. Travaux de la Section Belge du Programme Biologique International, pp. 581–99.

EEA: see European Environment Agency.

Einig, Klaus (1998), 'Ressourcenintensität der Stadt–Dem urbanen Metabolismus auf der Spur (Resource intensity of the city–tracing the urban metabolism), *RaumPlanung*, **81**, 103–9 (in German).

574 *References*

el Mahdi, Alia (1999), 'Material flow accounts: the case of Egypt', paper presented at The Material Flow Account Workshop, Cairo University, February 23, 1999.

European Environment Agency (EEA) (1999a), *Environment in the European Union at the Turn of the Century*, Copenhagen: European Environment Agency.

European Environment Agency (EEA) (1999b), 'Environmental indicators: typology and overview', *Technical report No 25*, Copenhagen: European Environment Agency.

European Environment Agency (EEA) (2000), 'Environmental signals 2000', *European Environment Agency Regular Indicator Report*, Copenhagen: European Environment Agency.

European Union (1999), *Presidency Summary of the Informal Meeting of the EU Environment Ministers and Environment Ministers of the Candidate Countries of Central and Eastern Europe and of Cyprus, July 23–25*, Helsinki.

Eurostat: Statistical Office of the European Communities (2000), *Economy-wide Material Flow Accounts and Derived Indicators. A Methodological Guide*, Luxembourg.

Fehringer, Roland and Paul H. Brunner (1997), 'Flows of plastics and their possible reuse in Austria', in Stefan Bringezu, Marina Fischer-Kowalski, René Kleijn and Viveka Palm (eds), *Proceedings of the ConAccount Workshop, January 21–23, 1997*, Wuppertal Special 4, Wuppertal, Germany: Wuppertal Institut, pp. 272–7.

Femia, A. (2000), 'A material flow account for Italy 1988', *Eurostat Working Papers*, 2/2000/B/8, Luxembourg.

Finnish Ministry of the Environment (FME) (1999), 'Material flow accounting as a measure of the total consumption of natural resources', *The Finnish Environment*, 287, Helsinki, Finland.

FME: see Finnish Ministry of the Environment.

Friege, Henning (1997), 'Requirements for policy relevant MFA–Results of the Bundestag's Enquête Commission', in Stefan Bringezu, Marina Fischer-Kowalski, René Kleijn and Viveka Palm (eds), *Proceedings of the ConAccount Workshop, January 21–23, 1997*, Wuppertal Special 4, Wuppertal, Germany: Wuppertal Institut, pp. 24–31.

Gardener, G. and P. Sampat (1998), 'Mind over matters: recasting the role of materials in our lives', *World Watch Paper 144*, Washington, DC: World Watch Institute.

Gerhold, S. and B. Petrovic (2000), 'Material Flow Accounts, material balance and indicators, Austria 1960–1997', *Eurostat Working Papers*, 2/2000/B/6, Luxembourg.

Gielen, Dolf (1999), 'Materialization Dematerialization–Integrated Energy and Materials Systems Engineering for Greenhouse Gas Emission Mitigation', Thesis, Delft University of Technology, Delft, The Netherlands (also Design for Sustainability Program publication no. 2).

Glenck, Emmanuel and T. Lahner (1997), 'Materials accounting of the infrastructure at a regional level', in Stefan Bringezu, Marina Fischer-Kowalski, René Kleijn and Viveka Palm (eds), *Proceedings of the ConAccount Workshop, January 21–23, 1997*, Wuppertal Special 4, Wuppertal, Germany: Wuppertal Institut, pp. 131–5.

Haberl, Helmut (1997), 'Biomass flows in Austria: integrating the concepts of societal metabolism and colonization of nature', in Stefan Bringezu, Marina Fischer-Kowalski, René Kleijn and Viveka Palm (eds), *Proceedings of the ConAccount Workshop, January 21–23, 1997*, Wuppertal Special 4, Wuppertal, Germany: Wuppertal Institut, pp. 102–7.

Hansen, Erik (1997), 'Paradigm for SFA's on the national level for hazardous substances in Denmark', in Stefan Bringezu, Marina Fischer-Kowalski, René Kleijn and Viveka Palm (eds), *Proceedings of the ConAccount Workshop, January 21–23, 1997*, Wuppertal Special 4, Wuppertal, Germany: Wuppertal Institut, pp. 96–101.

Hansen, Erik (1998), 'Experiences with SFAs on the national level for hazardous substances in Denmark', in Stefan Bringezu, Marina Fischer-Kowalski, René Kleijn and Viveka Palm (eds), *Proceedings of the ConAccount Conference, September 11–12, 1997*, Wuppertal Special 6, Wuppertal, Germany: Wuppertal Institut, pp. 115–8.

Hoffrén, J. (1999), 'Measuring the eco-efficiency of the Finnish economy', *Research Report 229*, Statistics Finland, Helsinki.

Hohmeyer, Olav, J. Kirsch and S. Vögele (1997), 'EMI 2.0–A disaggregated model linking economic activities and emissions', in Stefan Bringezu, Marina Fischer-Kowalski, René Kleijn and Viveka Palm (eds), *Proceedings of the ConAccount Workshop, January 21–23, 1997*, Wuppertal Special 4, Wuppertal, Germany: Wuppertal Institut, pp. 204–10.

Isacsson, A., K. Jonsson, I. Linder, Viveka Palm and A. Wadeskog (2000), 'Material Flow Accounts, DMI and DMC for Sweden 1987–1997', *Eurostat Working Papers*, 2/2000/B/2, Luxembourg.

Jimenez-Beltran, Domingo (1998), 'A possible role of material flow analysis within a European environmental reporting system–changing course in environmental information', in Stefan Bringezu, Marina Fischer-Kowalski, René Kleijn and Viveka Palm (eds), *Proceedings of the ConAccount Conference, September 11–12, 1997*, Wuppertal Special 6, Wuppertal, Germany: Wuppertal Institut, pp. 16–27.

Juutinen, Arrti and Ilmo Mäenpää (1999), *Time Series for the Total Material Requirement of Finnish Economy, Summary*, http://thule.oulu.filecoeflecoweb3.htm.

Kleijn, René, Arnold Tukker and Ester van der Voet (1997), 'Chlorine in the Netherlands Part I, An Overview', *Journal of Industrial Ecology*, 1(1), 95–116.

Kleijn, René, Stefan Bringezu, Marina Fischer-Kowalski and Viveka Palm (eds) (1999), 'Ecologizing societal metabolism. Designing scenarios for sustainable materials management', *Proceedings of the ConAccount Workshop November 21, 1998, Amsterdam*, CML report 148, Leiden University.

Koenig, Albert (1997), 'The urban metabolism of Hong Kong: an extreme example in the Asian region', *Conference Proceedings POLMET '97 Pollution in the Metropolitan and Urban Environment*, The Hong Kong Institution of Engineers, pp. 303–10.

Kohler, Nikolaus, U. Hassler and H. Paschen (eds) (1999), *Stoffströme und Kosten in den Bereichen Bauen und Wohnen* (Material flows and costs in the fields of construction and housing), Berlin, Heidelberg, New York: Springer Verlag (in German).

Liedtke, Christa, Holger Rohn, Michael Kuhndt and Regina Nickel (1998), 'Applying material flow accounting: eco-auditing and resource management at the Kambium Furniture Workshop', *Journal of Industrial Ecology*, 2(3), 131–47.

Maag, Jacob, E. Hansen and C. Lassen (1997), 'Mercury–Substance Flow Analysis for Denmark', in Stefan Bringezu, Marina Fischer-Kowalski, René Kleijn and Viveka Palm (eds), *Proceedings of the ConAccount Workshop, January 21–23, 1997*, Wuppertal Special 4, Wuppertal, Germany: Wuppertal Institut, pp. 283–7.

Machado, Jose A. and Norbert Fenzl (2000), 'The sustainability of development and the material flows of economy: a comparative study of Brazil and industrialized countries', paper presented for The Amazonia 21 Project, Federal University of Paraguay.

Mäenpää, Ilmo, Artti Juutinen, K. Puustinen, J. Rintala, H. Risku-Norja and S. Veijalainen (2000), *The Total Use of Natural Resources in Finland* (in Finnish), Helsinki, Finland: Ministry of the Environment, Finnish Environment 428.

Matthews, Emily, Christof Amann, Marina Fischer-Kowalski, Stefan Bringezu, Walter Hüttler, René Kleijn, Yuichi Moriguchi, Christian Ottke, Eric Rodenburg, Donald Rogich, Heinz Schandl, Helmut Schütz, Ester van der Voet and Helga Weisz (2000), *The Weight of Nations: Material Outflows from Industrial Economies*, Washington, DC: World Resources Institute.

Maxson, Peter A. and G.H. Vonkeman (1996), 'Mercury stock management in the Netherlands', background document prepared for the Workshop 'Mercury: Ban or Bridle It?', Institute for European Environmental Policy, Brussels.

Moldan, Bedrich, S. Billharz and R. Matravers (eds) (1997), *Sustainability Indicators: A Report on the Project on Indicators of Sustainable Development*, SCOPE 58. Chichester: John Wiley and Sons.

Mündl, A., Helmut Schütz, W. Stodulski, J. Sleszynski and M.J. Welfens (1999), *Sustainable Development by Dematerialization in Production and Consumption, Strategy for the New Environmental Policy in Poland, Report 3, 1999*, Warsaw: Institute for Sustainable Development.

Muukkonen, J. (2000), 'Material Flow Accounts, TMR, DMI and Material Balances, Finland 1980–1997', *Eurostat Working Papers*, 2/2000/B/1, Luxembourg.

Nordic Council of Ministers (1999), 'Factor 4 and 10 in the Nordic Countries. The transport sector – the forest sector – the building and real estate sector – the food supply chain', *TemaNord 1999*, **528**, Copenhagen, Denmark.

576 *References*

Obernosterer, Richard and Paul H. Brunner (1997), 'Construction wastes as the main future source for CFC emissions', in Stefan Bringezu, Marina Fischer-Kowalski, René Kleijn and Viveka Palm (eds), *Proceedings of the ConAccount Workshop, January 21–23, 1997*, Wuppertal, Germany: Wuppertal Institut, pp. 278–82.

Obernosterer, Richard, Paul H. Brunner, Hans Daxbeck, T. Gagan, Emmanuel Glenck, Carolyn Hendriks, Leo Morf, Renate Paumann and Iris Reiner (1998), *Materials Accounting as a Tool for Decision Making in Environmental Policy* (Case study report 1. Urban metabolism: The city of Vienna), Vienna, Austria: University of Technology, Institute for Water Quality and Waste Management, Department of Waste Management.

Odum, Howard T. (1996), *Environmental Accounting, Emergy and Decision Making*, New York: John Wiley.

OECD: see Organisation for Economic Cooperation and Development.

Orbach, Thomas and Christa Liedtke (1998), 'Eco-management accounting in Germany', *Wuppertal Papers*, **88**, Wuppertal Institut, Wuppertal, Germany.

Organisation for Economic Cooperation and Development (OECD) (1996a), *Meeting of OECD Environment Policy Committee at Ministerial Level. Paris, 19–20 February 1996*, OECD Communications Division.

Organisation for Economic Cooperation and Development (OECD) (1998a), *Towards Sustainable Development: Environmental Indicators*, Paris: OECD.

Organisation for Economic Cooperation and Development (OECD) (1998b), *Eco-Efficiency*, Paris: OECD.

Patel, Martin (1999), *Closing Carbon Cycles–Carbon Use for Materials in the Context of Resource Efficiency and Climate Change*, Thesis, Faculty of Chemistry, Utrecht University, Utrecht, The Netherlands.

Pedersen, O.G. (1999), *Physical Input-output Tables for Denmark. Products and Materials 1990. Air Emissions 1990–92*, Statistics Denmark, Copenhagen, Denmark.

Poldy, F. and B. Foran (1999), 'Resource flows: the material basis of the Australian economy', *Working Document 99/16*, Canberra Australia: Commonwealth Scientific and Industrial Research Organization (CSIRO), Wildlife and Ecology. (*http://www.dwe.csiro.au*).

Radermacher, W. and Carsten Stahmer (1998), 'Material and energy flow analysis in Germany – accounting framework, information system, applications', in Kimio Uno and Peter Bartelmus (eds), *Environmental Accounting in Theory and Practice*, Dordrecht, Boston, London: Kluwer Academic Publishers, pp. 187–211.

Reiner, Iris, C. Lampert and Paul H. Brunner (1997), 'Material balances of agricultural soils considering the utilization of sewage sludge and compost', in Stefan Bringezu, Marina Fischer-Kowalski, René Kleijn and Viveka Palm (eds), *Proceedings of the ConAccount Workshop, January 21–23, 1997*, Wuppertal Special 4, Wuppertal, Germany: Wuppertal Institut, pp. 260–3.

Richards, Deanna J., Braden R. Allenby and Robert A. Frosch (1994), 'The greening of industrial ecosystems: overview and perspective', in Braden R. Allenby and Deanna J. Richards (eds), *The Greening of Industrial Ecosystems*, Washington, DC: National Academy Press, pp. 1–22.

Schandl, Heinz (1998), 'Materialfluß Österreich; Die materielle Basis der österreicheschen Gesellschaft im Zeitraum 1960–1995', *Schriftenreihe Soziale Ökologie*, **50**, (Vienna, Interuniversitäres Institut für Forschung und Fortbildung (IFF)).

Schandl, Heinz and Walter Hüttler (1997), 'MFA Austria: Activity fields as a method for sectoral material flow analysis–empirical results for the activity field "Construction"', in Stefan Bringezu, Marina Fischer-Kowalski, René Kleijn and Viveka Palm (eds), *Proceedings of the ConAccount Workshop, January 21–23, 1997*, Wuppertal Special 6, Wuppertal, Germany: Wuppertal Institut, pp. 264–71.

Schmidt-Bleek, Friedrich B. (1994a), *Wieviel Umwelt braucht der Mensch? MIPS, Das Mass für ökologisches Wirtschaften* (How Much Environment for Human Needs?), Berlin, Basle, Boston: Birkhauser Verlag.

Schmidt-Bleek, Friedrich B. (1994b), 'Where We Stand Now: Actions Toward Reaching a Dematerialized Economy', Declaration of the First Meeting of the Factor 10 Club held in Carnoules, France, September 1994. (*http://www.techfak.uni-bielefeld.de/~walter/f10/*).

Schmidt-Bleek, Friedrich B., Stefan Bringezu, Friedrich Hinterberger, Christa Liedtke, J. Spangenberg, H. Stiller and M.J. Welfens (1998), *MAIA–Einführung in die Material-Intensitäts-Analyse nach dem MIPS-Konzept*, (MAIA–Introduction to Material-Intensity Analysis According to the MIPS Concept), Berlin, Basle, Boston: Birkhäuser.

Schütz, Helmut and Stefan Bringezu (1993), 'Major material flows in Germany', *Fresenius Environmental Bulletin*, **2**, 443–8.

Spengler, Thomas (1998), *Industrielles Stoffstrommanagement* (Industrial material flow management), Berlin: Erich Schmidt Verlag, (in German).

Stahmer, Carsten, Michael Kuhn and Norbert Braun (1998), *Physical Input-output Tables for Germany, 1990*, Eurostat Working Papers, 2/1998/B/1, Brussels: European Commission.

Statistics Finland (1999), *Finland's Natural Resources and the Environment 1999*, Helsinki, Finland.

Steurer, Anton (1992), *Stoffstrombilanz Österreich 1988*, Austria: Schriftenreihe Soziale Ökologie Band 26. Institut für Interdisziplinäre Forschung und Fortbildung der Universitäten Innsbruck, Klagenfurt und Wien.

Stigliani, William M. and Stefan Anderberg (1994), 'Industrial metabolism at the regional level: The Rhine Basin', in Robert U. Ayres and Udo E. Simonis (eds), *Industrial Metabolism: Restructuring for Sustainable Development*, Tokyo: United Nations University Press, pp. 119–62.

Tukker, Arnold (1998), *Frames in the Toxicity Controversy Based on the Dutch Chlorine Debate and the Swedish PVC Debate*, PhD thesis, Tilburg, Veenendaal, The Netherlands: Universal Press.

UKDETR: see United Kingdom Department of the Environment, Transport and Regions.

UNGASS: see United Nations General Assembly Special Session.

United Kingdom Department of the Environment, Transport and Regions (UKDETR) (1999), *Quality of Life Counts: Indicators for a Strategy for Sustainable Development for the United Kingdom: a Baseline Assessment*, London: Her Majesty's Stationary Office.

United Nations General Assembly Special Session (UNGASS) (1997), *Programme for the Further Implementation of Agenda 21*, Adopted by the Special Session of the General Assembly, New York, June 23–27.

Vaze, Prashant and Jeffrey B. Barron (eds) (1998), *UK Environmental Accounts 1998*, London: Her Majesty's Stationary Office.

Verfaillie, Hendrick A. and R. Bidwell (2000), *Measuring Eco-efficiency–a Guide to Reporting Company Performance*, Geneva, World Business Council for Sustainable Development.

Vitousek, Peter M., Paul R. Ehrlich, A.H. Ehrlich and P.A. Matson (1986), 'Human appropriation of the products of photosynthesis', *BioScience*, **36**(6), 368–73.

Voet, Ester van der (1996), *Substances from Cradle to Grave (Development of a Methodology for the Analysis of Substance Flows Through the Economy and the Environment of a Region – with Case Studies on Cadmium and Nitrogen Compounds)*, Molenaarsgraaf, The Netherlands: Optima Druk.

Voet, Ester van der, L. van Egmond, René Kleijn and Gjalt Huppes (1994), 'Cadmium in the European Community: A policy-oriented analysis', *Waste Management and Research*, **12**, 507–26.

Weizsäcker, Ernst-Ulrich von, Amory B. Lovins and L. Hunter Lovins (1997), *Factor Four: Doubling Wealth–Halving Resource Use: the New Report to the Club of Rome*, London: Earthscan.

Windsperger, Andreas, G. Angst and S. Gerhold (1997), 'Indicators of environmental pressure from the sector industry', Stefan Bringezu, Marina Fischer-Kowalski, René Kleijn and Viveka Palm (eds), *Proceedings of the ConAccount Workshop, January 21–23, 1997*, Wuppertal Special 4, Wuppertal, Germany: Wuppertal Institut, pp. 178–83.

Wolman, A. (1965), 'The metabolism of cities', *Scientific American*, September, 179–90.

World Business Council for Sustainable Development (WBCSD) (1998), 'WBCSD Project on Eco-Efficiency Metrics and Reporting', state-of-play report, M. Lehni, Geneva.

World Business Council for Sustainable Development (WBCSD) (1999), 'Measuring eco-efficiency with cross-comparable indicators', *WBCSD Executive Brief*, January (*http://www.wbcsd.ch*).

[7]

Towards an ecological-economic accounting of the provision-transformation-restitution cycle

Günter Strassert

1.Introduction: The relationships between the economic production and the environment

To demonstrate that "the economic process is entropic in all its m a t e r i a l fibers" (Georgescu-Roegen, 1984, 28) Georgescu-Roegen repeatedly used a consolidated flow-fund matrix as an analytical representation of "a stationary economy surrounded by its natural environment" (1971, 254) or of "the economic process in relation to the environment according to the energetic dogma" (1979, 1028; 1981, 56; 1982, 8) or simply "the relationships between the economic process and the environment" (1984, 27).

Table 1 is a modified version of this line of reasoning which corresponds more to input-output accounting.

Output / Input	Economic activities							Final use	Environment			
	M	E	K	C	F	D	R		W^s	W^f	W^g	D^e
M	x_{11}		x_{13}	x_{14}		x_{16}		f_1	w_1^s	w_1^f	w_1^g	d_1
E	e_{21}	e_{22}	e_{23}	e_{24}	e_{25}	$e_{26}\mid x_{26}$	e_{27}	f_2	w_2^s	w_2^f	w_2^g	d_2
K	x_{31}	x_{32}	x_{33}	x_{34}	x_{35}	x_{36}	x_{37}	f_3	w_3^s	w_3^f	w_3^g	d_3
C					x_{45}	x_{46}		f_4	w_4^s	w_4^f	w_4^g	d_4
F	$\mathbf{T_A}$					x_{56}		f_5	w_5^s	w_5^f	w_5^g	d_5
D							x_{67}	f_6	w_6^s	w_6^f	w_6^g	d_6
R	x_{71}					x_{76}		f_7	w_7^s	w_7^f	w_7^g	d_7
Mat. stores	x_1^m											
Environment												
M^s	x_1^s	$x_2^s\mid e_2^s$										
M^f	x_1^f	$x_2^f\mid e_2^f$										
M^g	x_1^g	$x_2^g\mid e_2^g$										

Table 1: A flow matrix for matter and energy representing the relationships between the economic production domain and the environment

The central matrix T_A represents the production domain of a set of seven economic activities (A_i) accomplishing the transformation of matter and energy. All material input comes from the environment, and the environment is the final destination of all transformed output.

The seven economic activities are distinguished as follows:

(A_1) M: Procurement of raw materials for processing through extraction of matter in situ

(A_2) E: Procurement of effective (available) energy (fuel) through extraction of energy in situ

(A_3) K: Production of capital goods: capital fund (X_k) and maintenance goods (servicing)

(A_4) C: Production of consumer goods

(A_5) F: Final production: immaterial goods (consumption in the broadest sense, e.g. self actualization or enjoyment of life)

(A_6) D: Disposal of garbojunk (including deposition)

(A_7) R: Recycling of garbojunk

Note that the stance of description taken here is one from within the economic domain. For implications deriving from a change in perspective see the next section.

To abbreviate, further explanatory comments refer to the following equalities that must always prevail:

(1) $x_1 + x_2 + x_1{}^m = f + w$: Matter balance (physical units)
with

(a) $x_1 = x_1{}^s + x_1{}^f + x_1{}^g$: Matter in situ for nonenergetic transformation in solid (s), fluid (f) or gaseous (g) condition

(b) $x_2 = x_2{}^s + x_2{}^f + x_2{}^g$ (mass units)

or $e_2 = e_2{}^s + e_2{}^f + e_2{}^g$ (energy units): Matter as energy in situ in solid, fluid or gaseous condition, e.g. coal, oil, gas)

(c) $x_1{}^m$: Input from material store (stock decumulation)

(d) $f = \sum_i f_i$: Stock accumulation, and in case of activity K also new equipment for the capital fund ($f_3 = x_k$) (investment). Other final use (export-imports) is assumed to be nil.

(e) $w_i = w_i{}^s + w_i{}^f + w_i{}^g$: Final waste before or after recycling in solid, fluid or gaseous condition

(f) $w = \sum_i w_i; i = 1,...,7$

The final material output of matter transformation by economic activities in an economy is waste. Waste generation is reduced by widening and deepening of the capital funds as far and as long as this activity (investment including material storing and servicing) is maintained.

(2) $c_2 = \sum_i d_i$; $i = 1,...,7$ Energy balance

with

(a) $c_2 = c_2^s + c_2^f + c_2^g$: energy units according to x_2 (see above (1) b)

(b) $d_i = c_{2i}$ $(i \neq 2)$: dissipated energy

(c) $d_2 = c_2 - \sum_{i \neq 2} c_{2i}$: dissipated energy

The final output of energetic transformation by economic activities is dissipated (unavailable) energy.

2. The provision-transformation-restitution cycle

As the above flow matrix (table 1) shows, the environment is both an emitter and a receptor. As an emitter, the environment provides the economic activities with the necessary material inputs. This so to say provision function of the environment represents the dictum that nothing can be produced out of nothing.

The concept of provision corresponds to a donor position (from the emitter's point of view) instead of the common acquisition position (from main stream economist's point of view) which covers all forms of environmental exploitation - as the concept of "exaction" (Perrings, 1987, 35) does.

After transformation the donor position is up to the actors of economic activities. What they received from the environment now they have to return, and that is the very point. The concept of restitution - hopefully - implies the quality aspect of returned outputs and is not to understand as "insertion" (Perrings, 1987, 35) which covers both the deliberate and accidental pollution associated with waste disposal.
A bioeconomist cannot stop here. "Environment" is not a black box but the term stands for an ecological system or ecosystem where the biotic community (all living auto- and heterotrophic populations) and the non-living surroundings (litho-, hydro- and atmosphere) function together (Odum, 1989, 27). The biotic community represents another production domain, i.e. the natural production domain of so-called bioactivities. For these activities (to be explained below) the above mentioned concepts are relevant, too: Transformation of matter and energy requires provision on the input side restitution on the output side.

According to the logic of input-output-accounting where one activity's input is another activity's output, and vice versa, provision and restitution or restitution and provision are the two sides of the same coin. This constitutes a cycle that I call the provision-transformation-restitution cycle (figure 1).

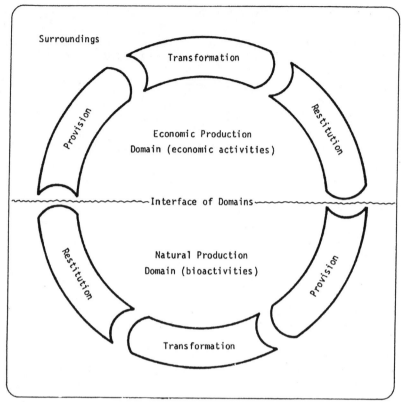

Figure 1: The provision-transformation-restitution cycle

On the right hand side of figure 1 provision of the bioactivities can be considered as recycling of restituted outputs from economic activities, and on the left hand side provision of the economic activities can be considered as recycling of restituted outputs from bioactivities.

These links are the essential working condition of any economic production domain. As a subsystem of a closed system (our global physical system) it is an open system because the closed system is not decomposable (Perrings, 1987, 18). In conclusion, "any subsystem operating within an indecomposable physical system will be limited by the effects of its actions on its environment. In a general sense, no one process can be thought to be independent of the rest" (ibid., 45).

This "rest" is nothing but the natural production domain with its set of bioactivities. If the provision of bioactivities is affected by the quantity and quality of the restitution output from economic activities, then - via transformation or non-transformation - the restitution output, its level and composition, from bioactivities is affected, too. And as soon as the provision of economic activities is affected the cycle is closed.

3.The relationships between the natural production and the environment

The upper halfcircle (fig. 1) corresponds to the accounting scheme dealt with at the outset (table 1). Now, it is tempting to look for an analytical representation of the relationships between the natural production and the environment using the same input-output framework. Such an attempt is made by table 2.

I felt encouraged in doing so by the initiatives of a group of ecologists who introduced input-output analysis into ecological studies (Hannon, 1973; Finn, 1976; Patten/Bossermann/Finn/Cale, 1976) and who are improving both the accounting in ecological systems and the model application (Hannon, 1979,1991; Fruci/Costanza/Leibowitz, 1982; Costanza/Hannon, 1989; Szyrmer, 1986, 1987)

Input \ Output	Bioactivities							Final use	Environment			
	P	H	C	SO(11)	SO(12)	SO(21)	SO(22)		M^s	M^f	M^g	e / D
P		y_{12}	y_{13}	y_{14}	y_{15}	y_{16}		f'_1	r_1^s	r_1^f	r_1^g	d_1'
H			y_{23}	y_{24}	y_{25}			f'_2	r_2^s	r_2^f	r_2^g	d_2'
C			y_{33}	y_{34}	y_{35}			f'_3	r_3^s	r_3^f	r_3^g	d_3'
SO(11)				y_{44}	y_{45}	y_{46}	y_{47}	f'_4	r_4^s	r_4^f	r_4^g	d_4'
SO(12)	T_B					y_{56}	y_{57}	f'_5	r_5^s	r_5^f	r_5^g	d_5'
SO(21)							y_{67}	f'_6	r_6^s	r_6^f	r_6^g	d_6'
SO(22)						y_{76}	y_{77}	f'_7	r_7^s	r_7^f	r_7^g	d_7'
Environment												
S	e											
M^s	m_1^s			m_4^s								
M^f	m_1^f			m_4^f								
M^g	m_1^g			m_4^g								

Table 2: *A flow matrix for matter and/or energy representing the relationships between the natural production domain and the (non-living) environment*

The central matrix T_B (table 2) comprehends in a consolidated form (again) seven activities (bioactivities: B_k, k = 1,...,7) which are pivotal components of the food web and can be distinguished as follows (Richards, 1987, 141, 154):

511

Grazing food chain:

(B₁) P: "Plants" (production of vegetal biomass: primordial production
         (photosynthesis) by photoauto- and heterotrophs)
(B₂) H: "Herbivores" (transformation of plant biomass (living tissue) into
         livestock of plant eaters
(B₃) C: "Carnivores" (transformation of prey livestock into predator livestock -
         including parasites)

Saprophaging food chain:

(B₄) SO(11): Soil organisms consuming dead organic matter of differnt condition
(B₅) SO(12): on soil level 1 and 2 of degradation and transformation

Biophaging food chain:

(B₆) SO(21): Soil organisms consuming living organic matter of different
(B₇) SO(22): condition on soil level 1 and 2 of degradation and transformation.

The general outcome of the grazing food chain is to enable life. The general result of both the saprophaging food chain and the biophaging food chain is decomposition, i.e. recycling of inorganic (mineral) substances (r_k^s, r_k^f, r_k^g). Cross feeding between these food chains creates the food web.

To keep clear the trophic and energy levels and its principally dependent organization the bioactivities are ordered in such a way that the matrix approaches a triangular representation.

Again, for the sake of brevity, further explanatory comments refer to the following equalities that must always prevail:

(1) $m_1 + m_4 = f' + r$ · Matter balance (physical units)
    with
    (a) $m_1 = m_1^s + m_1^f + m_1^g$: Matter in situ, i.e. inorganic substances in solid,
                                       fluid or gaseous condition

    (b) $m_4 = m_4^s + m_4^f + m_4^g$

         $= w^s + w^f + w^g$: Final waste from the economic production
                                       domain
    (c) $f' = \Sigma f'_k$; $k = 1,...,7$: Final use comprehends output storage in the
              k   sense of maintenance and growth of an organism.
                                       Other final use (exports-imports) is assumed to
                                       be nil
    (d) $r = \Sigma r_k$; $k = 1,...,7$: Remaining organic or inorganic material
              k   as restitution output to be stored or recycled
         $r_k = r_k^s + r_k^f + r_k^g$

512

If final use (f') is nil, the ecosystem stops working, i.e. recycling stops and r remains unused (is dumped). Equation (1) does not imply substitutability of f' and r, rather a complementary relation prevails, in its strongest (limitational) sense: $m_1 = [af'; br]$, a and b being constant parameters. Moreover, the composition of the final use vector $\underline{f}' = [f'_1,...,f'_k]$ and hence of the remainder vector $\underline{r} = [r_1,...,r_k]$ is dominated by complementary relations.

(2) $e = e_f + e_r + d'$ Energy balance (energy units)

with

(a) e   : solar energy input

(b) e_f, e_r : energy content of f and r (organic matter)

(c) $d' = \Sigma\ d'_k; k = 1,...,7$: dissipated energy

Solar energy is transformed into available energy which is stored in f and r, and unavailable energy which is dissipated. If used, stored energy also will dissipate and become unavailable.

4.A comprehensive accounting scheme

Finally, both tables (1 and 2) can be combined so that an accounting scheme for the complete provision-transformation-restitution cycle is achieved (table 3).

Table 3: An accounting scheme for the provision-transformation-restitution cycle

Each table comprehends three submatrices, P_A, T_A, R_A (table 1) and P_B, T_B, R_B (table 2), representing the provision of economic activities and bioactivities (P_A, P_B), the transformation of matter and energy (T_A, T_B), and the restitution by both sets of activities (R_A, R_B).

The linkage of both production domains is accomplished by means of two diagonal matrices (D_W and D_M). The first (D_W) transfers waste from the economic restitution account (row vector $w = [w^s, w^f, w^g]$) to the natural provision account (column vector $m' = [M^s, M^f, M^g]$), especially the solid waste (w^s) to the (first) decomposer activity B_4 (so that $w^s \leq m_4{}^s$). The second (D_M) transfers inorganic substances from the natural restitution account (row vector $m = [m^s, m^f, m^g]$) to the economic provision account (column vector $m' = [M^s, M^f, M^g]$), especially the solid raw material (r^s) to the economic activities A_1 and A_2 (so that $r^s \geq x_1 + x_2$).

5. Concluding remarks

Generally, accounting is a prerequisite to any modelling of economic and ecological systems. From a bioeconomic point of view, systems analysis should be as comprehensive as the real network of production activities calls for. The set of production activities comprehends both economic production activities and natural production activities of all living organisms as components of the food web (bioactivities). With regard to the transformation of matter and energy there is no principal difference between economic and natural production activities (production functions are isomorphic; e.g. Strassert, 1991). Any economic production domain represents a thermodynamically open system - in contrast to the fact that the major economic models of depletion and pollution involve a closed system. Every resource comes from somewhere and goes somewhere, "somewhere" being nothing else but another production domain which is generally subsumed unter the catch-all term of "environment". Whitout material interaction between both production domains matter could not circulate, and the described provision-transformation-restitution cycle could not take place. It is particularly this cycle that enables economic production in the long run, from what follows that further steps toward a comprehensive accounting will pay.

References

Costanza, R. and B. Hannon, 1989. Dealing with the "Mixed" Units Problem in Ecosystem Analysis. Wulff et al. (eds.) 1989. Network Analysis in Marine Ecology. Methods and Applications. Berlin: Springer, Ch. 5.

Finn, J., 1976. Measures of Ecosystem Structure and Function Derived from Analysis of Flows. J. theor. Biol. 56, 363-380.

Fruci, J., R. Costanza and S. Leibowitz, 1982. Quantifying the Interdependence Between Material and Energy Flows in Ecosystems. Third Int. Conf. on the State-of-the Art of Ecological Modelling, Colorado State University, Paper 241-250.

Georgescu-Roegen, N., 1971. The Entropy Law and the Economic Process. Cambridge, Mass.: Harvard UP.

Georgescu-Roegen, N., 1979. Energy Analysis and Economic Valuation. Southern Econ. J. 45, 1023-1058.

Georgescu-Roegen, N., 1981. Energy, Matter and Economic Valuation: Where Do We Stand? Daly, E., F. Alvaro and F. Umana (eds.), Energy, Economics, and the Environment. Boulder: Westview, 43-79.

Georgescu-Roegen, N., 1982. Energetic Dogma, Energetic Economics, and Viable Technologies. Advances in the Economics of Energy and Ressources. Greenwich, London: JAI Press. Vol. 4, 1-39.

Georgescu-Roegen, N., 1984. Feasible Recipes Versus Viable Technologies. Atl. Econ. J., 12, 20-31.

Hannon, B., 1973. The Structure of Ecosystems. J. theor. Biol., 535-546.

Hannon, B., 1979. Total Energy Cost in Ecosystems. J.theor. Biol., 80, 271-293.

Hannon, B., 1991. Accounting in Ecological Systems. Costanza, R. (ed.), Ecological Economics: The Science and Management of Sustainability. New York: Columbia UP, 234-252.

Patten, B., R. Bossermann, J. Finn and W. Cale, 1976. Propagation of Cause in Ecosystems. Patten, B. (ed.), Systems Analysis and Simulation in Ecology. New York: AP, 457-579.

Perrings, Ch., 1987. Economy and Environment. A Theoretical Essay on the Interdependence of Economic and Environmental Systems. Cambridge: CUP.

Richards, B.N., 1987. The Microbiology of Terrestrial Ecosystems. New York: Wiley.

Strassert, G., 1991. The metabolism of man as a production system. Unpublished paper.

Szymer, J., 1985. Measuring connectedness of input-output models:
1. Survey of the measures. Environment and Planning A. 17, 1591-1612.

Szymer, J., 1986. Measuring connectedness of input-output models:
2. Total Flow Concept. Environment and Planning A, 18, 107-121.

Szymer, J. and R. Ulanowicz, 1987. Total Flows in Ecosystems. Ecological Modelling, 35, 123-136.

Ulanowicz, R., 1983. Identifying the Structure of Cycling in Ecosystems. Math. Biosciences, 65, 219-237.

[8]

Mark T. Brown and Sergio Ulgiati

Emergy Evaluation of the Biosphere and Natural Capital

The measure of value called emergy is used to evaluate the flows of energy and resources that sustain the biosphere including the economy of humans. A donor system of value based on solar emergy required to produce things is suggested as the only means of reversing the logic trap inherent in economic valuation, which suggests that value stems only from utilization by humans. The stocks of natural capital and flows of environmental resources are evaluated in emergy and related to Global World Product. Several emergy indices are introduced as a means of evaluating sustainability of economies and processes. The total emergy flux of the biosphere is composed of 32% renewable flows of sunlight, tidal momentum and deep heat (it was 68% in 1950), and 68% slowly-renewable and nonrenewable flows. An index of environmental loading on the biosphere is shown to have increased about 4 times since 1950, while an index of global sustainability suggests that overall, sustainability of the global economy has precipitously declined.

INTRODUCTION

Geologic processes, atmospheric systems, ecosystems, and societies are interconnected through a series of infinitely different and changing relationships... each receiving energy and materials from the other, returning same, and acting through feedback mechanisms to self-organize the whole in a grand interplay of space, time, energy, and information. Processes of energy transformation throughout the biosphere build order, degrade energy in the process, and cycle information in a network of hierarchically organized systems of ever-increasing spatial and temporal scales.

Understanding the relationships between energy and the cycles of materials and information may provide insight into the complex interrelationships between society and the biosphere. Society uses environmental energies directly and indirectly from both renewable energy fluxes and from storages of materials and energies that resulted from past biosphere production. The actions of society, its use of resources and the load this resource use places on the biosphere are of great concern. Clearly it is imperative that perspective be gained concerning the interplay of society and environment to help direct planning and policy for the next millennium.

In this paper, emergy (1) is used to value flows of energy and materials, within the biosphere, including systems of humanity. When expressed in units of the same form of energy, systems of varying scales and organization can be compared and indices of performance can be calculated. Insight into the general behavior of systems may be gained through cross-scale comparison.

Flows of Energy Maintain Order

Systems of the biosphere are maintained by flows of energy that cycle materials and information. Without continual flows of input energy that build order, systems degrade away. It is through cycling that systems remain adaptive and vital. Materials or information sequestered in unreachable or unusable storages are of no value and often soon lose their importance or relevance.

Cycling allows for the continuous convergence and divergence of energy, materials and information. Processes of convergence build order, adding structure, reassembling materials, upgrading energy and creating new information. Processes of divergence disorder structure and disperse materials and information and allow concentrated energy to interact in amplifier actions with lower quality energies to maximize power flows.

The biosphere (Fig. 1) is driven by the flux of renewable energies in sunlight, tidal momentum, and deep earth heat. Human society draws energy directly from the environment, from short-term storages (from 10–1000 year turnover times) like wood, soils, and ground-water, and from long-term storages of fossil fuels and minerals. These energies and materials cycle through society's economy powering productive processes and building physical structure and storages of information. Feedback pathways exist throughout as do pathways of recycle, each diverging in reinforcement actions that carry materials and information back to sites of production and transformation.

In most systems, a significant portion of inflowing energy is degraded, with smaller amounts transformed into higher quality energies. Materials, on the other hand are mostly transformed and upgraded, only to recycle after their use, back through the environment. Information is created and recreated with each cycle in systems, driven by sources of energy and facilitated by material structure. In each cycle, through the process of convergence and divergence, information is validated for it is only through use that information can be maintained.

Environmental Resources and Natural Capital

Human society draws resources, and services from the environment. The resources are easily understood as things like fossil fuels, wood, water, fruit, animals, and so forth. Less easily understood and relatively difficult to quantify are environmental services such as waste assimilation, flood protection, or aesthetic qualities.

There is confusion in the literature concerning what is an environmental service, an environmental good, natural capital, or human released energy (2–5). The systems diagram in Figure 1 clarifies our meanings. Environmental services are represented by the flow labeled S from environmental systems to human society (6). The flows of environmental resources are labeled SR and N for Slowly Renewable and Nonrenewable, respectively. Renewability is a relative concept, since it depends on how quickly a material or energy is used compared to the speed at which it is generated. Wood, for instance, can be a renewable resource, if the rate of harvesting is matched with the regeneration rate. Fossil fuels and most mineral resources on the other hand are not renewable, even though they are being constantly regenerated, because their rate of use is much faster than the regeneration rate.

In this paper, we refer to energies as renewable or nonrenewable. Renewable energies to the biosphere are: sunlight (R_1), tidal energy (R_2), and deep earth heat (R_3). Renewable materials and energies used directly by society (renewable environmental resources) are those flows from storages of materials and energies that are used at rates slower than their generation rate (SR). Nonrenewable materials and energies used by society (nonrenewable environmental resources) are those flows from

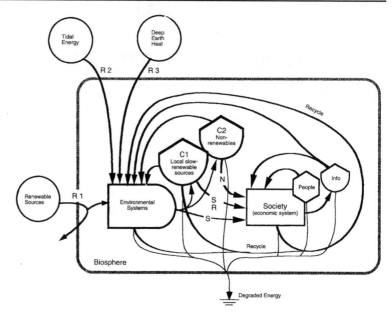

Figure 1. Systems diagram of the biosphere showing the inflow of renewable energies (R1, R2, and R3) environmental services (S), slow-renewable resource flows (SR), nonrenewable resource flows (N), the recycle of materials, and feed back of human energy and information. Info = information.

storages that are used at rates faster than their regeneration (N). We refer to them as "society released" materials and energies from storages of natural capital. The distinction between society released energy and environmental resources is difficult to make, since all flows used by humans are released by humans.

Natural capital is the storage of materials and energy from which environmental resources are drawn. In Figure 1, natural capital has been divided into two storages (C_1 and C_2). The first is the storage of plant biomass, soil organic matter, animals and water that is slowly renewable (C_1). The second is the storage of fossil fuels and minerals that are nonrenewable (C_2). We believe it important to maintain a difference between a storage as capital and a flow that is a flux of material or energy.

ENERGY AND EMERGY

Energy has been defined as the ability to do work, based on the physical principle that work requires energy input. Energy is measured in units of heat, or molecular motion... the degree of motion resulting in expansion and quantified in calories or joules (7).

Heat energy is a good measure of the ability to raise water temperature. However, it is not a good measure of more complex work processes. Processes outside of the window defined by heat engine technology, do not use energies that lend themselves to thermodynamic heat transfers. As a result, converting all energies of the biosphere to their heat equivalents reduces all work processes of the biosphere to heat engines. Human beings, then, become heat engines and the value of their services and information would be nothing more than a few thousand calories per day. Obviously, not all energies are the same and methods of analysis need reflect this fact.

Different forms of energy have different abilities to do work, and it is necessary to account for these different abilities if energies are to be evaluated correctly. A joule of sunlight is not the same as a joule of fossil fuel, or a joule of food, unless it is being used to power a steam engine. A system organized to use concentrated energies like fossil fuels cannot process a more dilute energy form like sunlight. Evaluation of energy sources is

system dependent. The processes of the biosphere are infinitely varied and are more than just thermodynamic heat engines. As a result, the use of heat measures of energy that can only recognize one aspect of energy, its ability to raise the temperature of things, cannot adequately quantify the work potential of energies used in more complex processes of the biosphere. As in thermodynamic systems where energies are converted to heat to express their relative values, in the larger biosphere system as a whole, energies should be converted to units that span this greater realm, accounting for multiple levels of system processes, ranging from the smallest scale to the largest scales of the biosphere, and accounting for processes other than heat engine technology.

Most valuation systems are based on utility, or what is received from an energy transformation process. Thus, fossil fuels are evaluated based on the heat that will be received when they are burned. Economic evaluation is based on the willingness to pay for perceived utility. An opposite view of value in the biosphere could be based on what is put into something rather than what is received. In other words, the more energy, time, and materials that are "invested" in something, the greater its value. This might be called a donor system of value, while heat evaluation, and economic valuation are receiver systems of value (8). A similar statement, i.e. that which is invested in something determines its value, is shared by Jørgensen (9), and recently by Svirezhev (10) using exergy accounting of ecosystems.

Emergy Basis of Value

A relatively new method of valuation, called Emergy Accounting (1) uses the thermodynamic basis of all forms of energy and materials, but converts them into equivalents of one form of energy, usually sunlight. Emergy is the amount of energy that is required to make something. It is the "memory of energy" (11) that was degraded in a transformation process. The units of emergy are emjoules, to distinguish them from joules. Most often emergy of fuels, materials, services etc. is expressed in solar emjoules (abbreviated sej). Emergy then, is a measure of the global processes required to produce something expressed in units of the same energy form. The more work done to produce something, that is the more energy transformed, the higher the emergy content of that which is produced.

To derive solar emergy of a resource or commodity, it is necessary to trace back through all the resources and energy that are used to produce it and express each in the amount of solar energy that went into their production. This has been done for a wide variety of resources and commodities and the renewable energies driving the biogeochemical process of the earth (12). When expressed as a ratio of the total emergy used to the energy of the product, a transformation coefficient results (called transformity whose dimensions are sej J^{-1}). As its name implies, the transformity can be used to "transform" a given energy into emergy, by multiplying the energy by the transformity. For convenience, in order not to have to calculate the emergy in resources and commodities every time a process is evaluated, previously calculated transformities are used.

There is no single transformity for most products, but a range. There is probably a lower limit, below which the product cannot be made, and there is some upper limit, although in theory, one could invest an infinite amount of fuel in a process and thus have an infinitely high transformity. Average transformities are used whenever the exact origin of a resource or commodity is not known or when not calculated separately. (Definitions of terms used in Emergy Accounting can be found in Appendix A).

Emergy measures value of both energy and material resources within a common framework. Transformities provide a quality factor as they account for convergence of biosphere processes required to produce something. Embodied in the emergy value are the services provided by the environment which are free and outside the monied economy. By accounting for quality and free environmental services, resources are not valued by their money cost or society's willingness to pay, which are often very misleading.

Emergy and Maximum Empower

Emergy accounting is a technique of quantitative analysis which determines the values of nonmonied and monied resources, services, and commodities in common units of the solar energy it took to make them (called solar emergy). The technique is based on the principles of energetics (13), system theory (14) and systems ecology (15). One of its fundamental organizing principles is the maximum empower principle (empower is emergy/time). Stated as simply as possible the maximum empower principle is as follows:

Maximum Empower Principle: Systems that self-organize to develop the most useful work with inflowing emergy sources, by reinforcing productive processes and overcoming limitations through system organization, will prevail in competition with others.

It is important that the term "useful" is used here. Useful work means using inflowing emergy in reinforcement actions that ensure and, if possible, increase inflowing emergy. Energy dissipation without useful contribution to increasing inflowing emergy is not reinforcing, and thus cannot compete with systems that use inflowing emergy in self-reinforcing ways. For example, drilling oil wells and then burning off the oil may use oil faster (in the short run) than refining and using it to run machines, but it will not compete, in the long run, with a system that uses oil to develop and run machines that increase drilling capacity and ultimately the rate at which oil can be supplied.

BALANCING HUMANITY AND NATURE

The biosphere is driven by renewable inputs of solar energy, tidal momentum, and deep heat each contributing to geologic, climatic, oceanic, and ecologic processes that are interconnected with flows of energy and materials and nonrenewable energies contained in vast storages that are exploited and released by society (Fig. 1). Within

Table 1. Flux of renewable and nonrenewable energies driving global processes, 1995.

Note	Source	Energy Flux (J yr^{-1})	Transformity* (sej J^{-1})	Solar Emergy Flux (E24 sej yr^{-1})	Emdollars# (E12 Em$)
	Global Renewable Energies				
1	Solar insolation	3.94 E24	1	3.94	3.57
2	Deep earth heat	6.72 E20	6055	4.07	3.69
3	Tidal energy	8.52 E19	16842	1.43	1.30
			Subtotal	9.44	8.56
	Society Released Energies (nonrenewables)				
4	Oil	1.38 E20	5.40 E04	7.45	6.75
5	Natural gas	7.89 E19	4.80 E04	3.79	3.43
6	Coal	1.09 E20	4.00 E04	4.36	3.95
7	Nuclear energy	8.60 E18	2.00 E05	1.72	1.56
8	Wood	5.86 E19	1.10 E04	0.64	0.58
9	Soils	1.38 E19	7.40 E04	1.02	0.93
10	Phosphate	4.77 E16	7.70 E06	0.37	0.33
11	Limestone	7.33 E16	1.62 E06	0.12	0.11
12	Metals	992.9 E12 g	1.0 E09 sej g^{-1}	0.99	0.90
			Subtotal	20.46	18.54
			TOTAL	29.91	27.10

* Transformities from Odum (1)
# Emdollars obtained by dividing Emergy in column 5 by 1.1 E12 sej $$^{-1} (Table 4).

1	Sunlight	Solar constant, 2 cal cm^{-2} min^{-1} 70% absorbed Earth cross section facing the sun = 1.278 E14 m^2 Energy Flux = (2 cal cm^2 min^{-1})(1.278 E18 cm^2) (5.256 E5 min yr^{-1})(4.186 J cal^{-1}) (0.7) = 3.936 E24 J yr^{-1}	(31)
2	Deep earth heat	Heat released by crustal radioactivity = 1.98 E20 J yr^{-1} Heat flowing up from the mantle = 4.74 E20 J yr^{-1} Energy Flux = 6.72 E 20 J yr^{-1}	(32) (32)
3	Tidal energy	Energy received by the earth = 2.7 E19 erg sec^{-1} Energy Flux = (2.7 E19 erg sec^{-1})(3.153 E7 sec yr^{-1}) / (1 E7 erg J^{-1}) = 8.513 E19 J yr^{-1}	(33)
4	Oil	Total production = 3.3 E9 Mt oil equivalent Energy Flux = (3.3 E9 t oil eq.) x (4.186 E10 J t^{-1} oil eq.) = 1.38 E20 J yr^{-1} oil equivalent	(34)
5	Natural gas	Total production = 2.093 E9 m^3 Energy Flux = (2.093 E12 m^3) x (3.77 E7 J m^3) = 7.89 E19 J yr^{-1}	(34)
6	Coal	Total production (soft) = 1.224 E9 t yr^{-1} Total production (hard) = 3.297 E9 t yr^{-1} Energy Flux = (1.224 E9 t yr^{-1})(13.9 E9J t^{-1}) + (3.297 E9 t yr^{-1})(27.9 E9 J t^{-1}) = 1.09 E20 J yr^{-1}	(34) (34)
7	Nuclear energy	Total production = 2.39 E12 kwh yr^{-1} Energy Flux = (2.39 E12 kwh yr^{-1})(3.6 E6 J kwh^{-1}) = 8.60 E18 J/yr elec. equivalent	(34)
8	Wood	Annual net forest area loss = 11.27E6 ha yr^{-1} Biomass = 40 kg m^2; 30% moisture Energy Flux = (11.27 E6 ha yr^{-1}) (1 E4 m^2 ha^{-1})(40 kg m^2) (1.3 E7 J kg^{-1})(0.7) = 5.86 E 19 J yr^{-1}	(18) (35)
9	Soil erosion	Total soil erosion = 6.1 E10 t yr^{-1} Assume soil loss estimate of 10 t ha^{-1} yr^{-1} and 6.1 E9 ha agricultural land = 6.1 E16 g yr^{-1} (assume 1.0% organic matter), 5.4 kcal g^{-1} Energy Flux = (6.1 E16 g) (.01) (5.4 kcal g^{-1})(4186 J kcal^{-1}) = 1.38 E19 J yr^{-1}	(16, 17)
10	Phosphate	– Total global production = 137 E6 t yr^{-1} Gibbs free energy phosphate rock = 3.48 E2 J g^{-1} Energy Flux = (137 E12 g) (3.48 E2 J g^{-1}) = 4.77 E16 J yr^{-1}	(36) (1; p125)
11	Limestone	– Total production = 120 E6 t yr^{-1} Gibbs free energy phosphate rock = 611 J g^{-1} Energy Flux = (120 E12 g) (6.11 E2 J g^{-1}) = 7.33 E16 J yr^{-1}	(36) (1; p47)
12	Metals	– Total global production of Al, Cu, Pb, Fe, Zn (1994) = 992.9 E6 t yr^{-1} = 992.9 E12 g yr^{-1}	(37)

the last several hundred years, the total inputs of energy released by society to the biosphere, from slowly renewable storages and nonrenewable storages, have grown to exceed the renewable ones. Table 1 lists the overall emergy values of the flows of emergy driving the biosphere, including those released by society. The energies released by society power machines and productive processes, creating structure and information that is fed back in autocatalytic pumping actions to increase power flows. Included in these flows are energies like wood and soils. Wood is sometimes considered a renewable energy input, however rates of deforestation and cutting exceed regrowth. The net loss of wood biomass is included in Table 1. Soil erosion has become a serious global problem. It is estimated that over 1/3 of all agricultural land is suffering erosional losses that threaten productive capacity (16, 17). Eroded soil is included as a slowly-renewable energy "released" by society, since it is lost to agricultural production in the future.

Total emergy driving the biosphere, including human society, in 1995 was 29.91 E24 sej, composed of 9.44 E24 sej from renewable inputs and 20.46 E24 sej from slowly- renewable and nonrenewable sources. Of the total emergy inputs to the global "economy", 68% are from slowly- and nonrenewable sources, while 32% are renewable. By far, the flows of nonrenewable fossil energies, including nuclear, dominate, comprising nearly 85% of the total released by society. Figure 2 is a graph of the changes in total global emergy flows since 1950, showing the steady yearly flux of renewable energies, and the increases in nonrenewables over the time period.

Emergy and the Global Economy

The global economy is driven by the interplay of both renewable and nonrenewable energy flows. Money circulating in the world economy is driven by emergy flows and can be related to emergy flux. By dividing the annual flux of emergy driving the world economy by the annual Gross World Product (GWP) a ratio of money circulating to emergy flux is calculated. GWP, measured in 1995 USD ($), for the years 1950, 1975, and 1995 was 4.9, 15.4, and 26.9 trillion dollars, respectively (18). Total emergy driving the world economy in those same years was 13.9 E24, 23.2 E24, and 29.9 E24 solar emjoules, respectively (Fig. 2). Thus, the emergy money ratio for those years was 2.8 E12 sej $^{-1}$, 1.5 E12 sej $^{-1}$, and 1.1 E12 sej $^{-1}$, respectively.

The ratio of emergy to money is, in essence, the fraction of total emergy required to circulate 1 dollar of GWP, with the assumption that the economy and biosphere are an integrated system. In 1995 the emergy per dollar ratio was 1.1 E12 sej $^{-1}$. This means that, on the average, 1.1 E12 sej were required inputs to the global economy for each dollar of GWP. The emergy per money ratio can be used to express emergy flows in equivalent monetary flows which we call emdollars (Em$). If a given emergy flow is divided by the emergy per money ratio the resulting quotient is emdollars, or the amount of GWP that results from the emergy flow (19). The emergy per money ratio can be calculated for any currency and for any transaction. For instance, we calculate emergy per money ratios for national economies and compare relative buying power (20), or for individual products and compare emergy advantage to the buyer (1), or for human services to evaluate emergy that supports service inputs to products and resources.

Figure 3 is a graph of the ratio of emergy to GWP (in constant 1995 USD) for the 45 years from 1950 to 1995. Using constant 1995 dollars reduces the effect of global inflation, yet there is still a declining trend in the emergy dollar ratio in Figure 3. The trend results from increasing participation of humans and their economies in the emergy flows of the biosphere. The decline in the emergy per dollar ratio of about 3% per year (equal to the growth of nonrenewable inputs to the global economy) represents a loss of buying power, since with each passing year, the amount of emergy that flows for each dollar of GWP is less. One might be tempted to suggest that a decline in emergy use per dollar of GWP means that the world economy is more efficient because less emergy is used for each dollar of GWP. On the other hand, we believe that it may mean that economic measures of inflation used to establish constant dollars, do not adequately account for inflation, and that a better measure might be the ratio of total emergy use to GWP (or in the case of a national economy, emergy use to GDP).

Emergy Values of Natural Capital

An emergy evaluation of global natural capital is summarized in Table 2. The natural capital accounted for in this paper is the main storages of resources within the global system. To some (3, 21, 22) the storages of "environmental re-

Figure 2. Emergy flows and Gross World Product (GWP) for the period 1950–1995, showing the increase in nonrenewable energy use and the constant renewable inflow. Estimated from energy data in Brown et al. (18) and calculated according to the methodology used in this paper.

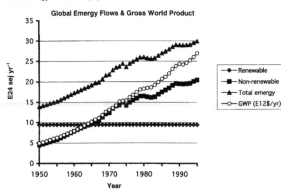

Figure 3. Global emergy dollar ratio for the period 1950–1995, showing the decline in purchasing power of money, even though the GWP has been corrected for constant 1995 dollars. Data from Figure 2.

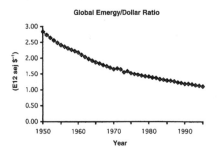

sources" (rows 1–4 in Table 2) are considered natural capital; storages that we consider slowly-renewable. We also consider the nonrenewable, fossil fuel resources, metals, and phosphorus as natural capital and these are given in the Table for comparison. Total emergy value of natural capital is 739.8 E25 sej, or about 6.85 quadrillion Em$. The largest storage of natural capital is freshwater that includes the polar ice caps (about 92%) groundwater (7.5%) and lakes, rivers, soil moisture, etc. (0.5%). Soil organic matter was the next largest storage of natural capital (2.1 quadrillion Em$). Plant biomass is valued at about Em$ 335 trillion, and animal biomass about Em$ 37 trillion. The storage of non renewables (based on estimated recoverable reserves as of 1996) is valued at about 1/4 that of the total storages or about Em$ 1.53 quadrillion. The storage of environmental resources (natural capital) from which environmental services are drawn is valued at about 600 times the flow. The storages of nonrenewable energies are about 360 times the present flows.

Emergy Based Indices of Sustainability

A definition of sustainability must include time. What is sustainable in one time period (during growth, for instance) may not be sustainable in the long run. The graph in Figure 4 illustrates different phases of growth and decline of a system. It could represent a human economy where there is growth, transition and decline of driving energy sources. Practices and processes that are characteristic during the growth phase may not be sustainable during transition or decline because they rely on nonrenewable energies that are diminishing. On the other hand practices that are sustainable during decline, because they have no reliance on nonrenewables, are probably not competitive with the dog-eat-dog competition that is characteristic of fast growing systems. Criteria for success in all systems (ecosystems with and without humans) during growth periods may be less based on efficiency and quality and more on speed. During times of transition and decline criteria for judging sustainability need to include several factors: *i)* the net yield of the process; *ii)* its environmental load, *iii)* its use of nonrenewables.

Several emergy indices have been defined and discussed elsewhere to illuminate these different aspects of sustainability (1, 20, 23–25). Using Figure 5 as a guide, several of these indices are defined as follows:

Percent Renewable (%Ren): The percent of the total energy driving a process that is derived from renewable sources (R/(R+SR+N)). In the long run, only processes with high %Ren are sustainable.
Emergy Yield Ratio (EYR): At the scale of the biosphere, the EYR is the ratio of the emergy of the output (Y = R + SR + N) divided by the emergy of nonrenewable inputs (N) that are used.
Environmental Loading Ratio (ELR): At the scale of the biosphere, it is the ratio of nonrenewable (N) and slowly-renewable emergy (SR) to renewable emergy (R) ((N + SR)/R). The ELR is an indicator of the load on the environment and might be considered a measure of stress due to economic activity.
Emergy Sustainability Index (ESI): An

index that accounts for yield, renewability, and environmental load. It is the incremental emergy yield compared to the environmental load and is calculated as the ratio of emergy yield to environmental load (EYR/ELR).

An Aggregate Measure of Yield and Sustainability

Maximum performance from human/biosphere interfaces and economic activities is facilitated when these processes yield net emergy and minimize their "load" on the environment. Load is used here as a general term to mean use or consumption, examples include use of land for agriculture, consumption of biological resources (wood), or waste assimilation by waterbodies. The greater the use of the environmental resources of an area the greater the load on the environment. If the load on the environment by human use is too great, reduced performance or even severe declines in function can occur (23).

The Emergy Sustainability Index (ESI) is a function of yield, renewability, and load on the environment (25). If a process has a negative net yield, by definition, it is not sustainable without continuing flows of invested emergy. At the same time, if a process depends entirely on nonrenewable resources, it is not sustainable; and finally, if a process places extreme load on the environment, it may cause damage that threatens long-term sustainability. Clearly an index that incorporates these aspects would shed light on sustainability issues and the fit of human economies with that of the biosphere.

Emergy Indices of Global, Regional, and Local Processes

Fitting the technological economy of humans to the global environmental self design is increasingly important as the flows of emergy released by humans dominate the global system. Ta-

Table 2. Global storages of natural capital, 1995.

Note	Name	Energy (joules)	Transformity* (E25 sej)	Emergy (E12 Em$, US)	Emdollars#
1	Fresh water	1.64 E23	1.82 E04	299.2	2770.4
2	Soil organic matter	3.10 E22	7.40 E04	229.4	2124.1
3	Plant biomass	4.16 E22	1.00 E04	41.6	385.2
4	Animal biomass	4.55 E19	1.00 E06	4.6	42.1
	Subtotal			574.8	5321.8
5	Coal	2.16 E22	4.00 E04	86.4	800.0
6	Crude oil	5.82 E21	5.40 E04	31.4	291.0
7	Natural Gas	5.28 E21	4.80 E04	25.3	234.7
8	Metals	1.74 E17g	1.0 E09 sej g⁻¹	17.4	161.1
9	Uranium	8.35 E20	1.79 E03	0.15	1.4
11	Phosphate rock	11.0 E15g	3.9 E09 sej g⁻¹	4.3	39.7
	Subtotal			165.0	1527.9
	TOTAL			739.8	6849.7

* Transformities from Odum (1).
# Emdollars obtained by dividing Emergy in column 5 by 1.10 E12 sej $⁻¹ (Table 3).

1	Fresh water	Total freshwater including ice caps = 33.28 E6 km³ Gibbs free energy of water = 4.94 E6 J m⁻³ Energy = (33.28 E15 m³)(4.94 E6 J m⁻³) = 1.644 E23 J	(38) (1; p. 295)
2	Soil organic matter	11.05 E9 ha woodland, crops, pasture, grassland Assume: 1 m deep, 1% organic content, 5.4 kcal g⁻¹ Energy = (9.32E13 m³) (1m) (1E6cm³ m³) (1.47g cm³) (.01org) (5.4kcal g⁻¹) (4186J kcal⁻¹) = 3.1 E22 J	(37)
3	Plant biomass	Total biomass = 1.841 E12 t dry wt. Energy = (1.841E12t) (1 E6g t⁻¹) (5.4 kcal g⁻¹) (4186 J kcal⁻¹) = 4.16 E22 J	(39)
4	Animal biomass	Total biomass = 2.013 E9 t dry wt. (1.015 E9 t on land, 0.998 E9 t in ocean) Energy = (2.013 E9t) (1E6g t⁻¹) (5.4 kcal g⁻¹) (4186 J kcal⁻¹) = 4.55 E19 J	(39)
5	Coal	Recoverable reserves = 5.19 E11 t coal eq. (hard coal) 5.12 E11 t coal eq (soft coal) Energy = (5.19 E11t) (27.9 E09 J t⁻¹) + (5.12 E09 J t⁻¹) = 2.16 E22 J	(34) (34)
6	Crude oil	Recoverable reserves = 1.39 E11 t oil Energy = (1.39 E11 t oil) x (4.186 E10 J t⁻¹ oil eq.) = 5.82 E21 J	(34)
7	Natural gas	Recoverable reserves = 1.4 E14 m³ Energy = (1.4 E14 m³) (37.7 E6 J m³) = 5.28 E21 J	(34)
8	Metals (Al,Cu,Pb,Fe,Zn)	Total recoverable reserves = 1.735 E11 t = 1.735 E17 g	(37)
9	Uranium	Recoverable reserve = 1.5 E6 t Energy = 1.5 E6t (1 E6 g t⁻¹) (0.007) (7.95 E10J g⁻¹) = 8.35 E20 J	(37)
10	Phosphate	Recoverable reserves = 11.0 E9 t = 11.0 E15 g	(36)

ble 3 summarizes the emergy indices for the biosphere in 1995, based on the data from Table 1. Figure 6 shows the change in these indices since 1950. The percent of total emergy flux in the biosphere that is renewable has declined from 68% in 1950 to 32% renewable today. The global ELR increased from 0.47 to 2.17, an increase in environmental stress of over 350%. Due to the simultaneous decline in the global emergy yield ratio, the global sustainability index has declined nearly 910% from 7.82 to 0.73.

Table 4 gives comparative indices for the globe and seven countries (Ecuador, Thailand, Chile, Mexico, USA, Italy, and Taiwan). Here, the Emergy Yield Ratio is more an index of "locally sustainable production", than a yield ratio. When the flows of the global or a national economy are used, the EYR divides total production by the emergy flux from nonrenewable resources and therefore expresses production per unit of nonrenewable investment.

The Emergy Sustainability index given in the last column of Table 4 is a measure of an economy's long-term global position relative to others. Low ESIs (USA, Taiwan, Italy) are indicative of economies that import a large fraction of their total emergy use and consume a relatively large percentage of total

emergy in the form of nonrenewable emergy. Sustainability of an economy is a function of renewable emergy flows, the extent to which it depends on imports, and its load on the local environment. While reliance on renewable resources and minimization of imports are important measures of sustainability, when they are combined with an index of environmental stress the aggregate measure, ESI, provides a multi-dimensional measure of long-term sustainability. The higher this index the more an economy relies on locally renewable energy sources *and* minimizes imports and environmental load. Sustainability can be measured at the global level, the regional or national level, or at the scale of individual economic activities (25).

EMERGY AND PUBLIC POLICY DECISION MAKING

The complex questions concerning the fit of humanity in the biosphere require that we look at things from a different perspective. Until very recently, the emergies released by humans were small, compared with the renewable driving emergy. Not so today. At the present time society releases about twice the emergy in slowly-renewable and nonrenewable resources than flows into the biosphere from renewable sources. Questions arise like: How best to fit humans and environment together? How do we develop an understanding of the workings of the biosphere with humans in it? How do we make decisions concerning the allocation and use of environmental services and natural capital? These are difficult questions and will require our concerted efforts. One thing is for sure, it cannot be done within a system paradigm that only recognizes/uses human-centered systems of valuation. When neoclassical economics is used to answer questions concerning fit, the answers inevitably are in favor of more development, greater use of resources, further exploitation of the environment. It may be time to question the reality created by humans that results from their utility theory of value.

Decisions at the scale of biosphere and society require a valu-

Table 3. Global emergy indices (1995).		
Name of Index	Definition (Fig. 4)	Index value[a]
Environmental Loading Ratio (ELR)	(SR + N)/R	2.17
Percent Renewable (%Renew)	R/(R + SR + N)	0.32
Emergy Yield Ratio (EYR)	(R + SR + N)/N	1.59
Sustainability Index (SI)	(EYR) / (ELR)	0.73
Emergy Dollar Ratio (E12 sej $[-1])	(R + SR + N)/ GWP[b]	1.10

a. Data from Table 1.
b. GWP = Gross World Product = 27.1 E12 $US (18)

Figure 4. Growth phases of an economic system showing early fast growth phase, a transition phase, and a phase of decline. Criteria for sustainability may differ depending on phase.

Figure 5. Simplified systems diagram of the biosphere showing the calculation of various emergy indices of sustainability.

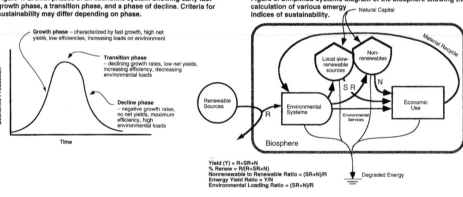

Figure 6. Graphs of the emergy indices of the biosphere for the years 1950, 1975, and 1995.

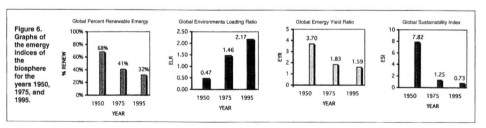

© Royal Swedish Academy of Sciences 1999
                                          http://www.ambio.kva.se

Table 4. Emergy Indices of national economies and the world economy (25).

Ref	Country	Total Emergy (sej yr⁻¹)	Renewable (R)	Emergy Flow (sej yr⁻¹) Slo-renewable (SR)	Nonrenewable (N)	%Renew[a]	Emergy Indices EYR[b]	ELR[c]	ESI[d]
1	Ecuador (1986)	9.64 E22	4.81 E22	4.21 E22	6.20 E21	50%	15.5	1.0	15.48
2	Thailand (1984)	1.52 E23	7.60 E22	2.70 E22	4.85 E22	50%	3.1	1.0	3.14
3	Chile (1994)	1.95 E23	6.81 E22	6.92 E22	5.78 E22	35%	3.4	1.9	1.81
4	Mexico (1989)	6.12 E23	1.39 E23	3.66 E23	1.08 E23	23%	5.7	3.4	1.66
5	WORLD (1995)	2.99 E25	9.44 E24	1.66 E24	1.88 E25	32%	1.6	2.2	0.73
6	USA (1983)	7.91 E24	8.24 E23	5.18 E24	1.90 E24	10%	4.2	8.6	0.48
7	Italy (1989)	1.27 E24	1.21 E23	3.57 E23	7.89 E23	10%	1.6	9.5	0.17
8	Taiwan (1990)	2.14 E23	2.13 E22	4.02 E22	1.52 E23	10%	1.4	9.0	0.16

Notes: a. Percent Renewable = R/(R+SR+N)
b. Emergy Yield Ratio = (R+SR+N)/N
c. Environmental Loading Ratio = (SR+N)/R
d. Sustainability Index = EYR/ELR

References: 1. (40), 2. (24), 3. (41), 4. (42), 5. This study, 6. (1), 7. (43), 8. (44).

ation system free of human bias. It is not surprising that development of resources, exploitation of global fisheries, and forests continues unimpeded when evaluated using economic value systems based on willingness-to-pay. The only things given value are those things that humans decide are valuable. The only values given things are human values. Neoclassical economic valuation cannot overcome the fact that its main underlying principle is that value is derived from utility and that utility is measured in human terms. Thus things must be useful to humans for them to have value. Recently, there has been much activity in the economic literature, especially in the "ecological economics" literature, concerning alternative methods of assigning economic values. Most of this activity is aimed at finding some way to "fix" economic theory to accommodate nonmarket goods. Unfortunately, economic values grounded in the neoclassical paradigm are based on human centered values, whether they be willingness-to-pay, contingency valuation, replacement cost measures, or other similar approaches (2, 3, 26–28). Money and the system of prices derived from economic theory have difficulty valuing environmental resources or natural capital correctly, and to make up markets or develop "pseudo-market based" measures by asking citizens what they are willing to pay, or what they are willing to accept, is not science, it is public opinion. Using "hedonic property price procedures" (3, 29) to value global ecosystems is tantamount to saying that because humans prefer to live on the southern coast of California, USA (based on property values), the marine ecosystems of southern California are more valuable to biosphere processes than other ecosystems where property values are lower. How is it possible that human preferences for a nice view and romantic sunsets has anything to do with ecological processes of the biosphere?

In another recent approach, Pimentel et. al. (5) have tried to evaluate total economic benefits of biodiversity in the USA and worldwide by pricing soil formation, waste disposal, pollination, ecotourism, and other items. The evaluation depends on prices derived from market values of equivalent services. For example, they value the environmental service of waste disposal (organic matter recycled by decomposers) based on the USD costs of collecting and disposing of organic wastes in USA cities. While they use biophysical data for their assessment of environmental services, the evaluation still relies indirectly on willingness-to-pay since economic price derived from market prices of equivalent services is a direct reflection of human value.

A biosphere perspective, one that seeks to balance humanity and environment, needs a valuation system free of human bias. We are not suggesting that humans are unimportant, instead we are saying that neoclassical economics (and its reliance on human utility values) has no place in the policy debates surrounding resource allocation and preservation of the biosphere. No amount of tinkering with the present economic paradigm can al-

**Box
Definitions**

Further discussion and definitions can be found in Odum (1); Brown and Ulgiati (25); Ulgiati et al. (23).

Energy: Sometimes referred to as the ability to do work. Energy is a property of all things which can be turned into heat and is measured in heat units (BTUs, calories, or joules).

Emdollar (or EM$): A measure of the money that circulates in an economy as the result of some process. In practice, to obtain the emdollar value of an emergy flow or storage, the emergy is multiplied by the ratio of total emergy to Gross National Product for the national economy.

Emergy: An expression of all the energy used in the work processes that generate a product or service in units of one type of energy. Solar emergy of a product is the emergy of the product expressed in equivalent solar energy required to generate it. Sometimes its convenient to think of emergy as energy memory.

Emjoule: The unit of measure of emergy, "emergy joule." It is expressed in the units of energy previously used to generate the product; for instance the solar emergy of wood is expressed as joules of solar energy that were required to produce the wood.

Nonrenewable Emergy: The emergy of energy and material storages like fossil fuels, mineral ores, and soils that are consumed at rates that far exceed the rates at which they are produced by geologic processes.

Production: Production measured in emergy is the sum of all emergy inputs to a process.

Renewable Emergy: The emergy of energy flows of the biosphere that are more or less constant and reoccurring, and that ultimately drive the biological and chemical processes of the earth and contribute to geologic processes.

Transformity: The ratio obtained by dividing the total emergy that was used in a process by the energy yielded by the process. Transformities have the dimensions of emergy/energy (sej J^{-1}). A transformity for a product is calculated by summing all of the emergy inflows to the process and dividing by the energy of the product. Transformities are used to convert energies of different forms to emergy of the same form.

© Royal Swedish Academy of Sciences 1999
http://www.ambio.kva.se

Ambio Vol. 28 No. 6, Sept. 1999

ter the logic trap of willingness-to-pay. Human preference cannot value ecological processes or environmental resources since these processes are outside the so called economic sphere.

Outlined in this paper is a method of valuation that is based on the principle that value is derived from what goes into something rather than on what one gets out of it. We have little difficulty in recognizing that the more effort we put into something, the more valuable it is. However, this is counter to the way most humans think about goods and services, and as a result difficult at first to accept. The question always arises, how can you say something has this or that value... what if it's not used... what if I don't want it... does it still have that value? Yes. Emergy is a biosphere value, it is the energy the biosphere invests in its goods and services (including the goods and services of society). The more that is invested, the greater the value (30).

The fact that humans now release more emergy than is inflowing from the renewable driving emergies, suggests that we, now more than ever, need to be good stewards of the biosphere. Our relationship to the biosphere changed in 1962 when the

emergy released by humans equaled and began to exceed the renewable driving emergies (Fig. 2). Our awareness began to shift as we began to see the effects of our numbers. Now as our nonrenewable energy supplies dwindle, our awareness must shift again. How do we live in a lower energy world? What is the economic paradigm that will help humanity to develop necessary symbiotic interfaces with the biosphere? We believe that it is not a human-centered valuing paradigm based on the flows of money, but is a biophysical paradigm, based on the flows of energy that drive and sustain all biosphere processes.

Emergy indicators show cause for alarm. Things are not getting better from a global perspective, they are getting worse. What is required is a concerted effort to understand society's place in the biosphere. Important to this undertaking are methods of analysis that produce synthesis and comprehension of wholeness. The biosphere is one system, that includes humans. We should use methods for quantification and valuing that recognize the whole, not just one end of the hierarchy, the human end. It may be time for a paradigm shift.

References and Notes

1. Odum, H.T. 1996. Environmental accounting. *Emergy and Environmental Decision Making.* John Wiley & Sons, NY.
2. Costanza, R., Cumberland, J., Daly, H., Goodland, R. and Norgaard, R. 1997. *An Introduction to Ecological Economics.* St. Lucie Press, Boca Raton, FL. 275 pp.
3. Costanza, R., d'Arge, R., de Groot, R., Farber, S., Grasso, M., Hannon, B., Limburg, K., Naeem, S., O'Neill, R., Paruelo, J., Raskin, R.G., Sutton, P. and van den Belt, M. 1997. The value of the world's ecosystem services and natural capital. *Nature* 387, 253–260.
4. Daily, G. (ed.). 1997. *Natures Services: Societal Dependence on Natural Ecosystems.* Island Press, Washington DC.
5. Pimenel, D., Wilson, C., McCullum, C., Huang, R., Dwen, P., Flack, J., Tran, Q., Saltman, T. and Cliff, B. 1997. Economic and environmental benefits of biodiversity. *BioScience* 47, 747–757.
6. Evaluated in this paper are the flows of environmental resources; we leave the more complex issues surrounding environmental services to a subsequent paper.
7. All energies can be converted to heat at 100% efficiency, thus it is relatively easy and accurate to express energies in their heat equivalents. The basic units of energy are the amount of heat required to raise a given amount of water a given number of degrees of temperature. Thus the calorie is the amount of heat required to raise 1 cm³ distilled water from 14.5°C to 15.5°C at the atmospheric pressure. A joule is equal to 4.187 calories.
8. While it might be argued that economics is an intersection of donor and receiver systems of value because price often reflects the costs of production (i.e what has gone into something) as well as willingness-to-pay, it remains that the purchase of a good or service is only consummated if the purchaser believes that he/she will receive value worthy of the price.
9. Jørgensen, S.E. 1992. *Integration of Ecosystem Theories: A Pattern.* Kluwer Acad. Publ., Dordrecht, Boston, 383 pp.
10. Svirezhev, Y. 1997. Exergy of the biosphere. *Ecol. Model.* 96, 309–310.
11. Scienceman, D. 1987. Energy and emergy. In: *Environmental Economics—The Analysis of a Major Interface.* Pillet, G. and Murota, T. (eds). Roland, Leimgruber, Geneva, Switzerland, pp. 257–276.
12. The solar emergy equivalent of tidal energy and deep heat were calculated based on analogous processes driven by sunlight that achieve the same result. While it is beyond the scope of the present paper, a complete discussion of assumptions and derivation of transformities for tidal energy and deep heat can be found in Odum, (1).
13. Lotka, A. J. 1922. Contribution to the energetics of evolution. *Proc. Nat. Acad. Sci. US* 8, 147–150.
14. von Bertalanffy. L. 1968. *General System Theory.* George Braziller Publ., New York, 295 pp.
15. Odum, H.T. 1994. *Ecological and General Systems: An Introduction to Systems Ecology.* Univ. Press of Colorado, Niwot, 644 pp.
16. Oldeman, L.R. 1994. The global extent of soil degradation. In: *Soil Resilience and Sustainable Land Use.* Greenland, D.J. and Szabolcs, I. (eds). CAB International, Wallington, UK, 561 pp.
17. Mannion, A.M. 1995. *Agriculture and Environmental Change: Temporal and Spatial Dimensions.* John Wiley & Sons, New York, 405 pp.
18. Brown, L.R., Renner, M. and Flavin, C. 1997. *Vital Signs 1997: The Environmental Trends that are Shaping Our Future.* W.W. Norton & Company, New York, 165 pp.
19. The emdollar value should not be considered an emergy based price for resources or services. Measuring natural capital and environmental resources in emdollars doesn't mean that these emdollars can buy them, as no markets exist for these items. Emergy drives the money flows, so emdollars actually express the amount of economic activity that can be supported by a given emergy flow or storage.
20. Brown, M.T., Odum, H.T., Murphy, R.C., Christianson, R.A., Doherty, S.J., McClanahan, T.R. and Tennenbaum, S.E. 1995. Rediscovery of the world: Developing an interface of ecology and economics. In: *Maximum Power: The Ideas and Applications of H.T. Odum.* CAS Hall (ed.). University of Co. Press, pp. 216–250.
21. Jansson, A.M., Hammer, M., Folke, C. and Costanza, R. (eds). 1994. *Investing in Natural Capital: The Ecological Economics Approach to Sustainability.* Island Press, Washington, DC.
22. Costanza, R. and Daly, H.E. 1992. Natural capital and sustainable development. *Conserv. Biol.* 6, 37–46.
23. Ulgiati, S., Brown, M.T., Bastianoni, S. and Marchettini, N. 1995. Emergy based indices and ratios to evaluate sustainable use of resources. *Ecol. Eng.* 5, 497–517.
24. Brown, M.T. and McClanahan, T. 1996. Emergy analysis perspectives of Thailand and Mekong River dam proposals. *Ecol. Model.* 91, 105–130.
25. Brown, M.T. and Ulgiati, S. 1997. Emergy based indices and ratios to evaluate sustainability: monitoring economies and technology toward environmentally sound innovation. *Ecol. Eng.* 9,51–69.
26. Pearce, D.W. and Turner, R.K. 1991. *Economics of Natural Resources and the Environment.* John Hopkins Univ. Press, Baltimore, 378 pp.
27. Cobb, C. and Cobb, J. 1994. *The Green National Product: A Proposed Index of Sustainable Economic Welfare.* University Press of America, New York.

28. Dixon, J.A. and Sherman, P.B. 1990. *Economics of Protected Areas.* Island Press, Washington DC, 234 pp.
29. Pearce, D. 1998. Auditing the Earth. *Environment* 40, 23–28.
30. Implicit in this statement is that processes are operating under the constraints of thermodynamics and the maximum empower principle which essentially suggests that processes which squander resources and do not feedback to improve the larger system performance, will not prevail in the long run. Humans may find themselves in such a precarious position if greater attention to the larger system is not forth coming in the near future.
31. Von der Haar, T.H. and Suomi V.E. 1969. Satellite observations of the earth's radiation budget. *Science* 169, 657–669.
32. Sclater, J.F., Taupart, G. and Galson, I.D. 1980. The heat flow through the oceanic and continental crust and the heat loss of the earth. *Rev. Geophys Space Phys.* 18, 269–311.
33. Munk, W.H. and McDonald, G.F. 1960. *The Rotation of the Earth: A Geophysical Discussion.* Cambridge Univ. Press, London, 323 pp.
34. British Petroleum, 1997. *BP Statistical Review of World Energy, 1997.* The British Petroleum Company, London, 41 pp.
35. Lieth, H. and Whittaker, R.H. 1975. *Primary Productivity of the Biosphere.* Springer-Verlag, New York, 339 pp.
36. USDI. 1996. *Mineral Commodity Summaries, January 1997.* US Department of Interior, Washington, DC.
37. World Resources Institute. 1996. *World Resources 1996–97.* Oxford University Press, New York.
38. Wetzel, R.G. 1975. *Limnology.* W.B. Saunders Co., Philadelphia, 741 pp.
39. Whittaker, R.H. and Likens, G.E. 1975. The biosphere and man. In: *Primary Productivity of the Biosphere.* Whittaker, R.H. and Lieth, H. (eds). Springer-Verlag, New York, pp. 305–329.
40. Odum, H.T. and Arding, J.E. 1991. *Emergy Analysis of Shrimp Mariculture in Ecuador.* Working Paper. Report to the Coastal Resources Center, University of Rhode Island, Narragansett, RI. Department of Environmental Engineering Sciences and Center for Wetlands, University of Florida, USA. 114 pp.
41. Brown, M.T. 1997. *Emergy Evaluation of Chile and Perspectives for Sustainable Development.* Working paper #97-014. Center for Wetlands, University of Florida, Gainesville, FL.
42. Brown, M.T., Green,P., Gonzalez, A. and Venegas, J. 1992. Emergy analysis perspectives, public policy options, and development guidelines for the coastal zone of Nayarit, Mexico. Volume 2: Emergy analysis and public policy options. *Final Report to the Government of Nayarit, Mexico.* Center for Wetlands and Water Resources, University of Florida, Gainesville, FL, USA. 217 pp.
43. Ulgiati, S., Odum, H.T. and Bastianoni, S. 1994. Emergy use, environmental loading and sustainability: an emergy analysis of Italy. *Ecol. Model.* 73, 215–268.
44. Huang, S.-L. and Odum, T.-H. 1992. The evolution and prospects of Taiwan's ecological economic system. Proceedings: *The Second Summer Institute of the Pacific Regional Science Conference Organization.* Chinese Regional Science Assoc. Taipei, Taiwan, RoC.
45. The material for this evaluation of biosphere services and natural capital was presented at a symposium held at the University of Geneva titled The co-action between living systems and the planet in September 1997. *The Co-Action between Living Systems and the Planet.* Greppin, H., Penel, C. and Degli Agosti, R. 1998 (eds). Printed by Rochat-Baumann, Imprimerie Nationale, Geneve.
46. First submitted 22 January 1998. Accepted for publication after revision 9 June 1999.

Mark Brown is assistant professor in the Department of Environmental Engineering Sciences and Associate Director of the Center for Wetlands, University of Florida. His address: Department of Environmental Engineering Sciences, PO Box 116450, University of Florida, Gainesville, FL 32611, USA.
E-mail: MTB@ufl.edu

Sergio Ulgiati is professor of environmental physical chemistry in the Department of Chemistry, University of Siena. His address: Dipartimento di Chimica, Universita' di Siena, Pian dei Mantellini 44, 53100 Siena, Italy.
E-mail: ulgiati@unisi.it

Part III
Greening the National Accounts

[9]

INTEGRATED ENVIRONMENTAL AND ECONOMIC ACCOUNTING: FRAMEWORK FOR A SNA SATELLITE SYSTEM

BY PETER BARTELMUS

United Nations Statistical Office

CARSTEN STAHMER

Federal Statistical Office, Germany

AND

JAN VAN TONGEREN

United Nations Statistical Office

National accounts have provided the most widely used indicators for the assessment of economic performance, trends of economic growth and of the economic counterpart of social welfare. However, two major drawbacks of national accounting have raised doubts about the usefulness of national accounts data for the measurement of long-term sustainable economic growth and socio-economic development. These drawbacks are the neglect of (a) scarcities of natural resources which threaten the sustained productivity of the economy and (b) the degradation of environmental quality from pollution and its effects on human health and welfare. In the present paper, the authors attempt to reflect environmental concerns in an accounting framework which maintains as far as possible SNA concepts and principles. To this end, the accounting framework is used to develop a "SNA Satellite System for Integrated Environmental and Economic Accounting" (SEEA). Environmental costs of economic activities, natural asset accounts and expenditures for environmental protection and enhancement, are presented in flow accounts and balance sheets in a consistent manner, i.e. maintaining the accounting identities of SNA. Such accounting permits the definition and compilation of modified indicators of income and expenditure, product, capital and value added, allowing for the depletion of natural resources, the degradation of environmental quality and social response to these effects. A desk study of a selected country is used to clarify the proposed approaches, to demonstrate their application in future country studies and to illustrate the quantitative effects of the use of modified concepts on the results of analysis.

1. INTRODUCTION

The discussion of environmentally sound and sustainable socio-economic development has received increased attention by the international community, stimulated in particular by the report of the World Commission on Environment and Development (1987). At its forty-second session, the General Assembly welcomed the Commission's report (resolution 42/187) and adopted an "Environmental Perspective to the Year 2000 and Beyond" which proclaimed "as the overall aspirational goal for the world community the achievement of sustainable development on the basis of prudent management of available global resources and environmental capacities" (resolution 42/186). Environmentally sound and

Note: The authors thank Hubert Donnevert and Stefan Schweinfest for their assistance on the present version. The views expressed by the authors are their own and not necessarily those of their respective institutions.

111

sustainable development will also provide the basic theme for the planned United Nations Conference on Environment and Development in 1992.

The need for clarifying this new development concept and for developing methodologies for its assessment and implementation has been recurrently stressed in international conferences, seminars and workshops. Joint workshops, organized by UNEP and the World Bank, examined the feasibility of physical and monetary accounting in the areas of natural resources and the environment and developed alternative macro-indicators of ecologically adjusted and sustainable income and product (Ahmad, El Serafy and Lutz, 1989). A consensus emerged in the workshops that enough progress had been achieved to link environmental accounting to the standard System of National Accounts, the SNA (United Nations, 1968), and to include certain aspects of environmental accounting in the ongoing revision of SNA.

National accountants and environmentalists reviewed a first draft of the present paper in a UNEP/World Bank-sponsored expert meeting (Paris, November 21-22, 1988). The experts at the meeting endorsed the idea of developing a satellite system of environmental accounts and discussed a variety of methodological and procedural questions. These questions should be resolved before preparing an internationally recommended manual of environmental accounting. The experts also requested that the revised SNA should elaborate on the approaches to incorporating environmental concerns in national accounts.

The immediate objective of the present framework is to serve as the basis for the preparation of a "SNA Handbook on Integrated Environmental and Economic Accounting" to be issued within the United Nations series of national accounting handbooks. The framework should also facilitate the consideration of environmental accounting in the revised SNA, possibly as part of a more general treatment of the concept of satellite accounts and with appropriate cross-referencing to the Handbook. The draft methodologies have been tested in pilot country studies, and will be distributed widely for comments and contributions.

The framework discussed in this paper is the basic structure for a "Satellite System for Integrated Environmental and Economic Accounting" (SEEA). It is presented in tabular form with an illustrative set of data and is described in some detail in the text. In section 2 the main objectives of environmental accounting as well as the general structure of the SEEA are described. Section 3 contains a description of the supply side of goods and services, focusing on environmental protection services and the supply of natural growth products. The accounting for the costs of environmental depletion and degradation, resulting from production and consumption, is the main issue of section 4. In this section, the authors also explain how these costs affect value added and final demand. One basic indicator, the Environmentally Adjusted Net Domestic Product or "Eco Domestic Product" (EDP) is presented in this context. In section 5 the flow accounts of sections 3 and 4 are complemented by the presentation of stock assets of tangible wealth that include natural assets and changes therein. In section 6 the possible extensions of the flow accounts to obtain welfare-oriented macro-indicators are discussed. Finally, some comparative analyses of the conventional and environmentally modified concepts are presented in section 7.

112

2. General Features of a Satellite System for Integrated Environmental and Economic Accounting (SEEA)

(a) *Objectives of Integrated Environmental and Economic Accounting*

The focus of traditional systems of national accounts on market and some related non-market transactions (except for imputations for "directly competitive" non-market production of goods and services) has effectively excluded the accounting for changes in the quality of the natural environment and the depletion of natural resources. These effects have been considered to be particularly relevant for the assessment of long-term sustained growth and development and of increases in "social welfare." The overall objective of environmental accounting is thus to measure more accurately the structure, level and trends of socio-economic performance for purposes of environmentally sound and sustainable development planning and policies. The attainment of this objective would facilitate both the systematic compilation and analysis of environmental and related socio-economic data and the formulation of alternative standard macro-economic variables for the analysis of environmental-economic interrelationships.

The current revision of the SNA (United Nations, 1990) presents a unique opportunity to examine how the various concepts, definitions, classifications and tabulations of environmental and natural resource accounting can be linked to or incorporated in the SEEA. It may appear premature, however, to radically change a well-established system of economic accounts that serves many different short-, medium-, and long-term socio-economic analyses. Further elaboration of the standards of environmental and natural resource accounting in a *SNA satellite system* of environmental accounts has therefore been proposed (Bartelmus, 1987). A similar view was expressed by the experts working on the current revision of the SNA (Lutz and El Serafy, 1989).

Satellite systems of national accounts generally stress the need to expand the analytic capacity of national accounting for selected areas of social concern in a flexible manner, without overburdening or disrupting the "core" system (Lemaire, 1987; Teillet, 1988; Schäfer and Stahmer, 1990). Typically, satellite accounts allow for the:

— provision of additional information on particular social concerns of a functional or cross-sectoral nature,
— linkage of physical data sources and analysis to the monetary accounting system,
— extended coverage of costs and benefits of human activities, and
— further analysis of data by means of relevant indicators and aggregates.

Accordingly, the following specific objectives can be formulated for the planned SEEA:

(i) Segregation and Elaboration of All Environment-Related Flows and Stocks of Assets of Traditional Accounts

Satellite accounts, in the narrow sense of detailed accounting for expenditures and revenues in major areas of social concern, were pioneered by France (Institute National, 1986a). There is now an increased interest in segregating all flows and stocks of assets in national accounts related to environmental issues and, in particular, in estimating the total expenditure for the protection or enhancement of the different fields of environment. One objective of this segregation is the identification of the increasing part of the Gross Domestic Product (GDP) which reflects the costs necessary to compensate the negative impacts of economic growth ("defensive expenditures") rather than increases in "true" (welfare-relevant) income (Hueting, Leipert, 1987; Leipert, 1989; and Olson, 1977).

(ii) Linkage of Physical Resource Accounting with Monetary Environmental Accounting and Balance Sheets

Physical resource accounts aim at covering comprehensively the total stock or reserves of natural resources and changes therein, even if these resources are not (yet) affected by the economic system.[1] The proposed accounting for these resources is considered the "hinge" by which comprehensive physical resource accounts could be linked to the monetary balance sheet and flow accounts. Another important method for analyzing the environmental-economic interrelationship in physical terms is the development of material/energy balances (Ayres, Kneese, 1969; Ayres, 1978; United Nations, 1976). This approach allows in particular the linkage of input-output tables with data on natural resource inputs, the description of the transformation of natural resources in the production process and the assessment of the generation of residuals of the economic activities (Isard, 1969; Leontief, 1973). Systems of environmental statistics such as those proposed by the United Nations (in preparation) should facilitate achieving compatibility between physical and monetary accounts by specifying those parameters that could be valued in monetary terms to obtain the figures required in environmental accounts. Non-monetary data in physical accounts are considered to be an integral part of the SEEA and will be fully elaborated in the Handbook on Integrated Environmental and Economic Accounting. However, the present framework will concentrate on the monetary stocks and flows of an environmental accounting system.

(iii) Assessment of Environmental Costs and Benefits

In contrast to the above-mentioned "narrow" satellite accounts, a broader framework for satellite accounting, covering additional "external" environmental costs and benefits, is proposed here. Taking the current state of knowledge and data availability into account, this framework focuses on expanding and complementing the SNA, with regard to two major issues, namely

—the use (depletion) of natural resources in production and final demand and
—the changes in environmental quality resulting from pollution and other impacts of production, consumption and natural events on one hand and environmental protection and enhancement on the other.

Possibilities of extending the framework for the analysis of environmental welfare effects, i.e. the "damage costs" of human health impairment, recreation and other aesthetic or ethical values, are also indicated.

---

[1]See e.g. the Norwegian approach to natural resource accounting (Alfsen, Bye and Lorentsen, 1987) or the more complex (including interactions in the biophysical environment) French "natural patrimony" accounts (Institute National, 1986).

(iv) Accounting for the Maintenance of Tangible Wealth

The recent discussion of the new paradigm of sustainable development stressed the need to fully account for the use of both man-made and "natural" capital in order to alert to possible non-sustainable growth and development scenarios. The proposed framework aims at extending the concept of capital to cover not only man-made capital, but also natural capital. Accordingly, SEEA will include additional costs for the depletion and degradation of these natural assets. It will also extend the concept of capital formation to capital accumulation which reflects additionally the deterioration of natural capital as a result of economic uses.

(v) Elaboration and Measurement of Indicators of Environmentally Adjusted Income and Product

The consideration of the depletion of natural resources and changes in environmental quality permits the calculation of modified macro-economic aggregates, notably the Environmentally Adjusted Net Domestic Product, short: Eco Domestic Product (EDP).

All these objectives can only be realized step by step. Initial emphasis in practical work should be on the improvement of physical environmental data and on linking them with national accounts as a prerequisite for the valuation of environmental effects.

(b) *Scope and Structure of the SEEA*

The proposed SEEA follows as far as possible the principles and rules established in the SNA (United Nations 1968, 1977, 1990). It is based on SNA's production boundary, follows its analysis of costs and outputs and incorporates the same accounting identities between supply and use of products and between value added and final demand. Information needed for environmental analysis is presented separately. In this manner, original (unadjusted) SNA data can be directly compared with environmentally adjusted statistics and indicators, facilitating the linkage with the central framework of the SNA. Such compliance and linkage with SNA aims at better integration of environmental variables into established economic analysis.

The very nature of a framework allows only the most important concepts and accounting procedures to be highlighted. Definitions, classifications, valuation principles, data sources and processing will be further elaborated on in the Handbook on Integrated Environmental and Economic Accounting. The Handbook will benefit from the experience gained in country studies and existing expertise at the national and international levels.

The present framework seeks to be flexible regarding alternative approaches to integrated environmental-economic accounting and analysis. The interrelationship between the environment and the economy is described as complete as possible. However, in line with the production boundary of SNA, phenomena that take place wholly within the environment, i.e. outside the economic system, are excluded. Such phenomena are probably better accounted for by the use of complementary biophysical resource accounts and systems of environment statistics and monitoring. Also, welfare effects from environmental quality degradation that affect "human capital," i.e. human health and welfare, are not accounted for in the present framework. However, as shown below (see section 6), a "window" to the analysis of environmental damage related to human welfare has been opened, facilitating further extension or alteration of the framework for such analysis.

The main emphasis of the proposed scheme is on the implications of the environment for production, value added, final and intermediate demand and tangible wealth. Therefore, the framework does not present complete accounts for all institutional sectors. Transactions related to income distribution and those concerning intangible assets, including exploitation rights, and also financial assets are excluded. A complete analysis of the interrelationships between the economy and the environment will call for an extended system of all institutional accounts, which shows not only the flows of goods and services, but also of income and finance.

In Table 1 the general structure of the system which consists of three basic components is illustrated. In Tables 1.1 and 1.2 the supply and use of goods and services is shown. The asset accounts with opening and closing assets and the items linking them are shown in Table 1.3. Tables 1.2 and 1.3 are connected via the accounts of capital accumulation. The component tables are further elaborated on in Tables 2, 3 and 5 as explained in sections 3 to 5.

The supply Table 1.1 contains an additional row which shows the involuntary "imports" of residuals (wastes etc.) of foreign economic activities which were transported to the domestic economy (-1.6). The use/value added Table 1.2 is extended by row as well as by column. In the table, we show not only the traditional GDP and NDP, but also further corrections due to the use of natural assets (depletion of natural resources, degradation of natural assets by residuals, agricultural and recreational use etc.). This use is valued with the costs which would have been necessary to keep the natural capital intact (ecological valuation; see below section 4c for an alternative approach in the case of "exhaustible" resources). These costs are interpreted as the decrease in value of the natural assets comparable to the consumption of man-made fixed assets. The deterioration of the natural assets could be caused by current production activities (59.8), consumption activities (household consumption 17.1) or by (scraps of) produced assets (5.1). The restoration activities of the government diminish the impacts of the economic activities on the natural assets (-5.0). The use of natural assets could affect the domestic nature (loss of ecological functions of the produced biological assets -0.9, natural non-produced assets -73.0) or—as far as the generation of residuals is concerned—could lead to transportation to the rest of the world (exports: -4.7). The value of the deterioration of the domestic as well as foreign natural assets caused by domestic sources ($59.8 + 22.2 = 82.0$) is used for estimating the environmentally adjusted Net Domestic Product (NDP), called Eco Domestic Product (EDP) (185.1) (see section 4c below).

The asset accounts (Table 1.3) show the produced assets (including cultivated biological assets) and the non-produced assets which contain only natural assets (wild biota, land, subsoil assets, water and air). Market valuation is applied except for the depletion and degradation values of natural assets shown in the

116

use/value added table (Table 1.2). These volume changes are valued with the (hypothetical) costs for maintaining them on the same overall quantity and quality level during the reporting period. The question of how such values could be integrated into the asset balances containing mainly market values is discussed in section 5.

3. Supply of Goods and Services

The supply table (Table 2) includes two elements: gross output, resulting from domestic production, and imports. Gross output is cross-classified by industries and type of product (good or service). Imports are classified by the same type of product as domestic gross output, so that the two elements of supply can be added together to obtain total supply by product. Furthermore, the involuntary "imports" of residuals of foreign economic activities are shown. This item could contain e.g. the unaccepted dumping of foreign wastes in national territories.

In Table 2 we show a breakdown of domestic production activities by environmental protection activities and other industries. The fully elaborated system will display a further breakdown by industries according to the International Standard Industrial Classification of all Economic Activities (ISIC) (United Nations, 1990a).

A major modification of the SNA is the separate identification of *environmental protection services* from other production activities for all industries. The separation is to facilitate the assessment of the importance of environmental activities in gross output, employment, other production costs, and in capital consumption. Environmental protection services comprise in principle all activities to maintain and enhance the quality of the natural assets. This could be achieved by avoiding environmental impacts of the economic activities (e.g. by using integrated or end-of-pipe technologies) or by restoring the natural environment already degraded or depleted. Environmental protection activities can be produced for third parties (external use) as main or secondary production activities of the establishments (36.2) or they can be used internally. The internal provision of environmental protection services is considered to be an "ancillary" activity which is not shown as separate output of the respective establishments in Table 2. The cost value of ancillary services is identified separately, however, in Table 3 as the total of intermediate consumption (17.9), consumption of fixed capital (4.8), compensation of employees (8.7) and net indirect taxes (0.3). These costs are balanced by a negative operating surplus (−31.7). It is not proposed to "externalize" the internal environmental protection activities within the SEEA in order to maintain close linkage with the SNA. For more comprehensive analyses of environmental expenditures and operations, ancillary activities could be externalized in supplementary tables.

The supply of products is disaggregated in Table 2 according to the three categories of natural growth products, external environmental protection services and other products only. A further breakdown of these categories needs to be developed, as far as possible in terms of the Central Product Classification (CPC) (United Nations, in prep.).

117

TABLE 1

SYSTEM FOR INTEGRATED ENVIRONMENTAL AND ECONOMIC ACCOUNTING (SEEA)

(Summary presentation)

Use/Value added (Table 1.2)	Total	Domestic Production (Industries)	Final Consumption Households	Final Consumption Government	Tangible assets (Table 1.3) Produced Except Natural	Produced Natural (biota)	Non-Produced Natural Assets	Rest of the World Exports/Imports	Flow of Residuals
Opening Stocks (Market Valuation)					991.3	83.1	1744.4		
						+(plus)			
Capital Accumulation					Produced Assets Except Natural 68.0	1.4	7.3	73.7	
Use of products Gross Domestic Product (GDP)	591.9	224.0 293.4	175.0	42.5					

Consumption of fixed capital	26.3							
Net Domestic Product (NDP)	267.1							
Use of natural assets (ecological valuation)	59.8	−1.6	17.1	−5.0	−23.0	−3.3	−73.0	−4.7
Environmental adjustment of final demand	22.2		−17.1		5.1	−0.9		
Environmentally Adjusted Net Domestic Product (EDP)	185.1				−5.1			

+(plus)

Supply/Origin (Table 1.1)			
Supply of products	591.9	517.4	
Origin of residuals	−1.6		74.5	−1.6

+(plus)

Adjustment of natural assets accumulation to market valuation			
Other volume changes (market valuation)	−25.3	0.9	81.2
Revaluation due to market price changes	138.1	12.6	22.8	382.8

=(equals)

Closing Stocks (Market Valuation)	1149.1	93.8	2165.5

119

TABLE 2
SUPPLY/ORIGIN

| | Total | Domestic Production (industries) | | | Imports | |
| | | Other industries | | | | |
		External Environmental Protection Activities	Internal Environmental Protection Activities	Other Activities	Products	Residuals
(1) Supply of products (goods and services)	591.9	36.2		481.2	74.5	
(1.1) Natural growth products	40.7			38.2	2.5	
(1.2) External env. prot. services	36.2	36.2			72.0	
(1.3) Other products	515.0			443.0		
(2) Origin of residuals	−1.6					−1.6
Σ Total supply [(1)+(2)]	590.3	36.2		481.2	74.5	−1.6

Natural growth products of agriculture, forestry and fishing (40.7) refer to those growth-based outputs that are controlled by human activities and can thus be considered as part of planned economic production. Natural growth in these products is treated as primary production which increases the stocks or fixed assets by the amount of growth taking place during the accounting period. On the other hand, those primary natural growth-based products that are largely harvested from the non-controlled natural environment (without human interference in the growth process, such as hunting, gathering of wild fruits, deep-sea fishing or the exploitation of tropical forests) are considered as either "free" inputs or, in case of "scarcities," as environmental depletion costs (see below, section 4) of the agriculture, forestry and fishing sectors. For example, in the case of free supply of fish to the fishing industry, the sector's output would not consist of live fish, but rather of fish landed and sold in the market-place.

4. USE AND VALUE ADDED

The use/value added table (Table 3) shows the use of products and (man-made as well as natural) assets as inputs of the domestic production activities or as components of final demand (final consumption, capital accumulation, exports). These data are supplemented with information on the value added of the different production activities. The use table is an instrument to distribute the total supply of goods and services from the supply table to its various destinations. However, the supply of environmental assets is not displayed in the supply table, but is shown as negative entries in the natural non-produced assets column of capital accumulation. In comparison to the traditional framework of the SNA, the use of natural assets is shown in additional rows and the capital accumulation of non-produced natural assets in an additional column.

(a) *Use of Goods and Services*

The first block of rows in Table 3 presents the use of products (goods and services) by intermediate consumption of economic activities and final demand, as supplied from Table 2 (591.9). This corresponds to the traditional use table in the SNA. The sum of the gross value added (293.4), the conventional Gross Domestic Product (GDP), is shown explicitly in Table 3. Subtracting the consumption of fixed capital obtains the Net Domestic Product (NDP) (267.1).

As indicated in section 3, the supply of natural growth products (40.7) stems from "controlled" production processes of agriculture, forestry and fishing only. These products are used as inputs into different economic activities (23.0), exported (5.0), consumed by private households (11.3), or may increase fixed capital or stocks (1.4). Stock increase results from the growth in products which are not used in the same period. Stock decrease is shown where naturally grown products of a former period are used for intermediate or final purposes. The increase of fixed capital on the other hand represents a growth in the remaining biomass that is not intended to be used up in intermediate or final consumption,

TABLE 3
Use Value Added

| | | Domestic Production (industries) | | | |
| | | | Other Industries | | |
	Total	External Environmental Protection Activities	Internal Environmental Protection Activities	Other Activities	Subtotal Domestic Production
(1) Use of products	591.9	15.9	17.9	190.2	224.0
(1.1) Natural growth products	40.7			23.0	23.0
(1.2) External envir. protection services	36.2			22.4	22.4
(1.3) Other products	515.0	15.9	17.9	144.8	178.6
Gross value added of industries [(9)-(1)]		20.3	−17.9	291.0	293.4
(2) Use of produced fixed assets (consumption of fixed capital)	0	1.3	4.8	20.2	26.3
Net value added of industries [(9)-(1)-(2)]		19.0	−22.7	270.8	267.1
(3) Use of natural assets (ecolog. valuation)	−1.6	6.3	4.6	48.9	59.8
(3.1) Quantitative depletion	0	0.3	0.4	16.8	17.5
(3.2) Degradation of land (except by residuals)	0	0.2		8.8	9.0
(3.3) Degradation by residuals	−1.6	5.8	4.2	23.3	33.3
Σ Total use [(1)+(2)+(3)]	590.3	23.5	27.3	259.3	310.1
(4) Environmental adjustment of final demand		1.8	2.1	18.3	22.2
Env. adj. net value added (EDP) of industries [(9)−(1)−(2)−(3)−(4) or (5)+(6)+(7)+(8)]		10.9	−29.4	203.6	185.1
(5) Compensation of employees		13.0	8.7	72.0	93.7
(6) Indirect taxes minus subsidies		2.0	0.3	34.1	36.4
(7) Net operating surplus		4.0	−31.7	164.7	137.0
(8) Eco-margin [−(3)−(4)]		−8.1	−6.7	−67.2	−82.0
(9) Total gross inputs/total total final demand [(1)+(2)+(3)+(4)+(5)+(6)+(7)+(8)]		36.2		481.2	517.4

				Final Demand				
Final Consumption		**Net Capital Accumulation**			**Exports**			
		Produced Assets		Non-Produced Assets			Sub-total Final Demand
Households	Government	Except Natural	Natural (biota)		Products	Residuals	
175.0	42.5	68.0	1.4	7.3	73.7		367.9
11.3			1.4'		5.0		17.7
8.8	5.0						13.8
154.9	37.5	68.0		7.3	68.7		336.4
		−23.0	−3.3				−26.3
17.1	−5.0	5.1	−0.9	−73.0		−4.7	−61.4
0.7			−0.9	−17.3			−17.5
0.8				−9.8			−9.0
15.6	−5.0	5.1		−45.9		−4.7	−34.9
192.1	37.5	50.1	−2.8	−65.7	73.7	−4.7	280.2
−17.1		−5.1					−22.2
175.0	37.5	45.0	−2.8	−65.7	73.7	−4.7	258.0

such as the trunks and branches of fruit trees or the breeding stock of livestock.[2]

External environmental protection services (36.2) are used for avoiding potential or restoring actual decreases in environmental quality. It is assumed in the numerical example that the environmental protection services of the government which are not sold on the market (government consumption: 5.0) are restoration activities whereas the other environmental protection activities (31.2) are avoidance activities and are bought by industries (22.4) and households (8.8). Environmental protection activities of the government for avoiding environmental degradation caused by its own production are assumed to be part of the internal environmental protection activities. Government environmental protection services services sold in the market are assumed to be intermediate consumption of industries or household consumption.

The other products (515.0) are used for intermediate consumption (178.6), final consumption (192.4), capital accumulation (75.3) and exports (68.7).

(b) *Use of Natural Assets*

Integrated environmental-economic accounting in the present framework focuses on the inclusion of costs, resulting from the quantitative depletion of natural resources and from the qualitative degradation of environmental quality by economic activities.

Depletion activities (at a total of 18.2) are shown in Table 3 to consist of depletion of natural assets by industries (17.5) and by households (0.7). As detailed in Table 5, they comprise the exploitation of natural resources such as sub-soil assets (mineral deposits) by mining and quarrying (-8.9), aquifers (-4.7) and biological assets (e.g. timber from tropical forests or fish stocks of inland and marine waters) by agriculture, forestry and fishing (-0.9, -3.7). The assumption is that scarcities in the availability of renewable (forest, fish, wildlife etc.) and cyclical (water) resources have been observed. Depletion costs are only estimated in these cases as far as the economic use of natural assets leads to imbalances in nature, i.e. if the depletion of biota exceeds the natural growth or the use of water exceeds replenishment of aquifers. The recording of corresponding negative amounts of tangible wealth reduction is discussed below in section 4d.

The other category of economic use of natural assets represents the environmental quality degradation of the environmental media of air, water and land by production and consumption activities. The degradation of land could be caused by improper agricultural practice (soil erosion, water logging, salinization), by excessive use for recreational purposes or by polluting the soil with wastes or waste-water. The main reason for degrading the quality of air and water is their use as a sink for residuals (wastes, pollutants) of economic activities. It has to be stressed that only the immediate influence on the environmental media is taken into account. The indirect effects by transboundary transport in the air or by transition from one environmental medium to another are not recorded in

---

[2]This treatment of natural growth processes in agriculture, forestry and fishing differs from the 1968 SNA recommendations, but may be adopted in the revised SNA.

the SEEA. These complex dynamics within the natural environment could be shown in supplementary data systems which should be linked with the SEEA. Furthermore, it should be noted that impacts of natural or man-made disasters are assumed not (or in some cases only indirectly) to be caused by economic use of environmental assets and are therefore excluded from the use/value added Table 3 but are included as a category (4) of asset volume changes in Table 5.

The net value of *degradation* is assumed to be equal to potential abatement (restoration) costs, required either to achieve the level of environmental quality at the beginning of the accounting period or at least a level specified by "official" environmental standards (Hueting, 1980). It is assumed that such standards reflect a technological solution to abating environmental quality degradation that can "reasonably" be expected to be applied by the different polluters. Obviously, such valuation does not measure actual environmental "damage" from pollution. A possible treatment of such welfare effects is discussed in section 5.

The environmental degradation is caused by production activities (9.0 plus 33.3), by consumption activities of households (0.8 plus 15.6), by man-made assets (5.1) and by imported residuals (1.6). Man-made assets have an effect on the natural environment by their residuals (e.g. scrapped machinery). A part of the environmental degradation is restored by government activities (−5.0). The remaining degrading impacts affect the domestic natural assets (−9.8, −45.9) and—as far as residuals are "exported"—the natural environment of the rest of the world (−4.7).

In Table 4, the value of the economic use (depletion as well as degradation) of domestic and non-domestic (foreign) natural assets and the corresponding impacts on the asset values are shown in a simplified balance sheet.

TABLE 4

ECONOMIC USE AND IMPACTS ON NATURAL ASSETS

Use of Natural Assets (environmental costs)		Impacts on Natural Assets (decrease of asset values)	
Domestic use		**Domestic environment**	
Depletion		Depletion	
industries	17.5	prod. natural assets	0.9
households	0.7	non-prod. natural assets	17.3
	18.2		18.2
Degradation		Degradation	
industries	42.3	non-prod. natural assets	55.7
households	16.4		
government	−5.0		
prod. assets	5.1		
		Environment of the	
Imports		**rest of the world**	
Degradation	1.6	Degradation	4.7
	60.4		60.4
	78.6		78.6

125

(c) *Environmental Adjustments of the Value Added*

Deducting the imputed costs of natural asset use (environmental costs) from net value added leads to a new value-added concept, termed here "environmentally adjusted net value added." The environmental costs represent the hypothetical costs for maintaining the natural assets at the same level during the reporting period. This concept reflects a "strong" or "narrow" sustainability concept which implies that future generations should receive a natural environment with a quantitative and qualitative level being at least comparable with the present situation (Bartelmus, in preparation; Blades, 1989; Daly, in preparation; Pearce, Markandya, Barbier, 1989 and 1990; and Pezzey, 1989). The international discussion of the last years has proved that it is not sufficient to sustain a constant level of total (man-made as well as natural) capital, denying substitution possibilities between these capital categories ("broad" or "weak" sustainability concept). The uncertainty of long-term impacts of economic activities on the natural environment and the increasing knowledge about irreversible damages of natural balances (climate change, ozone layer depletion etc.) has led to a more cautious risk-conscious attitude towards overburdening the natural environment. From this point of view, it seems necessary to maintain the natural assets treating them as complementary to man-made capital. The strong sustainability concept thus applies not only to the case of environmental quality degradation, but also to the maintenance of "stocks" of natural resources. In the case of subsoil assets, this approach seem to be questionable because the strong sustainability concept would lead to non-use of the resources, possibly causing severe world-wide economic problems. Instead, the objective could be to maintain a long-term optimal depletion rate, considering that new finds could only retard the shrinkage of the stocks. It has been proposed that the sustainability concept should be weaker in this case, and it would be sufficient to balance a decrease of the subsoil assets with an increase of other types of assets (with preference for permanent or renewable natural assets) to sustain the same income level in the future (El Serafy, 1989; Daly, in preparation).

The maintenance cost approach used for valuing the economic use of natural assets corresponds to the methods of national accounting for estimating the use of man-made fixed assets. The user costs of these assets are estimated with the costs necessary to keep the man-made fixed capital intact, i.e. to maintain the level of the assets at the same level during the reporting period. These costs which are called "consumption of fixed capital" or "depreciation" are also used to compile the net capital formation of the man-made assets in the accounting period.

As far as the natural assets have the character of *fixed assets*, treating the maintenance costs of natural assets in the same way as the depreciation of man-made assets seems plausible. However, distinguishing between assets that bear characteristics of fixed assets and those that are more in the nature of an *inventory* or *stock* (in this case, decrease of assets in the national accounts is booked as intermediate consumption and not as depreciation) is problematic because natural assets may exhibit simultaneously economic and environmental functions (Hueting, 1980). For instance, a timber tract represents a stock resource, but has also an important role in cleaning the air and regulating water balances.

Furthermore, it serves as habitat of animals and as recreational area. From an ecological point of view, the environmental media, i.e. land, water and air as well as the ecosystems can be considered as fixed assets. The maintenance costs of these assets should therefore be treated as depreciation. Further discussion seems to be necessary in the case of subsoil assets. They mainly have the character of inventory stocks of nature. Their depletion could therefore be treated as intermediate consumption.[3] For sake of simplicity of the present framework, the value of the depletion of these assets is not shown separately from the other environmental costs, but is also treated as decrease of a fixed asset.

Whatever the treatment of the environmental costs, as depreciation of natural assets or as intermediate consumption, their deduction from gross output affects the calculation of net value added. The gross value added of the industries remains unchanged in the SEEA. The environmental adjustments of the net value added (−82.0) comprise the imputed environmental costs connected with domestic production (−59.8), household consumption activities (−17.1) and the use of man-made assets (−5.1). These adjustments are called eco-margin which is introduced explicitly in order to permit the identification of all components of value added (including operating surplus) according to the conventional SNA concepts.

Impacts of household activities and of man-made *assets* on environmental quality are taken into account for correcting the net value added despite the fact that the respective environmental costs are not directly associated with production activities. Regarding households, their polluting activities could be viewed as non-market production of goods and services which produces "jointly" residuals like wastes and pollutants. In this case, the net value added of the households' production would be diminished by the imputed environmental costs of the households. This is achieved by shifting these imputed values (17.1) from final consumption to the totals of domestic production. A similar correction is made with regard to the environmental impacts of man-made assets, comprising additional imputed costs of the asset owners (5.1). These costs refer e.g. to pollution caused by controlled landfill and to the residues of unrecycled man-made assets. It is theoretically possible to transfer these costs to the different industries. In this case, their net value added would directly be affected. This procedure has not been applied in the SEEA in order to show separately the environmental costs caused by current production and man-made capital use. The shift of the environmental costs of households and man-made assets to the columns of domestic production is shown in Table 3 in the row "environmental adjustments of final demand." Net value added is thus corrected only for the totals of environmental protection activities (1.8 and 2.1) and of other activities (18.3).

In Table 3 we also record the components of value added, consisting of the compensation of employees, indirect taxes net of subsidies, net operating surplus and environmental costs equal to item (8) "eco-margin." Use of SEEA thus permits the analysis of these components of value added for the environmental

---

[3]See El Serafy (1989). However, the total depreciation approach is advocated by Harrison (1989) and Repetto (1989).

protection activities of the different economic sectors. Indirect taxes and subsidies, charged or granted as part of environmental protection policies, will be identified separately in the SEEA, reflecting the application of polluter- and user-pays-principles at the micro-economic level. Macro-policy makers on the other hand, might be concerned with the assessment of employment devoted to "defensive" environmental protection activities (total "environmental" renumeration of employees of 21.7 as compared to a total of other wages and salaries of 72.0).

The net operating surplus of the different production activities has not been environmentally adjusted in Table 3. The additional environmental costs are balanced by introducing the eco-margin. The idea is to facilitate the unequivocal linkage of the production accounts of the SEEA with the income accounts of the conventional SNA. Another possible presentation of the operating surplus could show an environmentally adjusted net operating surplus, but extend the table at the same time for identifying explicitly the non-adjusted gross and net operating surplus:

Environmentally adjusted net operating surplus	55.0
= Gross operating surplus	163.3
− Consumption of fixed capital	26.3
− Eco-margin	82.0

The total of the environmentally adjusted net value added is called Environmentally Adjusted Net Domestic Product or, short, Eco Domestic Product (EDP). EDP could be derived from GDP as follows:

Gross Domestic product (GDP)	293.4
− Consumption of fixed capital	26.3
= Net Domestic Product (NDP)	267.1
− (Imputed) environmental costs	82.0
= Eco Domestic Product (EDP)	185.1

(d) *Final Demand*

Final demand consists of final consumption, net capital accumulation and exports. Import and export flows are only slightly modified for environmental accounting. However, significant alterations are proposed for both final consumption and net capital accumulation to allow corrections of net value added while heeding the principle of accounting identities (see below, section 4e).

Imports and exports include flows of wastes which are not marketed, but transported to/from a foreign country or to the open sea. They represent either a degradation of the foreign natural media by exporting domestic residuals or of domestic media by importing residuals. They are estimated as negative values—costs for avoiding or restoring environmental quality degradation (exports: −4.7, imports: −1.6). The imports of residuals reduce the total value of imports and of the domestic natural assets (negative item in the column of net accumulation

128

of natural assets). The exports of residuals lead to an increase of the imputed environmental costs of the exporting industry which implies a reduced environmentally adjusted net value added of the exporting economic units and a reduction of the total value of the exports. Transboundary flows of residuals of the economic activities which are not transported by man but by environmental media (e.g. water, air), are recorded as degradation of the environmental media which directly receive the residuals. Their final destination is not taken into account.

The conventional final consumption of households (175.0) remains unchanged in the SEEA. The additional (imputed) environmental costs (17.1) which would have been necessary to avoid or which need to be incurred in order to restore a degradation of environmental quality by household activities (recreational use of land 0.8, pollution 15.6), or which represent the costs of depleting natural resources (firewood consumption 0.7) are shifted to domestic production.

The fully elaborated SEEA will comprise a further breakdown of the final consumption of households by environmentally oriented functions for identifying e.g. the environmental protection expenditures of the households and the expenditures required to compensate for the damages caused by environmental deterioration (health expenditures etc.).

Final *consumption of government* (42.5) is corrected by the environmental protection expenditures (−5.0) which are non-marketed and which are undertaken to avoid or restore a decrease of environmental quality caused by other economic units. These expenditures have the characteristics of an investment in environmental quality. Its value is shifted from the government final consumption to the capital accumulation of natural assets and diminishes the degradation of the natural assets which would have occurred if no restoration activities had taken place. The environmental protection activities of the government for own purposes (internal activities) and the additional (imputed) environmental costs of the government production activities are already recorded in the columns of domestic production. It is therefore not necessary to extend the concept of final consumption of government in the SEEA by taking into account imputed environmental costs.

The section on the *net accumulation of tangible wealth* in Table 3 differs considerably from the traditional incorporation of capital formation in a use table. The presentation of this part of final demand in Table 3 is limited to an asset classification by only three types of asset: produced biological (natural) assets, other produced assets, non-produced natural assets. A further breakdown of the capital accumulation is given in Table 5 which shows complete asset balances for the different types of assets. The following comments refer especially to the disaggregated version in Table 5. The capital accumulation concept of Table 3 corresponds to the (traditional) capital formation (item 2 of Table 5) and to the ecological valuation of volume changes of natural assets due to economic use (item 3.1 of Table 5). The valuation problem (market versus ecological valuation) and the other items of Table 5 are discussed in section 5.

In the SEEA, the asset boundary has been extended for including all natural assets which are actually or potentially used by economic activities or which could be affected by the residuals of economic production and consumption

TABLE 5

ASSET BALANCES OF NET TANGIBLE ASSETS

Monetary units

| | Total | Produced Assets | | Non-produced Natural Assets | | | | | |
| | | Produced Assets (except biological) | Produced Biological Assets | Non-produced Biological Assets | Land (landscape, ecosystems) | | Sub-soil Assets | Water | Air |
					Cultivated etc.	Uncultivated			
(1) Opening stocks (market values)	2818.8	991.3	83.1	65.4	1366.7	50.4	261.9		
(2) Net capital formation (use of products, market values)	50.4	45.0	−1.9		4.6		2.7		
(2.1) Gross capital formation	76.7	68.0	1.4		4.6		2.7		
(2.2) Consumption of fixed capital	−26.3	−23.0	−3.3						
(3) Volume change of natural assets due to economic use (market values)	36.0			−2.1	23.3	−5.0	19.8	0.0	0.0
(3.1) Ecological valuation									
(3.1.1) *Quantitative depletion*	−18.2		−0.9	−3.7			−8.9	−4.7	
(3.1.2) *Degradation of land (except by residuals)*	−9.8			−7.7	−2.1				
(3.1.3) *Degradation by residuals*	−45.9				−9.5	−3.1		−12.9	−20.4

(3.2) Adjustment due to market valuation								
(3.2.1) *Quantitative depletion*	8.1		0.9	1.6	33.1	2.1	0.9	4.7
(3.2.2) *Land use (except by residuals)*	35.2							
(3.2.3) *Degradation by residuals*	38.8				4.0	1.5	12.9	20.4
(3.3) Other volume changes (change of land use, new finds, new estimates etc.)	27.8				3.4	−3.4	27.8	
(4) Volume change by natural or multiple causes (market values)	−30.3	−25.3		1.3	−4.3	−2.0		
(5) Revaluation due to market price changes	533.5	138.1	12.6	11.1	331.0	11.8	28.9	
(6) Closing stocks (market values) [(1)+(2)+(3)+(4)+(5)]	3408.4	1149.1	93.8	75.7	1721.3	55.2	313.3	

131

processes. The extended asset concept comprises the following types of assets:

Produced assets
    Man-made assets (non-biological such as
        machinery and equipment, stocks of non-biological products)
    Natural assets produced by agriculture, forestry and fishing (fixed assets
        and inventory stocks)

Non-produced natural wild assets
    Wild biological assets
    Land (cultivated and uncultivated)
    Subsoil assets (developed and undeveloped proven reserves)
    Water (stored and unstored)
    Air

This classification distinguishes in particular between assets which are (economically) produced or not and which are man-made or natural. These two criteria are not identical because the (economically) produced biota are both produced and natural. In this case, the produced biota should only be subsumed under natural assets as far as they are living. A further breakdown is possible according to the degree of human influence on the natural environment (e.g. cultivated-uncultivated land, developed-undeveloped subsoil assets).

In Table 3, the net capital accumulation of *produced assets* is recorded mainly according to the conventional concepts of the SNA (gross capital formation: 68.0 and 1.4, consumption of fixed capital: −23.0 and −3.3). Only two minor deviations should be mentioned: The residuals of the produced assets which are loaded on the natural environment (e.g. scraps, pollution of controlled landfill) are valued with their avoidance costs (5.1) and shown in addition to the net capital formation. In a second step, these imputed costs are shifted to the industries of the responsible activities or, alternatively, to the industries as a whole [via the environmental adjustment row (4)]. In the case of produced biological assets, it might be necessary to estimate additional depletion costs (−0.9) if the economic activities of agriculture, forestry and fishing disturb the natural balances, e.g. if the amount of cut wood exceeds the natural growth and destroys the ecosystems of cultivated forests. In this case, the sustainability principle should be applied, and avoidance or restoration costs could be calculated.

The imputed depletion costs of *wild biota* (in Table 5: −3.7) are estimated only if depletion by economic activities (e.g. hunting, ocean fishing) and natural growth are not balanced. Depletion costs are thus estimated if depletion exceeds natural growth. The discussion of valuation of net depletion in this case has not been conclusive. One possible approach could be to value net depletion as the gross value added generated by the depleting activity. This would show value added foregone if the net depletion had been avoided. Another approach could be to assess the costs for compensating projects to restore the natural balances.

Net capital accumulation of *land* refers to the impacts of economic land use. The costs of developing land are treated in the conventional SNA as capital formation which normally leads—from an economic point of view—to an improvement of land quality and to increasing market values (in Table 5: 4.6).

From an ecological point of view, increasing economic use of land could cause a qualitative degradation of the land and the terrestrial ecosystems. The main reasons are restructuring (further economic development of cultivated land, cultivation of uncultivated land), intensive agricultural use (soil erosion etc.), recreational use (disturbing ecosystems) and use as a sink for residuals (such as pesticides and the pollution of controlled and uncontrolled landfill). In Table 5 degradation by residuals (−9.5 and −3.1) and by other economic activities (−7.7 and −2.1) are distinguished.

The degradation of land is valued as the cost to avoid (or at least mitigate) the negative impacts of economic activities or to restore the degraded areas, with a view to maintaining the terrestrial ecosystems in their present state. This valuation concept might differ widely from the market valuation. Changes in economic land use will often increase the market value of land, but at the same time could imply a decrease of the ecological quality of land.

Subsoil assets comprise the proven reserves of fossil and mineral assets. Proven reserves normally have to meet three criteria: high probability of existence (95 percent), exploitability with existing techniques and positive net return, i.e. the market price exceeds exploitation costs (Martinez *et al.*, 1987). Subsoil assets can be undeveloped or developed (established mines and other exploration facilities). The costs for developing subsoil assets (e.g. by exploration activities) have to be treated according to the conventional SNA as capital formation (Table 5: 2.7). The valuation of the depletion of subsoil assets has to reflect the future scarcity of the assets. Exploitation is mainly an economic and not an ecological problem because the immediate impacts on natural balances are usually low, with the notable exception of surface mining. The indirect impacts of subsoil depletion (e.g. losses of crude oil during transportation, pollution connected with energy consumption) are registered independently from the valuation of assets as environmental degradation from polluting economic activities.

Various methods have been proposed to value subsoil asset depletion (see Ward, 1982). Several authors suggest the use of the net operating surplus of the exploiting industry or a part of it. The proposal of El Serafy (1989) seems to be an approach tailored to the concept of sustainability. The idea is to estimate the depletion costs as the amount of money which should be invested to achieve a long-term constant flow of income, even after complete exploitation of the resources. This rule implies a substitution of the use of subsoil assets by other types of income generating activities and corresponds to a broad sustainability concept. The decrease of subsoil assets could be balanced, e.g. by increasing renewable (biological) assets or by the development of solar and wind energy sources instead of coal or crude oil. The value of subsoil depletion amounts to 8.9, in Table 5.

The economic use of *water* could lead to increasing scarcity (depletion) or to decreasing quality (degradation by residuals). Increasing scarcity of water will be observed if the economic abstraction exceeds the average natural inflow of water during the accounting period. In this case, net depletion could be valued as the value added, or part of it, generated by additional water use of the abstracting industries (−4.7). This value could represent the avoidance costs as in the case of wild biota. Further discussion is necessary to develop a generally accepted valuation method for water depletion. The degradation of water by residuals is valued as its avoidance (or restoration) costs (−12.9).

As described above (section 4b), the value of the degradation of *air* is its avoidance costs (−20.4).

In section 5 below, we describe a comprehensive system of balance sheets of tangible assets, including changes in volume not accounted for by capital accumulation in the use/value added table (e.g. effects of natural and other disasters).

(e) *Accounting Identities*

The national accounting identities between the totals of environmentally adjusted value added (plus imports) and final demand are maintained in the use/value added Table 3 by treating capital accumulation of natural assets as part of final demand. In Table 6 we show the transition from the conventional aggregates, according to the SNA, to the environmentally adjusted aggregates of the SEEA by using the numerical example (cf. Tables 2 and 3).

TABLE 6

ACCOUNTING IDENTITIES

Primary Inputs (value added, imports)		Final Demand (domestic, exports)	
Gross value added (Gross domestic product)	293.4	Domestic final demand (SNA concept)	294.2
− Use of produced assets (consumption of fixed capital)	26.3	− Consumption of fixed capital	26.3
− Use of natural assets for current production	59.8	− Government restoration costs	5.0
Environmental adjustment of final demand	22.2	+ Net capital accumulation of natural assets (−78.9 + 5.0)	−73.9
Environmentally adjusted net value added (Environmentally adjusted Net Domestic Product)	185.1	Environmentally adjusted domestic final demand	189.0
+ Import of products	74.5	+ Export of products	73.7
+ Import of residuals	−1.6	+ Export of residuals	−4.7
Environmentally adjusted primary inputs	258.0	Environmentally adjusted final demand	258.0

As already explained, the gross value added (293.4) is corrected by the consumption of fixed produced capital (26.3) and by the user costs of natural assets (current production 59.8, households 17.1, residuals of man-made assets 5.1). This obtains the environmentally adjusted net value added (185.1). The concept of imports is extended to additionally include imports of residuals (74.5 and −1.6). The total of the environmentally adjusted primary inputs (value added plus imports) is 258.0.

Domestic final demand (294.2) is corrected by the consumption of fixed produced assets (26.3) to achieve a net concept. The environmental restoration costs of the government (5.0) are treated as an increase of the value of natural assets and therefore reflected in the capital accumulation of natural assets. The value of depletion and degradation of natural assets by economic activities would have been −78.9 without government restoration activities. Taking these activities into account, the net capital accumulation amounts to −73.9 (−73.0 plus −0.9). The environmentally adjusted figures of total final demand (258.0) comprise the adjusted domestic final demand (189.0) and the export of products (73.7) and residuals (−4.7). This total is equal to the total of primary inputs.

5. Asset Balances of Tangible Wealth

As illustrated in Table 1, the section of the use/value added table on tangible wealth accumulation can also be viewed as an integral part of the asset balances. This is indicated in Table 1 by plus (+) and equal (=) signs, inserted between the four elements of the asset balances. This illustration shows an accounting identity between the closing stocks and the sum of opening stocks, net capital accumulation, adjustment of natural assets accumulation to market valuation, other volume changes and revaluation due to market price changes. This identity holds for man-made assets (produced, not natural):

$$1,149.1 = 991.3 + (68.0 - 23.0 + 5.1 - 5.1) + (-25.3 + 138.1),$$

for the (economically) produced natural assets:

$$93.8 = 83.1 + (1.4 - 3.3 - 0.9) + (0.9 + 12.6),$$

and for those non-produced natural assets which are used or affected by economic activities:

$$2,165.5 = 1,744.4 + (7.3 - 73.0) + (81.2 + 22.8 + 382.8).$$

The asset balance sheets are further elaborated on in Table 5. The asset classification has already been described in Section 4d. The volume and price changes of the assets during the reporting period are further disaggregated in Table 5, consisting of:

(2) Net capital formation (use of products);
(3) Volume change of natural assets due to economic use;
    (3.1) Ecological valuation,
    (3.2) Adjustment due to market valuation,
    (3.3) Other volume changes (market valuation),
(4) Volume change by natural or multiple causes;
(5) Revaluation due to market price changes.

The volume changes (2) and (3.1) reflect the net capital accumulation described in the use/value added table (Table 3 and Table 1.2), the adjustment due to market valuation (3.2) corresponds to the "adjustment of natural assets accumulation to market valuation" in Table 1.3. The other volume changes due to economic use (3.3) and the volume change by natural or multiple causes (4) are summarized under "other volume changes" in Table 1.3. The revaluation due to market price changes is presented in both tables under the same name.

The design of the asset balance sheets aims at introducing environmental aspects in the national stock accounts without disrupting the concepts of the conventional SNA balance sheets. As recommended in the International Guidelines on Balance-Sheet and Reconciliation Accounts (United Nations, 1977) and in chapter XI of the preliminary draft of the revised SNA (United Nations, 1990), the *opening* and *closing stocks* are valued at market prices or have values derived from market prices. Direct market valuation could be applied if the assets are marketed (some produced fixed assets like cars, inventory stocks of products, land). Indirect market valuation uses the net value concept (replacement costs minus cumulated depreciation) or tries—in the case of depletable natural assets like wild biota, subsoil assets or water—to estimate the assets by the discounted value of future net returns (future market prices minus all exploitation costs including a normal rent of capital).[4] It should be stressed that the SEEA does not aim at a complete market valuation of the non-produced natural assets. The market valuation should be limited to natural assets which are regularly depleted for market purposes (e.g. ocean fish, tropical wood and subsoil assets) or to assets which are directly marketed (uncultivated land in exceptional cases). The opening and closing stocks of the other non-produced natural assets have a market value of zero. In these cases, their volume changes are valued only if they are affected by economic activities.

Market valuation has also been applied in general for the *volume* and *price changes* during the accounting period. Net capital formation of produced assets [item (2) in Table 5] reflects the volume changes described in the conventional SNA framework. Some of the other volume changes of assets caused by economic, natural, non-economic and multiple (combination of these causes) activities and events [items (3) and (4) in Table 5] which had been part of the reconciliation accounts in the 1968 version of the SNA, will be integrated into the accumulation accounts which explain the changes in the balance sheets of the revised SNA at market values. Opening and closing stocks of these assets are also measured at market values. The transition to the level of the market values at the end of the accounting period (closing assets) is shown as item (5) in Table 5 (revaluation due to market price changes).

The connection between the SEEA and the conventional assets balance sheets is introduced by a breakdown of the volume change of natural assets due to economic use (item (3) of Table 5). As far as the economic use affects the natural balances and leads to a decrease of the value of the natural assets from an ecological point of view, the avoidance or restoration costs are estimated for maintaining the same qualitative and quantitative level of natural capital during the accounting period. These values are introduced in the extended use/value added table of the SEEA (see Table 3). This ecologically oriented valuation does not necessarily correspond to the market values due to the respective economic use. Therefore, an adjustment item is introduced which allows the transition to the market valuation of the asset balance sheets [item (3.2) of Table 5]. Volume

---

[4]The normal rent of capital refers to the produced assets which have been used for the exploitation of natural assets (e.g. trawlers for fishing and drilling instruments).

changes due to economic activities which do not directly deplete or degrade the natural assets (changes in land use, discoveries, etc.) are separately recorded and have market values [item (3.3) of Table 5]. In the SEEA, the analysis of the volume changes of the natural assets is focused on the economic uses. Therefore, no ecologically orientated valuation of the volume changes of natural assets due to natural or multiple causes (like wars and disasters) is applied, but market values of the volume changes are given.

It is not possible to describe the volume changes of the different types of assets in this overview article in detail. More detail on the extended asset balance sheets will be given in the SNA Handbook on Environmental Accounting. The following limited observations are thus only to facilitate a better understanding of the general scope and coverage of environmental assets in the SEEA.

The consumption of fixed capital (fixed produced assets) comprises only insurable risks of premature losses. Further losses by war or natural disasters are recorded under item (4) (−25.3).

The asset balances of the *biological assets* are relatively complicated because of the different concepts for describing the volume changes of produced and non-produced biota at market values. The natural growth of produced biota is treated as economic production (and gross capital formation) whereas the natural growth of non-produced biota is, as far as market values are associated to them, part of "(4) Volume change by natural or multiple causes" of Table 5. The depletion (due to economic use) of the produced biota is shown as decrease of stocks or consumption of fixed capital [item (2) of Table 5], whereas the depletion of non-produced biota is indicated under item (3). This different treatment implies that the net growth (natural growth minus depletion) of produced biota at market values is shown as net capital formation under item (2) (−1.9 = 1.4 − 3.3), while the net growth of non-produced biota equals the difference of the values under item (4) and item (3) (−0.8 = 1.3 − 2.1).

The ecological value of depleting produced biota (−0.9) reflects the ecological consequences of depleting cultivated biota beyond the economic use of these assets. If, for example, the wood of timber tracts is cut, the natural balance of forests could be disturbed as far as depletion exceeds natural growth. The necessary "ecological" costs could be estimated by the costs of compensating projects or by the additional value added generated by the net depletion (gross depletion minus natural growth). Further considerations are necessary to avoid double-counting if the depletion of produced biota exceeds their natural growth. In this case, the ecological valuation has to take into account that the (negative) net growth has already been valued at market values as (negative) capital formation.

The depletion of wild biota (−3.7) could be valued in ecological terms in a similar way. The natural balances could only be maintained if depletion and natural growth are balanced. That is, if the net depletion is positive avoidance or restoration costing refers to a reduction of the production (hunting, harvesting etc.) and a decrease of the corresponding value added, and the loss of ecological functions of the resource.

The valuation of the quality changes of *land* caused by economic activities might produce completely opposite results, depending on the economic or environmental point of view. Restructuring and development of land are normally connected with increasing market values, whereas their ecological effects could decrease the land values under environmental aspects. The development costs (4.6) are shown as capital formation. They reflect, together with the market value of the volume changes due to economic use (23.3, −5.0), the market value of all quantitative and qualitative volume changes of land caused by the different economic activities. The quantitative aspects of land use (changes in land use) are described under item (3.3) of Table 5 (3.5, −3.4). The qualitative component is shown under ecological aspects first (−7.7, −9.5, −2.1, −3.1) and adjusted to market valuation in a second step (33.1, 4.0, 2.1, 1.5). The qualitative changes do not only comprise the results of restructuring and development, but also excessive economic use, e.g. for agricultural purposes (often connected with soil erosion) and for recreation. Furthermore, the degradation by residuals is taken into account.

The ecological valuation of land degradation raises difficult estimation problems. In principle, the adequate avoidance or restoration costs to maintain the same level of land quality has to be estimated. Avoidance costs could comprise the decrease of value added in case of reducing excessive land use. Restoration costs could be the costs of compensation projects.

The opening and closing stocks of *subsoil assets* (proven reserves: developed and undeveloped) are valued with the discounted value of future net returns (i.e. revenues minus exploitation costs: 261.9, 313.3). New discoveries and changes in the economic conditions of exploitation which lead to new estimates of the proven reserves, are shown under item (3.3) of Table 5 (27.8). The exploitation costs do not contain the exploration costs (2.7) because they have already been included under item (2) of Table 5. The extraction (depletion) of these assets is estimated at "ecological" values (−8.9) and in a second step adjusted to market values (−8.9 + 0.9 = −8.0). These market values reflect the net prices of the depleted assets (current market price minus exploitation costs). The ecological valuation could comprise the costs for maintaining the level of natural capital (compensating projects to develop renewable or permanent assets) or of the total capital (man-made and natural).

The stock of *water* has normally no market values. Exceptions are stored water for drinking or irrigation purposes. The depletion of water is valued from an ecological point of view only if the average water stock is affected. This net depletion is valued with its avoidance costs [costs of reducing water use, e.g. by reducing agricultural production (−4.7)]. The avoidance cost approach can also be applied for valuing water degradation by residuals (−12.9).

The *air*, as a natural asset, has no market value. Therefore, the value of opening and closing stock is zero. For balancing the value of degradation by residuals (−20.4), a corresponding positive item has been introduced as an adjustment to market valuation.

6. Welfare-Oriented Measures of the Economic Use of the Environment

The concept of sustainability used in this paper is cost-oriented rather than welfare-oriented.[5] It reflects cost estimates which would be necessary to avoid, restore or replace decreases of environmental quantities and qualities during the reference period. Such an approach would normally suggest a greater effort at protecting the environment, as compared to estimating an economically optimal level of pollution. Optimality would require a balance of marginal costs of protection activities and of the (discounted) flows of marginal future environmental damages avoided. Because of underestimation, uncertainty and undervaluation (high discounting) of future damage, the optimality criterion will almost certainly present an amount of environmental deterioration which might be optimal from a micro-economic point of view, but not from a social point of view. In view of the uncertainties related to individual (marginal) evaluation and of prevailing societal and international concerns over long-term threats to critical life-support systems, the cautious concept of sustainability implicit in the cost values of the present framework, i.e. the maintenance (non-decrease) of environmental quality, appears to be a realistic approach. Under this aspect, the present cost approach also reflects (social) welfare aspects in its valuation of environmental degradation. Theoretical considerations, recently presented by Pearce, Markandya, Barbier (1990, especially p. 9), seem to support this approach.

Measurement and valuation problems of estimating the consequential damage (welfare losses) caused by environmental degradation are formidable. It is also difficult to associate unequivocally particular pollutants with health and welfare effects (for example, health damage caused by air pollution). One approach proposed to assess damage costs is to measure actual expenditures required for the elimination of the damage (Uno, 1989). Such expenditures could be shown separately in the SEEA as possible deductions under welfare aspects (Leipert, 1989). Another approach is to directly estimate health and welfare losses, including the impairment of recreational functions or aesthetic and ethical aspects of the environment. Some of these losses have been estimated by using the willingness-to-pay approach as an approximation of individual ("revealed") preferences or by other methods of contingent valuation (see OECD, 1989). Once comprehensive estimates of the value of damages become available, research projects could be undertaken to associate them with the polluting sectors. In this case, separate accounts should be established, which would allow a comparison of the actual and hypothetical avoidance cost on one hand and of the actual and imputed damage costs on the other. These comparisons would facilitate macroeconomic cost-benefit analyses, as proposed for example by Peskin (1989). Such additional accounts would permit further modifications of the components of final demand for the derivation of welfare-oriented measures (Bartelmus, 1987). In the SNA Handbook on Integrated Environmental and Economic Accounting, an approach will be discussed which could be derived from the cost-oriented measures of the SEEA by extending not only the asset boundary, but also the production boundary. This implies the introduction of the concept of environmental services "produced" by nature (see Peskin, 1989; Schäfer and Stahmer, 1989; and Stahmer, 1990).

---

[5]The question of welfare-oriented measures in national accounts is discussed in Drechsler (1976) and United Nations (1977a). The limits of accounting approaches to assets, the sustainability of economic growth, and possibilities of modeling the "feasability" of development programs are discussed in Bertelmus (in preparation).

7. APPLICATION OF THE FRAMEWORK: A DESK STUDY OF COUNTRY X

The environmentally modified concepts developed in the framework should stimulate alternative economic analyses and policies, based on an integrated assessment of environment-economy relationships. One aspect of such analysis is to focus on income available for spending on final consumption and new investments. Due to the consideration of environmental costs of production, environmentally adjusted income would generally be lower than income derived in traditional accounting. This *welfare* aspect of environmental accounting has received most of the attention in environmental studies of income and expenditure.

On the other hand, production cost and tangible asset and resource requirements of production reflect a *productivity* aspect of economic performance and environmental-economic analysis. Environmental accounting may result in values of value added generated and tangible assets used in each sector, that are different from the values of income and capital in traditional accounting. The reasons are the inclusion of cost due to environmental uses and of non-produced natural assets in broader concepts of cost and capital, respectively. Changed relations between value added and economic assets used in production might well lead to considerable re-assessment of the rentability and productivity of economic sectors from an environmental (accounting) point of view.

(a) *Economic and Environmental Features of Country X*

This analysis is done on the basis of an illustrative database, developed for the clarification of the above-described environmental accounting concepts and procedures. Only part of this database is reflected in Tables 1 to 5 above. The data describe the economic and environmental features of a realistic, but fictitious country "X" and are thus to a large extent fictive. There is however a basic core of data which was taken from the national accounts of an existing country. These core data include GDP by activity and expenditure categories, compensation of employees, indirect taxes (net of subsidies), operating surplus, output, intermediate consumption, capital formation and the consumption of fixed capital.

All other national accounts data, included in the framework, are elaborated on the basis of assumptions about the type of country, the circumstances under which traditional GDP is being generated in production, the effects of production on the environment, and environmental protection and response carried out by government, enterprises and individuals. These assumptions permit the breakdown of aggregate economic data which are part of conventional national accounts, but which could not be compiled from original data sets. Further assumptions about the environmental conditions of the country were made to obtain environmental data for calculating the environmentally adjusted concepts of income and expenditure.

The economic and environmental features of the fictive country X, as reflected in the data and assumptions, are described in the following. The country is a developing country with oil resources, agricultural production, exploitation of timber resources, and fishing activities in rivers, lakes and ocean.

(i) Tangible Wealth

Fixed assets consist of buildings, machinery and equipment, roads and other public structures, and also of livestock for breeding, draught and dairy, trees in orchards and grapevines in vineyards. As regards land, the assumption is that it is used mainly in agriculture for the cultivation of crops and rearing of livestock, in other services for dwellings and office buildings, and that it is owned as infrastructure by government (roads, dams and other structures).

(ii) Environmental Protection

Environmental protection activities are carried out in the country by all sectors. They are concentrated, however, in three sectors which are selling protection services: (a) "other services" which provide private waste disposal services, environmental consulting and recycling; (b) government, which provides sanitation services, and (c) trade and transport, which transports wastes to dumping areas and treatment and recycling plants. The environmental protection (sanitation) services offered by the government are sold to a very limited extent, the rest is assumed to be used by the government itself. The value of the cleaning activity is assumed to be equal to the cost (5.0). Households also purchase environmental protection services. These purchases (8.8) are presented as expenditure in the column of "household final consumption" in Table 3.

(iii) Mining Exploitation

The value of the mineral deposits of the country consists in particular of the value of oil reserves (opening stock in Table 5: 261.9). New deposits of oil were found as a result of exploration activities. This is presented in Table 5 as "Other volume change" (27.8), exceeding the amount of depletion ($-8.9+0.9$).

(iv) Natural Growth

The country has an important agricultural sector, a fishing industry which operates in rivers, lakes and the ocean, and timber tracts where wood is cut and replanted in a controlled exploitation activity. There are also minor wood collection activities in rural areas which are not controlled by any permits.

(v) Natural Disasters

During the period of accounting, the country suffered from a major earthquake which destroyed some of its infrastructure, particularly affecting roads owned by the government, machinery and equipment in the manufacturing sector, and dwellings and other buildings that are recorded as capital of the other service sector. The total value of destruction is included in Table 5 ("Volume change by natural or multiple causes:" -25.3).

(vi) Pollution

Pollution effects as a result of economic activities in the country are recorded in Table 3 in the row corresponding to qualitative degradation of land, water and air by residuals. In the case of air and water pollution, it is assumed that not only the domestic air and water were affected, but also those of neighboring countries (−4.7). Private households also cause pollution, which is assumed to consist of the effects of accumulated and illegally discharged wastes. The cost of this pollution (15.6) is reflected in the intersection of qualitative degradation by residuals and the household consumption.

(vii) Conversion of Tropical Forest to Commercial Use

Tropical rain forests are being converted to a limited extent to land for agriculture, urbanization and industrial development. This is recorded as change of land use in Table 5 (±3.4).

(b) *Comparative Analysis of the Economic Conditions of Country X, based on National and Environmental Accounts*

In Tables 7 and 8 we compare aggregates and indicators from traditional accounting with corresponding ones in environmental accounting. NDP is the main concept of national accounting and EDP is used as the environmental accounting alternative.

TABLE 7

ANALYTICAL MEASURES IN TRADITIONAL AND ENVIRONMENTAL ACCOUNTING:
RESOURCES AND USES

	Based on:		
	NDP	EDP	Percentage Difference
Macro-aggregates	(1)	(2)	(2)−(1)/NDP
Income/expenditure	267.1	185.1	−31
Final consumption	217.5	212.5	−2
% of final domestic uses	81	112	
Capital formation (accumulation) net	50.4	−23.5	−28
% of final domestic uses	19	−12	
Exports	73.7	69.0	−2
Minus: imports	74.5	72.9	−1

(i) Income and Expenditure

The income and expenditure analysis is done on the basis of the national accounts identity between income on one hand and domestic expenditure (final consumption, investment) plus exports minus imports on the other. The income and expenditure aggregates, based on Tables 2 and 3, are presented in Table 7.

In the case of traditional national accounting (column 1 of Table 7) the income concept is NDP, and the expenditure concepts are final consumption, net capital formation and exports minus imports. In the case of environmental acccounting (column 2), NDP is replaced by EDP, consumption by environmentally adjusted consumption and net capital formation by net capital accumulation. Environmentally adjusted consumption is derived from final consumption by deducting the improvement in the environment which is assumed to be equal to the government's net (accounting for clean-up of its own pollution) expenditure for environmental protection (5.0). Environmentally adjusted capital accumulation (−23.5) is arrived at by deducting from net capital formation (50.4) total environmental uses for all (produced and non-produced) asset categories (73.9).

The two sets of aggregate data present a very different picture of the economic situation of the country. Income is reduced drastically between NDP and EDP from 267.1 to 185.1, which represents a 31 percent reduction. Most of this reduction is caused by the modifications of the concept of capital formation to obtain a new concept of capital accumulation. Net capital formation changes from being positive (50.4) to a negative net capital accumulation of −23.5, which constitutes a reduction of income of 28 percent. The remaining 3 percent of the total reduction of GDP are explained by the difference between final consumption and environmentally adjusted consumption (−2 percent) and the decrease of exports minus imports (−1 percent) (see column 3, Table 7).

According to conventional national accounting, the country's domestic expenditure presents a healthy picture of capital formation of 19 percent of total expenditure. Environmental accounting indicates, however, that capital accumulation has been negative. The main factor explaining this result is the inclusion of non-produced assets into the asset boundary: the depletion of natural assets reduces the capital formation by a value of 18.2; a further reduction (−55.7, see Table 3) results from the degradation of land, water and air.

(ii) Income, Output and Capital

Production-related changes in environmental accounting, as compared to traditional national accounting, are elaborated on in the three sections of Table 8. In Table 8 we use figures for specific industries which are not shown in Tables 2 and 3 above, but which represent disaggregated (by economic sectors) figures of these tables. Section (i) of the table shows that there is a reduction in value added for the economy as a whole with EDP amounting to 69 percent of NDP. The impact differs from sector to sector, however. The largest reductions are in mining (52 percent) and agriculture (49 percent). In manufacturing, the reduction is 22 percent. Trade and transport also show a reduction of 14 percent due to the environmental cost of traffic pollution. All other sectors have lower reductions.

These differences are also reflected in the ratios of value added over output under NDP and EDP calculations in section (i) of Table 8. For the economy as a whole, the ratio falls from 52 percent to 36 percent. The largest drop is in agriculture from 77 percent to 39 percent, followed by mining (44 percent to 21 percent), trade and transport (61 percent to 52 percent), and manufacturing (34 percent to 27 percent). Other sectors show much lower reductions. Consequently, there are changes in the order of sector contributions to EDP as compared to NDP. Trade and transport is the largest contributor to both EDP and NDP. Manufacturing is the second largest and other services the third largest contributor to NDP. For EDP, however, this order is inverted. The weight of agriculture and mining in the economy is decreased whereas construction and government services increase in importance.

The other element of production cost, the use of economic wealth, is also affected by differences in coverage between traditional national accounting and environmental accounting. As shown in section (ii) of Table 8, produced assets, which are the capital element in national accounting, for the economy as a whole amount to only 38 percent of the total value of capital used, if non-produced assets are taken into account. For individual sectors the differences in coverage

143

TABLE 8

ANALYTICAL MEASURES IN TRADITIONAL AND ENVIRONMENTAL ACCOUNTING: INCOME, OUTPUT AND CAPITAL
(in percents)

Analytical Measures	Total	Agriculture	Mining	Manufacturing	Electr., Gas Water	Construction	Trade and Transp.	Other Services	Government Services	Environmental Adjustm.
(i)										
EDP as percentage of NDP	69	51	48	78	97	90	86	91	96	
Value added as percentage of output, based on:										
NDP	52	77	44	34	36	45	61	62	61	
EDP	36	39	21	27	34	41	52	57	59	
Value added as percentage of:										
NDP	100	12.1	12.6	16.7	0.8	7.1	26.2	14.5	9.9	
EDP	100	8.9	8.8	18.7	1.1	9.2	32.5	19.1	13.7	−12
(ii)										
Opening balance sheet: Ratio of produced assets/all assets, inclusive of non-produced assets	38	43	13	91	92	95	97	34	29	

Industries

Percentage changes between opening and closing balance sheets:									
Net capital formation and volume change due to econ. use (ecol. valuation)									
Produced assets	4	2	0	11	2	3	4	10	3
All assets, incl. non-prod. assets	1	−4	−2	10	2	3	4	3	1
Other volume changes in assets, net									
Produced assets	−2	0	0	−16	0	0	0	−5	−1
All assets, incl. non-prod. assets	0	0	8	−14	0	0	0	−2	−1
Revaluation and environ. value discrepancies									
Produced assets	14	15	13	13	15	13	12	15	15
All assets, incl. non-prod. assets	20	20	13	14	16	13	13	23	24
Total changes, net									
Produced assets	16	17	13	8	17	15	16	20	17
All assets, incl. non-prod. assets	21	17	19	10	18	16	16	24	24
(iii)									
Value added—capital ratios, based on:									
NDP	25	20	73	46	35	21	44	49	6
EDP	7	4	5	32	31	18	36	15	2

of economic wealth used in production is even more pronounced: particularly in the mining sector, produced assets are only 13 percent of the total value of assets used by economic activities.

Changes in coverage of assets also affect the change over time of economic wealth between opening and closing balance sheets. In section (ii) of Table 8, the total changes in assets are broken down into net capital accumulation (including ecologically valued volume change of natural assets due to economic use), other volume changes and valuation discrepancies due to market price changes and adjustments of ecological assets to market valuation.

The percentage change attributed to net capital accumulation is higher for produced assets (4 percent) than for all assets (1 percent). For other volume changes, however, this relationship is inverted. In the case of the traditional capital concept, other volume changes—due to earthquake damages—cause a reduction of produced assets (−2 percent), while economic wealth based on the broader concept roughly remains unchanged (0 percent). This inversion is mainly the result of the inclusion of new finds of subsoil assets (27.8, see Table 5) in the latter concept.

Discrepancies in valuation amount to 14 percent for produced assets, reflecting the average annual inflation in the country which was assumed to be 15 percent. In contrast to this, the value of all assets is increased by 20 percent. This is mainly due to the inclusion of the asset of cultivated land with its high price increases (331.0 on an opening stock of 1,366.7, see Table 5).

For the individual sectors a basic pattern can be described: total volume changes, defined as the sum of net capital accumulation and other volume changes, are approximately the same between the traditional capital concept and the broader economic wealth concept. There is a marked difference in the case of agriculture: In this sector, the volume of economic wealth increases by 2 percent (net capital accumulation of 2 percent plus other volume changes of 0 percent) when the narrower concept of produced assets is used, while it decreases by 4 percent (net capital accumulation of −4 percent plus volume changes of 0 percent) when volume changes in all assets are taken into account. The latter reduction is the result of the negative effects of land erosion, depletion and pollution (including acid deposition) on natural resources held by agriculture, forestry and fishing.

The combined changes in value added and economic wealth used in economic activities have considerable effects on the productivity or rentability of capital. The different effects on NDP- and EDP-based value added/capital ratios are presented in the last part (iii) of the table. For the economy as a whole, the ratio between value added and capital based on national accounting (NDP) is 25 percent; this is reduced to 7 percent if based on environmental accounting (EDP). For specific sectors, the differences are even larger. In mining, the value added/capital ratio based on NDP is 73 percent while for EDP it is only 5 percent. For agriculture, the ratio is reduced from 20 percent to 4 percent and for other services from 49 percent to 15 percent. These are significant changes in productivity or rentability indicators which might prompt a reassessment of investment policies as far as capital allocation to economic sectors is concerned. To the extent that environmental costs are also included in (internal) business

146

accounts, new EDP-based measures might also affect micro-economic investment decisions.

REFERENCES

Ahmad, Y. J., El Serafy, S., and Lutz, E. (eds.). *Environmental Accounting for Sustainable Development*, The World Bank, Washington, D.C., 1989.

Alfsen, K. H., Bye, T., and Lorentsen, L., *Natural Resource Accounting Analysis, The Norwegian Experience, 1978-1986*, Central Bureau of Statistics of Norway, Oslo, 1987.

Ayres, R. U., *Resources, Environment and Economics*, New York, 1978.

Ayres, R. U. and Kneese, A. V., Production, Consumption and Externalities, *American Economic Review*, Vol. 59, No. 3, 282-297, June 1969.

Bartelmus, P., Accounting for Sustainable Development, United Nations, Department of International Economic and Social Affairs, Working Paper No. 8, New York, 1987.

———, *Accounting for Sustainable Growth and Development: Structural Change and Economic Dynamics* (in preparation).

Blades, D. W., Measuring Pollution within the Framework of the National Accounts, in Ahmad, Y. J., El Serafy, S., and Lutz, E., 26-31, 1989.

Daly, H. E., Sustainable Development: From Concepts and Theory towards Operational Principles, *Populations and Development Review* (in preparation).

———, Sustainable Development: From Concepts and Theory towards Operational Principles, (in preparation).

Drechsler, L., Problems of Recording Environmental Phenomena in National Accounting Aggregates, *Review of Income and Wealth*, 22 (3), 239-252, 1976.

El Serafy, S., The Proper Calculation of Income from Depletable Natural Resources, in Ahmad, Y. J., El Serafy, S., and Lutz, E., 10-18, 1989.

Harrison, A., Environmental Issues and the SNA, *Review of Income and Wealth*, 35 (4), 377-388, December 1989.

Hueting, R., *New Scarcity and Economic Growth: More Welfare Through Less Production!* 1980.

Hueting, R. and Leipert, C., Economic Growth, National Income and the Blocked Choices for the Environment, Wissenschaftszentrum Berlin für Sozialforschung (discussion paper), Berlin, 1987.

Institut National de la Statistique et des Etudes Economiques *Les Comptes du Patrimoine Naturel*, Les collections de l'INSEE, Ser. C, 137/138, INSEE, Paris, 1986.

———, *Les Comptes Satellites de l'Environnement, Méthodes et Résultats*, Les collections de l'INSEE, Ser. C 130, INSEE, Paris, 1986a.

Isard, W., Some Notes on the Linkage of the Ecologic and Economic Systems, *Regional Science Association Papers*, 22, 85-96, 1969.

Leipert, C. National Income and Economic Growth: The Conceptual Side of Defensive Expenditures, *Journal of Economic Issues*, 23 (3), 843-856, 1989.

Leontief, W., National Income, Economic Structure and Environmental Externalities, in Moss, M. (ed.), *The Measurement of Economic and Social Performance*, Studies in Income and Wealth, Vol. 38, NBER New York, London, 565-578, 1973.

Lemaire, M. Satellite Accounting: A Solution for Analysis in Social Fields, *Review of Income and Wealth*, 33 (3), 305-325, 1987.

Lutz, E. and El Serafy, S., Recent Developments and Future Work, in Ahmad, Y. J., El Serafy, S., and Lutz, E., 88-91, 1989.

Martinez, A. R., Ion, D. C., De Sorcy, G. J., Dekker, H., and Smith, S., Classification and Nomenclature System for Petroleum and Petroleum Reserves, Twelfth World Petroleum Congress, Houston, 1987.

OECD Environmental Policy Benefits: Monetary Valuation, study prepared by D. W. Pearce and A. Markandya, Paris, 1989.

Olsen, M. The Treatment of Externalities in National Income Statistics, in Wingo, L. and Evans, A. (eds.), *Public Economics and the Quality of Life*, Baltimore, Md., 1977.

Pearce, D. W., Markandya, A., and Barbier, E., *Blueprint for a Green Economy*, London, 1989.

———, *Sustainable Development: Economy and Environment in the Third World*, London, 1990.

Peskin, H. M., A Proposed Environmental Accounts Framework, in Ahmad, Y. J., El Serafy, S., and Lutz, E., 65-78, 1989.

Pezzey, J., Economic Analysis of Sustainable Growth and Sustainable Development, World Bank, Environment Department Working Paper No. 15, Washington, D.C., 1989.

Repetto, R. and others, Wasting Assets: Natural Resources in the National Income Accounts, World Resources Institute, June 1989.

Schäfer, D. and Stahmer, C., Input–output Model for the Analysis of Environmental Protection Activities, *Economic Systems Research*, 1 (2), 203–228, 1989.
——, Conceptual Considerations on Satellite Systems. *Review of Income and Wealth*, 36 (2), 167–176, 1990.
Stahmer, C. Cost-Oriented and Welfare-Oriented Measurement in Environmental Accounting, paper presented at the Fifth Karlsruhe Seminar on Models and Measurement of Welfare and Inequality, August 12–19, 1990.
Teillet, P. A Concept of Satellite Accounts in the Revised System of National Accounts, *Review of Income and Wealth*, 34 (4), 411–439, 1988.
United Nations, *A System of National Accounts*, United Nations publication, No. E.69.XVII.3, 1968.
——, *Draft Guidelines for Statistics on Materials/Energy Balances*, United Nations Publication No. E/CN.3/492, 29 March, 1976.
——, *Provisional International Guidelines on the National and Sectoral Balance-Sheet and Reconciliation Accounts of the System of National Accounts*, United Nations publication, No. E.77.XVII.10, 1977.
——, *The Feasibility of Welfare-Oriented Measures to Supplement the National Accounts and Balances: A Technical Report*, United Nations Publication Series F, No. 22, New York, 1977.
——, *Revised System of National Accounts, Preliminary Draft Chapters, Provisional*, future ST/ESA/STAT/SER.F/2/Rev. 4, February 1990.
——, *International Standard Industrial Classification of all Economic Activities (ISIC)*, United Nations Publication, Series M, No. 4, Rev. 3, New York, 1990a.
——, *Concepts and Methods of Environment Statistics, Statistics of the Natural Environment—A Technical Report*, United Nations publication, in preparation.
——, *Central Product Classification* (CPC), United Nations publication, in preparation.
Uno, K., Economic Growth and Environmental Change in Japan–Net National Welfare and Beyond, in Archibugi, F. and Nijkamp, P. (eds.), *Economy and Ecology: Towards Sustainable Development*, 307–332, Dordrecht, 1989.
Ward, M., *Accounting for the Depletion of Natural Resources in the National Accounts of Developing Countries*, OECD Development Centre Publication, Paris, 1982.
World Commission on Environment and Development, *Our Common Future*, Oxford University Press, Oxford, 1987.

[10]

USA: Integrated economic and environmental accounting: lessons from the IEESA

J STEVEN LANDEFELD AND STEPHANIE L HOWELL

In April 1994, the United States Bureau of Economic Analysis (BEA) introduced a framework of Integrated Economic and Environmental Satellite Accounts (IEESAs) designed to cover the interactions of the economy and the environment. Modelled on the United Nations handbook on *Integrated Environmental and Economic Accounting*, they are constructed as satellite accounts to supplement, rather than replace, the existing accounts. This paper considers BEA's experiences in the development of the IEESAs, and suggests some lessons that may be useful for countries considering similar plans.[1] Over the years, the national economic accounts have benefited from discussion and critique of concepts, source data, and estimating methods. The same is to be expected for the IEESAs.

Background

Measures of economic activity such as gross domestic product (GDP) and national wealth shape perceptions and policies in profound ways. Better understanding of the critical interaction between the economy and the natural environment requires better measures of that relationship. However, the construction of accounts that illustrate these interactions involves a diversity of problems, including the controversial nature of the issue itself, theoretical approaches and data limitations. Countries attempting to move forward with environmental–economic accounts should carefully consider each of these issues in developing their research and implementation plans.

Determining the objective of the accounts is an obvious starting place, but one deserving of special mention, as the atmosphere surrounding environmental discussions lends urgency to this first step. The state of the environment has been a source of international concern for several decades, but approaches to its evaluation and maintenance or restoration still diverge widely, and the intensity of the emotions on all sides of the debate creates an atmosphere where any participation may imply advocacy of some form.

Economic vs welfare accounts

Since the founding of the US national accounts there has been an ongoing debate regarding the treatment of natural resources and the environment, as

K. Uno and P. Bartelmus (eds.), *Environmental Accounting in Theory and Practice*, 113–129.
© 1998 Kluwer Academic Publishers. Printed in Great Britain.

114   *J Steven Landefeld and Stephanie L Howell*

well as the treatment of a whole set of broader welfare-based measures of economic and social progress. One school, exemplified by Kuznets (1946), favoured development of a much broader set of welfare-orientated accounts that would focus on sustainability and address the externalities and social costs associated with economic development.[2] Another, exemplified by Jaszi (1971), insisted that the national accounts must be objective and descriptive and thus based on observable market transactions. Jaszi felt that, conceptually, the accounts should be extended to treat the economic discovery, depletion, and stocks of natural resources symmetrically with plant and equipment and other economic resources. The absence of observable market transactions and the wide uncertainty and subjectivity associated with such estimates led him to conclude, however, that they should not be included in the accounts.[3]

In the 1960s and early 1970s another more environmentally focused move to broaden the accounts arose out of concern about environmental degradation and fears that the world was running out of resources and approaching the 'limits to growth'.[4] Externalities associated with economic growth also prompted renewed interest in broader social accounting. Work by Nordhaus and Tobin (1973), among others, on adjusting traditional economic accounts for changes in leisure time, disamenities of urbanization, exhaustion of natural resources, population growth and other aspects of welfare produced indicators of economic well-being. However, the seemingly limitless scope, the range of uncertainty and the degree of subjectivity involved in such measures of non-market activities limited the usefulness of, and interest in, these social indicators. It was felt that inclusion of such measures would sharply diminish the usefulness of traditional economic accounts for analysing market activities. Attention subsequently focused on more readily identifiable and directly relevant market issues, such as the extent to which expenditures that relate to the protection and restoration of the environment (and other so-called defensive expenditures) are identifiable in the economic accounts.

The United Nations system of environmental and economic accounting

The development of the United Nations system of environmental and economic accounting (SEEA) and the use of supplemental, or satellite, accounts went a long way towards resolving the long-standing impasse between those who advocated broader sets of accounts and those concerned with maintaining the usefulness of the existing economic accounts. The supplemental accounts allowed conceptual and empirical research to move forward with estimates that can be linked to the existing accounts, but without diminishing their usefulness.

The SEEA, as described in the United Nations (1993a) handbook, is a flexible, expandable satellite system. It draws on the materials balance approach to present the full range of interactions between the economy and the environment. The SEEA builds on, and is designed to be used with, the System of

National Accounts (SNA) (Commission of the European Communities *et al.*, 1993). Like the 1993 SNA, the SEEA is primarily concerned with the implications of the environment for production, income, consumption and wealth.

The SEEA has four stages, each successively providing a more comprehensive accounting for the interaction between the economy and the environment. The four-stage presentation recognizes the need to develop concepts, to inventory and augment source data, and to adapt the implementation to differing analytical needs. The starting point is the 1993 SNA, which disaggregates, or provides additional detail on, environmentally related economic activities and assets. The second stage begins with the physical counterpart of the first stage. It maps, in physical terms, the interaction between the environment and the economy, providing the physical quantities to which prices are applied to derive the economic values included in the economic accounts. These physical accounts also provide a bridge to natural resource accounting and to materials and energy balances accounting. It then links the physical quantities to monetary values. The first two stages of the SEEA record the effects of the economy on nonproduced or environmental assets, either as other changes in the volume of assets or as changes in the distribution of income among the factors of production; these changes do not explicitly affect gross domestic product, final demand or net domestic product.

The third stage provides far more comprehensive and explicit measures of the interaction between the economy and the environment. It does so, first, by the use of alternative valuation techniques – that is, alternatives to the use of values tied to the market – and second, by the more explicit introduction of environmental effects on the measures of national production, investment, income, and wealth.

The fourth stage consists of further extensions of the SEEA. These extensions are provided for the purpose of 'opening a window on further analytical applications', and they will require further research. They include household production and the use of recreational and other unpriced environmental services in household production.

BEA's integrated economic and environmental satellite accounts

In constructing its IEESAs, BEA built on several key lessons from the social accounting experience of the 1970s and on the framework of the SEEA. First, such accounts should be focused on a specific set of issues. Second, given the kind of uses to which the estimates would be put, the early stage of conceptual development and the statistical uncertainties (even if the estimates are limited to the environment's effects on market activities), such estimates should be developed in a supplemental, or satellite, framework. Third, such accounts should not focus on sustainability or some normative objective, but should cover those interactions that can be tied to market activities and valued using market values or proxies thereof. Fourth, in keeping with the focus of the

116   *J Steven Landefeld and Stephanie L Howell*

existing accounts, the supplemental accounts should be constructed in such a manner as to be consistent with the existing accounts and thus allow analysis of the effects of the interactions between the environment and the economy on production, income, consumption and wealth.

The existing economic accounts do not provide normative data, and neither do the integrated economic and environmental accounts of the BEA. The IEESAs either report market values or proxies for market values. If a problem with property rights leads to the undervaluation and overexploitation of a resource, a set of integrated economic accounts will not reveal the right price or the correct level of stocks. They will, however, provide the data, for example, about changes in the value of the stocks and the share of income to be attributed to the resource, needed for objective analysis of the problem.

Scope

In accordance with the first criterion, BEA limited the IEESAs to those inter-actions that directly affect the economy and are thus relevant to the objective of economic accounts. From this standpoint, the environment can be thought of as consisting of a range of natural resource and environmental assets that provide an identifiable and significant flow of goods and services to the economy. The economy's uses of these productive natural assets and the goods and services they provide can be grouped into two general classes. When use of the natural asset permanently or temporarily reduces its quantity, this is viewed as involving a flow of a good or service, and the quantitative reduction in the asset is called depletion. When use of the natural asset reduces its quality, the qualitative reduction in the asset is called degradation. However, the use of natural assets describes only part of the interaction between the economy and the environment. There are also feedback effects, such as the reduction in the future yield of crops, timber, fisheries etc. from current pollution or overharvesting. Materials balance and energy accounting highlight both the use of the natural assets and the feedback effects from the use; thus, they capture the full interaction between the economy and the environment. In the case of environmental assets, the feedback is more complicated, with effects that often fall on other industries and consumers.

Integrated economic and environmental accounting aims to provide a picture of these interactions, both uses and feedbacks, between the economy and the environment. However, while this picture has numerous elements and is complex, by definition it does not cover many of the transformations and interactions within the environment itself, for example, the disposal of waste products from wild fish and mammals or the conversion of natural carbon dioxide into oxygen by plant matter on land and in the oceans.

Compliance with the first criterion resulted in accounts that were objective, rather than normative. They describe activities which bear upon the market in the monetary terms of the market, without implying any conclusions about whether the reflected situation is 'right'. Put simply, the IEESAs attempt to answer the analytical questions that are raised by the interactions of the economy and the environment, such as:

(a) The nation's wealth includes natural resources, such as oil and gas reserves and timber, that are used in production. At what rate are these resources being used?
(b) The income of producers in the mineral industries includes a return to the drilling rigs, mining equipment, and other structures and equipment engaged in them and a return to the mineral. What share is attributable to the mineral?
(c) Economic activity adds to the proved stock of natural resources by exploration and technological innovation. How much of the use of natural resources in production has been offset by these additions?
(d) Households, governments, and business all make expenditures to maintain or restore the environment. What share of their spending is for the environment?
(e) The economy disposes of wastes into the air and water, and the resulting degradation of the environment imposes costs, such as lower timber yields and fish harvests and higher cleaning costs. What are these costs? Which sectors bear them?

Structural features

In accord with the second criterion, the IEESAs have two main structural features. First, natural and environmental resources are treated like productive assets and only the economically productive aspects of the resources are considered. These resources, along with structures and equipment, are treated as part of the nation's wealth, and the flow of goods and services from them is identified and their contribution to production measured. Second, the accounts provide substantial detail on expenditures and assets that are relevant to understanding and analysing the interaction. Fully implemented IEESAs would permit identification of the economic contribution of natural and environmental resources by industry, by type of income and by product. Ultimately, accounts by region would add an important analytical dimension.

Productive assets

BEA's decision to treat natural and environmental resources like productive assets in the IEESAs is based on their similarity to man-made capital: for labour and materials are devoted to producing fixed assets, and they then yield a flow of services over time. For inventories, stocks are held pending further processing, sale, delivery, or intermediate use. An example of a fixed natural resource is trees; a natural resource inventory is livestock raised for slaughter.

118   *J Steven Landefeld and Stephanie L Howell*

Table 1. IEESA asset account, 1987 (billions of dollars). This table can serve as an inventory of the estimates currently available for IEESA. In decreasing order of quality, the estimates that have been filled in are as follows: For made assets, estimates of fixed reproducible tangible stock and inventories, from BEA's national income and product accounts or based on them, and pollution abatement stock, from BEA estimates (rows 1–21); for subsoil assets, the high and lows of the range based on alternative valuation methods, from the companion article (rows 36–41); and best-available, or rough-order-of-magnitude, estimates for some other developed natural assets (selected rows 23–35 and 42–47) and some environmental assets (selected rows 48–55) prepared by BEA based on a wide range of source data described in this article. The 'n.a.'--not available-- entries represents a research agenda.

	Row No.	Opening Stocks	Change — Total net (3+4+5)	Change — Depreciation Depletion Degradation	Change — Capital Formation	Change — Revaluation and Other Changes	Closing Stocks (1+2)
		(1)	(2)	(3)	(4)	(5)	(6)
PRODUCED ASSETS							
Made assets	1	11565.9	667.4	-607.9	905.8	369.4	12233.3
Fixed assets	2	10535.2	608.2	-607.9	875.8	340.2	11143.4
Residential structures and equipment, private and government	3	4001.6	318.1	-109.8	230.5	197.4	4319.7
Fixed nonresidential structures and equipment, private and government	4	6533.6	290.1	-498.1	645.3	142.9	6823.7
Natural resource related	5	503.7	23.1	-19.2	30.3	12.0	526.8
Environmental management	6	241.3	8.4	-7.0	10.5	4.7	249.6
Conservation and development	7	152.7	3.6	-4.4	5.3	2.7	156.4
Water supply facilities	8	88.5	4.8	-2.5	5.3	2.0	93.3
Pollution abatement and control	9	262.4	14.7	-12.2	19.7	7.3	277.1
Sanitary services	10	172.9	12.8	-5.6	13.7	4.8	185.8
Air pollution abatement and control	11	45.3	0.6	-4.1	3.5	1.3	45.9
Water pollution abatement and control	12	44.2	1.3	-2.5	2.6	1.2	45.5
Other /1/	13	8029.9	267.0	-478.9	615.0	130.9	8296.9
Inventories	14	1030.7	59.3	....	30.1	29.2	1090.0
Government	15	184.9	6.8	....	2.9	3.8	191.7
Nonfarm	16	797.3	62.4	....	32.7	29.7	859.7
Farm (harvested crops, and livestock other than cattle and calves)	17	48.5	-9.9	....	-5.5	-4.4	38.6
Corn	18	10.2	0.3	....	-1.1	1.4	10.5
Soybeans	19	5.0	-0.1	....	-1.0	0.9	4.9
All wheat	20	2.6	0.0	....	-0.2	0.2	2.6
Other	21	30.7	-10.1	....	-3.2	-6.9	20.6
Developed natural assets	22	n.a.	n.a.	n.a.	n.a.	n.a.	n.a.
Cultivated biological resources	23	n.a.	n.a.	n.a.	n.a.	n.a.	n.a.
Cultivated fixed natural growth assets	24	n.a.	n.a.	n.a.	n.a.	n.a.	n.a.
Livestock for breeding, dairy, draught, etc.	25	n.a.	n.a.	n.a.	n.a.	n.a.	n.a.
Cattle	26	12.9	2.0	n.a.	-0.3	2.3	14.9
Fish stock	27	n.a.	n.a.	n.a.	n.a.	n.a.	n.a.
Vineyards, orchards	28	2.0	0.2	n.a.	0.0	0.2	2.2
Trees on timberland	29	288.8	47.0	-6.9	9.0	44.9	335.7
Work-in-progress on natural growth products	30	n.a.	n.a.	....	n.a.	n.a.	n.a.
Livestock raised for slaughter	31	n.a.	n.a.	....	n.a.	n.a.	n.a.
Cattle	32	24.1	7.5	....	0.0	7.5	31.6
Fish stock	33	n.a.	n.a.	....	n.a.	n.a.	n.a.
Calves	34	5.0	0.9	....	-0.5	1.4	5.9
Crops and other produced plants, not yet harvested	35	1.6	0.3	....	0.1	0.2	2.1
Proved subsoil assets/2/	36	270.0 - 1066.9	57.8 - -116.6	-16.7 - -61.6	16.6 - 64.6	58 - -119.6	299.4 - 950.3
Oil (including natural gas liquids)	37	58.2 - 325.9	-22.5 - -84.7	-5.1 - -30.6	5.8 - 34.2	-23.1 - -88.3	35.7 - 241.2
Gas (including natural gas liquids)	38	42.7 - 259.3	6.6 - -57.2	-5.6 - -20.3	4.1 - 14.9	8.1 - -51.8	49.4 - 202.2
Coal	39	140.7 - 207.7	2.2 - -3.4	-5.4 - -7.6	4.4 - 6.3	3.2 - -2.1	143.0 - 204.2
Metals	40	* - 215.3	67.2 - 29.5	-0.2 - -2.2	2.2 - 9.2	65.2 - 22.5	38.5 - 244.8
Other minerals	41	28.4 - 58.7	4.3 - -0.8	-0.4 - -0.9	0.1 - 0.0	4.6 - 0.1	32.8 - 57.9
Developed land	42	n.a.	n.a.	n.a.	n.a.	n.a.	n.a.
Land underlying structures (private)	43	4053.4	253.0	n.a.	n.a.	n.a.	4306.3
Agricultural land (excluding vineyards, orchards)	44	441.3	42.4	n.a.	-2.8	45.2	483.7
Soil	45	n.a.	n.a.	-0.5	n.a.	n.a.	n.a.
Recreational land and water (public)	46	n.a.	n.a.	-0.9	n.a.	n.a.	n.a.
Forests and other wooded land	47	285.8	28.8	n.a.	0.6	29.4	314.6
NONPRODUCED/ENVIRONMENTAL ASSETS							
Uncultivated biological resources	48	n.a.	n.a.	n.a.	n.a.	n.a.	n.a.
Wild fish	49	n.a.	n.a.	n.a.	n.a.	n.a.	n.a.
Timber and other plants of uncultivated forests	50	n.a.	n.a.	n.a.	n.a.	n.a.	n.a.
Other uncultivated biological resources	51	n.a.	n.a.	n.a.	n.a.	n.a.	n.a.
Unproved subsoil assets	52	n.a.	n.a.	n.a.	n.a.	n.a.	n.a.
Undeveloped land	53	n.a.	n.a.	n.a.	n.a.	n.a.	n.a.
Water (economic effects of changes in the stock)	54	....	n.a.	-19.9	19.9	n.a.	....
Air (economic effects of changes in the stock)	55	....	n.a.	-38.7	38.7	n.a.	....
			n.a.	-27.1	27.1	n.a.	

n.a. not available
* The calculated value of the entry was negative.
1. The estimate for inventories differs from the NIPA estimate by the amount of government inventories added and cattle and calves shown separately. In full implementation of the IEESA account, farm inventories would include only harvested crops
2. The estimates in all columns result from the valuation method (see text for further discussion of the alternative methods) that produces the low and high estimates of opening stocks
NOTE. Leaders indicate an entry is not applicable

The distinction between fixed assets and inventories is not always clear, and each country will come to its own classifications. One example is the long-standing debate regarding the classification of mineral resources. Proved mineral reserves may seem to be similar to inventories – they are a set number of units waiting to be used up in production. Yet they also fit the classic characteristics of fixed capital – expenditures of materials and labour are needed to produce them, and they yield a stream of product over long periods of time. Further, like a fixed asset such as a machine, the number of units extracted from a new mine or field is uncertain and varies over time and the service life is used up in production. Finally, the treatment of mineral reserves as fixed assets serves equally well as a reminder of the reproducibility of proved reserves.

For these reasons, the IEESAs include these resources, along with structures and equipment, as part of the nation's wealth and give them the same treatment as fixed assets such as structures and equipment in the traditional accounts. This deals with three points of asymmetry between the treatment of mineral reserves and of structures and equipment encountered in traditional accounts. In traditional accounts: (1) depreciation is subtracted from profits to determine true, or sustainable, profits, but depletion is not; (2) depreciation is subtracted from GDP to estimate NDP, but depletion is not; and (3) additions to the stock of plant and equipment are added to GDP as capital formation, but additions to mineral reserves are not.

Detail

In the IEESAs, the standard economic accounting categories are disaggregated to show detail that highlights the interaction of the economy and the environment. For example, the expenditures detail shows spending by households, government and business to maintain or restore the environment. The asset detail shows environmental management (conservation and development, and water supply) and waste management projects (sanitary services, air and water pollution abatement and control) within the standard category of non-residential fixed capital.

The estimating requirements underlying these two main structural features of the IEESAs are apparent in the IEESAs tables, even when they are in skeleton form. Table 1, an asset account and Table 2, a production account, use modified forms of tables presented in the SEEA.

Accounts

Asset accounts

Integrated economic and environmental accounting requires the measurement of stocks and flows related to assets which are presented in an asset account. The IEESAs provide a complete accounting for the relevant assets: they show both stocks and flows associated with changes in those stocks. Table 1 provides for estimates of opening stocks, different kinds of changes in the stock and closing stocks. It also presents the non-financial assets that BEA would try to include in IEESAs asset accounts. These generally follow the subcategories of the 1993 SNA and the SEEA, but some of the subcategories are regrouped to broaden both the production boundary and the definition of assets. Non-financial assets are divided into made assets, developed natural assets and environmental assets. Made assets, which largely replicate the scope

120   *J Steven Landefeld and Stephanie L Howell*

Table 2.   IEESA production account, 1987 (billions of dollars).

		INDUSTRIES				Final consumption		FINAL USES (GDP)				
	Row no.	Agriculture, forestry, fisheries (1)	Mining, utilities, water, and sanitary services (2)	Other Industries (3)	Total (4)	Household (5)	Government (6)	Gross Domestic Capital Formation (7)	Exports (8)	Imports (9)	GDP (5+6+7 +8-9) (10)	Total Commodity Output (4+10) (11)
COMMODITIES												0.0
Made	1							933.0			#	#
Assets	2							933.0			#	#
Fixed assets	3							875.8			#	#
Environmental management	4							10.6			#	#
Pollution abatement and control	5							19.7			#	#
Other	6							845.5			#	#
Inventories	7							57.2			#	#
Government	8							30.1			#	#
Nonfarm	9							32.7			#	#
Farm	10							-5.5			#	#
Other	11	#	#	#	#	#	#		#	#	#	#
Environmental cleanup and waste disposal services	12	n.a.	n.a.	n.a.	n.a.	n.a.	n.a.		n.a.	n.a.	#	#
Other	13	n.a.	n.a.	n.a.	n.a.	n.a.	n.a.				#	#
Natural and environmental assets	14							n.a.			#	#
Fixed	15							n.a.			#	#
Cultivated biological resources: natural growth	16							n.a.			#	#
Proved subsoil assets	17							16.6 - 64.6			#	#
Developed land	18							n.a.			#	#
Uncultivated biological resources: natural growth	19							n.a.			#	#
Unproved subsoil assets	20							n.a.			#	#
Undeveloped land	21							19.9			#	#
Water	22							38.7			#	#
Air	23							27.1			#	#
Work-in-progress inventories (natural growth products)	24							n.a.			#	#
Total intermediate inputs	25	#	#	#	#							
VALUE ADDED												0.0
Compensation of employees	26	#	#	#	#							0.0
Indirect business taxes, etc.	27	#	#	#	#							#
Corporate profits and other property income	28	#	#	#	#							#
Depreciation of fixed made assets: structures and equipment	29	n.a.	n.a.	n.a.	-607.9							0.0
Environmental management	30	n.a.	n.a.	n.a.	-19.2							#
Pollution abatement and control	31	n.a.	n.a.	n.a.	-2.5							#
Other	32	n.a.	n.a.	n.a.	-585.1							#
Depletion and degradation of fixed natural and environmental assets	33	n.a.	n.a.	n.a.	n.a.							#
Growth products: fixed	34	n.a.	n.a.	n.a.	n.a.							#
Proved subsoil assets	35	n.a.	n.a.	n.a.	16.7 - 61.6							#
Developed land	36	n.a.	n.a.	n.a.	n.a.							#
Uncultivated biological resources	37	n.a.	n.a.	n.a.	n.a.							#
Unproved subsoil assets	38	n.a.	n.a.	n.a.	n.a.							#
Undeveloped land	39	n.a.	n.a.	n.a.	n.a.	n.a.						#
Water	40	n.a.	n.a.	n.a.	-19.9							#
Air	41	n.a.	n.a.	n.a.	-38.7							#
Gross value added (GDP) (rows 26+27+28+29+33)	42	n.a.	n.a.	n.a.	n.a.							#
Depreciation, depletion, and degradation (rows 29+33)	43	n.a.	n.a.	n.a.	n.a.							#
Net value added (NDP) (rows 42+43)	44	n.a.	n.a.	n.a.	n.a.							#
TOTAL INDUSTRY OUTPUT	45	#	#	#	#	#	#	#	#	#	#	0.0

n.a. Not available
These estimates will depend on the integration of the System of National Accounts and the System of Environmental and Economic Accounting as part of the overall modernization of BEA's economic accounts.
NOTE.-Leaders indicate that an entry is not applicable.
GDP Gross domestic product
NDP Net domestic product

of non-financial assets in traditional income and wealth accounts, are sub-divided into fixed assets and inventories. Developed natural assets are sub-divided into cultivated biological resources (both fixed and work in progress inventories), proved subsoil assets and developed land. Environmental assets are subdivided into uncultivated biological resources, unproved subsoil assets, undeveloped land, water and air (the last two in terms of the economic effects of changes in the stock).

Made and developed natural assets

To better highlight the interaction of the economy and the environment, Table 1 provides more detail on natural resource and environmentally related produced assets than the traditional income and wealth accounts. Within made assets, non-residential fixed capital is disaggregated into environmental management (conservation and development, and water supply) and waste management projects (sanitary services, air and water pollution abatement and control). Detail is also provided on farm inventories of finished goods. Within cultivated biological resources, Table 1 provides detail beyond that contained in the traditional accounts, such as cultivated fixed natural growth assets (for example, livestock), and categories not included in the traditional accounts (for example, trees on timberland). The treatment of proved subsoil assets and cultivated land in Table 1 differs from the SEEA treatment. Proved reserves are generally defined as those reserves that are proved to a high degree of certainty, by test wells or other test data, and are recoverable under current economic conditions and with current technology. In the SEEA, they are classified as non-produced assets. In Table 1, these assets, along with cultivated natural growth assets, are included in the category 'developed natural assets'. As will be illustrated in the production accounts, capital formation that adds to the stock of these assets, both by bringing undeveloped or uncultivated assets into the category of developed natural assets and by adding to their value within that category, is treated in a manner similar to capital formation that adds to the stock of structures and equipment.

This treatment was adopted because it is difficult to rationalize describing proved reserves and cultivated land as 'non-produced' natural assets when expenditures are required to prove or develop them. Agricultural land, for example, must be produced in that expenditures must be undertaken to convert uncultivated land areas into commercially valuable farmland, which yields a return over a number of years. Wetland areas, if they are to become farmland, must be drained and graded and cleared of vegetation. Unproved mineral reserves also require expenditure on test wells, engineering studies, and other exploration and development investments before they are recorded as proved reserves.

Similar treatment of these developed natural assets and made assets facilitates consistent treatment of capital formation of natural assets and more conventional capital formation, such as investment in structures and equipment. Under this treatment, as mineral reserves, for example, are proved, the total value of the produced assets – structures and equipment as well as the proved reserve's value – is included as capital formation. Similarly, as oil field machinery is depreciated, proved reserves associated with the machinery are depleted.

The other major difference between developed assets in Table 1 and in the comparable SEEA presentation is in the treatment of soil. In the SEEA, soil (that is, productive soil on agricultural land) is treated as separate from agricultural land. In Table 1, soil is a subcategory of agricultural land because the value of agricultural land is inseparable from the value of the soil. Available estimates suggest that the effect of soil erosion, or depletion, on agricultural productivity and land values in the USA is quite small. Nevertheless, though soil is not treated separately, it is shown separately because its erosion has a significant effect on environmental quality through its effect on water quality.

Environmental assets

Environmental assets include natural assets with significant economic value that differ from developed natural assets in that they are generally used as raw inputs into production in their natural state, either as intermediate products or as investments. For example, uncultivated biological resources, such as tuna harvested from the ocean, are included as environmental assets, whereas cultivated biological resources, such as rockfish raised on a fish farm, are included in developed assets. Other categories in environmental assets are uncultivated land, unproved subsoil assets, water, and air. The inclusion of unproved subsoil assets broadens the definition of subsoil assets to include reserves that, though unproved, have an economic value over and above that of other undeveloped land because of their location or geological characteristics. As capital expenditures are made to prove these properties, they move from non-produced to produced assets. This broader definition of subsoil resources will facilitate longer term planning and analysis of the use of mineral resources. The stock of proved reserves, like the stock of drill presses, can be expanded by additional investment; hence, firms will keep on hand the stock of reserves dictated by current market prices, finding costs, and interest rates. Thus, complete analysis of mineral resources requires consideration of un-proved, as well as of proved, reserves.

In a distinction similar to that between proved and un-proved subsoil assets, cultivated land such as agricultural land, parkland, and land underlying buildings is included in developed natural assets, whereas uncultivated land such as wetlands and forestland (not included as timberland) is included in environmental assets. The agricultural land must be developed before it can be used as farmland, whereas wetlands are used, for example, for flood control, in their natural state by the economy. Water, which is subdivided by type, and air also provide services to the economy in the form of recreational and waste disposal services.

Although these environmental assets differ from made and developed natural assets, investments that add to the stock of these assets, as noted below in the production accounts, are treated symmetrically with investments that add to the stock of structures and equipment and of developed assets. These investments, for example, include pollution abatement and control to improve the quality and waste disposal capacity of the air and water, or at least to offset the degradation/depletion (which is also recorded in the production account) occurring in the current period. The rationale for treating such expenditures as investment rather than costs is that they represent a decision by the economy to devote its resources to investments that improve air and water quality, rather than investments in structures and equipment.

Production accounts

The next step in integrating economic and environmental accounting is to combine the appropriate flows from the asset account with the flows in a production account. With this integration, the production account of the IEESAs explicitly includes the use of natural resources and environmental services in production through entries for depletion and degradation, and it explicitly includes the additions to the stock of natural and environmental assets through entries for investments that add to stocks of developed natural resources or that restore stocks of environmental assets.

Table 2 combines features of both the supply and use tables in the 1993 SNA. The table has four quadrants (one empty, except for a total) which are separated by double lines, a total column at the far right and a total row at the bottom. The left and right upper quadrants show the use of goods and services (commodities) named at the beginning of the rows, summing to total uses as measured by total commodity output. The left-hand upper and lower quadrants show the use of intermediate inputs and factors of production by the industries named at the top of each column, summing to total supply as measured by total output.

Valuation

The choice of a valuation approach was not a difficult one for BEA. While alternative methods such as maintenance cost and contingent valuation have attractive theoretical characteristics, they are not appropriate for BEA's purpose, and the associated practical difficulties outweigh their charms. In keeping with the goals and criteria stated above, market pricing was the optimal choice for the IEESAs. First, market pricing maintains objectivity by avoiding the bias that may be inherent in 'willingness to pay' surveys. Second, market pricing is consistent with conventional accounts, as well as the SEEA, and facilitates international comparability. Finally, market pricing is consistent with the limits placed on the included interactions because it values those interactions from the perspective of the market. This approach was not problem-free, however. The quality of the estimates released in 1994 varies with regard to the source data available and, as natural and environmental resources are rarely traded, market prices are often not available. Thus, the estimates recorded for 1987 in Table 1 should be regarded as rough order of magnitude, or best available, estimates.

When market prices or other source data were unavailable, BEA used the best available techniques to produce proxies of market values:

(a) The estimates of the value of vineyards and orchards are based on Federal Reserve Board estimates of the value of agricultural land and estimates of the acres of land in vineyards and orchards from the Bureau of the Census.
(b) The values of trees on timberland were estimated based on stumpage value estimates provided by the US Forest Service's Pacific Northwest Research Station. The stumpage value estimates are based on the concept of net rent to the timber stand (as distinct from the land underlying the forest) and are derived mainly from private market data on payments for logging rights. As such, they should correspond to the present discounted value of the timber sales from the tract less the costs of logging, access, transportation

124   *J Steven Landefeld and Stephanie L Howell*

and processing. All timber on commercially viable timberland in the United States, public and private, is included in this category.

(c) Sil estimates, obtained from the US Department of Agriculture (USDA), reflect the annual effect of soil depletion in terms of extra fertilizer costs and reduced productivity.

(d) The estimate of capital formation in recreational land is based on Federal Government maintenance and repair expenditures for parks; State and local expenditures are not available. It is assumed that these expenditures exactly offset the degradation/depletion of recreational land; in the case of recreational land, the only estimates available were of maintenance and repair expenditures. This assumption is made only so that both investment and degradation/depletion estimates are illustrated by the table and not to imply any judgment about the true value of degradation/depletion.[5]

(e) For environmental assets, the estimates are more uncertain than even the most uncertain estimates for developed land and proved reserves of subsoil assets. Indeed, most of this section of the table, especially that for renewable natural resources, is shown as 'not available'. No value is available for the stock of undeveloped land and its associated ecosystems, for unproved subsoil assets and for uncultivated biological resources (wild animals and fish, plants and forests).

(f) The SEEA does not recommend that the stock of air, which is truly a global common, or water be valued; instead, it recommends that valuation be limited to changes in these assets – their degradation and investments in their restoration. For these assets, Table 1 includes only aggregate values for the degradation of air and water and for expenditures to restore them or to prevent their degradation. The estimates in Table 1 for degradation of air and water quality, as well as for undeveloped land, are simply place markers which assume that maintenance exactly offsets degradation: they are aggregate estimates of the total costs of pollution of these media. The estimates for air, water and undeveloped land pollution are estimates obtained from the Environmental Protection Agency of the costs of public and private pollution control activities in the USA. Estimates of air pollution include the annualized costs of air pollution and radiation. Water pollution estimates are the annualized costs of maintaining water quality, including drinking water. Estimates of undeveloped land pollution are the annualized costs associated with the Superfund, toxic chemicals and pesticides.

Estimates

When market prices were not available, BEA tried to present a range of estimates reflecting various valuation techniques. In most cases, however, only one estimate, rather than a range, was available and many cells in Table 1 do not contain estimates. In general, the quality and availability of the estimates declines as one moves down the rows from produced to non-produced assets, reflecting the increasing conceptual and empirical difficulties in producing such estimates. The estimates may be best regarded as a measure of the work to be undertaken; they are presented here to serve as a road map for areas in which source data and estimating methods must be developed or improved.

The estimates presented in Table 2 are taken from Table 1. As indicated by 'n.a.', many valuation and measurement issues remain before an IEESAs production account can be completed. Further, work toward filling in the estimates would proceed in tandem with work on modernizing BEA's national accounts in line with the SNA. For example, treating expenditures on government structures, equipment, and inventories as capital formation implements a feature of the SNA. In the table, ' # ' indicates the estimates that would reflect both work toward the IEESAs and SNA-related changes.

The prototype estimates of mineral resources – the focus of the first phase of work released in 1994 – include stocks and flows in accounts that supplement BEA's national wealth accounts and National Income and Product Accounts (NIPAs). These prototype estimates provide a comprehensive picture of the stocks of natural assets and the changes in them. They also allow an examination of the practical consequences of several alternative methods of valuing the stock of resources, additions and depletion. The alternative methods – current rent (of which BEA used two variants), present discounted value, replacement cost and transaction prices – represent the Bureau's technical assessment of the best estimates and framework that are feasible with existing sources and methods. Some of the implications of these estimates are as follows:

(a) The value of additions has tended to exceed depletions. Since 1958, the value of the stocks of proved mineral reserves in the aggregate has grown in current dollars, while showing little change in constant (1987) dollars.

(b) Changes in the stocks of these productive assets over time have largely reflected changes in the resource rents. Increases in resource rents have been accompanied by greater investment in exploration and enhanced recovery technology. Decreases in rents of some resources have been accompanied by reduced exploration activity and the closing of marginal fields and mines.

(c) Proved mineral reserves constitute a significant share of the economy's stock of productive resources. Addition of the value of the stock of these mineral resources to the value of structures, equipment, and inventories for 1991 would raise the total by $471–916 billion, or 3–7%, depending on the valuation method used.

(d) The stocks of proved mineral resources are worth much more than the stocks of invested structures and equipment associated with the resources. In 1991, the value of the stock of subsoil assets was 2–4 times as large as

126   *J Steven Landefeld and Stephanie L Howell*

the value of the associated stock of invested structures and equipment and inventories.

(e) Valuing the effect of depletion and additions, as well as including the value of resource stocks, provides a significantly different picture of returns. Compared with rates of return calculated using income and capital stock as measured in the existing accounts, the IEESAs-based average rates of return on capital in the mining industry for 1958–91 are lower, at 4–5% rather than 23%. Rates of return for all private capital slip from 16% using measures in the existing accounts to 14–15% using IEESAs measures for the mining industries.

(f) Although the trends that emerge from the alternative methods are similar, the range of estimates is large. The highest estimates of stocks, depletion and additions were obtained from the current rent estimates based on capital stock values, and the lowest were from the current rent estimates based on average rates of return to capital.

Uses of the new accounts

The IEESAs will help to identify the use of the various natural and environmental resources, but because of offsetting changes it is difficult to say *a priori* whether there will be a net reduction or increase in their value overall. Indeed, it is not clear whether such a 'bottom line' estimate is even desirable. First, such an estimate may not be very informative. For example, while it is almost certainly true that the economic value of the stocks of some assets in the USA, such as bluefin tuna, is declining, the stocks of other environmental assets, such as timber stocks, have been increasing as planting and growth have more than offset harvests, fire and land conversions. Similarly, while losses of wetlands from development continue to outnumber gains from wetland restorations, increasing rates of investments in cleaner air and water since the mid-1970s appear to have resulted in net improvements in air and water quality; many of the measures of air and water quality, such as the ambient concentrations of air and water pollutants, have shown improvement. It is conceivable that when all entries in Table 2 (or if not all, at least enough more than at present to avoid risks of conclusions based on partial results) have been filled in, the table will show that IEESAs-NDP differs little from traditional NDP.

Second, it is not clear that the information reflected in a bottom line measure is always relevant. For example, as noted above in the case of mineral reserves, the stock of proven reserves varies with the rate of return and remains a fairly stable multiple of annual consumption; the mineral industries make expenditures to prove reserves to ensure a level of supply for a given or projected demand. Changes in proven reserves, therefore, have little to say about long-run sustainability. Instead, as the prototype IEESAs accounts illustrated, the changes in stocks of proven reserves and their prices over time have significant effects on rates of return, in the aggregate and by industry, and the structure of the accounts will allow the analysis of the secondary effects by type of income, type of investment and type of spending. Other effects that could be analysed include the impact of changes in minerals prices on the US terms of trade, the related measure of command-basis GNP (which reflects the resources over which a nation has command as a result of its exports and other income from abroad) as well as a wide range of issues including federal fees for grazing rights, water use, logging, mineral rights, fishing permits, and the impact of environmental regulations and emission taxes.[6] For a developed economy, such as that of the USA, this detailed information about the inter-action between the economy and the environment rather than normative mea-sures of our environmental welfare or long-run sustainability will provide the most valuable insights about the implications of different regulations, taxes and consumption patterns.

BEA's plan for natural resource and environmental accounting

BEA's plan calls for work on the IEESAs to be undertaken in conjunction with modernizing its economic accounts. BEA's national accounts are now under-going the first major redesign since the 1950s. The redesign, which will be along the lines of the 1993 SNA, will feature an integrated set of current and capital accounts, sector by sector. Fully developed capital accounts, along with balance sheets, are essential for a comprehensive set of economic accounts. The conceptual work on these accounts and the more specialized work on natural resources and the environment will be mutually supporting. Further, to make reasoned policy choices involving trade-offs among kinds of capital, one would want a view of the total capital stock, natural and made, consis-tently covered and appropriately valued.

BEA has developed a three-phase plan for the IEESAs. With the April 1994 issue of the *Survey of Current Business*, BEA completed the first phase of work. The overall IEESA framework is designed to build upon the existing national accounts and is in line with the guidance embodied in the new international SNA about a satellite system and the companion SEEA. In its initial work, BEA focused on mineral resources, consisting of oil and gas, coal, metals and other minerals with a scarcity value. The focus, in accordance with SNA rec-ommendations, is on proved reserves, the basis for valuation is market values, and the treatment given to mineral resources, which require expenditures to prove and which provide 'services' over a long timespan, is similar to the treatment of fixed capital in the existing accounts.

The second phase will incorporate renewable natural resources. Compared with the accounting for proved reserves of non-renewable resources, where the economic literature extends back over 50 years, valuation methods and con-cepts for many of the renewable resources are less well developed. Renewable natural resources are inherently more difficult to value than non-renewable

128   *J Steven Landefeld and Stephanie L Howell*

natural resources for several reasons: renewable resources, such as stocks or schools of wild fish, often have a commercial or production value as well as an amenity or a recreational value; often, ownership rights cannot be established, and they cannot be sold; and they are able to regenerate, so their use does not necessarily result in a net reduction in either their yield or the value of their stock.

These difficulties notwithstanding, there has been rapid progress in environmental benefit valuation for renewable natural resources in recent years as economists have tried to keep pace with regulatory, legal and policy needs for environmental damage and impact measures. Further work by BEA to translate these new concepts and measures into a consistent national framework would need to rely heavily on the expertise of other units within the US Government, for example, the National Oceanic and Atmospheric Administration, the Environmental Protection Agency, USDA, and the Department of Interior. The plan calls for work to extend the accounts to renewable natural resource assets, such as trees on timberland, fish stocks and water resources. Development of these estimates will be more difficult than for mineral resources because they must be based on less refined concepts and less data.

Building on this work, the third phase calls for moving on to issues associated with a broader range of environmental assets, including the economic value of the degradation of clean air and water, or the value of recreational assets such as lakes and national forests. Clearly, significant advances will be required in the underlying environmental and economic data, as well as in concepts and methods, and cooperative efforts with the scientific, statistical and economic communities will be needed to produce such estimates.

Lessons

Several lessons were learned in the process of developing the IEESAs that may be useful cautions for countries about to embark on a similar journey towards integrated economic and environmental accounts.

(a) First, the new accounts, like the conventional accounts, will only be worthwhile if they are used. Thus, consistency with the existing accounts through the use of market prices, and proxies thereof, and the treatment of natural resources and environmental assets symmetrically with economic assets remains an absolute requirement if they are to be used in conjunction with the existing accounts. In addition, if the new accounts are focused and based on the market-related concepts outlined in the existing accounts, many of the concerns related to the subjectivity and conceptual basis of earlier social accounting measures will be avoided.

(b) Throughout the development of the IEESAs, BEA looked outside its own work and built upon the economic and social accounting lessons of the past. BEA also relied on the expertise and data provided by natural resource and environmental and economic accounting experts in the USA and abroad. In this way, it avoided unnecessary 'reinventing' of the wheel.

(c) At the same time, BEA adapted that knowledge to its own needs to make the IEESAs appropriate for analysis of the specific concerns of the USA.

(d) When adequate source data were available, BEA presented a range of estimates to illustrate various methods and to emphasize the uncertainty associated with such accounts.

(e) In order to make its source data, methods and assumptions open and accessible, BEA published detailed information on source data and estimation methods.

(f) The limitation of the accounts to the interaction between the economy and the environment enabled BEA to apply a market approach consistently (though the exact approach and data availability remain issues for future work). If the accounts had extended to the noneconomic functions of natural resources and environmental assets, they would have been forced to incorporate inconsistent valuation methods that would preclude or at least complicate useful aggregation or comparison.

(g) The limitation to interactions between the economy and the environment also enabled BEA to construct its accounts upon a clear and consistent conceptual base. The advantages of this approach have been repeatedly revealed since the release of the prototype accounts. Most recently, the National Academy of Sciences has been able to begin its review of the accounts, as requested by Congress, with a clear understanding of the rationale for its structure and methods.

Notes

1. Copies of the two *Survey of Current Business* articles detailing the accounts are available on the Internet or by calling (202)606-9900.
2. In the last chapter, Kuznets (1996) notes that the result of the restriction of national income estimates to economic activities is that they 'neglect completely any consideration of such costs of economic activity as impinge directly upon consumers' satisfaction or the welfare of the community' and that errors of both omission and commission 'renders national income merely one element in the evaluation of the net welfare assignable to the nation's economic activity'.
3. Jaszi (1971) makes clear his belief that 'the tools we have available to construct a measure of output . . . cannot be used to construct a measure of welfare'.
4. This environmentalist school of thought has a long tradition both within and outside of economic circles. For example, US Vice President Gore (1992) goes beyond economic analysis in his comprehensive evaluation of the environment and society. Daly and Cobb (1989) use a more traditional economic approach in their development of the Index of Sustainable Economic Welfare. Cobb *et al.* (1995) use a similar approach in their calculation of a 'Genuine Progress Indicator' that adjusts GDP for household production, crime, and other welfare effects.
5. Phases II and III of BEA's work plan, described in the next section, include work, building on the damage assessment and recreational valuation literature, to construct estimates of the market value of recreational and environmental amenities.
6. For further discussion of the concept and measurement of command-basis GNP, see Denison (1981) or the *SNA* 1993 (Commission of the European Communities *et al.*, 1993 404–405).

[11]

Republic of Korea: SEEA pilot compilation

SEUNG-WOO KIM, JAN VAN TONGEREN AND
ALESSANDRA ALFIERI

Orientation and scope of environmental accounting in Korea

Following the success of an export-led growth policy during the 1970s and 1980s, the Korean environment began to face significant deterioration in the 1990s, due to a combination of rapid industrialization, population growth and urbanization. As in the past Korea had to pursue its economic development without a sufficient endowment of natural resources and technological accumulation, environmental concerns were not considered a priority in economic policy.

This chapter addresses the need to provide data to support policies which integrate governmental economic policies with environmental conservation. Based on international experiences and recommendations, the paper presents proposals for an environmental accounts framework which extends the present national (economic) accounts of Korea to reflect natural resource depletion and environmental degradation not valued in the market. The framework is based on the System of integrated Environmental and Economic Accounts (SEEA; United Nations, 1993a). It can be used to analyse the interactions between the environment and the economy (van Tongeren et al., 1994). Using the proposed framework of accounts, a pilot compilation of environmental accounts for Korea was carried out for the period 1985–1992. The project was funded by UNDP, implemented by the Korea Environmental Technology Research Institute (KETRI), and technically supported by the United Nations Statistics Division (UNSD) and the United Nations Department of Development Support and Management Service (DDSMS).

The accounts deal with economic causes of air and water pollution and the environmental protection activities required in response to these concerns. Also dealt with is the depletion of the stock of natural forests, selected minerals and fish; the latter analysis is extended beyond the boundaries of Korea by analysing the effects of economic activities in Korea on depletable natural assets in other countries. Land use issues, showing how forest and other non-economic land is absorbed by agricultural, built-up and recreational land, as a consequence of economic development of Korea, are also discussed.

The views expressed here are those of the authors and not necessarily those of their respective organizations.

K. Uno and P. Bartelmus (eds.), Environmental Accounting in Theory and Practice, 63–76.
© 1998 Kluwer Academic Publishers. Printed in Great Britain.

64   *Seung-Woo Kim, Jan van Tongeren and Alessandra Alfieri*

The framework includes selected national accounts data in monetary terms compiled by the Bank of Korea (1994), data in physical terms and imputed values of flows and stocks of natural assets, natural resource depletion and environmental degradation by industries. Data on environmental protection expenditures, implicitly included in the SNA aggregates, are presented separately as 'of which' elements.

This chapter presents a description of the accounting framework, the pilot compilation of environmental accounts based thereon, a preliminary analysis of the results of the compilation and suggestions for further work.

The accounting framework and its concepts

The accounting framework of the Korean environmental accounts, as for the SEEA, is the supply and use table of the 1993 System of National Accounts (SNA; Commission of the European Communities *et al.*, 1993). This table includes an integrated presentation of the supply and use and value added elements of the SNA. Supply includes output of industries and imports, and use covers intermediate consumption by industries, final consumption by households and government, exports and gross capital formation. Value added is presented in this framework as the difference between output and intermediate consumption of industries. To this central SNA framework, environmental accounts elements are added to obtain the SEEA framework presented in Figure 1 of Chapter 2. This chapter should be consulted for further details on the SEEA. Environmental accounts elements include data on the following:

(a) expenditures on environmental protection are made explicit as 'of which' items. They are reflected in intermediate consumption, capital formation and value added of industries, as well as in final consumption of households and the government;

(b) non-market uses of natural resources by industries and households, including depletion of minerals, as well as emissions, discharges or disposal of air and water pollutants and solid wastes by industries and households;

(c) output of industries and imports causing depletion of natural resources in the country and outside its borders are identified as an 'of which' category;

(d) asset accounts of non-produced natural assets including forests, minerals, fish, land, air and water.

The asset accounts for minerals, forests and fish include information on opening and closing stocks for each year and changes therein due to direct use, other economic decision or natural causes and changes in prices. Data on depletion, that is the value of the use of the resource above the sustainable level for renewable resources (forest and fish) and of the total use/extraction for non-renewable resources, are compiled. For water and air, only the cost of degradation is estimated. For land, the only imputed cost is that of degradation estimated as the cost of waste collection and treatment. All data are first compiled in physical terms and thereafter converted to monetary values, using unit values (see below). As there may be changes over time in the prices or nominal values of the assets, the asset accounts also include data on revaluation of the stock of natural assets.

The large data set covering the period 1985–92 consists of the central supply and use framework extended with environmental elements. It is supplemented with worksheets described in the next section. Two types of worksheets may be distinguished. The first contains economic data that are relevant to environmental analysis and are already included implicitly in the national accounts aggregates. These data refer to environmental protection expenditures, environmental charges and subsidies, and also to data on extraction products produced in Korea or imported. The second group of worksheets includes environmental data that are not covered by the national accounts, such as data on depletion, degradation and most data on the stocks and flows of asset accounts of non-produced assets. These data are generally specified in physical units and valued by applying unit net prices for depletion and unit 'best available technology' cost (current and levelized capital cost) for degradation. The latter method consists in estimating the imputed cost of treating the emissions, using the best available technology (e.g. construction and current expenses of waste and wastewater treatment plants, cost of scrubbers, filters, catalytic converters etc.).

Data, estimates and valuation

The 1985–1992 period allows the description of trends in economic development, environmental degradation and resource depletion. The Republic of Korea has well developed national accounts and economic statistics. However, data on environment and natural resources need to be further developed in order to improve the accounts and their analysis. The following describes the data used for the compilation of different elements of the SEEA framework.

Environmental protection expenses and environmental charges

As national accounts data, compiled annually by the Bank of Korea, do not provide enough information to identify environmental protection products and services in the economy, other data sources were used. *The Report on Mining and Manufacturing Survey* (National Statistical Office, Korea, 1987–1994) and *The Report on the Construction Work Survey* (National Statistical Office, Korea, 1986–1993b) were used to identify the supply and expenditure for environmental protection products and services for industries. For government and household expenditures, the *Government Revenue and Expenditures* (National Statistical Office, Korea, 1986–1993a) and *The National Survey of Family Income and Expenditures* (Ministry of Finance, Korea, 1985–1992)

66   *Seung-Woo Kim, Jan van Tongeren and Alessandra Alfieri*

reports were the main data sources. Environmental protection expenditures are identified by industry (Korean Standard Industrial Classification, KSIC), degradation/depletion categories and environmental media affected.

Different data sources, in particular *The Report on the Construction Work Survey, Korea Environmental Yearbook* (Ministry of the Environment, Korea, 1989–1994) and *Survey on Environmental Protection Expenditure by Manufacturers* (only for 1991 and 1992) (Ministry of the Environment, Korea, 1992) were used to identify capital formation for environmental protection by industries. Data on government investments in environmental protection equipment were estimated, based on the amount of grants and revenue shares allocated by the central government to local governments (six major cities and nine provinces).

Environmental charges include mainly plastic waste disposal charges. Environmental subsidies cover tax reduction and exemptions for industries installing pollution abatement and control facilities. Data are obtained from the *Korea Environmental Yearbook*.

Data on environmental protection are included in the following worksheets:

(a) supply and use table with economic data, based on Bank of Korea (1994) national accounts;
(b) output and intermediate consumption of environmental protection activities for manufacturing, construction, and community, social and personal services are obtained from several sources, notably *The Report on Mining and Manufacturing Survey, The Report on the Construction Work Survey* and *Korea Environmental Yearbook*;
(c) capital formation on environmental protection equipment by industry (user) and environmental subject area (air, water, wastes, land, noise);
(d) government gross fixed capital formation and current expenditures on environmental protection by environmental subject area;
(e) internal environmental protection expenditures by industry and environmental subject area (installation and clean-up of scrubbers, maintenance of waste and wastewater treatment plants etc.);
(f) environmental protection expenditures of households by type (water purifier, waste treatment fee, sewage fee, mineral water, septic tank, air cleaner, three-way converter etc.);
(g) emission charges by industry;
(h) export and import of environmental protection products;
(i) tax reduction for installing pollution abatement and control facilities;
(j) exports and imports of extraction products by type (minerals, forestry and fishery products).

Asset accounts for produced assets

Produced asset accounts are compiled using the *National Wealth Survey of Korea* which is carried out every 10 years by the National Statistical Office

(1989). The last survey took place in 1987. For the other years, Phyo *et al.* (1993) estimated fixed capital stock using the Perpetual Inventory Method and the Polynomial Benchmark Year Method. However, their estimates did not include fixed assets for large animals and plants which were added, using data published in the *Statistical Yearbook of Agriculture, Forestry and Fisheries* (Ministry of Agriculture, Forestry, and Fisheries, Korea, various years).

Asset accounts for non-produced assets

The non-produced asset accounts include land, mineral resources, fish, forest, water and air. Due to lack of data on aquifers and other groundwater, depletion of water resources is not included. However, degradation of water in terms of emissions of wastewater is estimated. Asset accounts for forest and fish are compiled in physical and in monetary terms. No cost for the depletion of the assets is included. The extensive programme of reforestation and protection of forest by the government and efficient forest management are the reasons why sustainable yield has not been exceeded and therefore no depletion has taken place. For fish, data on biomass, essential for the calculation of maximum sustainable yield (MSY), are available only for one species, yellow corvina. Marine fish stocks are known to be decreasing as the catches per unit efforts (CPUE) have generally decreased since the 1970s. Due to data limitation, no cost of depletion is allocated to the fishing industry.

Stock data for the compilation of physical and monetary asset accounts for non-produced natural assets are obtained from various statistical yearbooks and national publications. However, few data are available on flows beyond direct use (harvest/extraction), i.e. natural growth of biota, catastrophic losses due to natural and economic causes, discoveries etc.

Data on asset accounts for non-produced assets, included in separate worksheets, refer to the following:

(a) asset accounts for land, by type of land area (agricultural land, forest land, built-up land, other), in physical and monetary terms and also including land prices by type of land area (paddy field, dry field, housing site, commercial site, forest land, manufacturing site, other);

(b) monetary asset accounts for forest resources by species (conifer forest, deciduous forest, mixed forest), in physical and monetary terms and including net price data;

(c) asset accounts for fish resources, in physical and monetary terms, and including net price data;

(d) asset account for mineral resources by type of mineral (coal, iron ore, limestone, tungsten ore, copper ore, kaolin, gold, silver), in physical and monetary terms, and including net price and user cost data with different discount rates.

68   *Seung-Woo Kim, Jan van Tongeren and Alessandra Alfieri*

Emissions

The accounts for environmental degradation cover emissions in physical and monetary terms into air, water and land by industry. Emissions into air include CO, NO_x, SO_2 and TSP, into water the amount of BOD discharged, and into land the amount of wastes discharged. The cost of emissions is calculated using the maintenance cost in the form of 'best available technology' for treating the emissions. Emissions into air are distinguished by emissions from stationary sources (e.g. heating, electricity generation etc.) and mobile sources (vehicles) to take into account different treatment costs. In the first case, the costs of flue gas desulphurization (FGD) and of the use of selective catalytic systems (SCR) are estimated. For mobile sources, the cost of the three-way catalytic converters for gasoline vehicles and the electric heaters for diesel vehicles is compiled. BOD emissions are valued, using the levelized annual cost of construction of an activated sludge treatment plant of 20,000–100,000 tons/day capacity with 15 years of life expectancy and a discount rate of 10%, and adding the current costs. The cost of discharging waste is estimated on the basis of landfill costs.

Data on emissions are obtained from *The Annual Survey Report on the Industrial Waste Water Discharge* (Ministry of the Environment, Korea, 1986–1992, 1994) for water, *The Report on Energy Census* (Korea Energy Economics Institute, 1987, 1990, 1992) for air and *Korea Environmental Yearbook* for waste discharge.

Data on emissions are recorded in the following worksheets:

(a) amounts of general wastes emitted by type (briquette waste, other) and treatment (untreated, landfill), treatment cost per unit (alternatively based on landfill and incineration cost) and total social cost;

(b) air pollutants emitted by type (CO_2, NO_x, SO_2, TCP, HC), by industry and (in the transport sector) by type of emitting unit (passenger cars, jeeps, bus, truck, special equipment vehicles), in physical and monetary terms, also including the avoidance cost per unit of pollutant;

(c) environmental 'social' cost of emitting domestic and industrial waste water, in physical terms and monetary terms.

Analysis

A structural analysis of the data is presented in four tables. The tables emphasize differences between traditional analyses, based on economic data, and similar analyses carried out on environmentally adjusted aggregates. As the data base covers a 7-year period, it is possible to show how these structural analyses evolve over time. For the purpose of this paper only two years are compared (1986 and 1992) although a much larger data base is available. No effort is made to carry out growth analyses, as past experience has shown little difference between the growth rates of economic aggregates and environmentally adjusted aggregates.

Republic of Korea: SEEA pilot compilation 69

Table 1. Economic vs. economic–environmental analysis of main aggregates, 1992.

Economic analysis		Economic transactions related to natural assets as % of NDP						Economic-environmental analysis	
		Depletion			Degradation				
Concepts measured in economic analysis	(as % of NDP)	Forests	Minerals	Fish	Land	Air	Water	(as % of EDP)	Concepts measured in integrated economic-environmental analysis
NDP	100.00%							97.38%	**EDP (as % of NDP)**
of which: Environmental charges-subsidies	-0.05%				0.02%	0.00%	0.05%		
Value added of environmental protection industries	0.95%				0.32%	0.27%	0.36%		
Intermediate consumption/use of environmental protection products	1.74%				0.38%	0.66%	0.70%		
Use of natural assets (depletion & degradation) by industries	2.01%	0.04%			0.00%	1.96%	0.01%		
Final consumption of households	59.66%							61.88%	**Final consumption of households, adjusted for degradation impacts**
of which: Final consumption by households of environmental protection products	0.20%				0.04%	0.05%	0.11%		
Use of natural resources (degradation)	0.60%				0.01%	0.27%	0.33%		
Final consumption of government	12.01%							12.33%	**Final consumption of government**
of which: Final consumption by government of environmental protection products (*)	0.36%				0.29%	0.00%	0.05%		
Net fixed capital formation	29.44%							27.54%	**Net capital accumulation**
of which: Fixed capital formation on environmental protection equipment (**)	0.91%				0.23%	0.19%	0.49%		(Net capital formation adjusted for natural capital consumption, i.e. depletion and degradation)
Exports **less: Imports**	31.93% 33.04%							32.79% 33.52%	**Exports** **Imports**
of which: Imported products causing depletion in other countries	5.80%	0.44%	5.19%	0.17%					

(*) it includes cost of government expenditures on research and development and administration costs.
(**) it includes consumption of fixed capital on environmental protection equipment.

Economic vs. economic–environmental analysis of main aggregates

Tables 1 and 2 compare the conventional components of the net domestic product (NDP) (by expenditures) with those of environmentally adjusted net domestic products (EDP) taking into account costs of use of environmental assets. The percentages presented on the left-hand side refer to the breakdown of NDP, while those on the right-hand side reflect the breakdown of EDP. The differences between NDP and EDP analyses are explained by the economic transactions related to natural assets presented in the middle of the tables. These columns refer to the natural assets and environmental media that are the object of the study of this paper.

The following explains how the elements in the middle of the tables relate to the difference between the economic and environmental aggregates presented on both sides:

(a) NDP. Environmental charges less subsidies, value added of environmental protection industries, intermediate consumption/use of environmental protection products and uses of natural resources are identified as 'of which' elements of NDP. Environmental charges, value added of environmental protection activities and intermediate consumption/use of environmental protection products are identified, in the middle of the tables, according to the media they affect (land, air and water). The cost of uses of natural resources by industries refers to depletion of forests, minerals and fish, and

70   Seung-Woo Kim, Jan van Tongeren and Alessandra Alfieri

Table 2. Economic vs. economic-environmental analysis of main aggregates 1986.

Economic analysis		Economic transactions related to natural assets as % of NDP						Economic-environmental analysis	
		Depletion			Degradation				
Concepts measured in economic analysis	(as % of NDP)	Forests	Minerals	Fish	Land	Air	Water	(as % of EDP)	Concepts measured in integrated economic-environmental analysis
NDP	100.00%							95.87%	EDP (as % of NDP)
of which: Environmental charges-subsidies	-0.20%				0.00%	0.00%	0.00%		
Value added of environmental protection industries	0.53%				0.18%	0.05%	0.30%		
Intermediate consumption/use of environmental protection products	0.94%				0.30%	0.18%	0.46%		
Use of natural resources (depletion & degradation) by industries	3.08%		0.02%		0.00%	3.04%	0.01%		
Final consumption of households	61.37%							65.12%	**Final consumption of households, adjusted for degradation impacts**
of which: Final consumption by households of environmental protection products	0.11%				0.00%	0.00%	0.11%		
Use of natural assets (degradation)	1.06%				0.01%	0.47%	0.58%		
Final consumption of government	11.12%							11.60%	**Final consumption of government**
of which: Final consumption by government of environmental protection products (*)	0.20%				0.15%	0.00%	0.02%		
Net fixed capital formation	20.92%							17.51%	**Net capital accumulation** (Net capital formation adjusted for natural capital consumption, i.e. depletion and degradation)
of which: Fixed capital formation on environmental protection equipment (**)	0.66%				0.10%	0.08%	0.48%		
Exports	41.86%							43.67%	**Exports**
less: Imports	35.28%							36.80%	**Imports**
of which: Imported products causing depletion in other countries	6.06%	0.64%	5.32%	0.11%					

(*) it includes cost of government expenditures on research and development and administration costs.
(**) it includes consumption of fixed capital on environmental protection equipment.

degradation of land, air and water; it is deducted from NDP in the derivation of EDP.

(b) Final consumption of households. Two 'of which' elements are identified for final consumption by households of environmental protection services (e.g. fees for the collection of household waste) and use of natural resources by final consumers (generation of wastes and emissions into air and water). The latter is added to final consumption of households in order to arrive at an environmentally adjusted equivalent. This addition deviates from the practice of the SEEA, which suggests shifting this use as an additional deduction from NDP. It has been assumed here, however, that households effectively consume more than they pay for and therefore the shift is not applied, but instead final consumption is increased (see also below).

(c) Final consumption of government. Government expenditures on environmental protection services are identified separately as 'of which' elements. They do not affect any of the environmentally adjusted aggregates.

(d) Net fixed capital formation. Only fixed capital formation on environmental protection equipment is identified as an 'of which' element. It refers to the gross concept as no data are available on consumption of fixed capital on environmental protection equipment. It includes equipment for the treatment or prevention of emissions into the different media. Net capital accumulation is the environmentally adjusted equivalent of net capital formation. It is obtained by deducting the cost of uses of natural assets by industries and by final consumers from net fixed capital formation.

(e) Exports and imports. Imports of products causing depletion in other countries e.g. timber, minerals and fish products, are identified separately and allocated, in the middle of the tables, to depletion of forests, minerals and fish. The purpose is to show the dependency of the Korean economy on natural resources of other countries.

The middle parts of the tables contain information on economic transactions related to natural assets. However, as explained above, not all transactions constitute adjustments in the conversion from NDP to EDP.

The following conclusions can be drawn from the data presented in Tables 1 and 2:

(a) The overall structural relations between economic and environmental analysis between 1986 and 1992 reveal an increase in the share of EDP to NDP from 1986 (95.87%) to 1992 (97.99%) (see (c)). The two expenditure components that change between NDP and EDP analysis are final consumption of households with and without environmental adjustments, and net capital formation as distinct from net capital accumulation; all other concepts remain unchanged in the tables between economic and environmental analysis. In 1986, consumption of households (environmentally adjusted) increased by approximately 2% (61.88–59.66%) when comparing its shares in NDP and EDP, while the share of net capital accumulation as compared with net capital formation decreased by approximately 2% (29.74–27.54%). In 1992 these percentages were respectively +4% (65.12–61.37%) and +3.4% (20.92–17.51%).

(b) The main environmental impacts (use of natural assets), identified in the middle of the tables, are those on air by industries and, to a lesser extent, by households as consumers, and on water (discharge of wastewater) and land (disposal of solid wastes) by households. The total impact of households is approximately one-third that of industries. These impacts, however, decreased as a percentage of NDP between 1986 and 1992. Thus, the value of emissions into air (at maintenance cost) decreased from 3.04% of NDP in 1986 to 1.96% in 1992 by industries and from 0.47% in 1986 to 0.27% in 1992 by households. The value of wastewater discharge by households decreased from 0.58% in 1986 to 0.33% in 1992.

(c) Environmental protection efforts increased between 1986 and 1992. Thus, intermediate consumption/use of environmental protection products as a percentage of NDP increased from 1986 to 1992 (0.94% in 1986 and 1.74% in 1992), closing the gap with the environmental impacts as percentage of NDP (3.08% in 1986 and 2.01% in 1992). Fixed capital formation on environmental protection equipment also increased from 0.66% in 1986 and 0.91% in 1992; and value added of environmental protection activities increased from 0.53% in 1986 to 0.94% in 1992. However, data deficiencies limit the analysis. Intermediate consumption/use of environmental protection by industries includes imputed 'output' of environmental protection generated by ancillary activities of industries. Intermediate consumption of 'external' environmental protection products is not available and was estimated as the difference between the supply of environmental protection products (output and imports) and the exports and final consumption of government and households. It was impossible to allocate it to the industries and it is presented in Tables 3 and 4 in the row of 'Non-allocated' together with 'internal' environmental protection expenditures which could not be allocated to any particular industry.

(d) Depletion of mineral resources is very low in both years. This is not surprising, because Korea is not a natural-resources rich country. Rather, it uses natural resources of other countries, which is reflected in import figures. In order to determine the influence on the resource depletion of other countries, imports as a percentage of NDP are presented at the bottom left-hand side of the tables. In 1986, the import percentages for these products were 0.64% for forest, 5.32% for minerals, and 0.11% for fish in other countries, and were somewhat lower in 1992, except for fish (i.e. 0.44%, 5.19% and 0.17%, respectively). In evaluating these percentages one should take into account that these figure are not based on net rent or user cost valuations, but are the total value of the products at which they are purchased abroad; they do not reflect, therefore, the cost of depletion. Furthermore, these values do not change the main aggregate of EDP, because imports were already deducted in the derivation of NDP.

Contribution of industries to net product in economic and economic–environmental analysis

Tables 3 and 4 present an analysis of data by industries. These tables compare economic analysis, based on SNA concepts, with environmental analysis based on environmentally adjusted data as defined in the SEEA. The left-hand side of the tables shows the percentage distribution of NDP by industries and in the right-hand side a similar distribution of EDP. The middle parts show the impacts of economic activities on natural resources and the economic responses thereto. Three main ISIC categories of economic activities are included: (1) agriculture, forestry and fishing; (2) manufacturing, electricity, gas and water, and construction and (3) services. Of the latter, only two categories of selected activities are included (i.e. manufacture of chemical products; electricity, gas and water; construction; transport and communication; public administration and defence). The data in the middle of the tables are expressed as percentages of value added of each of the corresponding industries.

To illustrate the analysis of the tables, the 'slice' corresponding to electricity, gas and water, may be taken as an example. The contribution of this

Republic of Korea: SEEA pilot compilation 73

Table 3. Contribution of industries to net product in economic and economic–environmental analysis, 1992.

		Economic analysis	Economic transactions related to natural assets					Economic - environmental analysis
			% of net value added					
		% Distribution of NDP by industries	Current environmental protection expenditures (*)	Environmental charges - subsidies (**)	GFCF	Uses of natural assets	EVA	% Distribution of EDP by industries
Agriculture forestry and fishing	Total	7.69%	0.00%	0.01%	0.00%	0.35%	99.65%	7.86%
	Depletion							
	Land		0.00%	0.00%	0.00%	0.00%		
	Air		0.00%	0.00%	0.00%	0.35%		
	Water		0.00%	0.01%	0.00%	0.00%		
Mining	Total	0.37%	0.00%	0.01%	0.07%	11.78%	88.22%	0.33%
	Depletion					11.43%		
	Land		0.00%	0.00%	0.03%	0.00%		
	Air		0.00%	0.00%	0.00%	0.35%		
	Water		0.00%	0.01%	0.04%	0.00%		
Manufacturing, Electricity, gas and water, Construction *of which:*	Total	42.55%	0.00%	0.03%	0.29%	1.95%	98.05%	42.84%
	Depletion					0.00%		
	Land		0.00%	0.00%	0.07%	0.00%		
	Air		0.00%	0.00%	0.00%	1.95%		
	Water		0.00%	0.01%	0.22%	0.00%		
Manufacture of chemical products	Total	4.65%	0.00%	0.11%	0.35%	2.27%	97.73%	4.66%
	Depletion					0.00%		
	Land		0.00%	0.11%	0.03%	0.00%		
	Air		0.00%	0.00%	0.00%	2.27%		
	Water		0.00%	0.01%	0.32%	0.00%		
Electricity, gas and water	Total	1.83%	0.00%	0.00%	0.32%	16.79%	83.21%	1.56%
	Depletion					0.00%		
	Land		0.00%	0.00%	0.02%	0.00%		
	Air		0.00%	0.00%	0.00%	16.79%		
	Water		0.00%	0.00%	0.30%	0.00%		
Construction	Total	14.05%	0.00%	0.00%	0.32%	0.03%	99.97%	14.43%
	Depletion					0.00%		
	Land		0.00%	0.00%	0.16%	0.00%		
	Air		0.00%	0.00%	0.00%	0.03%		
	Water		0.00%	0.00%	0.16%	0.00%		
Services, total *of which:*	Total	50.18%	0.00%	0.00%	1.09%	0.23%	99.77%	51.40%
	Depletion					0.00%		
	Land		0.00%	0.00%	0.28%	0.00%		
	Air		0.00%	0.00%	0.00%	0.23%		
	Water		0.00%	0.00%	0.79%	0.00%		
Transport and communication	Total	6.13%	0.02%	0.00%	0.12%	1.60%	98.40%	6.19%
	Depletion					0.00%		
	Land		0.00%	0.00%	0.04%	0.00%		
	Air		0.02%	0.00%	0.02%	1.60%		
	Water		0.00%	0.00%	0.07%	0.00%		
Public administration and defense	Total	8.24%	0.02%	0.00%	5.71%	0.11%	99.89%	8.45%
	Depletion					0.00%		
	Land		0.00%	0.00%	1.32%	0.00%		
	Air		0.02%	0.00%	0.01%	0.11%		
	Water		0.00%	0.00%	4.29%	0.00%		
Non-allocated (% of the retail)	Total		99.04%	95.04%	26.85%	49.45%		
	Depletion							
	Land		100.00%	70.19%	25.58%	0.00%		
	Air		99.85%	0.00%	99.07%	50.13%		
	Water		100.00%	92.90%	0.03%	100.00%		
Total industries	Total	100.00%	1.74%	0.06%	0.91%	2.01%	97.38%	100.00%
	Depletion					0.04%		
	Land		0.38%	0.02%	0.23%	0.00%		
	Air		0.66%	0.00%	0.19%	1.96%		
	Water		0.70%	0.05%	0.49%	0.01%		

(*) Includes only internal environmental protection expenditures, external environmental protection expenditures are in Non allocated.

(**) Environmental subsidies appear only in Not-allocated.

74   *Seung-Woo Kim, Jan van Tongeren and Alessandra Alfieri*

Table 4. **Contribution of industries to net product in economic and economic–environmental analysis, 1986.**

		Economic analysis	Economic transactions related to natural assets					Economic - environmental analysis
		% Distribution of NDP by industries	% of net value added					% Distribution of EDP by industries
			Current environmental protection expenditures (*)	Environmental charges - subsidies (**)	GFCF	Uses of natural assets	EVA	
Agriculture forestry and fishing	Total	11.76%	0.01%	0.00%	0.01%	0.22%	99.78%	12.24%
	Depletion							
	Land		0.00%	0.00%	0.00%	0.00%		
	Air		0.00%	0.00%	0.00%	0.22%		
	Water		0.01%	0.00%	0.01%	0.00%		
Mining	Total	1.00%	0.02%	0.00%	0.02%	2.63%	97.37%	1.01%
	Depletion					2.47%		
	Land		0.00%	0.00%	0.00%	0.00%		
	Air		0.00%	0.00%	0.00%	0.15%		
	Water		0.02%	0.00%	0.02%	0.01%		
Manufacturing, Electricity, gas and water, Construction *of which:*	Total	40.25%	0.12%	0.01%	0.17%	2.77%	97.23%	40.82%
	Depletion					0.00%		
	Land		0.00%	0.00%	0.05%	0.00%		
	Air		0.00%	0.00%	0.00%	2.73%		
	Water		0.12%	0.01%	0.12%	0.03%		
Manufacture of chemical products	Total	5.12%	0.03%	0.09%	0.07%	1.92%	98.08%	5.23%
	Depletion					0.00%		
	Land		0.00%	0.08%	0.01%	0.00%		
	Air		0.00%	0.01%	0.00%	1.89%		
	Water		0.03%	0.00%	0.07%	0.03%		
Electricity, gas and water	Total	2.78%	0.01%	0.00%	0.01%	17.82%	82.18%	2.38%
	Depletion					0.00%		
	Land		0.00%	0.00%	0.00%	0.00%		
	Air		0.00%	0.00%	0.00%	17.82%		
	Water		0.01%	0.00%	0.01%	0.00%		
Construction	Total	7.24%	0.10%	0.00%	0.33%	0.12%	99.88%	7.54%
	Depletion					0.00%		
	Land		0.00%	0.00%	0.22%	0.00%		
	Air		0.00%	0.00%	0.00%	0.12%		
	Water		0.10%	0.00%	0.11%	0.00%		
Services, total *of which:*	Total	45.83%	0.04%	0.00%	1.01%	0.69%	99.31%	47.48%
	Depletion					0.00%		
	Land		0.00%	0.00%	0.07%	0.00%		
	Air		0.00%	0.00%	0.01%	0.69%		
	Water		0.04%	0.00%	0.93%	0.00%		
Transport and communication	Total	6.01%	0.02%	0.00%	0.05%	3.88%	96.12%	6.03%
	Depletion					0.00%		
	Land		0.00%	0.00%	0.01%	0.00%		
	Air		0.00%	0.00%	0.02%	3.88%		
	Water		0.02%	0.00%	0.02%	0.00%		
Public administration and defense	Total	7.20%	0.02%	0.00%	6.16%	0.38%	99.62%	7.48%
	Depletion					0.00%		
	Land		0.00%	0.00%	0.35%	0.00%		
	Air		0.00%	0.00%	0.06%	0.38%		
	Water		0.02%	0.00%	5.72%	0.00%		
Non-allocated (% of the total)	Total		92.79%	96.75%	19.60%	51.86%		
	Depletion							
	Land		100.00%	0.00%	50.96%	0.00%		
	Air		100.00%	0.00%	93.02%	52.51%		
	Water		85.30%	0.00%	1.22%	0.03%		
Total industries	Total	100.00%	0.94%	0.01%	0.66%	3.08%	95.87%	100.00%
	Depletion					0.02%		
	Land		0.30%	0.00%	0.10%	0.00%		
	Air		0.18%	0.00%	0.08%	3.04%		
	Water		0.46%	0.00%	0.48%	0.01%		

(*) Includes only internal environmental protection expenditures, external environmental protection expenditures are in Non allocated.

(**) Environmental subsidies appear only in Not-allocated.

industry to the NDP in 1992 was 1.83% while its contribution to EDP was 1.56%. The reduced contribution to EDP may be due to degradation impacts (emissions into air) caused by this industry, which amount in total to 16.79% of value added. On the basis of the available data and not taking into account the problem of non-allocation of cost to industries (see below), the economic responses by this industry to mitigate its environmental impacts are minor: environmental protection expenditures are negligible and environmental charges are not levied on this industry. Fixed capital formation on environmental protection equipment amounts to 0.32% of value added, of which 0.02% refers to environmental protection of land, and 0.30% to environmental protection of water. EVA (environmentally adjusted value added) as a percentage of net value added, presented in the middle of the tables, for this industry (83.21%) is below the average (97.33%) for all industries.

One of the difficulties in the analysis is the non-allocation to industries of all or large parts of some of the economic transactions and environmental impacts categories in the middle of the tables. Non-allocation, presented in the shaded row of the tables, is very serious for both 1986 and 1992. It is most serious in the case of environmental protection expenditures (1986, 92.79%; 1992, 99.94%) and environmental charges and subsidies (1986, 95.04%; 1992, 96.75%). It is somewhat lower, but still significant, for the use of natural resources (1986, 51.86%; 1992, 49.45%).

The conclusions drawn from the data presented in Tables 3 and 4, keeping in mind the large non-allocation of cost to industries, can be summarized as follows:

(a) As was already shown in Tables 1 and 2, there is an increase in the overall EVA/VA percentages for all industries between 1986 (95.87%) and 1992 (97.38%). The industries below these averages, in 1986, are electricity, gas and water and, in 1992, electricity, gas and water and mining. This might indicate that these industries have larger environmental impacts than the others.

(b) The average cost of natural asset use for all industries decreased between 1986 (3.08%) and 1992 (2.01%). This reflects similar decreases in the use of natural resources in manufacturing, electricity, gas and water, construction (1986, 2.77%; 1992, 1.95%) and in services (1986, 0.69%; 1992, 0.23%). However, at least for two industries the percentages were higher, i.e. mining (1986, 2.63%; 1992, 11.78%) and manufacture of chemical products (1986, 1.92%; 1992, 2.27%). This finding should be treated with some caution, as approximately half of the uses of natural resources was not allocated to industries.

(c) Total economic responses for all industries (current environmental protection expenditures, environmental charges, fixed capital formation on environmental protection equipment) increased between 1986 (1.61%) and 1992 (2.71%). This might explain the corresponding decrease in the cost of

76   *Seung-Woo Kim, Jan van Tongeren and Alessandra Alfieri*

the use of natural assets (3.08% in 1986 and 2.01% in 1992). In 1992, the cost of the use of natural resources (2.01%) was even lower than the total of economic responses (2.71%).

(d) Economic responses do not seem to be in proportion to their environmental impacts. Thus, for manufacturing, electricity, gas and water, and construction, environmental impacts in 1986 and 1992 were 0.3% and 0.32% and the economic responses were 2.77% and 1.95% respectively. In the case of electricity, gas and water the cost of natural asset use in 1986 and 1992 was 17.82% and 16.79%, and the economic response was 0.02% and 0.32% respectively. With regard to services, the cost of natural asset use in 1986 and 1992 was 0.69% and 0.23%, while the totals of economic responses in this industry were 1.05% and 1.09% respectively. The same 'unrelatedness' between economic responses and the use of natural assets can be observed in the case of construction, public administration and transport and communication. In most instances, however, the economic responses have increased between 1986 and 1992.

Future work

The pilot compilation of the SEEA was carried out using existing statistics. It identified data deficiencies, especially for environmental protection expenditures, water resources and fish. Moreover, the coverage of industries was limited to those for which data were available. Environmental protection expenditures were estimated from different data sources for the output and intermediate consumption. This led to a discrepancy between supply and use of environmental protection goods and services. Moreover, the data collected by the Ministry of the Environment and the Korean Development Bank were not consistent with the classification used in the national accounts (KSIC).

With regard to fish, the study shows that, on one hand, imports of fish have increased over the years, while on the other hand, catches per unit effort (CPUE) have generally decreased since the 1970s. Fish stocks appear to decrease rapidly. A more in-depth study for estimating fish biomass for different species, and hence sustainable yield and depletion, is needed to assess the significance of fish stock depletion.

The natural extension of the pilot compilation, in addition to improvement in data collection, would be the institutionalization of the compilation. The study was carried out with the assistance of United Nations Statistics Division (UNSD), by KETRI, a research institute within the Ministry of Environment. Support from other institutions such as the National Statistical Office (NSO) and the Bank of Korea (BOK), responsible for the compilation of national accounts, was limited. In order to ensure a continuation in the compilation of integrated environmental and economic accounts a coordinating institution, possibly the BOK or NSO, should build up on the experience gained from the pilot compilation of the SEEA.

[12]

TAKING THE ENVIRONMENT INTO ACCOUNT:
THE NAMEA APPROACH

BY MARK DE HAAN AND STEVEN J. KEUNING

Statistics Netherlands

The National Accounting Matrix including Environmental Accounts (NAMEA) shows environmental burdens that are consistent with the economic figures in the national accounts. In the NAMEA, the existing national accounts matrix has been extended with accounts in physical units. On the basis of the expected contribution of each polluting substance to a particular environmental problem, emissions are converted to theme equivalents. This results in six summary environmental indicators that are directly comparable to the conventional economic aggregates. In addition, this meso-level information system can be used as the core data framework for integrated analyses and forecasts of economic and environmental changes.

1. INTRODUCTION

In general, the value of commodities in the System of National Accounts (SNA) is based on actual payments and receipts for these commodities in the market place. In this way receipts always equal outlays, an important accounting practice that guarantees the system's consistency. This valuation method reflects the revealed preferences on markets and the preferences for public goods as the outcome of (democratic) decision-making processes. The present representation of pollution in the national accounts is based on this same starting point. If polluting companies are not actually charged for the resulting damage on the environment, there are no costs subtracted from Gross Domestic Product (GDP). This makes sense because these social burdens are not actually paid for by anyone and thus also not subtracted from factor payments to employees and capital suppliers of polluting companies. Analogously, free use of environmental functions, like swimming in a clean sea, does not lead to an increase in GDP. Similarly, unpaid household labour and leisure are not taken into account.

It can be concluded that the core SNA contributes to the understanding of the development of welfare, but does not provide a complete picture. Although welfare aspects such as Net National Income, employment and social security payments are part of the system, these aspects are not all reflected in a single indicator, for instance a national income adjusted for unemployment. A much more fruitful way to deal with the unpriced welfare issues is to expand the national

Note: Both authors are employed in the Department for National Accounts of Statistics Netherlands. Mark de Haan is a Research Assistant and Steven J. Keuning is Head of the Department. They would like to thank C. M. Baas, A. J. de Boo, P. R. Bosch, C. N. J. Beusekom, L. M. W. van Erk, B. Guis, J. A. P. Klein, C. S. M. Olsthoorn, L. H. M. Tromp and E. A. Zonneveld for the expertise provided. The views expressed in this paper are those of the authors and do not necessarily reflect the views of Statistics Netherlands.

accounts with non-monetary data on aspects of welfare, whereby for each aspect a separate indicator is constructed.[1] Changes in indicators can then subsequently be compared in overview tables. Examples can be found in Tables 4 and 5 of this paper. The NAMEA contains detailed information on the environment and converts this into a number of summary environmental indicators. In this way, indicators on the economy and the environment are reflected in a single accounting system. This is elaborated in the next section. Section 3 discusses on the environmental themes in the NAMEA framework. Section 4 gives an application of the NAMEA in which economic and environmental indicators are compared for various industries and consumption purposes. Finally, Section 5 winds up with other possible uses and discusses some aspects of the NAMEA's relationship to the interim Handbook on Integrated Environmental and Economic Accounting (SEEA) of the United Nations (1993).

2. AN AGGREGATE NAMEA

In the NAMEA, the National Accounting Matrix is extended with three accounts on the environment. A substances account (account 11 in Table 1), an account for global environmental themes (account 12) and an account for national environmental themes (account 13). These accounts do not express transactions in money terms but include information on the environment as it is observed in reality: that is in physical units.[2] In this part of the NAMEA, not only pollution generated by producers and consumers is presented, but also the accumulation of hazardous agents in the Dutch environment. This accumulation is equal to the domestic output of pollutants plus the balance of transboundary pollutant flows to and from other countries. In this statistical matrix, the value of these pollutant flows, expressed in guilders is equal to their transaction value in the economy, namely zero. In the environmental accounts, these trivial values are not reflected, but replaced by the corresponding physical units.

The other accounts in the NAMEA contain a brief overview of the regular transactions in the National Accounting Matrix (cf. Keuning and de Gijt, 1992).[3] Sometimes, actual transactions which are relevant to an environmental concern, are isolated and explicitly shown (see for instance account 1a in Table 1). In the NAMEA, receipts are reflected in the rows and outlays in the columns. Most of the accounts contain a balancing item in the column, defined as the difference between total receipts in the row, and the sum of total outlays in the column. These balancing items are doubly framed in the columns of the accounts in Table 1. In this way, column and row totals are equal for each account, a rule that guarantees the consistency of the accounting system. In order to emphasize that currency units and physical units cannot be added up, the physical units are positioned higher in the rows, and more to the left in the columns of accounts 2,

---

[1]See Keuning (1995) for an elaborate discussion on this issue.
[2]See Keuning (1993) for arguments against an imputation of hypothetical prices to physical flows within an accounting framework.
[3]These are standard ESA accounts.

3, 6 and 9. Table 1 is an aggregate presentation of the Netherlands NAMEA for 1991. The rest of this section gives a short description of this table.[4]

The first row and column contain the goods and services account. The intermediate and final use are presented in the row, and total domestic and foreign supply are presented in the column. Environmental cleansing services are reflected separately. In the NAMEA, two types of cleansing services are distinguished: internal and external environmental cleansing. External cleansing services are sold to other kind-of-activity units (intermediate consumption), to the government and to households (private consumption). These services are considered as production in the national accounts. An example is collection and incineration of waste by cleansing companies. Internal environmental cleansing services are produced by the same establishment that uses this service within its own production process. These internal services are in the national accounts identified neither as production nor intermediate consumption. In order to express the financial burdens of different industries on behalf of the environment, these expenditures are explicitly shown in the NAMEA.[5] Therefore, production as well as intermediate consumption are higher in the NAMEA than in the standard national accounts, but Net Domestic Product (NDP) and concomitantly all other balances do not change. A more detailed presentation of environmental cleansing services can be found in Table 6 of this paper. The column of the goods and services account also contains taxes on products (VAT, excises etc.) and trade and transport margins. Both of them make up the difference between the payments of users and the receipts of producers.

The second account is a specific consumption account, which reallocates consumption expenditures (matrix 1, 2) to consumption purposes (vector 2, 5). The latter are connected to specific pollution patterns (2, 11). Consumer goods that are purchased in order to protect the environment are presented separately. This concerns, for example, the extra costs of cars fitted with catalytic converters. These expenditures reflect the outlays of households for the protection of the environment (cell 2a, 5). Pollution generated by the government is in the NAMEA connected to government production and not to government consumption.

The third account shows in the row the production of goods and services, and in the column the intermediate use and value added. Other taxes on production are recorded on the a separate tax account (cell 8, 3) and consumption of fixed capital is directly put on the capital account (cell 6, 3), so that the balancing item in cell (4, 3) equals Net Domestic Product (NDP) at factor cost. In row 3 the production of goods and services is expanded with the concomitant emissions of unpriced pollutants (row-vector 3, 11). Table 2 gives detailed information on the agents emitted in all branches of industry. Vector (11, 3) contains information on a number of inputs in production processes for which no money is paid, and these are thus measured in physical units. Examples of these inputs are the extraction of natural resources and the amount of waste processed in incineration plants.

---

[4]The NAMEA's concept and application originated from Keuning (e.g. 1993); cf. also De Boo *et al.* (1993). De Haan *et al.* (1993) provides a more elaborate insight in the sources and methods for the actual compilation of the NAMEAs for the Netherlands.
[5]For a conceptual discussion on internal environmental costs, see De Boo (1995).

TABLE 1

A NATIONAL ACCOUNTING MATRIX INCLUDING ENVIRONMENTAL ACCOUNTS (NAMEA) FOR THE NETHERLANDS, 1991
(Account 1–10 in million Guilders)

ACCOUNT (classification)		Goods and services (Product-groups) Environ-ment 1a	Other purposes 1b	Consumption of households (Purposes) Environ-ment 2a	Other purposes 2b	Production (Branches of industry) 3	Income gene-ration (Primary input categories) 4	Income distri-bution and use (Sectors) 5	Capital 6	Taxes (Tax categories) Environ-mental taxes 8a	Other taxes 8b	Rest of the world Current 9
Goods and services (Product groups) Environmental cleansing services	1a	Trade and transport margins		Household consumption 24	-	Intermediate consumption 6305		Government consumption 1410	Gross capital formation			Export (fob)
Other goods and services	1b	-		710	321727	501783		76837	114818			293086
Consumption of households (Purposes) Environment	2a							Consumption of households 734				
Other purposes	2b							321727				
Production (Branches of industry)	3	Output, basic prices 7627	994861									
Income generation (Primary input categories)	4					Net Domestic Product, factor cost 429118				VAT not handed over to the government 1880		Wages from the rest of the world 820
Income distribution and use (Sectors)	5						Net National Generated Income, factor cost 430650	Property income and current transfers 573920		Taxes 3982	137518	Property income and current transfers from the rest of the world 60190
Capital	6					Consumption of fixed capital 61560		Net saving 72980				
Financial balance	7								Net lending to the rest of the world 17340			
Taxes (Tax categories) Environmental taxes	8a	Taxes less subsidies on products 907				Other taxes less subsidies on production 855		Taxes on income and wealth 2220	VAT on land and taxes on investment			Taxes from the rest of the world
Other taxes	8b	112	45787			2887		88730	992			1050
Rest of the world Current	9	Import (cif) 267386					Wages to the rest of the world 1170	Property income and current transfers to the rest of the world 67720		Taxes to the rest of the world 180		
Rest of the world Capital	10								Capital transfers to the rest of the world 2350			Current external balance -18710
Substances (CFCs and halons in 1000 kg, gas and oil in pj and other substances in million kg) CO_2	11a					Absorption of substances in production						Trans-border pollution to the rest of the world
N_2O	11b											
CH_4	11c											
CFCs and Halons	11d											
NOx	11e											488
SO_2	11f											159
NH_3	11g											113
P	11h											24
N	11i											581
Waste	11j					2645						
Gas	11k					2595						
Oil	11l					138						
Global environmental themes Greenhouse effect (GWP)	12a								Environmental indicators 188890			
Ozone layer depletion (ODP)	12b								3818			
National environmental themes Acidification (AEQ)	13a								156			
Eutrophication (EEQ)	13b								267			
Waste (KG)	13c								23761			
Loss of Natural resources (PJ)	13d								-759			
TOTAL		Supply, market prices 7739	1308941	Consumption of households 734	321727	Costs, basic prices 1002488	Allocation of generated income 431820	Current outlays 1206258	Capital outlays 135500	Tax receipts 3982	139558	Current receipts from the rest of the world 336436

Note: Due to rounding, totals do not always add up.

	Rest of the world Capital	Substances (CFCs and halons in 1000 kg, gas and oil in pj and other substances in million kg)												Global environmental themes		National environmental themes				TOTAL
						CFCs &									Ozone layer deple-		Eutro-		Loss of Natural Resour-	
		CO2	N2O	CH4	halons	NOx	SO2	NH3	P	N	Waste	Gas	Oil	Greenhouse effect	tion	Acidi-fication	phication	Waste	ces	
	10	11a	11b	11c	11d	11e	11f	11g	11h	11i	11j	11k	11l	12a	12b	13a	13b	13c	13d	
1a																					Commodity use, market prices 7739
1b																					1308941
2a		Emission of pollutants from household consumption																			Consumption of households 734
		36372	2	4		656	156	5	-	15	115	6663									
2b																					321727
3		Emission of pollutants from production																			Production, basic prices
		128040	59	724		4375	397	191	220	155	1257	19742									1002488
4																					Generated income 431820
5																					Current receipts 1206258
6	Capital transfers from the rest of the world 980	Other changes in natural resources										1836	138								Capital receipts 135500
7	Net lending from the rest of the world -17340																				0
8a																					Tax payments 3982
8b																					139558
9		Trans-border pollution from the rest of the world				93	99	27		20	415										Current payments to the rest of the world 336436
10																					Capital payments to the rest of the world -16360
11a															Allocation to global environmental themes 164412		Allocation to national environmental themes (accumulation of substances)				Destination of substances 164412
11b															61						61
11c															728						728
11d																5031					5031
11e																	158				646
11f																	136				295
11g																	134				247
11h																		166			190
11i																		1206			1787
11j																			23760		26405
11k																				-759	1836
11l																					138
12a																					Theme-equivalents global 188890
12b																					3816
13a																					Theme-equivalents national 156
13b																					287
13c																					23760
13d																					-759
	Capital receipts from the rest of the world -16360	Origin of substances													Theme-equivalents, global		Theme-equivalents, national				
		164412	61	726	5031	646	295	247	190	1787	26405	1836	138		188890	3816	156	287	23760	-759	

135

TABLE 2

DETAILED PRESENTATION OF THE ORIGIN AND DESTINATION OF MATERIAL FLOWS IN THE 1991 NAMEA FOR THE NETHERLANDS

	CO_2 11a	N_2O 11b	CH_4 11c	CFCs and halons 11d	NOx 11e	SO_2 11f	NH_3 11g	P 11h	N 11i	Waste 11j	Natural Gas 11k	Crude Oil 11l
	mln kg	mln kg		1000 kg			mln kg				pj	
Origin												
Household consumption expenditure (2)	36,372	2	4	656	156	5	—	15	115	6,663		
Own transport	14,672	2	—	—	135	4	—	—	39	120		
Other	21,700	—	4	656	21	1	—	15	76	6,543		
Production (3)	128,040	59	724	4,375	397	191	220	155	1,257	19,742		
Agriculture, hunting, forestry, fishing	10,260	33	534	—	36	2	215	131	1,117	1,190		
Mining and quarrying												
Crude petroleum and natural gas production	1,566	—	78	—	5	2	—	—	2	1,368		
Other mining and quarrying	357	—	—	—	—	1	—	—	—	—		
Manufacturing												
Food, beverage and tobacco industry	4,173	—	1	8	12	2	—	1	4	2,225		
Textile, wearing apparel and leather industry	357	—	—	160	1	—	—	—	—	61		
Wood, furniture and building materials industry	83	—	—	478	1	—	—	—	—	216		
Paper, paper products, printing and publishing industry	1,626	—	—	5	4	—	—	—	1	381		
Petroleum industry	11,843	—	—	—	22	76	—	—	9	56		
Chemical industry	20,307	17	3	1,626	41	22	4	14	25	3,099		
Rubber and artificial materials processing industry	1,487	—	—	720	3	—	—	—	1	41		
Manufacture of building materials, earthenware and glass products	2,335	—	—	50	14	5	1	—	5	378		
Manufacture of basic metals	6,097	—	—	15	12	14	—	—	4	308		
Manufacture of metal products and machinery	1,190	—	—	742	3	—	—	—	1	160		
Industrial manufacturing n.e.c.	992	—	—	472	2	—	—	9	16	123		

	(1)	(2)	(3)	(4)	(5)	(6)	(7)	(8)	(9)	(10)	(11)	(12)
Public utilities												
Electricity	38,781	—	—	—	68	35	—	—	21	149		
Other public utilities	75	—	96	—	1	—	—	—	—	485		
Construction	2,501	—	8	—	26	3	—	—	8	3,574		
Transport and storage	9,254	2	—	6	78	22	—	—	23	2,270		
Environmental cleansing and sanitary services	3,641	6	4	—	5	3	—	—	2	690		
Other services	11,115	1	—	93	63	4	—	—	18	2,968		
Capital (6)												
Rest of the World, current (9)	164,412	61	728	5,031	93	99	27	20	415		1,836	138
Total = column total 11	164,412	61	728	5,031	646	295	247	190	1,787	26,405	1,836	138
Destination												
Production (3)												
Crude petroleum and natural gas production										2,645	2,595	138
Environmental cleansing and sanitary services					488	159	113	24	581	2,645	2,595	138
Rest of the World, current (9)	164,412	61	728	5,031							2,595	138
Global environmental themes (12)	164,412	61	728	5,031	158	136	134	166	1,206	23,760	−759	0
National environmental themes (13)	164,412	61	728	5,031	646	295	247	190	1,787	26,405	1,836	138
Total = row total 11	164,412	61	728	5,031	646	295	247	190	1,787	26,405	1,836	138

The emissions of waste incineration plants are again taken into account in row-vector (3, 11). When sufficient data on the destination of recycled waste become available, this can also be reflected in vector (11, 3).

The fourth row contains different components of NDP (wages and salaries, employers' social contributions and operating surplus) and wages and salaries from abroad. Cell (4, 3) reflects the value added tax invoiced by sellers, but not handed over to the government, for various reasons. In the column of account four, the income flows are allocated to institutional sectors in the economy (financial and non-financial corporations, households and the government) and to the rest of the world. In the fifth account, income is (re-)distributed and used for consumption and saving. In account 6, net saving is converted into various types of capital formation. Account 7 presents the financial balances (net lending) of the total economy and the rest of the world. By definition, these balances add up to zero. Therefore the presentation of an (empty) column is not necessary.

Account 8 of the NAMEA is a separate tax account in which a variety of taxes are presented, such as taxes (minus subsidies) on products in sub-matrix (8, 1), other taxes on production in vector (8, 3) and taxes on income in vector (8, 5). In the detailed NAMEA, environmental taxes such as energy levies, levies on the pollution of surface waters and levies on waste water drain-offs are presented separately. The collection of tax receipts is reflected in the column of the tax account (row-vector 5, 8 and cell 9, 8b).

Accounts 9 and 10 represent transactions with the rest of the world. The row of the current account (9) contains not only imports of goods and services, but also the pollution that enters the Netherlands through the rivers or the air. In the column, outlays such as exports are presented, as well as the export of pollutants to other countries. Unfortunately, trans-border flows of waste are still missing due to lack of data. Cell (10, 9) reflects the current external balance of the rest of the world with the Netherlands. The figures show that the Netherlands managed to create a surplus for commodities as well as for pollutants.

Account 11 registers in the column the origin of ten types of pollutants. This pollution is caused by producers (row-vector 3, 11), consumers (row-vector 2, 11) and the rest of the world (vector 9, 11). Moreover this column registers additions to proven reserves and other changes in natural resources (vector 6, 11). The row of this account presents the extraction of natural resources (crude oil and natural gas) as well as the absorption of pollutants into the economic process. This concerns for instance, waste incineration (vector 11, 3). The rest of the pollutants is exported to other countries (vector 11, 9), or is reallocated to five environmental themes (sub-matrices 11, 12 and 11, 13) The use of natural resources is allocated to a sixth theme: loss of natural resources. Account 11 is expressed in kilograms or in petajoules (pj). Of course, the row and column totals of account 11 are equal.

3. Environmental Themes

The so-called "environmental themes" as presented in account 12 and 13 are adopted from the Netherlands' National Environmental Policy Plan (VROM, 1993). Environmental themes are used as an inventory framework of current environmental issues in the Netherlands. The column totals of account 12 and 13 reflect a weighted aggregation procedure. The weights reflect for each theme the potential relative stress on the environment of each substance. These aggregation methods are developed by the Dutch Ministry of the Environment (VROM) and are for the major part based on international research on the effects of different substances on environmental quality.[6]

Here, we present a brief overview of the environmental themes in the NAMEA. Changes in the concentrations of greenhouse gases in the atmosphere may result in climate changes. The following greenhouse gases have been incorporated in the greenhouse effect indicator: carbon dioxide (CO_2), methane (NH_4) and nitrous oxide (N_2O). CFCs and halons have also been mentioned as greenhouse gases but their contribution to the greenhous effect is inconclusive (IPCC, 1992). The relative contribution of each gas to the greenhouse effect can be expressed in CO_2 equivalents or so-called Global Warming Potentials (GWP). GWPs reflect the CO_2 concentration that would have had about the same effect on the radiating properties of the atmosphere as a particular concentration of another greenhouse gas. Table 3 reflects the compilation of the greenhouse effect indicator in the NAMEA.

TABLE 3

CONVERSION OF DUTCH GREENHOUSE GAS EMISSIONS INTO GWP, 1991

	Emission in mln kg	Global Warming Potential (GWP)/kg	Emission in GWP	%
CO_2	164,412	1	164,412	87
N_2O	61	270	16,470	9
CH_4	728	11	8,008	4
Total (account 12a)			188,890	100

A decreasing concentration of ozone in the stratosphere leads to a higher exposure to UV-B radiation, which may have negative effects on human health and ecosystems. Chlorofluorocarbons (CFCs) and halons are considered as catalysts in the reaction chains that lead to the depletion of stratospheric ozone.[7] The use of CFCs and halons is regulated by the Montreal Protocol which aims at a complete ban of CFCs in the year 1996. The ODP value is an indication of the degree to which a specific gas influences ozone concentrations in relation to CFC-11 (see VROM, 1992b).

Extensive deposition of acid substances leads to changes in the composition of soil and surface waters in the Netherlands. This process has already caused major damage to ecosystems, buildings and crops. The most important substances leading to acidification are nitrogen oxides (NO_x), sulphur dioxide (SO_2) and ammonia (NH_3). The potential contribution to acidification of each of these substances can be expressed in Potential Acid Equivalents (PAE). This measure reflects the amount of a substance that is necessary to form an acid with a certain

---

[6]See Adriaanse (1993) for a more detailed discussion.
[7]Carbontetrachloride and 1,1,1 trichloroethane also included in the compilation of the ozone depletion indicator. Data on HCFCs and methylbromide were too scarce to allow for their incorporation.

amount of H^+ ions. One acid equivalent equals $1/2$ mol (32 grams) SO_2, or 1 mol (46 grams) NO_2, or 1 mol (17 grams) NH_3 (Schneider and Bresser, 1988).

The excessive accumulation of nitrogen (N), phosphorus (P) and potassium (K) can lead to eutrophication. In turn, eutrophication may result in the loss of species, and a decreasing quality or even poisoning of drinking water. The NAMEA has only been focusing on nitrogen and phosphorus because of data availability. A preliminary common unit is used to aggregate both substances to one theme (see VROM, 1992a). Based on the average appearance of nitrogen and phosphorus in natural circumstances, a 1 to 10 ratio between nitrogen and phosphorus is assumed to arrive at Eutrophication Equivalents (EEQ).

The accumulation and removal of waste is a major environmental problem in most countries. Dutch environmental policy has been focusing on a reduction of the amount of waste generated (VROM, 1989). The theme-indicator therefore reflects the total amount of waste in millions of kilograms. Other aspects of particular waste flows such as the hazard of toxic chemical waste are not reflected in the waste indicator.

Finally, the net change in the combined proven oil and gas reserves during the reference year is reflected in the last indicator. This change is determined by the balance of extraction [$-(11k, 3)$ and $-(111, 3)$] and all other changes in proven reserves [cells (6, 11k) and (6, 111)].

The environmental themes lead to a limited number of physical environmental indicators. Account 12 in the NAMEA contains two environmental themes which are related to global environmental problems: the greenhouse effect and the depletion of the ozone layer. The corresponding indicators reflect the Netherlands' contribution to these global problems. Different accounting rules are applied to acidification, eutrophication and waste accumulation because these themes cause environmental damage within the national boundaries. For these problems information on the national accumulation of pollutants is relevant. This means: total domestic pollution plus import minus export of pollutants.

Most of the environmental themes allocate pollutants to certain environmental problems and are therefore an empirical reflection of highly complex cause-effect relationships in the environment. Many environmetal losses are the result of a combination of different types of environmental stresses. The actual environmental effects caused by a single environmental theme are in general difficult to measure. An objective determination of the relative seriousness of a particular environmental theme is even more troublesome. Social preferences are crucial in this respect. In the first pilot NAMEA (De Haan *et al.*, 1993), the theme indicators were based on the quotients of current environment pressures and their concomitant policy target, as stated in the Netherlands environmental policy plan (VROM, 1989 and 1992a). This plan reflected the official government policy and was formally approved by the Parliament. Policy endorsed norms are in our view the most acceptable weights if one wants to compile a single environmental pressure index. However, the user community, as reflected in the Dutch national accounts advisory board, was reluctant to mix statistics with politically determined targets.

At the most aggregate level, NAMEA presents the interrelation between macro-indicators for the economy (NDP, Net Saving, external balance) and the environment (environmental theme indicators). Underlying Table 1 a much more detailed information system is available, distinguishing for each account a number of categories. Table 2 presents more detailed information on substance flows in account 11 of the corresponding macro-table. The pollution from production is classified by industry branch. Pollution emitted by consumption is shown for two consumption purposes: (a) own transport and (b) other purposes.

4. COMPARING INDUSTRIES' AND HOUSEHOLDS' CONTRIBUTIONS TO ENVIRONMENTAL AND ECONOMIC INDICATORS

The indicators presented in Tables 4 and 5 are calculated by converting the emission data in the NAMEA into environmental stress equivalents and by aggregating these equivalents per theme. Table 4 shows that the emissions in the Netherlands as reflected in the NAMEA have on average decreased or increased significantly less than the Gross Domestic Product (GDP). The emission of pollutants which damage the ozone layer decreased by an average 12.4 percent per year. Other environmental indicators also show a decrease: eutrophication by 3.5 percent and acidification by 2.2 percent per year. The volume of waste, on the other hand, grew by 1.8 percent per year, while the emission of greenhouse gases increased by 2.0 percent. These percentage increases are, however, significantly lower than the volume increase of GDP between 1989 and 1991, i.e. 3.2 percent per year.

The average consumption growth equalled 3.8 percent between 1989 and 1991. In spite of this, consumers produced 2.1 percent less waste per year and emitted 4.9 percent less acid substances. The ozone layer depleting emissions were reduced by 12.3 percent yearly. However, the higher consumption did lead to more emissions of greenhouse gases (+2.9 percent) and eutrophicating substances (+2.5 percent) per year. These increases surpass the annual growth of the producers' emissions by industries (+1.8 percent and −4.0 percent respectively).

Remarkably, the relatively lower pollution due to consumption is nearly all accounted for by the lower emissions of cars and other forms of personal transport. In this consumption category emissions are down all along the line, while the consumption volume rose by nearly 3 percent per year. This is partly related to the increasing proportion of cars in the Dutch car fleet being fitted with catalytic converters since 1989. In spite of this decrease, in 1991 personal transport still caused 86 percent of the acidification due to consumption. Moreover it accounted for 41 percent of the greenhouse effect and 15 percent of eutrophication. In comparison, expenditure on personal transport made up only 9 percent of total consumer expenditure in 1991 (see Table 5).

In nearly all branches of industry which contribute significantly to the thinning of the ozone layer, eutrophication and acidification, the emission of pollutants which cause these problems dropped. The only exception was the emission of acidifying substances by the oil industry (+2.3 percent). The volume growth of value added was relatively high here too (+4.8 percent). The category "other manufacturing" realized the greatest reduction in damage to the ozone layer (−18.4 percent); this was mainly due to improvements in the manufacture of rubber and plastic products and in the metal products industry.

The decrease in the emission of eutrophicating substances was mainly caused by less emission by agriculture (−3.9 percent, with a production growth of 6.5

TABLE 4

AVERAGE ANNUAL VOLUME CHANGES 1990—91 FOR SOME ECONOMIC AND ENVIRONMENTAL INDICATORS

(%)	Economic Indicators			Environmental Indicators				
	GDP (factor cost)	Labour Volume	Consumption expenditure	Greenhouse Effect	Ozone Layer Depletion	Acidification	Eutrophication	Waste
Household consumption expenditure			3.8	2.9	-12.3	-4.9	2.5	-2.1
Own transport			2.8	-1.1	—	-6.3	-7.9	—
Other			3.8	6.0	-12.3	4.8	4.7	-1.7
Production	3.3	1.8		1.8	-12.4	-1.8	-4.0	3.2
Agriculture, hunting, forestry and fishing	6.5	-0.4		6.8	—	-1.5	-3.9	1.2
Mining and quarrying	4.8	0.0						5.2
Manufacturing	1.9	0.8		0.7	-12.5	-1.0	-3.0	4.4
Food, beverage and tobacco industry	3.7	0.3		2.0	—	—	—	9.0
Petroleum industry	4.8	0.0		0.3	—	2.3	—	—
Chemical industry	0.0	0.0		0.9	-3.1	-5.6	-13.6	3.2
Manufacture of basic metals	-1.9	-1.7		-3.8	-18.4	-2.2	—	
Other manufacturing of which	2.1	1.1		3.6		-1.3	—	1.5
Public utilities	3.2	-2.2		0.4	—	-7.0	—	
Electricity	2.2	-1.9		0.1	—	-7.7	—	
Construction	0.0	0.0		—	—			
Transport and storage	6.7	2.9		2.8	—	-0.5	—	-3.9
Environmental cleansing and sanitary services	1.9	3.8		2.7				5.0
Other services	3.3	2.5		1.1		-0.7		9.4
Total	3.2	1.8	3.8	2.0	-12.4	-2.2	-3.5	1.8

Note: — means contribution too small for a reliable estimate of change.

142

percent). Acidification also dropped in this branch of industry (−1.0 percent). This form of pollution was also down in electricity generation (−7.7 percent) and in the chemical industry (−5.6 percent). Electricity plants stabilized their emission of greenhouse gases while increasing value added by 2.2 percent. In some branches of industry the increase in waste generation and in the emission of greenhouse gases was higher than production growth. The amount of waste showed a strong growth in "other services" (9.4 percent), which includes commercial services, financial services, government etc., and in the food industry (9.0 percent). Between 1989 and 1991, the emission of greenhouse gases rose in nearly all the industries except the basic metals industry. The greatest increase was for agriculture and fishing (6.8 percent) and other manufacturing (3.6 percent).

Table 5 shows that in 1991 the share of "other services" in GDP is much higher than the contribution of this activity to the above-mentioned five environmental problems. Leaving aside the damage to the ozone layer this also holds for other manufacturing. Agriculture and fishing, the chemical industry and electricity plants show the reverse for most of the environmental problems.

It should be noted that in the NAMEA pollution is registered with the activity where the actual emission has taken place. For example, greenhouse gases emitted during electricity production for rail transport are not registered with the transport industry. Such indirect effects may, however, be calculated in a matrix multiplier analysis based on the NAMEA.

Table 6 contains an overview of pollution prevention expenditures of the government, households and branches of industry. As mentioned above, these expenditures can be subdivided into two types of services: internal and external cleansing services. The share of environmental cleansing services in government and household consumption expenditures slightly rose between 1989 and 1991. A major part of the external cleansing services provided to households is actually consumed and paid for by the government.[8] From 1989 to 1991, the average annual increase in expenditures on cleansing services by industries equalled 18 percent, which is much higher than the annual GDP growth rate. The percentages in Table 6 give the total environmental protection expenditures as a share of total household or government consumption, or as a share of total input costs per industry. The average share for all industries equalled only 0.5 percent in 1989 and rose slightly to 0.6 percent in 1991.

The shares vary among production activities, and these differences are generally not in conformity with the relative contributions to environmental themes. For instance, electricity generation spends 2.5 percent of total input costs on environmental protection in 1991, while this percentage is only slightly above average in agriculture and fishing. Related to this, the emission of greenhouse gases from electricity generation nearly stabilized, while the annual value added growth equalled 2.2 percent. Acid emissions from electricity generation were reduced by almost 8 percent. This combination of relatively high expenditures on environmental cleansing and a reduction in the contributions to environmental themes was also found in the basic metals industry. Here, the average decrease in emissions for all themes surpassed the reduction in value added and employment.

[8]Typically, waste collection is not directly paid for by households, but through taxation.

TABLE 5

CONTRIBUTIONS TO PRODUCTION AND CONSUMPTION ACTIVITIES TO GDP, EMPLOYMENT AND SOME ENVIRONMENTAL THEMES ACCORDING TO THE 1991 NAMEA FOR THE NETHERLANDS

(%)	Economic Indicators			Environment Indicators				
	GDP (factor cost)	Labour Volume	Consumption Expenditure	Greenhouse Effect	Ozone Layer Depletion	Acidification	Eutrophication	Waste
Household consumption expenditure				20	10	11	9	25
Production				80	90	89	91	75
Household consumption expenditure			100	100	100	100	100	100
Own transport			9	41	0	86	15	2
Other			91	59	100	14	85	98
Production	100	100		100	100	100	100	100
Agriculture, hunting, forestry and fishing	4	5		16	0	49	86	6
Mining and quarrying	4	0		2	0	1	0	7
Manufacturing	19	18		36	98	24	11	36
Food, beverage and tobacco industry	3	3		3	0	1	0	11
Petroleum industry	1	0		8	0	10	0	0
Chemical industry	3	2		16	44	7	6	16
Manufacture of basic metals	1	1		4	0	3	0	2
Other manufacturing	12	13		5	54	3	4	7
Public utilities, of which	2	1		26	0	9	1	3
Electricity	1	0		26	0	9	1	1
Construction	6	8		2	0	2	0	18
Transport and storage	6	5		6	0	9	1	11
Environmental cleansing and sanitary services	0	0		3	0	1	0	3
Other services	9	63		7	2	5	1	15

TABLE 6

Use of Internal and External Environmental Cleansing Services by the Government, Households and Branches of Industries in the Netherlands, 1989 and 1991

	1989				1991			
	Internal	External	Total Use as % of Input	Total Use as % of Consumption	Internal	External	Total Use as % of Input	Total Use as % of Consumption
	Mln Guilders							
Consumption expenditure	509	1,021		0.43	710	1,434		0.54
Government	–	999		1.39	–	1,410		1.80
Households	509	22		0.02	710	24		0.02
Total production	1,273	3,251	0.50		1,613	4,692	0.63	
Agriculture, hunting, forestry and fishing	26	198	0.51		30	262	0.66	
Mining and quarrying	14	112	0.77		14	138	0.67	
Crude petroleum and natural gas production	12	112	0.83		12	138	0.70	
Other mining and quarrying	2	–	0.13		2	–	0.14	
Manufacturing	563	1,240	0.61		695	1,622	0.74	
Food, beverage and tobacco industry	103	172	0.36		132	196	0.42	
Textile, wearing apparel and leather industry	114	13	1.44		135	16	1.60	
Wood, furniture and building materials industry	9	3	0.18		10	5	0.21	
Paper, paper products, printing and publishing industry	52	30	0.31		63	39	0.35	
Petroleum industry	20	233	1.24		28	249	1.27	
Chemical industry	71	456	1.10		101	717	1.80	
Rubber and artificial materials processing industry	6	2	0.09		11	4	0.15	
Manufacture of building material, earthenware and glass products	15	33	0.57		16	44	0.67	
Manufacture of basic metals	16	194	1.86		21	200	2.32	
Manufacture of metal products and machinery	62	97	0.43		74	141	0.51	
Industrial manufacturing n.e.c.	95	7	0.23		104	11	0.24	
Public utilities	10	274	1.41		10	298	2.56	
Construction	24	20	0.06		28	201	0.29	
Transport and storage	61	416	1.09		80	589	1.35	
Environmental cleansing and sanitary services	18	–	0.86		24	–	0.87	
Other services	557	991	0.38		732	1,582	0.49	
Total	1,782	4,272			2,323	6,126		

Note: Internal environmental cleansing services are included in total input (and output) in the NAMEA.

Concomitantly, environmental protection expenditures were high in relation to value added. Reverse patterns were found for transport and oil refineries. Here, above-average environmental expenditures were not combined with decreases in pollution. Nevertheless, growth rates of the contributions to environmental themes by oil refineries were lower than the value added volume increase. In conclusion, a straight-forward relationship between environmental protection expenditures and pollution reduction could not be determined at the industry level. Anyhow, the NAMEA may be a suitable framework for further research on this policy issue.

5. Other Applications and Future Extensions

The NAMEA system can be used for many purposes. For example, the indirect economic and ecological effects of consumption or exports can be shown. With the help of a Leontief-inverse, it is possible to estimate the pollution generated in all activities that contributed to the realization of one unit of final product. Detailed classifications of production activities and the concomitant pollutants are very important in this respect. Besides, the NAMEA can serve as a framework for applied general equilibrium models. These models can be used for calculating e.g. the effects of an energy tax on the environmental and economic indicators in the system. Another model application of the NAMEA is the estimation of a National income in a sustainable situation.[9]

It goes without saying that the NAMEA system itself does not contain separate entries for eco-value-added, eco-margins etc. which are found in the SEEA handbook of the UN (1993). A correctly adjusted NDP can only be the result of an explicit modelling exercise. Such an exercise should yield a different, but again fully consistent NAMEA. In order to facilitate a calculation of the full effects of pricing the environment, the NAMEA contains a complete accounting system. Some of the NAMEA accounts, such as an income distribution and use account are not yet included in the SEEA. The NAMEA contains a weighted aggregation of residuals by environmental problem. The SEEA also distinguishes residuals, but without a further aggregation by environmental problem. The NAMEA's link to pressure indicators by type of environmental problem is useful for two reasons: (1) environmental policies are usually formulated at that level and (2) much more data are available for pressures than for changes in states. It may be noted that NAMEA can be used *both* for the derivation of OECD-type aggregate indicators *and* for "green" income simulations. The most important difference between both systems is perhaps that the NAMEA starts from an expansion of the National accounts with the so-called substances accounts, while the SEEA focuses to a large extent on an expansion of the asset accounts in the SNA with accounts for non-produced natural assets.

At present, the conceptual and statistical development of the NAMEA continues. For instance, the number of environmental themes will be expanded when new information becomes available. This relates to e.g. other themes from the Netherlands' Environmental Policy Plan (the dispersion of toxic substances,

---

[9]In De Boer *et al.* (1994) such a simple optimization model based on the NAMEA is presented.

stench and noise nuisance and excessive use of ground water). Another expansion of the system is the decomposition of supply and use data in the NAMEA into physical units and average prices. A direct connection can then be made between the use of natural resources and the emissions of pollutants. This may lead to detailed research on material flows in production processes (see Konijn *et al.*, 1995). Table 2 reflects the most detailed emission data that are presently available. The research on material flows, for instance on energy balances, may lead to more detailed emission estimates in the near future.

Finally, research continues to integrate national accounts, environmental accounts and socio-demographic accounts in a single information system that also yields the core economic, social and environmental indicators for monitoring human development (Keuning, 1995; Keuning and Timmerman, 1995).

REFERENCES

Adriaanse, A., *Environmental Policy Performance Indicators*, Ministry of Housing, Spatial Planning and the Environment, VROM, The Hague, 1993.
CBS, *National Accounts 1993*, SDU Publishers, The Hague, 1994.
De Boer B., M. de Haan, and M. Voogt, What Would Net Domestic Product Have Been in a Sustainable Economy? Preliminary views and results, in *National Accounts and the Environment; Papers and Proceedings from a Conference*, London, March 16–18, 1994, Statistics Canada, National Accounts and Environment Division, Ottawa, 1994.
De Boo, A. J., Accounting for the Costs of Clean Technologies and Products, in *Conference papers from the Second Meeting of the London Group on Natural Resource and Environmental Accounting*, Washington, DC, March 15–17, 1995, U.S. Bureau of Economic Analysis Washington, DC, 1995.
De Boo, A. J., P. R. Bosch, C. N. Gorter, and S. J. Keuning, An Environmental Module and the Complete System of National Accounts, in A. Franz and C. Stahmer (eds.), *Approaches to Environmental Accounting*, Physica-Verlag, Heidelberg, 1993.
De Haan M., S. J. Keuning, and P. R. Bosch, Integrating Indicators in a National Accounting Matrix Including Environmental Accounts, NAMEA, in *National Accounts and the Environment; Papers and Proceedings from a Conference*, London, March 16–18, 1994, Statistics Canada, National Accounts and Environment Division, Ottawa, 1994.
IPCC, *The Supplementary Reports to the IPCC Scientific Assessment*, J. T. Houghton, B. A. Callander, and S. K. Varney (eds.), Cambridge University Press, Cambridge/London, 1992.
Keuning, S. J., An Information System for Environmental Indicators in Relation to the National Accounts, in W. F. M. de Vries, G. P. den Bakker, M. B. G. Gircour, S. J. Keuning, and A. Lenson (eds), *The Value Added of National Accounting*, Statistics Netherlands, Voorburg, 1993.
———, *Accounting for Economic Development and Social Change, with a case study for Indonesia*, Ph.D. thesis, Erasmus University Rotterdam, Rotterdam, 1995.
Keuning, S. J. and J. de Gijt, A National Accounting Matrix for the Netherlands, *National Accounts Occasional Paper*, No. 59, Voorburg, 1992.
Keuning, S. J. and J. G. Timmerman, An Information System for Economic, Environmental and Social Statistics: Integrating Environmental Data into the SESAME, in *Conference papers from the Second Meeting of the London group on Natural Resource and Environmental Accounting*, Washington, DC, March 15–17, 1995, U.S. Bureau of Economic Analysis, Washington, DC, 1995.
Konijn P., S. De Boer, and J. Van Dalen, Material Flows, Energy Use and the Structure of the Economy, *National Accounts Occasional Paper*, No. 77, Statistics Netherlands, Voorburg, 1995.
Schneider T. and A. H. M. Bresser, *Acidification Research 1984–1988*, Summary Report, Dutch Priority Programme on Acidification, nr. 00–06, RIVM, Bilthoven, 1988.
United Nations, *Intergrated Environmental and Economic Accounting*, United Nations, New York, 1993.
VROM (Ministry of Housing, Spatial Planning and the Environment), *Nationaal milieubeleidsplan* (National Environmental Policy Plan), VROM, The Hague, 1989.
——— *Thema-Indicatoren voor het milieubeleid* (Theme Related Indicators Supporting Environmental Policy), nr. 1992/9, VROM, The Hague, 1992a.
——— *CFC-Action programme, cooperation between government and industry*, Annual Report 1991, VROM, The Hague, 1992b.

———— Milieuprogramma (Environmental Programme) 1993–1996, voortgangrapportage, VROM, The Hague, 1992c.
———— *Nationaal milieubeleidsplan 2*, VROM, the Hague, 1993.

The following CBS publications were to compile the NAMEAs:

Animal Manure and Nutrients 1990 (floppy disk).
Costs and Financing of Environmental Control 1991–1992.
Emissions from the Combustion of Fossil Fuels in Furnaces 1980–1990.
Emissions by Road Traffic 1980–1990.
Environmental Statistics of the Netherlands 1993 (English publication).
Environmental Quarterly.
Industrial Costs for the Protection of the Environment 1992
Industrial Waste 1992.
Process Emissions 1980–1990.
Manure Production 1990.
Minerals in Agriculture 1970–1990; Phosphorus, Nitrogen and Potassium.
Municipal Waste 1991.
National Accounts 1993.
Phosphorus in the Netherlands 1970–1983.
Statistics of Water Quality Management and Control, Volume A :Discharge of Waste Water 1991, Volume B: Treatment of Sewage 1991.
Vehicle Wrecks 1989.

Part IV
Corporate Environmental Accounting

[13]

THE CORPORATE ENVIRONMENTAL ACCOUNTING SYSTEM:
A MANAGEMENT TOOL FOR FIGHTING ENVIRONMENTAL DEGRADATION*

ARIEH A. ULLMANN

St. Gall Graduate School for Economics, Business and Public Administration,
Switzerland

Abstract

Growing social costs and increasing criticism of prevailing accounting practices both on the macroeconomic and microeconomic level have recently led to efforts to expand the scope of accounting for better evaluation of an organization's behavior. CEAS provides corporate management as well as governmental authorities with a comprehensive assessment system of the annual environmental effects of a corporation's regular business activities. As a tool to control an economy's impact on the physical environment, it helps to achieve a better quality of life.

In recent publications evidence can be found of increasing criticism of the prevailing macro-economic as well as microeconomic accounting theories. If up until recently aspects such as the statistical accuracy of accounts were objected to, now even the basic assumptions of established theories are challenged. According to Kuhn (1962) this criticism could represent the beginning of a fundamental change in. paradigm. The criticism is based on a number of recent developments. In the last few decades the interdependence between different social activities and between different geographical regions have increased considerably, mainly due to a staggering change in man's capacity. Thus, the realm of economics has expanded remarkably as a growing proportion of an individual's daily life has been economized. This development is accompanied by a noticeable shift in public opinion concerning the relative importance of traditional economic goals in relation to other aspects of life. "Quality of life" instead of "standard of living" is a symbol of this broader outlook. Since the prevailing accounting theories restrict themselves to the traditional economic issues, the data generated by these theories are less relevant. As a result of this process new approaches are necessary to expand the scope of accounting.

In such an atmosphere of general criticism and discontent, it is of prime importance to keep in mind two basic aspects of any accounting theory: it is tied to a culture and it serves specific purposes. These two aspects can serve as guidelines for the development of new approaches.

The cultural background of any accounting theory can easily be seen by the terms and expressions used. Above all it is clearly visible in the section of reality subject to accounting. Gambling (1974, p. 48) describes this aspect most eloquently:

"It is important that not only the National Income accounts but also the underlying micro-accounts should measure what the people concerned are in fact interested in controlling. Thus there have been, in the past, communities that have derived genuine satisfaction from waging wars, building pyramids and similar costly and prima facie unrewarding activity. In the West it is convenient to construct macro-accounts in terms of sales, wages, profits, and the like, because it is assumed that our main interest lies in the consumption of transferable goods although this is not likely to be a universally correct assumption."

The goal orientation of accounting is illustrated in the progress achieved in macro-accounting as a result of the depression of the 1930's and the subsequent efforts to improve control over the economy (Abraham 1969; Studenski, 1958).

*The author would like to acknowledge the helpful comments of R. Müller-Wenk and of Ms B. E. Phiebig Ullman. An earlier draft of this paper was presented at the annual conference of the European Foundation for Management Development in Manchester, England in June 1975.

ARIEH A. ULLMAN

SHORTCOMINGS OF
CURRENT ACCOUNTING PRACTICES

On the macroeconomic level, the growth of social costs as undesirable second order consequences of the secular economic expansion in the West enlightens the fact that GNP is an insufficient gauge of a nation's achievements and well-being. The demands concerning the purpose of GNP have changed considerably since its first calculations. A modern welfare state is not only concerned with measuring the economy's efficiency but also with other aspects such as social justice, adequate supply of public goods, and the condition of the social and physical environment. Today efforts are being undertaken either to adapt the measurement of GNP to this new task (Nordhaus & Tobin, 1972; OECD, 1971) or to replace it by a system of social indicators (OECD, 1971a).

On the microeconomic level similar developments are noticeable. The pursuit of purely economic goals in the sense of profit-maximizing economic man does not only create diseconomies for society at large but in the long run also damages a company's reputation. Because traditional accounting practices neglect these aspects, difficulties arise when including the consequent "intangible" assets and liabilities in internal decision-making and in published reports. Hence, accounting no longer serves its purpose of providing the information necessary for an effective allocation of scarce resources and for the fulfilment of the organization's goals (American Accounting Association, 1966, p. 4). Above all, the prevailing accounting standards do not accomplish their purpose of reporting "on those activities of the enterprises affecting society", as they should according to a study group of the AICPA (1973, p. 66). For the last few years research has been undertaken to include some of these neglected aspects in accounting theories. Well-known examples are Human Resource Accounting (for an overview see Caplan & Landekich, 1974) and Social Accounting (see, e.g. Bauer & Fenn, 1972; Dierkes & Bauer, 1973; Dierkes, 1974). The latter covers a wide range of topics such as minority hiring, consumerism, employee safety and health, pollution, etc., issues that also fit under the key word of "corporate social responsibility" (McAdam, 1973, p. 12).

Various approaches to corporate social accounting have been advocated, namely: comprehensive as well as partial, monetary as well as nonmonetary, and input as well as output oriented systems (Bauer, 1973, p. 3). It is obvious that any combination of these approaches contains a number of advantages and disadvantages. Before developing a new system one should reflect on these aspects.

(1) A comprehensive system of social accounting accentuates the problem of aggregation. It is part of the basic axioms of accounting theory that aggregation is both possible and reasonable (Gambling, 1973, p. 26). However, the homogeneity necessary for aggregation is dubious in the case of a comprehensive system which combines economic effectiveness with such diverse topics as stated above. Besides, such an overall approach implies measurement standards general enough to embrace these topics. This inevitably would imply a loss in accuracy. In addition, such an approach requires consensus about the topics to be included and the relative importance attributed to each. Such a consensus, however, seems rather difficult to achieve (Bauer, 1973a, p. 402). Finally, studies about how to improve the quality of life indicate that one cannot easily substitute one area of vital importance by increasing the quality of another: more pollution can only be compensated for by more minority hiring within a certain tolerance limit.[1] A general denominator, inherent in any comprehensive system, might lead to attempts to increase a company's total social benefit record by promoting programs in the most accessible area while at the same time ignoring others with higher priority. In addition, such a procedure would indicate a step back to maximizing growth rates and sums instead of trying to achieve a balanced structure of goods and services delivered. The fallacy of maximizing behavior has received ample recognition in connection with the measurement of GNP.

(2) Monetarized approaches show severe shortcomings as indicated by the criticism that Linowes' SEOS (1972, p. 39) and Abt's Social Audit received (Dierkes, 1974, p. 102; Bauer, 1973, p. 3). Gray (1973, p. 315) emphasizes the fundamental problem:

---

[1] On the physiological level the importance of fulfilling a balanced combination of needs has long been recognized in the form of a "balanced meal". However, the application of the same to the psychological and sociological levels has been overlooked.

"The reason why it seems basically unsound to us to try to apply traditional business accounting to these 'externalities' is that prevailing accounting is married to and therefore bounded by the same limits as the prevailing theory of a market economy. Like that theory it focuses on the world of transactions. But the very problems we want this accounting to cover have become problems precisely because they lie outside the world of transactions."

An examination of the Social Audit of Abt Associates and of the German Steag AG (Schulte, 1974, p. 277; Dierkes, 1974, p. 78) clearly illustrates these difficulties.

(3) The selection between an input or an output oriented approach is closely connected with the two problem areas stated above. Generally, the financial costs involved in a program of corporate social responsibility are easier to compute than the resulting benefits. Hence, monetary input approaches are frequently chosen. The disadvantages of such an approach are well-known: an input approach reflects neither the adequacy nor the efficiency of the funds spent (American Accounting Association, 1973, p. 88).

THE CORPORATE ENVIRONMENTAL ACCOUNTING SYSTEM

In the midst of these problems a partial, nonmonetary and output oriented approach has been chosen. It deals only with the effects of a corporation's regular activities on the physical environment and measures them in nonmonetary units. By restricting itself to only one of the many important issues related to corporate social responsibility, the approach selected for the Corporate Environmental Accounting System (CEAS) is modest. However, by proposing a new, output oriented system to measure a company's impact on the environment, it is an ambitious approach.[2]

Underlying assumptions

Two basic hypotheses of equal importance represent the starting point of CEAS. On the one hand the current economic system of the West is clearly geared to growth. Paradoxically, even the current recession can be interpreted in this way. The ongoing zero growth period emphasizes the unsolved problems and accentuates the conflicts of interest. Hence, all efforts are directed toward restoring a steady rate of growth irrespective of second order consequences. On the other hand this growing economic activity unfortunately happens to take place on "spaceship earth", a partially closed system with a finite carrying capacity, with limited assimilative capabilities of its ecosystems and restricted amounts of non-renewable resources. Starting from a Materials Balance Approach (Ayres & Kneese, 1969, p. 282), taking into account the basic law of conservation of mass, it follows that one cannot deal with pollution alone, or with pollution and depletion of resources separately. Rather, these two factors, the major themes of the ongoing environmental debate, have to be considered as two manifestations of the same process. Within this frame of reference, growth in industrial output generally implies additional environmental stress: more pollution, increased consumption of resources. Since these aspects do not show up either in national or in corporate accounts, they are difficult to control. CEAS is an attempt to close this gap. It should provide both corporate management and public authorities with an information and assessment system.

The concept

CEAS is a system based on an input-output analysis of a corporation. It measures annual environmental effects connected with regular business operations: consumption of materials and energy, generation of solid waste, discharge of pollutants into air, water and soil.[3] Since there are many materials and various sorts of pollutants, a special account should be established for each.

It should be noted that not all types of environmental impacts are integrated into CEAS. For example, the problems connected with noise and land use are excluded, because they can easily be controlled by legal restrictions. It goes without saying that besides the proposed accounts new ones can easily be added if necessary.

The notion of an environmentally defined scarcity is of prime importance to CEAS. This type of scarcity is concerned on the one hand with the finite assimilative capacity of ecosystems and on the other hand with the limited amounts of non-renewable resources. This type of scarcity has very little in common with the market-type scarcity. The latter either does not include the

---

[2] A detailed description of CEAS was published as a working paper (Müller-Wenk & Ullmann, 1974).

[3] A somewhat similar approach has been proposed by Westman & Gifford (1973, p. 819).

environmentally defined scarcity at all, for instance in the case of the so-called free goods, or only includes a fraction of it, for instance increased exploration and mining costs when resources are dwindling. Two different types of environmental scarcity have to be distinguished. First, ecosystems show certain assimilative capacities and therefore are not damaged as long as man-made impacts do not exceed a certain critical emission rate. In this case the environmental scarcity denominates to what extent the regenerative capacity of ecosystems is used up due to the current rate of emissions. This type of environmental scarcity is called flow scarcity. Second, there is the so-called cumulative scarcity. Here, even the smallest impact aggravates the shortage. The consumption of a non-renewable resource is a good example. Depending on the type of impact, environmental scarcity is either defined on a world-wide basis or on a regional or national basis. For instance, compare the scarcity of mercury, which is relevant on the global level, to the scarcity of landfills needed for disposing solid waste, which is relevant to a given area.

By applying these two concepts of scarcity to each input and output a factor is obtained called the Equivalent Factor (EC). With regard to flow scarcity the EC is calculated as follows:[4]

$$EC = \frac{F}{F_c - F} \cdot \frac{1}{F_c} \quad ,$$

F is the current annual emission rate and F_c is the critical emission rate. If $F = F_c$, severe, irreversible damages occur. It is assumed that today F is in general smaller than F_c. If this assumption should not be valid, stricter measures than CEAS are required.

With regard to cumulative scarcity the EC is determined by the following formula:[5]

$$EC = \frac{nF}{R - nF} \cdot \frac{1}{R} \quad ,$$

F is the annual impact, R the known reserves, and n denominates the number of years for which R should last. n is a normative expression of a society's future orientation and responsibility for the unborn generations.[6] The EC is defined as long as $0 < nF < R$. It should be noted that R/F might be smaller than the time horizon set (n), so that the EC cannot be defined according to the proposed formula. In this case a special procedure has to be applied.

The EC's are to be established by the government and changed from time to time in order to allow for readjustments due to new developments of the environmental situation and in order to prevent undesirable inflexibility. With the use of the EC's it is possible to compare different environmental effects such as the consumption of energy with the consumption of other resources and with the emission of pollutants. This enables the company and the government introducing CEAS to assess the net environmental benefit of, for instance, installing air pollution abating equipment or of increasing recycling. Normally, this is a difficult task, since reducing air pollution levels often implies increasing water pollution; or, more recycling can lead to an increase in energy consumption of an organization so that the real benefit to the environment cannot be determined.

CEAS-units

First, the company measures its environmentally relevant inputs and outputs in physical units (tons, kWh, cbft, etc.). Second, by multiplying these amounts with the corresponding ECs and by adding up the resulting CEAS-units, a sum is obtained which reflects the total environmental impact produced by a company's business activities during one year.[7]

If materials are recycled, only the environmental effects connected with the recycling process are computed, for example the amount of energy required for transport and processing, or the pollution involved respectively. The value in CEAS-units of the material recycled is zero on the input side, because it was counted

---

[4] An example is given in Appendix A.

[5] An example is given in Appendix B.

[6] One should expect n to be at least 50, since the generation living now is certainly not interested in consuming non-renewable resources at such a rate that it would suffer in old age.

[7] An example is given in Appendix C.

when it entered the economic system for the first time. Thus, economical use of materials and recycling are reinforced.

FROM MICRO-ACCOUNTING TO MACRO-ACCOUNTING

Quotas

It cannot be ignored that the existing economic system might prevent a company from taking the measures required to minimize environmental impacts as indicated by the CEAS. Competition might coerce an enterprise to expand its sales and/or postpone investments beneficial to the environment. This can easily occur if competing companies are not concerned with the environmental effects they cause. Therefore, CEAS has to be linked to a system of quotas by which each company is given a certain sum of CEAS-units every year.

Then, the government, that is allocating the CEAS-units, is able to control the annual environmental impact produced by the economy. It is important to regulate only the total sum of a company's CEAS-units and — given certain emission standards — not that of a single account. Hence, an expanding company must save CEAS-units by choosing the measures which are best suited to its economic conditions and produce the biggest marginal benefit in CEAS-units saved.

Some special problems

Who should be subject to CEAS? It is suggested that all companies, private, public and state-owned, should install CEAS. Only private households and very small production entities (small farms, craftshops, and the like) should be excluded from this rule. Just as they are exempted, for practical reasons, from regular bookkeeping, the same should apply to CEAS. Therefore, the producers of goods which are sold to these CEAS-exempted entities, mainly producers of consumer goods, have to be charged for the environmental effects which result from the use of their products. As a consequence the average use of a number of consumer goods, for example cars or household appliances, must be assessed in terms of CEAS-units. This procedure does not place the producer of consumer goods at a disadvantage. However, it exercises a strong pressure for environmentally safer production and design of these products.

A second important question concerns the basis on which quotas should be established. There are a number of methods to distribute a limited quantity: assignment of an equal sum to each person or economic entity, distribution through market mechanism, by lottery, assignment according to priority or according to existing ownership. A close examination of the various mechanisms reveals that none of them are fully satisfactory. In consideration of the heterogeneity of the organizations subject to CEAS, and for pragmatic reasons such as minimum disturbance of the economic process, minimum implementation and maintenance costs, and conformity with prevailing legal conceptions, a distribution of the scarce CEAS-units according to existing ownership is favored. In other words, the allotment of the CEAS-units is made according to calculations of the companies' annual consumption in previous years.

A third problem encountered is the correct calculation and allocation of the environmental impacts computed, i.e. the avoidance of double-counting. Obviously, every company is only charged for the environmental effects it causes, with the exception of private households and small production entities as stated above. For pollutants and waste this concept creates no problems: Theoretically, the polluter is always identifiable. Concerning materials, however, several solutions are possible. Should the mining industry be charged or someone else in the economic process dealing with this material? From an environmental point of view it seems logical to charge at the point where dissipation occurs into the natural environment. There, according to the Laws of Thermodynamics, recovering is almost impossible. Thus, the producer of finished products will generally be charged, since these goods usually are distributed in the form of consumer goods. From an environmental point of view, however, distribution is equivalent to dissipation. For all other intermediate producers no charges for materials occur except for losses. In other words, CEAS is similar to the value-added tax system. For a proper functioning of the system, deliveries of goods to organizations subject to CEAS have to be accompanied by a certificate stating the composition of a product in regard to resources relevant to CEAS. It can be expected that by such a procedure a strong influence is exercised by the producers of finished goods on their suppliers to select materials with a minimum impact on the environment. Thus, reserves of scarce resources will be spared.

A company's CEAS-balance sheet therefore consists of three sections:[8]

(1) Environmental effects produced by the production process: materials and energy used, pollution and waste generated and dissipated, plus:

(2) Impacts due to the use of products sold to customers not subject to CEAS, minus:

(3) Materials, respectively material content of products sold to customers subject to CEAS.

Finally, very important questions arise since national economies are open systems and eco-systems transcend national border lines. If a country establishes CEAS, the logical strategy for a company with substantial environmental impact is either to move the production processes concerned abroad or to buy the corresponding semi-finished products from foreign suppliers.

Thus, the environmental impact is exported and the company's CEAS-balance sheet relieved. Such a restructuring of the economic process should be welcomed — not only from an environmental point of view but also in regard to the developing nations. Undoubtedly, these new host countries will be careful not to repeat the mistakes of the old industrialized economies.

If however negative side effects occur in the country introducing CEAS, importers could be charged for their imports in terms of CEAS-units as if the products were manufactured in the country. Exporters can be subject either to the same regulations as producers for the domestic market or special arrangements can be made. It is obvious that no general rule can be established, since the importance of exportation for the economy varies greatly from country to country.

A PROPOSAL FOR ACTION

It goes without saying that an all-embracing system such as CEAS cannot be implemented at once. Many questions remain to be answered, for instance regulations concerning mergers, lack of knowledge concerning environmental impacts, and undesirable spillover effects of CEAS. Therefore, a multi-stage procedure is proposed.

(1) In stage one CEAS should be tried out in different types of enterprises. Thus, it would be possible to refine the system on the basis of the

experience gained and to adapt it to the special needs of various industries.

(2) In stage two CEAS should be made compulsory for all companies with the exceptions indicated. It can be expected that the visualization of the companies' annual environmental impact will result in a change in the respective policies. At this stage implementation of the control system, required on the governmental level, should be tested.

(3) In stage three the companies subject to CEAS would have to publish an annual CEAS-balance sheet, while public authorities, similar to tax authorities, would gain access to the respective data.

(4) Finally, in stage four, an elaborated CEAS, based on the experience gained from the previous stages, would be introduced. Simultaneously, the government should try to persuade other governments to establish similar control systems.

THE STATE OF THE ART OF CEAS

Current research activities center around stage one. CEAS was established in collaboration with Roco Food Packing Co., Rorschach, Switzerland. A number of theoretical and practical problems were encountered; only the most important ones are mentioned below.

Since no official ECs were available, the ECs of the various resources had to be computed by the authors based on literature and statements of experts. This involved considerable work; it also indicated some gaps where no exact data were available. Substantial research is necessary concerning the amount of resources available and the effects of pollutants. It would, however, be fatal to wait until precise data are on hand. Regarding the magnitude of the problems and the risks involved immediate action is suggested despite the tentative character of certain data.

A very difficult problem arises from the weighing of the relative importance of world-wide and local effects. In the CEAS-balance sheet (Appendix C) the scarcity of a resource on a global basis was attributed the weight 1, whereas concerning the environmental effects on a local level, the respective ECs were multiplied by a factor denominating the regional importance, i.e. Switzerland's surface in relation to the earth's surface. By this procedure the results obtained are biased in so far as more importance is attributed to an environmental effect which is relevant on a

---

[8] See the example given in Appendix C.

world-wide basis than to one on a regional level. It can, however, be argued that, for instance, the degradation of a lake or the destruction of a local ecosystem, is of greater importance than, for instance, the depletion of mercury, since the latter can be substituted thanks to technological innovation whereas the former is vital to the people concerned and more difficult to restore. Clearly, there is no correct weighing possible. Any decision is obviously normative and has to be based on a democratic interplay of opinions. Consequently, the example given here should be understood as a preliminary proposal.

A practical difficulty encountered is the availability within the company of data required for CEAS. Since up until now these data were either not collected at all or classified according to criteria other than those of CEAS, they sometimes were difficult to obtain for the assessment of the company's previous environmental effects. Hence, the first step in implementing CEAS should be the rearrangement of the information flow according to the special needs of CEAS. In spite of these difficulties, the administrative expenditures involved for CEAS were small at the company level. At the governmental level the expenditures are more difficult to assess. They should, however, not exceed those necessary for the implementation and maintenance of the value-added tax.

RESULTS

One of the most desirable results from the practical work undertaken so far was the effect on top management of the presentation of the company's annual environmental impact. Top management was impressed by the amounts of gaseous and liquid emissions and loads of solid waste generated annually, and the amount of energy, materials and water used.

It remains to be seen whether a change of behavior will result from this. Further investigations showed that often neither top managers nor those on lower levels had an idea of a company's total environmental impact. Modifying a company's behavior thus seems to be a motivational as well as an informational problem. So, even if CEAS never gets beyond stage two, there is some hope that these modest steps will result in a company adopting a comprehensive policy to safeguard the environment.

BIBLIOGRAPHY

Abraham, W. I., *National Income and Economic Accounting* (Prentice-Hall, 1969).
American Accounting Association, *A Statement Of Basic Accounting Theory* (1966).
American Accounting Association, Report of Committee On Environmental Effects of Organizational Behavior. *The Accounting Review*, Vol. XLVIII (1973), Supplement, pp. 73-119.
American Institute of Certified Public Accountants. *Objectives of Financial Statements* (1973).
Ayres, R. U. & Kneese, A. U., Production, Consumption, and Externalities. *American Economic Review*, Vol. 59, No. 3 (1969), pp. 282-297.
Bauer, R. A. & Fenn, D. H. J., *The Corporate Social Audit* (Russell Sage Foundation, 1972).
Bauer, R. A., The State of the Art of Social Accounting, in Dierkes and Bauer (1973), pp. 3-40.
Bauer, R. A., The Future of Corporate Social Accounting, in Derkes and Bauer (1973a), pp. 389-405.
Caplan, E. H. & Landekich, S., *Human Resource Accounting: Past, Present and Future* (National Association of Accountants, 1974).
Dierkes, M. & Bauer, R. A., eds., *Corporate Social Accounting* (Praeger, 1973).
Dierkes, M. & Bauer, R. A., eds., *Die Sozialbilanz* (Frankfurt/M, 1974).
Gambling, T., *Societal Accounting* (Allen and Unwin, 1974).
Gray, D., One Way to Go About Inventing Social Accounting, in Dierkes and Bauer (1973), pp. 315-320.
Kuhn, T., *The Structure of Scientific Revolutions* (University of Chicago Press, 1962).
Linowes, D. S., Let's Get On With The Social Audit: A Specific Proposal, *Business & Society Review/Innovation* (Winter, 1972-73), pp. 39-49.
McAdam, T. W., How To Put Corporate Social Responsibility Into Practice. *Business & Society Review/Innovation* (Summer, 1973), pp. 8-16.
Meadows, D. *et al.*, *The Limits To Growth* (Earth Island, 1972).
Müller-Wenk, R. & Ullmann, A. A., *Die ökologische Buchhaltung* (St. Gallen, Zürich 1974).
Nordhaus, W. D. & Tobin, J., Is Growth Obsolete? *Economic Growth* (National Bureau of Economic Research, 1972).
OECD, *Environment and Growth in National Accounts* (1971).

OECD, *Working Group of Social Indicators, Social Indicators Development Program* (1971a).
Schulte, H., Die Sozialbilanz der Steag AG. *Betriebswirtschaftliche Forschung und Praxis*, No. 4 (1974), pp. 277–294.
Studenski, P., *The Income of Nations, Theory, Measurement and Analysis, Past and Present* (New York, 1958).
Westman, W. E. & Gifford, R. M., Environmental Impact: Controlling the Overall Level. *Science*, Vol. 181 (1973), pp. 819–825.

APPENDIX A

Computation of the EC of carbon monoxide for Switzerland:

$$F = 700{,}000 \text{ metric tons/yr}$$

$$F_c = \frac{(\text{air volume above Switzerland}) \cdot (\text{max. allowable concentration/m}^3)}{\text{average period of presence in the air}}$$

$$= \frac{205.10^{12} \text{ m}^3 \cdot 1 \text{ mg/m}^3}{0.1 \text{ yr}}$$

$$= 2{,}050{,}000 \text{ metric tons/yr}$$

$$EC = \frac{F}{F_c - F} \cdot \frac{1}{F_c} \cdot c^9 = 0.25 \cdot 10^6.$$

Taking into account that it is not of equal importance whether a certain amount of carbon monoxide is produced in a big or a very small country, the *EC* has to be weighed. The weighing factor for Switzerland is $8.04 \cdot 10^{-5}$.
Thus:

$$EC_{CO} = 20 \text{ CEAS-units/metric ton.}$$

APPENDIX B

Computation of the *EC* of tin:

$$F = 2.53 \cdot 10^5 \text{ lgtons}$$
$$R = 4.3 \cdot 10^6 \text{ lgtons}$$
$$n = 10^{10}$$

$$EC = \frac{nF}{R - nF} \cdot \frac{1}{R} \cdot c$$

$$= \frac{10 \cdot 2.53 \cdot 10^5 \text{ lgtons}}{4.3 \cdot 10^6 \text{ lgtons} - 10 \cdot 2.53 \cdot 10^5 \text{ lgtons}} \cdot 10^{12}$$

---

[9] For practical reasons a constant factor $c = 10^{12}$ was introduced.

[10] n is here 10. This does not imply that a time horizon of 10 yr is regarded as sufficient. It can mean that the resources known today are five times smaller than those which will be found in the near future.

Thus:

$$EC_{Sn} = 0.328 \cdot 10^3 \text{ CEAS-units/metric ton.}$$

The figures used here for F and R were given by the U.S. Bureau of Mines and listed in Meadows (1972, p. 56).

APPENDIX C

Abstract of the CEAS-balance sheet of Roco Food Packing Co., Rorschach, Switzerland, for 1973 (in CEAS-units):

Consumption of energy (electricity, gas, oil, etc.)	76,099
Consumption of materials (tinplate, plumber's solder, aluminium, glass, plastic, paper)	10,439,663
Solid waste	9
Sewage	30,545
Gaseous pollutants	12,913
Waste heat	515
Environmental effects caused by products sold to households (mainly solid waste)	222
Total	10,559,966
minus	
Deliveries of material to clients subject to CEAS	1,804,858
Net environmental impact	8,755,108

[14]

ACCOUNTING FOR ECO-EFFICIENCY

Stefan Schaltegger

SUMMARY

In this chapter the framework of environmental accounting is discussed, focusing on companies and the impact of their activities on the environment. First, *environmentally differentiated traditional accounting*, which is a part of traditional accounting, is discussed as a tool for measuring environmentally induced financial impacts in monetary terms. It is explained how, as the basis of most internal management decisions, it attempts to satisfy the needs of the external stakeholders of companies for financial information. The system of *ecological accounting* is then discussed as a tool for measuring the ecological impact of a company on the environment in terms of non-monetary physical units. This is followed by a discussion of *eco-efficiency*, which measures the economic performance of a company relative to the environmental impacts caused by its activities, together with an explanation of how the systems of traditional accounting and ecological accounting are integrated in eco-efficiency through the *Eco-rational Path Method* (EPM). All essential aspects of the above concepts are explained with the help of diagrams, tables and case studies, along with the concepts of *value added, environmental impact added,* etc.

ACADEMIC OBJECTIVES

After completing the chapter the reader should have a good understanding and working knowledge of the following:

- the concepts of value added, environmental impact added, environmentally differentiated accounting and ecological accounting and their respective sub-areas, and many other related topics and aspects;
- how the systems of traditional accounting and ecological accounting are integrated through the Eco-rational Path Method (EPM) to derive measures of eco-efficiency;
- the concept of eco-efficiency, its role and how it can be applied at the corporate level to assess the status of a company in terms of its economic performance relative to the environmental impacts of its activities.

ECO-EFFICIENCY AS AN OPERATIONAL MEASURE

Although the concept of *eco-efficiency* was first introduced and discussed in the literature by Schaltegger and Sturm (1990), it gained popularity only after the publication of the book entitled *Changing Course* by Schmidheiny (1992). Some other aspects of the concept and its limitations have been elaborated by Gladwin *et al.* (1995). In practice the term 'eco-efficiency' is used to convey different meanings with little precision. To begin with, therefore, it is important to clarify the concept of the term as it applies to the corporate level.

In general, efficiency is a measure of the output compared to the input. The higher the output for a given input, or the lower the input for a given output, the more efficient is an activity, product, company, etc. Since the purpose of any economic activity is to manage scarcity in the best possible manner, efficiency is a characteristic of economically rational management.

Efficiency is a dimensionless notion in its most general sense. While the units in which input and output are measured can differ depending on the subject matter, the dimensions of efficiency become concrete when the context is specified. In the business context, for example, if input and output are measured in financial terms, *profitability* becomes the measure of efficiency, commonly referred to as financial efficiency. Some of the measures of economic or financial efficiency are contribution margins, return on sales, return on assets, etc. Economic efficiency indicates whether, and for how long, social activities can be economically sustained. If, on the other hand, efficiency is measured in technological terms, then usually the focus is more on physical units such as kilograms. Technological efficiency is also called *productivity*. The ratio of the 'best possible' efficiency to the 'actually achieved' efficiency is called *X-efficiency* (Leibenstein, 1966). Efficiency is not confined to financial or technological dimensions, and different dimensions can be combined to calculate *cross-efficiency* figures such as the profit generated by each employee.

Using the definition of efficiency given above and appropriate units, the ecological efficiency of an activity can generally be expressed as the ratio of the desired output to what we will call the *environmental impact added* of that activity (Schaltegger and Sturm, 1990). Environmental impact added (EA) is defined as the sum of all the assessed environmental impacts caused by the activity. Thus,

$$\text{Ecological Efficiency} = \text{Desired Output}/ \text{Environmental Impact Added} \qquad (1)$$

This definition of ecological efficiency does not cover all aspects of sustainable development, however. The same is also true for value added (or added value). For example, the calculation of value added does not take into account an assessment of whether it was achieved by increasing the economic opportunities for the poor, if the products and services were oriented towards satisfying the basic needs of the workforce whose efforts led to the added value, and so on. It is clearly important to correlate environmental impact added with value added because no economic activity is without environmental impacts.

The management of a company is said to be ecologically efficient if the ratio of its products sold, or functions accomplished, to the resulting environmental impact added is high. Two different measures of ecological efficiency have been proposed in this context (Schaltegger and Sturm, [1992] 1994):

- ecological product efficiency;
- ecological function efficiency.

Ecological product efficiency is the ratio of a unit of the product (product unit) to the environmental impact added it would create over its whole life-cycle or a part thereof. That is,

$$\text{Ecological Product Efficiency} = \text{Product Unit}/ \text{Environmental Impact Added} \qquad (2)$$

Environmental improvements made by companies are often reported in communications on their total product efficiency (e.g. number of cars produced per unit of environmental impact). Product efficiency can be improved with a whole range of pollution prevention methods and strategies, including end-of-pipe devices, reduced input, substitution of resources, etc. Although in principle the improvement of product efficiency is desirable and to be recommended, some products will never be as ecologically efficient as others in meeting a certain demand. In meeting the demand for transportation, for example, a car will always be less ecologically efficient than a bicycle.

Ecological function efficiency takes a broader view compared with ecological product efficiency. It measures the environmental impact that will be caused, or has been caused, per unit of time in serving a specific function. Typically, a function could be defined as the transportation of a person over a certain distance. The alternative, which causes the minimum environmental impact in serving a given function, is said to have the highest ecological function efficiency, defined as

$$\text{Ecological Function Efficiency} = \text{Served Function}/ \text{Environmental Impact Added} \qquad (3)$$

Ecological function efficiency can be improved by substituting high eco-efficiency products for low eco-efficiency products (e.g. a bicycle instead of a car), by reducing the demand for the function to be served (e.g. use of carpools which lead to reduced demand for the use of private cars), by prolonging the life-span of products (e.g. longer corrosion guarantee for cars), and by improving product efficiency. Environmental interest groups often prefer to measure the environmental record of a product according to its overall ecological function efficiency (for example, the ecological function efficiency of a car in transporting a person over a given distance compared to that of a bicycle or public transport in performing the same function).

Both these measures of ecological efficiency – ecological product efficiency and ecological function efficiency – are useful, but their adequacy depends on their intended purpose. The ratios, given by equations (2) and (3), can be applied to different levels of aggregation, such as to a unit product, a strategic business unit, or to the total sales of a company. In this context it is important to consider total sales and the absolute environmental impact, because a large number of ecologically efficient products can be more harmful than a small number of ecologically inefficient products.

The cross-efficiency between the economic and ecological dimensions, or in other words the 'economic-ecological efficiency', is the ratio of the value added, created by a company, to the resulting environmental impact added (Schaltegger and Sturm, 1990). In most cases it makes sense to define it in terms of a relationship between some kind of economic performance and environmental impact as

Economic-Ecological Efficiency (eco-efficiency)
= Value Added / Environmental Impact Added
(4)

Economic-ecological efficiency is often referred to as 'eco-efficiency'. Clearly, the eco-efficiency of a product or activity will increase when its added value increases and/or its overall environmental impact decreases. Note that in equation (4) the measurement of neither the economic aspect nor the ecological aspect is fixed. The ratio of equation (4) should therefore be calculated by using such measures which provide the best information consistent with the aim of the analysis. If economic and ecological concerns are considered to have the same importance, then the numerator and the denominator should be given equal weighting as in equation (4). But, depending on their values, different groups are likely to assign different weightings to economic and ecological performance. Alternatively, as in the appraisal of investment on pollution prevention devices for example, the marginal product of eco-efficiency may be used representing the ratio of environmental improvement made per unit of extra cost (thus measuring cost-effectiveness).

Environmental indicators should always be set in the context of economic performance, because it would then be possible to assess the progress made by companies, products, nations, etc. with regard to their '*eco-efficiency portfolio*', shown in Figure 14.1. Environmental performance is plotted along the vertical axis of this figure, and the economic performance along the horizontal axis. The eco-efficiency portfolio shown in Figure 14.1 has four distinct areas:

- *Green stars* (upper right-hand corner) are sites, products, etc. with low environmental impact added and high economic performance. While low costs are achieved through integrated clean technologies, their environmental impact will already have been optimised during their development. Because they incur relatively low environmental impacts, there are markets where consumers are willing to pay a price premium for such environmentally friendly products. Costs savings as well as higher prices result in higher economic performance.
- '*Dirty cash cows*' (lower right-hand corner) result from strategies of quantitative growth. They are characterised by relatively high profitability and high environmental impact added. 'Dirty cash cows' are in danger of losing their profitability as soon as external environmental costs (economic externalities) are internalised, through the imposition of environmental taxes for example.
- *Green question marks* (upper left-hand corner) are environmentally friendly, but they achieve relatively low economic performance. In the long term they cannot prevail because of their economic weakness.
- '*Dirty dogs*' (lower left-hand corner) have high environmental impact added and a low or negative economic performance. They are economically uninteresting and cause enormous environmental damage. They should be eliminated, or improved both economically and ecologically.

Portfolios which bring environmental and economic data together are a very powerful analytical tool for assessing the relative eco-efficiency status of different production sites, products, companies, etc. They can also serve to benchmark environmentally 'good' competitors in relation to the company in

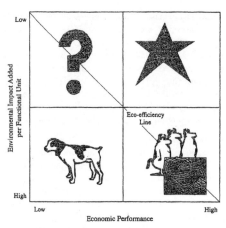

Figure 14.1 The eco-efficiency portfolio
Source: According to Schaltegger and Sturm, 1992

question (Ilinitch and Schaltegger, 1995). Also, once decisions have been taken on the basis of recorded and assessed data, appropriate strategies can be developed for making improvements. All movements above the eco-efficiency line, shown in Figure 14.1, represent improved eco-efficiency.

However, the definition of eco-efficiency is fraught with two major difficulties. First, how can environmentally induced financial impacts be considered and assessed when measuring economic performance? And second, how can environmental impact added be measured accurately?

ENVIRONMENTAL ACCOUNTING

Modern accounting, which began in the fifteenth century in northern Italy, has been the most important corporate system of information gathering and analysis for more than a hundred years. Because of continuing environmental degradation and the problems associated with it, increasingly greater importance is now being given to the gathering and analysis of information on environmental issues and problems. There is thus a growing need to adapt traditional accounting systems to this new situation. In order to assess the eco-efficiency of a company and its operations, the stakeholders of the company would

be interested in two main categories of information with regard to environmental issues and problems:

- environmentally induced financial impacts;
- environmental impacts of the company.

Given the different characteristics of these two categories, it is not surprising that many different perceptions and examples of 'environmental accounting' are now to be found (Schaltegger and Stinson, 1994). As a result, there is a correspondingly large, varied and growing body of literature on different aspects of what is generically called 'green accounting' (Adams, 1992; CICA, 1992; Epstein, 1995; Gray *et al.*, 1993; Gray, 1994; Gray and Laughlin, 1991; Price Waterhouse, 1991; Quirke, 1991; Rubenstein, 1994; Schaltegger *et al.*, 1996; Spitzer and Elwood, 1995).

According to the 'Tinbergen rule' though, which applies generally in economics and public policy, an instrument becomes inefficient and ineffective when it is used to pursue different aims that are not absolutely complementary (Tinbergen, 1968). None of the aims can be achieved effectively and efficiently under such circumstances. Therefore, different instruments should be applied to deal with non-complementary issues. With regard to accounting, this is why different accounting systems should be used to deal with different sets of issues. Every accounting system provides specific information for different groups of stakeholders. A stakeholder of a company is by definition an individual, or a group, who has an interest (stake) in the company and can influence, or is influenced by, the activities of the company and its policies. Stakeholders can be managers, employees, shareholders, suppliers and customers of the company, or they can be tax agencies, environmental pressure groups, neighbours, etc. Figure 14.2 shows important stakeholders and their interest in different *categories* and *systems* of accounting. In this figure the three important groups of stakeholders (management, shareholders and regulators) are shown vertically, and the traditional and ecological accounting systems horizontally.

As will be seen from this figure, both systems of accounting deal with environmental issues and are, therefore, part of 'environmental accounting'. The three areas, shaded in dark grey, represent the environmentally differentiated traditional accounting systems. As part of traditional accounting, they measure

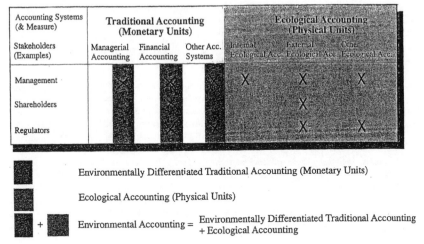

Accounting Systems (& Measure)	Traditional Accounting (Monetary Units)			Ecological Accounting (Physical Units)		
Stakeholders (Examples)	Managerial Accounting	Financial Accounting	Other Acc. Systems	Internal Ecological Acc.	External Ecological Acc.	Other Ecological Acc.
Management				X	X	X
Shareholders					X	
Regulators					X	X

■   Environmentally Differentiated Traditional Accounting (Monetary Units)

■   Ecological Accounting (Physical Units)

■ + ■   Environmental Accounting = Environmentally Differentiated Traditional Accounting + Ecological Accounting

Figure 14.2 Traditional and environmental accounting and their stakeholders

the environmentally-induced financial impacts of the company in monetary terms. The remainder of the traditional accounting systems, which do not deal with environmental issues, are represented by the unshaded areas.

Stakeholders are becoming increasingly more interested in environmental issues and problems, so traditional accounting systems should not only incorporate the financial impacts of environmental issues but should also be enlarged by including *ecological accounting systems*, or at least the essential aspects thereof. The systems of ecological accounting, shown in light grey in Figure 14.2, measure the ecological impact of a company on the environment. The measurements to be made for them, unlike those for environmentally differentiated traditional accounting, are in physical terms such as kilograms. It is necessary to distinguish between systems of ecological accounting and traditional accounting because:

- from a material point of view, the focus of ecological accounting is very different from that of traditional accounting. While the focus of ecological accounting is on environmental interventions, that of traditional accounting is on financial impacts;

- environmental information often stems from sources that are different from those which provide financial information;
- environmental information is often needed for different purposes, and by different stakeholders, than those requiring financial information;
- environmental information has different measures of quality and quantity (e.g. kilograms) than economic information (i.e. monetary units).

Since both the environmentally differentiated traditional accounting systems and the ecological accounting systems process environmentally induced information, they constitute, when taken together, what is generically called *environmental accounting* (Schaltegger *et al.*, 1996). As a sub-area of accounting, environmental accounting deals with:

- activities, methods and systems;
- recording, analysis and reporting;
- the environmentally induced financial impacts, as well as ecological impacts, of a defined economic system (e.g. a company, plant region, nation, etc.) Life-Cycle Assessment (LCA) may be seen as a special case of product-oriented environmental accounting.

The fact that traditional and ecological accounting systems are actually two different systems of accounting should not be an obstacle to the integration of their separate and individual results and information. Indeed, these results and information, when integrated, analysed and made available in a separate data stream, would facilitate both the calculation of eco-efficiency and decision-making by management and stakeholders.

Environmentally differentiated accounting

Ideally all impacts, including those on society and the natural environment, should be included in traditional accounting. Otherwise, since only a small part of the externalities are internalised, strategic management decisions may be based on incomplete information on past performance (thus influencing the expectations about the future) which may even be economically misleading in some cases (e.g. when external costs are internalised after a time-lag).

However, it would be even more misleading if the management were to internalise externalities in its traditional accounting, as long as this does not constitute a part of the actual economic effects on business. Traditional accounting is essentially a set of information systems for measuring the past economic performance of a company. A mixture of external and internal costs would therefore distort the actual figures and, consequently, they would no longer have the 'information value' necessary for making economic decisions.

Because of its legal obligation only to deal with actual internal financial impacts, traditional corporate accounting is concerned only with financial impacts that are internally relevant. Furthermore, in order to support economically rational decisions, these financial impacts need to be explicitly reflected in traditional accounting (i.e. differentiated from other financial impacts). Clearly, it is only with the proper management of information that shareholders and creditors can correctly assess the actual and potential economic consequences of environmental issues, adapt to the economic impacts of new environmental regulations, and conduct mutually fruitful discussions on how best to implement pollution prevention measures.

The system of traditional accounting is further divided into three sub-systems:

- traditional managerial accounting;
- traditional financial accounting;
- other traditional accounting.

Managerial accounting (also called management accounting or cost accounting) is the central tool and basis of most internal management decisions (for an introduction see Cowe, 1988; Horngren and Foster, 1987; Kaplan and Atkinson, 1989; Polimeni *et al.*, 1986) and is usually not required by external stakeholders (Figure 14.2). It deals with questions such as: What are the environmental costs and how should they be tracked and traced? How should environmentally induced costs (e.g. fines, fees, investments) be treated? Should they be allocated to products or counted as overhead costs? What are the responsibilities of a management accountant?

By contrast, financial accounting is designed specifically to satisfy the information needs of the external stakeholders (i.e. shareholders) of the company with regard to the financial impacts. Typical issues in financial accounting are whether environmentally induced outlays should be capitalised, or, what standards and guidelines should be adopted for the disclosure of (contingent) liabilities and what recommendations should be made on how to treat these liabilities in accounting. The financial result, produced at the end of the fiscal year, can change substantially depending on how environmental issues are dealt with.

'Other traditional accounting systems' is a term used to cover several additional and often more specific accounting systems such as tax accounting and bank regulatory accounting. Tax accounting is mandatory for all regular businesses because governmental tax agencies require their tax 'reports', whereas agencies such as bank regulatory agencies have special accounting and reporting requirements only for banks. Each of these traditional accounting systems deals with different aspects of how environmental issues influence organisations. The topics in other accounting systems vary. For example, tax accounting considers the effect of subsidies on pollution abatement devices, examines how the costs of landfill remediation can be deducted from taxes, and analyses the effects of accelerated depreciation on clean production technologies and the consequences of various environmental taxes (e.g. CO_2 tax). Environmental issues in other traditional accounting systems include insurance, product liability, mortgage, bank credits, etc.

To summarise, it is important to consider environmentally induced financial aspects in traditional accounting, because it is only by doing so that it becomes possible to make a correct calculation of the profitability and eco-efficiency of a company.

Ecological accounting

As we have pointed out earlier, traditional accounting systems should not only incorporate the financial impacts of environmental issues, but should also be enlarged by including *ecological accounting systems*, or at least the essential features thereof.

The systems of ecological accounting, shown in light grey in Figure 14.2, measure the ecological impact of a company on the environment. Also, as we have already pointed out, measurements to be made for them are in physical units unlike those for environmentally differentiated traditional accounting. Furthermore, like the traditional accounting systems, ecological accounting systems can also be divided into three sub-systems:

- internal ecological accounting;
- external ecological accounting;
- other ecological accounting.

Internal ecological accounting is designed to gather ecological information only for the purposes of internal management. It is complementary to traditional managerial accounting. Methods of measuring the impact of a company's products and processes on the natural environment are necessary for making good management decisions, as they are for monitoring pollution discharges and for calculating eco-efficiency. Account tracking material flows, energy use, and emissions are a core part of internal ecological accounting. Also, a system of internal ecological accounting, preferably a sophisticated one, is a necessary precondition for any environmental management system.

In *external ecological accounting*, which is the counterpart of traditional financial accounting, data are gathered and made available to the external stakeholders interested in environmental matters, including the general public, the media, shareholders, environmental funds and pressure groups. In the last ten years hundreds of companies have published such external environmental reports, thus giving the public at large an opportunity to scrutinise the environmental impacts of their activities. Many of these are extensive annual reports containing detailed information on pollutant discharges. A core question of external ecological accounting is the consolidation of environmental impact added of the different production sites of a company in its group report.

Other ecological accounting systems, which measure data in physical units, are a means for regulators to control compliance. They are necessary for the correct assessment of environmental taxes to be levied on CO_2, volatile organic compounds (VOC), etc. Clearly, such taxes to be paid by a company cannot be assessed without correct information on relevant pollutant discharges and emissions released by that company. Apart from the tax agency and the environmental protection agencies that are primarily interested in specific information on the discharges of specific pollutants, an increasing number and variety of stakeholders, such as banks (acting as money-lending agencies) and insurance companies, are now also asking for reliable information on the environmental impacts of companies. Clearly, ecological accounting is necessary for the calculation of eco-efficiency, because it permits the determination of the environmental impact added of companies, products, etc.

CALCULATION OF ECO-EFFICIENCY

Eco-efficiency may be calculated by internal as well as external stakeholders, but whereas the management can obtain necessary information for this from managerial and internal ecological accounts, external stakeholders have to rely on financial and external ecological accounts, or on other traditional and ecological accounting systems, for such information. For reasons of clarity, the calculation of eco-efficiency is explained in the following sections from an internal managerial perspective only. Further discussion on environmental accounting will be found in Schaltegger *et al.* (1996).

Environmentally corrected managerial accounting information

Managerial accounting is the central tool and basis of most internal management decisions (Cowe, 1988; Horngren and Foster, 1987; Kaplan and Atkinson, 1989; Polimeni *et al.*, 1986). It is defined as 'the identification, measurement, accumulation, analysis, preparation, interpretation, and communication of information that assists executives in fulfilling organisational objectives' (Horngren and Foster, 1987: 2).

Correct financial information, obtained or derived from managerial accounting, is a prerequisite for determining eco-efficiency. Information obtained from environmentally differentiated managerial accounting is often used in financial accounting for communication with external stakeholders. Other environmentally differentiated accounting systems also derive most of their information from managerial accounting. Given this central function of managerial accounting, it must provide correct information to support the most economic way of managing a company. As environmental issues continue to exercise increasingly greater influence on economic performance, it is clear that they must be considered with due rigour in managerial accounting. In order to calculate the profitability of products and the performance of production devices accurately, all environmentally induced costs and revenues, and other costs or revenues, must be tracked, traced and allocated correctly. In the past limited attention has been given to the calculation and allocation of environmentally induced costs. And pollution prevention and clean-up costs have often been considered as overhead costs and allocated to all products – even to the 'clean' products which do not incur such costs. As a result, the 'dirty' products and product groups have been internally cross-subsidised, while the profitability of clean products has been underestimated. Furthermore, management costs relating to machine occupation, personnel and raw materials have often not been considered in calculating the costs of waste generation.

Environmentally induced costs can be increased or reduced through environmental protection efforts. Additional costs can include fines, fees, clean-up costs, increased production of unwanted output, etc. On the other hand, savings may be made through the optimal use of resources, reduced unwanted output, less fines and fees, etc.

Environmentally induced revenues can be direct or indirect. Direct revenues include, for example, gains made from the sale of recyclables, increased sale of products, and higher prices of the products sold. Indirect effects are more intangible by comparison and can include, for example, enhanced corporate image, greater customer and employee satisfaction, transfer of know-how, and the development of new markets for environmentally benign products.

The main issues of managerial accounting are concerned with the tracking, tracing and allocation of environmental costs, as well as with investment appraisal. These issues are relevant to environmentally differentiated accounting, as they are to ecological accounting. Once the environmentally related financial impacts have been considered, managerial accounting enables a correct calculation of the financial performance indicators such as the contribution margin of products, return on net assets for different production sites, net present value of investment projects, etc.

Internal ecological accounting

Ecological accounting is that sub-area of environmental accounting which deals with the activities, methods and systems for recording, analysing and reporting the impacts of a defined economic system on the natural environment. It attempts to answer this question: how can environmental impact added be accurately measured?

Conceptually, the approach of internal ecological accounting corresponds to that of traditional managerial accounting. To this extent internal ecological accounting serves as:

- an analytical tool for detecting ecological weaknesses and strengths;
- a method which supports decisions on relative environmental quality and provides a basis for environmental measures and eco-efficiency;
- a tool to control environmental effects caused directly or indirectly;
- a neutral and transparent vehicle for internal communication (and also external in an indirect way).

Internal ecological accounting represents what is called a *satellite accounting system* whose purpose is to calculate the impacts of businesses on the environment. Measurements to be made for ecological accounting are expressed in physical terms, unlike in environmentally differentiated traditional accounting. The physical units to be used for this can be of a quantitative or qualitative nature, although preference is usually for the quantitative if at all possible. All environmental impacts originate from activities that are deemed to create value or utility. But these economic activities also cause *environmental intervention* such as emissions, use of resource, etc. which can be recorded in an inventory (e.g. an emissions inventory). However, given that almost all economic activities have impacts of varying intensity on nature, and that they inevitably cause complex and many hitherto unknown interactions, it is not possible to record all environmental interventions in an inventory.

Ecological accounting activities, which usually start with the investigation of individual stages of production, can be broadened to the analysis of products, sites and businesses. The *subject matter* of ecological accounting comprises the resources used, environmental interventions, and ecological assets. The resources used, to be considered in this context, include non-renewable material resources and energy carriers (e.g. ores, oil), as well as renewable material resources and energy carriers (e.g. wood, water).

Environmental interventions include material emissions and pollution in terms of substances, or compounds of substances such as CO_2, NO_x, VOC, as well as energy emissions in the form of heat, radiation, noise, etc. Ecological assets (meaning ecological capital goods) include land, forests, biodiversity, etc.

Internal ecological accounting deals with the recording of environmental interventions, and allocation and assessment of environmental impacts. In the context of *recording, tracking and tracing* of environmental interventions, the purpose of recording is to prepare an inventory in which all the environmental interventions are registered in physical terms. *Allocation* refers to the allocation of environmental impacts to products, processes and activities. It is actually a procedure for assigning environmental impacts to the individual stages of production, sites and the products which cause them. Impact *assessment*

is concerned with the determination of the relative severity of environmental interventions, and with the calculation of the environmental impact added. Impact assessment is a technical, quantitative, and/or qualitative process of classifying, characterising and assessing the effects of both resources consumed and pollutants released into the environment.

Recording

Quantified data are favoured in ecological accounting to measure the extent of environmental interventions (in terms of resources used, and material and energy emissions) and ecological assets (e.g. land, forests, water reserves, etc.). All internal and external accounting reports should contain quantitative data, together with necessary comments to facilitate their correct interpretation by the reader.

Ecological assets (e.g. forests, land) can be registered and described in what is called an 'eco-asset sheet'. Natural assets are seldom accounted for at the corporate level since only a few of the manufacturing companies own sizeable land assets or other natural resources. The *eco-asset sheet* is thus not a true counterpart of the financial balance sheet of a company. Rather, to put it simply, it is a 'photograph' of a company's natural assets on a given date, listing all the ecological assets the company owns or occupies on that date. The eco-asset sheet contains all the ecological assets of the company, including an inventory of the various species of flora and fauna inhabiting its land, forests, etc. Recently some companies (e.g. Dow Chemicals) have started to assign explicit monetary values to their ecological assets by, for example, establishing harvesting rights in rain forests. Though still 'raw', the eco-asset sheet is nevertheless a valuable tool which enables management to recognise both potential and manifest financial implications of their ecological assets. In the past many companies have underestimated the importance of the financial liability of their ecological assets.

The basic idea of the *environmental impact added statement* corresponds to the income statement in traditional accounting. Flows of material and energy inputs, as well as the resulting outputs into the natural environment, are recorded in these statements and assessed for each accounting period.

Environmental interventions can be accounted for only if they can be recorded, tracked and traced. The use of accounts to record and present financial flows is widely accepted. Therefore, given the need to find practical ways of dealing with data, and because efficient procedures for recording material and energy flows have already been established in traditional accounting systems, it would be sensible to use a similar procedure for ecological accounting, too. Clearly, data on environmental interventions will not be recorded in monetary terms in such a system (which is adapted from traditional accounting), but in physical terms in an 'input–output' account. In such a system of ecological accounting, first the material and energy flow diagrams must be prepared for the manufacturing processes. Information on material and energy flows needed for this can only be obtained from detailed observations of actual production. Table 14.1 shows a typical example of an 'input–output' account.

In the left-hand column of Table 14.1 all the material and energy inputs into production (natural resources, semi-manufactured goods, raw materials, etc.) are listed with an identification number. All desirable and undesirable material and energy outputs of production (desired output, emissions, waste, etc.) are shown on the right also with an identification number. The material inputs are divided into mineral resources, biomass, water, energy carriers and other materials. Energy carriers (e.g. oil) are registered as material resources.

Table 14.1 Typical example of an input–output account

Group 10 Material inputs	Group 20 Material outputs
100 Mineral resources	200 Products (environmental
101 Biomass	impact added carrier)
102 Water	201 Re- and downcyclats
103 ...	203 Emissions
104 Fossil energy carriers	2050 Landfill
1040 Crude Oil	2051 Water emissions
1041 Coal	20510 TOC
1042 Gas	20511 Sulphur
105 Regenerative energy	20512 Water
carriers	20513 ...
106 Materials	2052 Air emissions
1060 Polystyrol	20520 CO_2
1065 Re- and	20521 NO_x
downcyclats	20522 VOC
1066 ...	20523 ...

Source: Schaltegger and Sturm, [1992] 1994

The recording of energies should be separated from the registration of material flows in order to avoid double counting and confusion. According to the law of conservation of mass and energy, total mass and energy on the input side of the account must be the same as that on the output side. In other words, the left and the right sides of the ecological account must be in balance since neither mass nor energy can be destroyed. When there are too many items or activities to be accounted for, separate accounts can be opened for one or more of the items listed in the 'aggregate' account. That is, there could be a separate account for the oil used, another for CO_2 emissions, and so on.

Effluents can be transferred from one account to a subsequent account, or to the aggregate account, as in basic book-keeping, except that the transactions will be entered in kilograms. Following this procedure, the incoming and outgoing mass flows can be aggregated and defined according to their origin. This is analogous to a profit-and-loss account in traditional accounting.

Information on the quality of data is extremely important for the interpretation of results as well as for the search for better alternatives. Quality of data should be measured, calculated and estimated, and, if necessary, secondary data from the literature (e.g. an industry average) or from suppliers should be used. And data should be classified according to quality. Measured data usually reflect the specific situation in the best possible way. Nevertheless, it is helpful to scrutinise the methods used for data generation and collection in order to be able to assess the reliability and quality of data, and to determine how they compare with other data.

It makes no economic sense to aim for a full inventory of all mass and energy flows and, in any case, this goal can rarely be achieved. Methods of data collection usually take several years to develop, improving gradually until the marginal benefit of more detailed information matches the marginal costs of collection. Efficient collection and management of data certainly needs a computerised system, especially considering that the collection of high-quality data in sufficient quantity and detail is a burdensome and demanding task which has to be performed patiently and with great care.

Allocation

In managerial accounting, the purpose of *activity based accounting* is to calculate the total induced costs of an activity and of a cost carrier (product, product group, etc.). Activity based accounting is undertaken in order to determine exactly where a company generates its revenue from and where it loses money. There is a similar feature in internal ecological accounting, too. 'Ecological activity based cost accounting' aims to show where environmental interventions are caused and which products, product groups, etc. contribute most to the overall environmental impact added.

There is, however, a major difference between managerial cost accounting and ecological accounting. It is that, in the latter, environmental interventions are allocated before they are assessed. Usually they are assessed in a second stage, according to their relative environmental impact, in order to calculate the environmental impact added. In traditional cost accounting, on the other hand, no assessment is necessary because the monetary values (prices and costs) already constitute an assessment. Also, in analogy to managerial cost accounting, internal ecological accounting distinguishes between what are called environmental impact added centres, carriers, drivers, allocation rules and allocation keys, as described below.

Environmental impact added centres describe 'places' where material and energy are processed, or where the respective flows enter the natural environment. Examples of such centres are stages of production, production sites, incinerators, sewage plants, etc. 'Environmental impact added centre accounting' helps to identify the places where 'overhead environmental interventions' of jointly used clean-up facilities are actually created, or where they actually occur.

Environmental impact added carriers are analogous to cost carriers in traditional cost accounting. They describe a product, a product group, division, etc. that is seen to be responsible for creating value added as well as environmental impact added. Ideally, such carriers should correspond to the cost carriers, because it is only then that eco-efficiency can be calculated. 'Environmental impact added carrier accounting' identifies the products, processes or activities which cause the environmental interventions allocated to the environmental impact added centres. An analogue of this, to be found in managerial accounting, is the allocation of costs to the cost centres and to the cost carriers.

Environmental impact added drivers initiate environmental impacts. CO_2 emissions which cause the greenhouse effect, and VOC emissions which cause photochemical smog, are typical examples of these drivers.

Environmental impact added allocation rules formulate general procedures for ensuring the correct allocation of environmental interventions, while *environmental impact added allocation keys* describe the relationship between an environmental impact added carrier and the environmental interventions caused. If environmental interventions are caused jointly by the elements (e.g. scrubbers, sewage plants, etc.) of a multi-purpose clean-up facility, for example, then the individual intervention of each element must be traced and allocated to the carrier responsible (a typical example is given in Box 14.1). But, in order to do so as accurately as possible, representative environmental impact added drivers and allocation rules must be defined, and this calls for basically the same allocation procedure as in cost accounting. The importance of the chosen allocation rule becomes especially clear when its influence on the contribution margins of products, as well as on directing capital investments, is considered.

Impact assessment

Sometimes a complete inventory provides enough information in physical units to reveal what the main environmental problems are and where they are created. In such a case priorities for environmental protection, pollution prevention, etc. can be defined on the basis of the inventory. However, in most cases the inventory contains an enormous amount of unassessed and detailed information which cannot be accurately interpreted by management. An impact assessment of the inventory data is then necessary. Impact assessment is a technical, quantitative, and/or qualitative process of classifying, characterising and assessing the effects of the resources required and the recorded environmental loading. The ecological assessment of environmental interventions, which

---

BOX 14.1   A TYPICAL EXAMPLE OF ALLOCATION

With reference to the schematic representation of allocation given below, consider this problem: the waste waters of environmental impact added centre A (1 kg TOC/litre of water) and environmental impact added centre B (2 kg TOC/litre of water) are treated in a sewage plant. The water released into the river contains 0.090 kg of TOC/litre of water. How should the TOC discharged into the river be allocated to A and B, and to the environmental impact added carriers?

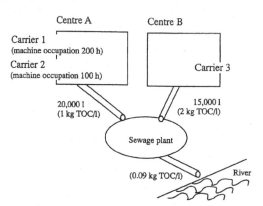

TOC released by environmental impact added centre A = 20,000 l × 1 kg/l = 20,000 kg
TOC released by environmental impact added centre B = 15,000 l × 2 kg/l = 30,000 kg
TOC discharged into the river = 35,000 l × 0.09 kg/l = 3,150 kg

Allocating with respect to the water load into the sewage plant,
TOC discharged by A into river = 3,150 kg × 20,000/35,000 = 1,800 kg
TOC discharged by B into river = 3,150 kg × 15,000/35,000 = 1,350 kg

Then, allocating on the basis of machine occupation time,
Allocation to environmental impact added carrier 1 = 1,800 kg TOC × 200/300 = 1,200 kg TOC
Allocation to environmental impact added carrier 2 = 1,800 kg TOC × 100/300 = 600 kg TOC
Allocation to environmental impact added carrier 3 = 1,350 kg TOC (the same as that for environmental impact added centre B)

---

often calls for the reduction of a multitude of physical measures to a few units (or even just one unit or index) of measurement, should be undertaken only after the aggregation of an environmental impact added centre (or an environmental impact added carrier) account has been made. The advantage of this approach is that different methods of assessment can be based on the same inventory data and compared with one another. For this reason ecological accounting is not restricted to the current level of knowledge about the harm caused by environ-

mental interventions, but it also allows for the application of new weightings at any time in the future.

In the literature there are many different approaches to *impact assessment*, as well as a host of variants that are adopted in practice.

Mathematically, environmental impact added is calculated by first multiplying the physical quantity of each emission released (e.g. CO_2, CH_4, etc.) by an appropriate weighting assigned to it (e.g. 1 to CO_2, 11 to CH_4). The results of all such multiplications, for all the relevant emissions, are then

---

BOX 14.2   IMPLEMENTATION OF ECOLOGICAL ACCOUNTING AT CIBA'S PIGMENTS DIVISION

Ciba's Pigments Division implemented the concept of ecological accounting in 1994. An interdisciplinary working group of six to eight staff members was established for the purpose. Its task was to introduce an environmental information system to meet the specific needs of the Division. The goal of the working group was to assess the relative positions of Ciba's different pigments and colours in the eco-efficiency portfolio as a basis for decision-making. After an intensive initial phase, the working group held monthly progress meetings.

The first step for the group was to identify the existing sources of information (production information system, information files prepared for the regulating agencies, etc.). One staff member was given the task of evaluating software with the object of improving the management of information. In order to establish a systematic and continuing environmental information system, the concept of ecological accounting was implemented for the key products of the division. The basic system, established after about one year, has since been continually upgraded. At present one part-time environmental manager is responsible for information collection, allocation and impact assessment. The results are discussed in annual management meetings, and used in making decisions on both environmental management and strategic management.

---

added to give the environmental impact added. The weighting of a given emission reflects its relative contribution to the overall environmental impact of the problem in question. When necessary, such individual contributions can be expressed in CO_2 equivalents, as in the case of greenhouse gases for example. Detailed discussion on this topic will be found in the literature on Environmental Impact Assessment (EIA) and in Schaltegger and Sturm ([1992] 1994).

The Eco-rational Path Method (EPM): integration of traditional accounting with ecological accounting

As will be seen from equation (4), eco-efficiency is the ratio of value added to environmental impact added, or the ratio of an economic performance indicator (e.g. contribution margin) to an ecological performance indicator. The calculation of eco-efficiency, therefore, requires the integration of economic information (flow of funds such as income, expense, revenues, costs, etc.), derived from traditional accounting, with environmental information (environmental interventions such as emissions, resource use, etc.) derived from ecological accounting. Figure 14.3 shows the process by which economic and environmental information can be integrated, and how the results of the process can be used in decision-making.

The Eco-rational Path Method (EPM), shown schematically in Figure 14.3, has been developed to meet this requirement for integration. It describes a

structured decision process to pilot the businesses of a company to eco-efficiency. EPM is a straightforward and practical procedure for integrating the economic dimension with the ecological dimension, shown respectively on the left and right of Figure 14.3. This process of integration distinguishes the three aspects; namely, *accounting*, *judgement* and *decision*.

In module I (Figure 14.3) the monetary results of managerial accounting, including environmental

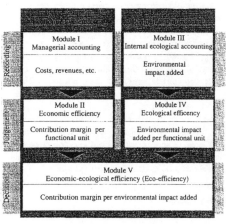

Figure 14.3 The Eco-rational Path Method
Source: Schaltegger and Sturm, 1994

compliance costs and earnings, are evaluated. Module III represents the evaluation of the ecological harm caused in units of environmental impact added, calculated from ecological accounting. An economic performance indicator is calculated in Module II as a measure of economic efficiency, such as Net Present Value (NPV), Return On Net Assets (RONA), or the Contribution Margin (CM). The key numbers needed for this will be found in any well-functioning managerial accounting system. For the allocation of environmentally induced costs, the environmental impact added caused by each cost centre must be known. Module IV calculates ecological efficiency in terms of environmental impact added per product, product group or some other functional unit. Modules II and IV are both steps in which data needed for making separate judgements on ecological or economic efficiency are supplied. All these four steps are integrated in Module V by combining the measures of economic and ecological efficiency, and by calculating the quotient of an economic performance indicator per environmental impact added (e.g. the monetary contribution margin created per environmental impact added of a product).

The 'factual' goal of integrating economic indicators with ecological performance indicators is to measure economic-ecological efficiency (eco-efficiency). Integration of environmental issues into the decision-making process in this way enables both the internal and external stakeholders to make decisions that would move matters towards the 'green cash cow' in Figure 14.1, so to speak. The 'political' purpose of integrating and weighting economic and ecological effects is to consider and meet the requests of different stakeholders. Depending on the need for information and the goals of stakeholders, economic performance or growth can be measured in terms of sales, revenues, contribution margin, net present value (NPV), etc. There is also a need for *project-related* financial and environmental information to support rational eco-integrated investment decisions.

CONCLUSIONS

Eco-efficiency is defined as the ratio of value added to environmental impact added, or, more generally, economic performance achieved per environmental

impact caused. To calculate eco-efficiency, environmental impact added, which is the sum of all environmental interventions caused and assessed according to their relative environmental impact, must be known. It is then correlated with value added, since no economic activity is without environmental impacts. Environmental accounting provides the information needed for determining both environmental impact added and eco-efficiency, while the Eco-rational Path Method (EPM) enables the integration of economic information with environmental information. Improvements achieved in eco-efficiency can be judged and compared visually from the eco-efficiency portfolios of different products, production sites, etc. Finally, the goal of eco-efficiency is to achieve high economic performance with low environmental impact added.

REFERENCES

Adams, J. (1992) *Accounting for Environmental Costs: A Discussion of the Issues Facing Today's Businesses*, Norwalk: FASB.

CICA (Canadian Institute of Chartered Accountants) (1992) *Environmental Accounting and the Role of the Accounting Profession*, Toronto: CICA.

Cowe, R. (ed.) (1988) *Handbook of Management Accounting* (2nd edition), Aldershot: Gower.

Epstein, M. (1995) *Measuring Corporate Environmental Performance*, Chicago: Irwin.

Gladwin, T., Krause, T. and Kennelly, J. (1995) 'Beyond Eco-Efficiency: Towards Socially Sustainable Business', *Sustainable Development* 3: 35–43.

Gray, R. (1994) 'Environmental Accounting and Auditing: Survey of Current Activities and Developments', *Accounting and Business Research* 24 (95): 285–286.

Gray, R. and Laughlin, R. (eds) (1991) 'Green Accounting, Special Issue of Accounting', *Auditing and Accountabilit. Journal* (AAAJ) 4: 3.

Gray, R., Bebbington, J. and Walters, D. (1993) *Accounting for the Environment*, London: Chapman Publishing.

Horngren, C. and Foster, G. (1987) *Cost Accounting. A Managerial Emphasis* (6th edition), Englewood Cliffs, Calif.: Prentice-Hall.

Ilinitch, A. and Schaltegger, S. (1995) 'Developing a Green Business Portfolio', *Long Range Planning*, No. 3.

Kaplan, R. and Atkinson, A. (1989) *Advanced Management Accounting*, Englewood Cliffs, Calif.: Prentice-Hall.

Leibenstein, H. (1966) 'Allocative Efficiency versus X-Efficiency', *American Economic Review*, 56: 392–415.

Polimeni, R., Fabozzi, F. and Adelberg, A. (1986) *Cost Accounting, Concepts and Applications for Managerial Decision Making*, New York: McGraw-Hill.

Price Waterhouse (1991) *Environmental Accounting: The Issues, the Developing Solutions*, New York: Price Waterhouse.

Quirke, B. (1991) 'Accounting for the Environment', *European Environment* 1 (5): 19–22.

Rubenstein, D. (1994) *Environmental Accounting for the Sustainable Corporation*, Westport, Conn.: Quorum.

Schaltegger, S. and Stinson, C. (1994) 'Issues and Research Opportunities in Environmental Accounting', Discussion Paper No. 9124, Basel: WWZ.

Schaltegger, S. and Sturm, A. (1990) 'Eco-Rationality' (in German: Ökologische Rationalität), *Die Unternehmung* 4: 273–290.

Schaltegger, S. and Sturm, A. ([1992] 1994) *Environmentally Oriented Decisions in Firms. Ecological Accounting Instead of LCA* (in German: Ökologieorientierte Entscheidungen in Unternehmen. Ökologisches Rechnungswesen statt Ökobilanzierung), Bern: Haupt (2nd edition).

Schaltegger, S. and Sturm, A. ([1995] 1996) *Eco-Efficiency through Eco-Controlling. For the Implementation of EMAS*

and ISO 14000, Zürich: Vdf (German version: Zürich/Stuttgart: Vdf/Schäffer–Poeschel).

Schaltegger, S., Müller, K. and Hindrichsen, H. (1996) *Corporate Environmental Accounting*, Chichester: John Wiley & Sons.

Schmidheiny, S. (1992) *Changing Course*, Frankfurt: Artemis & Winkler.

Spitzer, M. and Elwood, H. (1995) *An Introduction to Environmental Accounting as a Business Management Tool: Key Concepts and Terms*, Washington, DC: USEPA.

Tinbergen, J. (1968) *Economic Policy*, Freiburg: Rombach.

Vedsø, L. (ed.) (1993) *Green Management*, Copenhagen: Systime.

SUGGESTED READING

Schaltegger, S., Müller, K. and Hindrichsen, H. (1996) *Corporate Environmental Accounting*, London: John Wiley & Sons.

SELF-ASSESSMENT QUESTIONS

1　What is meant by 'eco-efficiency'? (Choose one or more.)
  (a)　Environmental impact caused in producing one unit of a product.
  (b)　The fastest way to achieve sustainable development.
  (c)　The economically cheapest approach to environmental protection.
  (d)　Value added created per unit of environmental impact added.
  (e)　Economic performance in relation to environmental impact added.
2　What is 'corporate environmental accounting'? (Choose one or more.)
  (a)　A system to account for the environmental impacts of floods, earthquakes, pollution, deforestation, etc.
  (b)　The basis of environmental auditing, because it provides all the information needed to complete the checklist of an environmental audit report.
  (c)　A sub-area of accounting which deals with the activities, methods and systems for the recording, analysis and reporting of the environmentally induced financial impacts as well as the ecological impacts of a defined economic system (e.g. a company, plant, region, nation, etc.)
  (d)　An attempt to account for all the aspects of sustainable development including environmental impacts, social development, and economic performance.
3　What are the main issues in ecological accounting? (Choose one or more.)
  (a)　To count the number of species in a geographical area and to draw a map showing their distribution.
  (b)　To calculate the monetary value of environmental degradation.
  (c)　To record, allocate and assess the environmental impacts of material and energy flows.
4　What is the idea of the 'Eco-rational Path Method (EPM)'? (Choose one or more.)
  (a)　The EPM is a strategic concept for more rational management of resource use.
  (b)　The EPM serves to integrate traditional accounting with ecological accounting in order to measure eco-efficiency.
  (c)　The EPM evaluates the financial impacts of environmental protection measures, thus supporting economically rational management.
5　Environmentally differentiated accounting (choose one or more)
  (a)　is not relevant for corporate environmental protection because it deals only with the financial aspects;
  (b)　is very important for corporate environmental protection because it improves corporate economic efficiency;
  (c)　is increasingly important for the economic performance of companies.
6　Calculation of eco-efficiency. Answer the following questions using the data given in the table below.

Environmental impact added carrier	Contribution margin (£) per unit	Environmental impact added of sales	Units (g) sold	Number of grams (g) needed to colour 1 m²
A	5	7,500	2,500	2.5
B	2	800	200	0.5
C	3	9,000	3,000	3.0

(a) What is the ecological product efficiency of the environmental impact added carriers A, B and C?
(b) What is the ecological function efficiency of the environmental impact added carriers A, B and C?
(c) What is the eco-efficiency of the environmental impact added carriers A, B and C (functional efficiency, product efficiency and eco-efficiency of total sales)?
(d) How can eco-efficiency be calculated if the environmental impact added carrier does not correspond with the cost carrier?

[15]

The KUNERT Group of Companies Worldwide at a Glance:

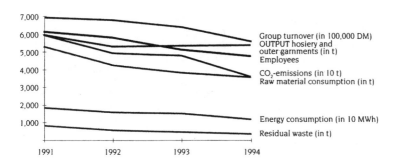

Group turnover (in 100,000 DM)
OUTPUT hosiery and
outer garnments (in t)
Employees

CO$_2$-emissions (in 10 t)
Raw material consumption (in t)

Energy consumption (in 10 MWh)

Residual waste (in t)

1991   1992   1993   1994

	1991	1992	1993	1994	+/–93/94
General Business Data[1]					
Employees	6,126	5,814	5,126	4,764	– 7%
Group turnover (millions of DM)	693	679	639	559	– 13%
Earnings after tax (millions of DM)	22.1	– 16.9	7.6	– 6.8	
Product-OUTPUT[1]					
Product-OUTPUT (in 1000 kg)	9,280	7,997	8,935	8,493	– 5%
OUTPUT hosiery a. outer garments (in 1000 kg)	5,963	5,318	5,328	5,394	– 1%
Packaging quota (in %)	32.4	32.0	29.3	25.9	
Raw materials, auxiliary and ancillary materials[1]					
Raw material consumption (in 1000 kg)	5,312	4,243	3,821	3,558	– 7%
Consumption of dyes (in 1000 kg)	172	106	114	91	– 20%
Quota of metal-free dyes (in %)	–	–	52.3	62.9	
Energy consumption and Emissions[1]					
Energy consumption (in GWh)	185	158	151	119	– 21%
Energy consumption per kg of product (kWh/kg)	44	50	48	49	+ 1%
NO$_x$-emissions (in 1000 kg)	164	135	139	101	– 28%
SO$_2$-emissions (in 1000 kg)	201	168	208	170	– 18%
CO$_2$-emissions (in 1000 kg)	59,357	49,605	48,081	36,110	– 25%
Water consumption and waste water[1]					
Water consumption (in 1000 m³)	672	531	495	429	– 13%
Water consumption per kg of product (l/kg)	159	167	158	176	+ 11%
Waste water (in 1000 m³)	488	388	376	339	– 10%
Solid waste[1]					
Solid waste total (in 1000 kg)	3,125	3,069	2,519	2,358	– 6%
Waste per kg of product (g/kg)	737	968	804	966	+ 20%
Hazardous waste quota (in %)	0.8	0.9	1.6	2.7	
Recyclables quota (in %)	62.8	73.7	76.2	77.0	
Residual waste quota (in %)	27.0	18.8	19.3	14.8	
Building rubble (in %)	9.3	6.6	2.9	5.5	

[1] Partially rounded values

Imprint

Publisher:	KUNERT AG, Immenstadt
Author/in charge of content:	Christian Wucherer
Internal Project Management:	Members of the environment working group: Klaus Beggel, Ulrich Daiss, Peter Frank, Gerhard Hofmann, Peer Quenzer-Hohmuth, Uwe Immoor, Rudolf Krebs, Ulrich Langenhorst, Arnim Lilienthal, Robert Martin, Michael G. Moeller, Hermann Niedolitschka, Hans Räth, Karl-Peter Schafheutle, Christian Wucherer
External Project Management:	Institut für Management und Umwelt, Augsburg: Prof. Bernd Wagner, Rainer Rauberger Tel. ++49/821/3490-272, Fax -273
Editor/Contact person:	Christian Wucherer
Sales:	KUNERT AG, Immenstadt, Sigrun Nickel
No. of copies:	15,000
ISSN:	0949-3662
Copyright:	KUNERT AG, Immenstadt
Address:	Julius-Kunert-Straße 49, D-87509 Immenstadt
Telephone:	++49/(0)8323/12-0
Telefax:	++49/(0)8323/12-389
Teletex:	832381 = KUNERT
Foreign Language Versions:	Last year's environmental report is also available in German, French and Dutch.
Translation into English	Aoife Kennedy, Brussels
·Phototypesetting:	Studio Siegl, Kempten
Reproduction:	Repro-Frick, Kempten
Printing:	Graphische Betriebe Eberl GmbH, Immenstadt
Jacket:	Printed on cardboard made of 90% recycled paper: water pan varnish
Contents:	Printed on 100% recycled paper

Front cover: Despite the need for hand washing by customers HUDSON and KUNERT have natural fibre collections - "HAUTE NATURE" and "100% NATURAL".

Back cover: One of the reasons KUNERT became committed to ecology was to protect the natural environment: the head office of the KUNERT group in Immenstadt in Allgäu.

Table of Contents

1) In the uniform system of accounts, STOCKS is abbreviated to S, INPUT to I and OUTPUT to O.
2) Pull-out with reply card in middle section

Preface by the CEO

An environment worth living in is indisputably one of the existential needs of the next generation. In the years ahead, consumers will make the transition from thinking in an environmentally aware way to acting in an environmentally aware way. Consumers will be requesting products that are not only to their liking and function perfectly but that are also socially responsible. This is the conclusion arrived at by resear-

This applies to textiles in the same way that it does to refridgerators, personal computers or cars. In a world of free competition, the informed consumer will become the driving force of environmentally sound production. By the time the children of today are grown, the ecological responsibility of the business world will probably be a central theme and an important factor in purchasing decisions.

Rainer Michel   Walter Traub   Hans-Jürgen Förster   Klaus Eberhardt

chers whose predictions of future global trends already proved correct in the nineties.

"Environmentally aware shopping" by consumers will "reward" firms that are socially and environmentally responsible. Every purchase will be the expression of a personal point of view as regards the environment. What governments take years to change through environmental legislation can be achieved in a few weeks or months by the consumers of the future using the laws of the market economy and environmental shopping.

In the textile sector, KUNERT has proved on several occasions, most recently with the results of its pilot project "Environmental Cost Management", that the interests of efficient production do not conflict but very often coincide with ecological objectives. Protecting the environment according to economic principles makes sense for businesses. Economics and ecology can work together in the market economy mechanism to strengthen our economy.

The KUNERT group of companies offers not only the individual chemical-free natural collections but an entire ecologically optimized range. This also includes articles made with synthetic fibres and dyes. Using the eco-balance and eco-controlling tools we are on course towards becoming an ecologically optimized business.

| 5

Some Points of Emphasis

Results of the Pilot Project "Environmental Cost Management"

If the results of the KUNERT pilot project were applied to the German economy, German industry could reduce their costs by tens of billions of Deutschmarks every year. One to two percent of an industrial firm's total costs could be cut. This is proven by the results of the one-year research project which used the example of the KUNERT factory in Mindelheim. Furthermore, the newly developed method combines environmental protection with every cost-cutting measure. The dominant cost factor of residual waste that causes environmental pollution is not the cost of disposal but the purchasing cost.

The new method, developed jointly by Kienbaum Unternehmungsberatung, Berlin, the Institut für Management und Umwelt, Augsburg, and the KUNERT group of companies, is a system that can be applied to all industrial companies. It makes it possible to identify the quantity and cost of non-value-adding residual materials at each production stage, something which is normally excluded from conventional accounting. The project was supported by the German Foundation for the Environment (Deutsche Bundesstiftung Umwelt).

Press conference: Presentation of the results of the pilot project "Environmental Cost Management" at the German Foundation for the Environment in Osnabrück. From left: Hartmut Fischer, Kienbaum Unternehmensberatung, Markus Strobel, Institut für Management und Umwelt, Rainer Michel, CEO of KUNERT AG, Fritz Brickwedde, Secretary General of the German Foundation for the Environment and Christian Wucherer, Head of KUNERT Environmental Controlling.

Group Review: Eco-balances

				Entry 1993	Entry 1994	Stock 31. 12. 1993
		INPUT				
S 1.		**Land" (m²)**		9,281	12,931	649,143
	1.1.	Sealed		3,323	636	68,606
	1.2.	Green		523	938	448,659
	1.3.	Built-over		5,435	11,357	131,878
S 2.		**Buildings" (m²)**		3,955	17,447	178,473
	2.1.	Production		0	1,210	73,709
	2.2.	Distribution and storage		3,695	16,059	87,569
	2.3.	Administration		260	178	17,205
S 3.		**Plant and Equipment (piece)**		1,321	1,436	16,542
	3.1.	Production machines		341	530	6,386
	3.2.	Office equipment		470	583	7,020
	3.3.	Office and comm. machines		421	277	2,806
	3.4.	Vehicle fleet		42	25	164
	3.5.	Technical facilities		47	21	166

			INPUT 1991	INPUT 1992	INPUT 1993	INPUT 1994	Stock 31. 12. 1994
I 1.		**Circulating goods (kg)**	15,771,320	12,006,223	12,421,796	11,055,912	–
	1.1.	Raw materials	5,311,896	4,243,238	3,821,006	3,558,124	697,183
	1.2.	Semi-finished a. finished goods	2,655,422	2,114,895	2,637,453	2,082,292	–
	1.3.	Auxiliary materials	5,954,169	4,115,455	4,345,438	3,936,325	–
	1.4.	Ancillary	1,849,833	1,532,635	1,617,899	1,479,171	–
I 2.		**Energy (kWh)**	185,039,982	157,709,097	150,682,651	118,986,313	N/A
	2.1.	Gas	15,749,655	20,536,032	19,892,297	16,570,184	N/A
	2.2.	Electricity	54,809,172	46,465,919	47,878,784	33,123,331	N/A
	2.3.	Fuel oil	97,754,180	71,677,150	59,416,240	47,262,590	497,616
	2.4.	District heating	1,615,625	2,391,466	5,595,680	5,586,418	N/A
	2.5.	Fuel	15,111,350	16,638,530	17,899,650	16,443,790	N/A
I 3.		**Water (m³)**	672,110	530,541	495,043	428,770	N/A
	3.1.	Tap water	451,936	338,583	303,852	281,275	N/A
	3.2.	Raw water	220,174	191,958	191,191	147,495	N/A
I 4.		**Air (m³)**	–	–	–	–	N/A

As a result of improved data collection in the KUNERT factories in Tunisia and Morocco the stock values in the land and buildings accounts have changed

Commentary

A comparison of INPUT and OUTPUT quantities over several years clearly indicates the success of eco-controlling. Over the years sustained reductions have been achieved in the quantities of material and energy INPUT as well as in the quantities of solid waste, waste water and air emissions.

Between 1991 and 1994, energy consumption fell by roughly 36%, water INPUT by roughly 36% and raw material consumption by 33%. The sharp fall in these INPUT

OUTPUT						
Stock 31. 12. 1994			**Exit 1993**	**Exit 1994**		
646,960			105,414	9,602	S 1.	Land[1] (m²)
65,750			13,435	2,692	1.1.	Sealed
448,386			54,322	340	1.2	Green
132,824			37,657	6,570	1.3	Built-over
185,369			1,569	17,923	S 2.	Buildings[1] (m²)
72,107			1,569	9,347	2.1.	Production
96,667			0	7,566	2.2	Distribution and storage
16,415			0	1,010	2.3	Administration
16,715			1,037	1,263	S 3.	Plant and equipment (piece)
5,943			554	973	3.1	Production machines
7,436			209	167	3.2	Office equipment
2,972			178	111	3.3	Office a. comm. machines
182			56	7	3.4	Vehicle fleet
182			40	5	3.5	Technical facilities
Stock 31. 12. 1994	**OUTPUT 1991**	**OUTPUT 1992**	**OUTPUT 1993**	**OUTPUT 1994**		
–	9,280,253	7,997,075	8,935,247	8,492,704	O 1.	Products (kg)
2,786,664	5,786,896	5,153,663	5,116,411	5,199,188	1.1	Hosiery
–	175,962	164,446	211,756	194,911	1.2	Outer wear
–	0	0	989,275	897,598	1.3	Transport packaging
–	3,007,958	2,561,693	2,617,805	2,201,007	1.4	Product packaging
36,398	3,124,629	3,069,063	2,519,252	2,357,988	O 2.	Waste (kg)
3,910	26,475	27,738	40,399	62,883	2.1	Hazardous waste
25,236	1,963,477	2,260,672	1,920,624	1,816,553	2.2	Recyclables
6,052	843,697	577,803	485,429	349,652	2.3	Residual waste
1,200	290,980	202,850	72,800	128,920	2.4	Building rubble
N/A	185,039,982	157,709,097	150,682,651	118,986,313	O 3.	Waste heat (kWh)
N/A	487,770	388,189	376,289	339,277	O 4.	Waste water (m³)
					O 5.	Air emission
N/A	163,521	133,058	138,828	100,548	5.2.1	NOₓ (kg)
N/A	200,632	167,702	207,872	170,132	5.2.2	SO_2 (kg)
N/A	59,356,556	49,605,355	48,080,685	36,109,594	5.2.3	CO_2 (kg)
N/A	–	–	121,614,000	96,895,400	5.2.4	Steam (kg)

values compare to a more modest fall of 10% in the OUTPUT of hosiery and outer garments over the four years: Over the same period, solid waste was reduced by a quarter while residual waste fell by 59%. Equally satisfactory were CO_2 and NO_x emissions, each falling by 39%. One disappointment, however, is the increase in hazardous waste. This can be partially attributed to improved recording, for example of electronic scrap material.

STOCK
S   1.   Land

No.	Type	STOCK 31. 12. 1993	ENTRY 1994	EXIT 1994	BESTAND 31. 12. 1994
S 1.	**Land[1] (In m²)**	**649,143**	**12,931**	**9,602**	**646,960**
1.1.	Sealed[1]	68,606	636	2,692	65,750
1.2.	Green[1]	448,659	938	340	448,386
1.3.	Built-over[1]	131,878	11,357	6,570	132,824

[1] The differences in stocks between 1993 and 1994 are due to improved collection of data.

Commentary

On the quantitative side, there were no significant changes in land stocks. On the qualitative side, in contrast, there were some serious findings. In KUNERT plant II, which has since been sold, dangerous waste left over from the past was discovered. In the 1950's the municipality of Rauhenzell had tolerated some small-scale dumping on the site by the owner of the plant at the time. After the industrial company went bankrupt the site was sold to KUNERT without any mention being made of the hazardous waste, which in the meantime had been covered over. The waste was first discovered in 1994 when soil analyses were being carried out as part of the sale negotiations.

In the former Hudson factory in Berlin small quantities of leftover waste containing PCP were discovered when a soil analysis was taken. It is not yet known how and when this pollution occurred.

The increased use of public transport by employees has come up against structural limits. The KUNERT factories are mainly in rural areas which are insufficiently served by public transport. Also, there was a large jump in bus company fares in 1993/94 as well as another organisational problem – diverse working hours – which had initially been underestimated. Increasingly flexible working hours and an extension of shift work means that fewer and fewer employees start and finish work at the same time. This has resulted in a trend, a negative one from the environmental protection point of view, towards using cars which allow people to be independent of timetables. Given the technology available today, an ecologically worthwhile alternative for employees in rural areas would be to use cars running on fuel that is low in noxious substances or free of them entirely.

The environmental-controlling function of the "company eco-balance" is still unsatisfactory for cases of transfer of stages of production. As a result of the closure of the KUNERT factory in Berlin consumption of texturing oils fell to nil - at least at first glance. In reality, the consumption of texturing oils was not reduced but simply transferred to the yarn manufacturers in the previous stage – no ecological improvement at all. KUNERT AG will try to incorporate this factor into the next environmental report by adding extra information to the eco-balance and by redefining the eco-balance guidelines.

Implementation of the goal of continuing renovation work in the sewage, pipework and storage systems can only start in 1995.

16|

S   2.   Buildings

Goals

- Ensuring that dangerous waste is not left over on land and that no sites with leftover contamination are bought.
- Reducing employee traffic between place of residence and place of work in the KUNERT group of companies.

No.	Type	STOCK 31. 12. 1993	ENTRY 1994	EXIT 1994	STOCK 31. 12. 1994
S 2.	**Buildings[1] (in m²)**	**178,473**	**17,447**	**17,923**	**185,369**
2.1.	Production[1]	73,709	1,210	9,347	72,107
2.2.	Distribution a. storage[1]	87,559	16,509	7,566	96,667
2.3.	Administration[1]	17,205	178	1,010	16,415

[1] The differences in stocks between 1993 and 1994 are due to improved collection of data.

Measures

- Thorough inspection of sites and buildings for waste left over from the past before they become KUNERT AG property.
- Continuation of inspection and renovation work in the sewage, pipework and storage systems.
- Inclusion of a permanent chapter "Traffic" in the KUNERT AG environmental report.
- Execution of a study on the subject "Reducing traffic between home and work by using 'information highways' and external workplaces in the home with online connection to KUNERT AG".
- Adapting the eco-balance guidelines so that transfers of production and the corresponding INPUT and OUTPUT quantities can be recorded.

Commentary

Following a review of the data for buildings delivered by the factories/marketing companies some corrections were made and data which had not been collected before was included. As a result the stock figures for buildings for 1994 are more accurate.

Under the new heat insulation regulation (Wärmeschutzverordnung), minimum environmental guidelines for new and renovated buildings have been in force since 1. January 1995 with the particular aim of keeping heat loss as low as possible. In the future, every building contract will have to be accompanied by proof of annual heat consumption. Depending on the building, there will be specific limit values which may not be exceeded.

A systematic ecological evaluation of all buildings in the group of companies has not yet been possible for reasons of personnel capacity. However, as part of rationalisation measures, optimization was carried out, particularly in the buildings in the supply and disposal plants. Examples can be found in the accounts "INPUT 2. Energy" and "OUTPUT 3. Waste heat".

The reduction of noise pollution has been achieved in conformance with the limit values laid down in legislation.

Goals

- Compliance with regulations for the transport and storage of hazardous goods.

Measures

- Further inspection of the transport routes as well as intermediate and final storage for hazardous goods in buildings as part of the staff training required by the Regulation on transport and storage of hazardous substances (Gefahrgutverordnung Straße – GGVS).

|17

S 3. Plant and Equipment

No.	Type	STOCK 31. 12. 1993	ENTRY 1994	EXIT 1994	STOCK 31. 12. 1994
S 3.	**Plant and Equipment[1] (piece)**	**16,466**	**1,439**	**1,263**	**16,718**
3.1.	Production machines	6,310	533	973	5,870
3.2.	Office equipment	7,020	583	167	7,436
3.3.	Office and communication machines	2,806	277	111	2,972
3.3.1.	Mainframes	23	4	3	24
3.3.2.	Visual display units/ Terminals	827	59	7	879
3.3.3.	Copiers	77	10	7	80
3.3.4.	Fax units	58	9	6	61
3.3.5.	Personal computers	224	55	13	266
3.3.6.	Printers	431	101	26	506
3.3.7.	Others	1,166	39	49	1,156
3.4.	Vehicle fleet	164	25	7	182
3.4.1.	Automobiles	133	17	6	144
3.4.2.	Station wagons and minibusses	20	8	1	27
3.4.3.	Trucks	11	0	0	11
3.5.	Technical machinery	166	21	5	182

[1] The differences in stocks between 1993 and 1994 are due to improved collection of data.

Commentary

The reduction in pressure steam facilities, semi-forming machines and knitting machines is partially attributable to the transfer of steps in the production process to supply firms. Cleaning machines using solvents containing CFCs were replaced by CFC-free machines in plants both at home and abroad. The decision in principle taken in 1994 to successively convert the KUNERT vehicle fleet, including the sales representatives' cars, to diesel cars of lower h.p. which consume less fuel, is proving worthwhile. Consumption is 30% lower than for petrol-driven cars.

The sales representatives have also been convinced of the quality of the new diesel technology. Rainer Michel, CEO, has sent a signal to all employees using company cars by switching from a petrol-driven Mercedes Benz 500 to a turbo diesel-engined 350 model.

The rapeseed diesel-engined VW Passat has become the most popular car in the KUNERT fleet. Performance, particularly at low revs, is better than that of the pure diesel-engined car. Now instead of petrol fumes the vehicle fleet is more likely to smell of "french fries". The medium-term future of the environment-friendly car lies in converting to cars fueled by solar hydrogen. In this respect KUNERT supports the strategic approach presented by BMW at the UN climate conference in Berlin. Using sulphur-free natural gas the technology of gas-driven cars can be developed to production level. In addition, natural gas gives Eastern European countries an opportunity to earn hard currency and thus makes a descisive contribution to building up the economy. At the end of 1995 KUNERT will be supplied with a natural-gas-driven test car by BMW so that this forward-looking environmental technology can be tested for suitability in the everyday business world.

Goals

- Further conversion of plant and equipment to resource and energy-saving technology and lower emissions by the end of 1996.

Measures

- Educating those taking decisions in purchasing, production and the vehicle fleet about KUNERT's environmental purchasing guidelines for production machines and cars.
- Carrying out tests on environment-friendly technology.
- Installing environment-friendly drawer-dyeing technology as well as high frequency drying techniques in other production sites in Germany and abroad before the end of 1997.
- Giving suppliers guidance on the environmental purchasing guidelines for plant and equipment by mid-1996, particularly for knitting, dyeing and packing machines.

| 19

INPUT

I 1. Circulating goods
1.1. Raw materials

No.	Type	INPUT 1993	INPUT 1994	STOCK 31. 12. 1994
I 1.1.	**Raw materials (in kg)[¹] yarns and fabrics**	**3,821,006**	**3,558,124**	**697,183**
1.1.1.	Polyamide[¹]	2,051,857	1,405,676	231,315
1.1.2.	Cotton[¹]	583,552	949,947	223,594
1.1.3.	Elasthan[¹]	388,347	268,409	27,037
1.1.4.	Wool / Polyamide[¹]	219,189	331,553	106,915
1.1.5.	Wool[¹]	145,267	146,252	28,069
1.1.6.	Wool / Cotton / Polyamide	91,834	145,398	32,187
1.1.7.	Wool / Polyacryl	67,140	82,044	10,756
1.1.8.	Viscose[¹]	10,423	13,376	18
1.1.9.	Polypropylene	15,663	20,734	15,708
1.1.10.	Acrylic yarn[¹]	228,434	162,404	11,846
1.1.11.	Other yarn[¹]	19,300	32,331	9,738

[¹] In the last environmental report the raw material input of yarn did not include woven fabrics. Input in the form of fabrics has thus now beed added

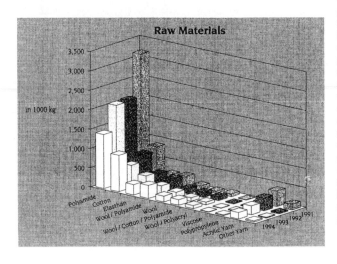

Raw Materials

in 1000 kg

Commentary

Consumption of the raw materials "yarns and fabrics" fell by another 7% in the group of companies compared to 1993. In contrast, the sub-accounts for natural fibre yarns showed increases:
- cotton + 63%
  and coloured yarns of natural fibre/ polyamide mix:
- wool/polyamide + 51%,
- wool/cotton/polyamide + 58%.

The fluctuations in raw materials are a reflection of the market. The trend is towards coarse knitted articles which means that both men's and ladies' socks are gaining ground while fine-knit tights are losing market shares. More extensive use was made of ecologically grown cotton for products in the KUNERT group of companies but limits were encountered. Firstly, the worldwide supply of ecologically grown cotton is still very limited and, secondly, the suppliers cannot guarantee the continuous supply of large quantities that would be necessary for the classic collections. In particular, only small quantities of the required combed cotton with long fibres is available and the raw material prices are almost 100% higher.

In the meantime, the German cotton exchange in Bremen has presented a study carried out by an independent institute on US cotton grown in the traditional way. It shows that the pesticide level in US cotton is minimal, lower even than the levels set for foodstuffs in Germany. KUNERT will be using this cotton, along with others, for the new one-size sock collection "Cotton 973".

With the methodological support of Prof. Bernd Wagner (University of Augsburg), the yarn supplier TWD (Textilwerke Deggendorf GmbH) drew up a product tree analysis for polyamide 6.6 (Nylon). The results are presented in full in the chapter "Product Tree Analysis". Methodological support of KUNERT suppliers in environmental management has resulted in more environmental commitment in the preliminary phase of textile finishing. In 1994, the Augsburger Kammgarnspinnerei (AKS) drew up a product tree analysis for DD double thread made of wool. In 1995, the Augsburg firm published its first environmental report with a full "company eco-balance" for the whole firm.

The use of natural enzymes for felt-free finishing of wool socks is still in its infancy and not yet ready for use in production.

Goals

- Compliance with the ÖKO-TEX-STANDARD 100 for all yarns (amount in kg) in the KUNERT group of companies.
- Testing the environmental impact of viscose yarns before mid-1996.

Measures

- Written guarantees from all yarn suppliers certifying that the ÖKO-TEX-STANDARD 100 has been complied with for all yarns delivered to KUNERT (purchasing condition).
- Spot-testing to check compliance.
- Environmental evaluation of "viscose".

|21

I   1.   Circulating goods
     1.2.   Semi-finished and finished goods

No.	Type	INPUT 1993	INPUT 1994
1.2.	**Semi finished and finished goods (in kg)** [1]	**2,637,453**	**2,082,292**
1.2.1.	Fine, plain articles [1]	1,437,082	1,205,858
1.2.2.	Knitted articles [1]	1,065,076	721,499
1.2.3.	Outer wear [1]	135,295	154,935

[1] The values for 1993 had to be corrected owing to a recording error.

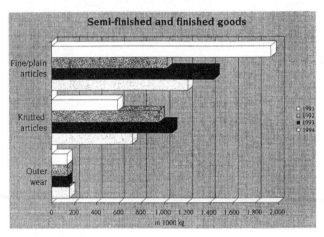

Semi-finished and finished goods

Commentary

In comparison to a overall production decrease of 22%, purchases of semi-finished and finished goods for hosiery fell by 15% for "fine, plain articles" and 32% for "knitted products". At the moment the growth area is "outer garments" with an increase of 15%. Following the revision of the Bedarfsgegenstände-Verordnung (Commodities regulation prohibiting the manufacture of commodities which may result in damage to health) all suppliers of semi-finished and finished goods were requested to guarantee that all deliveries comply with the conditions required by legislation. Since then guarantee declarations have been provided by almost all suppliers. If the declarations still lacking are not received by the end of October 1995, these suppliers will be deleted from the KUNERT group's list of suppliers. The implementation of the objective "creation of the organisational preconditions for short-term, fast, cost-effective textile testing processes" is still in the very early stages. Although tenders have been obtained from various testing institutes, they are anything but cost-effective, particularly in view of the high number of spot checks likely to be needed. In principle, all textile finishers and textile retailers are faced with this task. The "Gesamttextil" and "Gesamtmasche" manufacturers associations should also be called on to create the preconditions for cost-effective textile testing processes. A dispute among the experts over conclusive and recognised testing processes which allow the presence of illegal "carcinogenic amine" to be reliably proven has meant a delay in getting in binding tenders.

The "ecological INPUT-filter" does not yet function satisfactorily for the purchase of semi-finished and finished goods. There are no detailed purchasing terms that incorporate the results of the black list (especially dyes and chemicals). Also, internal training of the employees responsible and external training of suppliers has yet to be carried out. The tests of semi-finished and finished goods, which have only been partially carried out, should be integrated into the quality handbook as procedural instructions.

22 |

Goals

- Extension of control procedures to ensure compliance with the Commodities Regulation for semi-finished and finished goods purchased in the KUNERT group by the end of 1995.
- Compliance by suppliers with the "environmental purchasing guidelines" of the KUNERT group of companies.
- Respecting the ÖKO-TEX-STANDARD 100 for semi-finished and finished goods from the KUNERT group of companies.

Measures

- Deleting from the suppliers list any suppliers that do not provide a written engagement to comply with the Commodities Regulation by the end of October 1995.
- Working with Gesamtmasche and Gesamttextil in order to create the organisational conditions for cost-effective textile testing processes.
- Earmarking resources within the 1996 budget plan for textile testing processes.
- Updating and extending the environmental purchasing guidelines semi-finished and finished goods in cooperation with the buyers responsible.
- Drafting procedural instructions as part of the quality handbook for purchasing of semi-finished and finished goods as well as for implementing textile testing for the Commodities Regulation and the ÖKO-TEX-STANDARD 100.
- Training the buyers responsible in the environmental purchasing guidelines.
- Integrating the requirements of the Commodities Regulation into the purchasing terms for semi-finished and finished goods in the KUNERT group of companies.

|23

I   1.   Circulating Goods
1.3.   Auxiliary Materials
1.3.1.   Dyes

No.		Type	INPUT 1993	INPUT 1994	STOCK 31.12.1994
1	1.3.1.	**Dyes (in kg)**	**114,072**	**91,499**	**27,744**
	1.3.1.1.	Basic dye	888	1,215	1,486
	1.3.1.2.	Disperse dye	4,415	3,186	1,031
	1.3.1.3.	Direct dye[1]	2,443	3,847	2,061
	1.3.1.4	Metal-complex dye	34,268	18,308	7,258
	1.3.1.5.	Reactive dye for wool	1,073	870	714
	1.3.1.6	Reactive dye for cotton	38,094	39,666	8,089
	1.3.1.7	Acid dye	32,844	24,047	6,479
	1.3.1.8.	Natural dye	47	0	626
	1.3.1.9	Other dyes	0	360	0

[1]The accounts "Substantive dye" and "Indosol dye" have been combined as the account "Direct dye"

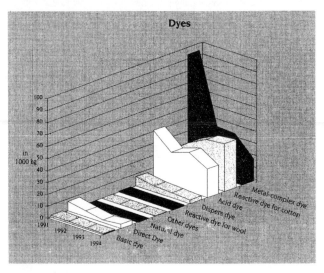

Commentary

The proportion of dyes containing heavy metals in total dye consumption was reduced by over 10 % in 1994. In the KUNERT group of companies, 63 % of the dyes used are free of heavy metals. However, it now seems that we have got as far as current technology allows. The numerous tests carried out with heavy-metal free dyes were only partially successful. An equal degree of colour fastness was achieved for the most part only with the half-form and dryer articles and the pastel shades which dye to good colour fastness using acid dyes. The retail trade and the consumers, however, are ever more demanding as far as the colour fastness is concerned. This may lead to a temporary rise in the use of metal complex dyes in 1995.

The "black list" database containing the almost 500 dyes and chemicals which are used in the KUNERT group has been improved with the help of outside experts and three new criteria have been added. The basis for the evaluation of all dyes and chemicals was the "Glat Model" developed in Switzerland. Following a series of waste water tests which showed higher than expected levels of dyes and chemicals with a "3" rating (i.e. black list) it is clear that the optimization of the materials used with respect to waste water will have to be pursued in the years to come.

Recycling of dye baths was the subject of a thesis. For five months experiments were carried out on "dyeing with a standing bath". The thesis was given support by external experts. The outcome was that recycling of dye baths is technically possible. However, the dyes used in the experiments had a high absorption rate so that only very small quantities of dye remained in the waste water. Recycling of dye baths with a high absorption rate does not make either economic or ecological sense. In addition, expensive collecting tanks and constantly large dye batches would have to be used.

Fairly limited progress was made in reducing the variety of articles. Following the concentration of production in the group in one production company as of 1996 further efforts will be made to streamline the variety of dyes.

The revised version of the Commodities Regulation issued in 1994 caused a furore. The legislator listed dyes with which it is prohibited to dye textiles because they deposit carcinogenic amine. Owing to the intensive preparatory work done in the area of "optimizing dyes with respect to waste water" these dyes had not been in use for years in the KUNERT group dyeing plants.

Goals

- Reducing the number of dyes on the black list that are graded "3" by 10% in 1995 and by a further 20% in 1996.
- Reducing the consumption of reactive dyes by 20% per kg of product dyed.
- Stabilizing the proportion of heavy metal dyes in overall dye consumption. The base taken is the 1994 level.
- Managing dye use with the aim of complying with the ÖKO-TEX-STANDARD 100 for all articles.

Measures

- Discussions with suppliers whose dyes have been put on the KUNERT group "black list". Requesting that alternatives be offered which would fall into grades "1" or "2" (KUNERT AG "green list").
- Ear-marking a budget for spot checks of the end product to ensure compliance with the Commodities Regulation or the ÖKO-TEX-STANDARD 100.

| 25

1.	Circulating Goods
1.3.	Auxiliary Materials
1.3.2.	Chemicals

No.	Type	INPUT 1993	INPUT 1994	STOCK 31. 12. 1994
1.3.2.	**Chemicals (in kg)**	**1,353,616**	**1,191,877**	**117,691**
1.3.2.1.	Levelling agent	89,427	70,062	12,908
1.3.2.2	Sodium chloride"	538,094	514,603	19,645
1.3.2.3	Lyes	68,658	82,724	8,716
1.3.2.4.	Oxidizing agent	20,398	10,344	1,571
1.3.2.5.	Aftertreatment agent	16,320	10,211	3,117
1.3.2.6.	Sodium sulphate	99,204	64,751	1,315
1.3.2.7.	Reducing agent	33,325	25,566	2,058
1.3.2.8.	Acids	143,403	118,026	19,762
1.3.2.9.	Detergent	72,654	67,815	12,995
1.3.2.10.	Softener	104,836	103,432	14,461
1.3.2.11.	Other Chemicals	167,297	124,343	21,143

" The full figure for INPUT of sodium chloride was not given in the last environmental report and has been corrected.

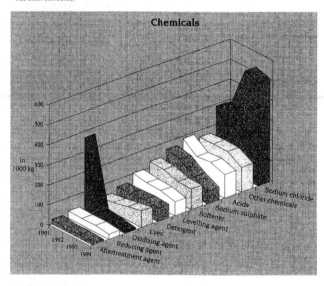

Chemicals

in 1 000 kg

Commentary

For many individual items the reduction in the use of chemicals was disproportionately higher than the reduction in production quantity. However, the continually high use of sodium chloride prevents this from being clear in the figure for total consumption.

The focus of 1994 was the ecological optimization of finishing chemicals with respect to waste water. The "black list" database was very helpful in this respect as it covers all of the chemicals used in the group of companies and classifies them into a "green list" (continued authorisation) and a "black list" (use in the future undesired). KUNERT was able to find replacement products for a whole series of chemicals that did badly in ecological evaluation. In addition, coordination between the KUNERT , Hudson and Burlington dye plant managers was facilitated by the clear database. It led to a series of coordination meetings and as a result the variety of chemicals was reduced. The results of the database also indicted a number of starting-points for optimizing finishing chemicals in coordination with the suppliers.

A thesis, supported by external experts, on the subject of softening agents brought some very interesting results to light. The absorption rates of some softeners in common use were considerably lower than the manufacturers' claims. This provides a definite starting-point for optimizing the finishing process and thus reducing the use of resources as well as waste water pollution. The thesis provided definite confirmation that controlling the pH value is a key factor in optimizing the finishing process. In Morocco and Mindelheim large-batch experiments to reduce the

26|

amount of common salt using when dyeing with reactive dyes proved promising. With the newly developed reactive dye the amount of common salt needed for dyeing could be reduced by two-thirds.

Goals

- Reducing the number of chemicals that have an ecological rating of "3" and are on the "black list" by 10% in 1995 and 20% in 1996.
- Controlling and, if necessary, optimizing finishing chemicals, so that the ÖKO-TEX-STANDARD 100 can be respected for all products.

Measures

- Instructing suppliers to find replacement products for the chemicals on the "black list" by the beginning of 1996.
- Instructing suppliers to find replacement products for chemicals for which compliance with the ÖKO-TEX-STANDARD 100 cannot be guaranteed.
- Reduction or extensive replacement of chemicals which on the basis of the waste water analyses have been identified as pollutants.
- Further training of dye plant managers and employees in optimization of finishing processes.
- Further training for employees concerned in the Regulation on transport and storage of hazardous substances (GGVS).

|27

I   1.   Circulating Goods
1.3.   Auxiliary Materials
1.3.3. Product Packaging

No.		Type	INPUT 1993	INPUT 1994
I	1.3.3.	**Product packaging total (in kg)**	**2,690,430**	**2,483,517**
	1.3.3.1.	Wrappers	816,593	672,080
	1.3.3.2.	Spool cards/inserts	729,854	711,747
	1.3.3.3.	Collapsible folding boxes/blanks	580,110	502,345
	1.3.3.4	Cartridges	7,408	6,080
	1.3.3.5.	Thigh-length panty girdle boxes	5,861	5,982
	1.3.3.6.	PP + PE polythene bags"	58,776	49,557
	1.3.3.7.	PP + PE film bag halves"	252,726	300,893
	1.3.3.8.	Embossed sheets	480	1,152
	1.3.3.9.	Transfer sheets	12,864	10,016
	1.3.3.10.	Rools	33,365	30,364
	1.3.3.11.	Plastic hooks	40,133	39,350
	1.3.3.12.	Adhesive labels	48,362	36,920
	1.3.3.13.	Sewn-on labels	103,898	117,031

" PE = Polyethylene, PP = Polypropylene

Goals

- Lowering the average proportion of packaging in the product to less than 25% by the end of 1996.
- Increasing the purity of the packaging product components, i. e. their ability to be recycled.

Measures

- Developing newer forms of packaging that have greater material purity and use fewer resources, particularly for articles in the lower price categories.
- Increasing the use of product packaging materials that are made up of pure components and can be recycled.
- Introducing advertising on packaging about the environmental friendliness of products, packaging and production technology in the KUNERT group of companies.

Commentary

There was a disproportionately large fall in the consumption of adhesive labels proving that progress is being made with printing the price directly on the packet. A lot of the measures initiated in 1992 and 1993 led to greater purity of the product components (i.e. recyclability) of packaging, while at the same time reducing the variety of materials. By refashioning labels, Hudson was able to reduce the number of types of labels by 33 variants (i.e. 40%). Polypropylene bags made of 100 percent regenerated PP material which were first used in Hudson are now used in KUNERT and Burlington. In the future all sock hooks will be marked indicating that the same material is in use at KUNERT, Hudson and Burlington. Not only product packaging but also the decoration materials and displays of the KUNERT GROUP OF COMPANIES have been marked with disposal instructions in several languages.

The planned use of multi-packs met with clear rejection in the retail trade, especially for the middle and higher price ranges.

1   1.   Circulating Goods
      1.3.   Auxiliary Materials
      1.3.4. Product Additions

No.	Type	INPUT 1993	INPUT 1994
1 1.3.4.	**Product additions total (kg)**	187,320	169,432
1.3.4.1	Sewn-in labels	5,039	5,662
1.3.4.2	Elasticated bands	28,499	38,083
1.3.4.3	Transflock appliques	613	217
1.3.4.4	Costume jewellery appliques	1,774	4,241
1.3.4.5	Gussets[1]	144,070	114,988
1.3.4.6	Decals	3,805	3,047
1.3.4.7	Cords	139	167
1.3.4.8	Metal clips and fasteners	100	220
1.3.4.9	Packaging paper	3,281	2,807

[1] In the 1994 environmental report stock figures were mistakenly shown as INPUT 1993 for the gusset Item. This has been corrected.

Commentary

Total consumption of product additions fell by 10% in 1994. With the help of the "ecological filter" in the central purchasing department it was organized that production additions that create "hazardous waste" will only be purchased in exceptional cases in the future. The possibilities for savings in materials have now been exhausted for the most part.

Goals

• Further improving the environmental friendliness of product additions.

Measures

• Instructions to suppliers of semi-finished and finished goods to use environment-friendly product additions, i. e. first and foremost materials made up of pure components which can be recycled.

| | 1. | Circulating Goods |
| 1.4. | Ancillary Materials |

No.	Type	INPUT 1993	INPUT 1994
I 1.4.	**Ancillary materials (in kg) (excluding office Materials)**	**1,617,899**	**1,479,171**
1.4.1.	**Oil and solvents (total in kg)**	**40,625**	**39,774**
1.4.1.1	Lubricants	32,523	34,000
1.4.1.2.	Engine and gearoil	5,850	3,921
1.4.1.3.	Compressor oil	440	778
1.4.1.4.	Solvents[1]	1,812	1,075
1.4.2.	**Transport packaging (total in kg)**	**1,577,274**	**1,439,397**
1.4.2.1.	Transport cardboard containers	1,531,103	1,404,926
1.4.2.2.	Hoop casing roll	5,329	5,563
1.4.2.3.	Wed adhesvie roll	14,808	14,515
1.4.2.4.	Clingwrap film	20,147	7,450
1.4.2.5.	PP-adhesive tape[2]	5,081	6,588
1.4.2.6.	Adress film	806	355
1.4.3.	**Office materials (sheet/piece)**	**37,466,520**	**30,163,383**
1.4.3.1.	**Paper total (sheets)**	**37,315,140**	**30,014,720**
1.4.3.1.1.	Recycling	2,141,414	908,619
1.4.3.1.2.	Chlorine free	34,926,330	28,941,773
1.4.3.1.3.	Conventional	247,396	164,328
1.4.3.2.	**Office supplies (piece)**	**151,380**	**148,663**
1.4.3.2.1.	Pencils	17,081	15,452
1.4.3.2.2.	Typewriter ribbon/correction band	2,884	2,568
1.4.3.2.3.	Computer material	2,493	3,559
1.4.3.2.4.	Foil and folders	86,100	102,122
1.4.3.2.5.	Files/briefcases	7,777	8,474
1.4.3.2.6.	Ring binder	14,345	11,210
1.4.3.2.7.	Register	2,548	1,776
1.4.3.2.8.	Other office supplies[3]	18,152	3,502

[1] In the 1994 environmental report, owing to an error in data collection, solvent-INPUT was given as 3,512 kg instead of the correct figure of 1,812 kg.
[2] PP = Polypropylene
[3] Other office supplies includes glues, metal articles (e. g. staples and clips), wooden articles (e. g. rulers) and any other articles not included elsewhere.

Commentary

The reduction in use of solvents was disproportionately high at 41 %, achieving the goal set out the previous year. On the other hand the reduction in production-related transport packaging was lower than expected at 9 %. The goal set out the previous year to achieve a very large reduction in transport packaging was attained for cling-wrap film (– 63 %) and address film (– 56 %), while the reduction in cardboard containers for transport was lower than the drop in production. The fall of 35 % in consumption of engine and gearoil is due to the sale of a total of 11 heavy goods truck trailers by KUNERT and Hudson.

The increase in compressor oil was caused by the installation of additional compressed air facilities. The development and implementation of measures to reduce the consumption of "office materials" and "other materials" were only partially successful. Nonetheless, this "beginning of the pipe" environmental management did help to reduce the relevant amounts of residual waste and recyclables. The variety of office articles was maintained at the very low level of 200 different articles.

Goals

- Further reducing specific consumption of ancillary materials that have particular environmental impact such as "solvents" and "transport packaging".
- Reducing consumption of paper, particularly paper dyed all the way through, as this complicates recycling.

Measures

- Study on the use of solvents in the factories and production stages and developing measures to save on solvents or replace them by environment-friendly substances.

| 31

I   2.   Energy

No.	Type	INPUT (in kWh) 1993	INPUT (in kWh) 1994	STOCK(in l) 31. 12. 1994
I 2.	**Energy total**	**150,682,651**	**118,986,313**	—
2.1.	Gas	19,892,297	16,570,184 [3]	—
2.2.	Electricity	47,878,784	33,123,331 [4]	—
2.3.	Fuel oil total	59,416,240	47,262,590 [3]	497,616
2.3.1.	Light fuel oil	23,063,560	17,060,650	416,016
2.3.2.	Heavy fuel oil	25,402,450	24,314,350	81,600
2.3.3.	Mixed fuel oil	10,950,230	5,887,590	0
2.4.	District heating	5,595,680	5,586,418	—
2.5.	Fuel total	17,899,650	16,443,790 [3]	0
2.5.1.	Conventional diesel	4,215,840	1,741,640	0
2.5.2.	Low-sulphur diesel fuel [1]	0	17,530	0
2.5.3.	Petrol [2]	6,315,710	5,713,950	0
2.5.4.	Outside carriers	7,368,100	8,970,670	—

[1] Since 1994 two vehicles using rapeseed diesel have been introduced.
[2] Owing to a recording error in the last environmental report incorrect values were given for 1993.
[3] Represents 6,771,963 kg of material.
[4] Represents 87,627,860 kWh of primary energy.

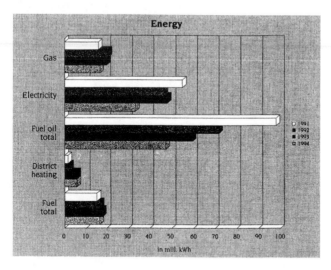

Commentary

Energy consumption in the KUNERT group of companies fell by 21 % in 1994. Given the analogous fall of 22 % in production this would seem to be self-evident. However, conventional business management shows that overheads, which include a part of energy costs, fall much less quickly than production quantity. If energy costs in the more limited sense of energy costs for production are considered, it is clear that there have been considerable savings as a result of efficient energy management and the introduction of new, energy-saving manufacturing technology in the factories of the KUNERT group of companies.

The reduction in the area of conventional diesel fuels is due mainly to the sale of the company truck trailers at KUNERT and Hudson. The conversion of the KUNERT vehicle fleet from petrol-driven to diesel-engined vehicles with catalytic convertors is making steady progress with the aim of reducing fuel consumption by one third. The initial results can already be seen in the figures for 1994. This trend should be translated into a significant fall in overall consumption in 1995 and 1996 (see also "S 3. plant and equipment").

per year were identified. Owing to the fact that significantly higher potential savings were identified in the areas of "rejects and reworking" and "readjustment and redyeing", the focus will initially be on developing measures in these areas.

The manufacturing technologies of "pre-boarding or pre-smoothing", "dyeing with drawer dyeing machines" and subsequently "drying with high frequency techniques", which were successfully tested in the KUNERT factory in Mindelheim have been introduced in the KUNERT factory in Morocco. As a result the factories in northern Africa are now also in a position to make further savings on energy in 1996.

Goals

- Reducing the environmental cost "waste heat" in the KUNERT factory in Mindelheim by the end of 1996 by reducing the energy INPUT (results of the pilot project "Environmental Cost Management").

Measures

- Developing measures to reduce the energy costs of the KUNERT Mindelheim factory by 5 % by the end of 1996.
- Applying these measures in other KUNERT group factories by the end of 1998.
- Paying particular attention to energy efficiency when purchasing plant equipment and technology; rational use of energy and low emissions being the most important factors.
- Improving procedures for determining the consumption of fuel.

|33

| 3. | Water |

No.	Type	INPUT 1993	INPUT 1994
3.	**Water total (in m³)**	**495.,043**	**428,770**
3.1.	Tap water	303,852	281,275
3.2.	Raw water (well / lake)	191,191	147,495

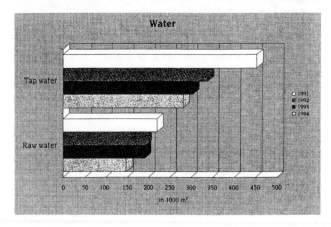

drum to the maximum. The malfunction in the control system was corrected immediately and will result in considerable savings in the dyeing plants in Mindelheim, Morocco, Hungary and Portugal.

Goals

- Reduction of consumption of drinking water per production unit in 1995.
- Reduction of water costs by 10 % per production unit by the end of 1996.

Measures

- Developing measures within the framework of the pilot project "Environmental Cost Management" in order to exploit the cost-saving potential calculated.
- Implementing the water-saving process optimization as part of the pilot project "Reducing waste water pollution".
- Applying the measures from both pilot projects (Waste water and Environmental cost management) in all dyeing plants in the KUNERT group of companies before the end of 1997.
- Water recovery in the KUNERT factory in Mindelheim as part of a research project under the Federal Ministry for research and Technology 1995/96 (see chapter OUTPUT 4. Waste water).

Commentary

The goal set out in the previous year's report of "reducing the consumption of drinking-quality water per unit of production" was not achieved. While total production (in kg) dropped by 22 % in 1994, the consumption of drinking water only fell by 7 % and total water consumption by 13 %. What is reflected here is the closure of the KUNERT dyeing plant in Immenstadt which up until 1993 used large quantities of raw water from a small alpine lake. The results of the thesis "dyeing with a standing bath" proved in laboratory tests as well as in production that significant quantities of water could be saved using this procedure. However, the high cost of purchasing collection tanks and the reduction in batch sizes from the same colour lot make it impossible for the technology to be put to cost-effective use at the moment. A secondary effect of the thesis, however, was a process optimization that led to water savings. In certain types of dyeing machines there was a malfunction in the automatic mechanism for water filling. Even with a small load, needing only a small quantity of water, the mechanism would fill the dyeing

| 4. Air

No.	Type	INPUT 1993	INPUT 1994
| 4.	**Air total (in m³)**	–	–
4.1	Air for air-conditioning units	3.,189,920,000	3,189,920,000
4.2	Air for burner systems[1]	90,210.202	71,839,377
4.3	Air for traffic	–	–
4.4	Air for compressed air	–	–
4.5	Air for other facilities	–	–

[1] On account of more comprehensive data collection there is a new value for 1993.

Commentary

The eco-balance account "air" is still in the construction and consolidation phase. Special filters in ventilation and air-conditioning systems that filter out dust and pollen from outside air minimize the level of the noxious substances in the INPUT air. This filters are maintained at regular intervals. There are no known cases of damage to health caused by air-conditioning systems in the KUNERT group of companies.

Goals

- Improving the completeness and consistency of data in the INPUT account "Air".
- Survey to collect data for additional sub-accounts, in particular "Traffic".

Measures

- Developing procedural instructions and extending the eco-balance guidelines to include data collection for "INPUT Air".

OUTPUT

Whereas the raw, auxiliary and ancillary materials entering the factories were recorded on the previous INPUT pages, the materials and energy that left the factories again in 1995, having been transformed, now follow on the OUTPUT pages.

O 1. Products

No.	Type	OUTPUT 1993	OUTPUT 1994	STOCK 31. 12. 1994
O 1.	**Products total (in kg)**	**8,935,247**	**8,492,704**	
1.1	Hosiery total	5,116,411	5,199,188	2,786,664
1.1.1	Fine, plain articles	2,845,310	2,762,880	1,469,213
1.1.2	Knitted articles	2,271,101	2,436,308	1,317,451
1.2	Outer wear	211,756	194,911	–
1.3	Transport packaging material[1]	989,275	897,598	–
1.4	Product packaging material	2,617,805	2,201,007	–

[1] Registered separately for the first time in 1993.

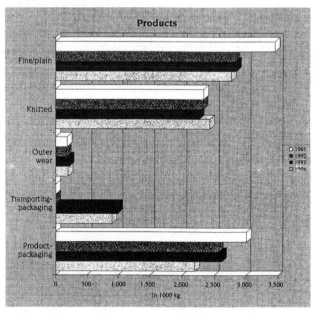

Products

Commentary

A clear shift has taken place over the last two years: whereas the "fine articles" area is declining, the "knitted articles" area, i. e. socks and knitted stockings, is expanding. The change is due to a change in consumer behaviour. Given that knitted articles require a lot less packaging that also explains the fall in product packaging by 16 %.

The variety of articles has been reduced. In particular, the variety of articles at KUNERT has been reduced by 15 % and, from 1993 to mid-1995, the variety of articles at Hudson fell by over 22 %. The variety of colours remained almost unchanged because the retail trade and consumers continue to expect this variety from a leading producer of brand-name hosiery. The proportion of dyes containing heavy metals in the total consumption of dyes was reduced by over 10 % in 1994. However, for some articles, increasing customer requirements for better colour fastness were not fulfilled. In 1995/96 these articles will once again be dyed using heavy metal dyes in order to guarantee the level of colour fastness demanded by the consumer.

36|

The "ÖKO-TEX-STANDARD 100" (Hohenstein Institute) has become increasingly important for the European textile industry. Increasing numbers of retailers, especially the big customers, are demanding that limit values be respected. Suppliers, in the meantime, have provided guarantees that this standard is respected for their raw, auxiliary and ancillary materials.

The German Commodities Regulation prohibiting the use of commodities that may result in damage to health lists dyes which are banned because they separate off carcinogenic amine. Thanks to the "ecological filter" at purchase these dyes have not been in use for years in own production in the KUNERT group of companies. Suppliers of semi-finished and finished goods have also given guarantees that they too will comply with the Commodities Regulation. Additional spot-checks will be carried out on residual stocks in storage.

The research project "Recycling of knitted goods" has been completed by the Institut für Textil- und Verfahrenstechnik in Denkendorf. The project identified a variety of ways of recycling knitted goods into filters, fibre-board and mould parts for the car industry. However, it also showed that the recycling process is very energy and resource-intensive. Recycling knitted goods requires the use of many different chemicals which in turn would cause environmental pollution. In addition, the return transport of the waste knitted goods would itself consume large quantities of energy and cause more air emissions. In conclusion: recycling of knitted goods does not make ecological sense given the technology available today.

Goals

- Compliance with the ÖKO-TEX-STANDARD 100 for all articles produced by the KUNERT group of companies.
- Closer involvement of environmental controlling in the marketing and product development decision-making processes.
- Reduction of the cost of residual materials in the area of "rejects and reworking" by 20 % in the KUNERT factory in Mindelheim by the end of 1995 and in all factories in the KUNERT production group by the end of 1996.

Measures

- Obliging all suppliers to comply with the ÖKO-TEX-STANDARD 100, particularly for yarns, dyes and chemicals as well as for any semi-finished and finished goods purchased.
- Deleting from the suppliers list any suppliers that do not guarantee compliance with the ÖKO-TEX-STANDARD 100 by the deadline of the end of 1996.
- Spot-checks to monitor compliance with the ÖKO-TEX-STANDARD 100 and provision of a budget for checks of this kind in 1996.
- Spot-checks to monitor compliance with the Commodities Regulation, in particular for semi-finished and finished goods purchased, and provision of an annual budget for this purpose from 1995 on.

- Deleting from the suppliers list any suppliers that do not provide a guarantee of compliance with the Commodities Regulation by the deadline of the end of October 1995.
- Developing process sequences, procedural instructions and purchasing guidelines as part of quality management which would ensure compliance with the Commodities Regulation and the ÖKO-TEX-STANDARD 100.
- Training employees in the stipulations of the Commodities Regulation by the end of 1995 and in those of the ÖKO-TEX-STANDARD 100 by the end of 1996, including the corresponding purchasing guidelines and procedural instructions. Provision of a training budget for 1995 and 1996.
- Implementation and continuation of measures introduced in the area of "rejects and reworking", "datasystems" and "waste water" until the end of 1995 (results of pilot project Environmental Cost Management).
- Permanent implementation of the newly developed time and organisation sequence for product development (results of pilot project Environmental Cost Management).
- Developing and implementing new cost-cutting measures to bring about 20 % reduction by mid-1996 in the residual materials cost potential in "readjustment and redyeing" in the KUNERT factory in Mindelheim.
- Transferring the cost-cutting measures in "readjustment and redyeing" to other factories in the KUNERT production group by the end of 1996.
- Making use of the KUNERT group's ecological advance within brand-name policy, advertising and sales promotions as well as on packaging.
- Further reduction of the variety of articles in 1996.

38

O 2. Wastes

No.	Type	OUTPUT 1993	OUTPUT 1994	STOCK 31. 12. 1994
O 2.	**Waste total (in kg)**	**2,519,252**	**2,357,988**	**36,398**
2.1.	**Hazardous waste (tot. in kg)**	**40,399**	**62,883**	**3,910**
2.1.1.	Solids	7,228	1,520	1,030
2.1.2.	Fluid hazardous waste	9,077	46,601	565
2.1.3.	Fluorescent lamps	1,792	1,291	656
2.1.4.	Capacitors containing PCB	2,731	3,018	118
2.1.5.	Batteries	422	451	69
2.1.6.	Waste medicaments	260	240	25
2.1.7.	Waste oil	11,506	3,315	2,170
2.1.8.	Electronic scrap material[2]	2,928	5,997	52
2.1.9.	Other hazardous waste[3]	4,455	450	75
2.2.	**Recyclables total (in kg)**	**1,920,624**	**1,816,533**	**25,236**
2.2.1.	Waste paper	274,917	260,739	3,136
2.2.2.	Corrugated board / cardboard	773,075	755,446	6,170
2.2.3.	Cover sheet	101,857	105,750	5,500
2.2.4.	Stocking waste	228,636	170,029	635
2.2.5.	Yarn waste	15,806	17,345	1,010
2.2.6.	Sewing waste	175,744	141,439	2,971
2.2.7.	Foil (PP+PE)[3]	47,121	56,464	850
2.2.8.	Cardboard cartridges	103,360	69,528	1,142
2.2.9.	Plastic cartridges	4,030	2,103	10
2.2.10.	Other synthetic materials	15,189	8,773	22
2.2.11.	Scrap metals	127,392	198,720	3,515
2.2.12.	Scrap glas	10,637	8,980	275
2.2.13.	Compostable waste[2]	10,150	1,465	0
2.2.14.	Other recyclables[1]	32,710	19,752	0
2.3.	**Residual waste (in kg)**	**485,429**	**349,652**	**6,052**
2.4.	**Rubble total (in kg)**	**72,800**	**128,920**	**1,200**
2.4.1.	Timber[1]	26,300	55,910	1,200
2.4.2.	Concrete, bricks, sand etc	46,500	73,010	0

[1] In the last environmental report 4100 kg of waste timber were erroneously included under other recyclables. This has been corrected.
[2] Recorded for the first time in 1993.
[3] PE = Polyethylene, PP = Polypropylene

Commentary

Residual waste fell by another 28 % compared to the previous year while hazardous waste increased by 56 %. A close look at hazardous waste reveals two reasons for this. Firstly, electronic scrap material increased by 105 % as a result of renovation work in the Burlington computer division in Schopfheim. Secondly, fluid hazardous waste increased by 413 %. This exceptional increase was in the Burlington dyeing plant in Hungary. In order to avoid additional waste water pollution 46,000 kg of dye and chemical sludge was disposed of as fluid hazardous waste in 1994. This waste comes from the monthly clean out of the equalizing tank in the heat recovery plant. In the future, when the planned waste water treatment plant has been installed the production of sludge can be avoided (see also chapter "O 4. Waste Water"). Had it not been for the sludge in Hungary the total figure for hazardous waste would have been roughly halved compared to 1993.

When the Administrative Union for Waste Management for Kempten, Oberallgäu, carried out spottests of the "residual waste" at KUNERT in 1994, it calculated a recyclables quota of 30 % and urged KUNERT to reduce the proportion of recyclables in residual waste to 0%. In order to reach the target set, KUNERT AG introduced an improved collection system for recyclables in the Immenstadt factory. The KUNERT

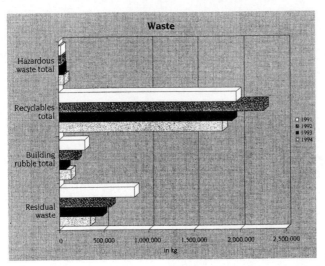

Goals

- Reduction of the residual waste quota (cf. environmental indicators) below 12 % by the end of 1997.
- Reduction of the hazardous waste quota to 0.8 % by the end of 1997.

Measures

- Introducing the new collection system in the KUNERT factory in Mindelheim by the end of 1995 and to other KUNERT factory locations where conditions allow for sound materials reclamation by the purchaser by the end of 1996.
- Extension of the environmental purchasing guidelines in order to limit the purchase of raw, auxiliary, ancillary materials or products that give rise to an OUTPUT of hazardous or residual waste.
- Development and implementation of measures required by the Recycling Act in coordination with the local Waste Management Union.

collection system sorts into four main groups of materials: recyclables, organic waste, residual waste and hazardous waste. In the offices there are residual waste containers and recyclables containers for paper quality A and B. All other material is disposed of by the employees at "their" recyclables island. Here, there are suitable containers for all types of waste produced in the various departments. In addition, there are organic waste containers in the kitchen to take food leftovers, coffee grinds, etc. The introduction of the new system was helped along by the use of notices over the recyclables islands and containers and an information brochure for employees informing them about the concept of collection systems for recyclables. The

positive effects can already been seen. The proportion of recyclables has risen, earnings from recyclables have risen and the amount of residual waste has dropped further.

The Administrative Union for Waste Management for Kempten, Oberallgäu, has successfully introduced the KUNERT model for disposing of the hazardous waste "fluorescent lamps" all over the Oberallgäu region. In addition to the commercial firms private households are also included. By way of this wide-ranging cooperation disposal is improved both in environmental and financial terms.

40

O   3.   Waste Heat

No.	Type	OUTPUT 1993	OUTPUT 1994
O 3.	**Waste heat total (in kWh)**	150,682,651	118,986,313

Commentary

During the pilot project "Environmental Cost Management" in the Mindelheim factory the potential for cost-cutting in energy emissions was studied ("other waste heat"). Going on this basis, targeted measures can now be developed to reduce the quotas of these cost potentials related to residual material costs.

The energy efficiency of the heat recovery installation in Mindelheim was improved by introducing a double-pipe waste water separation system for the rotary and drawer dyeing machines. Partial optimization of the control mechanism for the steam heating system in the KUNERT factory in Geyer and the installation of a radiant heating system for the goods compacting area is resulting in further energy savings.

In the KUNERT factory in Immenstadt the control mechanism for the air-conditioning system has been optimized and thus the loss of energy as heat reduced.

Goals

• Reduction of heat losses and the corresponding residual materials costs for "waste heat" in the KUNERT factory in Mindelheim by the end of 1996 and in the other dyeing and forming plants in the KUNERT production group by the end of 1998 (Pilot project "Environmental Cost Management").

Measures

• Developing further measures to reduce the loss of heat by mid-1996.

|41

O   4.   Waste Water

No	Type	OUTPUT 1993	OUTPUT 1994
O 4.	Waste water total (in m³)	376,289	339,277

Commentary

Waste water pollution has been significantly reduced since 1991. As regards the theoretical approach, the element of "beginning of the pipe management" most important in achieving this was the optimization of input materials with respect to waste water. During the pilot project "reducing waste water pollution", "hit lists" were drawn up for each of the ten most used dyes and chemicals. These input materials then went through an ecological assessment, and, if the results proved unsatisfactory, replacement substances were sought. Further ecological optimization of input materials was introduced by way of the "black list" project. Efforts were made in cooperation with the suppliers to find alternatives to dyes and chemicals with a "3" rating that are still in use and some alternatives have been identified. In parallel, the optimization of the dyeing and finishing processes is continuing – from installing pH-value control mechanisms in the dyeing machines as the basis for optimal process management to fully exhausting dyes and chemicals to reducing flocculent by 70 % in the KUNERT factory in Mindelheim. Besides reducing environmental pollution through better dosing of flocculent there is a cost saving

of DM 150,000 annually in the Mindelheim factory. A third strategic approach is the recycling of dyeing and finishing baths (see chapter 1.3.1 Dyes and 1.3.2 Chemicals) and the separation and recycling of waste water flows with heat recovery as the fourth strategy.

Optimizing the circulation of cooling water in the high frequency drying installation in the Mindelheim factory produced savings of DM 17,000 per year. Separating the baths on the rotary and drawer dyeing machines, the resulting improvement in the operation of the heat recovery installation and the installation of a neutralizing plant and cooling water recirculation for the rotary dyeing machines brought a further reduction in environmental pollution and costs. In Autumn 1995, a new waste water purification project, commissioned by the Federal Ministry for Research and Technology, will start under the project management of the Institut für Textil- und Verfahrenstechnik, Deggendorf. During this three-year project different filtering techniques for eliminating, recycling and disposing of dyes in an environment-friendly way will be tested. In addition, the project will study water recovery.

Proposals for waste water handling are currently being worked out in order to improve the unsatisfactory waste water situation in the KUNERT factory Temasa, Morocco, the Burlington factory in Mosonmagyaròvàr, Hungary and the KUNERT factory in Tunisia. The INPUT of dyes containing heavy metals fell by 10 % in 1994. This step forward on the INPUT side means, of course, that a further reduction in heavy metals pollution was achieved both at home and abroad. In the same way, the introduction of AOX-free dyes on the INPUT side led to a fall in the AOX level in waste water while at the same time reducing salt pollution.

Under various research projects tests of waste water from the dyeing plants were carried out giving results that were not entirely satisfactory. Some of the problem substances were identified in the course of follow-up analyses and measures to reduce or replace the dyes or chemicals in question have already been implemented.

Goals

- Further reducing waste water pollution in all factories of the KUNERT group of companies, in particular those with dyeing plants.
- Further reducing residual materials costs for waste water in the KUNERT factory in Mindelheim by the end of 1996.
- Recording waste water pollution by heavy metals in kg in the next eco-balance.

Measures

- Developing and implementing measures to reduce the waste water costs in the KUNERT factory in Mindelheim.
- Transferring the measures to reduce costs and pollution to other factories in the KUNERT group of companies.
- Reducing waste water pollution by continuing the pilot project and implementing the resulting measures by the end of 1996.
- Recovering and recycling water and chemicals (e. g. sodium chloride) in the framework of the project financed by the Federal Ministry for Research and Technology 1995/96.
- Provision of a budget for further waste water tests in order to identify and eliminate more of the substances polluting the water.
- Resolution of the unsatisfactory waste water situation in Morocco, Hungary and Tunisia by the end of 1996.
- Working out a method for recording water pollution by heavy metals (process-related emission factors).

O   5.   Air Emissions

No.	Type	OUTPUT 1993	OUTPUT 1994
O 5.1.	**Total quantity of air emissions (in m³)**		
5.1.1.	Air conditioning unit emissions	3,189,920,000	3,189,920,000
5.1.2.	Burner system emissions	–	–
5.1.3.	Traffic emissions	–	–
5.1.4.	Compressed air emissions	–	–
5.1.5.	Emissions from other systems	–	–
5.2.	**Total quantity of air pollution (in kg)**		
5.2.1.	NO_x[1]	138,828	100,548
5.2.2.	SO_2[1]	207,872	170,132
5.2.3.	CO_2[1]	48,080,685	36,109,594
5.2.4.	Water vapour[2]	121,614,000	96,895,400

[1] In 1994 for the first time it was possible to register air pollution caused by the electricity and district heating used by KUNERT group of companies. The figures for 1993 were adjusted so that the CO_2, SO_2 and NO_x values now cover emissions from KUNERT's own burner systems as well as emissions from external electricity and district heation production.

[2] Using a more accurate method, the water vapour emission value for 1993 has been recalculated, giving a new value.

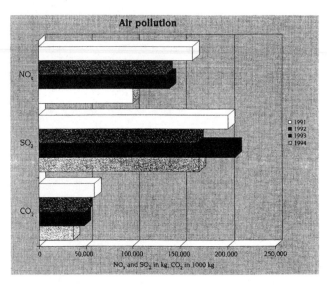

Air pollution

NO_x · SO_2 · CO_2

□ 1991 ■ 1992 ■ 1993 □ 1994

0 · 50,000 · 100,000 · 150,000 · 200,000 · 250,000

NO_x and SO_2 in kg. CO_2 in 1000 kg

Commentary

Another look at the INPUT account "2. Energy" reveals that the energy source with the lowest efficiency rate and thus the highest emissions was reduced by 31 %: electricity, as secondary energy, is produced mainly in coal-fired or nuclear power plants and must be transported over long distances. This causes emissions and loss of efficiency. Until now these "electricity" emissions have not been recorded in the "air emissions" account because they take place outside the factory walls. From 1994 on, CO_2, SO_2, NO_x emissions arising as a result of electricity or district heating obtained externally by KUNERT have been incorporated into the eco-balance. The values for previous years will be established and the balance corrected accordingly.

Distortions or "illusory improvements" in the eco-balance happen when production is transferred to supply companies, for example abroad. If the knitting and dyeing no longer takes place at KUNERT but in a far-away contract processing company the pollution caused is even greater – for instance because of the transport involved. The result does not improve the environment, it simply transfers the pollution elsewhere.

The natural gas pipe in Horb has been extended to the Hudson/SILKONA warehouse and forwarding centre. The incinerator in the KUNERT factory in Temasa, Morocco has been replaced by a shredding machine. All factories are being obliged to plant vegetation on factory grounds. The most recent example is the complete renovation of the employee car park and the areas around the administrative buildings at KUNERT headquarters in Immenstadt with the planting of vegetation that binds CO_2 and provides oxygen.

Goals

- Further reduction of flue gases (CO_2, SO_2, NO_x) by the end of 1996 (reference basis 1994).
- Identifying level of emissions from works and passenger traffic.

Measures

- Conversion of the burner systems in the Hudson/SILKONA warehouse and forwarding centre in Horb to natural gas.
- Reduction of energy INPUT with the aim of further reducing emissions of flue gases.
- Working out a procedure for determining traffic emissions.

45

Environmental Performance Indicators of the KUNERT Group Of Companies

No.	Type	1989	1990	1991	1992	1993	1994
A	**Production-specific ratios[1]**						
1.	Water consumption per kg product (l / kg)	–	166.7	158.5	167.3	158.0	175.6
2.	Energy consumption per kg product (kWh / kg)[2]	–	48.9	43.6	49.7	48.1	48.7
3.	Emissions per kg product[3]						
3.1.	NO_x-emissions (g/kg)	–	–	38.6	42.6	44.3	41.2
3.2.	SO_2-emissions (g/kg)	–	–	47.3	52.9	66.4	69.7
3.3.	CO_2-emissions (kg/kg)	–	–	14.0	15.6	15.3	14.8
4.	Waste per kg product (g / kg)[2]	987.06	781.56	736.93	967.78	804.26	965.84
4.1.	Hazardous waste (g / kg)	9.4	6.7	6.2	8.7	12.9	25.8
4.2.	Residual waste (g / kg)	345.2	335.7	199.0	182.2	155.0	143.2
4.3.	Recyclables (g / kg)	364.3	358.7	463.1	712.9	613.2	744.1
B	**Energy and Water Quotas**						
5.	Energy quotas[2]						
5.1.	Gas	6.5%	6.4%	8.5%	13.0%	13.2%	13.9%
5.2.	Electricity	28.4%	30.4%	29.6%	29.5%	31.8%	27.8%
5.3.	Fuel oil	57.1%	54.8%	52.8%	45.4%	39.4%	39.7%
5.4.	District heating	–	–	0.9%	1.5%	3.7%	4.7%
5.5.	Fuel	8.0%	8.4%	8.2%	10.6%	11.9%	13.8%
6.	Waste quotas[2]						
6.1.	Hazardous waste	1.1%	1.0%	0.8%	0.9%	1.6%	2.7%
6.2.	Recyclables	43.8%	55.1%	62.8%	73.7%	76.2%	77.0%
6.3.	Residual waste	55.1%	43.9%	27.0%	18.8%	19.3%	14.8%
6.4.	Building rubble	–	–	9.3%	6.6%	2.9%	5.5%
C	**Material ratios**						
7.	Proportion of heavy metal**free** dyes	–	–	–	–	52.3%	62.9%
8.	Average proportion of packaging in product	–	37.0%	32.4%	32.0%	29.3%	25.9%
D	**Emissions quotas[3]**						
9.	CO_2-emissions (g / kWh)	–	–	349.3	351.6	362.1	352.1
10.	NO_x-emissions (g / kWh)	–	–	0.96	0.96	1.05	0.98
11.	SO_2-emissions (g / kWh)	–	–	1.18	1.19	1.57	1.66

[1] The total figure for INPUT or OUTPUT including administration, storage, etc. is recorded and divided by the amount produced in the relevant time-period.
[2] Improved data collection resulted in some new values.
[3] Includes emissions from KUNERT's own burner systems and emissions arising from the production of electricity and district heat used by KUNERT.

46 |

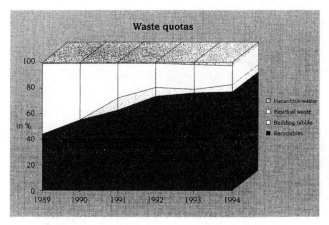

Waste quotas

□ Hazardous waste
■ Residual waste
□ Building rubble
■ Recyclables

Commentary

Efficient eco-controlling requires indicators which make it possible to compare the actual situation and the targets, to make comparisons over time with the values from previous years as well as comparisons between the other companies in the same branch. The validity of the absolute INPUT and OUTPUT figures recorded in the eco-balance may be affected by fluctuations in production and sales. With the help of the Institut für Management und Umwelt the KUNERT group of companies developed a system of performance indicators to make environmental trends and the eco-efficiency of the firm's activities clear using relative figures. It should be pointed out that these are gross figures and thus include energy consumption and waste production in places such as offices, the canteen and warehouses which are not directly affected by fluctuations in production.

A Production-specific ratios

In particular the production-specific ratios show how efficiently resources and energy have been used to manufacture the products because they present water and energy consumption as well as waste and emissions in relation to the amount produced in kg. In calculating these figures it is not the values of the OUTPUT balance account "1. Products" but the quantitites produced in the areas "knitting" and "dyeing" that are used. These are the two production areas using the most resources (yarns, dyes, chemicals, water/waste water) and energy (knitting, heating the dye bath to boiling point). The figures in the OUTPUT account "1. Products" cover by definition only the quantities that end up in the finished goods store, i.e. only finished goods and not the semi-finished products produced such as unfinished or dyed tights.

The figures clearly show that where production capacity is not fully exploited ecological efficiency in the use of resources and energy deteriorates. Eco-efficiency is best achieved when capacity is fully used because then the share of INPUTS and OUTPUTS in overall material and energy flows which does not directly contribute added value is reduced. First to be established were the specific NO_x, SO_2, CO_2 emissions. They include the emissions from KUNERT 's own burner systems and the emissions caused by the production of electricity and district heating that KUNERT buys elsewhere.

B . Energy and Waste ratios

Natural gas, which is more environment-friendly than fuel oil, accounts for an continually increasing share of the KUNERT group of companies' energy supply. The share of fuel oil in total energy consumption has continued to decline: in 1989 it was still 57.1 % but has in the meantime been brought down to 39.7 %. Owing to strong overall energy savings, the quota of fuel, which is declining in absolute terms, rose to 13.8 % in 1994. The comparison of waste quotas over several years brings the success of the KUNERT group in collecting and separating recyclables clearly to light. As a result, the residual waste quota fell from 55.1% in 1989 to only 14.8% today. At the same time, the proportion of recyclables which can be separated from the other

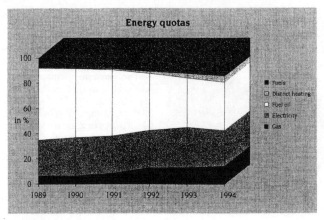

residual materials and recycled (profitably in part) has risen to 77 %. The building rubble quota does not indicate any particular development trend but rather reflects the strong variations in building activities from year to year. The sharp rise in the hazardous waste quota in 1994 is largely a result of disposal problems in the Burlington factory in Hungary: at the moment, large quantities of dye and chemical sludge are being produced because there is no suitable waste water treatment plant.

C. Material Ratios

The proportion of packaging in the product is in constant decline and is now 25.9%. Most of the pollution in the textile industry comes from the dyeing of fabrics and yarns. For this reason, one of the focusses of environmental management at KUNERT is on

reducing the proportion of dyes containing heavy metals. In this way, waste water pollution can already be avoided when dyes are being purchased (beginning of the pipe management). The evolution of the part of dyes containing heavy metals in total dye consumption should be made clearer by a new indicator. It shows that in 1994 almost 63 % of all dyes used contained no heavy metals, a 10 % rise on the previous year.

D. Emission Ratios

In the 1994 eco-balance CO_2, SO_2, NO_x emissions that result from the production of electricity and district heat used in KUNERT factories were recorded for the first time. The corresponding values for previous years were calculated retrospectively and the emission ratios were adjusted to take account of this. This explains the

big difference in the specific emission figures printed here and the figures published in earlier environmental reports which only took into account the emissions and energy consumption in KUNERT 's own burner systems. The jump in specific SO_2 emissions is a result of the inclusion of district heat: the Burlington factory in Hungary obtains district heat from a heat facility powered with heavy fuel oil.

Goals

- Further integration of the environmental performance evaluation into managerial decision-making.

Measures

- Extending the recording of performance indicators at factory level, e.g. waste quotas, energy quotas, production-specific indicators for each factory.
- Internal presentation and discussion of evironmental performance indicators as a means of setting objectives and as a management instrument.

Environmental Management and the EC Eco-Audit

It is expected that companies in Germany will be able to participate in the EC system for environmental management and the environmental audit (known as the Eco-audit or shortly EMAS Regulation) as from Autumn 1995. Companies that, on a voluntary basis, carry out an environmental audit, set up an environmental management system and inform the public by way of an environmental statement will, providing they meet all the requirements, receive a "certificate of participation" from an external expert. The company would then be able to use an official EC eco-audit logo on their letter heads and in non-product-specific advertising. The question is to what extent eco-controlling as practiced by KUNERT AG since 1990 already covers the requirements of the EC eco-audit.

The KUNERT eco-controlling model

Since 1990, KUNERT AG has had a group-wide, systematic eco-controlling system, which is continually developed and completed with new elements. Essentially, it covers the following elements which are relevant for participation in the EC eco-audit.

Company eco-balance

In an internal eco-balance the annual INPUT and OUTPUT of materials and energy (in kg and kWh) are systematically recorded as balance items, both for each individual factory and the group as a whole. In this way, the events in the company can be systematically checked for ecological weaknesses and dangers and comparisons can be made through significant indicators of performance. The data obtained makes it possible to target planning and to control and monitor material and energy flows within the company.

Environmental Report

The present environmental report which is published every year covers the following elements at group level:

- the environmental policy of the KUNERT group of companies,
- the company eco-balance,
- goals and measures for each individual balance item,
- environmental performance indicators,
- presentation of the environmental controlling system,
- information on priority themes.

The environmental report provides information for the public and also serves as an internal instrument for management and information in environmental controlling.

Eco-workgroups

The environment working group is a body that unites members from all factories and all staff levels in which current environmental protection problems in the company are discussed and solutions for these problems coordinated. Together with other small groups working on environmental priority projects, it does a great deal to ensure that environmental protection is perceived as a common responsibility throughout the company.

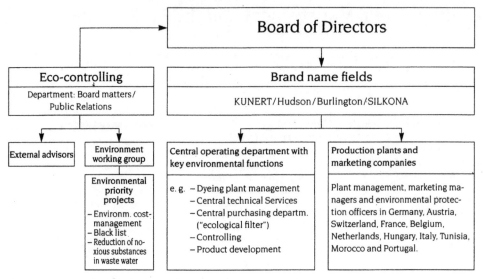

The company organisational structure of environmental management in the KUNERT group of companies.

Ecological Filter

The KUNERT group of companies has developed what is known as the "ecological filter" for purchasing. All dyes, chemicals and oils were recorded in a database and evaluated according to 18 ecological and human-toxicological characteristics. Undesirable substances were put on a "black list" (prohibition list) and substances that received continued authorisation on a "green list". The idea was to make it possible for the central purchasing department to filter out of the flood of incoming materials those raw, auxiliary and ancillary materials that are ecologically harmful. This is in keeping with the principle of "beginning of the pipe management", according to which environmental pollution should be prevented from the very beginning.

Environmental Cost Management

In the Mindelheim factory in 1994 and 1995 a pilot project on environmental cost management was carried out with the support of the German Foundation for the Environment. The aim was to investigate the costs arising from energy and material flows in order to uncover the cost-cutting potential of measures leading to both reduced costs and environmental pollution. To this end, actual costs, factors which push up costs and related environmental pollution aspects were studied in very comprehensive analyses.

50 |

Overlap – differences – measures

In the following diagram, the content of the two systems is compared.

Pilot Project EC Eco-audit at the KUNERT factory Mindelheim

In a pilot project at the Mindelheim factory, the following steps were carried out in order to prepare internally for participation in the EMAS-scheme and to also draw conclusions for other sites .

KUNERT Eco-controlling   EC-Eco-audit-Regulation

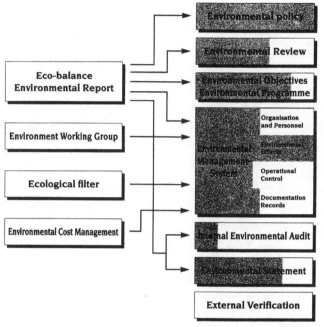

The shaded areas indicate the extent to which KUNERT Eco-controlling fulfills the requirements of the EC eco-audit regulation.

- With the help of internally-developed software the "initial environmental review" was carried out, sticking closely to the EC eco-audit regulation. Apart from monitoring the factory's level of environmental protection, it also checked compliance with the relevant environmental legislation (compliance audit).
- Environmental objectives and an environmental programme (goals and measures) were formulated specifically for Mindelheim as well as at group level.
- Some organisational details were clarified and training measures planned.
- Written work instructions in environmentally relevant areas were prepared.
- Environmental management documentation (handbook) specific to the site was produced.

KUNERT AG must decide whether participation in the EMAS-scheme with all the 11 locations is practicable. One argument in favour is that KUNERT AG, as a pioneer in environmental management and eco-auditing feels obliged to fulfill generally recognised European standards.

On the other hand, the benefit to be gained from additional external verification and EC statement of participation is fairly limited in comparison to the costs of preparation and external verification at all 11 sites.

Given that the budgetary resources and the conditions for verifica-

tion and registration were not in place by April 1995, KUNERT AG decided to carry out a pilot project in course of which all measures necessary for participation would be implemented on the Mindelheim site. On the basis of this experience the decision will be taken on whether to participate in the EMAS - scheme and to what extent.

The EC regulation places demands on the participating company, in terms of both materials/energy aspects and organisational aspects. The work done by KUNERT AG in the materials/energy area ("eco-balance") as a result of the eco-

controlling system established group-wide in 1990 and the pilot project "Environmental Cost Management" in Mindelheim goes far beyond the corresponding requirements in the audit regulation. Only on the organisational side is there a need for some additional measures.

The materials/energy part of the EC eco-audit

Around 400 employees work at the factory in Mindelheim. It is the high-tech centre of the group of companies owing to its highly modern plant and equipment. With the exception of knitting, all stages in the production of tights are executed there with partial international division of labour with other factories. Mindelheim, however, is purely a production plant: the level of administration is minimal and is normally dealt with in Immenstadt.

The production of a factory-specific production balance proved more complicated than expected because of the links throughout the group. In some cases data could only be obtained by measurements with representative reference weights and extrapolation.

INPUT 1993				OUTPUT 1993	
1.	**Circulating goods (kg)**	**2,191,381**	**1.**	**Products (kg)**	**1,954,244**
1.1.	Raw materials	–	1.1	Hosiery	1,100,066
1.2.	Semi-finished/		1.2.	Outer wear	–
	finished goods	1,133,256	1.3.	Transport packaging	268,005
1.3.	Auxiliary materials	950,116	1.4	Product packaging	586,173
1.3.1.	Dyes	26,110	**2.**	**Solid Waste (kg)**	**215,454**
1.3.2.	Chemicals	230,920	2.1.	Hazardous	
1.3.3.	Product packaging	691,740		waste	negligible
1.3.4.	Product additions	1,346	2.2.	Recyclables	155,774
1.4.	Ancillary materials	108,009	2.3.	Residual waste	59,680
1.4.1.	Oils/fats	586	**3.**	**Waste heat (kWh)**	**12,226,744**
1.4.2.	Transport packaging	107,423	3.1.	Waste heat: water	4,512,672
2.	**Energy (kWh)**	**12,226,744**	3.2.	Waste heat: air	7,714,072
2.1.	Gas	8,015,974	**4.**	**Waste water (kg)**	**49,322,400**
2.2.	Electricity	2,649,340		Water	49,322,400
2.3.	Fuel oil: extra light	1,561,430		Dyes	5,773
3.	**Water (kg)**	**61,653,000**		Chemicals	201,210
3.1.	Tap water	61,653,000	**5.**	**Air emissions (kg)**	**14,342,300**
3.2.	Raw water	–		NO_x	2,002
4.	Air (kg)	not recorded		SO_2	531
				CO_2	2,009,167
				Water vapour	12,330,600
		63,844,381			**66,041,381**

The site specific production balance for the KUNERT plant in Mindelheim.

52 |

The factory is not supplied with raw materials but exclusively semi-finished and finished goods (e.g. unfinished tights from the knitting factory in Immenstadt or goods for packaging). Water accounts for the largest part of INPUT. This illustrates the great environmental importance of the areas "water/waste water" in textile finishing.

Indicators of performance

A comparison of the Mindelheim factory's indicators of performance with those of the group as a whole clearly shows that Mindelheim is an above-average factory in environmental terms. Water and energy consumption per kilogramme OUTPUT of products is comparatively favourable even if comparisons between different stages in production have their limits.

Material efficiency indicates what percentage of the raw, auxiliary and ancillary materials used go into the product. The ratios for dyes and chemicals indicate what proportion of these materials go into the product. These ratios which were calculated only for the Mindelheim factory, make clear that only about 13 % of the chemicals (fabric softeners, etc.) and 78 %

of dyes go into the product. The rest leaves the factory in the waste water and is dealt with in the local authority's water treatment plant.

The very low values for specific air emissions (emissions per kWh) are due to the high proportion of natural gas in the energy INPUT. As a result, emissions of sulphur dioxide are way below average.

On the basis of the results of the eco-balance and of the pilot project on environmental cost management, the following measures were worked out:

Reduction of waste water quantities and the level of noxious substances in waste water:
- Pretreatment of the waste water in a neutralisation plant and exact dosing techniques reduced the input of flocculent substances by approx. two-thirds.
- Waste water is separated into a double pipe system according to its level of pollution and its temperature, thus allowing for heat recovery.
- As part of a thesis, study was undertaken into whether dyeing in a standing bath was possible for polyamide and polyurethane. This makes it possible to considerably reduce the input of water, dyes and chemicals since the waste water bath is reused for dyeing or finishing. Tests in the laboratory proved successful.
- In a programme supported by the Federal Ministry for Research and Technology over the next two years the installation of a nanofiltration system with membrane technology will be tested.

		MINDELHEIM SITE 1993	KUNERT AG 1993
Production-specific ratios			
Water consumption / OUTPUT product	l / kg	31,5	55,4
Energy / OUTPUT product	kWh / kg	6,3	16,5
Waste / OUTPUT product	kg / kg	0,11	0,28
Material ratios			
Packaging ratio	%	30,0	29,3
Material efficiency	%	89	75
Dye efficiency[2]	%	78	–
Chemicals efficiency[2]	%	13	–
Waste ratios			
Recyclables quota	%	72	76
Residual waste quota	%	28	19
Emissions quota[1]			
CO_2-emissions	g / kWh	164	252,5
NO_x-emissions	g / kWh	0,16	0,32
SO_2-emissions	g / kWh	0,04	1,68

[1] Only KUNERT burner systems.
[2] Recorded at factory level only.

|53

Reduction of production rejects:
- Errors in the production process result in rejects (waste) which are undesirable both from the ecological and economic point of view. By installing photosensors on the sewing machines, stepping up quality control in the early production stages, reducing the variety of articles and holding regular discussions on quality, the level of rejects was brought down in the Mindelheim factory. Since some measures have not yet been completed, the process of quantifying the improvements can only start in 1996.

The organisational part of the eco-audit

As regards organisation and form, the eco-audit regulation has certain requirements concerning the setting up of an environmental management system. In order to fulfill those requirements the following measures were developed:
- Using software specially designed for the purpose,the environmental review was carried out, sticking closely to the EC eco-audit regulation. Apart from the reviewing environmental protection performance in the company it also checked compliance with the relevant environmental legislation (compliance audit).
- An environmental programme (goals and measures) was formulated specifically for the Mindelheim site in addition to the group goals.
- A handbook was produced for the Mindelheim factory that fulfills the EC regulation's requirement for documentation on the environmental management system.
- A site-specific environmental statement was drafted.
- In the long term, the goal is to develop the information system further in order to integrate and relate environmental data to cost accounting. Care will be taken to cover all relevant material flows (products, outgoing residual material flows and internal cyclical work e.g. reworking). In this way, cost-cutting potential can be consistently exploited through environmental management measures.

Pilot Project Conclusion

KUNERT AG welcomes the EC eco-audit regulation. The regulation forces the issue of industry's responsibility and initiates a process of continuous improvement of environmental protection in business. It presents a framework for environmental management systems without specifying exactly how such a system should be set up. In this way room is left for innovation and for practice-related solutions individual to the company. There is however a danger of a tendency to bureaucratize environmental management. If KUNERT AG decides to participate in the EC system with all ist 11 sites it would entail producing eleven handbooks and eleven environmental statements every three years as well as paying eleven times verification fees for external verifiers. An eco-controlling system integrated into the management – such as KUNERT has implemented until now – represents a "slimmer" alternative to the EC eco-audit with its costly documentation and external verification. Nonetheless, KUNERT AG will implement the internal measures required for participation of other sites in the EC-scheme up to preparing the environmental statement. Whether or not all locations actually go through verification by an environmental verifier will depend on whether the related fees are set at a level that makes financial sense for industrial firms.

54 |

Results of the pilot project "Environmental Cost Management"

Each kilogramme of "solid waste", each cubic metre of "waste water" and each kilowatt-hour of "waste heat" not only pollutes the environment but also considerably reduces company earnings. The company pays several times for these unused material and energy flows:

1. in purchasing for raw, auxiliary and ancillary materials,
2. in production for machine hours, productive wages, energy, transport, storage, etc. and,
3. in disposal of solid waste, waste water and air emissions.

Also, if no noxious substances are bought on the INPUT side they do not have to be disposed of at high cost later. The opportunities for environmental management in the future lie in a new approach: moving away from "end of the pipe" towards "beginning of the pipe" thinking. Purchasing plays a key role here as an economic and ecological filter.
These key realizations within KUNERT environmental management were the starting point for a one-year "Pilot Project Environmental Cost Management" completed in May 1995. KIENBAUM-Unternehmensberatung, Berlin, the Institut fur Management und Umwelt, Augsburg and KUNERT AG worked together on a study of the KUNERT factory in Mindelheim. The aim of the one-year project was to systematically develop unexploited cost-cutting potential and introduce measures to reduce costs.

Thanks to the exemplary nature of the project and the prospect of its results being widely transferable to other companies, it was supported by the German Federal Foundation for the Environment.

The objective of the project was to develop new methods of environmental cost management, going beyond the pragmatic approaches previously adopted, which would;

- reduce solid waste, waste water and energy consumption through integrated environmental protection and reduce the factory's costs.
The main focus here was on optimizing the flows of energy and materials, from INPUT through all production stages to OUTPUT.
- set up an environmental cost management system in the KUNERT group of companies which would allow all significant opportunities for environmental protection and cost-cutting to be systematically registered and exploited and to continue this in the future.

In the KUNERT factory in Mindelheim, 400 people are employed mainly in producing, dyeing, forming and packing fine tights. The production process is energy and waste water-intensive. In addition, large quantities of the packaging end up as waste. On the other hand, air emissions are low.

1. Developing Material Flow Transparency

The first step was to achieve transparency in the material flows. For every stage in the production process, materials and energy flows were systematically recorded according to the INPUT-OUTPUT system.
This work was done in close co-operation with both business management and technical sides in the factory and involved all levels of the hierarchy from group manager to factory manager. This ensures that the results are sound, widely accepted and lead to an active commitment to the environment throughout the company's departments. The environmentally harmful flows of energy and materials at the Mindelheim factory currently amount on a yearly basis (1993) to 215,454 kg solid waste, 48,336 m^3 waste water and 7,714,072 kWh air emissions. Air pollution amounts to 531 kg SO_2, 2,002 NO_x and approx. 2 mill. kg CO_2. The waste water is polluted by 206,395 kg of dyes and chemicals. Taking into account the waste water loading (excluding the water part) it emerges that around 47 % of the raw, auxiliary and ancillary materials go into the product, 35 % into the product packaging and 18 % leave the factory as waste material or waste water.

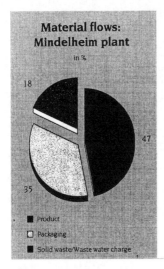

**Material flows:
Mindelheim plant**

in %

18

47

35

■ Product
□ Packaging
■ Solid waste/Waste water charge

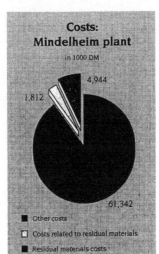

**Costs:
Mindelheim plant**

in 1000 DM

4,944

1,812

61,342

■ Other costs
□ Costs related to residual materials
■ Residual materials costs

3. Developing Cost-cutting Measures

In Autumn 1994, the cost and quantity analyses were presented to the Board of Directors and a programme of measures to develop cost-cutting potential was proposed.

Because the budget for the project was limited both financially and temporally not all the measures could be tackled. Three areas were chosen in which measures to simultaneously reduce costs and pollution were to be implemented. As the most cost-intensive area, priority was given to the largest cost potential "rejects and reworking". Two workgroups were set up to deal with this area. The first group had the task of improving the data system for production so as to ensure long-lasting transparency of the material flows. The second group had the task of improving the quality of articles in all production stages from product development to packaging in order to reduce the reject rate and increase the number of articles in the highest quality grade.

A third group dealt with the residual material cost potential "waste water" which was chosen as a second cost-intensive area.

2. Allocating the Costs

The next step was to allocate costs to the material and energy flows. In the Mindelheim factory in the reference year 1993, total costs were of the order of DM 68 million. Of that, DM 4.94 million or 7.25 %, were non-value-adding costs (related to "residual materials" in solid waste, waste water, air emissions, etc.). Added to that were costs related to residual materials of the order of DM 1.8 million.

For purposes of comparison: the average proportion of residual material costs in German industry is between 5 % and 15 %.

The actual disposal costs only accounted for a tiny part of the residual materials costs established at the Mindelheim factory. The dominant cost factor was not the disposal fees but the purchasing cost of the residual materials. This means that environment-friendly avoidance of residual materials is considerably more profitable than previously thought in industry.

In the Mindelheim factory, rejects – that is tights which end up in the waste basket during production because of quality defects – represent the largest block of costs among the residual materials. For this sub-area alone "rejects and reworking" amounted to total costs of DM 1.2 million. Around DM 1 million of this was the purchasing costs for yarns, dyes and chemicals.

56|

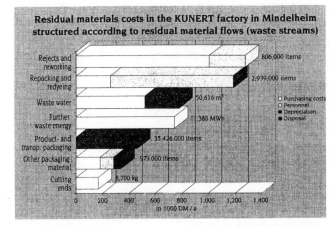

Residual materials costs in the KUNERT factory in Mindelheim structured according to residual material flows (waste streams)

Conclusion

Going on the experience of the project participants, there is a cost-cutting potential of 5 % to 15 % on total costs for industrial firms contained in the costs of non-value-adding waste streams. Using environmental cost management companies are certain of saving 1 to 2 % of total costs. This represents millions for firms and billions for the national economy. The dominating cost factor in environmentally harmful residual materials is not the cost of disposal but the purchasing value. These non-value-adding costs are scarcely, or only partially, made clear in current data-processing programmes used in business administration and accounting – certainly not, in any case, with quantities and costs allocated to them for each stage in production.

This cost-cutting potential cannot be developed on an ad-hoc basis. Environmental cost management requires an interdisciplinary approach. All departments and the employees responsible from the most diverse levels of the hierarchy must be involved in the collection of data and the development of measures. The subsequent adjustment phase lasts one to three years and has to compete with other priorities in the company.

By the end of April 1995, a programme of measures had been worked out and partially implemented bringing savings of DM 800,000. The newly developed environmental cost management system was integrated into the existing company structure: into production, controlling, quality management, and environmental management. The cost-cutting potentials in other areas not yet dealt with will be developed over the coming years. Environmental Cost Management will be applied to other factories in the KUNERT group of companies where it proves worthwhile and effective.

The goal is to realize 20 % of the environmental cost-cutting potential, i. e. 1 to 2 % of total costs in the Mindelheim factory and in other factories in the KUNERT group of companies. This represents millions of Deutschmarks in savings and at the same time a reduction in environmental pollution.

Environmental cost-cutting measures that have proved their worth in one factory can be transferred to other factory locations. The same applies as generally applies for the eco-balance: if all German companies were to tackle this cost-cutting potential through effective environmental cost management it would be the greatest ever boost for investment into the environment in the German economy.

After the results of the pilot project can any doubt remain about whether environmental protection according to economic principles is practicable for firms? Combining economics and ecology according to market economy principles for the benefit of our economy is possible.

Developing measures in interdepartmental working groups

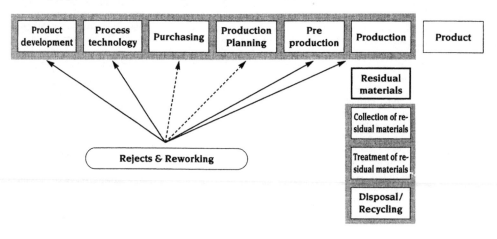

Product Tree Analysis

The internal product balance of a pair of "smooth and soft" fine tights laid the foundation in 1993 for life-cycle environmental product assesssment using the product tree analysis. The manufacturing process of one of the main products of the KUNERT group of companies was traced throughout its internal production life cycle, and the ingoing and outgoing material and energy flows balanced against each other throughout all processing stages.

As a result of the product balance for "worsted yarn" by the Augsburger Kammgarnspinnerei AG and another for a dye by Ciba-Geigy GmbH study had been done into the preliminary phases of tights production. The product balance for the main raw material used by KUNERT AG, nylon (polyamide 6.6.), carried out by Textilwerke Deggendorf (TWD) has now added a further building block to comprehensive assessment of the environmental impact throughout the life cycle of a pair of "smooth and soft" fine tights.

Product Balance for 1000 kg Polyamide

The following product balance gives information about the material and energy flows involved in producing 1000 kg of polyamide grey yarn, the most important raw material in the KUNERT group of companies. This amount represents the primary raw material for approx. 50,000 pairs of "smooth and soft" tights which is the basic article studied (see Environmental Report 1993).

When 1000 kg of polyamide(6.6) grey yarn is produced there is approx. 42 kg (4.2 %) of waste, mainly yarn ends and spinning cake which are produced when the raw material granulates are spun. Of the preparatives needed for the spinning process, 85 % remain on the grey yarn and are emitted during the subsequent phases (texturing, knitting, forming and dyeing). The remaining 0.9 kg (15 %) is lost during production – 6 % as fluid loss (during spraying) and 0.3 kg as vapour in air emissions. The 36.67 kg of spinning bobbins, the main ancillary material used, does not become waste until the texturing process which follows. The product and transport packaging amounts to between 11.2 % and 17.2 % of total weight depending on the size of the spool.
In order to manufacture 1000 pairs of "smooth and soft" tights 80 % polyamide yarn is used as the main raw material or 18.66 kg of the amount balanced above. It is

INPUT		OUTPUT	
1. Raw material		**1. Products**	
Granulates	1036.5 kg	1.1 Grey yarn PA 6.6.	994.8 kg
2. Auxiliary materials		1.2 Spinning preparatives	5.2 kg
Spinning preparatives	6.1 kg	**2. Auxiliary materials**	—
3. Ancillary materials		**3. Ancillary materials**	36.67 kg
3.1 Spinning bobbins	36.67 kg	**4. Waste**	
3.2 Nozzle parts	0.07 kg	4.1 Yarn ends / spinning cake	41.7 kg
3.3 Oils and separating agents	0.41 kg	4.2 Waste chips;	
3.4 Nitrogen	0.334 m³	Steel / Aluminium scrap	0.07 kg
4. Energy		4.3 Waste oil	0.1 kg
(Engines, heating devices,		4.4 Spinning preparatives	0.6 kg
air-conditioning unit)	1,837 kWh	**5. Waste heat**	1,837 kWh
5. Water(1 kg = 1 l)	620 kg	Noise (winding)	90 dB
6. Air		**6. Waste water** (1 kg = 1 l)	620 kg
Compressed air	2,533.4m³	**7. Air emissions**	
		7.1 Oil and other	
		preparatives	0.61 kg
		7.2 Air	2,533.4 m³
		7.3 Nitrogen	0.334 m³
Materials in total	**1,700 kg**	**Materials in total**	**1,700 kg**
Energy in total	**1,837 kWh**	**Energy in total**	**1,837 kWh**

assumed here that the polyamide yarn used for the gusset which comes from a different grey-yarn manufacturer has the same production structure as the TWD-produced polyamide yarn used for the leg section. The texturing and making-up of the finished yarn is not expressed in figures in the table above because it has already been included as texturing in the former KUNERT factory in Berlin in the previous balance which has been used as a basis.

Thus, specific energy consumption of 34.3 kWh (= 1837 kWh / 1000 kg * 18.66 kg) from the manufacture of the grey yarn polyamide can be added to internal energy consumption of 482 kWh from the internal balance. Grey yarn manufacture thus represents, from an energy point of view, approx. 7 % of consumption in the entire manufacturing process right up to the finished pair of tights. The energy content of the basic raw material, polyamide-granulates (oil-based) has not yet been taken into account here. Recalculated for the reference amount of 1000 pairs of "smooth and soft" tights an additional 0.8 kg of production waste must be added, about 10 % of which is waste at KUNERT. Specific water consumption on the other hand, an extra 11 litres per 1000 pairs, is quite low compared to KUNERT 's internal water consumption (mainly for dyeing and forming) of 4000 cubic metres.

Ways of bringing about improvement in cooperation with the suppliers (yarn) and the manufacturers (fine tights) becomes clear in the analysis of product and transport packaging: it was established that if big 4.2 kg spools are used for making up instead of the smaller 2.2 kg spools 35 % of the packaging material can be spared.

Goals

- In-depth analysis of the sub-balances still missing in the product life-cycle – from the manufacture of the raw material through retailing and on to use and disposal by the end consumer.

Measures

- Inclusion of transport and important preliminary and subsequent phases in the internal product balances.
- Adherence to the priority guideline for packaging (PP-cling-wrap, spool card, cover sheet).
- Development of a methodology for including the post-factory phases in the product life cycle (retailing, use, disposal).

The KUNERT Group of Companies

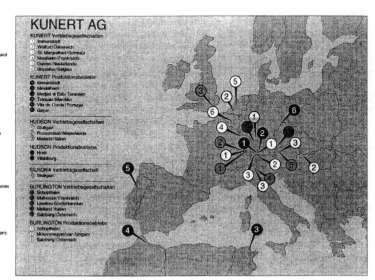

KUNERT sales companies
1 Immenstadt
2 Wolfurt/Austria
3 St. Margarethen/Switzerland
4 Molsheim/France
5 Duiven/Netherlands
6 Bruxelles/Belgium
KUNERT factories
1 Immenstadt
2 Mindelheim
3 Medjez el Bab/Tunesia
4 Tetouan/Morocco
5 Vila do Conde/Portugal
6 Geyer

HUDSON sales companies
1 Stuttgart
2 Roosendaal/Netherlands
3 Milan/Italy
HUDSON factories
1 Horb
2 Vilsbiburg

SILKONA sales companies
1 Stuttgart

BURLINGTON sales companies
1 Schopfheim
2 Mulhouse/France
3 London/Great Britain
4 Milan/Italy
5 Salzburg/Austria
BURLINGTON factories
1 Schopfheim
2 Mosonmagyaróvár/Hungary
3 Salzburg/Austria

The KUNERT AG is a customer-oriented hosiery company. The brand names and their quality form the main focus of its sales policy. Four brand names in controlled competition with each other – KUNERT , HUDSON, BURLINGTON and SILKONA – operate on a Europe-wide basis.

Besides hosiery, outer garments are also marketed. Private-label products for hosiery round off the range of branded products.

The manufacturing stages in production are carried out in accordance with the principle of international division of labour, in Central Europe if they are decisive for quality and capital-intensive, and in cheaper countries if they are wage-intensive.

All production, all human action is linked to a greater or lesser extent, to adverse effects on the environment. While giving the priority to the market, KUNERT AG wishes to produce with as little harm as possible to the environment and combine economy and ecology.

KUNERT AG would like to be fair to its staff, customers, shareholders, suppliers and all those in contact with KUNERT AG, and would like to gain their sympathy.

Conclusion

Prof. Dr. Bernd Wagner, University of Augsburg

In publishing the current report KUNERT AG is presenting its sixth consolidated group eco-balance. The eco-balance instrument is firmly established in the company and has become a permanent component of the management process. This could only happen in so far as the concept, apart from bringing ecological success, also brought economic success. In some cases these successes can be measured and proven, for example the reduction in consumption of raw materials, energy, water or in the reduction in the amounts of packaging or waste. In some cases, however, it is difficult to express the successes in figures, e.g. the beneficial effect for the company image or the increase in employee motivation. Other successes which cannot really be measured are the preventive kind, e.g. when a firm is able to adapt without any problems to new external requirements such as the Commodities Regulation whereas in other companies without environmental management, major restructuring of production is necessary.

Although at the beginning, KUNERT AG was the lone pioneer, a wide movement has now started in Germany and beyond its borders. There is hardly a major company in Germany to be found that does not publish an environmental report. The methodology of the internal eco-balance, i. e. the INPUT-OUTPUT analysis, has been widely adopted as a means of structuring and presenting environmental reports. Nonetheless, the methodology of the internal eco-balance is still at the dynamic development stage (the development of the commercial balance has still not been not finalized after decades of work). The first methodological recommendations to introduce some standardization are however being developed, e.g. for example by the Umweltbundesamt (Federal Environmental Agency) in its new "Eco-controlling" handbook or by the various ministries for the environment (e.g.in the states of Baden-Württemberg and Bavaria) with their environmental management guidelines.

In its comparison of 100 environmental reports world-wide, the 1994 UNEP study made particular mention of the KUNERT AG eco-balance INPUT-OUTPUT analysis. The association for environmental management in banks, savings societies and insurance firms has just presented a first draft of a standardized accounts framework for an eco-balance for service industries.

Continuous further development of the methodology will make it more efficient, not only for internal management but also for inter-firm comparisons - "benchmarking". On account of its wide-ranging previous experience, the KUNERT group of companies is still a significant participant in this process and continues to spearhead some individual development lines. Included in these is the further improvement of the concept of environmental cost management. Expressing environmentally relevant facts – levels of consumption or savings for example – not only as physical amounts but also economically speaking as costs is the key to future integration of environmental management into business policy. The development of environmental performance indicators is also likely to provide considerable impetus to business management, as it is shown in the corresponding chapter in this report.

However, one of the preconditions in order to be able to establish and use these indicators effectively is an eco-balance database. In many firms this does not yet exist.

Environmental reporting is also receiving another Europe-wide push boost through the EC eco-audit regulation. The regulation does not specifically demand an eco-balance drawn up according to the method presented above. However, in a somewhat unsystematic way, scattered throughout the text of the regulation, it asks for information on the majority of the balance items. It has proved helpful, not only in KUNERT AG, to offset the lack of structure in the regulation by using the systematic eco-balance approach. Using the eco-balance the regulation, which is generally criticised for being unclear and over complex, becomes easier to manage and more systematic. This helps those dealing with the regulation within the firm and also makes for easier inter-firm comparisons. The eco-balance facilitates access to the unstructured regulation text, as well as to complex environmentally relevant situations in the firm. It provides a system for stucturing both the environmental report and the EC regulation's environmental statement.

[16]

Environmental cost accounting and auditing

Peter Letmathe
Assistant Professor, Ruhr-Uni Bochum, Bochum, Germany
Roger K. Doost
Professor, School of Accountancy, Clemson University, Clemson,
South Carolina, USA

Keywords
Environmental impact,
Sustainable development,
Hazardous materials,
Environmental audit, Law, Waste

Abstract
An environmental cost accounting
system is a flow- and decision-
oriented extension of traditional
cost accounting systems. It is
based on cause-and-effect
analysis which helps to assign the
costs of environmental impacts
correctly to their perpetrators.
This article attempts to
demonstrate how to use an
environmental cost accounting
system for internal and external
audits and performance
improvements. The generated
information is appropriate to see if
objectives and targets are
achieved. High amounts of
environmental impacts point to
inefficiencies in the production
area. Their elimination can help
accomplish both ecological and
business goals of a company.

Introduction

The currently high consumption of goods and services falls short of the vital necessity for sustainable development. West European countries seem to be further ahead with regard to the environmental matters as compared to the USA. For example, the German Federal Environmental Agency (1997) emphasizes the following alarming trends:
- Increase in mean global air temperatures by 0.3 to 0.6"C since the end of the nineteenth century.
- Sea level rise of between 10-25 centimeters over the last 100 years.
- Depletion of the stratospheric ozone layer.
- Accelerating species extinction.
- Continued erosion and rapid loss of fertile soil.
- Pollution and overfishing of the seas.
- Gradual over-taxation of the earth system through anthropogenic loads.
- A change of the direction of the Gulf Stream which can result in chaos of the whole world climate.

The total estimated damage caused to the natural environment in one day according to the German Federal Environmental Agency (1997) is given by:
- the destruction of 55,000 hectares of tropical forest;
- the reduction of arable land by 20,000 hectares;
- the extinction of 100 to 200 species;
- emission of 60 million tons of carbon dioxide into the atmosphere.

Extension of traditional cost accounting systems to account for environmental impacts and their costs started towards the end of the 1970s in Germany. In 1979, two guidelines of the Bundesverband der Deutschen Industrie (1979) and of the Verein Deutscher Ingenieure

(1979) were published which included rules on how to calculate the business costs of environmental protection. These guidelines helped companies to comply with their reporting requirements for public statistics in Germany. But this approach was not decision-oriented and, therefore, not suitable for systematic environmental management. Hence, many companies tried to achieve legal compliance and to satisfy the interests of their stakeholders mostly through self-designed management methods.

During the 1980s and 1990s, the German government introduced a number of new regulations in the environmental area. As a result, the legal compliance costs for waste water purification and for filtering emissions increased substantially. Further, the costs of many undesired byproducts such as hazardous waste and waste water increased in many cases by several hundred percentage points. This development motivated many companies to look closer at the costs of their output flows, and many case studies about cost reduction through environmental protection were published. Gege (1997), who is a representative of an environmentally-oriented association of enterprises (BAUM), estimated in 1997 that companies could reduce by 5 per cent their total costs with a decision-oriented environmental management system. These systems should include reliable data about the costs of material and energy. Gege's book contains about 1,000 examples on how companies achieved cost reduction through environmental protection. Klassen and McLaughlin (1996) see a significant impact of environmental management on firm performance. As key advantages, they mention cost reduction because of technological changes and reduced material and energy consumption. Eco-labeling of products can result in a substantial gain in the marketplace.

Letmathe (1998) provides more systematic environmental cost accounting approaches,

Managerial Auditing Journal
15/8 [2000] 424–430
© MCB University Press
[ISSN 0268-6902]

The current issue and full text archive of this journal is available at
http://www.emerald-library.com

Peter Letmathe and
Roger K. Doost
*Environmental cost
accounting and auditing*

Managerial Auditing Journal
15/8 [2000] 424–430

which were developed in this decade. He focuses not only on the correct accounting for the costs of environmental protection but also considers the costs of environmental-related flows of materials and energy. The overall goal is to accomplish both business goals and improvements in the area of environmental protection (see Hansen and Mowen, 1999, ch. 12).

The flow- and decision-oriented perspective of environmental cost accounting supplements the more process-oriented way of thinking of most companies. This is especially advantageous if costs of materials, processes, and products have an impact in other areas, e.g. cost of waste disposal and spoilage. Environmental cost accounting shows the real costs of inputs and the business processes and ensures cost-efficient legal compliance. In addition, the results can be applied in other areas, e.g. for measuring quality and service costs.

Environmental audits examine the whole environmental management system. The main goals are to check legal compliance and to find inefficiencies which can reduce both the amount of environmental impacts and cost. An appropriate information base does not only decrease the necessary efforts to carry out the audit, it improves the results of the audits as well. This paper shows how an environmental cost accounting system works and how it can improve the results of performance-oriented audits.

Purpose of environmental cost accounting

An environmental cost accounting system is a flow-oriented cost accounting system which is based on a systematic cause-and-effect analysis. Especially output-related costs, e.g. for emissions, waste disposal and waste water are assigned correctly to the inputs which cause them. In traditional cost accounting systems, these costs are treated like other overhead costs and allocated arbitrarily. For example, emissions, waste disposal and waste water costs may be accumulated and prorated arbitrarily among the various cost centers regardless of which ones caused those costs to occur in the first place. This procedure does not include any incentives for the cost centers to reduce environmental impacts and their costs. Ansari *et al.* (1997) argue that the correct assignment of environmental costs to their perpetrators can help reduce costs in other areas too. A high amount of waste is very often a sign of inefficiencies in business processes. For example, spoiled production

not only increases costs of waste disposal, it also leads to higher costs of manufacturing because of additional material, labor, and overhead which goes to spoiled goods.

Environmental costing accounting contributes to an internal pricing system which evaluates inputs, processes and products with their real costs. This procedure creates both a decision-oriented information base for the environmental management system and for planning, control and supervision of material and energy flows. Therefore, environmental cost accounting is an appropriate instrument to ensure legal compliance with lower costs. It integrates environmental aspects in all areas of planning which use cost data automatically. Besides, environmental data improve the understanding of the business processes. For example, companies which have data about output flows are often surprised about the volume of their waste flows and the costs which are related to them. This information can help find measures and change the attitude of the organization to environmental protection (see Ansari *et al.*, 1997).

To achieve this, it is necessary to extend the existing cost accounting system. But management will only agree with such an extension if benefits of the additional information are higher than the costs to get them. Hence, the integration of the traditional and the environmental cost accounting systems must be justified. Opportunities to extend and adjust the system to meet changing business requirements facilitate the decision to introduce such a system. To run such a system, it is not necessary that the cost area managers be very knowledgeable about cause-and-effect of environmental costs. The internal prices, which include costs of environmental impacts, are the main incentives to reduce environmentally-related costs.

The systematic consideration of the environmental impacts also makes sense for organizations with a defensive environmental strategy. Even if an organization does not have the explicit goal of protecting the environment and only reacts according to the environmental regulations, there is considerable potential for more success in achieving the traditional company objectives such as, maximizing profits or higher level of market share.

Structure of an environmental cost accounting system

To identify and to assign environmental costs correctly, the complex cause and effect of

Peter Letmathe and
Roger K. Doost
*Environmental cost
accounting and auditing*

Managerial Auditing Journal
15/8 [2000] 424–430

environmental impacts should be considered. The following approach emphasizes the task of cost accounting to deliver information for planning, control and supervision of business processes. Figure 1 shows the structure of this environmental cost accounting system.

Only if flows of material and energy are recorded and evaluated with their realistic costs, environmental costing can help control these flows in an appropriate way. To achieve this target, five steps which are partly carried out simultaneously are required:

1 At first, the EMS-group has to identify environmental impacts of its organization. This is also one of the requirements of the ISO 14001 standard. Normally, most of the impacts are related to materials including storage, production, and distribution. The cause and the kind of environmental impacts should be documented. In this step, the EMS-group has to decide which of the environmental impacts are of high or low significance. Only the high-significance impacts will be considered and evaluated in an environmental cost accounting system.

2 The next step is to figure out which flows of material and energy are causing the significant environmental impacts. If possible, the impact of one item of a material or energy source should be measured. A single material can cause different environmental impacts. For example, chlorofluorocarbons contribute to the greenhouse effect and to the depletion of the ozone layer.

3 To be able to calculate environmental costs, the quantities of material and energy have to be determined. For the purpose of planning, it is useful to implement environmental bills of materials and energy and to assign them systematically to inputs, processes and products. To control the flow of material and energy, their actual volume can be compared with the standard quantities. This procedure is not only appropriate to reduce environmental impacts, inefficiencies which lead to higher cost and/or quality problems can also be avoided.

4 After accounting for their quantities, the flow of material and energy should be evaluated with their realistic costs. Only a realistic assignment can prevent that environmental cost be underestimated

Figure 1
The concept of an environmental cost accounting system

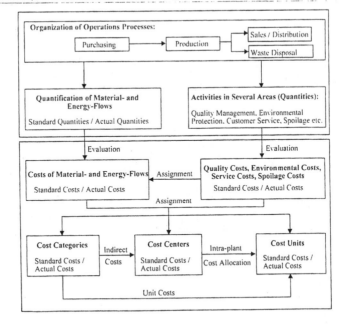

Peter Letmathe and
Roger K. Doost
*Environmental cost
accounting and auditing*

Managerial Auditing Journal
15/8 [2000] 424–430

systematically. Besides the purchase cost, other costs may also be relevant. Examples are costs for the treatment and logistical handling of purchased goods or waste.

5 Finally, the environmental costs have to be assigned correctly to their causing objects like input, processes and products. This will be carried out according to the bills of material and energy which were mentioned in step 3. Internal prices are the result of adding all cost components of a single material and energy sources. These internal prices can be used for planning and control of inputs, processes, products and environmental impacts.

Bills of environmental impacts
All environmental impacts can be traced back to flows of material and energy. To assign them correctly to their perpetrators three different kinds of environmental impacts can be distinguished:

1 Input-related environmental impacts are directly caused by the use of an input, like the carbon dioxide emissions as the result of burning coal, oil or other fossil energy sources. Input-related environmental impacts are independent of the process in which the input is inserted.

2 Process-caused environmental impacts cannot be assigned to a single input. They are a consequence of carrying out a specific process. They are caused by a combination of inputs, like emission which depends on the temperature of a process.

3 Product-caused environmental impacts can be traced back to a product but not to a single input or process. An example is the energy use during the consumption phase or the waste after the product's use.

To investigate the flows of materials and energy, these information sources may be of interest:
• The manufacturer of the machine which is needed to carry out the production process knows the materials and energy sources which are required to run it. Additionally, he/she can give details about technological efficiency and the spoilage rate. Customers, who already work with this technology, can provide further information.
• The quality manager knows about the existing and potential sources of quality problems. Statistical quality control provides information about the optimum specification of materials and other process parameters to meet the quality standards of the organization.

• Scientific literature gives further details about the productivity and specific risks of a production technology. Such information is extremely valuable if an organization wants to introduce a technologically new process.
• The environmental management gathers data about environmental impacts of the organization. Its experience and knowledge can contribute to the estimation of material and energy flows and the process risks as well.
• Communication with the organization's stakeholders can reduce conflict of interests. Ideally, members of the stakeholder groups have knowledge which can lead to a more environmentally friendly and cost efficient production.

As a result, bills of materials and energy can be generated. This information can then be used to plan environmental impacts in advance and to control the level of impacts during the production phase. If there are significant differences between the standard and actual environmental impacts, then corrective action should be taken.

Bill of environmental impacts of an input
The bill of environmental impacts of an input (see Figure 2) includes all environmental impacts which can be traced back to a single material or energy source. This means that the amount of environmental impact does not depend on the process in which the input is used. In this step, all the input-related environmental impacts have to be assigned to the input which caused them.

Bill of environmental impacts of a process
The bill of environmental impacts of a process (see Figure 3) contains environmental impacts which are caused if a process is carried out. The total environmental impacts of a process are the sum of both the direct process-related and the input-related environmental impacts. The direct process-related environmental impacts cannot be assigned to a single input. The input-related environmental impacts can be calculated through the multiplication of input-coefficients of the process with the

Figure 2
Bill of environmental impacts of an input

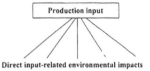

Direct input-related environmental impacts

Peter Letmathe and
Roger K. Doost
*Environmental cost
accounting and auditing*

Managerial Auditing Journal
15/8 [2000] 424–430

input-related environmental impacts per unit of the considered input. The input-related environmental impacts are given by the bills of environmental impacts of the inputs.

Bill of environmental impacts of a product

With the bill of environmental impacts of a product (see Figure 4) significant environmental impacts can be assigned correctly to a product. The environmental impacts of a product contain the direct product-related environmental impacts and all input-and process-related impacts which are caused through the processes and inputs to manufacture the product.

The described bills of environmental impacts give a company the opportunity to plan, control and supervise its environmental impacts much more systematically. If the actual environmental impacts, e.g. represented through the amount of emissions or waste water, are higher than the standard impacts, these indicate inefficiencies in the business processes. Also legal compliance can be achieved much better with appropriate data. But because the

environmental impacts are only measured in quantities, there is no way to ensure legal compliance and the accomplishment of business goals cost efficiently. Therefore, the calculation of internal prices of material and energy sources is the next logical step to create a decision-oriented information base.

Internal pricing

The recorded quantities of material and energy need to be evaluated with their realistic costs. In addition to the purchase costs, other cost components are often relevant (see Figure 5):

- Treatment costs result from the separation, refinement, and cleaning of used materials or undesired residuals like waste, waste water, and emissions.
- Logistic costs include the costs of storage and transportation as well as costs for security measures to avoid accidents and uncontrolled environmental impacts.
- In Europe, many manufacturers have to take back their old products (see Epstein, 1996) after usage. An example is the new European regulation which obliges all car manufacturers to take back all old cars from the year 2005. The amount of cost depends on the ability to dismantle and recycle the products. Processes which improve the reusability of the products can reduce such costs.
- Costs of environmental risks are determined by financial risks which are uncertain with regard to their occurrence and their amount. Examples are liability risks of high environmental impacts (see Rubenstein, 1994). The costs of environmental risks can be estimated through the expected value minus or plus a security charge.
- Supervision costs are incurred on the documentation and control of harmful substances and waste to achieve legal compliance. The costs for the EMS documentation are also included in this category.
- Additional control costs may be used to set incentives to reduce the use of a material which causes considerable environmental impact. They help to control the use of material and energy according to the environmental objectives and targets in the environmental program. It is also conceivable to consider the externalities of material and energy use.

The internal prices (Figure 5) change the relative prices of inputs, processes and products. The result indicates the substitution of harmful material through

Figure 3
Bill of environmental impacts of a process

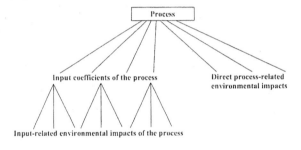

Figure 4
Bill of environmental impacts of a product

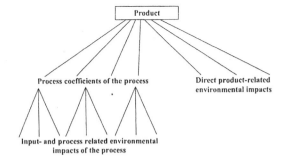

Peter Letmathe and
Roger K. Doost
*Environmental cost
accounting and auditing*

Managerial Auditing Journal
15/8 [2000] 424–430

other substances which are less harmful and result in lower costs.

Auditing and environmental costs

Environmental cost accounting provides information for planning, control and supervision. All areas which use cost data automatically integrate the extended information into their own planning system. Besides, information from an environmental cost accounting system can be used for investment decisions, for launching new products, etc. The bills of environmental impacts can be integrated in production planning and control systems.

To examine how environmental cost accounting can deliver useful information for auditing, it makes sense to distinguish between internal and external audits. External audits or third-party audits are carried out to review the management system by an independent external auditor or registrar. The most common external audits are the ISO 9000 and ISO 14001 audits which review the quality management or environmental management system. Both audits are conducted to see if the management system meets the requirements of the relevant standards. Although they are formal and not result-oriented standards, appropriate data can support the work of the registrar. Data about input and output flows of material and energy show if the business processes are properly documented. The ISO 14001 (see Clemens, 1996) standard is dedicated to continual improvement as the overall goal of environmental management systems. To accomplish this, the organization has to define concrete objectives, targets, and measures to achieve them. Concrete measures and targets can include the reduction of waste, waste water, and emissions. If these outputs are accounted for through the environmental cost accounting system, it would be much easier to compare the current flow with the flow in the next period. This gives the organization the opportunity to

review its improvements. To retain ISO 14001 or ISO 9000 certification, external audits must be repeated frequently (see Culley, 1998). Especially the way the organization documents and supervises its improvements may be viewed with much interest.

Internal audits can be carried out to prepare for external audits for the mentioned standards. They are also conducted to ascertain compliance with management's goals. These audits can use the information base of an environmental cost accounting system in the same way as the external audits. The more work is done through continuous and systematic review of the company's environmental measures by the internal auditors, the less time, effort, and money need to be spent by the external auditors in this area.

Another kind of audit is performance auditing. Performance audits measure the current performance of the organization and try to identify potentials for improvement. Performance audits can also be a basis for defining objectives, targets and measures which should be attained in the future. To achieve an adequate level of a performance audit, companies need to review (Cushing, 1994) their:

- organizational arrangements to ascertain that proper division of responsibilities exist to achieve the organization's goals;
- system planning to make sure about the adequacy of system development projects to handle the complexities of the proposed cost system;
- personnel policies to ascertain the presence of proper standards for hiring, training, and assigning of personnel to handle the tasks necessitated as a result of new requirements;
- financial controls to make certain about the adequacy of responsibility accounting and reporting procedures for measuring costs and variances attributed to various operations and cost flows; and
- computer operations to ascertain about proper data processing capabilities in terms of equipment, software, and personnel.

For these tasks to be accomplished, comprehensive information is needed which is based on a cause-and-effect-analysis. Very often, a high volume of waste, waste water and emissions is the result of inefficiencies. Inefficiencies can also be pointed out by high variations of the amount of undesired byproducts. Hence, performance audits should prioritize areas/cost centers which are responsible for most of the environmental impacts. For example, a high amount of wasted heat can indicate the need for investment in a heat recovery system. A

Figure 5
Calculation of internal prices for material and energy flows

	Purchase costs
+	Treatment costs
+	Logistics costs
+	Take back costs for recycling and disposal of old products
+	Costs of environmental risks
+	Documentation and supervision costs
+	Additional control costs
	Internal price of a material or an energy source

Peter Letmathe and
Roger K. Doost
*Environmental cost
accounting and auditing*

Managerial Auditing Journal
15/8 [2000] 424–430

high volume of fresh and waste water usage can be reduced by a closed-loop cycle. Spoilage can be avoided through technical and organizational measures or substitution of materials. Waste can be separated and at least a part of it recycled. Another way is to reduce the costs for waste disposal through more efficient processes. This leads also to lower purchase costs for raw material. Because management is focusing on overall costs and not only on purchase cost, it can make more informed decisions.

A self-audit and inspection by the internal audit department is often a necessity to satisfy Environmental Protection Agency (EPA) requirements and reduce potential additional external costs. The Environmental Protection Agency (EPA, 1998) has published a self-audit preparation guide for organic coating facilities which covers the following areas:
- air emissions;
- wastewater management;
- hazardous materials/waste management;
- solid waste management;
- community right-to-know;
- pollution prevention.

The first three areas are audited with the help of several checklists which includes the inspection of the following areas:
- records to review;
- physical features to inspect;
- responsibilities of supervisors and managers;
- supervisor's and manager's management of the considered area and resource recovery;
- organic finishing facilities.

The reviewed records include data about the amount of emissions, wastewater, and waste. These flows can be reviewed much easier if an environmental cost accounting system provides the appropriate data. If the inspectors see that these data are in compliance with the inspected physical features, the whole inspection can be accelerated. Where continuous supervision of significant environmental impact is present, the EPA finds few, if any, violations. The recording of material and energy flows documents the responsible handling of environmental issues and is therefore a good basis for demonstrating the organization's environmental compliance.

Conclusion

An environmental cost accounting system that is based on a cause-and-effect relationship is necessary. It is needed for better identification and proper charging of environmental related costs. Such a system

not only helps the company in terms of performance improvements, but it provides a very important road map for internal and external auditors in their endeavors to determine the entity's compliance with company policies as well as environmentally related laws. Improvements achieved as a result of creation and monitoring of an effective environmental cost accounting system can help the company achieve its goals, comply with environmental laws, and contribute to the health of the ecology for our generation as well as generations to come.

References
Ansari, S., Bell, J., Klammer, T. and Lawrence, C. (1997), *Measuring and Managing Environmental Costs*, Irwin, Chicago, IL.
Bundesverband der Deutschen Industrie (1979), *Anleitung zur Bestimmung der Betriebskosten für den Umweltschutz in der Industrie*, Köln.
Clemens, R.B. (1996), *Complete Guide to ISO 14001*, Prentice-Hall, Englewood Cliffs, NJ.
Cushing, R. (1994), *Accounting Information Systems*, Addison-Wesley, New York, NY.
Culley, W.C. (1998), *Environmental and Quality Systems Integration*, Lewis, Boca Raton, LA.
Environmental Protection Agency (EPA) (1998), *Self-audit and Inspection Guide for Facilities Conduction Cleaning, Preparation, and Organic Coating of Metal Parts*, EPA, Washington, DC.
Epstein, M.J. (1996), "Accounting for product take back", *Management Accounting*, August, pp. 29-33.
Gege, M. (1997), *Kosten senken durch Umweltmanagement*, Vahlen, München.
Hansen, D.R. and Mowen, M.M. (1999), *Management Accounting*, 5th ed., South-Western, Cincinetti, OH.
Klassen, R.D. and McLaughin, C.P. (1996), "The impact of environmental management on firm performance", *Management Science*, Vol. 42, pp. 1199-214.
Letmathe, P. (1998), *Umweltbezogene Kostenrechnung*, Vahlen, München.
Rubenstein, D.B. (1994), *Environmental Accounting for the Sustainable Coperation*, Quorum, Westport, CT and London.
Verein Deutscher Ingenieure (1979), *VDI-Richtlinie 3800 – Kostenermittlung für Anlagen und Maßnahmen zur Emissionsminderung*, Düsseldorf.

Further reading
Epstein, M.J. and Birchard, B. *Counting What Counts: Turning Corporate Accountability to Competitive Advantage?*
Federal Environmental Agency (Germany) (1997), *Sustainable Germany*, Berlin.
Gallhofer, S. and Haslam, J. (1995), "Worrying about environmental auditing", in Lehman, G. and Owen, D. (Eds), *Social and Environmental Accounting, Special Edition of Accounting Forum*, Vol. 19, pp. 205-18.

Part V
Policy Use and Analysis

[17]

National Accounts and Environmental Resources

KARL-GÖRAN MÄLER
Stockholm School of Economics, Box 6501, S-113 83 Stockholm, Sweden

Abstract. In the paper, optimal growth theory is used to derive the appropriate definition of the net national product concept, when there are environmental resources and environmental damage to take into account. The basic conclusions are that conventional defined NP should be corrected by deducting environmental damage and adding the value of the net change of all resources.

Key words. National growth theory, national accounting systems.

Introduction

National income accounts as we now know them, came into use in the 40s. At that time, they were constructed with the objective of aiding macroeconomic policy analyses. As the prevailing macroeconomic school at that time was Keynesianism, it was natural that the accounting system was designed to give information on the balance between total supply and total demand, on savings and investment in reproducible capital, and on international relations. This system is still very valuable for that purpose. However, the gross national product measure has been used for many other purposes too, the most usual one as a welfare measure. There have been many criticisms against this use of GNP, the argument being that GNP is a gross concept and should be replaced by net national product NNP. However, even if depreciation is deducted from GNP, the NNP measure may still be a bad measure of welfare and in particular in connection with natural and environmental resources. This note is only concerned with the net national product as a welfare measure in connection with these resources. Moreover, this note is only concerned with a theoretical analysis of an appropriate conceptual framework for measuring aggregate welfare. Very few remarks will be offered on the implementation aspects and it is my view that the system described can hardly be implemented one hundred percent. We will have to continue relying on physical and other special indicators to a large extent in order to judge the performance of the economy with respect to the use of environmental resources. In spite of this, it is hoped that this theoretical inquiry will shed light on the problems with the present accounting system.

There are three main criticisms against the present national accounting framework:

Environmental and Resource Economics 1: 1—15, 1991.

(i) defensive expenditures, i.e. expenditures for measures individuals undertake in order to reduce the impact of environmental damage, are now included in the final demand but should be deducted,

(ii) neither the value of environmental degradation to households nor to firms are deducted in computing the net national income,

(iii) the change in the value of stocks of environmental resources is not included in the accounts.

We will in this short note discuss these points in a very simple but sufficiently general model. We will find that point (i) is not valid, and that (ii) and (iii) are partly valid.

The Model

Let there be two environmental resources y_1 and y_2. y_1 is a flow resource which is available in each time period in the quantity y_{1o}. We can think of it as clean air or clean water. In each time period it can be used as input in production processes (waste disposal). The amount of use as input is denoted z_1. The remaining amount

$$y_1 = y_{1o} - z_1$$

is then an index of the purity of air or water.

The other resource is a stock resource y_2. Let the resource use be z_2 and assume that the resource has a linear growth function. Thus

$$\frac{dy_2}{dt} = m(q_3, l_3)y_2 - z_2.$$

Here we have assumed that the growth of the resource can be affected by management, represented by the use of the produced good q_3 and labour l_3. q_3 can be thought of as input of fertilizers in forestry or agriculture. Dasgupta[1] defines an environmental resource as "resources which are regenerative but potentially exhaustible". Therefore, y_2 is an environmental resource in this sense. It can stand for the stock of standing timber, the population of a certain fish species, but also for the asset of clean water or clean air.

Assume that there is only one good produced and that the production function can be written

$$q = f(l_1, k_1, s_1, z_2, y_1, y_2),$$

where l_1 is the amount of labour employed, k_1 the stock of reproducible capital and s_1 the quantity of residuals generated. This is quite a general formulation, implying that not only the harvesting of the stock resource, z_2, but also the stock itself may affect production. In most cases it would be

National Accounts and Environmental Resources 3

natural to assume that $\partial f/\partial y_2 = 0$. Furthermore, it is also assumed that the flow of environmental services, y_1, may affect production. The firm can also buy pollution control services from special pollution control firms. Their production function is

$$z_1 = g(s_1, l_2, k_2).$$

Here l_2 and k_2 is the amount of labour employed and the capital stock in the pollution control sector. This implies that only the firm is generating pollutants. However, it would be quite easy to extend the model to include household generation of pollutants.

Assume that the households can improve their environment by "defensive" expenditures, that is by using goods for extra insulation, cleaning etc. Let the household production function be

$$y = \varphi(y_1, q_2, l_4),$$

where q_2 is the input of purchased goods, and l_4 is the input of own labour. One could easily introduce a stock of household capital into this production function, but it would not give any further insights (the inclusion of investments in such a stock in an accounting framework will be touched upon later).

Finally, let the household utility function be

$$u = u(q_1, y, y_2, l_5),$$

where q_1 is the consumption of goods and services, and where l_5 is the free time available for recreation. Obviously we have

$$q = q_1 + q_2 + q_3 + I_1 + I_2,$$

where I_i is the gross investment in sector i. This means that

$$\frac{dk_i}{dt} = I_i - \delta_i k_i, \quad i = 1, 2.$$

Assume that the labour supply is exogenous and equal to $\bar{l}$, that is

$$l_1 + l_2 + l_3 + l_4 + l_5 = l.$$

If r is the rate of interest, a dynamic competitive equilibrium can be represented as the solution to the following intertemporal optimization problem:

$$\text{Max} \int_0^\infty e^{-rt} u(q_1, \varphi(y_1, q_2, l_4), y_2, l_5) \, dt$$

s.t.

$$q_1 + q_2 + q_3 + I_1 + I_2 = f(l_1, k_1, s_1, z_2, y_1, y_2)$$
$$z_1 = g(s_1, l_2, k_2)$$
$$y_1 = y_{1o} - z_1$$
$$l_1 + l_2 + l_3 + l_4 + l_5 = \bar{l}$$
$$\frac{dk_i}{dt} = I_i - \delta_i k_i$$
$$\frac{dy_2}{dt} = m(q_3, l_3)y_2 - z_2.$$

The current Hamiltonian value for this optimization problem is

$$
\begin{aligned}
H = {} & u(q_1, \varphi(y_1, q_2, l_4), y_2, l_5) \\
& -p(q_1 + q_2 + q_3 + I_1 + I_2 - f(l_1, k_1, s_1, z_2, y_1, y_2)) \\
& -v_1(y_1 + z_1 - y_{1o}) + a(z_1 - g(s_1, l_2, k_2)) \\
& -w(l_1, + l_2 + l_3 + l_4 + l_5 - \bar{l}) + \mu_1(I_1 - \delta_1 k_1) + \mu_2(I_2 - \delta_2 k_2) \\
& + v_2(m(q_3, l_3)y_2 - z_2).
\end{aligned}
$$

Necessary conditions for an optimum are obtained by maximizing H with respect to $l_1, l_2, l_3, l_4, l_5, s_1, z_1, z_2, q_1, q_2, q_3, I_1, I_2, y_1$.

For future reference, the conditions are (if we assume an interior maximum)

$$u'_{q_1} - p = 0; \qquad u'_y \varphi'_{q_2} - p = 0;$$
$$u'_y \varphi'_{y_1} + pf'_{y_1} - v_1 = 0; \qquad u'_y \varphi'_{l_4} - w = 0; \qquad u'_{l_5} - w = 0;$$
$$p - \mu_1 = 0; \qquad p - \mu_2 = 0; \qquad pf'_{l_1} - w = 0;$$
$$ag'_{l_2} - w = 0; \qquad pf'_{s_1} - ag'_{s_1} = 0;$$
$$v_1 - a = 0; \qquad v_2 m_{l_3} - w = 0; \qquad v_2 m_{q_3} - p = 0;$$
$$pf'_{z_2} - v_2 = 0; \qquad pf'_{y_1} - v_1 = 0.$$

Let $v^c_{y_1} = u'_y \varphi'_{y_1}$, that is, the marginal utility of degradation of the flow resource, and let $v^p_{y_1} = p f'_{s_1}$, that is, the marginal productivity of the flow resource. Then $v_1 = v^c_{y_1} + v^p_{y_1}$. Let $v_{pc} = ag_{s_1}$. Then v_{pc} can be interpreted as the price of pollution control. Finally, let $v^c_2 = u'_{y_2}$ be the household's marginal valuation of the stock resource and $v^p_2 = p f'_{y_2}$ the marginal productivity of the stock resource (as distinct from the input z_2) in production.

The stock prices μ_1, μ_2 and v_2 are determined from the differential equations

$$\frac{d\mu_1}{dt} = -\frac{\partial H}{\partial k_1} + rk_1$$

$$\frac{d\mu_2}{dt} = -\frac{\partial H}{\partial k_2} + rk_2$$

$$\frac{dv_2}{dt} = -\frac{\partial H}{\partial y_2} + ry_2.$$

Note that we can also write

$$u_1(t) = \int_t^\infty e^{-r(\tau - t)} p(\tau) f'_{k_i} \, d\tau, \text{ and}$$

$$\mu_2(t) = \int_t^\infty e^{-r(\tau - t)} v_1(\tau) g'_{k_2} \, d\tau.$$

The prices μ_i can therefore be interpreted as the present value of the future return on a marginal increase in the present capital stock. As we will soon see, v_2 can be interpreted as the present value from a marginal increase in the stock resource.

In the same way we have that

$$v_2(t) = \int_t^\infty e^{-r(\tau - t)} (u'_{y_2} + p f'_{y_2}) \, d\tau.$$

Along the optimal path, the Hamiltonian is

$$H^* = u(q_1, \varphi(y_1, q_2, l_4), y_2, l_4) + \mu_1 \frac{dk_1}{dt} + \mu_2 \frac{dk_2}{dt} + v_2 \frac{dy_2}{dt}.$$

Net National Welfare Measure

The Hamiltonian along the optimal trajectory is the national welfare measure in utility terms we are looking for. The linear support of the Hamiltonian along the optimal path is the exact correspondence to the net national welfare measure NWM. It measures the current utility of consumption (of produced goods and services and environmental services) and the present value of the future utility stream from current stock changes. This follows because the stock prices measure the present value of the future contributions to welfare from a marginal increase in the stocks.

The meaning of the linearization requires some further comment. We take the prices along the optimal trajectory, that is the optimal prices, and evaluate all quantities — output, environmental variables, etc., at those prices. No real economy is on the optimal trajectory and one could perhaps ask why we should bother about optimal prices in this connection. The reason is that if the underlying feasibility set is convex, the optimal prices are the only prices that will yield an estimate of the welfare measure that in all circumstances will indicate a true welfare increase or decrease. Thus, with the convexity assumption, the use of optimal prices will give the correct indication of welfare changes, irrespective of whether the economy is on the optimal trajectory or not. It follows that the prices must in general be accounting prices and not actual market prices. Let X be the vector of arguments in the Hamiltonian (except prices) and let X_t^* be a point at the optimal trajectory at time t. We now consider a small pertubation. The value of the Hamiltonian at this new point is the net welfare measure NWM or

$$\text{NWM} = H(X_t^*) + u_{q_1}q_1 + u_y(\varphi_{y_1}y_1 + \varphi_{q_2}q_2 + \varphi_{l_4}l_4) + u_{y_2}y_2$$
$$+ u_{l_5}l_5 + \mu_1 \frac{dk_1}{1d_t} + \mu_2 \frac{dk_2}{2d_t} + v_2 \frac{dy_2}{2dt}$$

By using the necessary conditions for an optimal trajectory, this can be written:

$$\text{NWM} = p(q_1 + q_2 + q_3) + \mu_1 \frac{dk_1}{dt} + \mu_2 \frac{dk_2}{dt} \qquad \text{(conventional NP)}$$

$$-pq_3 - w(l_1 + l_2 + l_3) + v_1^c y_1 + v_2^c y_2 + v_2 \frac{dy_2}{dt} \qquad \text{(adjustments)}$$
$$+H(X_t^*).$$

The three first terms correspond to the conventionally measured net national product, in that they include the total output for consumption q_1, the total defensive expenditures in households (and public sector) pq_2, the total input of produced goods in enhancing the growth of the environmental asset and the net investment in the stocks of reproducible real capital. This conventional net national product should then be corrected in various ways:

(a) Wages in the production of goods should not be part of the net national product, the intuitive reason being that on the margin, people are indifferent between taking a job on the labour market or being free and spending the time on recreation or on their own work.

(b) Current defensive expenditures pq_2 should not be deducted from net national income in order to avoid double counting when the value of environmental services $v_{y_1}^c$ is included. If we would have introduced household capital, then household net investments to protect *future* environment should have been included.

(c) The value of input goods used to enhance the stock of environmental assets should be deducted from conventional net national product.

(d) The value of the flow services should be included but valued at households marginal valuation $v_{y_1}^c$. The damage to production should not be deducted from NNP, the reason being that this damage has already been accounted for by pq_1.

(e) The value of the current direct use of the stock resource should be included, but valued by the household's marginal valuation and its value in production should not be included.

(f) The value of the change in the stock (not the change in the value of the stock) should be included. Anticipated capital gains are not parts of national income.

(g) The change in the stock resource should be valued at a price reflecting the future value of the stock, both as a source of inputs to production, z_2, as a direct source of utility to household, and as a source of productivity in production. We have

$$\frac{dv_2}{dt} = (r - m)v_2 - (v_2^c + v_2^p), \quad \text{and}$$

$$v_2 = pf_{z_2}.$$

This means in particular that

$$v_2(t) = \int_0^\infty e^{-(r-m)(\tau-t)}(v_2^c + v_2^p)\,d\tau,$$

that is the accounting price on the stock resource is equal to the present value of the future gains from the stock.

(h) There is a constant term $H(X_t^*)$ which is not affecting the value of the perturbation. It reflects the wealth of the society and we will come back to a further discussion of this term later. It is obvious that it will not in any way affect the effects on NWM from present economic activities and we will therefore in the mean time neglect it.

Conclusion (a) may be startling. The intuitive reason is as follows. Assume that individuals are free to choose their labour supply, that the labour market is in equilibrium and that the opportunity cost of working is the vacation time that must be given up. On the margin, no individual would get better from an increase in the labour supply. As national welfare is a linear approximation of the true welfare, it follows that labour income should not be included. This shows the importance of being clear of the use of the accounts. For macro-economic analysis, labour income is obviously one of the most important variables. If we want a measure of welfare, labour income should not be included (giving the assumptions on a perfect labour market). Thus, there is a need to keep the established accounts for giving a basis of macroeconomic analysis and supplementing them with accounts that take labour and environmental resources into account. Note that we have not included the perhaps most important asset — human capital. If human capital would have been

8

included in the model and if parts of wages are return on human capital, then these parts should be included in the NWM-concept. That part of the wage bill that corresponds to "raw labour" should be subtracted from the value of the total output in order for the NWM to provide a good measure of individual welfare.

In the sequel, we shall, for simplicity disregard the arguments presented above and keep to the established procedures of including wages in NWM.

Social Accounting Matrix

These results can be represented in a social accounting matrix for this simple economy. For simplicity we will neglect the term $H(X_i^*)$. Let $I = I_1 + I_2$ and $q = q_1 + q_2$. Moreover, let $v^c = v_1^c y_1 + v_2^c y_2$ represent the total consumer valuation of the two environmental resources and let $v^p = v_1^p y_1 + v_2^p y_2$ be the corresponding value of the resources in the production (except for the value of the first resource for waste disposal and the value of the second resource as an input). Finally let V_i be the surplus of revenues over wages, pollution control expenditures, depreciation, and implicit environmental costs in sector i and let $V = V_1 + V_2$. V_i can be interpreted as the net return on capital.

A Social Accounting Matrix

	H	L	C	Prod.	Poll. C.	$S-I$	Env.
H		wl	V				V_e
L				wl_1	wl_2		wl_4
C				V_1	V_2		
Prod	$p(q_1 + q_2)$					I	pq_3
Poll. C.				$v_{pc}s_1$			
$S-I$	S			$\delta_1 k_1$	$\delta_2 k_2$		
Env.	v^c			$v^p + v_2 z_2$	$v_1^p z_1$	$v_2^* dy_2/dt$	

Here it has been assumed that there is an environment authority that buys labour and produces goods to enhance the growth of the environmental asset. Now interpret the first column as the total final demand, except capital investments, that is, let the public sector be included. We see that the national welfare measure is given by the sum of the first column. It includes current expenditures on goods and environmental services, $p(q_1 + q_2) + v^c$, plus net savings S. As the row sum is equal to the column sum, it follows that national welfare also equals the value added $wl + V$ and the implicit value of all environmental resources V_e. This implicit value of the environment equals the value of the environment to the households v^c, to the firms v^p as a flow of unspoilt resources and as a stock, to the firms $v_2 z_2$ as an input, to the firms for waste disposal, and the net investment in the stock resource $v_2(dy_2)/dt$

less expenditures on enhancing the growth of environmental assets. The net savings S equals net investment in reproducible capital and investment in the environmental asset,

$$S = I - \delta_1 k_1 - \delta_2 k_2 + v_{d2} \frac{dy_2}{dt}.$$

The national welfare measure can now be written

$$NWM = p(q_1 + q_2) + v^c + I + v_2 \frac{dy_2}{dt} = wl + V + V_e.$$

Apparently, it is quite important to separate the household valuation from the importance of the resources in production. The use of the resources in production is reflected in net national income through profits and outputs, while the household valuation is not included in such a way. The value of stock changes, on the other hand, should include both the direct consumer and the indirect production marginal valuations. Local air pollution is an example of the former resources, as a high ambient concentration this year may mean nothing for the ambient concentrations next year. Regional air pollution may offer an example of the stock resource. Sulfur emissions will be deposited as sulfates and if the deposition is in excess of the "critical load", an accumulation will take place leading to long term damage. In the first example, only the direct damage to the consumers should be included while in the second example, the present value of all future damage due to the excess deposition this year should be included in the accounts.

We could easily extend the accounting framework above to include foreign trade and transboundary environmental effects. It is easily seen that the standard identity between the balance of trade and domestic financial savings will be valid in this extended framework.

Let us return to our national welfare measure concept

$$NWM = p(q_1 + q_2) + v^c + S.$$

Another way of writing it is

$$NWM = p(q_1 + q_2) + v_1^c(y_{1o} - z_1) + v_2^c y_2 + S.$$

Now assume that $y_{1o} = 0$ (which simply means that we have chosen a zero point for the scale by which the flow resource is measured) and that $v_2^c = 0$. Let us also forget, without any consequences for the generality of the argument, about the use of goods and labour for enhancing growth in the environmental stock resource. Then we have

$$NWM = pq - ED + S$$

$$= pq + (I - \delta_1 k_1 - \delta_2 k_2) - ED - \left(-v_2 \frac{dy_2}{dt} \right).$$

10   *Karl-Göran Mäler*

where ED is the environmental damage $-v_1^c z_1$. This new measure differs from the conventional net national product definition in that we have deducted the environmental damage ED and the degradation of the stock $(-v_2 dy_2/dt)$. Thus, the general conclusion is that the conventional net national income should be adjusted in two ways:

deduct current environmental damage as valued by households,

deduct the value of the degradation of stocks with a price reflecting future value of the stock.

Environmental Damage

How do we estimate the environmental damage (or equivalently the value of the environmental services $v_1^c y_1$)? In spite of remarkable progress in estimating the monetary value of environmental damages during the last ten years, it is clear that we are far from a situation where we can estimate them routinely. In view of that, it has often been suggested that the defensive expenditures are a proxy for the environmental damage. Thus, instead of subtracting the environmental damage, one should subtract the defensive expenditures. However, defensive expenditures in general are very bad estimators of environmental damage. Only if the defensive expenditures are a perfect substitute to the environmental services can this approximation be defended (see, for example, Mäler, 1985). In most cases defensive expenditures will have no relations whatsoever with the true damage cost. Thus, this procedure can hardly be seriously considered.

As a more interesting alternative has been suggested that one should specify environmental targets — maximum ambient concentration of SO_2, minimum dissolved oxygen levels in a stream, minimum recreational possibilities for a community etc. In general it is much easier to estimate the cost of achieving these targets than to estimate the loss from not achieving them. The cost of achieving the targets could then be used as a crude approximation of the true social value. If all marginal willingness to pay curves and all marginal abatement cost curves have the usual curvature, we will by following this procedure obtain estimates that are biased downward. Even if the estimates are biased, there is some satisfaction in that the direction of the bias is uniform. However, the bias may differ substantially from one environmental problem to another.

The decision on the environmental targets is a political one. Political beliefs could also be expressed in marginal valuations. Thus, if the politicians after public discussions could decide on the marginal value of environmental improvements, these marginal values could be used to estimate the environmental damage cost.

Last but not least, the art of estimating damage cost functions is rapidly improving. For many environmental problems, values of damage cost can be found — values that can be used in a satellite system of accounts.

Sustainable Income

We can now adapt Weitzman's analyses (Weitzman, 1976) of the welfare significance of national product. In fact, it is possible to show that NWM as defined above is the maximum consumption that can be allowed if future consumption should be prevented from decreasing. First note that

$$\frac{dH^*}{dt} = \frac{\partial H^*}{\partial k_1}\frac{dk_1}{dt} + \frac{\partial H^*}{\partial k_2}\frac{dk_2}{dt} + \frac{\partial H^*}{\partial y_2}\frac{dy_2}{dt}$$

$$+ \frac{\partial H^*}{\partial \mu_1}\frac{d\mu_1}{dt} + \frac{\partial H^*}{\partial \mu_2}\frac{d\mu_2}{dt} + \frac{\partial H^*}{\partial v_2}\frac{dv_2}{dt}$$

$$= r\mu_1 \frac{dk_1}{dt} + r\mu_2 \frac{dk_2}{dt} + rv_2 \frac{dy_2}{dt} = r(H^* - u^*),$$

where u^* denotes the utility along the optimal path. This is a differential equation in H^* with the solution

$$H^*(t) = r \int_t^\infty u^* c^{-r(\tau - t)} dt.$$

Thus

$$\int_t^\infty H^*(t)\, e^{-r(\tau - t)} d\tau = \int_t^\infty u^*(\tau)\, e^{-r(\tau - t)} d\tau.$$

The present value of the constant utility stream H^* is thus equal to the maximum present value of the utility stream. Thus $H^*(t)$ is the maximum current utility that can be sustained forever, that is, H^* (or NWM $= H^*$) is a measure of sustainable income (in utility terms).

Sustainable Development

As we have shown that NWM is a measure of sustainable income, it follows that sustainable development can be defined as such a development in which NWM never decreases. Thus

> Economic development is sustainable if and only if utility is non-decreasing over time.

From the analysis in the section above, it is seen that

$$\frac{d\,\text{NWM}}{dt} = r\left(\mu_1 \frac{dk_1}{dt} + \mu_2 \frac{dk_2}{dt} + v_2 \frac{dy_2}{dt}\right).$$

12   *Karl-Göran Mäler*

If follows that if we define the total stock of capital as

$$K = \mu_1 k_1 + \mu_2 k_2 + v_2 y_2,$$

development will be sustainable if and only if K is non-decreasing at constant prices. Thus, sustainable development requires that the total stock of capital, defined in a special way (first introduced by Solow (1986)), is non-decreasing. However, there is nothing in the preceding analysis that suggests that a sustainable development defined in this way is feasible. If, for example, $m = 0$, that is if the stock resource is an exhaustible resource, and if the substitution elasticity between this stock resource and capital is less than one, the value of the stock resource relative the other capital prices will be such that K always will be decreasing. This has been analysed in Dasgupta and Heal (1981). In particular, that would mean that the sustainable income is zero. On the other hand, if technical progress is introduced in the model, even in this situation, sustainable development may be feasible.

One particular aspect of this is Hartwick's rule which says that sustainable development is achieved when the competitive rents on exhaustible resources are invested in reproducible capital.[2] It is easily seen that our (or rather Solow's) formulation yields a generalization of Hartwick's rule to the case of renewable resources.

It follows from above that

$$H(X_t^*) = rK_t^*,$$

that is H^* is equal to the total return on all capital at time t. This means that the NWM can be written

$$\text{NWM} = rK^* + p(q_1 + q_2 + q_3) + \mu_1 \frac{dk_1}{dt} + \mu_2 \frac{dk_2}{dt} \qquad \text{(conventional NP)}$$

$$-pq_3 - w(l_1 + l_2 + l_3) + v_1^c y_1 + v_2^c y_2 + v_2 \frac{dy_2}{dt}. \qquad \text{(corrections)}$$

This can reasonably be interpreted as the net national product NP.

Unanticipated Changes

The analysis so far has been based on the assumption that the future is known with full certainty. Assume now that there is no reason to reject the assumption of perfect foresight, but that in time period t' there is a completely unanticipated change in a resource stock or in technology (or in world market prices which can be represented as a change in the production function).[3] From period 0 to t', NWM will develop as above up to t' (although we have to assume that the prices used to compute NWM are Arrow–Debreu prices or shadow prices computed so as to reflect the "value" of goods and services and resources in different states of the world).

In t' there will, however, be a shift in the parameters, and therefore also in the optimal path from t' onwards. Thus, NWM will shift in t', and unanticipated capital gains at t' will be included.

In case there is uncertainty about future resource stocks, technology and prices, it can be shown that (Dasgupta and Heal, 1974; Dasgupta and Stiglitz, 1976) essentially the same thing will happen. The difference is that the discount rate r now also must include a risk premium. Thereby the uncertainty of the future will be taken into account. When an unanticipated change takes place, there will be a change in NNI and the economy will follow a new path till the next unanticipated changes are realized.

Thus, it becomes quite important to identify anticipated changes in prices, stocks and technology from unanticipated changes, as this will affect the way NWM should be computed. This conclusion is strengthened if one considers changes in world market prices for goods produced in our economy. If such changes are correctly anticipated, they can be represented in our model as shifts in the production function, that is as technical progress (although in this case technical progress may be negative). Capital gains arising from these price changes should not be included in NWM. Their importance has already been capitalized in other prices and therefore already been included in the net national income concept. Unanticipated gains, on the other hand, have by their definition not been capitalized and should therefore be included in a correct measure of national welfare measure.

Conclusions

In this paper, an attempt has been made to create an analytical framework for a discussion on how to include environmental resources in national accounting systems. It was found that the conventional Net National Product measure should be adjusted in the following ways:

(i) the flow of environmental damage should be deducted from conventional NNP,

(ii) the value of the net change in the stocks of all assets and not only man made capital should be added to conventional NNP,

(iii) investments in the enhancement of stocks of natural resources should be treated as intermediary products,

(iv) existing wealth, as the return on the total stock of assets in the economy should be added.

With these adjustments, there is no need to deduct defensive expenditures or to make any other similar adjustment.

The Net Welfare Measure, so constructed, can be interpreted as the sustainable income, in the sense that it gives the maximum feasible constant flow of consumption.

Furthermore, this maximum flow can be interpreted as the return on the total wealth in the economy.

14 *Karl-Göran Mäler*

Acknowledgements

This article is to a very large extent the product of several discussions with Partha Dasgupta and some of the conclusions presented here have already been published in two appendices in our joint paper Environment and Emerging Development Issues. In a very true sense, he should be regarded as a coauthor of the paper, but he has not seen it and is therefore absolved from any errors that, in all probability, may still exist. I am also very grateful to two anonymous referees who have given very useful comments on the original manuscript. After I completed the manuscript I came across an interesting article by Hartwick (1990) who has basically used the same approach that I have. I am grateful to John Hartwick for useful comments on an earlier version of the manuscript.

Notes

[1] See Dasgupta (1982), p. 14.
[2] See Hartwick (1977), (1978) and Dixit, Hammond, and Hoel (1980).
[3] The following discussion is based on Dasgupta and Mäler (1990).

References

Ahmad, J. J., E. Lutz, and S. El Sarafy (1989), *Environmental Accounting for Sustainable Development*, World Bank, Washington D.C.

Bartelmus, P. and J. W. van Tongeren (1988), *SNA Framework for Environmental Satellite Accounting — Draft Proposals*, UNSO.

Bartelmus, P. (1988), *Accounting for Sustainable Development*, Working Paper No. 8 Department of International Economic and Social Affairs, United Nations.

Dasgupta, P. (1982), *Control of Resources*, Basil Blackwell, Oxford.

Dasgsupta, P. and G. Heal (1974), 'The Optional Depletion of Exhaustible Resources', *The Review of Economic Studies*, Symposium on the Economics of Exhaustible Resources.

Dasgupta, P. and K.-G. Mäler (1990), Environment and Emerging Development Issues, WIDER.

Dasgupta, P. and G. Heal (1981), *Economic Theory and Exhaustible Resources*, Cambridge University Press.

Dasgupta, P. and J. Stiglitz (1976), Uncertainty and Resource Extraction Under Alternative Institutional Arrangements, IMSSS Technical Report 1979, Stanford University.

Devarajan, S. and R. J. Weiner (1988), *Natural Resource Depletion and National Income Accounts*, unpublished.

Dixit, A., R. Hammond, and M. Hoel (1980), 'On Hartwick's Rule for Regular Maximum Paths of Capital Accumulation and Resource Depletion', *Review of Economic Studies* **45**, 551—6.

Hartwick, J. (1977), 'Intergenerational Equity and the Investing of Rents from Exhaustible Resources', *American Economic Review* **66**, 972—4.

Hartwick, J. (1978), 'Substitution among Exhaustible Resources and Intergenerational Equity', *Review of Economic Studies* **45**, 347—54.

Hartwick, J. (1990), Natural Resources, National Accounting and Economic Depreciation, *Journal of Public Economics*, forthcoming.

Mäler, K.-G. (1974), *Environmental Economics — A Theoretical Inquiry*, The Johns Hopkins University Press.

Mäler, K.-G. (1985), 'Welfare Economics and the Environment', in *Handbook of Natural Resource and Energy Economics*, eds. A. V. Kneese and J. L. Sweeney, North-Holland.

Peskin H. (1989), *Accounting for Natural Resource Depletion and Degradation in Development Countries*, Environment Department Working Paper No. 13, The World Bank.

Repetto, R., W. Magrath, M. Wells, C. Beer, and F. Rossini (1989), *Wasting Assets Natural Resources in the National Income Accounts*, World Resources Institute.

Solow, R. W. (1986), 'On the Intertemporal Allocation of Natural Resources', *Scandinavian Journal of Economics* **88**(1).

Weitzman M. (1976), 'On the Welfare Significance of National Product in a Dynamic Economy', *Quarterly Journal of Economics* **90**.

[18]

ENVIRONMENTAL REPERCUSSIONS AND THE ECONOMIC STRUCTURE: AN INPUT-OUTPUT APPROACH

Wassily Leontief *

I

POLLUTION is a by-product of regular economic activities. In each of its many forms it is related in a measurable way to some particular consumption or production process: The quantity of carbon monoxide released in the air bears, for example, a definite relationship to the amount of fuel burned by various types of automotive engines; the discharge of polluted water into our streams and lakes is linked directly to the level of output of the steel, the paper, the textile and all the other water-using industries and its amount depends, in each instance, on the technological characteristics of the particular industry.

Input-output analysis describes and explains the level of output of each sector of a given national economy in terms of its relationships to the corresponding levels of activities in all the other sectors. In its more complicated multi-regional and dynamic versions the input-output approach permits us to explain the spatial distribution of output and consumption of various goods and services and of their growth or decline — as the case may be — over time.

Frequently unnoticed and too often disregarded, undesirable by-products (as well as certain valuable, but unpaid-for natural inputs) are linked directly to the network of physical relationships that govern the day-to-day operations of our economic system. The technical interdependence between the levels of desirable and undesirable outputs can be described in terms of structural coefficients similar to those used to trace the structural interdependence between all the regular branches of production and consumption. As a matter of fact, it can

* This paper was presented in Tokyo, Japan, March 1970 at the International Symposium on Environmental Disruption in the Modern World held under the auspices of the International Social Science Council, Standing Committee on Environmental Disruption.

Peter Petri and Ed Wolff, both members of the research staff of the Harvard Economic Research Project, have programmed and carried out the computations described in this paper. For their invaluable assistance I owe my sincerest thanks.

be described and analyzed as an integral part of that network.

It is the purpose of this report first to explain how such "externalities" can be incorporated into the conventional input-output picture of a national economy and, second, to demonstrate that — once this has been done — conventional input-output computations can yield concrete replies to some of the fundamental factual questions that should be asked and answered before a practical solution can be found to problems raised by the undesirable environmental effects of modern technology and uncontrolled economic growth.

II

Proceeding on the assumption that the basic conceptual framework of a static input-output analysis is familiar to the reader, I will link up the following exposition to the numerical examples and elementary equations presented in chapter 7 of my book entitled *"Input Output Economics"* (Oxford University Press, N.Y. 1966).

Consider a simple economy consisting of two producing sectors, say, Agriculture and Manufacture, and Households. Each one of the two industries absorbs some of its annual output itself, supplies some to the other industry and delivers the rest to final consumers — in this case represented by the Households. These inter-sectoral flows can be conveniently entered in an input-output table. For example:

TABLE 1. — INPUT-OUTPUT TABLE OF A NATIONAL ECONOMY (IN PHYSICAL UNITS)

Into From	Sector 1 Agriculture	Sector 2 Manufacture	Final Demand Households	Total Output
Sector 1 Agriculture	25	20	55	100 bushels of wheat
Sector 2 Manufacture	14	6	30	50 yards of cloth

The magnitude of the total outputs of the two industries and of the two different kinds of inputs absorbed in each of them depends on, (1) the amounts of agricultural and manufactured goods that had to be delivered to the final consumers, i.e., the Households and, (2) the input requirements of the two industries determined by their specific technological structures. In this particular instance Agriculture is assumed to require 0.25 ($= 25/100$) units of agricultural and 0.14 ($= 14/100$) units of manufactured inputs to produce a bushel of wheat, while the manufacturing sector needs 0.40 ($= 20/50$) units of agricultural and 0.12 ($= 6/50$) units of manufactured product to make a yard of cloth.

The "cooking recipes" of the two producing sectors can also be presented in a compact tabular form:

TABLE 2. — INPUT REQUIREMENTS PER UNIT OF OUTPUT

Into From	Sector 1 Agriculture	Sector 2 Manufacture
Sector 1 Agriculture	0.25	0.40
Sector 2 Manufacture	0.14	0.12

This is the "structural matrix" of the economy. The numbers entered in the first column are the technical input coefficients of the Agriculture sector and those shown in the second are the input coefficients of the Manufacture sector.

III

The technical coefficients determine how large the total annual outputs of agricultural and of manufactured goods must be if they are to satisfy not only the given direct demand (for each of the two kinds of goods) by the final users, i.e., the Households, but also the intermediate demand depending in its turn on the total level of output in each of the two productive sectors.

These somewhat circular relationships are described concisely by the following two equations:

$$X_1 - 0.25X_1 - 0.40X_2 = Y_1$$
$$X_2 - 0.12X_2 - 0.14X_1 = Y_2$$

or in a rearranged form,

$$0.75X_1 - 0.40X_2 = Y_1$$
$$-0.14X_1 + 0.88X_2 = Y_2 \qquad (1)$$

X_1 and X_2 represent the unknown total outputs of agricultural and manufactured commodities respectively; Y_1 and Y_2 the given amounts of agricultural and manufactured products to be delivered to the final consumers.

These two linear equations with two unknowns can obviously be solved, for X_1 and X_2 in terms of any given Y_1 and Y_2.

Their "general" solution can be written in form of the following two equations:

$$X_1 = 1.457Y_1 + 0.662Y_2$$
$$X_2 = 0.232Y_1 + 1.242Y_2. \qquad (2)$$

By inserting on the right-hand side the given magnitudes of Y_1 and Y_2 we can compute the magnitudes of X_1 and X_2. In the particular case described in table 1, $Y_1 = 50$ and $Y_2 = 30$. Performing the necessary multiplications and additions one finds the corresponding magnitudes of X_1 and X_2 to be, indeed, equal to the total outputs of agricultural (50 bushels) and manufactured (100 yards) goods, as shown in table 1.

The matrix, i.e., the square set table of numbers appearing on the right-hand side of (2),

$$\begin{bmatrix} 1.457 & 0.662 \\ 0.232 & 1.242 \end{bmatrix} \qquad (3)$$

is called the "inverse" of matrix,

$$\begin{bmatrix} 0.75 & -0.40 \\ -0.14 & 0.88 \end{bmatrix} \qquad (4)$$

describing the set constants appearing on the left-hand side of the original equations in (1).

Any change in the technology of either Manufacture or Agriculture, i.e., in any one of the four input coefficients entered in table 2, would entail a corresponding change in the structural matrix (4) and, consequently, of its inverse (3). Even if the final demand for agricultural (Y_1) and manufactured (Y_2) goods remained the same, their total outputs, X_1 and X_2, would have to change, if the balance between the total outputs and inputs of both kinds of goods were to be maintained. On the other hand, if the level of the final demands Y_1 and Y_2 had changed, but the technology remained the same, the corresponding changes in the total outputs X_1 and X_2 could be determined from the same general solution (2).

In dealing with real economic problems one takes, of course, into account simultaneously the effect both of technological changes and of anticipated shifts in the levels of final deliveries. The structural matrices used in such computations contain not two but several hundred sectors, but the analytical approach remains the same. In order to keep the following verbal argument and the numerical examples illustrating it quite simple, pollution produced directly by Households and other final users is not considered in it. A concise description of the way in which pollution generated by the final demand sectors can be introduced — along with pollution originating in the producing sectors — into the quantitative description and numerical solution of the input-output system is relegated to the Mathematical Appendix.

IV

As has been said before, pollution and other undesirable — or desirable — external effects of productive or consumptive activities should for all practical purposes be considered part of the economic system.

The quantitative dependence of each kind of external output (or input) on the level of one or more conventional economic activities to which it is known to be related must be described by an appropriate technical coefficient and all these coefficients have to be incorporated in the structural matrix of economy in question.

Let it be assumed, for example, that the technology employed by the Manufacture sector leads to a release into the air of 0.50 grams of a solid pollutant per yard of cloth produced by it, while agricultural technology adds 0.20 grams per unit (i.e., each bushel of wheat) of its total output.

Using $\bar{X}_3$ to represent the yet unknown total quantity of this external output, we can add to the two original equations of output system (1) a third,

$$0.75X_1 - 0.40X_2 \qquad = Y_1$$
$$-0.14X_1 + 0.88X_2 \qquad = Y_2$$
$$0.50X_1 + 0.20X_2 - \bar{X}_3 = 0 \qquad (5)$$

In the last equation the first term describes the amount of pollution produced by Manufacture as depending on that sector's total output, X_1, while the second represents, in the same way, the pollution originating in Agriculture as a function of X_2; the equation as a whole simply states that X_3, i.e., the total amount of that particular type pollution generated by the economic system as a whole, equals the sum total of the amounts produced by all its separate sectors.

Given the final demands Y_1 and Y_2 for agricultural and manufactured products, this set of three equations can be solved not only for their total outputs X_1 and X_2 but also for the unknown total output $\bar{X}_3$ of the undesirable pollutant.

The coefficients of the left-hand side of augmented input-output system (5) form the matrix,

$$\begin{Bmatrix} 0.75 & -0.40 & 0 \\ -0.14 & 0.88 & 0 \\ 0.50 & 0.20 & -1 \end{Bmatrix} \qquad (5a)$$

A "general solution" of system (5) would in its form be similar to the general solution (2) of system (1); only it would consist of three rather than two equations and the "inverse" of the structural matrix (4) appearing on the right-hand side would have three rows and columns.

Instead of inverting the enlarged structural matrix one can obtain the same result in two steps. First, use the inverse (4) of the original smaller matrix to derive, from the two-equation system (2), the outputs of agricultural (X_1) and manufactured (X_2) goods required to satisfy any given combination of final demands Y_1 and Y_2. Second, determine the corresponding "output" of pollutants, i.e., $\bar{X}_3$, by entering the values of X_1 and X_2 thus obtained in the last equation of set (5).

Let $Y_1 = 55$ and $Y_2 = 30$; these are the levels of the final demand for agricultural and manufactured products as shown on the input-output table 1. Inserting these numbers on the right-hand side of (5), we find — using the general solution (2) of the first two equations — that $X_1 = 100$ and $X_2 = 50$. As should have been expected they are identical with the corresponding total output figures in table 1. Using the third equation in (5) we find, $X_3 = 60$. This is the total amount of the pollutant generated by both industries.

By performing a similar computation for $Y_1 = 55$ and $Y_2 = 0$ and then for $Y_1 = 0$ and $Y_2 = 30$, we could find out that 42.62 of these

60 grams of pollution are associated with agricultural and manufactured activities contributing directly and indirectly to the delivery to Households of 55 bushels of wheat, while the remaining 17.38 grams can be imputed to productive activities contributing directly and indirectly to final delivery of the 30 yards of cloth.

Had the final demand for cloth fallen from 30 yards to 15, the amount of pollution traceable in it would be reduced from 17.38 to 8.69 grams.

V

Before proceeding with further analytical exploration, it seems to be appropriate to introduce the pollution-flows explicitly in the original table 1:

TABLE 3. — INPUT-OUTPUT TABLE OF THE NATIONAL
ECONOMY WITH POLLUTANTS INCLUDED
(IN PHYSICAL UNITS)

From \ Into	Sector 1 Agriculture	Sector 2 Manufacture	Households	Total Output
Sector 1 Agriculture	25	20	55	100 bushels of wheat
Sector 2 Manufacture	14	6	30	50 yards of cloth
Sector 3 Air pollution	50	10		60 grams of pollutant

The entry at the bottom of final column in table 3 indicates that Agriculture produced 50 grams of pollutant and 0.50 grams per bushel of wheat. Multiplying the pollutant-output-coefficient of the manufacturing sector with its total output we find that it has contributed 10 to the grand total of 60 grams of pollution.

Conventional economic statistics concern themselves with production and consumption of goods and services that are supposed to have in our competitive private enterprise economy some positive market value. This explains why the production and consumption of DDT is, for example, entered in conventional input-output tables while the production and the consumption of carbon-monoxide generated by internal combustion engines is not. Since private and public bookkeeping, that constitutes the ultimate source of the most conventional economic statistics, does not concern itself with

such "non-market" transactions, their magnitude has to be estimated indirectly through detailed analysis of the underlying technical relationships.

Problems of costing and of pricing are bound, however, to arise as soon as we go beyond explaining and measuring pollution toward doing something about it.

VI

A conventional national or regional input-output table contains a "value-added" row. It shows, in dollar figures, the wages, depreciation charges, profits, taxes and other costs incurred by each producing sector in addition to payments for inputs purchased from other producing sectors. Most of that "value-added" represents the cost of labor, capital, and other so-called primary factors of production, and depends on the physical amounts of such inputs and their prices. The wage bill of an industry equals, for example, the total number of man-years times the wage rate per man-year.

In table 4 the original national input-output table is extended to include labor input or total employment row.

TABLE 4. — INPUT-OUTPUT TABLE WITH LABOR
INPUTS INCLUDED
(IN PHYSICAL AND IN MONEY UNITS)

From \ Into	Sector 1 Agriculture	Sector 2 Manufacture	Households	Total Output
Sector 1 Agriculture	25	20	55	100 bushels of wheat
Sector 2 Manufacture	14	6	30	50 yards of cloth
Labor inputs (value-added)	80 ($80)	180 ($180)		260 man-years ($260)

The "cooking recipes" as shown on table 2 can be accordingly extended to include the labor input coefficients of both industries expressed in man-hours as well as in money units.

In section III it was shown how the general solution of the original input-output system (2) can be used to determine the total outputs of agricultural and manufactured products (X_1 and X_2) required to satisfy any given combination of deliveries of these goods (Y_1 and Y_2) to final Households. The corresponding

TABLE 5. — INPUT REQUIREMENTS PER UNIT OF OUTPUT
(INCLUDING LABOR OR VALUE-ADDED)

From \ Into	Sector 1 Agriculture	Sector 2 Manufacture
Sector 1 Agriculture	0.25	0.40
Sector 2 Manufacture	0.14	0.12
Primary input-labor in man-hours (at $1 per hour)	0.80 ($0.80)	3.60 ($3.60)

total labor inputs can be derived by multiplying the appropriate labor coefficients (k_1 and k_2) with each sector's total output. The sum of both products yields the labor input L of the economy as a whole.

$$L = k_1 X_1 + k_2 X_2. \qquad (6)$$

Assuming a wage rate of $1 per hour we find (see table 5) the payment for primary inputs per unit of the total output to be $0.80 in Agriculture and $3.60 in Manufacture. That implies that the prices of one bushel of wheat (p_1) and of a yard of cloth (p_2) must be just high enough to permit Agriculture to yield a "value-added" of v_1 ($= 0.80$) and Manufacture v_2 ($= 3.60$) per unit of their respective outputs after having paid for all the other inputs specified by their respective "cooking recipes."

$$p_1 - 0.25 p_1 - 0.14 p_2 = v_1$$
$$p_2 - 0.12 p_2 - 0.40 p_1 = v_2$$

or in a rearranged form,

$$0.75 p_1 - 0.14 p_2 = v_1$$
$$-0.40 p_1 + 0.88 p_2 = v_2 \qquad (7)$$

The "general solution" of these two equations permitting to compute p_1 and p_2 from any given combination of values-added, v_1 and v_2 is,

$$p_1 = 1.457 v_1 + 0.232 v_2$$
$$p_2 = 0.662 v_1 + 1.242 v_2 \qquad (8)$$

with $v_1 = \$0.80$ and $v_2 = \$3.60$ we have, $p_1 = \$2.00$ and $p_2 = \$5.00$. Multiplying the physical quantities of wheat and cloth entered in the first and second rows of table 4 with appropriate prices, we can transform it into a familiar input-output table in which all transactions are shown in dollars.

VII

Within the framework of the open input-output system described above any reduction

or increase in the output level of pollutants can be traced either to changes in the final demand for specific goods and services, changes in the technical structure of one or more sectors of the economy, or to some combination of the two.

The economist cannot devise new technology, but, as has been demonstrated above, he can explain or even anticipate the effect of any given technological change on the output of pollutants (as well as of all the other goods and services). He can determine the effects of such a change on sectoral, and, consequently, also the total demand for the "primary factor of production." With given "values-added" coefficients he can, moreover, estimate the effect of such a change on prices of various goods and services.

After the explanations given above, a single example should suffice to show how any of these questions can be formulated and answered in input-output terms.

Consider the simple two-sector economy whose original state and structure were described in tables 3, 4, 5 and 6. Assume that a

TABLE 6. — STRUCTURAL MATRIX OF A NATIONAL
ECONOMY WITH POLLUTION OUTPUT AND
ANTI-POLLUTION INPUT COEFFICIENTS INCLUDED

Inputs and Pollutants' Output \ Output Sectors	Sector 1 Agriculture	Sector 2 Manufacture	Elimination of Pollutant
Sector 1 Agriculture	0.25	0.40	0
Sector 2 Manufacture	0.14	0.12	0.20
Pollutant (output)	0.50	0.20	
Labor (value-added)	0.80 ($0.80)	3.60 ($3.60)	2.00 ($2.00)

process has been introduced permitting elimination (or prevention) of pollution and that the input requirements of that process amount to two man-years of labor (or $2.00 of value-added) and 0.20 yards of cloth per gram of pollutant prevented from being discharged — either by Agriculture or Manufacture — into the air.

Combined with the previously introduced sets of technical coefficients this additional information yields the following complex structural matrix of the national economy.

The input-output balance of the entire economy can be described by the following set of four equations:

$$0.75X_1 - 0.40X_2$$
$$= Y_1 \quad \text{(wheat)}$$
$$-0.14X_1 + 0.88X_2 - 0.20X_3$$
$$= Y_2 \quad \text{(cotton cloth)}$$
$$0.50X_1 + 0.20X_2 - X_3$$
$$= Y_3 \quad \text{(pollutant)}$$
$$-0.80X_1 - 3.60X_2 - 2.00X_3$$
$$+ L = Y_4 \quad \text{(labor)}$$
$$(9)$$

Variables:

X_1 : total output of agricultural products
X_2 : total output of manufactured products
X_3 : total amount of eliminated pollutant
L : employment
Y_1 : final demand for agricultural products
Y_2 : final demand for manufactured products
Y_3 : total uneliminated amount of pollutant
Y_4 : total amount of labor employed by Household and other "final demand" sectors.[1]

Instead of describing complete elimination of all pollution, the third equation contains on its right-hand side Y_3, the amount of uneliminated pollutant. Unlike all other elements of the given vector of final deliveries it is not "demanded" but, rather, tolerated.[2]

The general solution of that system, for the unknown X's in terms of any given set of Y's is written out in full below

$$X_1 = 1.573Y_1 + 0.749Y_2 - 0.149Y_3$$
$$+ 0.000Y_4 \quad \text{Agriculture}$$
$$X_2 = 0.449Y_1 + 1.404Y_2 - 0.280Y_3$$
$$+ 0.000Y_4 \quad \text{Manufacture}$$
$$X_3 = 0.876Y_1 + 9.655Y_2 - 1.131Y_3$$
$$+ 0.000Y_4 \quad \text{Pollutant}$$
$$L = 4.628Y_1 + 6.965Y_2 - 3.393Y_3$$
$$+ 0.000Y_4 \quad \text{Labor}$$
$$(10)$$

The square set of coefficients (each multiplied with the appropriate Y) on the right-hand side of (10) is the inverse of the matrix of constants appearing on the left-hand side of (9). The

[1] In all numerical examples presented in this paper Y_4 is assumed to be equal zero.
[2] In (6) that describes a system that generates pollution, but does not contain any activity combating it, the variable X_3 stands for the total amount of uneliminated pollution that is in system (8) represented by Y_3.

inversion was, of course, performed on a computer.

The first equation shows that each additional bushel of agricultural product delivered to final consumers (i.e., Households) would require (directly and indirectly) an increase of the total output of agricultural sector (X_1) by 1.573 bushels, while the final delivery of an additional yard of cloth would imply a rise of total agricultural outputs by 0.749 bushels.

The next term in the same equation measures the (direct and indirect) relationship between the total output of agricultural products (X_1) and the "delivery" to final users of Y_3 grams of uneliminated pollutants.

The constant -0.149 associated with it in this final equation indicates that a reduction in the total amount of pollutant delivered to final consumers by one gram would require an increase of agricultural output by 0.149 bushels.

Tracing down the column of coefficients associated with Y_3 in the second, third and fourth equations we can see what effect a reduction in the amount of pollutant delivered to the final users would have on the total output levels of all other industries. Manufacture would have to produce additional yards of cloth. Sector 3, the anti-pollution industry itself, would be required to eliminate 1.131 grams of pollutant to make possible the reduction of its final delivery by 1 gram, the reason for this being that economic activities required (directly and indirectly) for elimination of pollution do, in fact, generate some of it themselves.

The coefficients of the first two terms on the right-hand side of the third equation show how the level of operation of the anti-pollution industry (X_3) would have to vary with changes in the amounts of agricultural and manufactured goods purchased by final consumers, if the amount of uneliminated pollutant (Y_3) were kept constant. The last equation shows that the total, i.e., direct and indirect, labor input required to reduce Y_3 by 1 gram amounts to 3.393 man-years. This can be compared with 4.628 man-years required for delivery to the final users of an additional bushel of wheat and 6.965 man-years needed to let them have one more yard of cloth.

Starting with the assumption that Households, i.e., the final users, consume 55 bushels of wheat and 30 yards of cloth and also are ready to tolerate 30 grams of uneliminated pollution, the general solution (10) was used to determine the physical magnitudes of the intersectoral input-output flows shown in table 7.

The entries in the third row show that the agricultural and manufactured sectors generate 63.93 (= 52.25 + 11.68) grams of pollution of which 33.93 are eliminated by anti-industry pollution and the remaining 30 are delivered to Households.

VIII

The dollar figures entered in parentheses are based on prices the derivation of which is explained below.

The original equation, system (7), describing the price-cost relationships within the agricultural and manufacturing sectors has now to be expanded through inclusion of a third equation stating that the price of "eliminating one gram of pollution" (i.e., p_3) should be just high enough to cover — after payment for inputs purchased from other industries has been

met — the value-added, v_3, i.e., the payments to labor and other primary factors employed directly by the anti-pollution industry.

$$p_1 - 0.25p_1 - 0.14p_2 = v_1$$
$$p_2 - 0.12p_2 - 0.40p_1 = v_2$$
$$p_3 \qquad\quad - 0.20p_2 = v_3$$

or in rearranged form,

$$0.75p_1 - 0.14p_2 \qquad = v_1$$
$$-0.40p_1 + 0.88p_2 \qquad = v_2$$
$$\qquad\quad - 0.20p_2 + p_3 = v_3. \qquad (11)$$

The general solution of these equations — analogous to (8) is

$$p_1 = 1.457v_1 + 0.232v_2$$
$$p_2 = 0.662v_1 + 1.242v_2$$
$$p_3 = 0.132v_1 + 0.248v_2 + v_3. \qquad (12)$$

Assuming as before, $v_1 = 0.80$, $v_2 = 3.60$ and $v_3 = 2.00$, we find,

$$p_1 = \$2.00$$
$$p_2 = \$5.00$$
$$p_3 = \$3.00$$

The price (= cost per unit) of eliminating pollution turns out to be $3.00 per gram. The prices of agricultural and manufactured products remain the same as they were before.

TABLE 7. — INPUT-OUTPUT TABLE OF THE NATIONAL ECONOMY
(SURPLUS POLLUTION IS ELIMINATED BY THE ANTI-POLLUTION INDUSTRY)

Inputs and Pollutants' Output	Sector 1 Agriculture	Sector 2 Manufacture	Anti-Pollution	Final Deliveries to Households	Totals
Sector I Agriculture (bushels)	26.12	23.37	0	55	104.50
	($52.24)	($46.74)		($110.00)	($208.99)
Sector 2 Manufacture (yards)	14.63	7.01	6.79	30	58.43
	($73.15)	($35.05)	($33.94)	($150.00)	($292.13)
Pollutant (grams)	52.25	11.68	−33.93	30 ($101.80 paid for elimination of 33.93 grams of pollutant)	
Labor (man-years)	83.60	210.34	67.86	0	361.80
	($83.60)	($210.34)	($67.86)	($361.80)	
Column Totals	$208.99	$292.13	$101.80	$361.80	

$p_1 = \$2.00$, $p_2 = \$5.00$, $p_3 = \$3.00$, $p_4 = \$1.00$ (wage rate).

Putting corresponding dollar values on all the physical transactions shown on the input-output table 7 we find that the labor employed by the three sectors add up to $361.80. The

wheat and cloth delivered to final consumers cost $260.00. The remaining $101.80 of the value-added earned by the Households will just suffice to pay the price, i.e., to defray the costs of eliminating 33.93 of the total of 63.93 grams of pollution generated by the system. These payments could be made directly or they might be collected in form of taxes imposed on the Households and used by the Government to cover the costs of the privately or publicly operated anti-pollution industry.

The price system would be different, if through voluntary action or to obey a special law, each industry undertook to eliminate, at its own expense, all or at least some specified fraction of the pollution generated by it. The added costs would, of course, be included in the price of its marketable product.

Let, for example, the agricultural and manufacturing sectors bear the costs of eliminating, say, 50 per cent of the pollution that, under prevailing technical conditions, would be generated by each one of them. They may either engage in anti-pollution operations on their own account or pay an appropriately prorated tax.

In either case the first two equations in (11) have to be modified by inclusion of additional terms: the outlay for eliminating 0.25 grams and 0.10 grams of pollutant per unit of agricultural and industrial output respectively.

$$0.75p_1 - 0.14p_2 - 0.25p_3 = v_3$$
$$-0.40p_1 + 0.88p_2 - 0.10p_3 = v_2$$
$$- 0.20p_2 + \quad p_3 = v_3. \tag{13}$$

The "inversion" of the modified matrix of structural coefficients appearing on the left-hand side yields the following general solution of the price system:

$$p_1 = 1.511v_1 + 0.334v_2 + 0.411v_3$$
$$p_2 = 0.703v_1 + 1.318v_2 + 0.308v_3$$
$$p_3 = 0.141v_2 + 0.264v_2 + 1.062v_3. \tag{14}$$

With "values-added" in all the three sectors remaining the same as they were before (i.e., $v_1 = \$.80$, $v_2 = \$3.60$, $v_3 = \$2.60$) these new sets of prices are as follows:

$$p_1 = \$3.234$$
$$p_2 = \$5.923$$
$$p_3 = \$3.185$$

While purchasing a bushel of wheat or a yard of cloth the purchaser now pays for elimination of some of the pollution generated in production of that good. The prices are now higher than they were before. From the point of view of Households, i.e., of the final consumer, the relationship between real costs and real benefits remain, nevertheless, the same; having paid for some anti-pollution activities indirectly he will have to spend less on them directly.

IX

The final table 8 shows the flows of goods and services between all the sectors of the national economy analyzed above. The structural characteristics of the system — presented in the form of a complete set of technical input-output coefficients — were assumed to be given; so was the vector of final demand, i.e., quantities of products of each industry delivered to Households (and other final users) as well as the uneliminated amount of pollutant that, for one reason or another, they are prepared to "tolerate." Each industry is assumed to be responsible for elimination of 50 per cent of pollution that would have been generated in the absence of such counter measures. The Households defray — directly or through tax contributions — the cost of reducing the net output of pollution still further to the amount that they do, in fact, accept.

On the basis of this structural information we can compute the outputs and the inputs of all sectors of the economy, including the anti-pollution industries, corresponding to any given "bill of final demand." With information on "value-added," i.e., the income paid out by each sector per unit of its total output, we can, furthermore, determine the prices of all outputs, the total income received by the final consumer and the breakdown of their total expenditures by types of goods consumed.

The 30 grams of pollutant entered in the "bill of final demand" are delivered free of charge. The $6.26 entered in the same box represent the costs of that part of anti-pollution activities that were covered by Households directly, rather than through payment of higher prices for agricultural and manufactured goods.

The input requirements of anti-pollution activities paid for by the agricultural and manufacturing sectors and all the other input requirements are shown separately and then combined in the total input columns. The figures entered in the pollution row show ac-

270   THE REVIEW OF ECONOMICS AND STATISTICS

TABLE 8. — INPUT-OUTPUT TABLE OF A NATIONAL ECONOMY
WITH POLLUTION-RELATED ACTIVITIES PRESENTED SEPARATELY

	Agriculture			Manufacture			Anti-pollution	Final Deliveries to Households	National Totals
	Wheat	Anti-pollution	Total	Cloth	Anti-pollution	Total			
Agriculture	26.12 ($84.47)	0	26.12 ($84.47)	23.37 ($75.58)	0	23.37 ($75.58)	0	55 ($177.87)	105.50 ($337.96)
Manufacture	14.63 ($86.65)	5.23 ($30.98)	19.86 ($117.63)	7.01 ($41.52)	1.17 ($6.93)	8.18 ($48.45)	.39 ($2.33)	30 ($117.69)	58.43 ($346.07)
Pollutant	52.25	−26.13	26.12	11.69	−5.85	5.84	−1.97	30 ($6.26 paid for elimination of 1.97 grams of pollutant)	
Labor (value-added)	83.60 ($83.60)	52.26 ($52.26)	135.86 ($135.86)	210.34 ($210.34)	($11.70)	($222.04)	($3.93)		361.8 ($361.80)
Totals Costs	($254.72)	($83.24)	($337.96)	($327.44)	($18.63)	($346.07)	($6.26)	($361.80)	

$p_1 = \$3.23,\quad p_2 = \$5.92,\quad p_3 = \$3.19.$
$v_1 = \$0.80,\quad v_2 = \$3.60,\quad v_3 = \$2.00.$

cordingly the amount of pollution that would be generated by the principal production process, the amount eliminated (entered with a minus sign), and finally the amount actually released by the industry in question. The amount (1.97) eliminated by anti-pollution activities not controlled by other sectors is entered in a separate column that shows also the corresponding inputs.

From a purely formal point of view the only difference between table 8 and table 7 is that in the latter all input requirements of Agriculture and Manufacture and the amount of pollutant released by each of them are shown in a single column, while in the former the productive and anti-pollution activities are described also separately. If such subdivision proves to be impossible and if, furthermore, no separate anti-pollution industry can be identified, we have to rely on the still simpler analytical approach that led up to the construction of table 3.

X

Once appropriate sets of technical input and output coefficients have been compiled, generation and elimination of all the various kinds of pollutants can be analyzed as what they actually are — integral parts of the economic process.

Studies of regional and multi-regional systems, multi-sectoral projections of economic growth and, in particular, the effects of anticipated technological changes, as well as all other special types of input-output analysis can, thus, be extended so as to cover the production and elimination of pollution as well.

The compilation and organization of additional quantitative information required for such extension could be accelerated by systematic utilization of practical experience gained by public and private research organizations already actively engaged in compilation of various types of input-output tables.

MATHEMATICAL APPENDIX

Static-Open Input-Output System with Pollution-Related Activities Built In

Notation

Commodities and Services

$1, 2, 3, \ldots i \ldots j \ldots m, m+1, m+2, \ldots g \ldots k \ldots n$
   useful goods   pollutants

Technical Coefficients

a_{ij} — input of good i per unit of output of good j (produced by sector j)

a_{ig} — input of good i per unit of eliminated pollutant g (eliminated by sector g)

ENVIRONMENTAL REPERCUSSIONS AND ECONOMIC STRUCTURE   271

a_{gi} — output of pollutant g per unit of output of good i (produced by sector i)

a_{gk} — output of pollutant g per unit of eliminated pollutant k (eliminated by sector k)

r_{gi}, r_{gk} — proportion of pollutant g generated by industry i or k eliminated at the expense of that industry.

Variables

x_i — total output of good i

x_g — total amount of pollutant g eliminated

y_i — final delivery of good i (to Households)

y_g — final delivery of pollutant g (to Households)

p_i — price of good

p_g — the "price" of eliminating one unit of pollutant g

v_i — "value-added" in industry i per unit of good i produced by it

v_g — "value-added" in anti-pollution sector g per unit of pollutant g eliminated by it.

Vectors and Matrices

$A_{11} = [a_{ij}] \qquad i, j = 1, 2, 3, \ldots, m$

$\left. \begin{array}{l} A_{21} = [a_{gi}] \\ A_{12} = [a_{ig}] \end{array} \right\} \begin{array}{l} i = 1, 2, 3, \ldots m \\ g = m+1, \ m+2, \ m+3, \ldots, n \end{array}$

$A_{22} = [a_{gk}] \qquad g, k = m+1, \ m+2, \ m+3, \ldots, n$

$Q_{21} = [q_{gi}] \qquad \begin{array}{l} i = 1, 2, \ldots m \\ g = m+1, \ m+2, \ldots n \end{array}$

$Q_{22} = [q_{gk}] \qquad g, k = m+1, \ m+2, \ldots, n$

where $q_{gi} = r_{gi} a_{gi}$

$\qquad\quad q_{gk} = r_{gk} a_{gk}$

$$X_1 = \left\{ \begin{array}{c} x_1 \\ x_2 \\ \cdot \\ \cdot \\ x_m \end{array} \right\} \quad Y_1 = \left\{ \begin{array}{c} y_1 \\ y_2 \\ \cdot \\ \cdot \\ y_m \end{array} \right\} \quad V_1 = \left\{ \begin{array}{c} v_1 \\ v_2 \\ \cdot \\ \cdot \\ v_m \end{array} \right\}$$

$$X_2 = \left\{ \begin{array}{c} x_{m+1} \\ x_{m+2} \\ \cdot \\ \cdot \\ x_n \end{array} \right\} \quad Y_2 = \left\{ \begin{array}{c} y_{m+1} \\ y_{m+2} \\ \cdot \\ \cdot \\ y_n \end{array} \right\} \quad V_2 = \left\{ \begin{array}{c} v_{m+1} \\ v_{m+2} \\ \cdot \\ \cdot \\ v_n \end{array} \right\}$$

PHYSICAL INPUT-OUTPUT BALANCE

$$\left[\begin{array}{c|c} I - A_{11} & -A_{12} \\ \hline A_{21} & -I + A_{22} \end{array} \right] \left[\begin{array}{c} X_1 \\ \hline X_2 \end{array} \right] \quad \left[\begin{array}{c} Y_1 \\ \hline Y_2 \end{array} \right] \tag{15}$$

$$\left[\begin{array}{c} X_1 \\ \hline X_2 \end{array} \right] = \left[\begin{array}{c|c} I - A_{11} & -A_{12} \\ \hline A_{21} & -I + A_{22} \end{array} \right]^{-1} \left[\begin{array}{c} Y_1 \\ \hline Y_2 \end{array} \right] \tag{16}$$

INPUT-OUTPUT BALANCE BETWEEN PRICES AND VALUES-ADDED

$$\left[\begin{array}{c|c} I - A'_{11} & - Q'_{21} \\ \hline - A'_{12} & I - Q'_{22} \end{array} \right] \left[\begin{array}{c} P_1 \\ \hline P_2 \end{array} \right] = \left[\begin{array}{c} V_1 \\ \hline V_2 \end{array} \right] \tag{17}$$

$$\left[\begin{array}{c} P_1 \\ \hline P_2 \end{array} \right] = \left[\begin{array}{c|c} I - A'_{11} & - Q'_{21} \\ \hline - A'_{12} & I - Q'_{22} \end{array} \right]^{-1} \left[\begin{array}{c} V_1 \\ \hline V_2 \end{array} \right] \tag{18}$$

Supplementary Notation and Equations Accounting for Pollution Generated Directly by Final Consumption

Notation

Technical Coefficients

$a_{gy,(i)}$ — output of pollutant generated by consumption of one unit of commodity i delivered to final demand.

Variables

y_g^* — sum total of pollutant g "delivered" from all industries to and generated within the final demand factor,

x_g^* — total gross output of pollutant g generated by all industries and in the final demand sector.

$$A_y = \left\{ \begin{array}{cccc} a_{m+1, \, y(1)} & a_{m+1, \, y(1)} & \cdots & a_{m+1, \, y(m)} \\ a_{m+2, \, y(2)} & a_{m+2, \, y(2)} & \cdots & a_{m+2, \, y(m)} \\ \cdot & \cdot & & \\ \cdot & \cdot & & \\ a_n \, y_1 & a_n \, y_2 & \cdots & a_n \, y_m \end{array} \right.$$

$$Y_2^* = \left\{ \begin{array}{c} y^*_{m+1} \\ y^*_{m+2} \\ \cdot \\ \cdot \\ y_n^* \end{array} \right\} \qquad x_g^* = \left\{ \begin{array}{c} x^*_{m+1} \\ x^*_{m+2} \\ \cdot \\ \cdot \\ x_n^* \end{array} \right\}$$

In case some pollution is generated within the final demand sector itself, the vector Y_2 appearing on the right-hand side of (15) and (16) has to be replaced by vector $Y_2 - Y_2^*$, where

$$Y_2^* = A_y Y_1. \tag{19}$$

The price-values added equations (17), (18) do not have to be modified.

Total gross output of pollutants generated by all industries and the final demand sector does not enter explicitly in any of the equations presented above; it can, however, be computed on the basis of the following equation,

$$X^* = [A_{21} : A_{22}] \left[\begin{array}{c} X_1 \\ \hline X_2 \end{array} \right] + Y_2^*. \tag{20}$$

[19]

GREEned National STAtistical and Modelling Procedures: the GREENSTAMP approach to the calculation of environmentally adjusted national income figures

Roy Brouwer

CSERGE, University of East Anglia, UK

Martin O'Connor

C3ED, Université de Versailles–St Quentin en Yvelines, France
e-mail: Martin.OConnor@c3ed.uvsq.fr

Walter Radermacher

Statistical Office of the Federal Republic of Germany (Statistisches Bundesamt), Wiesbaden, Germany

Abstract: The paper gives an overview of the GREENSTAMP Project (GREEned National STAtistical and Modelling Procedures) which, during 1994–1996, developed results and recommendations concerning empirically and theoretically robust methods for greening national accounts. The recommended approach centres on methods for quantifying economic opportunity costs associated with meeting specified environmental performance standards. In this perspective, a 'greened GDP' is a hypothetical measure of a performance potential, viz., an estimate of the level of output (or of consumption, or of national income, etc.) that a national economy would be able to achieve while simultaneously respecting specified environmental quality and resource husbandry requirements. The GREENSTAMP approach is modular, establishing linkages with different categories of data and analyses. First, information is organized in so-called satellite environmental accounts, which describe the state of the environment according to chosen categories and measures (largely non-monetary), and which establish links between economic activity sectors and environmental change in terms of the pressures acting on each environmental category. Second, cost information is obtained through various levels of analysis (firms and households, sectors and macro-economic aggregates) about the economic resource requirements – such as investments needed or consumption foregone – that would be necessary in order to reduce a specified environmental pressure. Environmental defensive expenditures, pollution avoidance cost curves, and macroeconomic comparative static and dynamic scenario modelling are among the applicable cost concepts and tools. In this cost-effectiveness perspective, the value of environmental assets and services is not estimated in monetary terms directly. Rather, estimates of the costs – at various scales of analysis and timeframes – of specified improvements in environmental performance are considered in relation to scientific, political and economic judgements about the importance of the environmental functions, services and assets in question.

Keywords: avoidance cost curves, cost-effectiveness, dynamic models, environmental standards, GREENSTAMP, national accounts, statistical methods, sustainable national income.

8   *R. Brouwer, M. O'Connor and W. Radermacher*

Reference to this paper should be made as follows: Brouwer, R., O'Connor, M. and Radermacher, W. (1999) 'GREEned national STAtististical and Modelling Procedures: the GREENSTAMP approach to the calculation of environmentally adjusted national income figures', *Int. J. Sustainable Development,* Vol. 2, No. 1, pp. 7–31.

1   Prologue

In this paper we give an overview of the outcomes of a research project, known as the GREENSTAMP Project, funded by the European Commission during 1994–1996, whose purpose was to develop recommendations for useful ways in which national accounting systems can be adapted and exploited to construct indicators of macroeconomic performance vis-à-vis the environment.[1] The main task was to appraise options for the definition and estimation of environmentally adjusted national income figures (henceforth 'greened GDP' for short). This goal has to be viewed against the backdrop of a wider concern that national accounting systems be developed as sources of information for evaluating policy and investment alternatives in the pursuit of economic, social and environmental sustainability goals.

There have been many perspectives developed on the questions of greened GDP and indicators for sustainability. We outline thus the overall approaches that the GREENSTAMP project developed, and the reasons why we consider them best practice. Section 1 summarizes the central analytical perspectives and empirical analysis approaches, and Section 2 presents the main research and policy recommendations of the project itself.

The research project set out initially to resolve a set of methodological and practical problems with identifying and quantifying 'environmental costs', consisting of environmentally defensive expenditures and avoidance costs. The idea was that, having once established how to calculate these expenditures and costs, they could be estimated for any real economy on a sector-by-sector basis. Then, when these costs were subtracted from traditionally measured national income (GDP), the resulting environmentally adjusted national income figure would provide policy-makers with a better compass for macroeconomic performance evaluation.

In the course of the project, the identification and quantification problems were recognized to form just one part of a much more complex issue. Investigating the range of existing proposals for adjusting GDP brought to light a remarkable diversity of propositions about what makes GDP a useful policy indicator (or not), and about what the role could be of an environmentally adjusted GDP figure in policy decision-making processes (e.g. Aaheim and Nyborg, 1995; Cobb and Cobb, 1994; Daly, 1989; Faucheux and Froger, 1994; De Haan and Keuning, 1996; Hueting, 1989; Hueting *et al.*, 1995; Peskin, 1991; Peskin and Lutz, 1993; Stahmer, 1995). The project at this stage became very much a process of reflection and clarification around existing work, as well as the development of some original ideas and applications.

One point that emerged very clearly from these reflections was the need to distinguish fundamentally between different contexts and scales of measurement and aggregation. In brief, for the study of a national economy we can distinguish (at least) the following levels: the 'micro-micro' level of individual households and firms; an economic 'sector' of activity as defined in national statistical systems; the national macroeconomic level measured by aggregates of sectoral activity.

Within the GREENSTAMP project itself, detailed investigations were made of environmental defensive expenditures and of firm-level reporting practices on environment-related investments and expenditures (see Brouwer and Leipert in this issue). Rigorous statistical procedures were developed and tested empirically for the construction of abatement cost functions for emissions of various nitrogen compounds in the national economy of Germany (see Riege-Wcislo and Heinze in this issue). The experiences gained in the calculation of avoidance costs for these specific pollutants confirmed on an empirical basis the theoreticians' worries that calculations based on sector-by-sector statistical information could not, on their own, be an adequate basis to come to a meaningful adjustment of a macroeconomic aggregate like GDP to obtain a sustainability indicator.

This conclusion led necessarily to a reconsideration of the role that avoidance costs information should play in the construction of an adjusted GDP figure. We may, in retrospect, summarize the evolution of our thinking as follows. Most proposals for adjusting GDP, including the ones coming initially from project participants, have sought to turn a short-term indicator derived from a periodic accounting system of the economy in the past (namely GDP), into a long-term indicator of (potential) economic and environmental success. This transformation is achieved, in theory, by a process of 'correcting GDP'. Typically, this is taken to mean putting prices on the 'depreciations' of natural capital that are the sources of flows of goods and services from nature. In this way the intertemporal scarcity of environmental assets (natural resources, ecosystem services, etc.) is factored into to the modified national product figure. The calculation of a 'greened GDP', sometimes also supposed to be a 'sustainable national income' figure, by making deductions from current period GDP, is the main example of this approach.

After making an appraisal of the numerous difficulties, both theoretical and practical, in making inventories of environmental services and their possible depreciation and in estimating a set of shadow prices that might be proposed to induce market actors to behave in a sustainable way, the GREENSTAMP project abandoned this deduction-based approach. The project's perspective shifted from delivering estimates based on welfare-theoretic 'optimizing' criteria, to estimation procedures of long-term economic performance potential based on cost-effectiveness relative to 'satisfycing' criteria in an explicit scenario perspective.

A satisfycing approach seeks a 'good' result while acknowledging that uncertainties, complexities and the variety of principles for judgment make it impossible to decide what is 'the best'. Cost-effectiveness analysis in environmental policy seeks to estimate a 'least cost' way of achieving specified environmental goals. For our project, the objective became to develop procedures for the definition and empirical estimation of prospects for maintaining national income at high levels while simultaneously respecting a specified set of goals representing long-term maintenance of key environmental services. We consider this satisfycing approach to constitute 'best practice' for providing macroeconomic policy-relevant information concerning efficient and equitable use of the environment.

The project's objective thus became more complex than initially envisaged. On the one hand, it is proposed that the national accounting system should continue to support traditional accounting uses, such as defining the money value of national output, sectoral statistics, employment, and so on. On the other hand, in relation to environmental and

10   *R. Brouwer, M. O'Connor and W. Radermacher*

economic sustainability concerns, systematic information on the state of the environment, on environmental 'pressures' and on technical potentials for pressure abatement should be developed, but we do not propose the simple calculation of a greened GDP. Rather than environmentally adjusted national accounts being used as merely a descriptive instrument permitting calculation of a 'corrected' macroeconomic indicator, they should be developed as a policy support databank for a variety of analyses and modelling purposes aimed at clarifying prospects of ecological–economic sustainability.

2   Methodological overview

2.1   *Economic theory, environmental science and statistical practice*

The call for sustainable development at all scales (North–South, European Union, national and sub-national levels) signals the emergence of a set of policy preoccupations quite distinct from the post-World War Two fiscal management and macroeconomic performance preoccupations that were the backdrop for the original systems of national accounts. The new requirement is for use of national accounts statistics to explore long-term environmental prospects as well as economic performance prospects. This new application of national statistics is emerging within political contexts where conflicts emerge and must be resolved between competing economic and environmental interests, between people holding different value systems and different principles of judgement, and also between different representations of future states and visions of the world.

The approach to calculation of environmentally adjusted national income figures that we adopt seeks to respond to four broad sets of considerations in an integrated manner:

- *Scientific adequacy*: do the description and evaluation methods deal well with the important features of the natural world and of the ecological, technological and social change processes in question?

- *Social adequacy*: do the methods furnish information in ways that respond to stake-holders' needs and that support social processes of decision-making?

- *Economic rationality*: do the suggested choices or courses of action that emerge from the valuation, statistical analysis and modelling procedures respect economic efficiency, in the sense of appearing to be reasonably cost-effective ways for moving in the desired directions or for arriving at the envisaged outcomes?

- *Statistical adequation*: can the methods and measurements proposed be implemented in conformity with established quality standards in statistical work, within the budgets available for this work?

No one of these four criteria, on its own, is enough to judge the adequacy of an approach to development of macroeconomic indicators for sustainability. Work in this domain must, therefore, consist of a process of tuning theory, statistical concepts, actual measurement and the corresponding interpretation and use of results. In the GREENSTAMP project, when it has turned out that a theoretical concept is not applicable to the situation being analysed, or that it cannot be measured in a reliable way, then we have abandoned it as inadequate for offering policy guidelines.

2.2 Economic and ecological dimensions of sustainability

We summarize in this section the perspective on sustainability that underpins our work, and the way it assigns complementary roles to monetary and non-monetary information in sustainability analyses, and then we present in a synthetic way our favoured approach to defining an environmentally adjusted national income. We have adopted an ecological economics perspective (cf. Faucheux and O'Connor, 1998), suggested in Figure 1, from which point of view economic resource management must fulfill two complementary functions:

- The delivery of an ecological welfare base through assuring maintenance of critical environmental functions and amenity (lower portion of the diagram), and

- The delivery of an economic welfare base through production of economic goods and services (upper portion of the diagram).

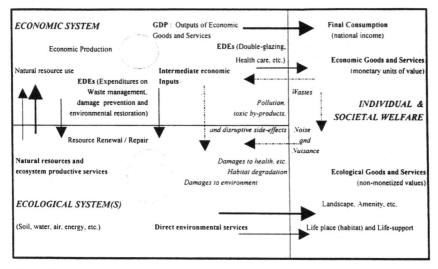

Figure 1

In this perspective, a basic design criterion for 'greening' national accounts should be to furnish an information base allowing cost-effectiveness in the allocation of economic resources for the pursuit, over time, of economic and environmental output goals. This means information sets covering production and exchanges of economic goods and services (including final consumption), changes in the state of the environment, and the economy–environment interfaces that bear on these two domains. The question is, how should monetary and non-monetary information be applied?

Many contributions on the construction of environmentally adjusted accounts have suggested procedures for making monetary estimates of the value of environmental benefits and damages, in order to quantify natural capital depreciation in monetary terms (e.g., El Serafy, 1989; Pearce and Atkinson, 1993; Repetto, 1989). Our study does not endorse this angle of attack for the calculation of a greened GDP.

Ecological as well as economic goods and services contribute to human welfare, and for analysis purposes they may be treated as complementary but in a relation that is asymmetric. Environmental quality is a primary support for human welfare and for sustainable economic activity. Policies aimed at safeguarding this primary support function – that is, meaning to commit scarce resources in order to maintain or recover the desirable level of environmental quality – correspond to a kind of 'social demand' for maintenance of environmental functions. In economics it is habitual to ask, is the value of the benefit obtained, or of the loss avoided, worth the investment of economic goods and labour needed to obtain it? Yet this 'demand' for environmental quality, which will include provision for future generations and a demand for protection from environmental harms, cannot easily be expressed as a value in monetary terms. Even if such estimates can be made, the numbers obtained often have very large error bars (if this is the right terminology!) and can be highly sensitive to underlying parameter assumptions (e.g., concerning possibilities and elasticities of substitution, endowment and income distribution, technological progress prospects). So the application of traditional cost–benefit analysis aimed at identifying a Pareto-efficient allocation of resources is difficult, rather indeterminate and controversial. Many environmental decisions involve problems of risk distribution, management of uncertainties, and conflict of interests that cannot be dealt with very well as cost–benefit 'optimizing' problems. Attempts to put monetary values on environmental benefits and damages that are spread over time, and whose significance is sometimes as much ethical as biophysical, are often quite artificial (O'Connor, 1997a, 1997b).

To avoid misunderstandings, let us agree that, for project appraisals and localized cost–benefit policy problems, the monetization of environmental benefits/damages can be extremely useful. However, the purposes of macroeconomic performance analysis require that a very large range of environmental performance concerns be considered simultaneously. The indeterminacies and controversies inherent in some of these matters – such as climate change impacts, risks and benefits of nuclear and genetic modification technologies, health dangers of toxic wastes and pesticide residues – are sufficiently great that they give rise to the phenomenon of 'horse and rabbit stew'. In a process of aggregation involving monetary estimates for possible climate change impacts, the precise data that we have for some domains of economic activity and performance potential will simply be swamped.

For this reason (among others), we recommend that, for macroeconomic environmental performance purposes, statistical work in monetary units should be confined to the stocks and flows of produced economic goods and services (the upper portion of Figure 1), but not be generalized to environmental functions and services (the lower portion). At macroeconomic levels of analysis, the best operational specification for a society's 'demand for environmental quality' will be in non-monetary terms, through defining environmental standards that express the society's priorities for the delivery of the ecological welfare base to both present and future generations.

We know, furthermore, that any society's environmental performance goals will involve compromises that will be the product of explicit and implicit negotiations. The debates over priority-setting may, in some cases and to some extents, be aided by attempts to quantify in monetary terms the relative welfare significance of natural resources and of different environmental amenities, life-support functions and other services. Nonetheless, for the various reasons already mentioned, we have concluded that in empirical work supporting the calculation of environmentally adjusted national income figures, *full monetary valuation of environmental benefits and deterioration is not needed and should not be the objective.*

Multi-criteria decision-support approaches that bring together cost-effectiveness frameworks with non-monetary information on environmental changes contained in satellite accounts, will be an effective way to organize the information needed to calculate macroeconomic performance indicators adequate for the purposes wanted – a single-period greened GDP, or a time-series of greened GDPs, or several scenario time-series of greened GDPs. Also, the matrix structures of environmental satellite accounts linked to the monetary national accounts in aggregate or sector-by-sector can be an effective and highly communicative way for presenting the costs and benefits associated with environmental policy and other development options. A multi-criteria perspective thus provides for the presentation of information for discussion and support of decision-making procedures in ways that do not yield a unique ranking of options, but that help make explicit the sorts of social choices and ecological and economic trade-offs that underpin the macroeconomic aggregates and time-series that are constructed.

2.3 Defining an environmentally adjusted national income

The intuitive idea of an environmentally adjusted national income figure (a greened GDP) is quite simple. It is an estimate of the level of output (or of consumption, or of national income, etc., depending on the exact measure proposed) that a national economy would be able to achieve while simultaneously respecting the environmental quality and resource husbandry requirements for sustaining welfare levels in the long term.

Although the idea seems simple, good empirical estimations of greened GDP and, by extension, of a sustainable national income (SNI) are not simple matters, for several reasons. First, the estimations do not involve only the measurement of a level of real aggregated economic activity, rather they are inferences about what is or might be feasible for the future. Second, there are a lot of differences of opinion, including social/ethical value judgments as well as scientific uncertainty, about the ecological and economic determinants of feasibility — technological change possibilities and risks, new natural resource discoveries, the resilience and stability of ecosystems, the importance of biodiversity conservation, and so on.

In the course of the GREENSTAMP project, we distinguished and discussed three main approaches to the calculation of an environmentally adjusted national income figure considered as a macroeconomic indicator for sustainability. These are:

- Estimation of an environmental net national product (ENNP) as defined in neoclassical models of growth-with-natural-capital, and interpretation as an estimate for an SNI. The ENNP can, in theory, be estimated through making deductions from the economy's GDP, these deductions representing the depreciation of capital stocks, including economic (produced or machine) capital, human capital, and, most importantly in this context, natural capital.

- Estimation of an environmentally adjusted GDP figure as proposed by Hueting *et al.* (1992), through making deductions from conventional GDP representing the economic costs of achieving independently specified environmental quality and conservation standards (e.g., costs associated with pollution emission reductions) sufficient for achieving long-run sustainability of all important environmental functions.

14   *R. Brouwer, M. O'Connor and W. Radermacher*

- Estimation of a greened GDP and, by extension, of an SNI based directly on
  empirically calibrated modelling of a national economy in order to calculate feasible
  economic output subject to respect for environmental quality (ecological–economic
  sustainability) norms.

The first approach depends strongly on imputation of monetary values to all flows of
benefits and damages from natural resources and environmental functions during present
and future periods of economic activity. The second and third approaches, by contrast, do
not monetize the social demand for environmental goods and services. Rather they
designate environmental sustainability standards in non-monetary terms (e.g. critical
thresholds for pollutants).

It may also be noted that both the first and second approaches are consistent, each in
their own way, with a neoclassical welfare theoretic interpretation of the environmentally
adjusted national product figure as an aggregate indicator for overall welfare
optimization. By contrast the third approach, based on modelling, estimates a 'shadow
GDP' – an aggregate measure of a feasible economic output – without any particular
welfare-theoretic significance. In the modelling approach, economic output and
environmental quality are dealt with as complementary but incommensurate objectives,
so no welfare aggregation across ecological and economic domains is needed.

After careful review of theoretical and empirical estimation issues, we have
concluded that that the first approach, the production of a figure for greened GDP
obtained through deductions of 'natural capital depreciation' from conventional GDP,
and, more particularly, interpretation of this figure as an estimate for SNI, is theoretically
erroneous and – in view of definitional and estimation problems – largely illusory for
providing a meaningful indicator for sustainability (see, in particular, the discussions in
Asheim, 1994; Faucheux, Muir and O'Connor, 1997; Pezzey, 1997).

Turning to the second approach, we are in sympathy with Hueting's (1980, 1996)
arguments for defining economic adjustment costs associated with respect of
environmental sustainability standards defined in non-monetary terms. This was indeed
the starting point for the GREENSTAMP project in 1994. However, the approach laid out
by Hueting *et al.* (1992), although it avoided some of the difficulties associated with
quantifying in welfare-theoretic terms the significance of complex and far-reaching
environmental changes, did not in our view resolve adequately the methodological
problems involved in (a) defining environmental quality standards and priorities, and (b)
estimating economic opportunity costs associated with meeting sustainability standards.
In particular, the subtraction of avoidance costs (including defensive expenditures
actually made and also the 'costs' that would hypothetically be incurred to respecting the
sustainability standards) from real national income figures is not, in our view, a
satisfactory procedure for estimating the feasible national income for a (hypothetical)
sustainable economy.

We thus favour the third approach, which is to make estimates of environmentally
adjusted national income using multi-sector national economic models. This approach
unites several sorts of analytical and statistical work, including: (1) avoidance-cost
analysis at firm and branch/sectoral level which is the basis for calculating the resource
implications of a (hypothetical) reduction of a specific environmental pressure (such as
CO_2 emissions, or a heavy metal residue); and (2) whole-economy multi-sectoral
modelling, either dynamic simulation or comparative static. In the full GREENSTAMP
Project Final Report (Brouwer and O'Connor, 1997b), we set out to demonstrate how

these several sorts of analysis can be brought together in a way that can provide useful information on requirements and prospects for achieving sustainability. The papers contained in this issue, several of which are based directly on components to the GREENSTAMP final report, are contributions to this demonstration task.

2.4 Cost-effective resource management to maintain environmental functions

Hueting has for many years put forward an approach to the definition of a gNNP that is close to the 'strong sustainability' perspective that specifies the sustaining of environmental services through safeguarding the functionality of the ecosystem structures that furnish them (Hueting, 1989; Hueting *et al.*, 1992, 1995). The essential reasoning is as follows.

*   First, physical standards are defined for environmental pressures, at levels that provide for the long-run maintenance of the key environmental functions (e.g. drinking water quality, climate stability, forest health and regeneration, fisheries stock health, and so on).

*   Second, in order to satisfy these standards, remedial measures are required (e.g. technical pollution abatement measures, substitutes for non-renewable natural resources, measures aimed at replacing environmentally detrimental activities by alternatives that are not dangerous to the environment). Estimates are made of the monetary costs of the actions (investments of produced capital, labour, etc.) that are needed to implement such measures — that is, the economic costs. For each environmental function needing protection or restoration, the idea is to identify the minimum economic costs to be borne in order to move from current environmental use levels to sustainable use levels.

*   Finally, these costs for all categories of environmental functions are added together, say *CAS*, and this total is deducted from the conventional NNP, say *Y*, to yield $Y^* = Y - CAS$.

The result of this adjustment calculation was originally called a 'sustainable national income' (Hueting *et al.*, 1992). Subsequent reflection has showed that this procedure probably gives a much too pessimistic view of the sustainability potential of the economy. In effect, the 'cost' components, *CAS*, constitute an aggregation of the opportunity costs in terms of consumption (economic output valued in present prices) that would have to be foregone (either not produced or invested in environmental protection measures) to achieve the specified environmental standards. The above analysis is actually quantifying the policy trade-off between:

1   Depleting/degrading environmental functions (critical natural capitals) by not making the adjustments required to satisfy the norms; and

2   Foregoing consumption and/or using up economic capital if the resource use commitments were made that are needed to respect the norms.

A valid interpretation of the sum of these 'costs of achieving sustainability' would be as an indicator of 'distance-from-sustainability' of the present pattern of economic activity (see Faucheux and Froger, 1994; Faucheux, *et al.*, 1994; and Ekins and Simon in this issue). But the adjusted figure *Y** is probably significantly lower than the national income that could be obtained, and maintained durably, while respecting the norms. The economic expenditures and foregone production aggregated together in *CAS* are not net reductions in economic activity. Rather, the 'correction' measures the magnitude by which current activity would have to be reoriented in order to respect the norms.

These observations suggested the need for developing further the Hueting approach in order to formulate a more rigorously valid concept of an SNI. The feature to be preserved is the principle of respecting critical use levels of environmental functions – in effect defining standards for the preservation of environmental functions for future generations. The deficiency to be overcome is that the Hueting method as initially put forward (Hueting *et al.*, 1992) does not actually estimate what would (or might) be the national income generated along a sustainable time-path.

The following modifications to the Hueting calculation procedures and interpretation have thus been proposed (see also Brouwer *et al.*, 1996). First, when 'indirect' (inter-sectoral) effects and 'structural' measures, such as changes in volumes of sectoral activity (including final consumption), are to be considered, the economic costs associated with implementing environmental protection measures to the desired standards can more consistently be estimated by means of an economic multi-sector equilibrium model. This sort of approach specifically takes into account the 'indirect' or inter-sectoral effects of measures taken on the relative prices and levels of sectoral activity and also, thus, the reallocation of resources between sectors (see also De Boer *et al.*, 1994).

Thus, for example, one can aim to calculate a figure for SNI defined as an estimate, under specified assumptions, for the level of national consumption that is technologically feasible for an economy while respecting the sustainability standards. This indeed becomes the definition that we propose for a greened GDP, that is:

- An estimate of a hypothetical national economic product that would be obtainable for the accounting period or periods in question, subject to the condition that the economy is respecting a specified set of environmental standards.

It is important to note that (i) this definition may be applied retrospectively to evaluate (counter-factually) a real present or past situation, or it may be applied speculatively towards the future; in the latter case (ii) it provides for the construction of time-series of greened GDP figures (on a period by period basis); and, most importantly, (iii) it allows that more than one greened GDP (environmentally adjusted national product figure) might be calculated, or more than one time-series might be calculated, as a function of the environmental standards specified.

We emphasize that a greened GDP, as we define it, usually does not measure actual economic performance or welfare delivery. Rather it offers an estimate based on multi-sector economic modelling (or somesuch, see discussions below), of the level and composition of environmentally respectful economic output that, for each accounting period being considered, may be feasible with currently known technology or under hypotheses about future technological innovation.

De Boer *et al.* (1994) have emphasized the necessity to clarify the numerous assumptions of a scenario character that must be made in order to estimate a 'greened' or 'sustainable' national income in this 'strong sustainability' perspective. We reiterate this point, and add that, by highlighting the 'scenario' character of the various technological, economic, demographic, lifestyle (etc.) hypotheses being made, the speculative character of the analyses is kept clearly in mind.

Turn now to the nature of the information that is 'integrated' in any effort at estimation of a greened GDP defined in this way. Within any economic system, trade-offs will exist between production output and environmental maintenance and enhancement goals. These trade-offs are not simple to quantify, because they can involve a range of quite different sorts of choices and time-frames, including for example (see also Hueting *et al.*, 1992):

- Expenditures within production sectors to improve efficiency of resource use or to reduce specified polluting emissions per unit of output, through changes to technologies employed within any given production sector;

- Changes to particular natural resources or physical locations of environmental exploitation, including exploitation of renewable resources and respect of maximum sustainable yields or assimilation capacities;

- Replacement of products or activities by alternatives judged to be less noxious for the environment, that is, changes to products and consumption patterns (which may in part reflect responses to relative price changes, in part changes in consumer preferences and also changes in income distribution and in population).

So, in analyses seeking to quantify policies and opportunity costs for meeting sustainability goals, it can be necessary to treat these different sorts of adjustments in distinct ways. Private and public sector actions may involve investments over widely differing time-frames. Any analysis must make clear which technological possibilities are considered in calculations, which categories of environmental pollution or ecological change are being dealt with under prevailing policy and research funding priorities, and so on.

The cost-effectiveness approach, as initially developed by Baumol and Oates (1971) in the context of the implementation of environmental quality standards for pollution control, takes a performance standard as given and aims to identify the way of attaining it that involves the least expenditure of scarce economic resources. In effect this is a type of partial equilibrium analysis. In reality, of course, the process is much more complicated. First of all, the standard setting is partly dependent on initial estimates about the probable magnitude of these costs (very expensive adjustments are unlikely to be politically feasible). Further, the costs and their incidence can be very sensitive to the time-frame for implementation. (It is obvious, for example, that phasing in pollution emissions standards over a 10–20 year period can be integrated with renewal of manufacturing technologies and with the turnover of a big part of the road vehicle fleet.) It is also true that costs can be highly path-dependent (for example, 'lock-in' to specific technological choices, incompatibilities between different technological or infrastructure investment options). Finally, the least-cost criteria may be modulated by concern for the distribution of the burdens of adjustment.

From a partial equilibrium theoretical point of view, the most cost-effective or least-economic-cost way of achieving pollution abatement is found by ranking the marginal costs of (sets of) possible measures sequentially according to increasing magnitude, resulting in a marginal cost curve for the firm or sector. In practice many difficulties arise when trying to construct this cost curve, related in part to the problem of defining time-scales of implementation and in part to the limited availability of statistical information (see Radermacher *et al.*, and Riege-Wcislo and Heinze, both in this issue). Moreover, technical measures alone may appear to be insufficient to respect a chosen environmental standard. So-called structural measures, that is measures aimed at reducing the volume of environmentally harmful economic activity, are desirable if not inevitable. The question then becomes whether it is not more cost-effective to take structural measures only, or a combination of technical and structural measures. This question can be given a coherent response only in the framework of a scenario approach, that makes explicit hypotheses about the timing of various policy and investment responses.

Broadly speaking, a multi-sector model-based cost-effectiveness approach can be developed in two ways:

- First, an ex-post modelling of the economy, taking into account the possible economy-wide effects of the (hypothetical) introduction of currently available technical measures or options to reduce environmental pressures in one economic sector, based on the actual structure and institutional setting of the economy (Schäfer and Stahmer, 1989).

- Second, an ex-ante modelling of a dynamic path of the economy, in which social responses and technological development to reach environmental standards are taken into account.

Thus, useful calculations of greened GDP figures can be based on comparative static modelling or on dynamic modelling. In the case of dynamic modelling, the model output is a time-series for the aggregate national product that is attainable while respecting, for each period, the specified sustainability guidelines. Such figures are potentially valuable inputs into policy debates, but certainly they are not the basis in themselves for policy choices. The figures obtained will depend on, among other things the environmental standards imposed. Given that uncertainties are quite large, and that the range of different effects of a decision extends to many different ecological, social and economic domains, the processes of standard setting, statistical estimation and aggregation to produce such figures involve a whole range of caveats and contingencies. This implies the construction not one but many greened GDP figures, usually in the form of time-series.

In this issue, the papers by O'Connor and Ryan and by Schembri present a multi-sectoral Structural Economy–Environment Simulation Modelling (SEESM) approach, which allows development of scenarios of feasible (or, at least, conceivable) economic futures including their consequences for selected environmental pressures. In this approach, information on available technical measures that, at a different level of analysis, may be used in calculating the direct costs of technical measures, is a key data source for postulates about Leontief sectoral coefficient changes over time. It thus becomes crucially important to specify the time-scales over which technical and structural changes (adjustments in sectoral activity levels, including environmental pressure abatement efforts) are postulated to take place (see, also, the dynamic input–output modelling by Duchin and Lange, 1994; and the modular modelling approach of Meyer and Ewerhart, 1996).

In the SEESM perspective, it is understood that the (sustained) delivery of environmental functions implies, through the intermediary of the policy obligation to respect specified environmental pressure norms, some constraints on delivery of economic goods and services. These restrictions might take the form of constraints on the technologies utilized or in terms of constraints on levels of production and consumption and (hence) energy, water or other natural resource use or pollutant emissions. The dynamic intersectoral modelling means that the 'trade-offs' can be investigated in terms of changes in levels of sectoral activity from period to period, changes in consumption patterns, in labour requirements, and so on. Scenarios can be developed to simulate alternative policies, and to obtain estimates of the environmental benefits achievable from technological changes, or the significance of changes in final consumption and of depollution and environmental restoration activity to achieve a desired normative situation.

Although such modelling cannot represent or resolve fine-grain layers of policy evaluation, it is a useful tool for laying out major issues of economic feasibility and policy trade-offs. Scenario modelling in this sense is a decision-support tool, which helps build a platform of agreed understandings upon which stakeholders can state their interests and lay out their claims. Indeed, the decision support information of most value is not found in the aggregate figure themselves, but in the richness of information through comparison of the different model outputs and scenarios.

3   Recommendations from the GREENSTAMP project

Within the GREENSTAMP project, four major methodological research areas were distinguished, as reflected in the structure of the *Final Project Report* (Brouwer and O'Connor, 1997b). These were: (a) review of the theoretical and statistical basis for deriving sustainability indicators; (b) defensive expenditures; (c) the construction of avoidance cost curves; (d) micro-macro aspects of environmental–economic accounting. Keeping in mind this four-way division, we provide a synthetic set of recommendations deriving directly from the project work, and also mention some fields of further research that we judge as very important though they were not specifically addressed within our own project.

3.1   Methodological perspectives

There are a range of different concepts of, and ways of estimating, an environmentally adjusted national product (greened GDP). For the construction of useful macroeconomic performance indicators, we recommend adoption of the following definition based on a macroeconomic cost-effectiveness perspective :

> **R.1**   An environmentally adjusted national product (greened GDP) is the value (in money units) of the highest ('best') feasible economic production for the accounting period in question, subject to the condition that the economy is respecting a specified set of environmental standards.

As discussed in Section 2, this definition may apply to a real or model situation, and it provides for the construction of time-series of greened GDP figures on a period-by-period basis. Moreover, it allows that more than one greened GDP might be calculated, or more than one time-series as the case may be, as a function of the environmental standards specified.

> **R.2**   Useful calculations of greened GDP figures can be based on comparative static modelling or on dynamic modelling.

In particular, scenario modelling work permits the quantification of the feasibility space for possible future national economic trajectories, including the calculation of time-series for environmentally adjusted national income, based on explicit hypotheses about acceptable pollution emissions levels, the available natural and manufactured resources,

20   *R. Brouwer, M. O'Connor and W. Radermacher*

consumption patterns to be maintained or changed, and technological options. This sort of approach provides, in our view, a richer and empirically more robust information base for appraisal of macroeconomic and sectoral policy options than can be provided by an indicator based on subtracting imputed money values of natural capital stocks from GDP.

3.2   European contexts for statistics collection and implementation

The EU through the Commission (EC, 1993; EUROSTAT, 1994) and the Parliament has committed member countries to the production of modified national accounts that allow measures of economic performance to be put in relation with information on environmental change. In December 1994 the EC in its Report COM(94) 670 Final (EC 1994) set out a plan for analysis and implementation over several stages for the development of systems of environmental indicators and green accounting in Europe. The European Parliament, in its resolution A4-0209/95, affirmed the general elements of the action plan, while requesting some fine tuning, such as provision for the specificity of each country's environmental preoccupations within a common framework and an environmental accounting framework that allows actual and potential causes of environmental deterioration to be identified. Three stages of green accounting were envisaged:

- The systematization of environmental pressure information through agreeing on accounting framework conventions (ESEA) and through implementing a common system of environmental pressure indices (ESEPI);

- The creation of a set of integrated economic and environmental indices (ESI);

- Implementation of methods for placing monetary values on natural resources and environmental deterioration categories, permitting full integration of economic and environmental accounts in monetary terms.

Recent work, including our project, has made clear that the greening of national accounts is not only a question of economic theory and of accounting concepts, but also a question of data availability and information technology. The good organization of data processing, the improvement of statistical services by means of standardization and the documentation of data quality by meta-information (pedigree of data, reliability etc.) is essential. A precondition for further progress is the organization of a 'cost-effectiveness information system' close to the sectoral structure of input–output tables of national accounting. The European activities ESI, ESEPI and ESIS under the leadership of Eurostat, are good starting points for this purpose. We recommend:

> **R.3**   The available economic and technical data-sets should be organized and linked in such a way that they can readily be used for both the calculation of direct economic costs (e.g., changes of weights within the distribution of available techniques) and the multi-sectoral economic modelling (e.g., changes of the average production technique).

> **R.4**   In addition to ESI and ESEPI, some European countries and Eurostat have started developing an Emission Structure Information System (ESIS). We recommend that these sorts of initiatives be continued.

> **R.5**   It would be useful to pool current experience, at present fragmented across Europe, concerning the estimation of sector-by-sector and pollutant-by-pollutant avoidance cost curves. This could be promoted through an EC DG-XII Concerted Action or research programme accompanying measure.

R.6 Country applications of model-based calculations of environmentally adjusted national income figures (that is, comparative static or scenario time-series of greened GDP figures) must be carried out for several different EU countries in order to gain real experience with the diversity of environmental-economic conditions and with the adequacy (or not) of country data bases and information formats for the calculation of greened GDPs.

In the GREENSTAMP project itself, based on the cost-effectiveness approach, a procedure for the construction of abatement cost curves (ACCs), showing the direct effects of technical abatement measures, was developed and empirically tested for various nitrogen compounds. The empirical work demonstrated that a fully adequate official comprehensive database for construction of ACCs is not yet available in Germany, the country of application. The required information originates in different (economic and technical) spheres and institutional sources, each with their own data classification and categorization systems, which have to be brought together. The final aim in the ACC estimation procedure is to have results for the 'homogeneous production processes' as the statistical accounting unit.

Following the lines set out in the *Manual on The Construction of Abatement Cost Curves* (Riege-Wcislo and Heinze, 1996) produced in the course of the GREENSTAMP project (and subsequently adapted for publication in this issue: see Radermacher *et al.*, and Riege-Wcislo and Heinze), the necessary time to construct one ACC for one pollutant is approximately three-quarters of a person-year. In the German empirical study, only the direct microeconomic effects of abatement measures have been estimated. To get to macroeconomic results, as are required for the linking of the data with the national accounts, a more comprehensive modelling approach is needed. In the future, statistics offices can offer basic data about abatement costs for selected environmental pollutants, which then have to be linked with modelling calculations by research institutes. In view of the limited financial resources and the generally poor data situation (relative to the immense complexity of the pollution and environment domain), a full coverage of all processes, products and environmental themes seems unreachable. With the help of a statistical selection procedure (the details of which have still to be developed), a sample of environmental pressures and of polluting economic sectors should be chosen, including the most important environmental pressures and harmful economic processes with a high technical abatement potential. The proposed methodology for calculating ACCs with integrated techniques/changes of production processes may then be implemented empirically.

Having made this assessment of statistical feasibility, the roles that we have identified for statistical offices in greened national accounts preparation are:

1 Estimations of the direct costs of cost-effective responses to environmental deterioration on a sector-by-sector and pollutant-by-pollutant basis involving the use of available technologies under existing economic conditions;

2 The information base for estimations of the indirect effects of cost-effective responses on the individual economic sectors and the economy as a whole, based on the available information in statistical offices about the input–output structure of a nation's economy in a certain accounting year (that is, with the help of ex-post modelling using fixed Leontief coefficients).

These two suggestions do not exhaust all possibilities. They are, however, enough to demonstrate the basis for implementing our 'cost-effectiveness' perspective on resource

22   *R. Brouwer, M. O'Connor and W. Radermacher*

management for sustainability. The information obtained in the two categories mentioned can furnish preliminary indications of the required economic re-orientations in order to respect environmental standards.

In addition, we recommend the development of scenario modelling that goes beyond the simple compiling of statistics and exploitation of ex-post data (such as in the NAMEA framework), to the quantification ex-ante of the feasibility space for possible national economic trajectories. This is work properly carried out by research institutions, in cooperation with policy and statistics agencies (for example, as reported in O'Connor and Ryan, and in Schembri, both in this issue). Scenario modelling work permits the quantification of the 'feasibility space' for possible future national economic trajectories, including the calculation of time-series for environmentally adjusted national income (that is, time-series for future greened GDPs) based on explicit hypotheses about the environmental quality (ecological–economic sustainability) standards to be respected, the available natural and manufactured resources, consumption patterns to be maintained or changed, and the available technological options.

We emphasize that the figures obtained in each of these three analysis categories have to be interpreted cautiously.

- First, there is often a lack of information about possible interactions (synergy or incompatibilities) between technical measures included in the direct cost calculations.

- Second, estimates of direct costs usually focus on a particular type of pollutant emission or environmental quality goal, whereas in reality there are often interactions between environmental pollutants that make estimation of environmental damage strongly site-specific. Although several careful studies are proceeding, we still seem to be far away from being able to calculate cost-effective responses in a rigorous way for a set of complicated environmental problems. These estimation difficulties also carry over to the calculations of indirect (cross-sectoral) effects associated with environmental policy implementations.

- Third, the statistical data for the costs and the technical measures to reduce environmental pressures stem from different data sources, and often these sources do not correspond with the economic sectors distinguished within the usual SNA. Integrating this information in a meaningful and useful way is perhaps the most important task that can be organized by Statistical Offices.

3.3   Environmental defensive expenditures

The GREENSTAMP project dealt intensively with the question of which role the environmental protection expenditures should play in an environmentally adjusted GDP (see, especially, Liepert, 1989; Brouwer and Leipert, in this issue; the literature discussion goes back to Kuznets, 1948; Herfindahl and Kneese, 1973; and others). This role depends generally on the objective of the adjustment procedure and correspondingly on the interpretation of the environment-related expenditures in the adjusted domestic product.

In this area, the first question that we have addressed is: for the purposes of greened GDP estimation, what is the right way to take account of the welfare significance of the flows of environmental goods/services during the accounting period? The issue to be surmounted is that real GDP, as traditionally measured, rises as a result of increased production that disregards the environment, and rises still further when environmental damages are then mitigated through further economic activities. This is a perverse characteristic of GDP as a macroeconomic performance indicator.

The interpretation of certain expenditure categories as (environmentally) defensive expenditures, or EDEs, is rooted in the debate about analytical deficiencies of the conventional GDP as an economic welfare measure. It has sometimes been proposed that, in order to 'correct' the GDP as a performance indicator, deductions from the conventionally measured GDP should be made for the EDEs aimed at maintaining or improving the level of environmental services (or reducing harm). In effect, this procedure would involve a reclassification of the EDEs as intermediate goods/services in national accounts systems, whereas they have conventionally (for essentially pragmatic reasons) been included in final consumption.

On the one hand, if environmental or natural capital is considered as a factor of production, this reclassification procedure makes sense. However, such a correction is difficult to implement in statistical practice, because it is very difficult to draw the line between expenditures conducted for defensive reasons as opposed to productive reasons, or in tandem with productivity-gain objectives.

On the other hand, if the environmental goods/services in question are regarded as themselves contributing directly to welfare, the deductions should not be made in a periodic accounting procedure. One question that then arises from a welfare-theoretic point of view, is how to construct a welfare measure that aggregates the value of environmental goods/services together with the conventional consumption of economics goods and services.

In this project, we have adopted the convention that economic and ecological sources of welfare should be treated as complementary but not commensurate. We note that the positive environmental effects of environmental protection expenditures are not monetarized in the existing SNA and are, consequently, not represented as a separate output category in the GDP volume figure. This is actually consistent with our cost-effectiveness framework, where a greened GDP figure or time-series is considered simply as an indicator of feasible economic activity and there is no compelling welfare-theoretic reason to quantify EDEs separately for the adjustment to national income figures. So we conclude:

> **R.7** The environmental outputs of environmental protection activities should not be monetarized for macroeconomic accounting purposes. (There are also statistics quality reasons for this, to considering the well-known uncertainties and degree of arbitrariness of monetary estimates of many environmental damages and benefits.)

On the other hand, environmental functions and services should be identified in qualitative or multi-criteria terms for their welfare significance, even if they do not need to be evaluated in monetary terms. It is necessary and urgent to supplement the data on monetary environmental protection expenditures (and costs) by physical data. Useful information about the environmental effects of actual environmental protection expenditure is only obtained when this information can be linked to physical environmental indicators. So we further recommend:

> **R.8** The current European initiatives for EDE data collection should be pursued, and high priority should be given to defining ways that this information can really be used in environmental policy priority-setting and policy evaluation.

24   *R. Brouwer, M. O'Connor and W. Radermacher*

R.9   In particular, Eurostat should pave the way for including environment-orientated in-process modifications (integrated environmental protection measures) in the SERIEE data system on environmental protection expenditure. It is well-known that these measures are becoming increasingly important in the environmental management strategy of enterprises, substituting more and more the dominating role of end-of-the-pipe measures.

R.10   Eurostat should work out with high priority the 'natural resources use and management account' foreseen as a part of SERIEE.

Measures taken by enterprises to increase the efficiency of energy and materials use in production processes are becoming more and more important. These measures are often included in the environmental cost accounting of enterprises. In many cases they are the most important integrated option for reducing environmental pollution induced by the production process. They are not included in the Environmental Protection Expenditures Account (EPEA) of SERIEE, because they do not fulfill the causa finalis criterion. So it seems necessary and urgent to develop an operational concept and classification of this type of measure and to record reliable data as well. Otherwise SERIEE will publish data on environmental protection expenditures in the near and further future that are less and less representative of the total array of efforts to reduce pollution and material and energy consumption.

Also, we have a few observations about terminology. In some accounting approaches, guided by a notion of 'optimizing' resource allocation (where marginal cost is equal to marginal benefit obtained), information on EDEs is considered as a proxy for the money value of environmental degradation that is being avoided or repaired or compensated for. Of course, this is valid only to the extent that the EDEs reflect real marginal benefits. For several reasons, including the diffuse nature of environmental damages and services, free-rider behaviour, limited expenditure budgets of economic actors, irreversibilities, lack of information and so on, EDEs will often relate to a very incomplete set of benefits to be regained or damages to be avoided.

We do not favour the interpretation of EDE or 'avoidance cost' information as a proxy measure for the value of environmental services maintained or regained. Rather, we place the emphasis directly on the quantification of economic costs that are, or that would be necessary to reach or regain desired environmental quality. This is considered the most appropriate way to deal with environmental deterioration in a periodic accounting system.

Calculations of the costs of improving environmental quality or avoiding environmental degradation depend crucially on the environmental quality to be reached serving as a standard for these cost calculations. The reference level proposed in the existing SEEA is that the nation's domestic economic activities during the actual period should not impair the environmental quality as it exists at the beginning of the period. Of course other reference standards are thinkable. For example, in the *Sustainable National Income* project at Statistics Netherlands, ecological sustainability standards are established for a number of environmental problems in a scientific way within specified uncertainty ranges. Contrary to the standard advocated in the SEEA, this sustainability standard does not refer to the state of the environment at the beginning of some accounting period, but to an ecologically sustainable state – that is, the sustainable rate and type of use of environmental systems and their products and services.

The two categories of costs – prevention costs actually incurred and potential prevention costs not undertaken by the actors while justifiable from a social welfare or sustainability point of view – directly complement each other. In any one period, without the activities financed by the actual prevention expenditures the degradation of the environment would have been higher than is actually the case. However, if a zero-degradation or stronger sustainability standard is the reference point, then additional avoidance and restoration costs would be needed to fill the gap between the environmental quality actually reached and the more ambitious period standard. Estimates of these additional costs of avoidance and restoration must be made through inferences based on data about available technologies or lifestyle changes and so on – the various estimates of direct and indirect costs as discussed elsewhere.

3.4 Environmental performance and reporting at firm level

One of the key tasks of our project was to investigate the extent to which information at the firm or 'micro' level on environmental pressures and abatement prospects can become a useful data source for green national accounting purposes. Our investigations of the empirical estimation of cost curves and of the data requirements for modelling confirm the importance of such information. At the same time, our research shows that enterprise-level monitoring, quality control and reporting practices produce information that is extremely heterogeneous. There is not a simple 'translation' from this heterogeneous information to the technological database and cost-accounting categories relevant to calculations of greened GDP.[2] In addition, much information is commercially sensitive, which can limit its accessibility to researchers.

> **R.11**   It is useful to distinguish two different senses in which environmental consequences of economic activity are 'taken into account' or internalized. The first is a qualitative sense of internalization that is reflected in the information categories and reporting purposes of economic actors. The second is the attempt to produce quantitative indicators at sectoral and national levels.

In qualitative terms, a direct parallel can be drawn between the normative interest in greened GDP as an indicator of prospects for national economy activity to respect defined environmental norms (including sustainability-related standards), and the increased attention within the private sector for documenting company environmental performance and product environmental quality (for example eco-reporting, best available technology, ISO 14000 protocols). The macroeconomic accounting adjustments and the new firm reporting practices are two different ways in which the burden of proof is being shifted from relative neglect of environmental consequences of economic activity towards the obligation to take the 'best reasonable measures' in favour of environmental quality.

However, the 'bridge' between firm-level (micro) data and the statistical categories for greened national accounting (macro) is not a simple passage of collection and aggregation. In fact, this key finding is common to the three different domains of our project empirical work – the estimation of abatement cost curves, the classification and estimation of environmental defensive expenditures, and environmental information at firm level.

Let us summarize the micro–macro link from the point of view of constructing national accounts and of calculating figures for environmentally adjusted national income (greened GDP). The required information comes from many different economic and technical domains, each having their own classification systems. Data about emissions and about major raw materials and energy inputs is usually available at an aggregated level for firms, sectors and the economy as a whole. This sort of data then has to be

26   *R. Brouwer, M. O'Connor and W. Radermacher*

supplemented by very detailed and disaggregated technical information (where available) about abatement measures and their costs. Such data often derive from various research projects, some within the private sector, much of it within publicly funded institutions. Thus there is a big gap between this detailed but fragmented information on the one hand, and statistically useful figures for abatement potential and costs for representative firms or sectors on the other hand. Bridging this gap depends on the cooperation of researchers, technicians and process managers, and statisticians to share their specialized knowledge and arrive at mutual understanding of their contrasting needs.

There is not a simple accounting or reporting procedure to ensure this 'bridge' between technical-economic research, firm information and statistical figures. What is most important is to encourage a permanent interaction based on the assertion of a public interest in the production and dissemination of high quality information on technical potentials for abatement at firm level, and the costs involved.

> **R.12**   We recommend that work should be encouraged involving partnerships between private sector actors, researchers and policy-makers, to further define how this reorientation of priorities and reporting conventions at 'micro' level can be promoted and exploited for more effective policy-making for sustainability in the public domain. A permanent interaction between researchers, statisticians, public policy-makers and private sector stakeholders is essential for good progress in this field.

The production and sharing of information can be promoted by publicly funded clearing houses such as the European Environment Agency, and by giving a high profile to specialized datasets with particular policy importance (such as BATNEEC information as provided for under recent EC Directives). In addition, the development of internationally recognized standards and quality certification, through public policy and corporate protocols (such as the ISO 14000 series) can promote the process of 'internalization through information'.

Empirical data at the 'micro' levels (that is, technical research data and firm-level information) is an essential input for construction of abatement cost curves. It is also needed as underlying data for the more comprehensive modelling work required to calculate the economy-wide effects of changing production patterns brought about by introducing emission abatement techniques on a large scale. As already discussed elsewhere in the report, the economy-wide modelling must be developed on a basis of hypotheses about rates and types of technical change and final consumption change, on a sector-by-sector and pollutant-by-pollutant basis. These hypotheses reflect knowledge about new technologies available or in prospect (process efficiency improvements, new products) and judgements about the responses of economic actors (firms, financial intermediaries and households) to the new technological opportunities, policy signals, and so on. In these behavioural respects also, a permanent interaction between researchers, statistical offices, policy-makers and a variety of producer and consumer stakeholders is a pre-requisite for quality and pertinence of work.

3.5   Further work and the evolving character of policy analyses

Our approach to defining environmentally adjusted macroeconomic indicators emphasizes the pragmatic and evolving character of policy-oriented analyses. Environmental and technological-prospect datasets will never be comprehensive in the sense of responding to all analytical or policy-evaluation needs. Modelling approaches are important and, in particular, ex-ante scenario modelling has a major role for the exploration of domains of possibility and constraints on the development of a national economy through time. Yet in the face of data limitations and the indeterminacies of future studies, some results will be less robust than others. The task is not to pursue an illusion of precision, but to understand the quantified results and the uncertainties in a dialectical way. Scenario modelling approaches do not lead to one unique figure for an 'environmentally corrected national income' (greened GDP) for a nation but, rather, to many sets of time-series for possible greened GDPs. As already mentioned, the information of most value is not found in the aggregate figures themselves – which are always open to alteration through changing assumptions – but in the richness of information and understanding obtained through the work of construction and comparison of the different model outputs and scenarios.

By way of conclusions, we want to mention some fields of further research that were not specifically addressed within our own project but that we consider to be particularly important for the tuning of national accounts systems for sustainability policy concerns.

The empirical results presented in our project (notably in Part II of the final report) relate mainly to one broad category of environmental pressures: atmospheric pollutant emissions related to fuel combustion (e.g., CO_2, NO_x, SO_x), and also some other nitrogen compounds. We have insisted that, faced with the range and complexity of environmental problems, pragmatic answers must be found for the following questions. Which types of environmental pressure are most relevant? Which industrial or other productive activities are important? How can we ensure representativeness and significance if, within a reasonable budget, data collection and analysis is limited to relatively small samples?

In future work, avoidance cost curve estimation and scenario analyses should be widened in scope to cover also the environmental pressures arising in such categories as: heavy metal emissions; chemical pollutant emissions from agricultural practices (such as nitrates, phosphates and pesticides) into land and water systems; and others.

Some applied work has already been carried out in some EU countries, for example within the NAMEA framework in the Netherlands (De Haan, 1996; CBS, 1996; Keuning, 1996). The integrated land cover data based on satellite measurements that is managed by the European Environment Agency, and the water accounts being developed in several European countries, are further examples of highly valuable information sets. However, experience with the use and articulation of the various information sets is as-yet fragmented, and there will be advantages to be gained through pooling knowledge.

The quantification for macroeconomic modelling purposes of different sorts of environmental pressure can pose a diversity of problems. For example, the doses of chemical pollutants entering water systems from agriculture depend on a variety of local factors, including the particular agricultural practices, rainfall patterns, the dynamics of water transport on the surface, in rivers and underground, and any adjacent non-agricultural land and water resource uses. Development of an adequate database and incorporation in the simulation model of environmental standards information relating to agricultural soil and water quality targets, poses a number of challenges for the modelling specifications and empirical calibration.

Another dimension that has not been addressed in detail within our project is the international dimension of environmental pressures. We have noted (in Chapter 7 of the full report, Brouwer and O'Connor, 1997b) that issues such as climate change and large-scale deforestation must be treated with proper regard to their global political-ecological

28   *R. Brouwer, M. O'Connor and W. Radermacher*

scale. An important task for policy-scenario studies and green accounting is to represent not only the volumes of international trade in different categories of goods and services but also the corresponding 'trade' – actual or imputed by origins – in environmental burdens. A purely national focus could lead to quite erroneous conclusions.

A highly developed country with a significant component of service industries, banks, insurances and so on, may look perfectly sustainable in a separated national ecobalance because it imports its needed (depletable) primary materials and energy and has succeeded in exporting the polluting production industries. Statistical trends over the last 30 years are, in fact, widely in accordance with such a pattern of unequal development: an increasing amount of total international trade combined with a decreasing share of imports of raw materials into the industrialized countries and a decreasing share in toxic pollutants. For example, in Japan, relatively more aluminium is imported today from countries such as Canada where hydroelectricity is very cheap than in the 1970s. Similarly, Japan has for some time been developing hydroelectric power in countries such as Brazil and Indonesia. A part of the pollution and ecological damage associated with Japan's economic dynamism is, in effect, being shifted offshore.

In addition to environmental statistics for nationally registered environmental pressures (such as energy resource exploitation, forest cutting, fish catch, pollutant emissions and land-use changes), the corresponding effects have to be calculated which are linked with imports and exports of raw materials and goods. A number of analysis tools are being actively developed which can respond to this need. Ecological 'rucksacks' can – in principle – be calculated by a combination of lifecycle analysis (for the pressures of the excavation and production of energy and raw materials) and input–output analysis (for the international trade of goods, which are already composed of different raw materials). Because international input–output tables that are up-to-date and of high quality are not available, this sort of work is still in a quite early state of development. Yet outlines are already clear. In Germany, for instance, some groups including the Wuppertal Institute have established a working group for cooperation in material and energy flow accounting, including international trade. Elsewhere, preliminary analyses have been conducted for a range of countries to quantify the 'ecological footprints' left by production and consumption in rich countries, in terms of land area, water and photosynthesis requirements, compared with the availability of these resources in the producing and consuming countries. The 'sink' capacity of different regions of the planet for carbon dioxide emissions, compared with the anthropogenic sources of this gas, has recently become the object of international debate. (It has been argued that the industrialized countries have appropriated the environmental services in an historically inequitable way, in this sense taking from their less developed neighbours as well as imposing a cost on future generations.)

Finally, it may be mentioned that the international or trans-boundary transactions of capital in various forms (mostly electronically transmitted) greatly outweigh in money value, for any given period (a day, a month, a year), the flows of tangible goods and services. In the context of national income measures and their interpretation, increased attention should be given to international capital movements and their driving roles for national economic activity and, by transmission effects, environmental pressures at national and international levels.

These suggestions are by no means exhaustive. They simply signal some important fields for analysis, the data requirements for which should be integrated within greened national accounting systems. These brief remarks also highlight the point made throughout this project, that quantitative results from sectoral studies or macroeconomic multi-sector modelling scenario analyses exploring prospects for economic and environmental sustainability, must be interpreted in an open-ended way. The insights that can be obtained are among the many inputs to policy debate. Indicators must not be taken out of context of the assumptions, measurement frameworks and appraisal purposes within which they are constructed.

Endnotes

1   This paper is adapted from the *Final Summary Report* (Brouwer and O'Connor, 1997a) for the project 'Methodological problems in the calculation of environmentally adjusted national income figures', carried out during 1994–1996 for the European Commission Directorate General XII under Contract No. EV5V-CT94-0363, under the coordination of Peter Bosch and Roy Brouwer (Statistics Netherlands – Central Bureau voor de Statistiek). The final report was prepared principally by Roy Brouwer (CBS) and Martin O'Connor (C3ED), in extensive consultation with Walter Radermacher (Statistisches Bundesamt, Germany) and other members of the GREENSTAMP project team, and with technical assistance from Sarah Dwyer (C3ED). In addition to the CBS, the C3ED and the BD, the GREENSTAMP project partners included the Wuppertal Institute for Climate, Environment and Energy in Wuppertal, Germany, and Christian Leipert of the Institute für Ökologische Wirtschaftsforschung, Berlin, Germany.

2   For detailed discussions, refer to Part IV of Brouwer and O'Connor (1997b), which is based on intensive information on firms' environmental reporting practices compiled by researchers at the Wuppertal Institute (under the leadership of Eberhard Seifert) and an interpretative framework for classification of firms' environmental strategies adapted from Faucheux, O'Connor and Nicolaï (1997, 1998).

References

Aaheim, A. and Nyborg, K. (1995) 'On the interpretation and applicability of a 'green national' product', *Review of Income and Wealth*, Vol. 41, No. 1.

Asheim, G. (1994) 'Net national product as an indicator for sustainability', *Scandinavian J. of Economics*, Vol. 96, pp.257–265.

Baumol, W.J. and Oates, W.E. (1971) 'The use of standards and prices for protection of the environment', *Swedish J. of Economics*, Vol. 73, pp.42–54.

De Boer, B., De Haan, M. and Voogt, M. (1994) 'What would net domestic product have been in an environmentally sustainable economy?', in *National Accounts and the Environment*, Papers and Proceedings from a Conference of the London Group, 16–18 March 1994, London.

Brouwer, R and O'Connor, M. (1997a) Final Summary Report of the research project No. EV5V-CT94-0363, Methodological Problems in the Calculation of Environmentally Adjusted National Income Figures, in 2 volumes, produced by the C3ED for the DG-XII of the European Commission.

Brouwer, R. and O'Connor, M. (1997b) Project Final Report of the research project No. EV5V-CT94-0363, Methodological Problems in the Calculation of Environmentally Adjusted National Income Figures, in 2 volumes, produced by the C3ED for the DG-XII of the European Commission.

Brouwer, R., O'Connor, M. and Radermacher, W. (1996) 'Defining cost effective responses to environmental deterioration in a periodic accounting system' in Proceedings of the Third Meeting of the London Group on Natural Resource and Environmental Accounting (held at Stockholm, 28–31 May 1996), Statistics Sweden, Stockholm.

CBS (1996) 'Accounts and indicators for the economy and the environment; the 1986–1992 NAMEAs' (in Dutch), Statistics Netherlands, Voorburg/Heerlen.

30   *R. Brouwer, M. O'Connor and W. Radermacher*

Cobb, C.W. and Cobb, J.B. Jr. (1994) *The green National Product. A proposed index of sustainable economic welfare*, University Press of America, Lanham, MD.

Daly, H.E. (1989) 'Towards a measure of sustainable social net national product', in Ahmad, Y.J. *et al.* (Editors) *Environmental Accounting for Sustainable Development*, The World Bank, Washington, DC., pp.8–9.

Duchin, F. and Lange, G.M. (1994) *The Future of the Environment: Ecological Economics and Technological Change*, Oxford University Press, New York.

El Serafy, S. (1989) 'The proper calculation of income from depletable natural resources', in Ahmad, Y. *et al.* (Editors) *Environmental Accounting for Sustainable Development*, The World Bank, Washington, DC.

European Commission (1993) *Towards sustainability; a European Community programme of policy action in relation to the environment and sustainable development*, Publication 93/C138.

European Commission (1994) Directions for the EU on Environmental Indicators and Green National Accounting, Communication to the Council and the European Parliament, COM(94)670 Final.

EUROSTAT (1994) SERIEE 1994 Version, Luxembourg.

Faucheux, S., Muir, E. and O'Connor, M. (1997) 'Neoclassical theory of natural capital and 'weak' indicators for sustainability', *Land Economics*, Vol. 73, No. 4, pp.528–552.

Faucheux, S. and Froger, G. (1994) 'Le 'Revenue National Soutenable': est-il un indicateur de soutenabilité?', *Revue Francaise d' Economie*, Vol. 9, No. 2, pp.3–37.

Faucheux, S., Froger, G. and O'Connor, M. (1994) 'The costs of achieving sustainability: the differences between environmentally corrected national accounts and sustainable national income as information for sustainability policy', *Discussion Papers in Environmental Economics and Environmental Management*, University of York, UK.

Faucheux, S. and O'Connor, M. (Editors) (1998) *Valuation for Sustainable Development : Methods and Policy Indicators*, Edward Elgar, Cheltenham.

Faucheux, S, O'Connor, M. and Nicolaï, I. (1997) 'Economic globalisation, competitiveness, and environment', *Globalisation and Environment: Preliminary Perspectives*, OECD, Paris, pp.101–141.

Faucheux, S; O'Connor, M. and Nicolaï, I. (1998) 'Globalisation, competiveness, governance and environment: what prospects for a sustainable development?', in Faucheux. S., Gowdy, J; and Nicolaï, I. (Editors) *Sustainability and Firms: Technological Change and the Changing Regulatory Environment*, Edward Elgar, Cheltenham, UK.

De Haan, M. and Keuning, S.J. (1996) 'Taking the environment into account: the NAMEA approach', *Review of Income and Wealth*, Series 42 No. 2 (June 1996).

De Haan, M. (1996) 'An input-output calculation of avoidance costs', contribution to the fourth biennial meeting of the international society for ecological economics (ISEE), Boston, 4–7 August 1996.

Herfindahl, O.C. and Kneese, A.V. (1973) 'Measuring social and economic change: benefits and costs of environmental pollution', in Moss, M. (Editor), *The Measurement of Economic and Social Performance, Studies in Income and Wealth*, Vol. 38, pp.441–508.

Hueting, R. (1980) *New scarcity and economic growth; more welfare through less production?*, North-Holland Publishing Company, Amsterdam.

Hueting, R. (1989) 'Correcting national income for environmental losses: towards a practical solution', in Ahmad, Y. *et al.* (Editors), *Environmental Accounting for Sustainable Development*, The World Bank, Washington, DC.

Hueting, R., Bosch, P. and De Boer, B. (1992), *Methodology for the Calculation of Sustainable National Income*, WWF International Publication.

Hueting, R., De Boer, B., Bosch, P. and Van Soest, J.P. (1995) 'Estimating sustainable national income', in W. van Dieren (Editor), *Taking Nature into Account*, Copernicus, Springer-Verlag, New York.

Hueting, R. (1999) 'The Parable of the Carpenter', Paper prepared for the workshop *Valuation Methods for Green National Accounting: A Practical Guide*, co-organized by The World Bank, the UN Statistical Office, and the ISEE, held at Washington DC., March 1996, revised version forthcoming in the *International Journal of Environment and Pollution*, Vol.12.

Keuning, S.J. (1996) *Accounting for Economic Development and Social Change*, IOS Press, Amsterdam.

Kuznets, S. (1948) 'National income and economic welfare' in Kuznets, S. (Editor), *Economic Change*, London, p.192ff.

Meyer, B. and Ewerhart, G. (1996) 'Modelling towards eco domestic product', contribution to *International Symposium on Integrated Environmental and Economic Accounting in Theory and Practice*, Tokyo, 5–8 March 1996.

O'Connor, M. (1997a). 'Internalization of environmental costs: implementing the polluter pays principle in the European Union', *Int. J. Environment and Pollution*, Vol. 7, No. 4, pp.450–82.

O'Connor, M. (1997b) 'Environmental valuation: from the point of view of sustainability', in Dragun, A. and Kristin (Editors) *Sustainability and Global Environmental Policy*.

Pearce, D. and Atkinson, G. (1993) 'Capital theory and the measurement of sustainable development: an indicator of 'weak' sustainability', *Ecological Economics*, Vol. 8, No. 2, pp.85–103.

Peskin, H.M. (1991) 'Alternative environmental and resource accounting approaches', in Constanza, R. (Editor), *Ecological Economics, the Science and Management of Sustainability*, Columbia University Press, New York.

Peskin, H.M. and Lutz, E. (1993) 'A survey of resource and environmental accounting approaches in industrialized countries', in Lutz, E. (Editor), *Towards Improved Accounting for the Environment*, The World Bank, Washington, DC.

Pezzey, J. (1997) 'Sustainability constraints versus 'optimality' versus intertemporal concern, and axioms versus data', *Land Economics*, November 1997, Vol. 73, No. 4, pp.448–66.

Repetto, R. (1989) *Wasting Assets: Natural Resources in the National Income Accounts*, World Resources Institute, Washington, DC.

Riege-Wcislo, W. and Heinze, A. (1996) 'Manual on the construction of abatement cost curves, methodological steps and empirical experiences' produced in the course of the GREENSTAMP project (and subsequently adapted for publication in this issue (see the papers by Radermacher *et al.*, and Riege-Wcislo and Heinze).

Schäfer, D. and Stahmer, C. (1989) 'Input–output model for the environmental protection activities', *Economic Systems Research*, Vol.1, No.2, p.203–228.

Stahmer, C. (1995) 'Environmental accounting and the system of national accounts', in van Dieren, W. (Editor) *Taking Nature into Account; A Report to the Club of Rome*, Springer-Verlag, New York.

[20]

Whither economics?
From optimality to sustainability?*

PETER BARTELMUS

Environment, Energy and Industry Statistics Branch, United Nations Statistics Division, Room DC2-1650, New York, NY 10017, USA

ABSTRACT. Environment and economy interact. Most economists and economic policy makers have tended to neglect this interaction as 'external' to mainstream market economics. The question is whether environmental externalities have reached a level where they overwhelm optimality and efficiency in resource allocation. Sustainability in growth and development has been advanced as a criterion for dealing with the social costs of environmental impacts. The article examines how this criterion can be operationalized for assessing the significance of environmental concerns in economic analysis and policy. Indicators of economic and ecological sustainability are defined and compiled for selected countries. Based on these indicators, operational paradigms of 'eco-nomics' and 'sustainable development' are advanced.

1. Economics out of sync?

Bashing economics for wrong diagnoses and misleading policy advice has a tradition. The oil crises of the 1970s, social upheaval following structural adjustment in developing countries, the chaotic transition from centrally planned to market economies, and conspicuous environmental externalities cast doubt on the predictive and advisory capability of conventional analysis. Perhaps the most eloquent critique of one of the basic tenets of economics, namely, optimal resource use under ideal conditions of atomistic markets, was launched by Galbraith (1986).[1] More recently, as part of a growing literature of 'discontent', the apparent resurgence of *laissez-faire* economics has been castigated on account of its indifference to reality: for-

---

* The author is a staff member of the United Nations Statistics Division (UNSD). The views expressed here are his own and not necessarily those of the United Nations. The Index of Material/Energy Intensity (IMEI) was compiled by Donald Shih, Officer-in-charge of the Environment Statistics Section of UNSD; the figures and tables were prepared with the assistance of Kathleen Suite, Statistics Assistant. The extensive comments and suggestions of three (anonymous) reviewers helped to streamline the paper and are gratefully acknowledged.

[1] It is quite curious that Galbraith's attack on the fundamentals of widely taught and applied economics has brought about so little change in economic analysis. Galbraith (1986) himself points out that this is due to an alliance of 'mature' corporations and the state; both hide their common goals of economic growth and power behind the screen of allegiance to—powerless—perfect competition.

P. Bartelmus

malistic rigour appears to be favoured at the expense of real-world vision (Ehrlich, 1994; Heilbroner and Milberg, 1995; Kuttner, 1997).

Mainstream economists seem to ignore or deny the mounting critique of economic fundamentals, in particular of 'rational' microeconomic behaviour in perfectly competitive markets, ensuring optimality in the allocation of scarce resources. Others argue that action based on an ideal situation might contribute to achieving this situation, possibly by a 'sequence of policy reforms' (Dasgupta, 1994: 42), or that 'economics in a vacuum' might still throw light on complicated problems (Samuelson and Nordhaus, 1992: 295). As long as nothing drastic happens, we can probably live with the 'semi-fiction' (Solow, 1992: 10) of perfect markets.

At the same time, drastic things do happen. Environmental phenomena that were characteristically dismissed as 'external' to market economics may have reached a scale where they undermine policy analysis based on conventional economics by generating 'social' costs in excess of 'private' benefits of income and consumption. A frequently cited example is the case of Kiribati, a Pacific Ocean island living off its phosphate deposits. Depletion of these deposits terminated all mining activities in 1982, and GDP dropped to less than half of its average level of the previous four years (OECD, 1985). Dismissing this issue as the concern of a small island will not do either. Industrialized countries may have dumped a good deal of increasing environmental problems on financially starved developing countries. Importing natural resources (e.g. of fish and timber) and translocating unsafe and polluting industries can be seen as the export of depletion and degradation to the 'Third World' under the cloak of market liberalization.

Other, notably global, phenomena such as climate change, ozone holes, land degradation and species extinction appear to 'swamp economic values in a sea of externalities', rendering economics 'useless' for dealing with these phenomena (Martinez-Alier, 1987: xii, xiv). As one of the leading green economists puts it, the planetary boat might sink if overloaded by pollution and depletion, however optimal the distribution of its load (Daly, 1989). This picture conveys the impression that economics of optimal resource allocation has become irrelevant as it is overridden by the transgression of vital environmental limits.

If environmental phenomena were independent of economic activity, there would be no need to trouble economic analysis. Environmental issues could be addressed by environmental policies, and economics could pursue its own objectives without risk of impairing the achievement of its own and other domains' objectives. Environment and economy interact, however. Policy failures in both environment and development have been traced back to the neglect of this interdependence by compartmentalized line ministries and agencies (WCED, 1987).

Much of the discussion of the relevance of environmental phenomena for economic performance and development is still unsubstantiated, however. How close are we to life-threatening environmental limits? Is the planetary boat sinking? Does the economic system head for self-destruction as it undermines its environmental support systems (Brown *et al.*, 1993)? Is sustainable growth just a bad oxymoron (Daly, 1991), or a *sine qua non* for development (Boutros-Ghali, 1995)?

Environment and Development Economics

In support of the non-sustainability of current patterns of production, consumption and economic growth, reference is typically made to[2]

- *climate change*: 1–3.5°C global warming, caused by greenhouse gas emissions (1995 assessment by the Intergovernmental Panel on Climate Change);
- *biomass appropriation*: 40 per cent of annual net primary productivity used up by consumption of organic material and destructive land use (Vitousek *et al.*, 1986);
- *ozone layer depletion*: ozone layer in 1993 at an all-time low of 90 Dobson units, with the ozone hole 15 per cent larger than in previous years (Brown *et al.*, 1994), caused by the use of CFCs and halons in refrigeration, insulation and packaging;
- *land degradation and desertification*: 500 billion tons of top soil lost since 1972 (Brown *et al.*, 1993); 5 million hectares lost annually to desertification;
- *biodiversity*: one-quarter of species in danger of extinction; 5,000 to 150,000 species lost annually, caused by destruction of biomes and habitat by agriculture, deforestation, pollution and other land uses;
- *deforestation*: 16.8 million hectares lost annually from logging and land clearance for agriculture and settlement;
- *energy*: 90 years of proved recoverable (mineral) reserves, 243 years of proved reserves in place, and 800 years of total (including additional estimated) reserves left (United Nations, 1992).

Obviously, answers cannot be found by simply listing disparate indicators, expressed in so many degrees of global warming, Dobson units of ozone depletion or hectares of advancing deserts. An operational definition of sustainability is needed, capable of combining or comparing all these phenomena, among each other and with the costs and benefits of related economic activities. This article explores the possibilities of quantifying environment–economy interaction by means of comparable (integrative) measures, uses the underlying concepts for operational definitions of sustainability in growth and development, presents first statistical results, and reaches conclusions on the relevance of mainstream economic analysis and on the need to introduce new paradigms.

2. Operationalizing sustainability: a dichotomy of approaches
To achieve integration of environmental concerns and economic objectives, both 'economists' and 'environmentalists'[3] looked into their

---

[2] Where not otherwise specified, the source is UNEP (1992).

[3] To use a crude distinction, for purposes of exposition, between advocates of mainsteam neoclassical economics and advocates of holistic views of the human environment. The latter views have been expressed in particular by 'deep ecologists' who emphasize the need for a comprehensive, religious and philosophical world-view and the intrinsic equality of all species (Naess, 1976; Devall and Sessions, 1985). In a similar vein, reference is made to 'environmental economists'. Of course, neither the existing schools of thought nor their representatives may fully fit into this simplified categorization.

P. Bartelmus

analytical toolkits so as to apply them to the other field. In doing so, they imposed their own values, with the result of distinctly different views of sustainability in growth and development.

Environmental economists thus seek to incorporate scarce environmental goods and services into their economic (monetary) value system. Their premise is that the environment can be treated as a commodity because this is how individuals perceive it. Consumers can therefore be prompted to reveal their preferences for environmental services or dispreferences for service losses in money terms. In the absence of markets, supply and demand curves for this classical public good can at least be imagined, if not simulated.

To this end, the concept of economic value is broadened to include the use of natural resources and environmental functions of waste absorption, as well as the non-use values, i.e. option or existence values, derived from the knowledge about preserved ecosystems or species (Munasinghe, 1993). A variety of valuation techniques to capture these values have been developed for cost–benefit analyses of the environmental impacts of projects and programmes. Several of these valuations were incorporated in methodologies of 'green' national accounting (Bartelmus, 1997). Some environmental economists go further into 'analysis', advocating the introduction of—shadow-priced—environmental welfare effects into national income or net national product (Mäler, 1991; Pearce, 1994).

Environmentalists contest the notion that the environment can be treated as a commodity. People see, or should see, the environment from a cultural or ethical point of view as an indivisible social good. Toward such a good, people express attitudes or moral convictions (see, e.g., Doob, 1995) rather than preferences in terms of economic costs and benefits. It is repugnant to see the value of a public good or national heritage subjected to the 'willingness to pay' which in reality might reflect an 'ability to pay' (Jacobs, 1994: 80). The question is not how to generate economic value for an underpriced commodity, but how to prevent being 'colonized by the economy' through misleading economic valuation (van Dieren, 1995: 7).

Since, according to this reasoning, the real value of nature cannot be expressed in monetary terms, new indicators or indices of the 'quality of life' (OECD, 1973), 'human development' (UNDP, 1995) or 'sustainable development' have been advanced.[4] Aggregation of the different facets of these concepts would have to be done by appropriate weighting of the quantifiable aspects of priority concerns and/or related activities and results. Such indicator selection and weighting bears the risk of representing the values and parameters of the index-builders and might thus reflect the priorities of environmentalist mindsets, preferences and data frameworks—colonizing the economy?

The result is a distinct dichotomy in measuring and analysing the interactions between environment, economic performance, growth and development. The dichotomy is based on two different 'world-views' of the role of the natural environment in human life. They can be broadly

---

[4] See, for a brief literature review of quality-of-life indicators, Fergany (1994); an overview of indicators of sustainable development is given by Bartelmus (1994b).

Environment and Development Economics

characterized as the advocacy of (1) *economic sustainability*, aiming at the long-term preservation of economic output, income or consumption, i.e. economic growth, and (2) *ecological sustainability*, focusing on the preservation of human populations in a given territory, endowed with limited natural assets. Ecological sustainability represents an application of the ecological concepts of carrying capacity and optimum sustained yield of bioproductive systems (Odum, 1971) to the general use of nature by humans, notably for life support. Economic sustainability is production- and consumption-oriented, while ecological sustainability is focused directly on people and their needs. As a consequence, the role of the environment is differently perceived, either as a requisite for economic growth or as the provider of essential consumer services or amenities.

Figure 1 presents this dichotomy between economic values and measures (in shaded boxes) and physical or non-monetary concepts and measures (in white boxes). Use is made of a generic process of supply, use and users of goods, services and amenities from nature, the economy and the social system. This presentation permits the further categorization of sustainability of supply, use and users, and a possible distinction between the sustainability of economic (supply and use) and human (users/populations) development. The distinction is a useful reminder that the ultimate objective of sustainability is, not human activity, but human beings themselves.

Monetary measures in Figure 1 include those compiled in extended national accounts such as the United Nations (1993a) system of integrated environmental and economic accounting (SEEA). These measures are de-

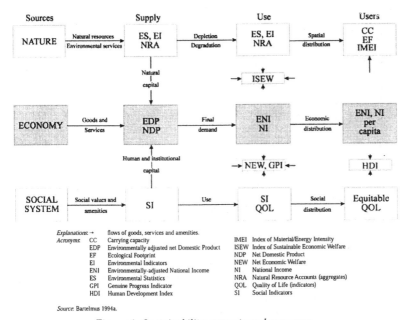

Explanations: →	flows of goods, services and amenities.		
Acronyms:	CC	Carrying capacity	IMEI	Index of Material/Energy Intensity
	EDP	Environmentally adjusted net Domestic Product	ISEW	Index of Sustainable Economic Welfare
	EF	Ecological Footprint	NDP	Net Domestic Product
	EI	Environmental Indicators	NEW	Net Economic Welfare
	ENI	Environmentally-adjusted National Income	NI	National Income
	ES	Environmental Statistics	NRA	Natural Resource Accounts (aggregates)
	GPI	Genuine Progress Indicator	QOL	Quality of Life (indicators)
	HDI	Human Development Index	SI	Social Indicators

Source: Bartelmus 1994a.

Figure 1. *Sustainability concepts and measures.*

P. Bartelmus

rived indeed by imposing monetary values on environmental concerns. As a result, conventional economic indicators such as national income and product, capital, investment, saving or consumption are modified to obtain 'green' aggregates, in particular an environmentally adjusted net domestic product (EDP; see section 3). Non-monetary measures of ecological sustainability include the carrying capacity (CC) of a territory, which measures the sustainability of human populations in a particular geographic area, and its inverse, the ecological footprint (EF), which measures the land area affected by an inhabited area beyond immediate occupation (Rees and Wackernagel, 1994). Further attempts at capturing ecological sustainability include the development of frameworks or lists of social and environmental indicators (SI, EI), possibly combined into indicators of sustainable development, and the above-mentioned indices of the quality of life (QOL) or human development (HDI).

The capability of both monetary and physical indicators to measure significant aspects of economic and ecological sustainability is explored in the following sections. Other proposals attempt to measure the basically non-operational generic notion of sustainability, defined as non-declining welfare (Pezzey, 1989), by adding 'desirables' to and deducting 'regrettables' from per capita national income or consumption. These indices are typically compiled outside a systematic framework and suffer from lack of transparency in index composition and compilation, and arbitrariness in scope, coverage, weighting and valuation; they are therefore not further discussed here.[5]

3. Measuring economic sustainability

Economic theory and accounting already use a narrowly defined 'sustainability' criterion when considering the depreciation or consumption of *produced* capital. The rationale is to distinguish clearly between income and capital to avoid consuming the capital base of income generation.[6] The use of financial or produced capital for consumption, without replacement or reproduction is clearly non-sustainable in the long term. Focusing on produced capital, the—national—accounting argument is more neutral in justifying the netting-out of 'capital consumption'. It refers to the need to avoid double-counting in the aggregation of economic output: the inputs of produced goods and services, including capital services (reflected in the

---

[5] Figure 1 displays some of the better-known indices in between the physical and monetary data streams, notably the measure of net economic welfare (NEW; Samuelson and Nordhaus, 1992), the Index of Sustainable Economic Welfare (ISEW; Daly and Cobb, 1989), and the ISEW-based Genuine Progress Indicator (GPI; Cobb *et al.*, 1995).

[6] This time-honoured distinction can be traced back to Adam Smith (1776, cited by El Serafy, 1989) who advanced the notion of 'neat revenue' which can be consumed by the inhabitants of a country 'without encroaching upon their capital'. This concept was restated 160 years later by Hicks (1946: 172) as a 'guide for prudent conduct ... to give people an indication of how much they can consume without impoverishing themselves'. Similarly, national (disposable) income can be distinguished from 'net worth' in national accounts conventions with certain assumptions about the composition of net worth (see CEC *et al.*, 1993, para. 8.15).

Environment and Development Economics

'wear and tear' of capital goods), are deducted from gross output to obtain net value added and its sum total, net domestic product (NDP).

By opening the asset boundary of national accounts to non-produced natural assets, the SEEA makes use of Hicks's prudency argument (see note 6). The costing of natural resource inputs and waste absorption services is justified by their scarcity and necessity for production. Using the extended national accounts concepts, the sustainability of economic performance can now be operationally defined as the maintenance of produced *and* natural capital, used in the production of goods and services. More comprehensive analyses of the sustainability of production and growth would have to take into account further factors of production, i.e. human and institutional capital, as well as effects of technological progress, substitution among production factors and material inputs, changes in consumption patterns, and impacts of natural disasters.

Setting aside the difficult-to-measure human and institutional capital and the erratic impacts of catastrophes, the question remains *how much* capital maintenance is needed, given the possibilities of substituting scarce natural capital by applying environmentally sound, clean and resource-saving production and consumption techniques. 'Weak sustainability' would assume that scarce natural assets can be replaced by other production factors, and overall (total) capital maintenance is a sufficient measure of sustainability. Complementarities in natural asset use would require 'strong sustainability', i.e. the full conservation of natural capital categories. 'Sensible sustainability' has been advocated as a criterion that takes both complementarity and substitution possibilities into account (Serageldin and Steer, 1994).

The different 'strengths' of sustainability are reflected to some degree in the green accounting aggregates calculated according to different valuation methods. Three basic valuations are proposed by the SEEA. They are (1) market valuation of economic natural assets and their changes, (2) maintenance costing of environmental degradation and destruction, and (3) contingent valuation of damage resulting from degradation and destruction.

Market valuation is applied to 'economic (natural) assets', whose extraction or harvest yields economic gains (CEC *et al.*, 1993, para. 10.2). Market valuation focuses therefore on the income generation capacity of natural assets whose products of minerals, fish or timber are sold in the market. Discounting the value of expected net revenues obtains a market value of the natural assets and their consumption. From a microeconomic point of view, the change in economic value of a reproducible or renewable (natural) asset calls for making a cost allowance that permits the replacement of the asset at its market value.[7] This is a strong-sustainability criterion, as it refers to the income generation capacity of the particular

---

[7] Under certain conditions (perfect competition, optimal resource use, full substitutability of production factors), the net rent per unit, i.e. the 'net price', can be used as a proxy for obtaining the change-in-present-value depreciation cost. See, for a discussion of the underlying assumptions in this case, and also of other valuation methods, Bartelmus (1997).

P. Bartelmus

natural asset only. An alternative is the 'user cost allowance' (El Serafy, 1989) which retains only part of the net income generated from the sale of asset outputs. It aims at a permanent income stream from investing this allowance in any kind of production activity or even financial markets. Clearly the objective of income maintenance reflects a weak-sustainability concept, without regard to the future composition of capital at the micro- or macroeconomic levels.

Maintenance valuation is introduced in the SEEA in order to cost environmental externalities in addition to the depletion of natural resources. Focusing only on 'economic' assets (in the SNA sense) would be a radical reduction of economic analysis, excluding scarce resources only because they are not traded in markets.[8] Environmental maintenance costs are defined as the costs that one would have had to incur in order to avoid the deterioration of the environment by current production and consumption activities (during the accounting period). These costs are similar to depreciation allowances made to replace worn-out fixed capital; they are the costs required to maintain environmental sink and (re)source capacities. This is a strong-sustainability concept calling for the full conservation of an environmental asset. The justification is that uncertainty about possible long-term hazards and irreversibilities of environmental impacts may indeed call for a high degree of risk aversion, i.e. the maintenance of at least the present level of environmental quality in most cases (United Nations, 1993a, para. 53). In other cases, compliance with appropriate emission standards would have to be costed, allowing for safe uses of environmental capacities.

Contingent valuation is hardly applicable in routine—national—accounting, from both a data availability and a theoretical[9] point of view. On the other hand, it could be used for estimating demand for particular environmental protection programmes, based on the revealed dispreferences for environmental damage. In theory, acceptance of compensation for environmental damage could be interpreted as weak sustainability of welfare generation in terms of income maintenance, while the willingness to pay for conservation of particular environmental assets would point to a preference for strong sustainability or full conservation of these assets.

In practice, i.e. in country projects implementing the SEEA, for market valuation the simpler 'net price method' has been generally applied, either alone or in combination with maintenance costing. The result is the compilation of two environmentally adjusted indicators of overall economic performance: EDP1, representing strong sustainability of economic assets, and EDP2, representing strong sustainability of both economic and environmental assets.

[8] Indeed, the SNA itself introduces public goods production and consumption with the argument of 'market failure' (CEC *et al.*, 1993, paras. 9.84, 9.92). This is clearly a value judgment about what *should* be included in the accounting system. It seems to be a small step from here to argue the inclusion of another public good, the environment, at least in 'satellites' of the core accounts, even if the scarce environmental services are offered by nature rather than a social institution.

[9] Contingent valuation which includes consumer surplus when assessing the willingness to pay for a particular good or service is inconsistent with the market price valuation applied to economic 'transactions' in national accounts.

Environment and Development Economics

Table 1. *Net domestic product (NDP) and environmentally adjusted net domestic product (EDP) in case-studies of green accounting (lowest and highest percentages)*

Country	EDP1[a]/NDP(%)	EDP2[b]/NDP(%)
Costa Rica (1970–89)[c]	89–96	
Mexico (1985)	94	87
Indonesia (1971–84)[c]	69–87	
Japan (1985/90)	98/99.6	97/98
Korea, Republic of (1985–92)[d]	100	96–98
Papua New Guinea (1986–90)	92–99	90–97
Philippines (1988–92)[d, e]	96–99.5	
Thailand (1970–90)[d]	96–98	
Ghana (1991–3)[c, d]	85–89	75–83
United Kingdom (1980–90)[f]	95–100	

Sources: Costa Rica: Solórzano *et al.* (1991); Mexico: van Tongeren *et al.* (1991); Indonesia: Repetto *et al.* (1989); Japan: Oda *et al.* (1996); Korea: Kim *et al.* (forthcoming); Papua New Guinea: Bartelmus *et al.* (1992); Philippines: Domingo (1996); Thailand: Bartelmus and Tardos (1992); Ghana: Powell (1996); United Kingdom: Pearce *et al.* (1993).
Notes: [a]EDP1 is NDP, adjusted for natural resource depletion only. [b]EDP2 is NDP, adjusted for natural resource depletion *and* environmental quality degradation. [c]Concept adjusted to United Nations (SEEA) methodologies. [d]Preliminary estimates. [e]Soil erosion not yet covered. [f]Oil and gas depletion only.

Table 1 presents these aggregates as obtained from pilot studies of natural resource and environmental accounting. The studies provide information about the significance of natural capital in production and income generation by comparing EDP with NDP. An effort was made to adjust those indicators that were compiled outside the national accounts framework (Indonesia, Costa Rica, United Kingdom) to SEEA concepts. However, as indicated in the table notes, comparability is still impaired by remaining differences in concepts, methods, valuations and coverage of environmental phenomena.

All SEEA applications have taken a cautious approach, leading to undercoverage and underestimation. This may explain some of the rather modest share of depletion and degradation cost in economic performance, especially in the industrialized countries of Japan and Korea.[10] While these countries hardly extract or harvest domestic natural resources, other (developing) countries show more significant effects on their natural capital. Indonesia, Costa Rica and Ghana have been exploiting their natural resources at rates of 10–30 per cent of their NDP (see EDP1/NDP column of

[10] Current (annual) cost and production measures do not allow for past accumulation of environmental impacts and low current levels of resource stocks, due to past exploitation. Alternative concepts and measures of 'environmental debt' have been proposed to this end (Hueting and Bosch, 1994; National Institute of Economic Research and Statistics Sweden, 1994), but are not directly comparable (like 'cost') to current income and production. Such measures also point to the need for further analysis of the 'responsibilities' of these countries for environmental deterioration in other countries (through natural resource imports and translocation of polluting industries).

P. Bartelmus

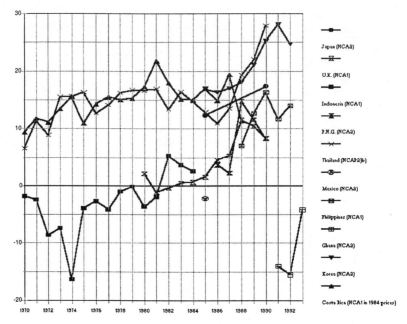

Note: ^a Net capital accumulation (NCA) is defined as net capital formation minus environmental
cost; NCA1 refers to net capital accumulation covering natural resource depletion costs
only; NCA2 covers depletion and degradation costs.
^b Elements of NCA1 and NCA2 (low coverage).

Figure 2. *Sustainability of growth (net capital accumulation*^a *in per cent of NDP).*

Table 1). Probably more important than the overall national aggregates—
for structural and sectoral policy and management—are the environmental costs generated by economic sectors. Here the case-studies show
that depletion costs generated by forestry and mining reduce conventional
value added by over 70 per cent in Mexico and Thailand.

Another way of looking at the (non-)sustainability of economic performance or growth is to assess a nation's ability to generate new capital
after taking produced and natural capital consumption into account.
Figure 2 presents net capital accumulation (NCA; net capital formation
minus natural capital consumption) in per cent of NDP. Indonesia and
Ghana (with provisional figures) exhibit non-sustainable growth patterns
of disinvestment. Mexico is a possible candidate as far as a one-year result
can tell. As already mentioned, the sustainability index for other countries
might be overly optimistic due to undercoverage of environmental depletion and degradation, notably in the (preliminary) Thai study.

4. The limits of growth: assessing ecological sustainability
As discussed above, pricing the priceless for economic sustainability has
been deemed 'repugnant' by some environmentalists. Others consider it irrelevant. If indeed ultimate limits in the assimilative capacities of the

Environment and Development Economics

environment and the availability of natural resources are transgressed, continuous functional relationships in conventional economics become meaningless in a system 'riddled with threshold effects' (Perrings, 1995: 63). This situation can only be argued outside standard economic analysis as a case of non-sustainable throughput of energy and materials. Such throughput turns low-entropy mass into high-entropy waste (Georgescu-Roegen, 1971), cutting through the circular economic flow system. Optimal allocation, relative scarcity of resources and perceived economic equilibria lose relevance in Malthusian economics of limited 'scale' of resource flows where absolute scarcities dominate the field (Daly, 1989).

In this situation, sustainability or non-sustainability has to be defined as compliance or non-compliance with capacity limits of natural systems. Attempts have been made to demonstrate the prevalence of these limits in terms of biomass appropriation (Vitousek *et al.*, 1986) or by means of carrying capacity assessment (FAO *et al.*, 1982; World Bank, 1985), i.e. the ecological sustainability of human populations (see section 2 above). Carrying capacity is usually measured by the number of people a territory can sustain indefinitely, or for a specified time period, at particular standards of living. The problems with carrying-capacity measures lie in assumptions about minimal or desirable standards of living, current and future technologies that may affect the use of available resources, the time horizon of the analysis, and trade with other territories that render the concept inapplicable except at the global level (Cohen, 1995).

Data on material throughput expressed as material intensities of economic activities are more readily available. They have been used to compile proxy indices for pressures on carrying capacities, i.e. of ecological (non-)sustainability. Declining average material and energy intensities in industrialized countries were thus taken as a sign of declining impacts on the environment. Economic growth is considered to be effectively 'delinked' from the environment in this case (Jänicke *et al.*, 1989). A later study found, however, that a process of 'relinking' seems to be underway in these countries since the mid-1980s (de Bruyn and Opschoor, 1997).

Figures 3 and 4 show the results of similar calculations for selected materials in the industrialized and developing countries for which case-studies of environmental accounting were carried out (except Ghana and Papua New Guinea, for which data were not available). The only difference is that material input is related to gross domestic product (GDP) rather than population. The reason is that material inputs are more closely related to production (patterns) than to changes in final demand, i.e. final consumption or income per capita. The figures present trends in an 'Index of Material/Energy Intensity' (IMEI) as defined in Figure 3, note (a). The IMEI does indicate a degree of relinking (i.e. an upward movement) of environmental pressures with economic performance for the three industrialized countries of Japan, USA and UK during the 1980s. However, this trend does not seem to continue into the 1990s. For the developing countries, two patterns of IMEI development can be observed. The newly industrializing countries (NICs) of the Republic of Korea, Thailand and Indonesia (and less dramatically Mexico) show trends of increasing IMEI as a possible result of rapid economic growth. By contrast, the Philippines

P. Bartelmus

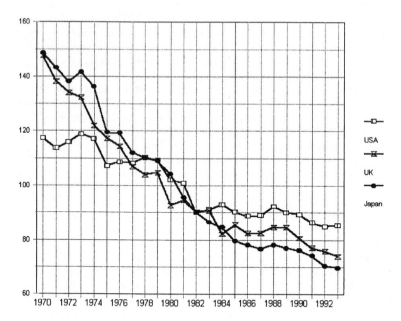

Note: [a] Average (for all selected materials) percentage deviation from the average consumption of
each material per GDP (1970–93, in constant prices). Materials included are cement, steel,
freight (rail and road: net tkm and vehicles in use) and energy. See, for a detailed
description of the concepts and method of the index calculation, Jänicke *et al.* (1989) and de
Bruyn and Opschoor (1997).
Source: UNSD data bases.

Figure 3. *Index of Materials/Energy Intensity (IMEI)*[a] *in selected industrialized
countries (1970–93).*

and Costa Rica exhibit fairly erratic changes in material and energy use in
the 1970s and early 1980s. More recently, they seem to follow the material
intensity trend (increase) of the NIC economies.

The calculations suffer from the general drawbacks of any physical indicator aggregation, i.e. arbitrary weighting and indicator selection. In the case
of IMEI, different environmental impacts produced by different material inputs are given equal weights, possible substitution of materials is not
accounted for and the effects of environmental protection are not always reflected in reduced material intensities. Also, and as pointed out by one of the
anonymous reviewers, a declining IMEI may be indicative of both an increase in the absolute level of throughput (though relatively lower than the
increase in GDP) and an absolute decrease in throughput. De Bruyn and
Opschoor (1997) describe these outcomes as 'weak' and 'strong' delinking or
'dematerialization', respectively. All these processes and activities would
have to be further examined in more detailed analyses before any policy
conclusions could be reached. Such loss of direct usability in policy-making
and analysis is another drawback of physical indicators.

The results of monetary environmental accounting and physical IMEI

Environment and Development Economics

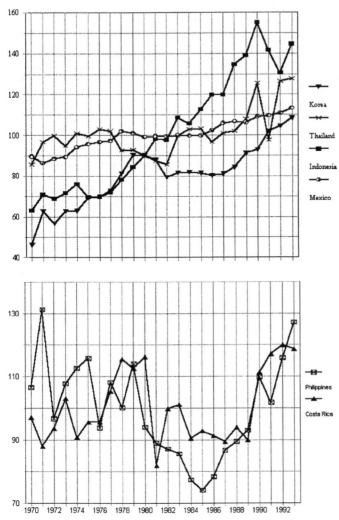

Note: ª see Fig. 3.

Figure 4. *Index of Materials/Energy Intensity (IMEI)*ª *in selected developing
countries (1970–93).*

calculation are hardly comparable. In principle, non-sustainabilities of
negative or reduced capital accumulation (because of natural capital consumption) should be reflected in physical material production and
consumption patterns. In practice, the empirical results of IMEI compilations do not convey a clear picture of sustainability or non-sustainability
of economic growth, and the many assumptions underlying the index calculation make it difficult to derive policy conclusions. So far, it does not

P. Bartelmus

seem to be possible, therefore, to link unequivocally overall physical indices such as the IMEI to EDP or NCA trends.

What can be concluded from the limited studies available to date is that
at least for some, in particular natural-resource-dependent, countries, non-
sustainable growth patterns and denial policies, based on conventional
economics and indicators, cannot be ruled out. At least those countries
would have to take urgent action to reorient their economic and environmental policies towards greater integration and sustainability. This could
be achieved along the lines of new paradigms of economic performance,
growth and development, discussed below.

5. Towards operational paradigms: eco-nomics and sustainable development

The above results confirm the occurrence of non-sustainabilities of economic performance, brought about by environmental impacts. The
question remains whether these impacts, in addition to other, notably mo-
nopolistic, market imperfections, are grounds enough to change radically
conventional economic planning and policy-making. Ultimate answers to
this question can probably not yet be found with the incomplete and imperfect data sets available.

There are, however, at least two immediate benefits of the methodological data work carried out so far, especially in the field of environmental
accounting. One is the provision of more operational definitions of sustainability, consistent with standard economic indicators. The other is a
clearer demarcation between what can be incorporated into a monetary accounting framework and corresponding empirical analysis, and what has
to be assessed by supplementary or alternative indicator systems. Using
this demarcation, two basic paradigms of 'eco-nomics' (coined by Postel,
1990) and 'sustainable development' can be distinguished. The former
focuses on environmental cost internalization into conventional micro-
and macroeconomics; the latter endeavours to comply with social and environmental norms while catering to economic (growth) objectives.

5.1. Eco-nomics: cost internalization and sustainable growth

Eco-nomics can be seen as overcoming the widespread neglect of environmental concerns in conventional market economics. Treating
environmental effects of economic activities as 'external' to mainstream
market economics might be one reason why environmental policy has frequently been relegated to peripheral agencies or departments. When
environment–economy interactions could not be overlooked any more,
and calls for integrating environmental and economic policies intensified
(WCED, 1987; United Nations, 1993b), the obvious response was to resur-
rect Pigovian taxes and similar market instruments as a means of cost
internalization at the microeconomic level (see, e.g., Dorfman and
Dorfman, 1993, ch. 3). The idea is to maintain fundamentals of conventional economics such as competitive markets and optimizing behaviour
by establishing individual property rights over public (environmental)
goods and/or applying fiscal and other incentives of cost internalization
such as effluent charges, tradable pollution permits, or deposit-refund sys-

Environment and Development Economics

tems. Households and enterprises are thus prompted into accounting for environmental costs in their plans, programmes and budgets without impairing the allocative efficiency of the market.

Integrated environmental and economic accounting permits the measurement of the hypothetical (since actual environmental impacts did take place) environmental depletion and degradation cost. These are the costs at which internalization instruments should be set initially and realistically, referring to the best available technologies that could have prevented environmental impacts from current economic activity. The aggregate of EDP and its elements and components thus account for the missed-opportunities cost of not having prevented environmental depletion and degradation. Such costing of environmental sins in consumption and production should facilitate the translation of public declarations in support of sustainability into commitments to environmental protection (expenditure) and 'a specifiable amount of productive investment' (after allowing for natural capital consumption) (Solow, 1992, p. 20).

The ultimate effects of initial cost internalization on economic aggregates would have to be modelled according to prevailing price elasticities and technological (production) structures. As a result, hypothetical aggregates such as an 'optimal net domestic product with regard to environmental targets' (Meyer and Ewerhart, 1996) or a 'maximum NDP generated in an economy in which the burden on the environment is reduced to a sustainable level' (de Boer *et al.*, 1994) can be determined. In fact, it can be shown that under certain, quite restrictive and probably unrealistic, conditions of perfect competition, full substitution of production factors and optimal (resource-use) behaviour, such modelling would ensure both maximum output and the long-term sustainability of consumption (Solow, 1974; Hartwick, 1977; Dasgupta and Mäler, 1991). These models can be seen as attempts to accommodate externalities while at the same time reconciling conventional economic analysis with criteria of intergenerational equity (defined as long-term maintenance of per capita consumption).

Overall, economic growth would have to be redirected from GDP maximization towards (more) sustainable growth which can be defined as positive trend in EDP. The assumption underlying this definition is that the allowances made in EDP calculations for the consumption of produced capital and the depletion and degradation of natural capital can and will be invested in capital maintenance, taking into account that trends of depletion and degradation can be offset or mitigated by technological progress, substitution, discoveries of natural resources and changes in production and consumption patterns.[11]

5.2. Sustainable development: from sustainability to feasibility

Costing economic sustainability by incorporating environmental depletion and degradation into national accounts does not capture the 'things that

[11] Other factors such as the effects of natural disasters, changes in the productivity of human capital, or high inflation and indebtedness also affect the sustainability of economic growth. The allowance for produced and natural capital consumption in the above definition reflects therefore only a 'more sustainable' growth concept that requires further refinement (modelling) (Bartelmus 1994a: 70).

P. Bartelmus

most people think should not be for sale' (Kuttner, 1997: 300). Those 'things' encompass non-economic amenities and values, offered by nature and social institutions, both operating outside the market system. Public institutions may offer political freedoms, security, equity in the distribution of income and wealth, and cultural values. In addition, the disruption of environmental services may cause the loss and impairment of human and non-human lives, as well as inequities in the distribution of these effects within and among nations, and between current and future generations.

Rational and explicit policy analysis would have to specify these needs and values in terms of minimum targets or standards and maximum limits or thresholds, exogenous to the economic exchange system. Those standards and limits may include

- standards of living;
- limits of natural resource capacities;
- pollution and contamination standards;
- limits of the carrying capacity of bioproductive systems;
- distributional standards for income, wealth (including natural assets) and environmental impacts; and
- other cultural, political, social or demographic standards and targets.

Assessing the achievement of these targets and the compliance of human activities with norms and standards is not possible with the above-discussed measures of economic performance or growth. This is because prices or preferences expressed in money terms do not reflect relative scarcities and social priorities and preferences in these areas. For instance, real interest rates might discount much more strongly (over a relatively short period of time) the financial future than social preferences would indicate for the welfare of future generations.

A broader concept of 'development' is needed to overcome the dichotomy between economic and ecological sustainability and to address simultaneously economic objectives and non-economic targets and norms. An operational definition of 'sustainable development'[12] that takes explicit account of economic and non-economic standards and targets has been proposed to this end as 'the set of development programmes that meets the targets of human needs satisfaction without violating long-term natural resource capacities and standards of environmental quality and social equity' (Bartelmus, 1994a: 73).

The consideration of standards, targets or norms turns the question of economic sustainability, defined above operationally as capital maintenance, into one of compliance with social goals or norms. Individual preferences for goods and services, more or less efficiently revealed by markets, may thus be overridden by social fiat, however democratically

---

[12] Sustainable development was popularly defined by the Brundtland report *Our Common Future* (WCED, 1987: 43) as 'development that meets the needs of the present without compromising the ability of future generations to meet their own needs'. The definition fails, however, to specify what are the human needs; omits to clarify the timeframe for the analysis of future generations' needs; and does not even mention the environment as the current key concern in sustainability.

Environment and Development Economics

such fiat may have been achieved. Market valuation could be replaced by social *evaluation*, and sustainability by *feasibility* of human activity in terms of non-violation of social norms. To the extent that such standard-setting affects market exchange, a radical change in economic analysis would be required: from a focus on individual preferences to those of 'society', the 'government' or 'expertocracy'. The invisible hand of the market would be overruled by the visible one of the standard-setter(s).

This can be demonstrated by an illustrative model of the size of the 'feasibility space' of interdependent activities (Bartelmus, 1979). This space is generated by limited capacities, standards and norms. Figure 5 shows this for the simple two-commodity economy of food (x_1) and shelter (x_2) production and consumption. Society has to face in this model minimum needs for food ($\bar{c}_1$) and shelter ($\bar{c}_2$), maximum production capacity limits ($\hat{x}_1$ and $\hat{x}_2$) and maximum environmental limits of natural resource availability ($\bar{x}_r$) and pollution ($\bar{x}_p$). The minimum and maximum constraints delimit the shaded area of the economy's feasibility space. Of course, other distributional issues such as the trade-off between intra- and intergenerational equity, i.e. poverty and long-term sustainability of consumption (Solow, 1993), would have to be dealt with in a second-stage 'political space' of decision-making.

Within the feasibility space, conventional micro- and macroeconomic strategies can be played out, aiming at maximum economic efficiency or growth. Outside this space, normative/political criteria overrule economic ones. A wide, open space means that traditional production, consumption and investment activities are hardly affected by social and environmental concerns. In other words, if there is a lot of slack in the feasibility con-

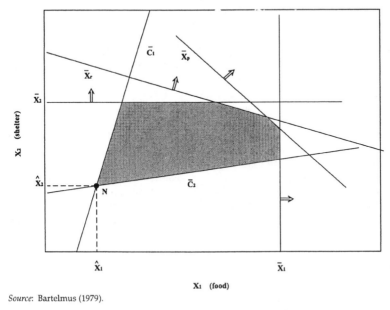

Source: Bartelmus (1979).

Figure 5. *Feasibility space of sustainable development.*

P. Bartelmus

straints, it will be economics as usual. A largely reduced space, on the other hand, would reveal that markets cannot account for significant interference of non-economic values with conventional economic decision-making. This would indeed end economics as we know it, since socio-political restrictions would surely limit the functioning of markets and market-based economic growth. The neglect or denial of standards and targets of sustainable development might lead in this case to the replacement of development by uncontrolled 'developments' such as poverty-induced riots, war over access to natural resources, eco-terrorism, surge in ecological refugees and other social strife. Since market prices cannot alert to approaching these situations, it would indeed be 'foolhardy to find out the hard way' (Perrings, 1995: 63), i.e. with a *laissez-faire* attitude.

New, environmentally beneficial, technologies could be a saviour, potentially widening the feasibility area. This is indicated in Figure 5 by arrows pushing capacity and environmental constraints 'outward'. The shift of constraints would be reflected in changed technical relations between pollution and natural resource use, and production and consumption. Such a transition from 'limits to growth' to the 'growth of limits' (MacNeill, 1990) might buy some time but cannot be expected to be the cure for all social woes. Moreover, uncertainties in predicting technological progress and environmental impacts present a high risk for relying totally on technology and market expansion and liberalization.

6. Outlook: towards a long-term vision of sustainable development

Instruments of eco-nomics, i.e. of environmental cost internalization by economic agents, have been applied successfully, especially in northern European countries, after 'languishing as arcane concerns of academic environmental economists' (Ekins, 1996: 31). Implementation problems, including the monitoring of environmental impacts, the measurement of marginal damage costs and the short-sightedness of short-lived administrations, seem to have made the use of market instruments more of a tool for revenue-raising than for changing microeconomic behaviour (OECD, 1989). In addition, acute and high-risk environmental phenomena such as the depletion of atmospheric ozone would have to be tackled by immediate regulative action rather than through time-lagged 'marginal' prompting by economic (dis)incentives. The use of these instruments is thus still in an experimental phase. Experimentation, notably with a more realistic setting of these instruments—at a level determined by measurements of environmental cost in consistency with national accounts concepts and indicators—is perhaps the most promising way to achieve economic sustainability in the short and medium term.

Non-economic objectives, such as intergenerational fairness, and potentially irreversible threshold effects on life-support systems call for guarding against violation of social goals and environmental limits in current and future economic activity. This may indeed require sacrificing short- and medium-term efficiency for the sake of incorporating 'vital' standards into long-term economic planning and policy-making. Positive and normative economics would thus be merged by explicitly introducing standards and norms into economic analysis—anathema to many economic scientists (see, e.g.,

Environment and Development Economics

Caldwell, 1982: 4 and part II; or Samuelson and Nordhaus, 1992: 9, 295). However, such merging is unavoidable in real-world politics. Much of the irrelevance of economics might thus be the consequence of the prevailing positivist approach of 'puzzle-solving in ignorance of the wider methodological, social and ethical issues' (Funtowicz and Ravetz, 1991: 138).

Sustainable development was shown above to be the widely advocated paradigm capable of incorporating these wider issues in an integrative vision of environment and economy. Implementation of such a paradigm cannot be achieved through short-term market clearance. A first step towards implementation is to make vision visible: the above-described illustrative model of a feasibility space might serve this purpose by setting economic activities into a framework of explicitly stated goals and standards. The next step of quantifying the model would be more difficult. For instance, in order to apply the tools of activity analysis, norms and standards have to be formulated in units of means (inputs) and ends (outputs) of activities which in turn would have to be fully reflected by some functional, quantifiable and realistic, relationship between inputs and outputs. Such analysis might be usefully tackled by collaborative research of positivist and normative economists.

Beyond analysis, social 'compacts' need to be established between decision-makers and stakeholders to achieve the setting of and compliance with norms and standards in economic planning and decision-making. At the national level, such compacts could be negotiated between government and civil society on a voluntary basis, or would have to be enforced by law and regulation. The chances for effective implementation of social compacts and long-term planning for sustainable development seem to be slim, in the wake of market euphoria brought about by the downfall of central planning. Also, entrenched 'asymmetries in power and knowledge' (Kuttner, 1997: 285) and uncertainties about the extent, location and timing of environmental impacts are not conducive to the adoption of an overarching visionary approach like sustainable development by 'introvertive' (Heilbroner and Milberg, 1995: 101) economists.[13]

The answer to 'whither economics?' may well have to come from the next generation of potential eco-nomists. To cite a recent communication to the author from a Canadian eighth-grade study group, enquiring about how to maintain the Earth's productivity for future generations:

> It is our responsibility as the Earth's next peoples to be held accountable for what is, and what will happen to our Earth if we do not take care of it.[14]

---

[13] Achieving consensus through direct negotiation might be easier at the local or community level—an argument for implementing participatory grass-roots strategies of 'ecodevelopment'; see, for a review of these bottom-up approaches and their links to central planning and policies, Bartelmus (1994a). Much of the generic discussion of sustainable development applies also at the local level and is therefore not pursued here.

[14] Beth Hall, Gladstone Elementary School, Gladstone, MB (for the Sustainable Development Group).

P. Bartelmus

References

Bartelmus, P. (1979), 'Limits to development—environmental constraints of human needs satisfaction', *Journal of Environmental Management* **9**: 255–269.

Bartelmus, P. (1994a), *Environment, Growth and Development: The Concepts and Strategies of Sustainability*, London and New York: Routledge.

Bartelmus, P. (1994b), *Towards a Framework for Indicators of Sustainable Development*, Department for Economic and Social Information and Policy Analysis, Working Paper Series No. 7, New York: United Nations.

Bartelmus, P. (1997), *The Value of Nature: Valuation and Evaluation in Environmental Accounting*, Department for Economic and Social Infomation and Policy Analysis, Working Paper Series No. 15, New York: United Nations.

Bartelmus, P. and A. Tardos (1992), 'Integrated environmental and economic accounting for Thailand: a feasibility study' (restricted).

Bartelmus, P., E. Lutz and S. Schweinfest (1992), *Integrated Environmental and Economic Accounting: A Case Study for Papua New Guinea*, Environment Working Paper No. 54, Washington, DC: The World Bank.

Boutros-Ghali, B. (1995), *Agenda for Development*, New York: United Nations sales publication (E.95.V.16).

Brown, L.R. *et al.* (1993), *State of the World 1993*, London and New York: W.W. Norton.

Brown, L.R., H. Kane and D.M. Roodman (1994), *Vital Signs 1994*, New York and London: W.W. Norton.

Caldwell, B. (1982), *Beyond Positivism: Economic Methodology in the Twentieth Century*, London: Allen and Unwin.

Cobb, C., T. Halstead and J. Rowe (1995), 'If the GDP is up, why is America down?', *The Atlantic Monthly*, October: 59–78.

Cohen, J.E. (1995), *How Many People Can the Earth Support?*, London and New York: W.W. Norton.

Commission of the European Communities (CEC), International Monetary Fund, Organization for Economic Cooperation and Development, United Nations and World Bank (1993), *System of National Accounts 1993*, New York: United Nations sales publication (E.94.XVII.4).

Daly, H.E. (1989), 'Steady-state and growth concepts for the next century', *in* F. Archibugi and P. Nijkamp, eds., *Economy and Ecology: Towards Sustainable Development*, Dordrecht, Boston and London: Kluwer.

Daly, H.E. (1991), 'Sustainable growth: a bad oxymoron', *Grassroots Development* **15**(3).

Daly, H.E. and J.B. Cobb, Jr (1989), *For the Common Good: Redirecting the Economy towards Community, the Environment, and Sustainable Future*, Boston, MA: Beacon Press.

Dasgupta, P. (1994), 'Optimal versus sustainable development', *in* I. Serageldin and A. Steer, eds., *Valuing the Environment*, proceedings of the First Annual International Conference on Environmentally Sustainable Development, Washington, DC: The World Bank.

Dasgupta, P. and K.-G. Mäler (1991), *The Environment and Emerging Development Issues*, Beijer Reprint Series No. 1, Stockholm: Beijer.

de Boer, B., M. de Haan and M. Voogt (1994), 'What would net domestic product have been in an environmentally sustainable economy? Preliminary views and results', *in* Statistics Canada, ed., *National Accounts and the Environment: Papers and Proceedings from a Conference* (London, 16–18 March 1994), Ottawa.

de Bruyn, S.M. and J.B. Opschoor (1997), 'Developments in the throughput–income relationship: theoretical and empirical observations', *Ecological Economics*, **20**: 255–268.

Devall, B. and G. Sessions (1985), *Deep Ecology: Living as if Nature Mattered*, Layton, UT: Peregrine Smith.

Environment and Development Economics

Domingo, E.V. (1996), 'Adaptation of the UN system of environmental accounting: the Philippine experience', paper presented at the Special IARIW Conference on Integrated Environmental and Economic Accounting in Theory and Practice, Tokyo, 5–8 March 1996.

Doob, L.W. (1995), *Sustainers and Sustainability: Attitudes, Attributes, and Actions for Survival*, Westport, CT: Praeger.

Dorfman, R. and N.S. Dorfman, eds. (1993), *Economics of the Environment: Selected Readings*, 3rd edn, New York and London: W.W. Norton.

Ehrlich, P.R. (1994), 'Ecological economics and the carrying capacity of earth', *in* A.M. Jansson, *et al.*, eds., *Investing in Natural Capital*, Washington, DC: Island Press.

Ekins, P. (rapporteur) (1996), *Environmental Taxes and Charges, National Experiences and Plans* (Report of the European Workshop, Dublin, 7–8 February 1996), Luxembourg: European Communities.

El Serafy, S. (1989), 'The proper calculation of income from depletable natural resources', *in* Y.J. Ahmad, S. El Serafy and E. Lutz, eds., *Environmental Accounting for Sustainable Development*, Washington, DC: The World Bank.

Fergany, N. (1994), 'Quality of life indicators for Arab countries in an international context', *International Statistical Review* 62(2): 187–202.

Food and Agriculture Organization (FAO), United Nations Fund for Population Activities and International Institute for Applied Systems Analysis (1982), *Potential Population Supporting Capacities of Lands in the Developing World*, Rome: FAO.

Funtowicz, S.O. and J.R. Ravetz (1991), 'A new scientific methodology for global environmental issues', *in* R. Costanza, ed., *Ecological Economics: The Science and Management of Sustainability*, New York: Columbia University Press.

Galbraith, J.K. (1986), *The New Industrial State*, 4th edn, New York: Mentor.

Georgescu-Roegen, N. (1971), *The Entropy Law and the Economic Process*, Cambridge, MA: Harvard University Press.

Hartwick, J.M. (1977), 'Intergenerational equity and the investing of rents from exhaustible resources', *American Economic Review*, 67(3): 972–974.

Heilbroner, R. and W. Milberg (1995), *The Crisis of Vision in Modern Economic Thought*, Cambridge University Press.

Hicks, J.R. (1946), *Value and Capital*, 2nd edn, Oxford University Press.

Hueting, R. and P. Bosch (1994), 'Sustainable national income in the Netherlands: the calculation of environmental losses in monetary terms', paper submitted to the 'London Group' meeting on Natural Resource and Environmental Accounting, Washington, DC, 15–17 March 1995.

Jacobs, M. (1994), 'The limits of neoclassicism: towards an institutional environmental economics', *in* M. Redclift and T. Benton, eds., *Social Theory and the Global Environment*, London and New York: Routledge.

Jänicke, M. *et al.* (1989), 'Structural change and environmental impact', *Intereconomics* Jan.–Feb.: 24–35.

Kim, S.-W., A. Alfieri, P. Bartelmus and J. van Tongeren (forthcoming), *Pilot Compilation of Environmental-Economic Accounts for the Republic of Korea*.

Kuttner, R. (1997), *Everything for Sale: The Virtues and Limits of Markets*, New York: Knopf.

MacNeill, J. (1990), 'Meeting the growth imperative for the 21st century', in D.J.R. Angell *et al.*, eds., *Sustainable Earth: Responses to the Environmental Threat*, London: Macmillan.

Mäler, K.-G. (1991), *National Accounts and Environmental Resources*, Beijer Reprint Series No. 4, Stockholm: Beijer.

Martinez-Alier, J. with K. Schlüpfmann (1987), *Ecological Economics, Energy, Environment and Society*, Oxford and Cambridge, MA: Blackwell.

P. Bartelmus

Meyer, B. and G. Ewerhart (1996), 'Modelling towards eco domestic product', paper presented at the Special IARIW Conference on Integrated Environmental and Economic Accounting in Theory and Practice, Tokyo, 5–8 March 1996.

Munasinghe, M. (1993), *Environmental Economics and Sustainable Development*, World Bank Environment Paper No. 3, Washington, DC: The World Bank.

Naess, A. (1976), 'The shallow and the deep, long-range ecology movement, a summary', *Inquiry* **16**: 95–100.

National Institute of Economic Research and Statistics Sweden (1994), *SWEEA, Swedish Economic and Environmental Accounts*, preliminary edition.

Oda, K. *et al.* (1996), 'The system of integrated environmental and economic accounting for Japan, trial estimates and remaining issues', paper presented at the Special IARIW Conference on Integrated Environmental and Economic Accounting in Theory and Practice, Tokyo, 5–8 March 1996.

Odum, E. P. (1971), *Fundamentals of Ecology*, Philadelphia, PA: Saunders.

Organisation for Economic Co-operation and Development (OECD) (1973), *List of Social Concerns Common to Most OECD Countries*, Paris: OECD.

OECD (1985), 'Treatment of mining activities in the system of national accounts' (note by the Secretariat, DES/NI/85.4).

OECD (1989), *Economic Instruments for Environmental Protection*, Paris: OECD.

Pearce, D.W. (1994), 'Valuing the environment: past practice, future prospect', *in* I. Serageldin and A. Steer, eds., *Making Development Sustainable: From Concepts to Action*, Environmentally Sustainable Development Occasional Paper Series No. 2, Washington, DC: The World Bank.

Pearce, D.W. *et al.* (1993), *Blueprint 3*, London: Earthscan.

Perrings, C. (1995), 'Ecology, economics and ecological economics,' *AMBIO* **24**(1): 60–63.

Pezzey, J. (1989), *Economic Analysis of Sustainable Growth and Sustainable Development*, Environment Department Working Paper No. 15, Washington, DC: The World Bank.

Postel, S. (1990), 'Toward a new "eco"-nomics', *World-Watch* **3**(5): 20–28.

Powell, M. (1996), 'Integrated environmental and economic accounts for Ghana', paper presented at the Special IARIW Conference on Integrated Environmental and Economic Accounting in Theory and Practice, Tokyo, 5–8 March 1996.

Rees, W.E. and M. Wackernagel (1994), 'Ecological footprints and appropriated carrying capacity: measuring the natural capital requirements of the human economy', *in* A. Jansson *et al.*, eds., *Investing in Natural Capital*, Washington, DC, and Corelo, CA: Island Press.

Repetto, R. *et al.* (1989), *Wasting Assets: Natural Resources in the National Income Accounts*, Washington, DC: World Resources Institute.

Samuelson, P.A. and W.D. Nordhaus (1992), *Economics*, 14th edn, New York: McGraw-Hill.

Serageldin, I. and A. Steer, (1994), 'Epilogue: expanding the capital stock', *in* I. Serageldin and A. Steer, eds., *Making Development Sustainable: From Concepts to Action*, Environmentally Sustainable Development Occasional Paper Series No. 2, Washington, DC: The World Bank.

Solórzano, R. *et al.* (1991), *Accounts Overdue: Natural Resource Depreciation in Costa Rica*, San José: Tropical Science Center; Washington, DC: World Resources Institute.

Solow, R.M. (1974), 'Intergenerational equity and exhaustible resources', *Review of Economic Studies*, Symposium: 29–46.

Solow, R.M. (1992), *An Almost Practical Step toward Sustainability*, Washington, DC: Resources for the Future.

Solow, R.M. (1993), 'Sustainability: an economist's perspective', in R. Dorfman and N.S. Dorfman, (eds.), *Economics of the Environment—Selected Readings* (3rd ed.), New York and London: W.W. Norton.

Environment and Development Economics

United Nations (1992), *1990 Energy Statistics Yearbook* (sales no. E/F.92.XVII.3).

United Nations (1993a), *Integrated Environmental and Economic Accounting* (sales no. E.93.XVII.12).

United Nations (1993b), *Report of the United Nations Conference on Environment and Development, Rio de Janeiro, 3–14 June 1992*, vol. I: *Resolutions Adopted by the Conference* (sales no. E.93.I.8).

United Nations Development Programme (UNDP) (1995), *Human Development Report 1995*, Oxford University Press.

United Nations Environment Programme (UNEP) (1992), *Saving our Planet: Challenges and Hopes*, Nairobi: UNEP.

van Dieren, W., ed. (1995), *Taking Nature into Account*, New York: Springer-Verlag.

van Tongeren *et al.* (1991), *Integrated Environmental and Economic Accounting: A Case Study for Mexico*, Environment Working Paper No. 50, Washington, DC: The World Bank.

Vitousek, P.M., P.R. Ehrlich, A.H. Ehrlich and P.A. Matson (1986), 'Human appropriation of the products of photosynthesis', *Bioscience* 36(6): 368–373.

World Bank (1985), *Desertification in the Sahelian and Sudanian Zones of West Africa*, Washington, DC: The World Bank.

World Commission on Environment and Development (WCED) (1987), *Our Common Future*, Oxford University Press.

Name Index